Baseball's First-Year Player Draft,
Team by Team Through 1999

Baseball's First-Year Player Draft,
Team by Team
Through 1999

by
W. C. MADDEN

McFarland & Company, Inc., Publishers
Jefferson, North Carolina, and London

Library of Congress Cataloguing-in-Publication Data

Madden, W.C.
   Baseball's first-year player draft, team by team through 1999 /
by W.C. Madden.
      p.   cm.
   Includes index.
   ISBN 0-7864-0960-6 (illustrated case binding : 50# alkaline paper) ∞
   1. Baseball draft — United States — History.   2. Baseball players —
United States — Registers.   I. Title.
   GV880.25.M33   2001
   796.357'0973 — dc21   00-56090

British Library cataloguing data are available

Manufactured in the United States of America

Cover image © 2001 John Olerud; photograph by Kenny Keiffer.

McFarland & Company, Inc., Publishers
  Box 611, Jefferson, North Carolina 28640
    www.mcfarlandpub.com

Contents

Abbreviations

AK: Alaska
AL: Alabama
ANA: Anaheim Angels
AR: Arkansas
ARZ: Arizona Diamondbacks
ASU: Arizona State University
ATL: Atlanta Braves
AZ: Arizona
BAL: Baltimore Orioles
BOS: Boston Red Sox
CA: California
CC: Community College
CHC: Chicago Cubs
CHW: Chicago White Sox
CIN: Cincinnati Reds
CLE: Cleveland Indians
CO: Colorado
COL: Colorado Rockies
CT: Connecticut
DC: District of Columbia
DE: Delaware
DET: Detroit Tigers
DR: Dominican Republic
FL: Florida
FLA: Florida Marlins
FSU: Florida State University
GA: Georgia
HI: Hawaii
HOU: Houston Astros
HS: High School
IA: Iowa
ID: Idaho
IL: Illinois
IN: Indiana
JC: Junior College
KCR: Kansas City Royals
KS: Kansas

KY: Kentucky
LA: Louisiana
LAD: Los Angeles Dodgers
LSU: Louisiana State University
MA: Massachusetts
ME: Maine
MD: Maryland
MI: Michigan
MIL: Milwaukee Brewers
MIN: Minnesota Twins
MN: Minnesota
MO: Missouri
MON: Montreal Expos
MS: Mississippi
MT: Montana
NC: North Carolina
ND: North Dakota
NE: Nebraska
NH: New Hampshire
NJ: New Jersey
NM: New Mexico
NV: Nevada
NY: New York
NYM: New York Mets
NYY: New York Yankees
OAK: Oakland Athletics
OH: Ohio
OK: Oklahoma
ON: Ontario
OR: Oregon
PA: Pennsylvania
PHI: Philadelphia Phillies
PIT: Pittsburgh Pirates
PR: Puerto Rico
RI: Rhode Island
SC: South Carolina
SD: South Dakota

SDP: San Diego Padres
SEA: Seattle Mariners
SFG: San Francisco Giants
STL: St. Louis Cardinals
TAM: Tampa Bay Devil Rays
TEX: Texas Rangers
TN: Tennessee
TOR: Toronto Blue Jays
TX: Texas
UCLA: University of California–Los Angeles
UNC: University of North Carolina

UNLV: University of Nevada–Las Vegas
USC: University of Southern California
UT: Utah
VA: Virginia
VT: Vermont
WA: Washington
WAS: Washington Senators
WI: Wisconsin
WV: West Virginia
WY: Wyoming

Preface

I owe the deepest gratitude to my wife for making this book possible. Without her help and patience it would never have been written. Some fellow Society for American Baseball Research members were of great assistance. Patrick Stewart labored long boring hours on lists of players and dug up research on former players for the book. Then Helena Guzman typed up that information for the book. SABR member Phillippe Cousineau from the Canadian Embassy in Rabat was of invaluable assistance in putting together the Montreal Expos chapter. I'd also like to thank SABR members Charlie Bevis and Ira Fischbein for contributing information. Several members of the Indiana Bulls, a local team that travels the country to help prospective players, helped to provide names and interviews, particularly Cliff Selery and Dave Taylor. An old friend of mine, Bob Bellone, a reporter for the *Tampa Tribune*, helped with some research and information as well. And thanks to Baseball Hall of Fame researchers in the Giamatti Research Center, particularly Tim Wiles. Their facilities were great and the people there very helpful. It's a baseball researcher's dream come true.

While I took the bulk of photos for the book, many of the photos came from Marty Orr and Jackie Dowling, who volunteered many photos from their collections. And thanks to Jolene McMeens for providing some great photos from the West Coast. As a former reporter, I was accustomed to being stonewalled occasionally from getting information. Such was the case with this book, but even more so. I sometimes felt like Rodney Dangerfield, who used to joke about not getting any respect. Authors are

not treated like the working press by most baseball teams. They are not given the same access as TV, radio or newspaper reporters. Getting credentials to have access to players was sometimes like pulling teeth. Of the 30 major league teams I requested media passes from for spring training, only a few responded favorably. The teams who gave me passes were the Florida Marlins, Philadelphia Phillies, Pittsburgh Pirates, Seattle Mariners and Toronto Blue Jays. A newspaper in Florida helped me get into one camp as one of their reporters. I also wrote many teams for photographs of draft picks from years past and only a few responded, including the ones previously mentioned. I graciously thank those media relations people for allowing me in their camp for a day or two. I'd also like to thank the Indianapolis Indians who gave me a pass for the season, which allowed me to get interviews from many players at the Triple-A level.

Major League Baseball graciously gave me permission to use any information off their web site, which proved very helpful. Most everything in this book was obtained from two or more sources, including a number of online sources. The greatest amounts of information came from team media guides and websites, newspaper articles, *The Sporting News*, *Baseball Weekly*, Microsoft Corp. and first-hand interviews with hundreds of players and baseball management personnel.

During my review of the draft lists, I even came across an interesting name: William Madden. That's my birth name. He never made it to the majors either. Neither did Joe Madden, who was picked by the San Francisco Giants in that first draft. And Andrew Madden, a first round

1

Author W. C. Madden by Janice Madden.

choice with Boston, developed arm problems early and never got past Class A ball. Only three Maddens have made it to the majors so far. I was also surprised to find a draft pick from my high school graduating class: Tom Lundgren of Rolling Meadows who graduated from Forest View High School in 1965.

I quit a full-time job to finish this book. I hope it was worth it. If you get some enjoyment and information from the book, it will be.

Introduction

When I started out to write this book about the first-year player draft, I thought about a title. The Yankees had quite a dynasty going before the draft began in 1965. And I knew Don Mattingly had never played in the World Series. So I surmised that the draft had accomplished some measure of success in bringing some competitive balance to baseball, which was one of its original intentions. "The Great Equalizer" was my first title candidate. But after months of research and interviews, I began to waver on the title.

I concluded that free agency had ruined the balance in baseball. The process did not take place overnight, for free agency was not much of a factor at first. The reason: collusion. The owners surpressed the free agency market by not bidding competitively on players. Big contracts were few and far between. This forced many players to resign with their own team rather than go before an open market where bidding could be more like an auction.

By the mid–1990s, the competitive balance the draft had brought began to erode. Weathered by free agency and baseball's becoming a world sport, the scales began to tip again to teams that had the most money and could buy their way to a championship. When the Florida Marlins won the World Series in 1997, it was obvious that powerful owners with lots of money could buy themselves a championship using free agency almost exclusively.

The Marlins began drafting players in 1992. By the 1997 season, only a few of the drafted players had gained enough experience to be able to play for the team and contribute to the championship. The rest were free agents or players acquired in trades.

In 1999 the New York Yankees won their third World Championship in four years. They have returned to their old domineering form because of free agency, not because of the draft.

Many of the small-market teams have had losing seasons since the strike-shortened 1994 season, including the Athletics, Brewers, Blue Jays, Expos, Phillies, Pirates and Twins. The Angels, Athletics, Brewers, Royals and Tigers haven't been in a World Series since the 1980s. The Astros and Expos have never been in a World Series.

The dictionary defines "draft" as a selection of personnel from a group for some particular purpose or duty. To prospective baseball players it means a lot more than that. It can mean fame and fortune. Americans, Canadians and Puerto Ricans who don't get drafted face a tougher road to get to the majors. They have to try out for a team in order to get signed. Back in the good ol' days of baseball long before the first-year player draft, teams discovered many of their players by holding tryout camps. Then teams began employing more scouts to seek out players and tryouts began to dwindle. When the draft came about, the frequency of tryout camps declined even more. Then along came the Major League Scouting Bureau to hold tryout camps throughout the land. Since teams were paying for this service, some teams completely dropped tryout camps from their vernacular. They began to send their scouts to the MLB tryouts to get a close look at prospects or simply wait for the reports that the bureau would provide.

In 1999, the Bureau held tryout camps from June 7 to June 28. Camps were scattered all over the country, but none were listed on their website for Canada or Puerto Rico where the draft extends to as well.

On the June 23, the Bureau held a tryout in Richmond, Indiana, at McBride Stadium, home of the Richmond Roosters, an independent minor league team. Players were told to report at 8:30 a.m. to register for the tryout, but registration didn't begin until after 9 a.m., which was sort of like going to a doctor's appointment early and waiting 30 minutes before seeing him.

A little after 9 a.m., Bureau area scout Mike Childers greeted the players. "If you're a drafted player, you can't participate in this camp," he told the 70 some players sitting in the warm sun in the rightfield box seats. "If you've been released from a team, you can participate. If you're injured, do not participate. High school players still in the tournament can't participate." The state finals were not being held until the weekend, so players from those eight Indiana schools were automatically ruled out. That would make it difficult for those players to participate in any Bureau tryouts, since there were few left and none scheduled for the area. And the Bureau wanted players to try out in their area according to one mother. Her son had gone to a Bureau tryout in West Virginia. After he tried out, he was told to come to Richmond to try out again because that was where the Ohio scout would be. "He tried out and they couldn't place him because he's from Ohio, so he was sent here," she explained. That wasn't explained on the Internet website that lists the tryout camps. Perhaps he should have been told that prior to wasting his time at the tryout. What difference did it make who evaluated him? The report was for the 30 major league teams and not for the Bureau.

The hopeful youngsters filled out the card they were given. They were assigned a number and that is how they would be graded. That made the evaluations more impartial. The scout explained the grading system. Grades 2 through 8 would be used with 5 being the major league average.

First was the 60-yard dash. Every player was sent down the outfield gauntlet, which had scouts and timers lined on both sides. One scout rooted for players as if it were a competition between two racers. What would impress the scouts? "If we saw someone run 6.3, we'd all shit," said the scout from a major league team.

Scouts from four teams were also at the tryout. "Then we'd ask him how old he was and if he was still in school." The best time was 6.6 seconds. The worst time was posted by a player that looked like a refugee. He ran it so slow that it looked like the race of the tortoise and the hare.

Then the young men were split up into their respective skills. Outfielders were evaluated by their ability to throw to third base and home. The infielders were checked for their fielding and how good they could throw to first base. Catchers were clocked on throws to second base.

Pitchers were evaluated for fastballs and curveballs. A bureau scout, who remains nameless because Childers wouldn't reveal his name, put a radar gun on each throw. A Richmond Roosters scout put his gun on the players as well. He was looking for right-handed pitchers who threw in the high 80s or left-handed hurlers who could manage a little less. Lefty John Hensley, a soon-to-be senior at the University of Indianapolis, was lighting up the gun in the mid-80s and gathered some attention. He was drafted in 1996 after he graduated from Fountain Central High School. Tampa Bay had picked him in the 61st round and considered him as a draft-and-follow. He didn't sign and went on to junior college then regular college. Now he was hoping to get drafted again after his senior year. Perhaps he should have signed the first time, because the Devil Rays would have worked on his strengthening and taught him more about pitching than what he could get in college.

Not lighting up the gun was Mark Squire, a senior from Wright State University, He was a submarine pitcher who had 15 saves during the year and 35 over his college career. His idol was Dan Quisenberry. "It's so frustrating, because you don't know what they're looking for," he explained about the tryout.

After the arm throwing events, the Bureau made their cuts so they wouldn't have to look at everyone hitting the ball. The players who couldn't run under seven seconds or throw for nothing were sent packing. That left the Bureau scouts just 18 players to view in the batting cage. The batting practice was held just like they do in the majors, so the scouts would get a good comparison of the hitters. Bat speed, power and stance were important. Several of the players knocked the ball out of the independent minor league park or hit the billboards in the outfield. One left-handed hitting black catcher was really impressive as he sent ball after ball over the rightfield fence. He was by far the best hitter of the group.

After the tryout, Chris Williams had some good news for a buddy of his, Steve Harris. Both impressed the Richmond scout enough to get an offer to play. Williams had set the school record for doubles (20) in a single season during his senior year at Murray State University. Harris had broken the school record for home runs (26) and tied the conference record. He would have broken the conference record had he not passed a runner who had gone back to tag up at first base. "I wasn't paying attention," Harris explained. "I was watching the ball and running hard." Ironically, the player he ran past was drafted for the major leagues and he wasn't. It was hard for his parents to understand that fact. They had gone through two days of frustration waiting for a call from a major league team that never came. The Colorado Rockies had told them they were going to draft their son, but they had changed their mind. One person had told them their son had been listed on their board to be picked in the 10th round. For some reason they will never know, his name was erased. "It's a lot of politics," his father said, dismissing the issue.

Since the draft began 35 years ago, only a few major leaguers can trace their roots to a tryout camp. Dan Driessen came from a tryout camp, according to a high school coach at the tryout. Jeff Treadway was also signed out of a tryout. There are undoubtedly more; otherwise, nobody would be conducting tryouts anymore.

Today's tryouts are a look at the bottom of the barrel, but there's always a chance not all the apples have gone rotten. Some teams have given up on the process. The Yankees don't bother anymore. They can afford not to. Other teams have decided tryouts aren't worth it, either. Both Chicago teams don't hold open tryouts. On the other hand, a few teams, like the Cincinnati Reds, hold tryout camps all over the nation in an effort to find that one player that everyone has missed. A few teams only hold them in their local area, which may be more of a public relations effort than anything else.

Another term used for tryouts is "cattle calls," because some teams will look at hundreds of players in a day or two and sign anyone who they think has potential. Tim Darmody was with Cal State Fullerton when he was invited to a tryout with the California Angels. "They cut everyone so quickly," he recalled. But he made it to the second day of the tryout before he was given the axe. The Angels signed two players out of the 300 or so players who came.

While most tryouts last a couple of hours, some go on for days. The Montreal Expos held a three-day tryout in California in 1999. The Expos also have a scout that attends a week-long school in Florida. Unlike the free tryouts, the school costs more than $500 to attend. Some players have been signed out of the school, while others considered it a waste of their time.

One of the problems with teams holding the tryouts is their lack of communicating those opportunities to prospective players. Only a couple of teams posted the tryout to their website and none of them advertised in the baseball newspapers. They did distribute news releases to the areas in which they were having them and local newspapers published the information. Only a couple of players came to one tryout held by the Texas Rangers and it was rained out. It was not rescheduled, which was disappointing to one of the players who had driven all that way for a tryout that never materialized.

Another problem with the tryouts that one team scout explained was that a lot of the good players who really qualify as prospects for the majors are already involved with summer leagues or independents. It's often better for the scouts to look at the those particular teams than waste their time with tryouts. But there's always that one in a thousand chance a player may be good enough to play in the majors someday. So tryouts will continue as long as there is baseball.

Part I

The First-Year Player Draft

A History

The push for a draft in Major League Baseball finally came to shove because bonuses were getting out of hand for owners. With no limit imposed on signing bonuses after the bonus rule was discontinued in the late 1950s, some teams began to bid heavily on prospects. Six-figure bonuses began to become commonplace in the 1960s. Bob Bailey received a record $175,000 bonus in 1961. Then in June 1964, the Los Angeles Angels signed Rick Reichardt, an outfielder from the University of Wisconsin, for $205,000. Those dollar amounts were a high price to pay for teams in those days, because they weren't generating the dollars they do nowadays from television and other sources.

The second purpose of the draft was to bring some parity to the leagues. The Yankees had long enjoyed dominance in the American League over other teams. In the National League, the Los Angeles Dodgers and San Francisco Giants, who had moved from New York, were the dominant forces. Occasionally, another team might rise to the top for a season, but their fame was always short-lived. The hope was the draft would change all that and give other franchises a chance to win a world championship or at least get to the World Series.

Owners decided something must be done and authorized commissioner Ford Frick and the league presidents to come up with a draft proposal. When the proposal came to a vote, many of the National League teams voted in favor of it and many of the American League teams voted against it by the same margin like some bills in Congress. The vote was shelved until the winter meeting after the 1964 season. The concern among some owners was that the draft could cost baseball its antitrust status, but teams were convinced otherwise and the measure was passed 13–7 at the winter meetings.

The First-Year Player Draft Rule went into effect on May 1, 1965, over the objections of a few franchises. One team director called it "communistic," a favorite term of the era due to the cold war with Russia. Another questioned its legality.

Commissioner Frick started the first draft like a court scene as he used a gavel to open the proceedings at Commodore Hotel in New York City on June 8, 1965. The clubs drafted in reverse order of their 1964 finish and the American League had the right to go first. The Kansas City Athletics started the draft process by selecting Rick Monday from Arizona State University. Monday had been offered a $20,000 bonus by the Dodgers when he completed high school. The A's gave him $104,000 to sign. The first round took just 28 minutes.

Unlike today where representatives pick the draft for the parent clubs and later assign players to wherever they chose, the players were picked for the minor league teams affiliated with the parent clubs. Each Class AAA team was entitled to two players. Each of the 20 major league teams had one Triple-A team, so rounds two and three were devoted to selecting players for that team.

The proceeding went along smoothly the first day except when the Dodgers announced a wrong player and withdrew the name from the third round. The cross-town Angels decided they wanted the player a round later.

After the third round, the Class AA draft was next. Instead of picking in reverse order of the major league team, the process went in the reverse order of the Double-A team's finish. Double-A teams got to select four players.

Class A was last and teams again picked in the reverse order of their finishes and not the major league club. There was no limit on how many players they could select for these teams. The draft did not extend down to rookie leagues.

A total of 826 players were selected over two days. Teams picked mostly high school players and 43 percent came from colleges. The Houston Astros picked the most players (72), while the Boston Red Sox picked the fewest (20).

Teams had until 15 days before the winter meeting to sign the players they drafted. Those who went unsigned would be put into a special phase of the draft. Players not drafted could be signed by any club. Teams could even draft four-year college freshmen and sophomores.

A special draft was set up in August 1965 for American Legion baseball players. A total of 11 boys were selected in that draft, which made the process a waste of time in comparison with the regular draft. The Dodgers again screwed up in this draft when they selected two players who had already been drafted in June. Apparently, they were the only players on their list, so they ended up picking no one.

Ken Holtzman was the first draftee to make it to the majors. He was drafted in the fourth round in June and was called up in September by the Cubs. The first drafted player to be inducted in the Hall of Fame was Johnny Bench, a second-round pick in the first draft.

The second draft came in January 1966 so that players who were drafted would only be committed to a team for a six-month period. This maneuver by Major League Baseball was used to appease players and those opposed to the draft. The draft was now split into two phases: regular and secondary. The regular phase was for high school graduates, junior college players and players who had reached their 21st birthday. The secondary or special phase offered teams those players who had been previously selected in the draft, but still hadn't signed and were newly eligible. The secondary draft order was out of the hat. Football and basketball players were popular picks during the 1966 draft. Most were made for publicity purposes because some players were already committed to the other sports. Getting them to sign a baseball contract was probably wishful thinking. The Dodgers drafted Mike Garrett, a great running back and Heisman Trophy winner from USC. The Yankees took Fred Biletnikoff, a quarterback from Miami University. And the Reds grabbed Archie Roberts, a Columbia quarterback. None of those players signed. The Senators turned to basketball and drafted Davidson's Dick Synder, who had been drafted by the St. Louis Hawks of the National Basketball Association. The A's drafted Cazzie Russell, a University of Michigan basketball star and the first player taken in the NBA draft. Russell hadn't played a game of baseball during his college career. The last American Legion draft was held in September 1966 and only eight players were selected.

A new rule went into effect for the regular phase of the draft in 1967. Teams could no longer draft an undergraduate player (freshman or sophomore) from a four-year university. Teams continued to draft NFL prospects. The Mets selected Ken Stabler, who went on to a long career as a quarterback. They also picked Arnie Chonko, an Ohio State linebacker. The Yankees, who got the first pick for the first and only time in draft history, took a record 74 players in the June draft.

In the January 1968 draft, a third of the players drafted were from California, showing how popular the sport was among youth in the state. Surprisingly, the Astros picked only six players in the January draft. But the owners had a lot of interests at the time: a soccer team, a hockey team, an amusement park and a circus.

During the January 1970 draft, Commissioner Bowie Kuhn warned teams not to tamper with draft picks by talking to someone who was picked by another team. MLB came out with a rule requiring teams to contact players within 15 days of the draft and sign them within six months. The contract rule would have some dire consequences for some teams 26 years later. Pittsburgh selected 30 players in the January regular draft, which was the most ever for January. And one club actually drafted a player who had been dead for a week.

The telephone was first used in January 1971 to reduce travel costs for the teams. Limiting the number of players drafted was first talked about in the June draft because clubs weren't signing late picks anyway. The talk finally became reality in 1992.

The Major League Scouting Bureau began in 1974 as 17 clubs put up about $120,000. The result was the firing of more than 250 scouts by teams to cut down on expenses. Large scouting staffs became a thing of the past and part-timers or bird-dogs wouldn't be needed as much. However, some teams became dissatisfied with the Bureau and have since hired back many of the positions they cut back on originally.

A rule change in 1976 allowed all college players between their junior and senior year to be eligible for the draft regardless of their age. The free agency ruling came about in July 1976 in an agreement worked out between the owners and players. Players with six years of major league service gained free agency status. A player could declare himself free to play with any team once his contract expired. As a result, 281 players signed multi-year contracts in 1977, and only 11 free agents changed teams after the 1977 season.

The owners introduced compensation picks in 1978 as a way to penalize teams for signing free agents. The Red Sox were affected by this decision the most as they signed three free agents, therefore losing their first three picks in the process.

The teams who signed free agents and forfeited a draft pick were:

- Boston Red Sox for signing free agents Jack Brohamer, Dick Drago and Mike Torrez
- California Angels for signing Merv Rettenmund
- Chicago White Sox for signing Ron Blomberg
- Los Angeles Dodgers for signing Terry Forster
- Milwaukee Brewers for signing Ray Fosse
- Montreal Expos for signing Ross Grimsley
- New York Mets for signing Elliott Maddox
- San Diego Padres for signing Oscar Gamble
- Texas Rangers for signing Mike Jorgensen

The teams who lost free agents and were compensated included:

- Baltimore Orioles for Elliott Maddox, Ross Grimsley and Dick Drago
- Chicago White Sox for Oscar Gamble and Jack Brohamer
- New York Yankees for Ron Blomberg and Mike Torrez
- Oakland A's for Mike Jorgensen
- Pittsburgh Pirates for Terry Forster
- San Diego Padres for Merv Rettenmund
- Seattle Mariners for Ray Fosse

Signability had been an issue for a long time with the draft and it came to a head in 1979. The Phillies didn't draft Bill Bordley because he wanted too much money and a West Coast team. Instead, they drafted and signed Mark Davis. The Reds went ahead and drafted Bordley in the first round of the January Secondary Phase and he threatened a lawsuit. The

commissioner's office stepped in and helped the Reds arrange a trade to the San Francisco Giants to pacify Bordley's desires and avoid a lawsuit.

For the first 15 years of the draft, high school players were preferred over college players. The pendulum began to swing the other way in the 1980s. College players got more attention the first two rounds than the high school prospects in 1981. Thirty-six of the 52 players chosen in first two rounds were out of college. Ten years before no college players were even drafted until the second round. The first time an agent represented a draft pick was also in 1981. Ron Darling had his agent represent him, so some teams avoided signing. He was the ninth player taken overall in the June regular draft. Today, agents are commonplace. Most players in the first round have an agent, called an "advisor," to represent them in the negotiation process.

Membership in the Major League Scouting Bureau became mandatory in 1983. Teams had to contribute to the bureau whether or not they would use the reports. And some didn't. However, most teams use the bureau as another valuable source of information. Today the Bureau provides reports and videotape on prospects to all teams.

The best players in the United States and the world, for that fact, were to play in the Olympics for the first time as baseball was a demonstration sport in 1984. Teams who picked American players wouldn't have their services for the summer. The team consisted of 30 players, 22 of which were eligible for the draft. Fifteen of the 22 were taken in the first round. Slugger Mark McGwire was one of those Olympians and was drafted by Oakland. The others included Drew Hall (Cubs), Cory Snyder (Indians), Pat Pacillo (Reds), Don August (Astros), Scott Bankhead (Royals), Norm Charlton (Expos), Mike Dunne (Cardinals), John Hoover (Orioles), Gary Green (Padres), Shane Mack (Padres) and Oddibe McDowell (Rangers).

The January 1985 draft was the first draft of foreign-born players attending school in the United States. As a result, four Canadians were taken in the process. That year qualifies as one of the best drafts ever as it was loaded with talent and some of those players ended up in the majors as all-stars, MVPs and future Hall of Famers.

While the 1984 draft scooped up some good talent from the 1984 Olympic baseball squad, several players on the team went back to finish up their degree before signing up for baseball the following year.

In the June 1985 draft, Montreal chose Pete Incaviglia, the best hitter in college history. He had a resounding .464 batting average, 48 homers and 143 RBI at Oklahoma State. He refused to sign with the Expos because he wanted to play for another team. These demands led the Expos to sign Incaviglia to a Major League contract and trade him immediately to the Texas Rangers. That led Major League Baseball to change the draft to not allow teams to trade players until one year after signing.

The January draft marked its last year in 1986. The reasons it was begun in the first place had all but vanished with free agency. Only one draft a year would be needed and no secondary round would be necessary. A new rule was put in force that gave teams a compensation pick when they were unable to sign a first-round selection or lost a player due to free agency. If a team signed a Type A free agent — a player who is ranked in the top 30 percent as determined by the Elias Sports Bureau — it would lose either its first- or second-round pick to the team it acquired the free agent from. If the team getting the free agent was in the top half of the standings, it would surrender its top pick, otherwise, its second round pick. The team losing the Type A player also gets a compensation pick, which is granted between the first and second round. If a team signed a Type B free agent — a player ranked among the top half (but not the top 30 percent) of players at his position — the club losing the free agent receives the signing club's draft pick, but no compensation pick. For a Type C player, the club losing the free agent gets a compensation pick between the second and third round. The Red Sox first benefited from the new rule in the 1987 draft.

In 1989 players from all U.S possessions were included in the draft. This rule had the largest impact on players from Puerto Rico, who had previously been scouted heavily and were free to sign with any team. Baseball had already added players from foreign countries who attended high school or college in the United States. Canada was soon added to this growing list of players coming under the draft.

The 1990 draft included two Class AA clubs, the Erie Sailors of the New York–Penn League and the Miami Miracle of the Florida State League. Rule IV draft regulations permitted minor league clubs to participate. Erie made one selection, while Miami made 16.

In 1992, Colorado and Florida were allowed to participate in the draft although they wouldn't begin playing until the next season.

Several agents in 1996 used a little loophole in the rules to get free agency for their draft picks. First there was Bobby Seay. He claimed the White Sox hadn't made a legitimate offer within the 15-day period after the draft. The White Sox tried to make offers to Seay's parents but were referred to Scott Boras, his advisor. Then they contacted Boras who didn't want to talk to the Sox unless they made an offer for more than what the Sox could afford. The White Sox could have requested a hearing, but chose not to. "What the White Sox did wrong was not fight it and go all the way," said Grady Fuson, Athletics scouting director. Several other players and agents followed suit, including A.J. Hinch from the A's. Fuson recalls telling Hinch, "We aren't going to bother you until after the Olympics." Hinch agreed with the decision, but later had second thoughts. "I don't think he had any intention of taking this through." Others who were granted free agency included Travis Lee, John Patterson and Matt White after they filed similar grievances. The new expansion teams took the golden opportunity to sign the players, but they paid millions to do so. The Arizona Diamondbacks paid Lee $10 million.

The draft moved into the computer age when the first round was broadcast live over the Internet for the first time in 1998. Television coverage could be the next step. That year also marked the first year that the draft was limited to 50 rounds.

In recent drafts, many teams decided it was best to try and wheel and deal before the draft began to try and cut down on bonus money or get a jump on other teams. The illegal practice has caught some players by surprise and made some parents furious. Teams are only allowed to offer a deal to the first pick in the draft. The player, who wanted to remain anonymous, was not selected until the sixth round. The player refused to name the team who tried to circumvent the rules, but so many teams do it that Major League Baseball must feel powerless to enforce the rules.

In 1999, a new rule allowed 21-year-old players to be drafted even if they haven't completed their junior year of college. At least one player was drafted using that new rule. The 1999 draft was peculiar for some teams. For the first time in the history of the draft, a team had four first round picks. The Orioles received those picks as compensation for losing free agents. In all, the Orioles had seven picks out of the first 50 players due to compensation. Here is the entire order of selection for the 1999 First-Year Player Draft:

First Round

1. Tampa Bay
2. Florida
3. Detroit
4. Arizona
5. Minnesota
6. Montreal
7. Kansas City
8. Pittsburgh
9. Oakland
10. Milwaukee
11. Seattle
12. Philadelphia
13. Baltimore
14. Cincinnati
15. Chicago (AL)
16. Colorado
17. Boston (from Anaheim for Mo Vaughn)
18. Baltimore (from St. Louis for Eric Davis)
19. Toronto
20. San Diego (from Los Angeles for Kevin Brown)
21. Baltimore (from Texas for Rafael Palmeiro)
22. Chicago (AL) (from New York Mets for Robin Ventura)
23. Baltimore (from Cleveland for Roberto Alomar)
24. San Francisco
25. Kansas City (from Boston for Jose Offerman)
26. Chicago (NL)
27. New York (AL)
28. San Diego
29. San Diego (from Houston for signing Ken Caminiti)
30. St. Louis (from Atlanta for signing Brian Jordan)

Sandwich Picks for Type A Players

31. Arizona (for Devon White signing with Los Angeles)
32. Kansas City (for Jose Offerman signing with Boston)
33. Seattle (for Mike Timlin signing with Baltimore)
34. Baltimore (for Roberto Alomar signing with Cleveland)
35. Chicago (AL) (for Albert Belle signing with Baltimore)
36. St. Louis (for Brian Jordan signing with Atlanta)
37. Los Angeles (for Scott Radinsky signing with St. Louis)
38. Texas (for Todd Stottlemyre signing with Arizona)
39. San Francisco (for Jose Mesa signing with Seattle)
40. Boston (for Mo Vaughn signing with Anaheim)
41. San Diego (for Kevin Brown signing with Los Angeles)
42. Houston (for Randy Johnson signing with Arizona)
43. Kansas City (for Dean Palmer signing with Detroit)
44. Baltimore (for Eric Davis signing with St. Louis)
45. Chicago (AL) (for Robin Ventura signing with New York Mets)
46. St. Louis (for Delino DeShields signing with Baltimore)
47. Texas (for Will Clark signing with Baltimore)
48. Boston (for Greg Swindell signing with Arizona)
49. San Diego (for Ken Caminiti signing with Houston)
50. Baltimore (for Rafael Palmeiro signing with Texas)

51. San Diego (for Steve Finley signing with Arizona)

Second Round

52. Tampa Bay
53. Florida
54. Kansas City (from Detroit for Dean Palmer)
55. Houston (from Arizona for Randy Johnson)
56. Minnesota
57. Montreal
58. Kansas City
59. Pittsburgh
60. Oakland
61. Milwaukee
62. San Francisco (from Seattle for Jose Mesa)
63. Philadelphia
64. Chicago (AL) (from Baltimore for Albert Belle)
65. Cincinnati
66. Chicago (AL)
67. Colorado
68. Anaheim
69. Los Angeles (from St Louis for Scott Radinsky)
70. Toronto
71. Arizona (from Los Angeles for Devon White)
72. Texas
73. New York (NL)
74. Cleveland
75. San Francisco
76. Boston
77. Chicago (NL)
78. New York (AL)
79. San Diego
80. Houston
81. Atlanta

Sandwich Picks for Type C Players

82. St. Louis (for Tom Lampkin signing with Seattle)
83. Los Angeles (for Brian Bohanon signing with Colorado)
84. New York (NL) (for Armando Reynoso signing with Arizona)

Third Round

85. Tampa Bay
86. Florida
87. Detroit
88. Boston (from Arizona for Greg Swindell)
89. Minnesota
90. Montreal
91. Kansas City
92. Pittsburgh
93. Oakland
94. Milwaukee
95. Seattle
96. Philadelphia
97. Seattle (from Baltimore for signing Mike Timlin)
98. Cincinnati
99. Chicago (AL)
100. Colorado
101. Anaheim
102. St. Louis
103. Toronto
104. Baltimore (from Los Angeles for signing Alan Mills)
105. Texas
106. New York (NL)
107. Cleveland
108. San Francisco
109. Boston
110. Chicago (NL)
111. New York (AL)
112. San Diego
113. Houston
114. Atlanta

Fourth Round

115. Tampa Bay
116. Florida
117. Detroit
118. Texas (from Arizona for signing Todd Stottlemyre)
119. Minnesota
120. Montreal
121. Kansas City
122. Pittsburgh
123. Oakland
124. Milwaukee
125. Seattle
126. Philadelphia

127. St. Louis (from Baltimore for signing Delino DeShields)
128. Cincinnati
129. Chicago (AL)
130. Colorado
131. Anaheim
132. St. Louis
133. Toronto
134. Los Angeles
135. Texas
136. New York (NL)
137. Cleveland
138. San Francisco
139. Boston
140. Chicago (NL)
141. New York (AL)
142. San Diego
143. Houston
144. Atlanta

Fifth Round

145. Tampa Bay
146. Florida
147. Detroit
148. San Diego (from Arizona for signing Steve Finley)
149. Minnesota
150. Montreal
151. Kansas City
152. Pittsburgh
153. Oakland
154. Milwaukee
155. Seattle
156. Philadelphia
157. Texas (from Baltimore for Will Clark)
158. Cincinnati
159. Chicago (AL)
160. Colorado
161. Anaheim
162. St. Louis
163. Toronto
164. Los Angeles
165. Texas
166. New York (NL)
167. Cleveland
168. San Francisco

169. Boston
170. Chicago (NL)
171. New York (AL)
172. San Diego
173. Houston
174. Atlanta

Rounds Six to Fifty

175. Tampa Bay
176. Florida
177. Detroit
178. Arizona
179. Minnesota
180. Montreal
181. Kansas City
182. Pittsburgh
183. Oakland
184. Milwaukee
185. Seattle
186. Philadelphia
187. Baltimore
188. Cincinnati
189. Chicago (AL)
190. Colorado
191. Anaheim
192. St. Louis
193. Toronto
194. Los Angeles
195. Texas
196. New York (NL)
197. Cleveland
198. San Francisco
199. Boston
200. Chicago (NL)
201. New York (AL)
202. San Diego
203. Houston
204. Atlanta

A National League club selects first in even-numbered years, and an American League club selects first in odd-numbered years. The clubs take turns selecting players in reverse order of their won-loss records at the close of the previous regular season, with National and American League clubs alternating selections.

Bonuses Getting Out of Hand

The increase in bonus money to sign players was one of the key factors that led to the first-year player draft originally. After the bonus rule went away in 1957, bonuses paid to players steadily swelled. In 1957, Bob Taylor received $108,000 from the Braves. The Orioles exceeded that figure the next year by giving Dave Nicholson $120,000. The Cubs upped the ante in 1960 by doling out $130,000 to Danny Murphy. The following year, Bob Bailey received $175,000 from the Pirates. And a year before the draft, the Angels broke the $200,000 barrier when they signed Rick Reichardt for $205,000.

When the draft began in 1965, the bonus balloon burst. No longer could players go to the highest bidder. They could negotiate with only one team. Still, the A's needed to go over $100,000 to sign Rick Monday, which was half of the previous high. The plan had worked.

Bonuses were held in check until agents came along in the 1980s to help players with the negotiation process. In 1981 only one player, pitcher Ron Darling, had an agent representing him after being drafted in the first round. Now most first rounders have an agent or an advisor. Technically, players with any college eligibility left can't have an agent per se, because they would lose their eligibility if they signed a contract with an agent. That issue is skirted by players letting an agent call himself an advisor and not signing any kind of contract. Of course, the player and advisor probably have an understanding that once the player does sign a contract with the team, the advisor turns into an agent again.

Bonuses began to escalate in the 1980s, and by the early 1990s, million-dollar signing bonuses became commonplace for the first pick. Rich teams created the inflation by giving out large bonuses to players. For example, the New York Yankees gave left-handed pitcher Brien Taylor more than a million dollars in 1992 after he graduated from high school. Now bonuses have taken off like the bull market. Nearly every player in the first round in 1999 got at least a million dollars.

Agents have become smart and learned how to effectively negotiate with the teams. For example, agents learned about the incentive bonus plans that teams would offer with hard-to-negotiate players and parents. The plan calls for a player to get bonuses for moving up the levels of baseball and getting to the majors. They have to be on the active list at the next level for 90 days before getting the bonus, so a September call-up would not qualify. Bonuses typically escalate. Many incentive bonus plans call for the player to get $1,000 for moving up to Class AA, $1,500 for Class AAA and $5,000 for the majors.

Major League Baseball tried to curb the rising costs of bonuses by creating a rule in 1992 that allowed clubs to own players' rights for five years after they were drafted. The reason they gave was to help players go to college. The union saw it otherwise, fought it and won. The rule was overturned by an independent baseball arbitrator.

Before the draft, players had no idea how they stacked up with other players. The draft now puts a number on their value. "I don't like the way it [the draft] slots the players for agents," commented Tim Perpura, the assistant general manager for the Houston Astros. "We do all the work and the agents benefit from that."

The recent high bonus packages have raised a lot of eyebrows among not only the executives in baseball, but the players themselves. "It causes problems when you have major league players who are playing every day in the big leagues and don't make the millions," said Perpura. He has heard a lot of players comment on the draft, such as: "What the hell have they proven?"

Some players are a little upset with draft picks getting bonuses as high as $4 million without playing a day in professional ball. "What these guys are getting these days is outrageous!" blurted Chris Holt, a pitcher with the Astros. "It's a lot to give an unproven player. Some of those guys are getting more than those guys in the All-Star Game. You can't blame the kids for going out and getting it."

Astros teammate Russ Johnson agreed: "It's gotten ridiculous with some of the money. Nowadays they're just giving handouts. The game is all messed up on the financial side."

Some major league players earn barely above the minimum salary of $200,000 and many draft picks these days are getting more than that in bonus money. "They're making more money than some of the guys in the big leagues," observed Pirate pitcher Jason Schmidt. "These guys should not get more money than the guy that put the time in. That's my personal opinion."

Mike Walker, a 13-year professional player, concurred with Schmidt: "My personal opinion, I don't think anybody out of high school or college is worth $6 million. I really don't think anyone is worth $1.5 million. There's no 18 year old or 20 year old worth that kind of money. He's done nothing for professional baseball. If you're that good you're going to make the money in the big leagues. Yes, they deserve something for being possibly the best players coming in the draft — millions of dollars, no. If that's the case, what does he have to work for. Here's $6 million kid. Gee I don't have to do anything the rest of my life. That's why a lot of these number 1 picks are getting hurt or they're just falling on their face because they have nothing to work for."

Gary Thurman, a first round pick by the Royals, saw a situation similar to what Walker was describing. A draft pick who got nearly a million-dollar bonus was ready to quit after one season. "They begged him to stay because of all that money they had invested in him," Thurman explained.

Not all players think the bonuses are too high. Sean Casey, who received a healthy bonus when he was drafted in the second round in 1995, felt a little different than Walker. "I guess I have a lot of mixed emotions," he explained. "I guess more power to him to get what he can get. Not to play a game and get $10 million, more power to him."

Some players share Casey's opinion because of where we live — America, which is the land of opportunity and great wealth. With some business executives making billions, the millions made by players seems small in comparison.

Many players and executives agree that the signing bonuses are getting out of hand. The money spent on bonuses could be used to give more money to minor league players and increase their quality of life. "I think one great injustice that is going on right now is our first-year players are making $850 a month for a five-month period. I think that's really unfortunate," explained Perpura.

Minor league players don't get a large minimum salary like the major league players, because they are not part of the player's association. But the draft is tied to collective bargaining, so the players' union would have to concur with any change to it, such as a salary bonus cap like the National Basketball Association. "I think we're headed to changes, because of the finances of it," observed Chuck LaMar, Tampa Bay Devil Rays general manager. "We're starting to pay astronomical bonuses in our sport and yet our players might be two, three and four years away from the major leagues. It's a very high-risk business."

Some executives in baseball feel a cap is needed on bonuses because small-market teams can't afford to play the high premiums that some of the players and their agents are seeking. Such was the case with the highly publicized J.D. Drew situation. Drew was drafted in the first round by the Philadelphia Phillies in 1997 and his agent, Scott Boras, wanted the Phillies to cough up $10 million in bonus money. The Phillies wouldn't, so Drew played independent ball for a season before he was put back in the draft the following season.

Boras, like most agents, would oppose a salary cap on bonuses because they eventually become the winners in the situation as well. "Amateurs' values should not be dependent on unilateral rules imposed by the major-league teams," Boras wrote for ESPN Sportszone. "History shows such trust would be misplaced. The clubs have reaped the benefits of the current draft system for more than 30 years. Now they should pay fairly. It is time for a change through collective bargaining."

Not only do agents press for higher bonuses, but so do parents. "Every mom and dad thinks their son should get a million dollars," commented Bob Turzilli, an Atlanta scout for a quarter of a century.

After a salary cap of a million dollars was put on drafted rookies in the National Basketball Association in 1998, the baseball players' association came out and said it would oppose any kind of salary cap for professional baseball players. So if the owners try and institute a salary cap, they will undoubtedly find a lot of opposition from the union.

A cap puts a restriction on free enterprise, but so does a draft for that fact. Free enterprise really has nothing to do with the situation. A company can pay a salaried person anything they want if both parties agree to it.

Sports agent Jeff Borris wrote that small-market teams should move or go out of business instead of looking for help through revenue sharing or salary caps. Even if the franchises were moved to bigger markets, some markets would still be larger than others.

A structured salary for the minor leagues may be a better answer, suggested Tampa Bay scouting director Dan Jennings. He suggested a plan that would pay $25,000 to a Class A player, $50,000 for Class AA and $75,000 for Class AAA players. That would insure a pay raise for each player as they climbed up the ladder. A structured salary would eliminate the "greed factor," he explained.

And if the draft was eliminated, there would be no assurance than bonuses would go down. On the average they would likely go up. In any case, getting a handle on the escalating bonuses will certainly be a challenge for teams in the future.

Draft Is Highway to Majors

For some major league players, baseball began when they could throw a ball. At five, their father entered them in T-ball where they swatted at a ball on a rubber stand. They wore a T-shirt and a hat that indicated they were on the Yankees, or Cubs. Or their beginnings were a more modest as they fashioned a stick and ball and played the game on the street in front of the house. Then it was on to Little League where they got their first taste of what the draft would be like. They tried out for a position in front of managers who would pick them for the majors or send them packing to the minors or to some other league. After that it was some sort of advance league for teenagers. And they took up the sport in high school, working their way up to the varsity team and earning a letter on their jacket.

The first-year player draft process usually starts for players when they reach high school, although some scouts actually begin to get wind of a talented player in Little League, Babe Ruth or some pre–high school league.

In high school, players on the varsity squad get surveyed by the scouts, so if a freshman lands on the team, he can get exposed to scouts for four years. Exposure is the key, because if a scout doesn't see a player and evaluate them, they can't draft them. The more a player is seen by scouts,

the more he has a chance of getting picked. Because scouting is somewhat subjective, not every scout looks at every player like every other scout. Some scouts are looking for players with particular skills, because their team needs that type of player. For a position player, scouts typically look at five tools: running speed, arm strength, hitting with consistency, fielding and hitting with power. For a pitcher, the pluses are for a fastball with movement, a good curveball, a smooth delivery, control and poise. Some teams really delve into the makeup of a player and give out psychological tests, such as the Minnesota Multiphase Personality Index or Athletic Motivation Inventory. The scouts will also talk with the manager, coaches and the parents to find out more.

The process can become grueling for really good players who attract attention. Joe Lawrence, who was drafted by the Toronto Blue Jays in the first round in 1996, remembered one game where there were 12 general managers and 70 scouts from major league teams and colleges in the stand. "I'd come home from school and they'd be waiting in the driveway," he explained, adding that he felt they should have been more discreet. He actually changed the number on his jersey to hide from some scouts. He was heavily scouted for both football and baseball. And agents came after him like flies on a dead raccoon. "I don't know how I handled it," he said. "I was bombarded."

Lawrence was also bombarded by agents. The movie *Jerry McGuire* starring Tom Cruise was no exaggeration on how aggressive agents can be sometimes. High draft picks get called time and time again by some Jerry McGuires looking for big commissions later when the player makes it to the majors. "It's probably more solicitous and more competitive than anything I've ever seen," said David Taylor, an agent and attorney from Indianapolis. Taylor knows a

Tom Mastny

lot of good agents, but there are some bad apples out there. "There's no gate to keep anyone out," he explained. "There are no requirements to become or remain an agent."

Then there's the opposite situation — a player who is playing for a small school in a small town who would like to get drafted but scouts aren't coming to see him. Tom Mastny, a six-foot-six right-handed pitcher from Zionsville, Indiana, was one of those players. He had put up some impressive numbers in high school, but he went unnoticed by the scouts.

A player first becomes eligible for the draft once they are a senior in high school. If they are drafted before they actually graduate or before their team finishes playing in any state tournaments, they must wait until after graduation or the playoffs before signing. A team may decide to draft the player and follow him for a year before signing him. This is called a draft-and-fol-

low. If the player still decides not to sign after a year, he goes back into the draft pool for the next year. If he goes back into the pool and the same team wants to draft him again, they have to get his permission. This rule allows players to get away from a team they don't want to be drafted by, which gives them a little freedom of choice. Now, let's say the freshman at this junior college gets drafted, but he decides to attend his sophomore year. Once he finishes his sophomore year, he can either sign with the team that drafted him or go on to a four-year university. They he would be eligible to be drafted again after his junior year. Then if he decides not to sign, he can attend his senior year and be eligible again after he graduates from college, unless he's a fifth-year senior or goes on to graduate school. It's rare for college juniors to complete their senior year after being drafted because they lose any leverage they had once they graduate. But some players are good enough that it doesn't make a difference. Those are few and far between. This could go on forever as long as the player decides to go to college, but we will stop here. When the draft was every six months, some players were drafted as many as six or seven times. Now, three times is more realistic. An exception to the above rule is if the player has reached age 21. Once they have reached 21, they can be drafted regardless of what year they are in college.

"It's not what you know, it's who you know" many times plays a significant role for people in getting jobs in the business world. Baseball is similar to a certain extent, but the saying has to be changed to: "It's not how good you are, it's who you are." Many relatives of major leaguers get picked for the draft or get elevated in the selection process because teams realize they are related to someone previously in the game. The players have shown they have some talent, but because they are related to someone in the game, they may get a littler higher consideration. Or they are drafted only to get them a baseball scholarship to a school. After the draft, the relationship won't count for much of anything. Only skill will get the player to the majors and a successful career there.

On the day of the draft, most clubs will call the players they have selected to give them the good news and make them an offer for a contract. An offer is required within 15 days of the draft or the player becomes a free agent. If the team cannot notify the player, they may call the university the player attended. "I've heard stories about players who the teams couldn't find," said Brett Johnson, who once worked as an intern for the Sports Information Office at the University of Kentucky.

NCAA rules say a player cannot embrace an agent until after college. Many players do though, but teams usually don't make an issue over it and the NCAA can hardly enforce it. To avoid legal problems with the NCAA, they call their agents "advisors." But we all know who the advisor is and what they are after. Most agents want 2 to 5 percent piece of the actions. Some don't want anything until after a player reaches the majors, while others sap money off the players all the way up to the time they make the majors. If the agent is a bonafide agent as recognized by the Player's Association, they can't collect any money until the player reaches the majors.

For most American players, the first-year player draft is the expressway to the majors.

Is Parity Coming to an End?

The second reason the draft was implemented in 1965 was to bring some equality to the league. Several teams in baseball had gone decades without even an appearance in the World Series. By the early 1990s, the competitive balance the draft had brought began to erode like the coliseum in Rome. Weathered by years of free agency and baseball becoming a world sport, the scales began to tip more again to teams who had the most money and could buy their way to a championship.

Free agency came about in the mid-1980s and baseball tried to adjust to the situation by implementing compensation picks to teams losing players to free agency. Most teams were compensated with a pick between the first and second round, so compensation players became known as sandwich picks. The players picked up as compensation began appearing in the majors in the early 1990s and haven't made the impact that baseball had hoped for. Giving up draft picks as compensation doesn't seem to be the answer, because a team is losing a proven player and getting just prospects in return. The prospects may never get to the majors. If money had been put in the formula as compensation as well, the team losing the free agent would get something more tangible that it could use later. The money could be used to purchase a free agent. Instead, baseball imposed a luxury tax. Padres manager Bruce Bochy felt a strong type of revenue sharing was needed. "We need to have a little more of a level playing field," he explained. "You have to give the smaller-market clubs a chance."

When the Florida Marlins won the World Series in 1997, it was obvious that a powerful owner with lots of money could buy themselves a championship using free agency almost exclusively. The Marlins didn't begin drafting players until 1992. By 1997, only a few of the drafted players had achieved enough experience to be able to play for the team and contribute to the championship.

In 1999 the Yankees won their third World Championship in four years. The team included several high-priced free agents former draft picks, high-priced free agent foreigners and just a few of their own draft picks. The team was not built from the bottom up. It was more like from the top down.

In another example from that year, Jerry Colangelo spent big bucks on several free agents to bring a winner to Arizona before the draft could take any effect on the team. The strategy worked as the franchise went from last place in 1998 to first place in 1999 on the strength of the free market.

However, spending a lot of money on a team is not necessarily going to assure a winning team. The Baltimore Orioles threw a lot of money at players in 1998 and finished with a losing record. They then began 1999 like an expansion team and had achieved one of the worst records in baseball by the time April ended. And getting squashed by Cuba in early May didn't help matters either.

Signs that the natives were getting restless appeared during the 1999 season when Kansas City fans wearing T-shirts that read "Share the Wealth" showed up when the Yankees came to town. The protest was organized by radio station KCTE to bring attention to the growing disparity between big market teams like the Yankees and small market teams like Kansas City.

About 3,000 fans loaded the left-field bleachers for the game. When the Yankees came to bat, they turned their backs. Then they chanted "share the wealth" and "Let's go Royals." In the fourth inning they all filed out, which

took nearly 15 minutes. One protester held a sign that read "George Steinbrenner — Death of Baseball."

If more fans get into the act, baseball could have itself a revolution of sorts. If anything, fans like voters carry a lot of power in numbers and can influence changes in baseball more than just a few voices. More changes to the draft are bound to come about to bring more equality to the game in order for franchises to compete successfully. However, no matter what restrictions are imposed, it is doubtful Major League Baseball will ever achieve total parity. The rich franchises will always have the upper hand somehow.

"It's my belief there'll never be parity," said Dan Jennings, the Tampa Bay scouting director.

The Future of the Draft

With bonuses escalating and parity dwindling, some changes in the draft seem likely, but drastic changes are usually slow to come. "I think the draft needs reform," said Texas scouting director Chuck McMichael. "It's no longer assisting the teams who finished last the year before." Several scouting directors agree with McMichael and changes are inevitable to go along with the changing times. "We're going to have to do something," concurred Chet Montgomery, a special assistant to the Pittsburgh general manager. Here are a few revisions that baseball executives are mulling over with the draft.

International Draft

Major League Baseball did a study of opening day rosters in 1998 and found that players came from 17 different countries. About 20 percent of the players came from countries other than the United States. The most came from the Dominican Republic, where all teams are recruiting players. Other countries included Cuba and other islands in the Caribbean, Panama, Mexico, Venezuela, South Korea, Japan and Australia.

Baseball is emerging in many other countries now that the sport is part of the Olympics. Certain players have put some countries on the baseball map. Hensley "Bam Bam" Meulens, who signed a contract with the Yankees in 1985,

was the first player from Curacao, an island 25 miles off the coast of Venezuela, after he was called up to the Braves. Pitcher Dennis Martinez made Venezuela famous when he was referred to in the movie *Under Fire* with Nick Nolte.

The only country the draft affects right now is Canada; however, the draft also applies to foreigners who attend American schools. That is why some players from other countries have already been drafted.

When baseball became an Olympic sport in 1984, the game became more global than in the past. "I see more happening in Europe in five to 10 years," said Texas Rangers scouting director Chuck McMichael. "There are other countries that are now starting to produce."

Some major league teams have expanded their scouting staffs internationally to scoop up some of this talent before other teams can. Small market teams, however, can't afford to hunt all over the world for talent.

Opinions about an international draft run the gamut.

"I'm on the fence with an international draft," McMichael admitted. "I see so many problems with an international draft."

Pat Daugherty, vice president of scouting at Colorado, favors an international draft. "The prices are going off the wall," he explained. "That's because agents are traveling to international markets to recruit players themselves. It would level the playing field for all clubs."

Tim Perpura, the assistant general manager of the Astros, is not in favor of an international draft. He would not like to see any draft for that fact.

"The way the salaries are escalating, an international draft is the only way we can control bonuses," said Atlanta Braves scout Sherrard Clinkscales. He thinks an international draft would give small market teams a better chance at winning.

A lot of American players are in favor of an international draft because foreigners would then be in the same boat as them. "I think everyone should be in the draft," said Tom Davy, a player with the Toronto Blue Jays.

ESPN's Peter Gammons explained on *Baseball Tonight* that an international draft would likely hurt foreign players. He pointed to Puerto Rico as a prime example of that. The draft expanded to Puerto Rico in 1989 and not one good player has come out of that country since, because now teams can't develop players at a younger age like they were doing before. "Owners that want the Dominican Republic subject to the draft should understand how much development takes place at the age of 16 and 17 in baseball complexes in that country," he explained.

Is an international draft around the corner? "You can almost bet on that happening," commented Montgomery.

Trading Draft Picks

Many of the other professional sports allow teams to trade draft picks, but baseball has never allowed it. In fact, teams are not allowed to trade a draft pick until one year after signing. This restriction came about when Pete Incaviglia demanded to be traded or else not sign a contract with Montreal after being drafted by the team.

Trading draft picks would likely be more beneficial to smaller market teams, because they are currently trapped in a Catch-22 situation. A small-market team cannot afford to spend millions of dollars in bonus money, so they are avoiding drafting some players because they know they won't be able to offer them enough money to sign them. Take the J.D. Drew situation that occurred in 1997. His agent, Scott Boras, figured he could

get about $10 million for the prospect, but the Phillies drafted him and didn't want to pay that kind of money. So Drew didn't sign and the Phillies lost out. The Phillies were compensated with a first-round pick the next year, but the fact remains they couldn't afford to pay the player they had picked. And compensation doesn't fully make up for what the Phillies lost. In fact, a team could get caught in a loppy-de-loop.

College Players Only

One idea suggested by Tim Bogar, a player with the Houston Astros, would be to eliminate the drafting of high school players. "If they did, there wouldn't be so much pressure on the kids," he explained. In that manner, the minors could be reduced to one team per level, he recommended. The draft would then be more like the NFL or NBA, who draft mostly college players.

Signing Bonuses

The draft is tied to the collective bargaining process, so any changes to it must also be approved by the Players Association. This will make it tough for baseball to put a salary cap on drafted players like the National Basketball Associations has imposed. However, other changes could win the approval of the players.

Other Changes

The draft is currently held in early June when some high school and college players are still playing with their school team. The answer would be to move the draft to July, suggested Terry Wetzel, scouting director for the Kansas City Royals.

The baseball draft went on the Internet in 1999, but it has never been televised. "I think they should televise it like basketball and football," said James Clark, an outfielder with the Seattle Mariners.

Atlanta scouting director Paul Synder would like to retain rights of players for a longer time when they attend college. Currently, a team only retains the rights of a player until a week before the next draft. "I'd like to give players a chance to reconsider," he explained. Instead of a draft-and-follow program that lasted one year, it could go for three or four years.

Part II

The Draft by Team

Part II is organized by league and then by current team name as of 1999:

American League

Anaheim Angels

Baltimore Orioles

Boston Red Sox

Chicago White Sox

Cleveland Indians

Detroit Tigers

Kansas City Royals

Minnesota Twins

New York Yankees

Oakland Athletics

Seattle Mariners

Tampa Bay Devil Rays

Texas Rangers

Toronto Blue Jays

National League

Arizona Diamond-
backs

Atlanta Braves

Chicago Cubs

Cincinnati Reds

Colorado Rockies

Florida Marlins

Houston Astros

Los Angeles Dodgers

Milwaukee Brewers

Montreal Expos

New York Mets

Philadelphia Phillies

Pittsburgh Pirates

St. Louis Cardinals

San Diego Padres

San Francisco Giants

The appendix provides a list of all players selected in the first-year player draft since 1965. Full information (round, name, position, birthplace, school, year and team the player debuted in the majors, number of years with that team, number of years in the majors) is provided on draft picks who appeared in the major leagues. For example:

> *1— Jim Spencer, 1b; B: Hanover, PA; Andover HS, Glen Burnie, MD; 1968 CAL (6) (15)*

AMERICAN LEAGUE

Los Angeles/California/Anaheim Angels

The Angels franchise began operation four years before the first-year player draft began. At that time was known as the Los Angeles Angels. Right after the draft began, the team changed its name to California Angels when owner Gene Autry moved the team to Anaheim Stadium. It took nearly two decades before the franchise became a contender, and the team still has yet to get to the World Series. The Angels won its first division championship in 1979 under Jim Fregosi, yet the team fell short in the League Championship Series. Then Gene Mauch guided the team to two other division crowns, but the team again failed to win the LCS. In 1997, the franchise changed its name to Anaheim Angels. They are affectionately known as the Halos.

Many of the Angels' good picks over the years, especially pitchers, charged out of the gate like they were going to be great finds only to poop out in the stretch and finish poorly. A look at the three first-place teams shows that the team

had few of its own draft picks in the mix. The 1979 and 1982 teams had just a couple of players that were California bred, while the 1986 team had a handful of original picks: Wally Joyner, Chuck Finley, Devon White, Kirk McCaskill and Dick Schofield. The team also made some poor trades along the way that didn't help much. The Angels really haven't relied on the draft that much in trying to be a winner. It has perhaps tried to rely too much on veteran talent rather than building from within.

The Angels have dipped into the free agent market a lot over the years and have traded many of their own draft picks. For example, Richard Dotson, Alan Wiggins, Paul Sorrento, Dennis Rasmussen and Dave Engle were all drafted by the Angels and traded to other teams before they ever got a shot at the majors. And all of these players went on to many years of service with other teams. Or the team has had a hair trigger on some players and traded them long before they matured. Willie Aikens, Thad Bosley, Dante Bichette, Tom Brunasky and Rance Mulliniks all came up with the Angels, but spent just a year or two with the team before getting traded.

The Angels have gotten away from trading some of its best prospects in the 1990s. The roster now has many players — Garrett Anderson, Darin Erstad, Jason Dickson, etc. — that came up through the Angels farm system. The result is a second-place finish in 1998.

Over the years, the Angels have concentrated heavily on proven college players from four-year universities rather than the raw talent of high school players. Only 20 percent of their picks in 1998 were from high school.

The Angels have a larger than average scouting department, which is headed by Bob Fontaine, Jr. The department covers the United States and Canada with 18 area scouts, four supervisors and two national crosscheckers. They have seven scouts looking at the major leagues, which is one of the largest efforts in the majors. They have a presence in the international market, too. Besides an academy in the Dominican and a presence in Mexico, they are scouring the Far East for players. The Angels have given up on holding open tryouts for players who weren't drafted.

In 1999, the Angels didn't have a first-round pick due the signing of free agent Mo Vaughn. Half of the 49 picks in 1999 were pitchers. A breakdown of the 21 players picked by the Angels included 29 collegiate players, 12 community college players and eight high schoolers.

Best Draft Picks

The best draft pick in Angels' history has to be **Chuck Finley**, a first-round pick in the January 1985 draft secondary phase. The left-handed hurler from Northeast Louisiana University was 3-1 with five saves in Class A Salem his first year. After not allowing an earned run in 10 relief appearances with six saves to start the 1986 season, the Angels brought him up to the majors as a reliever. In 1988, he was turned into a starter for the team. His best seasons so far came in 1990 and 1991 when he had identical 18-9 records for the Halos. Finley has been the

Brian Anderson, drafted by the Angels. (Photograph by Marty Orr.)

ace of the staff during the 1990s and appeared in two All-Star games. He has compiled a 153-129 record in 13 seasons with the Angels.

Another proficient pitcher who was an Angels original was **Andy Messersmith**, a first-round pick in the June Secondary Phase in 1966. Two years later he was pitching in the majors for California. By 1971 he was a 21-game winner for the Angels and was named to his first All-Star team. The following season he slumped due to arm injuries, and the Angels decided to trade him to the Dodgers. He rebounded the following season and was back up to 20 wins again in 1974. He got out of the blocks quickly in 1974 to earn the starting spot in the All-Star game with his 11-2 mark before the break. His 20 wins helped the Dodgers to win a pennant and the League Championship Series. He didn't have much success in the World Series and the Athletics went on to their third straight championship. When he refused to sign a contract the next season, he helped set the stage for free agency. A bidding war for his services ensued and the Braves ended up playing him $1.75 million for a multi-year deal.

Pitcher **Frank Tanana** helped the Angels to the playoffs in 1979. The first-round pick

Mark Sweeney with Cincinnati, drafted by the Angels. (Photograph by Marty Orr.)

from 1971 pitched eight seasons for California. The starter's best year with the Angels came in 1976 when he was 19-10. He led the league in strikeouts in 1975. He had another great year in 1977 as he led the league in ERA with 2.54 and shutouts with seven. Tanana was traded in 1981 to Boston in a multi-player trade. He went on to pitch 20 seasons in the majors.

Kirk McCaskill, a fourth-round pick in 1982 from the University of Vermont, was a starting pitcher for seven seasons with the Angels. He spent three years in the minors before getting called up in 1985. In his sophomore year, he helped the Angels to the League Championship Series with a 17-10 mark, but he was clobbered in the playoffs with two losses. After two off years, he was 15-10 in 1989 with a 2.93 ERA. After leading the American League in losses with 19 in 1991, he was shown the door. The free agent signed with the White Sox and pitched for five more seasons.

The Angels selected pitcher **Jim Abbott** from the University of Michigan in the first round in 1988. He went off to pitch in the Olympics before beginning his professional career. In the championship game, the left-handed hurler, who lacked a right hand, threw a seven-hitter in a 5–3 victory over Japan to win the gold for the United States. The following year Abbott became the 15th draft pick to go directly to the majors. He pitched four seasons with the Angels and got better each year, but California didn't give him much run support. Despite an excellent 2.77 ERA in 1992, his record was 7-15. The Angels traded him to the Yankees in 1992. He returned to California in 1995 in a trade with the White Sox. Then in 1996, he had lots of trouble getting hitters out and his ERA ballooned to 7.48, resulting in a 2-18 record, the most losses in the American League. The Angels released him after spring training in 1997 and he sat out the season. He made a comeback in 1998 with the White Sox, pitching his way up through the minors and back to the majors where he was 5-0. The comeback showed Abbott's determination in overcoming adversity. His disability never stopped him from being an excellent fielder, and he got his first hit as a batter in 1999 with Milwaukee before being released again.

Three was a lucky number for one Angels player. **Wally Joyner**, a third-round pick in 1983, spent three seasons in the minors. He was an Eastern League all-star in 1984. In his first season in the majors, Joyner came out of the blocks so quickly that he became the first rookie to start in an All-Star Game since the fans began voting. By the break he had slammed 20 homers, knocked in 73 RBI and was hitting .313. After the Midsummer Classic, he melted under the summer sun and hit just two more homers the rest of the season and ended with 100 RBI, still an amazing stat for a rookie. He bettered that the next season when he knocked in 117 RBI, second to Jose Canseco. California became "Wally's World" for five more seasons before he signed a free agent contract with Kansas City, who later traded him to San Diego where he helped the Padres to the World Series in 1998.

Three times was the charm for **Gary DiSarcina**, a sixth rounder in 1988. He was called up three times to California before he finally stuck for good in 1991 after a great season at Edmonton where he hit .310 and was the Pacific Coast League's best shortstop, going 29 games without an error. In his rookie season, he had the second most hits on the club and led the American League in assists, total chances and errors. His best season with the bat so far came in 1995 when he batted .307. He was also named to an All-Star game in his first decade with the team.

The Angels pulled the trigger too quickly on **Tom Brunansky** when they traded him along with Mike Walters for Doug Corbertt and Rob Wilfong. Brunansky, a first rounder in 1978, won a spot in the outfield on Opening Day in 1981; however, he lasted only a month on the team and was sent back to Triple-A to improve on his .152 average. He did just that by hitting 22 homers and 10 triples for Salt Lake City. "Bruno" was sent to the Minnesota Twins the next year where he found the indoor stadium much to his liking as he hit two inside-the-park homers to go along with 18 others in his rookie season. His 32 homers helped the Twins to the World Series in 1987. During his 13-year career, he hit 271 dingers and was named to the All-Star Team once.

Devon White, a sixth round pick in 1981, helped his progress in the minors when he was named to the California All-Star Team in 1984. He got a call up to the majors the next September, but failed to hit his weight. The next September he showed he was ready for the majors and the Angels made him a regular after that. In his rookie season, he knocked a career high 24 homers. By 1988 he was earning Gold Gloves in the outfield and did so seven more times in his career, which was still going at this writing. He also has been named to two All-Star games. After a disappointing 1990 season, the Angels traded him to Toronto, where he rebounded back to his old form.

The Angels traded **Rance Mulliniks** after he was hitting just .147 in his third season with the team. The excellent fielding infielder was a couple of years away from maturing in the majors. He wasn't given a full-time job until he was traded to Toronto where he was given the third base job. Mulliniks had his career year in 1984 when he batted .324. He led the American League in fielding his position that year, although he didn't pick up a Gold Glove. He

helped the Blue Jays to the League Championship three times during his 16-year career in the majors.

Included in that trade with Mulliniks to Kansas City was **Willie Mays Aikens**, a powerful hitter. After going to the Royals, he helped the team to the World Series where he hit four homers over the six-game series. He continued to hit double-digit homers over the next three seasons. After the 1983 season, he was arrested for drug possession and plea bargained his way to a one-year sentence. Commissioner Bowie Kuhn reinstated him and he stayed two more seasons in the majors before he sent back to the minors. Then he went to the Mexican League where he clobbered the pitching with a .454 batting average, 46 homers and 154 RBI in one season.

The Mulliniks/Aikens trade has to go down in Angels history as one of its worst trades. For Mulliniks and Aikens, the Angels got Al Cowens, pitcher Todd Cruz and pitcher Craig Eaton. They kept Cowens for a couple of months before dealing him to Detroit for Jason Thompson, who they kept for just two seasons. Eaton and Cruz never pitched a game for the Halos.

Another poor trade that the Angels made involved two of their own draft picks — Richard Dotson and Thad Bosley — for Brian Downing, Chris Knapp and Dave Frost with the White Sox.

Richard Dotson was a promising prospect in the Angels minor league system when he was shipped to Chicago. He helped the Southsiders to the League Championship Series in 1983 when he had the best season of his career as he led the league in winning percentage, .759, with a 22-7 record on the season. He was named to the All-Star Team that year and was a candidate for the Cy Young Award. His effectiveness deteriorated after that season. By 1986 he had the most losses in the American League with 17. In all, he pitched 11 seasons in the majors with a 111-113 record.

Thad Bosley was another player the Angels held on to for just one season before trading him. The fourth-round draft pick was the best player in the Angels minor league system in 1976 when he stole 90 bases and was named California League's Most Valuable Player. The following season the Angels brought him up and he hit .297. The Angels traded him the next season to the White Sox. Bosley was often injured and went to several teams before finding his best role — a pinch hitter. With the Cubs, he helped them to a division championship in 1984 and twice led the National League in pinch hits.

The Angels drafted **Paul Sorrento** in the fourth round in 1986. After three seasons in Class A, the Angels traded him in a multi-player deal with the Twins. He shined the next season and was named Southern League all-star at Double-A Orlando. The Twins called him up that year. In 1991, he made it to the majors for good after being named Pacific Coast League Player of the Week honors when he hit .524 one June week. He was traded to Cleveland for a couple of hurlers and there he became a better hitter. He helped the Indians to the World Series in 1995. Then he slugged a career high 32 homers in 1996.

Tim Salmon was a third round pick in 1989 out of Grand Canyon University. He was a great player in the minors and picked up all sorts of accolades, including Triple-A Player of the Year. He didn't disappoint the Angels when they raised him to the majors in 1993. He was named Rookie of the Year after hitting 31 homers in his rookie season. In seven seasons with the Angels, he had clubbed 179 homers and knocked in over 100 RBI twice.

Long Shots

Coming from a small college can have its drawbacks because scouts aren't going to pay as much attention. The result is that some players get drafted late or not at all. In 1989, **Chad Curtis** played with Grand Canyon College and slugged 19 homers while hitting .369. He established an NAIA record by scoring six runs in one game on April 15. The result was a 45th round pick in the draft. He signed with the California Angels and went to Mesa where he hit .303 and was promoted to Class A Quad City. The following season he was second in the league in batting average (.307) and stolen bases (64), which sent him quickly up the ladder to Triple-A in 1991. He again racked up some good numbers and was picked for the Triple-A All-Star

Team. Then he went to winter ball in Venezuela and was named Most Valuable Player. The Angels had seen enough and put him on the Opening Day roster in 1992. He led American League outfielders in assists in his first season. The following year he avoided the sophomore jinx and improved on all of his numbers. After three seasons with the Angels, he was traded to Detroit. Then he went to the Dodgers, Indians and Yankees.

Another long shot that made the roster as a regular was **Damon Easley**, a 30th round pick out of Long Beach Community College in 1988. Unlike most 30th round picks, he breezed

Damon Easley with the Detroit Tigers; he was drafted by the Angels in the 30th round in 1988. (Photograph by Marty Orr.)

through the minors in three-and-a-half years and arrived at the Angels in 1992. After four seasons with the Angels, he was traded to the Tigers for pitcher Greg Gohr. Easley has found Tiger Stadium more to his liking and hit a career-high 27 homers in 1998.

Dante Bichette was a 16th round pick in

the 1984 draft and progressed slowly through the minors. Not until he got to Triple-A Edmonton did he begin to shine and hit .300 on the season with 13 homers. The following season he got a call to the Angels and became a regular in 1990. He showed he had a great arm by throwing out 12 runners that season and hit 15 homers. The Angels traded him to Milwaukee for an over-the-hill Dave Parker. Bichette stayed two years for the Brewers before being traded to the Rockies where he found the high air more to his liking. He hit a career high 40 homers in 1995, and he knocked in more than 100 four years running. That earned him three trips to the All-Star Game.

The Angels took a chance at **Tony Chavez** with their 50th round pick in the 1992 free-agent draft. The right-handed reliever responded well and rode a roller coaster through the minors until he found success at Triple-A Vancouver in 1997. After saving 15 games, the Angels called him up in September 1997. He allowed only one run in seven innings that month, but the Angels sent him back to Vancouver for the 1998 season. Perhaps he'll get another shot later. He's already beat the odds.

Disappointments

The Angels have had good success with their first pick in the June regular drafts, because they have signed mainly proven talent out of college. However, there have been some disappointments.

The first disappointment for the Angels came in the second draft. They picked **Jim De-Neff** from Indiana University. The shortstop got as far as Triple-A. The same fate came to **Mike Nunn**, a high school catcher who was a first-round pick in 1967.

The Angels couldn't sign their first-round pick in June 1969. **Alan Bannister** decided to go on to college and later played 12 seasons in the majors with five other teams.

Billy Taylor, a first round pick in 1973, never got past Class A. He was an outfielder out of high school.

In 1983, the Angels picked **Mark Doran** first. The outfielder from the University of Wisconsin peaked at Triple-A.

The latest disappointment in the Angels camp is **Jeff Schmidt**, a first-round pick from 1992. The right-handed pitcher from the University of Minnesota was a real loser in the minors, compiling a 10-41 record in seven season. The Angels gave him a call up in 1996. The result was disgusting: 7.88 ERA. The Angels tried him as both a starter and reliever, but decided to let him go in October 1998. He signed with the Indians.

Undrafted Player

Pitching is the most sought after commodity in the draft. **Bryan Harvey** was not drafted after high school and he dropped out of the University of North Carolina at Charlotte. However, Angels bird dog scout Alex Cosmidis gave Harvey a try out in 1984 and liked what he saw. The right-hander went on to become a stopper for the Angels and sign a $15.5 million multi-year contract in 1992. Then he signed a $4.5 million contract with the Marlins in 1995 before an arm injury diminished his value and prevented him from playing in 1996.

Where Are They Now?

The Angels gave up on **McKay Christenson** before they ever saw him play in the minors. The 1994 first rounder was dealt to the White Sox after he spent two years in Japan to complete his Mormon mission. The outfielder made his debut in 1999 out of spring training. He jumped all the way from Class A.

P.J. Forbes was drafted in the 20th round in 1990 by the Angels. "I was just hoping to be drafted," explained the second baseman who had graduated from Wichita State University. The long shot didn't get much of a bonus. "If you wanna play baseball, you don't worry about that," he explained. After six years in the Angels organization and not getting a shot at the majors, he signed with Baltimore. In 1998, he finally got a cup of coffee with the Orioles when Roberto Alomar went on the disabled list for 15 days. In 1999, he was assigned to the Triple-A Rochester Red Wings again.

The manager at Rochester also got his beginnings with the Angels. Manager **Dave**

Dave Machemer, drafted by the Angels. Pictured as manager of the Rochester Red Wings.

Machemer was drafted by the Angels in the fourth round in 1972. He recalled that his bonus was $10,000 for signing. He also got $1,000 when he got to Double-A, $1,500 at Triple-A and $5,000 at the major league level. His last year of schooling at Central Michigan would also be paid. His name was put in the record book when he got his call to the majors and hit a home run in his first at bat. That was in 1978. He called playing quits in 1982 when he was with the Toledo Mudhens. After a short hiatus, he came back to become a manager and instructor for several teams.

Ron Jackson, a second-round selection in June 1971, played with the Angels for seven seasons during his 10-year major league career. He turned to coaching after playing and was the first base coach with the Brewers in 1999.

Another former player who turned to coaching was **Bryan Price**, an eighth round choice in 1984. Price underwent shoulder surgery in 1987 and was granted free agency later that year. He signed with the Mariners and got as far as Triple-A before turning to coaching pitching with the Mariners' system.

Thad Bosley is now the first base coach with the Oakland Athletics. He was originally drafted by the Angels in the fourth round of the 1974 draft and made his major league debut with California in 1977.

The Angels first-ever draft pick, **Jim Spencer**, now owns a trophy and awards manufacturing business in Sykesville, Maryland. He won two Gold Gloves in the majors, but couldn't

hit well enough to stay at first base. The Angels tried to convert him to an outfielder before shipping him to Texas for Mike Epstein in 1973.

Best Draft

No year jumps out because a lot of the players who were drafted by the Angels didn't stay there long. In 1981 the Angels picked a couple of players who helped them to the playoffs: Dick Schofield and Devon White.

The year 1995 is starting to shape up as a great draft because Darin Erstad and Jarrod Washburn have been very successful thus far.

Worst Draft

Probably, 1973 was the worst year for the Angels. Only two players that were drafted ever made it to the majors and they only lasted one season. The draft of 1969 was also discouraging for California. They drafted Alan Bannister first and couldn't sign the high school shortstop. They also drafted Jim Wohlford out of high school and he wouldn't sign either. The second baseman went on to a long major league career. Only two players from all of the draft picks that season made it to the majors with the Angels.

All in the Family

Rance Mulliniks is the son of minor league pitcher Harvey Mulliniks. He upstaged his father by making it to the majors and playing 16 seasons there.

Among the 1998 picks were two sons with an Angels connection. The Angels picked **Bradley Downing**, the son of former Angels outfielder Brian Downing. They also chose **Mario Mendoza**, the son of former major leaguer and current Angels Lake Elsinore Single-A manager Mario Mendoza.

The White Sox could never be accused of nepotism because they allowed Anaheim to draft and sign shortstop **Joshua Shaffer**, the son of Chicago White Sox scouting director Duane Shaffer. Shaffer was the 26th round pick in 1998 by the Angels.

In 1999, the Angels drafted **William Curtis**,

the younger brother of New York Yankee out-fielder Chad Curtis, and **Garry Templeton, Jr.**, the son of former major leaguer and current Angels Double-A Erie manager Garry Templeton.

On the Roster

Seven is a lucky number in craps and it has been a lucky number for the Angels, who got **Jim Edmonds** in the seventh round of the June 1988 draft. The outfielder has shown up on Plays of the Week with regularity with his fantastic catches that earned Gold Gloves in 1997 and 1998. He didn't start out to be a power hitter, but has developed into one and hit a career high 33 four baggers in 1995. Injuries have hurt his career though.

Jim Edmonds of the Angels.

Jason Dickson, a sixth round pick in 1994, proved himself in three short seasons in the minors to get a call from the Angels in 1996. The next year he was named to the All-Star Game in his rookie season. His record was more impressive before that game than it has been since. He was 13-9 in 33 starts in his rookie year, but had a little slump in his sophomore season as his ERA went up to 6.05 and his record was 10-10.

Darin Erstad, California's first pick in the 1995 draft, was the first player selected overall. The University of Nebraska student played both baseball and football, and was named to the All-Academic Team as well. The Angels wasted little time with him in the minors and elevated

him to the majors in his second professional season. He responded with a .284 average and has been an excellent player ever since. He's a pure hitter and looks to get better and better in the future.

Troy Percival, a sixth round pick in the 1990 draft, was converted from catching to pitching in 1991. It turned out to be a great move as the right-hander became the team's stopper in 1996. Because he throws hard, he has always been a reliever and got his first call to the Angels in 1995 when he appeared in 62 games as a setup man. After four seasons with Anaheim, he has saved 108 games with a 2.77 ERA. He has appeared in one All-Star Game thus far.

Mike Holtz was selected in the 17th round in 1994 and played just two-and-a-half seasons before getting the call. The left-handed hurler from Clemson University made his debut with the Angels in 1996 and now has three seasons under his belt as a middle reliever.

Nineteen ninety-eight marked the debut of **Jarrod Washburn**, a second round pick in 1995, with the Angels. The left-handed hurler showed he could pitch in the majors by compiling a 6-3 mark over 11 starts. He could have earned himself a start in the regular rotation.

Todd Greene, a 12th round pick from 1993, had rotator cuff surgery in 1998 and it ended his days as a full-time catcher. He moved into a backup role at catcher and designated hitter.

Justin Baughman, a fifth round pick from 1995, played three seasons at Class A before skipping over Double-A on his way to his major league debut in 1998. But a broken leg in the Mexican League over the winter sidelined him for 1999 and may end his career.

The Angels wasted no time bringing **Troy Glaus** to the majors for a try in 1998 after spending a team record $2.25 million on the first round choice in 1997. Glaus didn't sign until September 1997, so 1998 was his first year as a professional. However, the third baseman hit a paltry .218 in 1998 in the majors. Glaus became the regular third baseman for the Angels in 1999.

Christopher Pritchett was a second round selection in 1991 and was twice an all-star in the minors before getting a call up in 1996. He was sent back to the minors for two more seasons before a call to Anaheim again in 1998. The first baseman has hit .288 in the minors

Garrett Anderson, selected by the Angels in the fourth round of the 1990 draft, was first called up to the majors in 1994 after hitting .321 at Triple-A Vancouver. Anderson has shown that the .300 average was no fluke and has averaged .299 in five seasons with Anaheim.

Future Stars?

Since **Scott Schoeneweis**, a third round pick in 1996, has already overcome cancer and Tommy John surgery, making it to the majors was probably an easier task. The left-handed pitcher from Duke University joined the club on the last day of spring training in 1999. The starter was 26-16 in the minors.

Another 1996 draft pick who seems to be in line for a major league job is **Jason Dewey**. The draft-and-follow 26th round long shot has been a good hitter and has a good arm. He could be a 2001 major league player or sooner.

The draft of 1996 also produced **Marcus Knight**. The seventh round selection was an Arizona League all-star in his first season when he hit .291.

Matt Wise made the all-star team in Class A his first year in professional ball after going 9-1 with a 3.25 ERA. The right-hander was a sixth round pick in 1997. He had a little more trouble in Double-A in 1998.

Another pitcher from the 1997 draft was **Heath Timmerman**, a third rounder. The right-

handed hurler had a 7-13 season at Class A in 1998, but his ERA was just 4.30.

A long shot from the Class of 1997 doing well was 21st round pick **Mike Colangelo**. After beginning at short-season Cedar Rapids, he was promoted to Class A Lake Elsinore and hit a whopping .379. The outfielder hits line drives to all fields and has great speed.

To show how desperate major league teams are for left-handed pitching, you can turn to the 15th round pick of the Angels in 1999. **Sean Brummett** had just a 5-6 record with a 6.00 ERA at Indiana State University when he was picked. However, Brummett had a 90 mph fastball, slider, changeup and potential. "I'm excited! I'm ready to go," he said the day after the draft. His best game in college was against Murray State when he threw a complete game and had a dozen strikeouts. The scouts must have been at that game. Brummett was not drafted after he completed high school in Brookston, Indiana. He played the outfield in his freshman year before becoming a starter the next two seasons. The Angels will try and turn him into a winner.

The Angels picked consensus All-American right-hander **Seth Etherton** in the first round in 1998. He was unimpressive at Double-A in his rookie season in the pros as he was 1-5 with a 6.14 ERA.

Anaheim continued their emphasis on pitching in 1999 when they selected right-hander **John Lackey** out of Grayson County Junior College as their first pick. The second round selection was 10-3 with a 4.23 ERA. He was named to the All-Northern Texas Athletic Conference and All-Region 5 first teams. "I was real excited to hear I was drafted by the Angels," said Lackey. "It's an opportunity that every little kid wants when growing up and I was really excited when I heard I went in the second round."

Baltimore Orioles

In the 35-year history of the draft, the Orioles have won the pennant or their division nine times, which is eight times more than the club did in the 35 years before the draft. Of course most of those 35 years before the draft they were

the lowly St. Louis Browns, which had a habit of finishing last. The Browns only won the pennant in 1944 when everyone else was off to war. The Orioles didn't benefit from any draft picks in winning the World Series in 1970, because

Jeffrey Hammonds, Cincinnati Reds. Drafted by the Orioles. (Photograph by Marty Orr.)

those players were just then showing up in the majors. The 1979 World Series team had several of its own draft picks that contributed greatly to the Orioles. Draft picks also were partially responsible for the Orioles winning the World Series in 1983. The Orioles made some great picks during the 1970s, but chose poorly in the 1980s which resulted in some poor teams.

In recent times, the Orioles have abandoned the slow-cooking development of minor league players in favor of signing some high-priced free agents, which helped the club to a first-place finish in 1997. After the dismal fourth-place finish in 1998, owner Peter Angelos went out and signed a quartet of free agents: Albert Belle, Will "The Thrill" Clark, Delino DeShields and Charles Johnson. Less than a fourth of their 40-man roster is made up of Baltimore originals.

The Orioles strategy has changed several times over the history of the draft depending on who's in charge at the top. In recent years, it has been to draft the best athlete available, regard-

less of position, with a preference on the high school player. In the early rounds, the emphasis has been on pitching; whereas, in later rounds, Baltimore looks to fill certain positions.

Baltimore is developing a new philosophy thanks to Tony DeMacio, who took the job of scouting director in 1999. The 1999 draft was a bit unusual for Baltimore because the club had seven picks out of the first 50 due to compensation. DeMacio called it an "aberration" because it was such a departure from the norm. The Orioles took pitchers with the first two picks, followed by two outfielders, then two more pitchers and lastly a middle infielder. "We concentrated on the middle of the diamond," he explained.

The new director, who came to Baltimore with experience serving in the Atlanta, Cleveland and Chicago Cubs organizations, hopes to turn Baltimore back around to a winning franchise like it used to be. He likes players with high ceilings and all the tools. "We're looking at kids who can play the game. Kids that can't do without baseball," he commented. "Makeup is becoming so much more important now." He also prefers young high school arms to veteran college pitchers. "I want to develop some depth in the organization." The Baltimore farm system was short on left-handed pitching, so DeMacio concentrated on that for his first draft. The first pitcher he ever scouted was Tom Glavine, so he knows what to look for.

Long shots didn't seem to have much of a chance until recent times, as several prospects were well down the list of picks. A couple of picks beyond the 30th round are now on the 40-man roster.

With the rounds down to 50 now, the 1,000-1 shots won't get a chance whatsoever. And DeMacio would like to cut down the number of rounds down further to 40. "Make it more elitist," he said. He also believes in the draft-and-follow rule and used that option on about a dozen players in 1999.

Baltimore has an average size scouting staff with 15 area scouts, four crosscheckers and five international scouts. It is concentrating its overseas efforts in Aruba, Venezuela, the Lower Antilles, Curacao and the Dominican Republic.

If all goes well for Baltimore in the future,

draft picks will figure more in the mix and a combination of veterans and draft picks will bring a championship back again to Baltimore.

The Orioles were the first team in the 35-year history of the draft to have four true first-round picks in 1999, not including supplemental choices. In addition to their own selection (No. 13), they received extra draft picks as compensation for the free agent signings last winter of Eric Davis (St. Louis, 18th & 44th), Rafael Palmeiro (Texas, 21st & 50th) and Roberto Alomar (Cleveland, 23rd & 34th). The Orioles had more picks in the top 50 selections than any team in the draft and the most in franchise history. The Orioles lost their selections in rounds 2 through 5 for the free agent signings of Albert Belle (Chicago, 2nd), Mike Timlin (Seattle, 3rd), Delino DeShields (St. Louis, 4th) and Will Clark (Texas, 5th). Drafting and signing all those players would provide a challenge for Baltimore's budget. "Overall we are happy with the progress that we have made in our efforts to get our draft picks in the fold and we will continue to work toward that end," said general manager Frank Wren.

Best Picks

One of the best draft picks made by the Orioles was a favorite son —**Cal Ripken, Jr.** His father was part of the organization at the time, but that didn't assure he'd be picked by the Orioles. The Orioles wouldn't even tell Senior if they were picking his son. Ripken was known more for his pitching than fielding in high school. Scouts felt he was too big — 6-foot-2 — to play short. Shortstops were historically short and fast. He was neither. The scouts also liked him as a pitcher and he was considered a two-way shot to make it to the majors. The Orioles waited until the second round to choose Junior. They gave him a $20,000 bonus in 1978. He signed rather than going off to college. Little did the Orioles know he would be such an "Iron Man" and break Lou Gehrig's record. Ripken finally broke the consecutive-game streak himself on Sept. 20, 1998, at 2,632 games. Like Gehrig, he will end up in the Hall of Fame someday.

Another draft pick who turned out be a gem was **Eddie Murray**. The team selected him in the third round in the 1973 draft and he didn't disappoint them. By 1977 he was a regular on the team and named as the American League Rookie of the Year. The following season he was named to the All-Star Team. He played 13 seasons for Baltimore and 21 in the majors before retiring after the 1997 season. Murray is best of five brothers to play professionally. With 504 career home runs, a spot in the Hall is waiting for him.

One of the best free-agent draft picks in Orioles history was **Mike Mussina**. Baltimore first drafted him in June 1987 as an 11th round selection out of Montoursville High School. He declined and went to Stanford University. The Orioles didn't give up on the pitcher and picked him again in the first round of the 1990 draft. This time the opportunity was too good for him to pass up and the Orioles are glad he did. Mussina roared through the minors like a twister and found himself in the starting rotation the next season with Baltimore. After nine seasons in the majors, he has compiled a 131-69 record. He won his third Rawlings Gold Glove Award in 1998. He has been named to four American League All-Star teams.

Don Baylor, a second-round pick in 1967, turned out to be a hard-nosed player as evidenced by breaking season and career marks for being hit by pitches. His trip through the minors included the highest honor — Minor League Player of the Year. He became an Orioles regular in 1972 and helped the team to two American League East titles. With free agency looming, Baltimore traded him to Oakland. Then he signed with the Angels and became the league's top designated hitter. His banner year came in 1979 as he was named to his only All-Star team performance and won the league's MVP honor. By the time his playing career ended in 1988, he had played in three World Series with three different teams: Boston, Minnesota and Oakland. In 1993 he became the manager of the Colorado Rockies.

A year after Baylor was picked, the Orioles selected **Al Bumbry** in the 11th round. After serving in Vietnam, he came up to the Orioles in 1972. In his first season, he hit .337 on the season with a league tying 11 triples to earn the American League Rookie of the Year Award. Bumbry roamed the Baltimore outfield until

1984 and helped the team to four division crowns, two American League titles and a World Series. When he left for San Diego in 1985, he was Baltimore's all-time basestealer with 254 thefts. After playing, he turned to coaching.

Bobby Grich was a first round pick in 1967 and signed for $40,000. After batting .336 and hitting 32 home runs in the minors in 1971, he came up with Baltimore the next season. He became a free agent in 1976 and signed a five-year contract with the Angels for $1.69 million. His career changed the next year when he hurt his back lifting an air conditioner and suffered a herniated disk. The injury limited his mobility in the field and he went from a potential Hall of Famer to just another ball player. The Angels named him to their Hall of Fame though. He won four Gold Gloves and led the league in several fielding categories during his career.

Mike Flanagan was first drafted by the Astros in the 15th round in 1971, but he chose to attend the University of Massachusetts. After setting the school record for strikeouts and going 12-1, the Orioles picked him in the seventh round in 1973. Flanagan became the first third-generation Major League baseball player — contrary to popular belief that the Boones were first — when he made it to the Orioles in 1977 as a September call-up. His grandfather, Ed "Sleepy" Flanagan, came up to the majors in 1887, and his father by the same name, pitched for Boston from 1947 to 1952. The lefthander became a consistent winner for the Orioles. In 1979 he had a career best 23-9 record to lead the league and earn the Cy Young Award. A tired elbow and other injuries slowed him after that and he was traded to Toronto in 1987. He returned to the Orioles as a nonroster invitee in 1991 and finished his career with the team.

Mike Boddicker, a sixth round pick in 1978, was one of the leading pitchers for the Orioles during the 1980s. His first full year in the majors came in 1983 and he helped the team to the pennant with a 16-8 record. Then he won a game in the League Championship Series and the World Series. The following season he led the American League with 20 wins. Boddicker pitched nine seasons for the Orioles before being traded to Boston for Curt Schilling and Brady Anderson.

Doug DeCinces, a third rounder in 1970, came up with the Orioles as a utility infielder. When Brooks Robinson retired, DeCinces got the job at third base. In 1977 he led the league third baseman in assists and double plays. He also smashed 28 homers. He helped the Orioles to the World Series in 1979. His good defense continued, but his performance with the bat slid and he was traded to the Angels. He became an All-Star in 1983.

An Orioles compensation pick who turned out to be a good pitcher but for another team was **Pete Harnish**, who was a third-team All-American with Fordham University. Baltimore picked him in the 1987 draft and by the next season he was pitching in the majors. Harnish had a losing record with the Orioles, but he went on to a winning mark with the Astros. The right-handed hurler then had losing marks with the Mets before rebounding with the Reds in 1998 with a 14-7 record. He recorded a one-hitter in 1999 in helping the Reds compete for the pennant.

Long Shots

Steve Finley, a 13th round selection in 1987, was good enough to make the Orioles' starting lineup on Opening Day in 1989 after being a nonroster invitee in spring training. Injuries played havoc with his performance that first season in the majors. He played another season with Baltimore before he was traded to Houston. He's been a solid player ever since and won two Gold Gloves. The excellent fielder and .275 career hitter helped the Padres get to the World Series in 1998.

Another 13th round pick to make it in the majors was **Mike Oquist**. The right-handed pitcher had an up-and-down trip the Orioles as he bounced between Triple-A and the majors over three seasons. He was granted free agency in 1995 and signed with the Padres for a season before heading to Oakland, who put him in the regular rotation in 1998.

Brad Pennington, a 12th round pick in 1989, has followed a similar path as Oquist. Also a pitcher, Pennington cracked the Orioles' lineup in 1993, like Oquist. The left-handed reliever has had an up-and-down career as well. His ERA has fluctuated wildly, down one day and up the next. For example, after a 12.00 ERA with Baltimore in 1994, he was sent back down to the minors. He was traded to the Reds where he ballooned to 12.27 ERA at Class AAA Indianapolis. Then with Boston the next season he had a 2.77 ERA before being claimed on waivers with California where his ERA rose to 12.27. In 1998 he signed with Tampa Bay.

Terry Crowley, a 15th round choice in 1966, became a great pinch hitter during his career. He wasn't with the Orioles long as he was sent to Texas for $100,000 in December 1973. He returned to Baltimore in 1976. His most famous pinch hit came in 1982, when he hit a grand slam in the ninth inning against Kansas City. In his 15 years in the majors he picked up 108 pinch hits, sixth on the all-time list.

David Segui, an 18th round selection in 1987, earned a promotion to the big leagues in 1990 after batting .349 in Triple-A. The Orioles decided to deal him in 1993 to the Mets for Kevin Baez and pitcher Tom Wegmann, neither of whomever played for the Orioles. It was a lousy trade. Segui became a .300 hitter with 20 homers per season by 1997 with Montreal and Seattle.

Rick Krivda was a 23rd round pick in 1991 and he was with the Orioles by 1995. He's been up and down like a yo-yo since then.

The Orioles would like **Ryan Minor** to become a major star at third base. The 33rd round pick out of the University of Oklahoma in 1996 was elevated from Double-A to the majors in the September call-ups in 1998. He started at third the night Cal Ripken decided to end his record of consecutive games at 2,632. Minor's fielding ability was rewarded in 1997 when he won the Brooks Robinson Minor League Player of the Year Award. And he can hit. He smashed 24 homers in 1997 and 17 in 1998 in the minors.

Disappointments

Baltimore had its fair share of bombs over the years from the their first round picks in the June regular draft.

The Orioles got off to a slow start in the draft when they chose pitcher **Scott McDonald** in the first draft. He only got as far as Double-

A. The following year shortstop **Ted Parks** was their first pick and he bombed at Triple-A.

Go directly to the majors, do not go to the minors and collect $75,000. This is the Monopoly game **Mike Adamson** played in 1967. The first player taken in the secondary phase of the June 1967 draft was sent directly to the majors by the Orioles. The 19-year-old right-handed pitcher had gone 8-3 with the USC with a 2.20 ERA. His direct flight to the majors didn't last long. After appearing in three games and losing one, he was give a return flight to the minors. The Orioles brought him back twice more in the next two years, but Adamson never won a game and ended up with a 7.46 ERA.

Because of their good finishes in the early 1970s, the Orioles didn't get to choose until late in the first round. They got the last pick in 1970 and choose **James West**, a catcher out of high school. He only got as far as Class A. The Orioles did an instant replay in 1972 and got the same result. **Ken Thomas**, a catcher out of high school, peaked at Class A.

Dallas Williams, a first-round pick in 1976, received $60,000 bonus and got a cup of

Dallas Williams, drafted by the Orioles.

coffee in the majors and hit just .079 in 20 games in the majors. The same held true the next year when **Drungo Hazewood**, an outfielder, was picked in the first round. He played eight games in the majors. The Orioles' poor luck continued the next year as well. **Robert Boyce**, a third baseman, only got as far as Class A.

Baltimore got the last pick in the first round in 1980 and chose **Jeff Williams** out of high school. The outfielder peaked at Triple-A. Such was the case with **Joe Kucharski**, a right-handed pitcher in 1982.

The Orioles didn't get first round selections in 1979 and 1981 due to free agent signings.

Nineteen eighty-three was a waste as well when the Orioles picked **Wayne Wilson**. The right-handed pitcher out of high school didn't get past Class A. The following year Baltimore picked another pitcher, **John Hoover**, who got a cup of coffee in the majors.

Brad DuVall was the choice in the first round in 1987 and the pitcher didn't sign.

Mark Smith, a first round choice in 1993, fell below the Orioles' expectations, so he was traded. Smith was given a couple of tries with Baltimore before he was dealt but his performance wasn't good enough. Smith did better with Pittsburgh in 1997, then he fell below the Mendoza Line in 1998.

Some draft picks never made it to the majors because of illness not related to baseball at all. **Joel Stephens** was a ninth-round pick by the Orioles in the 1995 draft. He spent three seasons in Class A ball. Then he was diagnosed with colon cancer in November 1997. But that didn't necessarily mean an end to his baseball career. Another Baltimore player, Eric Davis, contracted the disease and recovered to return to the Orioles and play again. Stephens tried to work his way back to baseball, but finally succumbed to the disease on Sept. 30, 1998. Darryl Strawberry of the New York Yankees also contracted the cancer at the end of the 1998 season forcing him out of the playoff picture.

Those Who Wouldn't Sign

The Orioles have drafted several players who wouldn't sign and went onto very successful careers with other teams as a result.

In the first draft, the team selected **Carlton Fisk** in the 48th round, but he went to college and later signed with the Red Sox. The All-Star catcher played 24 seasons in all with Boston and the White Sox.

A few years later the Orioles selected **Dave Kingman**, but he wouldn't sign.

Another home run power hitter the Orioles drafted but didn't sign was **Dave Winfield** in 1969. The outfielder waited to sign with the

Padres. In all he played 22 seasons in the majors and hit 465 career home runs. He might just end up as another draft pick in the Hall of Fame. He won't be eligible until 2001.

Cecil Fielder also showed promise of hitting home runs, so the Orioles picked him in the 1981 draft. Fielder waited to be drafted by the Blue Jays. But not until he went to the Tigers did he reach his prime. With a physique reminiscent of Babe Ruth, Fielder busted 50 homers in 1990 to lead the American League.

The Orioles also missed out on **Glenn Davis** and **Kevin Gross** in 1979. The two high schoolers went on to college and signed elsewhere.

Baltimore's strong pitching staff may have been even stronger had **Rick Honeycutt** signed out of high school in 1972. But he didn't. And one of the latest misses was Jamie Navarro in 1986.

The Orioles apparently weren't too interested in **Mike Shebek**, a junior from Ball State University. The Indianapolis native had a losing record (5-12), but the Baltimore scout had seen him at his best when he threw a one-hitter. Shebek had an 88-mph fastball and some other good pitches, so he was marginally acceptable. The Orioles picked him in the 38th round of the 1986 draft and didn't get a hold of him until two weeks after the draft. Shebek didn't even know he had been picked. The Orioles gave him until the next day to decide and offered him $3,000 and money to finish his degree. Shebek declined.

"They [Orioles] wanted me to pick up some velocity," he was instructed for his senior year. Ball State baseball coach Pat Quinn took Shebek under his wing and decided to call all his pitches in his senior year. In a game against Toledo University, the hurler got clobbered and lost 10–9 thanks to 39 straight fastballs called by the coach. "That was the beginning of the end," Shebek explained. He got his fastball up to 92, but the Orioles didn't draft him after his senior season. Nor did any other team. He went to a Kansas City tryout in Chicago, where the scout said he would sign any pitcher who threw 88 mph. Shebek accomplished that, but the Royals didn't sign him. Now the Carmel, Indiana, resident makes and sells pool covers for a living while playing in the Men's Adult Baseball League and only dreaming about pitching in the majors.

Best Draft

Because **Cal Ripken** was picked in 1978, that year is about the best Baltimore has done in the draft. That was also the year that **Mike Boddicker** was chosen in the sixth round. The Orioles had two compensation picks that year for losing Elliott Maddox and Ross Grimsley to free agency. One pick was **Larry Sheets** who made it to the big leagues as an outfielder. Also, making it to the majors from that draft were **Bob Bonner** and **Don Welchel**, but neither had much success.

Nineteen eighty-eight is also turning out to have been an excellent draft for Baltimore. Pitchers **Gregg Olson** and **Arthur Rhodes** came out of that draft and have turned out quite well.

Worst Draft

The Orioles have been snake bit twice in the draft. In 1966 and again in 1974, Baltimore had only one player each of those years make it to the majors.

All in the Family

Besides Cal being drafted as a favorite son, his brother, **Billy Ripken**, was also drafted by the Orioles in the 11th round in 1983. Billy put on an Oriole uniform for the first time in 1987.

Baltimore picked **Pete Rose II** in the 12th round of the 1988 draft hoping he would follow in the footsteps of his father, who had broke Ty Cobb's all-time hit record and seemed headed to the Baseball Hall of Fame until he was banned from baseball for gambling. The Oak Hills High School graduate accepted Baltimore's offer and reported to Class A ball the following season. After failing to show much in two seasons, the Orioles traded him to the White Sox. Then the Indians took him from the White Sox in the Rule V minor league draft in late 1991. Rose idled in Class A like a car in a traffic jam, so the Indians released him in 1994. The White Sox again picked him up. He played most of the 1995 season at Class A South Bend where he was be-

Pete Rose II was drafted by the Orioles. Here he is shown with the Indianapolis Indians. (Photograph by Jackie Dowling.)

ginning to show signs of improvement with the bat. The young Rose finally moved up to Double A in 1996. He was granted free agency after the 1996 season and signed with his hometown Cincinnati Reds, where his father played for 19 seasons. The Reds assigned him to Double A Chattanooga where he found consistent home run power for the first time in his career, knocking out 25 homers in 112 games to earn a promotion to Triple A Indianapolis. In September 1997, the Reds called up the third baseman, which improved attendance for the final month during a dismal season. Rose played in 11 games and hit just .143. The next year found him back in Indianapolis, where he played inconsistently. In one game he allowed a runner to score when he threw the ball over the first baseman's head and into right field. The Reds decided to release him in favor of Aaron Boone at third base. A disgruntled Rose kept his hopes alive signing with Nashville, another Triple A team. He was soon released and signed with New Jersey, an Independent. His career seemed over by the end of the season, but the Dodgers invited him to its spring training camp as a favor to his father. Rose didn't make the team.

Jerry Hairston, Jr., became a third generation major leaguer in 1998 when he took to the field for the Orioles. He became the fourth member of the Hairston family to reach the majors. His father, Jerry, played 14 years mostly with the White Sox. His grandfather, Sam, played four games with the 1951 White Sox and his uncle, Johnny, played three games with the Cubs in 1969.

Greg Zaun, a 17th round pick in 1989, is the nephew of former Orioles catcher Rick Dempsey.

Baltimore drafted **Tim Raines, Jr.,** in 1998 in the sixth round. He is an outfielder like his dad, who was with the Athletics in 1999 and never played in Baltimore. Junior has speed like his father, too.

Where Are They Now?

Terry Pollreisz, a sixth round pick in the 1969 January Secondary Phase, turned to coaching high school and college ball after playing. Then he came back to managing in professional ball in 1998 with the Mariners' short-season Class A–Everett.

Another Orioles player who turned to coaching after playing is **Blaine Beatty**, a ninth rounder in 1986. The hurler got a couple of cups of coffee in the majors with the Mets but couldn't stick. After a try with the Pirates, he turned to coaching for them and is now with the Williamsport Crosscutters, a rookie team.

John Selby, a first-round pick in the 1977 January Regular Phase, played seven seasons with the Orioles before going to the Dodgers, for whom he now coaches first base.

Dallas Williams, a first rounder, turned into a hitting coach in the White Sox farm system after his playing days and completed his ninth season with the organization in 1999.

On the Roster

With Baltimore out of the pennant race in September 1998, they called up several players to give them some exposure to the major leagues.

Jerry Hairston went from Class A all the way to the Orioles in 1998 and did it in fine fashion. After hitting .302 on the season with 34 doubles, 6 triples, 10 homers and 70 RBI, he got the September call. The all-around infielder could become the team's utility fielder in the future before slipping into a regular role.

The Orioles gave a look-see at **Chris Fussell** in a September call-up in 1998, too. The ninth round pitcher in 1994 started a couple of games and got rocked. He began his pro career on a great note as he was 9-1 in rookie ball. Then he was named as a Class A All-Star but suffered a sore shoulder. After a shaky 1-8 performance in 1996, he has improved greatly. He's projected as a starter someday for the team.

A third September call-up in 1998 was **Calvin Pickering**, a 35th round pick in 1995. The first baseman was an Eastern League all-star in 1998, a season in which he slammed 31 homers and batted .308. His brief call produced two home runs in nine games, so he showed he can hit the long ball in the majors as well.

Ryan Minor also got the call in 1998 and batted a whopping .429 in his nine games. The 3rd baseman was originally a 33rd round choice in 1996. He was a South Atlantic League all-star at third in 1997.

Arthur Rhodes, a second round pick in 1988, has become a long-time pitcher with the Orioles. Selected out of high school, he proved himself in Double-A in 1991 as he was picked as an Eastern League all-star and MVP. That led him to get his first call to Baltimore that same season. The Orioles kept trying him out in the majors as a starter until they found out he was better used as a reliever in 1996, a season in which he went 9-1. The next year he went 10-3. His record with Baltimore so far is 40-32.

Rocky Coppinger, a 19th round pick in 1993, has had two careers with the Orioles. He first worked his way up to the Orioles in 1996 and was 10-6 with a 5.18 ERA. The next season he had elbow and shoulder surgery which sent him all the way back to rookie ball. He worked his way back up the farm system in two seasons and made it back to the Orioles, but this time as a reliever.

Jesse Garcia, a 26th round pick in 1993, made the roster out of spring training when

Delino DeShields went on the disabled list. He had moved up to Triple-A in 1998 where he hit .294. At spring training in 1999 he made just one error.

The Orioles added **Gabe Molina**, a 21st round pick in 1996, to the 40-man roster in 1999. The right-handed reliever saved 24 games at Double-A in 1998. He got a call to the majors on May 1, 1999, when pitcher Heathcliff Slocumb was released. Baltimore was looking at him as their closer because he picked up 24 saves for Bowie and was named as the Orioles minor league pitcher of the year.

Future Stars?

Tommy Davis, a second round pick out of the University of Southern Mississippi, was called up in May 1999 when catcher Lenny Webster went on the disabled list. Davis steadily progressed up the minors and has a good bat as he averaged .277 in the minors. Originally drafted as a third baseman, he moved to first base and then to catcher. The move has obviously paid benefits.

The Orioles drafted and signed the first African-born player in 1997 for $500,000. **Ntema Ndungidi**, taken in the first round (36th overall), was born in Zaire and moved to Montreal when he was three. The compensation pick from the Yankees signing David Wells showed promise in the rookie leagues, but has a long way to go to get to the majors.

Brian Falkenborg, a second round pick in 1996 out of high school, has yet to break out of Class A after three seasons in the minors. However, he's still young and developing. He's more of a finesse pitcher than a thrower.

A promising left-handed pitcher picked by the Orioles in the third round in 1997 is **Matt Riley**. The young hurler with a keen fastball manufactured 136 strikeout victims in 83 innings while turning out a 1.19 ERA in Class A in 1998.

The Orioles are hoping **Darnell McDonald**, a first round pick in 1997, keeps developing like he did in his first year in the minors. He batted .260 with seven homers at Class A. And he can field with the best of the outfielders, too.

Larry Bigbie was surprised when he was

Larry Bigbie. (Photograph courtesy of the Baltimore Orioles.)

picked in the first round in 1999. "I really wasn't expecting the first round," the Ball State University outfielder explained. "It's very stressful. You don't know where you stand."

His selection by the Orioles was a little déjà vu. When he first started playing the game at age six, he played on the Orioles and he still has the shirt to prove it.

Bigbie was a late bloomer in baseball as he was a better quarterback at Hobart High School, Indiana. "I had more offers to play football in college than baseball," he admitted. He wasn't drafted by baseball, either. When he began playing baseball in college, the infielder was converted to an outfielder. Then he started to put on some weight to that six-foot-four frame and hit a whopping .419 with 17 homers and 54 RBI in his senior season to get Orioles scout Mark Ziegler's attention amongst others.

The weekend after the draft he hadn't signed yet and was leaving that matter to his agent, but he was looking at becoming a millionaire. He didn't seem too concerned about that though. "I just want to go and have a solid year," he said. Nor did he care whether he got a major league contract. "You go out and play good and they're going to send you up whether its negotiated or not." He signed a week later.

The Orioles very first pick in the first round in 1999 was **Mike Paradis**, a right-handed pitcher who was headed to the College World Series to pitch for Clemson. He was 6-1 on the year with a 4.43 ERA. Paradis was selected in the seventh round by Oakland in 1996, but he decided to go to college. "We were really happy to get Mike Paradis with the 13th pick," said Orioles General Manager Frank Wren. "He's a power sinkerball pitcher, throws in the low 90s and has a sharp slider. We like his stuff and he fits the profile of a Camden Yards pitcher."

With their second selection of the first round, which was the 18th pick overall, the Orioles drafted left-handed hurler **Richard Stahl**. The high school senior went 11-0 with a 2.40 ERA in 15 games. He struck out 146 batters in 79 innings. Both Paradis and Stahl were scouted by Lamar North, the Orioles' longtime scout in the Georgia–South Carolina area. "Richard Stahl has an above average fastball, a good breaking ball and he is a good athlete for a big, 6-7 left-handed pitcher, so he should be an imposing figure out on the mound," Wren said.

With their final first round pick and the 23rd selection overall, the Orioles chose **Keith Reed.** The outfielder batted .398 with 17 homers and a school-record 79 RBI for Providence College, who advanced to the NCAA tournament in their final season of collegiate baseball. Reed, a right-handed hitter, was the Big East Conference Player of the Year and was a second team All-America selection by Collegiate Baseball.

In the supplemental round in 1999, the Orioles selected left-handed ace **Josh Cenate** as the 34th pick of the draft. Cenate was 13-1 with a 0.71 ERA in 15 pitching appearances for Jefferson High School. He had 179 strikeouts and only 21 walks in 89 innings pitched this season, allowing 35 hits. He had a 34-4 career record in four years in high school. The Orioles signed him a month after the draft. "He has a great arm and outstanding mound presence," said Wren. "Hard throwing left-handed pitchers who also possess a knowledge of pitching is a rare commodity and Josh fits that description."

The Orioles selected another left-hander, **Scott Rice**, with the 44th selection of the draft. He went 6-2 with two saves and a 3.32 ERA for Royal High School this spring. He struck out 72 batters and walked 41 in 54.2 innings this year, allowing 46 hits.

With their final selection in the supplemental round, the Orioles chose shortstop **Brian Roberts** from the University of South Carolina with the 50th overall selection. He batted .353 with 12 home runs and 36 RBI for the Gamecocks and led the NCAA with 67 stolen bases. He transferred this season from the University of North Carolina, where his father, Mike Roberts, was head coach for 21 years.

Boston Red Sox

The Red Sox got off to a great start with the draft as they had at least one of their number-one picks make it to the majors the first four years of the draft, including Billy Conigliaro, Ken Brett and Carlton Fisk. In fact, they had significant selections the first decade of the draft. The Sox only made 20 picks the first draft, the lowest of any team, but made them count. Good drafts have resulted in the Red Sox finishing first in the American League East five times and two World Series appearances. In the 35 years before the draft, the Sox had finished in first just twice in 1946 and 1967.

The draft had a profound effect on the 1975 World Series team. Boston original draft picks on that team included Rick Burleson, Cecil Cooper, Dwight Evans, Carlton Fisk, Bill Lee, Fred Lynn and Rick Miller. Evans was the only player from the 1975 team to make it to the next series appearance in 1986. He was joined by many other Boston originals: Wade Boggs, Mike Greenwell, Jim Rice, Dave Stapleton, Oil Can Boyd, Roger Clemens, Bruce Hurst, Al Nipper and Bob Stanley.

In 1993, the Red Sox revamped their minor league, player development and scouting system to provide skilled young talent for their major league team. That tree began to bear fruit in 1998 and helped the team reach the playoffs as a wild card; however, the Sox were eliminated in

Andy Abad, with Pawtucket. He was drafted by the Red Sox in 1993, 16th round. (Photograph by Marty Orr.)

the first round to keep up with the Curse of the Bambino Theory. The Sox have had a winning team each year since 1993.

The Red Sox made scouting and signing the local New England talent a priority and that is beginning to pay off. Catcher Steve Lomasney, a fifth round choice from 1995 from Peabody, Mass., and pitcher Jeff Taglenti, a seventh round pick in 1997 from Walpole, Mass., are fine examples of that effort.

"Fans have witnessed the importance of our efforts in preparing and executing during the June Free Agent Draft," said general manager Dan Duquette. "Our V.P. of scouting, Wayne Britton, and his staff continue to do an outstanding job in scouting, drafting and signing the best young players."

The Sox have traded a lot of their own drafted talent to meet more immediate needs in recent years. "I can think of ten prospects that they've traded over the past year," commented Pawtucket player Jim Chamblee in May 1999. He was a 12th rounder himself in 1995.

The Red Sox have tried to go after pitchers, shortstops and centerfielders in the draft in

recent drafts that finally paid off with Nomar Garciapara. They like right-handed power hitters because of the Green Monster in left field. And they prefer position players with power rather than defensive gems.

The scouting staff consists of 14 area scouts and two national crosscheckers, which is fairly small in comparison with other teams. In comparison, the team has taken a more aggressive approach to scouting in the international arena. In 1998, Korean righty Jin Ho Cho made his debut. Cho, along with right-handed pitching prospect Sun Woo Kim, played for the Korean National team and both were signed by the Boston international scouting staff. Tomokazu Ohka was obtained from the Japanese professional league and was promoted to Triple-A in 1999 after going 8-0 in Double-A. The Red Sox also scouted and signed highly-sought infielder Julio Guerrero, 17-year-old brother of Wilton and Vladimir, from the Dominican Republic.

The team still believes in holding tryout camps to scout some players who may have been missed in the draft. Camps are held throughout the United States.

Best Picks

The Red Sox began the first draft by selecting **Billy Conigliaro** as its very first pick. The choice seemed logical. His brother, Tony, was already a star for the Red Sox. As the fifth overall selection in the draft, he received a reported $60,000. Billy worked his way up to the majors by 1969 and joined his brother in the outfield. The two outfielders made a great combination for the Sox, but the fairy tale ended when the Red Sox traded Tony to the Angels. Both brothers' careers made a downturn after that. Billy was also traded to the Brewers after the 1971 season. He didn't like his playing time with the Brewers, so he walked off the team in the middle of the season. Oakland bought his contract. He injured a knee there and his career soon ended.

One of the early picks in the draft who turned out to be a real winner later was **Carlton Fisk**. Chosen in the first round (fourth overall) of the 1967 draft by the Sox, Fisk also had been selected in the first draft by the Orioles in the

48th round, but he chose to go to college. When Fisk was a rookie in 1972, a scout said he was a "fair receiver with strong arm, but needs experience." Fans certainly liked him and he was named to the All-Star Team in his rookie season. He also won a Gold Glove. He culminated the season as the first player ever to win the Rookie of the Year unanimously. He cemented his place in Sox folklore with his dramatic homer off the left-field foul pole in the sixth game of the 1975 World Series. "Pudge" played with the Red Sox until 1980. In 1981 he went to the White Sox where he finished out his career. He retired in 1993 after 24 seasons and 2,226 games to break the major league record. He also broke home run records by a catcher with 376. Fisk appeared in 11 All-Star games during his career. He earned just one Gold Glove. His name went on the ballot for the Baseball Hall of Fame in 1998, but he did not get enough votes that year to get inducted.

Cecil Cooper, a sixth-round pick in 1968, would have been the regular first baseman for the Red Sox had a legend not been playing there — Carl Yastrzemski. Cooper was first called up to the majors in 1971 yet he wasn't a permanent fixture until the 1974 season. After a poor showing in the 1975 World Series, the Sox traded him to Milwaukee for Bernie Carbo and George Scott. The regular playing time resulted in his maturity as a hitter and he twice led the league in doubles and RBI. He was named to five All-Star teams with the Brewers. However, he never won a Gold Glove.

Ben Oglivie, an 11th round pick in 1968, played just three seasons in Boston before he was traded to Detroit for Dick McAuliffe after he hit a paltry .218. The over-the-hill McAuliffe did worse the next season when he hit just .210 and was out of baseball the next year. Meanwhile, Oglivie began becoming a hitter and averaged .270. He soon started hitting homers and really came into his own when he went to Milwaukee. There he slammed 41 dingers in 1980 and tied Reggie Jackson for the league lead for four baggers. He was named to three All-Star teams. By the time his 16-year ended he had hit 235 homers. After his playing career ended in Japan, he became a scout for the Brewers and is now a hitting coach for the Pirates' Class A Hickory Crawdads.

The Red Sox picked **Dwight Evans** out of high school in the fifth round of the 1969 June draft. He got his first call to the Sox in 1972 after being named International League's Most Valuable Player. He was there to stay by the next season. The great outfield defender showed the world his skills when he made a classic catch into the right-field stands to rob Joe Morgan of a home run during the 1975 World Series. The following season he earned his first Gold Glove and notched seven more of the famed gloves over his career, which only ranks behind Willie Mays, Roberto Clemente and Al Kaline. "Dewey" was no slouch behind the plate, either. He slammed a total of 366 homers over his two decades in the majors. The three-time All-Star spent 19 of those seasons with the Sox.

Rick Burleson, a first-round selection in the January 1970 secondary phase, was a tough player and a tough out during his 13 years in the majors. An excellent fielding shortstop with good range and a cannon arm, he won a Gold Glove and set a record for the most double plays (147) in 1980. He also set a record for most assists in a game by a shortstop (15). After seven years with Boston, he was traded to the California Angels. The three-time All-Star displayed toughness when he bounced back from a torn rotator cuff to become the American League Comeback Player of the Year in 1986. A year later he retired in Baltimore.

The Red Sox made **Jim Rice** its first-round pick in 1971 and he didn't disappoint them. He played his whole 16-year career with Boston and was named to nine All-Star teams. His 382 career home runs ranks behind only Ted Williams and Carl Yastrzemski in Boston's history. Rice's best season came in 1978 when he hit 46 homers and knocked in 139 RBI to earn Most Valuable Player honors. Rice finally got his chance to play in the World Series in 1986. He made the most of it by batting .333 against the Mets. After his playing career ended he became a hitting instructor with the Red Sox, first in the minors then in the majors. He has been considered for the National Baseball Hall of Fame since 1995 and has earned more votes each year. Boston inducted him in their own Hall of Fame in 1995.

Bob Stanley was one of the best relievers

for the team to come out of the draft. The first round pick in the June 1974 secondary round pitched 13 seasons for the Red Sox. During that span, he appeared in 637 games and saved 132. He twice led American League relievers in victories and twice in loses. He filled every pitching role during his time and ended up with a 115-97 record. He was named to two All-Star Games.

Another first round pitcher who played alongside Stanley was **Bruce Hurst**. Hurst was a starter for Boston for nine seasons in the 1980s. The ace of the staff won two of the three games he started in the 1986 World Series, but it was not enough as the Sox lost the Series in seven games. He was named to the All-Star Game in 1987. His best season with the Red Sox was his last when he went 18-6. The following season he went to San Diego where he led the National League with 10 complete games in route to a 15-11 record. He ended his 15-year career ended with the Rangers and a 145-113 record.

Seven turned out to be a lucky number for Boston in the 1976 June regular draft. They selected **Wade Boggs** out of high school. After six years in the minors, the Sox elevated the .300-plus hitter to the majors and he soon showed he could hit over .300 there, too. By the next season, Boggs was leading the league in average and did so four more times with the Sox. He was named to eight straight All-Star teams beginning in 1985. He batted .290 in a losing effort in the 1986 World Series, but he earned a ring 10 years later as a member of the Yankees. One of the game's most consistent hitters went to Tampa Bay in 1998 where he batted .280 on the season.

Eighteen major league teams today are regretting they didn't draft **Roger Clemens** in the 1983 draft. He was the 19th player taken and the Red Sox benefited from their foresight. The University of Texas pitcher joined the Sox staff the following season. He had his breakout season in 1986 to lead the Red Sox to the World Series. His 24-4 record earned him Cy Young and Most Valuable Player awards. His only shortfall that season was not earning a World Series ring. "The Rocket" played 12 seasons for the Sox and was named to five All-Star teams and won three Cy Young awards. Twice he has tied the major league record for most strikeouts in a game with 20, both in a Red Sox uniform. In fact, he tied the immortal Cy Young in career victories with Boston and 38 complete game shutouts before leaving for the Toronto Blue Jays. In 1998, he added his fifth Cy Young Award to his mantel.

Another pitcher who has turned out to be quite a strikeout artist who was a Boston original is **Curt Schilling**. Drafted in the second round of the January 1986 draft, the right-hander was traded while he was still in the minors to Baltimore. Then he spent a year with Houston before landing in Philadelphia, where he has made a name for himself. He became the ace of the staff in leading the team to a pennant with a 16-7 record. Then he was named as the Most Valuable Player in League Championship Series. He also added a victory in the World Series that year. He became the National League strikeout leader in 1997 and 1998. Schilling set the National League strikeout record with 319. He was named to three straight All-Star games starting in 1997.

In that trade with Schilling was another budding star and Red Sox draft pick, **Brady Anderson**. Baltimore decided to keep the outfielder and he has turned in some great performances for the team. He set American League record for

Wade Boggs, drafted by the Red Sox. Shown here with the Devil Rays. (Photograph by Marty Orr.)

most consecutive stolen bases without being caught, 34, in 1994–1995. Then he had his finest season in 1996, hitting .297 with 117 runs, 37 doubles 50 home runs, 110 RBI and 21 steals. He's been named to three All-Star teams thus far.

The Red Sox also traded **Jeff Bagwell**, a fourth round pick in 1989, while he was still in the minors to the Houston Astros for pitcher Larry Anderson. Houston brought him up to the majors the following season and he captured the National League Rookie of the Year Award, getting 23-of-24 first-place votes. Then in 1994 he was named National League MVP, the first player in Houston franchise history to win the award. He also became the first player in the history of the Houston franchise to hit 30-or-more home runs in four seasons and in three consecutive years.

Mo Vaughn played three seasons at Seton Hall University batting .417 with a school-record 57 home runs and 218 RBI in his college career. He hit 28 home runs as a 1987 freshman to break the school single season mark. His Omega Psi Phi fraternity brothers gave him the nickname "Hit Dog." The Boston Red Sox selected Vaughn in the first round (23rd pick) of the June 1989 draft. He made his major league debut, June 27, 1991, starting at first base against the Yankees. Vaughn was named to the All-Star Team in 1995 during a breakout season in which he hit 39 homers and 126 RBI to lead the Sox to a first-place finish in the American League East. His efforts won him the Most Valuable Player Award at the end of the season. Vaughn was also named to All-Star teams in 1996 and 1998 with the Sox. He became a free agent in 1998 and signed with the Angels.

Nomar Garciaparra may someday replace Joe Cronin as the best-ever shortstop in Boston history the way he has played already. The first-round pick in 1994 moved quickly through the farm system and first appeared with the Sox in September 1996. The following year he hammered American League pitchers for a major league record 30 homers to earn Rookie of the Year honors. He also had a 30-game hitting streak, another rookie record. The rookie was also named to the All-Star Team. One Boston sportswriter called him the best Sox infielder in

Jeff Bagwell was drafted by Boston in the fourth round in 1989.

50 years. No sophomore slump for this shortstop. He bettered his first season by batting .323-36-122 and helping the Sox to the League Championship Series. By the way, Garciaparra decided baseball was his calling at age five and decided he was going to be a major leaguer someday. That day has come.

Long Shots

Bill Lee, a 22nd round pick in 1968, quickly moved through the minors and was in Boston by 1971. The lanky lefty was made part of the starting rotation in 1973. He responded with a 12-4 record by the All-Star break, which earned him a spot on the All-Star Team. He finished the season with 17 wins, which was how many games he won the next two years as well. Lee was such a character that he earned the nickname "Spaceman." He ran into trouble with management, which resulted in him being traded to Montreal. There he left the club when teammate Rodney Scott was traded.

The 1980 draft produced two long-shot pitchers for the Red Sox: **Oil Can Boyd**, 16th round, and **Tom Bolton**, 20th round.

Boyd, whose real first name is Dennis, came out of Jackson State University and got his first appearance with the Red Sox in 1982. The following season the showy, skinny right-hander became a starter on the staff. The Red Sox suspended him in 1986 after he got upset for being left off the All-Star Team. The following season he helped the team to the League Championship Series with his 16-10 record. He won a game in the LCS, but lost his only World Series performance. Blood clot problems in his shoulder limited his effectiveness after that season. He became a free agent in 1990 and signed with Montreal. His career ended in 1991.

Bolton, on the other hand, was drafted out of high school and took longer to get to the majors as he was not called up until 1987 as a reliever. In 1990 the Sox turned him into a starter and he responded with a 10-5 record to help Boston to the playoffs. He relieved in two games in the LCS and held the Athletics scoreless. Bolton was with Boston for six seasons before going on to Cincinnati, Detroit and Baltimore.

The Red Sox may have given up on **Joel Bennett** a little too soon. Originally drafted in the 21st round in 1991 from East Stroudsburg University, the pitcher was released in 1996. Undaunted by the release, Bennett signed with Newburgh, an independent team in the Northeast League. After going 6-0 with a 0.79 ERA, the right-hander signed with the Orioles. The six-foot-one pitcher began 1998 at Triple-A Rochester and couldn't lose. He was 10-0 with a 3.64 ERA when the Orioles called him up. After seven years and three months, he was finally in the majors.

Chico Walker was a 22nd round pick. The 1976 selection first got a call to Boston in 1980. After three other short stints with the Red Sox, he signed with the Cubs. The utility fielder played a decade in the majors.

Disappointments

While the Red Sox have had some good number-one picks over the years, they had some real duds as well from the June regular draft.

The first disappointment for the Red Sox came after they appeared in the 1967 World Series, because they got the last pick in the draft, who was **Tom Maggard**. The outfielder/catcher out of high school made it only to Triple-A before succumbing to an insect bite. He died in 1974 after being bitten by an undetermined bug.

The Sox number one pick in 1969 was **Noel Jenke**, who made it as far as Triple-A until turning to the National Football League and playing four years there. He was also drafted by the National Hockey League.

The following year, Boston couldn't sign shortstop **Jimmy Hacker** after picking him in the first round. Another shortstop, **Joel Bishop**, was picked two years later in the first round and he couldn't get past first base (Class A).

Boston signed **Eddie Ford** in 1974 after drafting him in the first round. He made it as far as Triple-A. The same was true of **Otis Foster** the following year. The first rounder got as far as Triple-A before calling it quits in 1980.

Andrew Madden, a first-round choice in 1977, developed arm problems early and never got past Class A ball.

The Sox lost their first-round picks from 1978 through 1980 as a result of signing some high-class free agents. They made up for those losses by having three first-round picks in the 1982 draft. However, of those three draft picks, only Sam Horn made it to the majors with the Sox and he was a bust with a .232 average. Boston also didn't get a first-round pick in 1990 for signing Tony Pena. And they lost first-round privileges in 1992.

Two of the three first-round picks in the 1982 draft were complete busts. Right-handed pitcher **Rob Parkins** (18th overall) underwent surgery immediately after signing and was lost for the year. He failed at Class A. He tried a comeback at age 28, but never materialized in the majors. First baseman/outfielder **Jeff Ledbetter** did him only one level better. Ledbetter had shattered the all-time collegiate mark with 42 homers in one season and 97 in his college career. That was 33 more than the previous career mark. Ledbetter never achieved the home run success in the minors and was released by the Red Sox in 1985 at his own request. He tried to come back with the Cardinals, but was miserable as well. **Dan Gabriele**, a first-round pitcher in 1985, made it to Double-A before injuring a wrist.

Boston gambled on signing **Dan McMurtry** and lost. The first rounder chose to go to the University of Michigan and play football. He was later drafted by the National Football League.

The Red Sox had high hopes for **Greg Blosser**, who they had drafted in the first round (16th overall) in 1989. The outfielder showed some progress by hitting more than 20 home runs in the minors. Blosser was called up in 1993 and 1994 with the team, but each time he failed to hit major league pitching. He went 3 for 39 for an .077 average. He was granted free agency in 1995 and was signed by the Orioles, who released him the next season. Then he was signed by the Devil Rays in 1996. Blosser had a disappointment himself when his brother, a third rounder with the Royals in 1995, died in a car crash in 1998.

The latest setback for the Red Sox was **J.J. Johnson**, a first-round pick (37th overall) in 1991. The outfielder out of high school hadn't progressed very far in five seasons, so the Sox traded him to the Twins. After eight seasons, he was only at Double-A ball with the Twins.

Best Draft

The Red Sox had several good years, and 1976 stands out as the best, because several of those players ended up on the 1986 World Series team. The first pick was left-handed pitcher **Bruce Hurst**, who pitched eight seasons for the Red Sox. He won two of the three games that Boston won in the Series. **Glenn Hoffman**, a second round choice out of high school, played the infield for seven seasons in Boston. Fifth rounder **Mike Smithson** came up to the majors with Texas, but played the last two seasons of his career with Boston. The best find of the 1976 draft was **Wade Boggs**, who was also drafted out of high school. Boggs was part of that 1986 squad as well as LCS in 1988 and 1990. Ninth rounder **Gary Allenson** was mostly a backup receiver to Carlton Fisk with the Sox for six seasons. **Reid Nichols**, a twelfth round pick, was also with the Sox for half-a-dozen seasons as an outfielder. And long shot **Chico Walker** played four seasons with the Sox as a utility player.

Worst Draft

Nineteen seventy-eight was a lost year for the Red Sox, but that was somewhat of their own making. They lost their first three picks as compensation to other teams for free agents. Only two of the players—**Brian Denman** and **John Lickert**— selected ever made it to the majors for a total of 10 games.

Not much better was the 1992 draft in which three players made it to the majors, but none made any impact.

Where Are They Now?

Not every Dominican comes into professional baseball as a free agent. **Luis Ortiz** was born in Santo Domingo, but attended Union University in Tennessee. He became eligible for the draft and Boston picked him from Baptist University in the 1991 draft. He first came up with the Red Sox in 1993, but was traded to the Rangers in 1994. He played some Japanese ball in 1987 and signed with the Brewers in 1998.

DeMarlo Hale, a 17th round selection in the 1983 draft, is now manager of Trenton Thunder (Class AA). He spent four years in the club's minor league system.

Another former player who turned to coaching after playing is **Mike Goff**, a 21st round selection in 1984. He played in the Red Sox systems for five seasons, but never got to the majors. A back injury ended his playing career.

Glenn Hoffman, a second round selection in 1976, played nine seasons with the Boston and turned to coaching after his playing career ended. In 1999 he was the third base coach for the Dodgers, the team he went to play with after leaving the Red Sox.

Carlton Fisk rejoined the Red Sox as a special assistant to the general manager in 1999.

Steve Lyons is now a sports broadcaster for the Fox Network.

Ones Who Got Away

The Red Sox picked several players over the history of the draft who ended up playing significant time with other teams.

Boston picked **Amos Otis** in the fifth round in the first draft out of high school. The following year he was drafted off a minor league roster by the New York Mets. Refusing to play third early in 1969, he missed out on a World Series opportunity and was traded to the Royals after the season for Joe Foy. The Mets certainly got the worst of that deal as Foy never played in the majors, while Otis became a five-time All-Star with the Royals. He was one of the first players inducted into the Royals Hall of Fame.

Geoff Zahn was chosen in the fifth round of the 1967 January Secondary Phase and wouldn't sign. He went on to a 13-year career pitching career with Minnesota and California.

Roy Smalley was a two-time selection in 1971 and 1972, but he wouldn't sign and went on to a 13-year career with other teams.

The Sox picked **Gary Redus** in the 17th round in 1978, but he waited until the next season to get selected by the Reds in the 15th round before signing.

Dave Magaden was the 12th pick out of high school in the 1980 draft and he ended up going to college and waiting until 1983 before signing with the Mets in the third round.

The Sox missed out on two good pitchers in 1984. They selected **Derek Lilliquist** in the 15th round and **Jack McDowell** in the 20th round. Both players went to college and turned out to be first-round picks in 1986 with Atlanta and the White Sox, respectively.

All in the Family

Chris Cannizzaro, Jr., whose father spent 13 years in the big leagues, was caught in the ninth round in 1983.

The Red Sox selected **Marc Sullivan**, son of general manager Haywood, in the June 1979 draft.

The Red Sox have nothing against nepotism as witnessed by them selecting three players with Boston connections in 1999: **Brady Williams**, son of Red Sox Manager Jimy Williams; **Joe Kerrigan, Jr.**, son of Sox pitching coach Joe Kerrigan; and **Jordan Remy**, son of former Sox infielder and current TV broadcaster Jerry Remy.

Best Undrafted Player

One of the best undrafted local players Boston found was right-handed **Ken Ryan**. Signed in 1986 after he was not drafted out of Seekonk High School, he sat at Class A for five seasons before he moved up in the farm system. The reliever first came to Boston in 1992 and was up three more times before being traded to the Phillies. In his best season with the Sox he saved 13 games. In Philadelphia he relieved in 62 games with eight saves in 1996.

On the Roster

The Red Sox had more than a dozen of their own draft picks on their 40-man roster entering 1999, which was more than most teams and shows how important the draft is to the team.

The two veteran draft picks of the team were infielders **Tim Naehring** and **John Valentin**, who were both drafted in 1988 by Boston. Naehring first came up with Boston in 1990, but Valentin has played more games since being called up in 1992. Valentin moved over to third base in 1998 when Naehring was recovering from reconstructive surgery on his elbow from an injury in 1997. Valentin hit 23 homers in 1998 and went errorless for a 65-game stretch in helping the Red Sox to the playoffs.

One of the best compensation picks for the Red Sox has been **Scott Hatteberg**. He was a "sandwich" pick in 1991 as compensation from the Royals signing free agent Mike Boddicker. Hatteberg was captain and Most Valuable Player for Washington State, which won the Pac-10 all three years he played there. He was also a member of the U.S. team at the Goodwill Games. He became the team's regular catcher in 1997 and hit a solid .277.

Long shots on the roster included **Michael Coleman** and **Ronald Mahay**, both 18th round picks. Mahay was drafted as an outfielder in 1991 and got a call up in 1995, but he was just average for an outfielder. The next season he switched to pitching and started the process all over again. The lefty only took two seasons to get to the majors again in 1997. And he got another call in 1998. On the other hand, Coleman, an outfielder, got a call up in 1997 to Boston, but was unimpressive and spent the next season at Triple-A.

Brian Barkley, a fifth-round pick in 1994, is a left-handed pitcher who first got a call up in September 1998. He will have to finesse his way into the majors as he's not an overpowering pitcher.

Two catchers on the roster were **Scott Hatteberg** and **Steve Lomasney**. Hatteberg became the team's regular receiver in 1997, while Lomasney may someday replace him there but was still developing into a hitter in 1999.

Trot Nixon, a first round pick in 1993, has been up to Boston for two September calls and may break through in 1999. He also earned a start in the League Championship Series. Back problems have held him back, but in 1998 he hit 23 homers in Triple-A while batting .310. The outfielder has good bat speed and foot speed as he stole 26 bases in 1998.

Donnie Sadler can also play the outfield, but Boston used him at second base in 1998 when they brought him up early in the season. The 11th round pick in 1994 may serve in a utility role in Boston's future. He's regarded as the most athletic player in the system.

The 1995 seventh round selection **Cole Liniak** has moved quickly through the Boston system and displayed home run power expected of a third baseman in 1998 when he whacked 17 at Triple-A. He may be the next regular Boston third baseman.

Lou Merloni, a 10th round pick in 1993, finally got his opportunity to play with the Red Sox in 1998. The second baseman proved himself and may have more of a future in Boston in the future.

Brian Rose, a third round pitcher, was the International League all-star starting pitcher in 1997 when he went 17-5 in Triple-A, but he was not as impressive in the majors with Boston in 1998 and was sent back to Pawtucket for more seasoning. Rose signed with the Red Sox out of high school in 1994 instead of going to Michigan. "If it wasn't for being drafted by the Red Sox, I'd probably be in Ann Arbor at school right now," Rose wrote a fan during a chat on the Internet.

Left-handed pitcher **Robert Ramsey**, a

Jim Chamblee, a Red Sox draft choice, shown here with the Pawtucket Red Sox.

seventh rounder in 1996, may soon be with the Red Sox. After a 12-6 record and 3.49 ERA in 1998 at Double-A Trenton, the starter could be called up to the majors at any time.

Future Stars?

Dernell Stenson, a third round pick in 1996, showed he had legitimate home run power in 1998 when the left-handed outfielder slugged 24 dingers in Double-A. He was voted top hitting prospect by Eastern League managers. Then he hit .299-4-20 in the Arizona Fall League.

The first round pick of the 1997 draft, **John Curtice**, struck out more than a batter per inning in his first full season in the minors. The southpaw has a fastball in the mid–90s and is working on his other pitches. The high school pick is still a few years away from the majors.

The next long shot who may be headed to the majors is **David Eckstein**, a 19th round selection in 1997, who was scouted and signed by Luke Wrenn. A batting average over .300 in Class A sent him on to Double-A Trenton in 1999. Then he was selected for the Double-A Association All-Star Game after being selected as the Player of the Month in May. The second baseman was hitting .326 when he was named to the game.

Another long shot who was doing well in 1999 was **Jason Norton**, a 16th rounder from 1998 who was scouted by Joe Mason. He was named South Atlantic League Pitcher of the Week after throwing a complete game shutout, improving to 7-3 on the season. The right-handed pitcher had struck out 101 while walking only 19 on the season by mid–July.

Jim Chamblee, a 12th round pick in 1995, has moved up to Triple-A after four seasons in

the minors. The tall second baseman — six-foot-four — was sporting long sideburns with Pawtucket and hitting long home runs to help his progress toward the top.

The Sox hoped to strengthen their outfield in the next century when they selected **Rick Asadoorian** in the first round in 1999. "He's got confidence in his ability," Britton said. "If I had his tools and ability, I'd have confidence, too." Boston plans on turning him into a centerfielder. Asadoorian has the proverbial total package of skills. He can hit for both average and power and is a gazelle in centerfield with a rocket right arm. The Massachusetts boy batted .500, piled up 41 RBIs, and scored 35 runs. His raw numbers are impressive by themselves, but what makes Britton and the Red Sox most enthusiastic about their new selection is his maturity and his intangibles. Asadoorian was scouted by Ray Fagnant.

Boston's second pick in the 1999 draft was **Brad Baker**, a high school pitcher from Massachusetts. The supplemental pick who was the 40th player taken in the draft, is six-foot-two and throws a fastball, curve and change.

Marshall McDougall of Florida State, who made history, belting six consecutive home runs in one game against Maryland, was the 26th round pick in 1999. He went 7-7 to set NCAA records with six home runs, 16 RBI, and 25 total bases. He was named ACC Player of the Year and led the team with a .429 batting average, 266 at bats, 97 runs, 114 hits, 25 HR, 96 RBI, an .820 slugging percentage, a .503 on-base percentage. He is also 19 for 21 in stolen base attempts.

Chicago White Sox

The draft has helped the White Sox be a competitor over the last 30 years in comparison to the 35 years before the draft. The Sox were competitive in the 1950s and '60s, but finished only first once in 1959, the last time they were in the World Series. After a slump in the 1970s, the Sox returned to prominence and have finished first three times in their division.

The 1983 team that finished first in their division, but lost in the League Championship Series to Baltimore, had only a couple of Sox originals, including Harold Baines, Brit Burns and Mike Squires.

The White Sox then had a run of great first-round picks in the late 1980s when they chose Jack McDowell, Robin Ventura, Frank Thomas and Alex Fernandez in successive drafts starting in 1987. These players helped lead the team to a first-place finish in 1993 and 1994. Also, on that team were White Sox draft picks Ron Karkovice, Jason Bere, Scott Radinsky, Bobby Thigpen and others. The Sox also had some great picks from other teams on that squad to have a good mix of veterans and young players.

The Sox have failed to protect some of their draft picks over the years and lost several to Rule 5, the minor league draft. For example, John Hudek, a 10th round pick in 1988, and Buddy Groom, a 12th round pick in 1987, were both lost to Detroit to the December draft of minor leaguers not protected by the 40-man roster.

The Sox have also traded some draft picks before they ever made it to the majors. For instance, Johnny Ruffin, a pitcher drafted in the fourth round in 1988 was traded to the Reds for Tim Belcher in July 1993. The strategy behind that trade was to get somebody right away to help the team win the pennant and it worked. The Sox traded Randy Velarde to the Yankees because they didn't need a catcher right away.

The Sox seem to prefer more experienced college players in the first round. Five or six players taken in the first round in 1997 were from college. The Sox received five sandwich selections in 1997 for having free agents who signed with other teams. The Sox generally take the best players when they draft. "You have your needs, but you go for the best available," explained Brian Porter, White Sox baseball operations.

After losing Albert Belle and Robin Ventura to free agency, the White Sox went into a youth

Bobby Seay was drafted by the White Sox in the first round, the 12th pick.

rebuilding mode for the 1999 season. As a result, they became youngest team in the American League. Young draft picks Jeff Abbott and Greg Norton were expected to replace the veterans who had left. Manager Jerry Manuel was trying to instill a team concept to take some of the pressure off the rookies.

The White Sox had five picks in the first round in 1999 and they chose all pitchers. The Chicago White Sox selected pitchers with 14 of the club's first 15 picks during the initial day of the 1999 first-year free-agent draft. The Sox had six picks among the draft's first 66 selections, taking five power pitchers. "This was a pitching strong draft and we tried to take advantage of what the draft had to offer," said Duane Shaffer, scouting director. "I was very pleased with the talent we found among the top picks available to us, but I was just as pleased with how deep were able to go and still find quality players."

The size of the scouting department is one of the smallest in baseball. The Sox have just 13 area scouts, three regional supervisors and a national crosschecker. On the international market, the Sox have only three scouts and a Latin America coordinator. They used to have an academy in Venezuela, but it was moved to the Dominican Republic. They haven't done much scouting in the Pacific Rim, either. "We don't have the resources to go to Asia," said Porter. The Sox don't hold tryout camps, but rely on reports from the Major League Scouting Bureau.

Best Picks

Carlos May, the younger brother of Lee May, was Chicago's first draft pick to make significant contributions to the team. The first-round pick in the second draft was American League Rookie of the Year in 1969 when he hit 18 homers in 100 games. His career nearly ended that first season as he was injured when a mortar misfired when he was stationed at Camp Pendleton. However, the Marines fixed him up and he was able to rebound to baseball. May never really improved much upon his rookie year and the White Sox traded him to the Yankees in 1976 for pitcher Ken Brett and outfielder Rich Coggins. He appeared in the World Series for the Yankees, but was hitless. The Yankees sold him the next year to the Angels. He retired at the end of the season and became a postal worker in Chicago.

Another player who peaked early with the White Sox was **Terry Forster**, a second round pick in 1970. Drafted out of high school, he got a call to the Sox the next season. In his rookie year in 1972, he saved 29 games to finish behind Sparky Lyle for most saves in the American League. Two years later he led the league in saves with 24 and was named Fireman of the Year. He suffered an injury the next season and the Sox traded him to Pittsburgh for Richie Zisk. Forster went on to the Dodgers and appeared in two World Series with Los Angeles before his career ended with the Angels in 1986.

Rich Gossage was the other player to be sent to Pittsburgh for Zisk in the Forster trade. He was picked the same year as Forster, but in the ninth round. After being named as the Midwest League's Pitcher of the Year, the Sox called him as a reliever in 1972. He was 7-1 as a reliever in his first season. However, Gossage suffered the next season and was sent back to the minors. He pitched most of 1974 in the majors as a reliever. The next season he took over the roll of stopper from Forster and led the league with 26 saves to become the Fireman of the Year. That led him to be named as the first reliever to the All-Star Game. He stayed one year in Pittsburgh before going to the Yankees for six seasons. He became the oldest player in the majors in 1994 with Seattle and became the third pitcher to pitch in more than 1,000 games. His career ended with 310 saves, fourth highest in history.

Bucky Dent made a big dent in the majors as a player and manager. He was originally drafted in the first round of the June 1970 Secondary Phase and became Chicago's starting shortstop in 1974. He finished second in the Rookie of the Year voting with his slick fielding and hitting .275. After three more seasons with the Southsiders, he was dealt to the Yankees, where he became famous. The fame came from his excellent fielding and clutch hitting in the League Championship Series and World Series. He was named the Series Most Valuable Player. He led American League shortstops in fielding three times during his playing career. After playing he turned to managing and became the skipper for the Yankees a couple of times. He left the Yankees to become a coach with the Cardinals, which was the first team to draft him.

Harold Baines, a first round pick in 1977 out of high school, took just three years in the minors before getting the call to Chicago in 1980 as a starter. In his third season with the team he knocked in 105 RBI, the youngest player to accomplish that with the Sox. The following year he helped the Sox in the League Championship Series with clutch hitting. He set a major league mark for game-winning RBI with 22. The Sox traded him in 1989 to the Texas Rangers in a multi-player trade involving Sammy Sosa. In all, Baines was named to six Midsummer Classics during his career.

Doug Drabek was originally an 11th round pick in 1983 with the Sox. He was the player to be named later in a trade with the Yankees the next year. Drabek first came up to the majors with the Yankees in 1986, who sent him packing to Pittsburgh at the end of the season in a multi-player trade. He started off disastrously with the Pirates in 1987 when he was 1-8 with a 4.79 ERA before the All-Star break. However, the right-hander turned things around and was named Pitcher of the Month in August when he was 5-0. Drabek won the Cy Young Award with the Pirates in 1990 when he led the league in wins with 22 in helping the Pirates to the League Championship Series. He helped the Pirates to the LCS three years running. In 1994, he was named to the All-Star team when he jumped to

a 10-5 start with Houston. The Sox got him back in 1997 as a free agent. He was 12-11 with the Southsiders that season. He then signed with Baltimore in 1998 where he struggled through a 6-11 season that led to his retirement.

The best reliever in White Sox history so far is **Bobby Thigpen**. The fourth round pick in 1985 out of Mississippi State was a starter in the minors and had a losing record when he was called up to the Sox in 1986. He showed the Sox he was better as a stopper, but it took another season before the team was convinced. In 1988 he broke the White Sox record with 34 saves. His breakthrough year came in 1990. He was saving games at a record pace, so he was named to the All-Star game and pitched one scoreless inning. By early September, he broke the major league record of 46 saves by Dave Righetti. He ended the season with 57 saves and four wins. In fact, he had a say in 65 percent of Chicago's wins on the year. His career tailed off after that, but he ended up with 201 saves lifetime.

When Carlton Fisk was finished with his long career, **Ron Karkovice** was there to take over the starter's spot. The first-round pick in 1982 was first called up in 1986 and kept being called up each season until he became a permanent fixture in the 1990s. He led receivers in the American League in throwing out thieves and helped the White Sox to the League Championship Series in 1993. That year he hit 20 homers as well. Karkovice played with the Sox until retiring in 1997.

Jack McDowell, a pitcher on that 1993 squad, was also a first rounder. Drafted in 1987, the White Sox gave him the express elevator to the majors and he received a call to the majors that first season. He responded with a perfect 3-0 record. But the following season he slumped to a 5-10 mark, so his elevator went back to the minors for a season. "Black Jack" became a better pitcher for the experience and became a real asset for the team after that. In 1993 he hit the top floor of his career with a 22-10 mark and was given the Cy Young Award. However, he was hit hard in the championship series by the Blue Jays and lost the two games he started. The Sox traded him to the Yankees after the 1994 season.

Frank Thomas may be the first White Sox draft pick to be admitted to the Baseball Hall of

Fame once his career is over. The first-round pick from 1989 out of Auburn University spent less than two seasons in the minors before the White Sox promoted him to the majors. By 1993 he was the American League's Most Valuable Player and a big reason the White Sox made it to the championships, but the Blue Jays wisely pitched around him. The "Big Hurt" continued his torrid pace the following season and was named MVP again. Then he was the batting champion in 1997 when he batted .347. He also had 35 homers and 35 doubles that season. The five-time All-Star had an off season in 1998 when he hit just .265; however, he continued to hit home runs and slammed 29. Among active players, he ranked fourth in the majors. The clutch hitter has knocked in more than 100 runs each full season he has been in the majors. By mid-1999, he broke the 300 home run mark and was back in the .300 hitting grove.

Another first-rounder on that 1993 team was **Robin Ventura**. The third baseman was first drafted in 1989. After being named a Southern League all-star, the White Sox gave him a September call up that first year and he became a permanent fixture. The slick-fielding Ventura grabbed his first Gold Glove in 1991 and began hitting double-digit home runs as well. He scooped up four more Gold Gloves in the next seven seasons with the Sox. Then he became a free agent and signed with the New York Mets.

Long Shots

It didn't hurt **Mike Squires** to have a dad who was a scout for the White Sox. He was picked by the team in the 18th round in 1973. But Squires showed he didn't need any help after that and proved himself by being named as the Southern League's Most Valuable Player in 1975, which led to his first promotion to the Big Leagues that season. He wasn't going to become famous as a great hitter, so the Sox found other ways to use the left-handed first baseman. Manager Tony La Russa put him behind the plate in 1980 to become the first left-handed catcher in 22 years in the majors. Then La Russa used him at third base in 1983, which made him the first left-handed third baseman in some 50 years.

Squires even won a Gold Glove Award playing first for the Sox in 1981.

Randy Velarde, a 19th round draft in 1985, spent two years in the White Sox farm system before being traded to the Yankees who first called him up to the majors in 1987. The following season the middle infielder was shuttled between Columbus and New York five times. Still he was named an all-star in the International League. He was in the bigs to stay in 1990 with the Yankees. Then he was granted free agency in 1995 and signed with the Angels. Through the 1998 season he had a .268 average in the majors.

The White Sox traded pitcher **Joe Borowski**, a 32nd round pick in 1989, in 1991 for Pete Rose, Jr. Rose never amounted to much, but Borowski was called up to the majors in 1995 with the Braves. He's also been with the Yankees and Brewers as a reliever.

Jason Bere was just a 36th round pick in 1990 and had about as much chance of making it to the majors as a meteor hitting the earth. The pitcher out of junior college received a $2,000 signing bonus and a plane ticket to

Jason Bere, pictured here with Cincinnati, was drafted by the White Sox. (Photograph by Marty Orr.)

rookie league. When he first reported to rookie ball, he was "shocked" a little with the higher draft picks there. "High picks don't stay there long," he explained. They moved up quickly, and he was able to compete better with the remaining pitchers. The velocity of his fastball increased to the mid–90s the next season and he began getting hitters out with more consistency at Single-A. His breakthrough season came in 1992 as he went all the way from Single-A to Triple-A. After a 5-1 start at Nashville the next season, the Sox made him a starter and he helped them to the League Championship Series with his 12-5 record. He also got to start one game in the series, but got no decision in a game won eventually by the Sox. The following season he got off to a great start and was named to the All-Star Game and ended up the season with a 12-2 record. His brief baseball career was at a pinnacle. There was only one way for it to go — down — and it did like a meteor. The following season he began experiencing elbow problems and fell to an 8-15 record sending him back to the minors. Tommy John surgery was necessary to fix his pitching elbow. His career began all over again. After a 3-7 start in 1998, the Sox and released him in July. He was picked up by the Reds and finished the season with a 3-2 mark in Cincinnati. In 1999, he started in Cincinnati, but was sent back to Triple-A in mid-season.

Disappointments

The Sox have a long list of casualties from the first round of the June regular draft.

The Sox got off to a disappointing start in the first draft. They chose **Ken Plesha**, a local boy who attended Notre Dame, and the catcher only got as far as Class A. Their 1967 first round draft pick was **Dan Haynes**, a third baseman who peaked at Triple A. The Sox continued their every-other-year poor pick as they chose another local player, **Ted Nicholson**. The third baseman never got past first base in the baseball world.

In 1971, the Sox had a first in draft history. They had the first pick in the draft and chose **Danny Goodwin**, who became the first player in draft history not to sign a contract. The catcher from nearby Peoria decided to attend Southern University instead. The following year

the Sox picked **Mike Ondina** in the first round. The high school outfielder got to Triple-A before he nose dived.

The Sox took a local favorite **Larry Monroe** in 1974. The right-handed pitcher from the northwest suburbs only got a cup of coffee in the majors. Another coffee drinker in the majors was **Rick Seilheimer**, a first round catcher in 1979. **Kurt Brown**, a first rounder in 1985, was another catcher who bombed out at Triple-A. The next year the Sox picked **Grady Hall** and the left-handed hurler met the same fate.

The Sox failed to sign first-round pick **Steve Buechele** in 1979 and in those days there was no compensation for not signing a number one. Buechele attended Stanford University and was drafted by the Rangers in 1982. He ended up playing for the crosstown Cubs for four seasons.

The latest first-round failure was **Eddie Pearson**, who was drafted in 1992. The Sox gave the first baseman seven seasons before they gave up on him and let him become a free agent. He hit a mere .270 in the minors, which wasn't enough to earn a first baseman's job in the majors.

Best Draft

The year 1970 turned out to be a very good one for the White Sox as Terry Forster, Rich Gossage, and Bucky Dent were selected, but 1990 was better from top to bottom. Alex Fernandez was the first choice that year and he pitched seven seasons for the Sox. Another pitcher, James Baldwin, was a fourth round pick and he was still pitching for the Sox in 1998. Ray Durham was next choice in that draft and he turned out to be a starting second baseman for the Sox. A long shot from that class of 1990 was Jason Bere, a 36th round selection, who pitched five seasons for the Southsiders.

Worst Draft

The years 1984 and 1985 each produced just one player who reached the majors and neither had much impact on the team.

Where Are They Now?

Julio Vinas, a 33rd round pick in 1991, was granted free agency in 1997 after making it to Triple-A. The long shot signed with the Pirates then with the Orioles. In 1999 he was still trying to find a way to the majors with the Rochester Red Wings. When he was drafted, he had a letter of intent to go to Notre Dame. "If I had to do it over again, I would've gone to Notre Dame," he reflected. Although he hasn't been in the majors yet, he got a taste of it with the White Sox when they played the Cubs in the Windy City Classic before interleague play was introduced. In his first at-bat, he stroked a home run. Now he'd like to get the chance to do the same in the majors.

Mitch Lukevics, a second-round pick in the 1975 draft, pitched for six seasons in the White Sox farm system before he decided coaching was an easier route to the majors. He became a pitching coach first in the White Sox system and now with the Devil Rays' minor league system.

Bucky Dent, a first round pick in the 1970 June Secondary Phase, is now the dugout coach for the Texas Rangers. He also owns a baseball school in Delray Beach, Fla.

Ones Who Got Away

The White Sox picked **Warren Cromartie** out of high school in 1971, but he didn't sign. Instead, he waited until the Expos drafted him in the first round in 1973 before signing.

Andy McGaffigan was a fifth round pick in the January regular phase of the 1976 draft. Instead, he signed with the Yankees after they picked him.

The Sox chose **Gary Gaetti** in the 1978 June secondary phase. He went on to Northwest Missouri State University and was drafted in the first round by Minnesota in 1979. The third baseman ended up in Chicago in 1998, but on the northside with the Cubs. The Sox also lost **Tim Teufel** to the Twins. And the Cubs also hosted another of the Sox draft picks, **Calvin Schiraldi**, who was an 18th rounder in 1980 out of high school, but he didn't sign until the Mets picked him in the first round in 1983.

All in the Family

Jerry Hairston had more connections with the majors than United Airlines has to Chicago. His father, Sam, was the first black player ever signed by the White Sox. His brother had played with the Cubs in 1969. Another brother had played in the minors with the Sox. He was scouted and signed by his father as well after he was picked in the fourth round in June 1970. He was first called up to the Sox in 1973. The outfielder could never quite stick with the Sox and they sold him to the Pirates, who shipped him to Mexico where he spent four seasons in the Mexican League. The Sox took him back in 1981 and he became a pinch hitter for the team. In fact, he led the league in pinch hits with the Sox. His son was drafted by the Orioles in 1997 and made his major league debut in 1998 to give the family the distinction of being a third-generation baseball family. Then the Sox selected Scott Hairston, a shortstop out of high school.

Bruce Tanner, son of Pittsburgh manager Chuck Tanner, was taken in the fourth round in 1983. He is now a pitching coach with the Nashville Sounds in the Pirates' farm system.

Dan Monzon, Jr., son of Dan Monzon, who played two seasons with the Twins, was drafted in the 43rd round in 1989. He never made it to the majors like his dad, at least not yet.

On the Roster

With the White Sox in a retooling mode starting the 1999 season after ridding themselves of some high-priced players, several draft picks got their chance with the team out of spring training.

David Lundquist, a fifth-round pick in 1993, made the White Sox out of spring training in 1999 after six years in the minors. The right-hander began as a starter in the minors before he was converted to a relieving role in 1997 following elbow surgery. He saved 12 games in 1998.

Jeff Liefer, a first rounder in 1995, made the team out of spring training, too. He slammed 22 homers in 1998 in Double-A and Triple-A. Liefer shared first-base duties with

Jeff Liefer, drafted by the White Sox in the first round in 1995. (Photograph by Marty Orr.)

Paul Konerko, another first rounder, at the beginning of the 1999 season as well as playing the outfield.

The Sox also elevated **Mark Johnson** to the majors in 1999 in a backup role. The first-round pick in 1994 got his first call-up with the Sox in 1998 for eight games. The left-handed hitter averaged .245 in the minors and is a highly regarded defensive catcher.

Jim Parque, a first-round supplemental pick in 1997, was hustled through the system and got his call to the White Sox in 1998 after just 21 games in the minors. He was an All-American at UCLA in 1997 to earn the first round selection. The lefthander went from Single-A to Triple-A in three months in his rookie season. Then the Sox invited him to spring training in 1998, which gave him enough experience in their opinion. He earned a spot in the regular rotation after jumping to a 7-5 record.

Another pitcher seeing his first action in 1995 was **James Baldwin**, a fourth-round pick in 1990 out of high school. He was a Midwest League all-star in 1992, led the Southern League in ERA in 1993 and led the American Association in strikeouts in 1994. *The Sporting News* named him American League Rookie Pitcher of the Year in 1996 when he compiled an 11-6 mark. After a tough season in 1997, the right-hander came back with a 13-6 mark in 1998.

One of the veterans on the Sox is **Ray Durham**, a fifth-round pick in 1990. The second baseman was an all-star at Triple-A in 1994, which shot him into the majors the next season. He's no all-star, but he's been a consistent performer for four seasons at second base, averaging .273 and increasing his power numbers each season. In 1998, he hit a career high 19 dingers.

Mike Sirotka, a 15th round pick in 1993, also made his first performance in 1995 with the Sox after being named an all-star the year before at Class A South Bend. The lefty hurler from LSU was up and down like a yo-yo for three seasons before earning a spot in the regular rotation in 1998. He led the team with 14 wins in 1998 and had five complete games.

Greg Norton, a second round pick in 1993 out of the University of Oklahoma, led third basemen in fielding percentage in 1995. He got his first call to the majors in 1997 after leading the American Association in slugging percentage at .534, while clubbing 26 homers and 27 doubles. He earned a regular spot on the team in 1998 playing first base, but he moved back to third base to start the 1999 season.

Carlos Castillo, a third-round selection in the 1994 draft, has bounced back and fourth from the minors since 1997 as a reliever. The right-handed high school draft pick was a starter his first few seasons in the minors, but has been used mainly in middle relief since then.

Jeff Abbott was a two-time all-star in the minors before becoming a regular outfielder for the Sox in 1998, but the fourth round pick was sent back to the minors in 1999 for more experience.

Future Stars?

Long shot **Mario Valdez**, a 48th-round pick in 1993, would probably be in the majors if there wasn't such a logjam at first base in Chicago. The Mexican-born player did get a call in 1997 for 54 games with the Sox, but he hit just .243 with one homer, which didn't earn him a spot. He rebounded in the minors in 1998 with a .330 average and 20 homers.

When Robin Ventura left the Sox, it left a big gap at third base that fifth-round pick **Joe Crede** would like to fill one day. The 1996 draft pick hit a whopping .315 with 20 homers in 1998 to earn Most Valuable Player honors in the Carolina League. That earned him a promotion to Double-A. "He has a chance to be a special player," said general manager Ron Schueler.

Aaron Myette was one of the six first-round picks in 1997, and he has made excellent progress in the minors, going 20-10 his first three seasons. The Canadian right-hander with a mid–90s fastball moved up to Double-A in 1999, so he could get a call to the majors soon.

The White Sox had six picks in the first round in 1999 and spent one of their picks on **Rob Purvis** out of Bradley University. The

Rob Purvis, drafted by the White Sox in 1999. (Photograph courtesy of Rob Purvis.)

right-handed pitcher had a disgusting year in college with a 2-8 record, but his ERA was just 3.28. "We didn't play real well," he explained. "I'm not going to bad mouth my team though." Run support had been a problem.

Scouts told him that he reminded them of John Wetteland. But he really compares himself to John Smoltz. The Tipton, Indiana, native was first drafted out of high school by the Giants in the 49th round after going 32-3 with a ERA around 0.50. About the only thing his team didn't do was win the state championship.

Purvis felt he was going to go even higher in the draft, but he tore up his middle finger, had a dead arm for three games and didn't do real well in a tournament to lower him to a compensation pick. "If I sign and when I sign, it's time to go out and prove it," he said. He signed about a month after he was drafted. His agent got him $800,000 and one of the first things he did was buy a car for his folks. The small-town boy was now on his way to the big city.

The first player taken in 1999 was another pitcher: **Kip Wells** of Baylor. The 16th pick went 13-4 with a 3.71 ERA and 135 strikeouts for the Bears. "We are extremely pleased to be able to draft Kip with our selection," said Duane Shaffer, scouting director. "He's a big, strong right-handed power pitcher who we think will be a tremendous addition to our organization."

The right-hander struck out a season-high 12 on April 5 vs. Kansas and reached double figures five times in his 19 starts. He went 10-2 over his final 12 decisions and posted a 2.15 ERA in his last 12 outings. "I'm very excited about being selected by the White Sox," Wells said. "Even though you have an idea about how things will happen, you are still kind of shocked once it finally does. I'm happy the White Sox thought I could help their organization, and I can't wait to get started."

The Chicago White Sox selected pitcher **Jason Stumm** with the 15th pick in 1999. Stumm, 18, went 10-0 with an 0.81 ERA and 94 strikeouts for Centralia High School. "We were very impressed by Jason's arm strength and tremendous makeup," said Shaffer. "His fastball is explosive and caught everyone's attention. It was one of the best high school fastballs I saw this year."

"To be the White Sox first pick is a real honor," said Stumm. "I know the White Sox are a young team, and I hope that I can get to Chicago soon because the Sox have a bright future."

Another pitcher taken in the first round in 1999 was **Matt Ginter**, the 22nd pick in the first round for the Sox in 1999. Ginter, 21, was 8-7 with a 4.37 ERA and 102 strikeouts for Mississippi State. He became the fourth pitcher in Mississippi State history to post two 100-strike-out seasons. "We are very happy to be able to select a pitcher of Matt's ability and experience," Shaffer said. "He has a plus slider, and we think it can develop into an impressive 'out pitch' at the major league level."

"I wanted to go to an organization where pitchers move along quickly," said Ginter. "The Sox are an organization that gives young guys that opportunity. I'm excited. This couldn't have been a better day."

Cleveland Indians

The draft didn't help the Indians out of their 40-year funk until the club came up with a new formula called "Blueprint for Success." Designed in 1990 to revitalize the farm system, the results of that formula began to show up in 1994 when the Indians finished second. Also, contributing to the surge from pretender to contender was a new stadium and a move to the Central Division.

The Indians have drafted better in recent times then in the past as well, which has been one of the reasons they became a power in the 1990s. The Indians had their fair share of good picks before the late 1980s, but overall their drafts were relatively weak. Then in 1987 they picked Joey Belle, who later changed his named to Albert. He zipped through the minors and was with the Tribe by 1989. At that time the city was still known more as a mistake by the lake instead of a contender since the draft began.

That situation began to change with the arrival of veteran scout Chet Montgomery, who left Cincinnati after a couple of decades when Marge Schott took over. In his first year as director, he failed to sign Calvin Murray, the team's first round pick. Murray decided not to sign and go to the University of Texas. "We had reports that he was going to sign," he explained his decision.

Since the team had already forfeited its second-round pick, the media condemned Cleveland as having the worst draft in all of baseball. It was one of the things that led to his demise at Cleveland after two years as director. He also had a rift with another person in the organization, too. "It wasn't a good situation to be in," he explained. Chet was offered a national cross-checking position. However, Larry Doby in Pittsburgh offered him a player development job and he left the Indians.

The "poor" draft in 1989 actually turned out to be very good. Because it takes years for draft picks to make it to the majors and then usually a couple of more years before they reach their peak, judging a draft within a year or two is premature. After a decade, the results of the 1989 draft can now be evaluated more clearly. Murray was later selected in the first round by the Giants in 1992. By the end of 1998 he was still in the minors after six seasons. Overrated? As a first-round pick, he should have made it to the majors by now. Jerry Dipoto was picked third in the draft. The left-handed hurler made it to the majors in 1993. Alan Embree, another left-hander pitcher, was taken in the fifth round and he made it to the Indians in 1992 before coming back to stick for good in the majors in 1995. Curt Leskanic was an eighth rounder and the right-handed pitcher climbed to the majors in 1993 with Colorado. Probably the strongest player to come out of that draft was thirteenth round pick Jim Thome. He first got to Cleveland in 1991 and became an impact player in 1994. Brian Giles wasn't taken until the 17th round. It took him until 1995 to make it to the majors. In 1997 he became a starting outfielder for the Indians. Even Robert Person, a 25th round selection, made it to the majors in 1995 with the Mets.

Another seven draft picks made it from the

1990 draft, but with not as good results. First rounder Tim Costo made it to the majors in 1992 with Cincinnati. Darrell Whitmore was picked in the second round and made it to the majors with the Florida Marlins in 1993 and has spent three seasons in the sun. Third-round pick Jason Hardtke made it to the Mets in 1996 and has three seasons in the majors. David Bell was a seventh-round selection and came up with the Tribe in 1995 and has been up in the majors ever since with three different teams. Likely the best so far out of that draft is Dave Mlicki in the 17th round. The pitcher first came up with the Indians, but was traded to the Mets. He has been in the majors for six seasons. Steve Gajkowski was taken in the next round and he took until 1998 to rise up to the majors with Seattle in 1998. Even 51st round selection Carlos Crawford made it to the Phillies in 1996 for a brief appearance.

A total of 13 players have made it to the majors so far from those two drafts when Montgomery was director. Judging a draft early is like judging how a baby will turn out — impossible. Montgomery is not bitter over the matter. "I don't hold any grudges," he said. He's now doing well in Pittsburgh scouting the major leagues now.

Montgomery was replaced in Cleveland by Mickey White, who lasted only two years as well. "There was so much paranoia there, you were destined to fail," explained White, now the scouting director for the Pirates. He too had some good picks which helped the Indians, but he never had a chance to see them develop. So far, 14 players from those two drafts have made it to the majors, including Manny Ramirez, Chad Ogea and Dave Mlicki.

The middle-market Indians then started signing some of their young players to long-term contracts before they became free agents. This saved them money in the long run and helped them retain their players in their prime. "We've had a tremendous run of offensive players," said general manager John Hart. But the pitching staff lacked some talent, so the Indians have traded some of their good draft picks who were fielders for pitching. For example, with Jim Thome at first, the Indians dealt Sean Casey to the Cincinnati Reds for pitcher Dave Burba.

The Indians' strategy now with the draft is to take the "best player available," regardless of whether or not they are in high school or college, according to Brad Grant, the assistant director of scouting. The scouting director going into 1999 was Josh Burns, who replaced Lee MacPhail in 1998.

The Indians have an average size scouting department. It is made up of a national cross-checker, three regional scouting directors, 17 full-time area scouts, 16 part-timers and 40 associate or bird dog scouts. Internationally, they concentrate their efforts in the Dominican, Venezuela and Panama. If the draft became international, they wouldn't be prepared for it. They'd have to expand their international staff. Their latest non-drafted free agent who has come via free agency from the Dominican is Bartolo Colon, who was named to the All-Star Team in 1998. Cleveland still believes in open tryouts for players and holds them all over the country during the summer trying to find that one gem.

Being a middle-market team, Cleveland can afford to spend some money on draft picks and free agents, which they have done in the past. They wouldn't like to see any changes in the draft right now. Why should they? They have done well in the '90s.

Best Picks

The first great pick the Indians made was **Buddy Bell**, a lowly 16th round pick in 1969. He was picked as a second baseman, but he was switched to third base in the minors. Good move. He wasn't that impressive when the Indians brought him up in 1972, but he soon showed his talents and was picked for the All-Star Game in his sophomore season. It was the first of five appearances he would make in the Midsummer Classic. Bell was just ripening at third base when the Indians traded him to Texas. Big mistake. He began picking up Gold Gloves and turned into a clutch hitter, as he knocked in a career-high 101 RBI. In all, he garnered six Gold Gloves. He didn't put up enough numbers for consideration in the Hall of Fame, but he still garnered eight votes when he became eligible.

Chris Chambliss was sought after by many teams and was drafted several times before he signed with the Indians in January 1970. The first-round pick made his debut with the Indians in May the following year. By the end of the season he had nine homers, 48 RBI and batted .275 to earn Rookie of the Year honors. However, he failed to live up to what the Indians wanted out of him, so he was traded to the Yankees in 1974. He consistently hit double-digit homers every season. New York then dealt him to Atlanta in 1980. His 20 homers in 1982 helped the Braves to a division title. In 1985 he became a pinch hitter and contributed to baseball for a couple of more seasons.

Dennis Eckersley was a third-round pick in 1972 out of high school and he wasted no time getting to the majors. Three years later he became a starter for the Indians and went 13-7 to earn the *Sporting News* American League Rookie Pitcher of the Year. Thirteen was the number of wins again for him in his sophomore season with the Tribe. "Eck," as he was sometimes called for short, made a name for himself in 1977 when he threw a no-hitter, which led him to being named to the All-Star Game. The Indians decided to trade him to Boston in a multi-player trade. Another mistake. He won 20 games the next season for the Red Sox then 17 the season after that. After two off-seasons, he was more true to form and was named to the Midsummer Classic again. That number 13 came up again as he was 13-13 on the season. After a couple of seasons with the Cubs, he went to Oakland and began pitching in relief. His sidearm delivery was tougher on batters for short stints than over a long hauls like a starter. He began saving games for the A's. In 1988, he was nothing short of spectacular. He compiled a major league high 45 saves and was named as the best reliever in baseball and second in Cy Young voting. Eck was more brilliant in the League Championship Series as he picked up all four saves in Oakland's sweep of his former Boston Red Sox. Kirk Gibson ruined the stellar season with a dramatic homer off him in Game 1 of the World Series, which was won by the Dodgers. Eckersley made up for his poor showing the next season by helping the A's to a world championship. Over his career, he was named to six All-Star games and retired in 1998 with 197 victories, 390 saves and a 3.50 ERA.

Albert Belle, drafted by the Cleveland Indians in 1987. (Photograph by Marty Orr.)

Albert Belle, a second round pick in 1987, helped launch the Indians from obscurity into a championship team with his prolific home runs and RBI. Before the draft, he set LSU career records in seven offensive categories, including 49 homers and 172 RBI. Scouted and signed by Red Gaskill, he was first called up the majors in 1989 and made the club as a regular in 1991. By 1993 he was the American League RBI leader. Belle became the league's home run and RBI leader in 1995 to help his team win the division. He was the RBI leader in 1996 as well to again help the Indians win the division. Off the field, Belle was the Cleveland Indians' Roberto Clemente Award nominee in 1993 and 1994 and the club's Branch Rickey Award nominee in 1994 for his efforts in the community. He became a free agent in 1996 and signed with the rival White Sox where he played for two seasons. His 152 RBI in 1998 was the sixth highest total in baseball since 1949, while his 399 total bases were the most in the American League since Jim Rice had 406 in 1978. Belle had 316 homers by the end of 1998, and he signed with Baltimore for the 1999 season.

Thirteen has turned out to be a lucky number for **Jim Thome**. Selected in the 13th round in 1989, Thome has made quite a mark in Cleveland and has helped the team to four division championships in a row. He got his first call to the majors in 1991 after being named to all-star teams in the minors. His first full season with the Indians came in 1994, which coincides with Cleveland's rise to the top of their division. He has hit 20 or more home runs every season since then and has been named to three All-Star teams. He has played well in the postseason. His 12 career postseason home runs ties him for fifth all-time with Yogi Berra. And one of his dingers was a grand slam, only the third in ALCS history. He won the Silver Slugger Award at third base in 1996 when he clouted 38 homers and 116 RBI.

Another recent draft pick who has turned out to be one of the best picks ever for the Indians is **Manny Ramirez**, a first-round selection in 1991. He spent three seasons in the minors and was an all-star twice and Most Valuable Player in his rookie season in the Appalachian League. His rookie season came in 1994 and he finished second in Rookie of the Year voting. The powerful hitter has hit double-digit homers each of his professional seasons and was averaging 30 bleacher balls a year in the majors. His three grand slams in one season allowed him to join Andre Thornton, Al Rosen, and Tris Speaker as the only Indians to hit three slams in one season. In 1997, he tied a Major League record with eight homers in five games. He was also awarded the 1997 Cleveland Baseball Writers Man of the Year Award. He has been named to three All-Star teams so far and had totaled 154 homers by the end of the 1998 season.

Charles Nagy, a first-round pick in 1988, has become the team's most winningest pitcher in the 1990s with 104 victories to his credit. He was named Indians Minor League Pitcher of the Year in 1990 when he was 13-8 at Double-A Canton-Akron, where he was named Double-A All-Star. That was enough for the Indians, who called him up after that. After a great start in 1992, he was named to the All-Star team. He had an off-season the next year when he caught shingles, a painful skin disease, at the beginning of the season and ended the year with shoulder surgery. He rebounded from that and had his best season in 1996 when he started the season

with an 11-1 record to get another All-Star invitation. He finished the season second in the American League with a .773 winning percentage (17-5 record).

Long Shots

Ron Hassey was picked in the 18th round in 1976 and spent nearly that many years in professional ball. The catcher first came up to the Indians in 1978 and became the backup the next season. He fought off any sophomore slump by hitting for a .318 average. Hassey played seven seasons with Cleveland before going on to the White Sox, Yankees, Athletics and Expos. He retired in 1991 with a .266 batting average and two appearances in the World Series.

John Lowenstein was also an 18th round pick. He was drafted as a shortstop, but became a utility fielder for the Indians for eight seasons. He played nearly every fielding position and designated hitter. He played another eight years with Texas and Baltimore. His career year came in 1982 when he batted .320 and hit 24 homers.

The Indians saw tremendous speed in **Damian Jackson**, and picked him in the 44th round in 1991 fresh out of high school. The infielder showed he had great promise by stealing a lot of bases in the minors and hitting more than .250. He quickly worked his way up to Triple-A, and Cleveland called him up in 1996. The Indians brought him up again for eight games the following season before dealing him to Cincinnati in a swap of pitchers. However, the promising shortstop would have to try and displace MVP shortstop Barry Larkin, unless the Reds traded the high-priced player. The Reds did shop Larkin around in 1998, but didn't get an offer they liked. Meanwhile, Jackson played at Indianapolis for most of the season, where he hit .261 and stole 25 bases. The young player threw a few temper tantrums at Victory Field when he played poorly on the field. Then he got a September call from the Reds. The Reds traded him in the offseason to the San Diego Padres, who made him a regular, but the rookie made a lot of mistakes and errors in his first year in the majors.

Having been the Indians' 17th round draft pick in 1989, **Brian Giles** is used to overcoming large odds. Giles did just that, advancing a level each season between 1989 and 1994. Because the Indians outfield has been loaded with stars the past three years, Giles spent most of 1995 and half of 1996 at the Triple-A level. The Indians finally unloaded him to the Pirates in 1999 and he was making quite a name for himself there.

Disappointments

The Indians have had many disappointments early in the draft, which is one of the reasons the draft didn't help them much until the 1990s.

Ray Fosse, Cleveland's first-ever draft pick in 1965, became a disappointment through no fault of his own. Seemingly destined for stardom, he was injured by the aggressive Pete Rose in a memorable home plate collision to end the 1970 All-Star Game. He played six seasons with the Indians before being traded to Oakland.

The Indians failed to sign their first-round pick in the June Regular Draft the next year. **John Curtis** decided to go to Clemson University for a couple of years and sign with Boston in 1968.

In 1968 the Indians drafted **Robert Weaver** in the first round. The shortstop out of high school failed to get past Double-A. Their first pick the next year only made it one level higher; **Alvin McGraw**, an outfielder out of high school, peaked at Triple-A.

Steve Dunning became the second draft pick to get a promotion directly to the majors in 1970. The second player taken overall in the 1970 June draft signed for $60,000. The 21-year-old Stanford Indians righthander won his first game with the Cleveland Indians. That was a great start, but Dunning would find himself in the minors a year later after going 12-23 with the Tribe. He was bounced around baseball like a pinball game, ending up with eight organizations in nine years. He spent time in the majors with Texas, California, Montreal and Oakland over seven seasons. He ended up with a dismal 23-41 record and 4.56 career ERA.

The Indians' 1971 first pick was another pitcher, **David Sloan**. The righthanded pitcher out of high school failed to go beyond Double-A.

When the Indians selected **Glen Tufts** in the first round in 1973, they hoped he would turn out to be like another baseball star from his hometown of Bridgewater, Mass.—Hall-of-Famer Mickey Cochrane. Tufts certainly showed the potential. One scout liked his "old-fashioned country swing." He began clouting homers in his last year in Little League. At Bridgewater Raynham High School, he got better and better. His batting averages were .565, .530 and .524 his last three years of high school, respectively. But what impressed the scouts and fans most was his monumental 400-foot blasts. And he could pitch. He was 6-0 in his senior year. The Indians picked him fifth overall and gave him a bonus $60,000. The money seemed like a good investment at the time. However, a team never knows when fate will play a part in preventing a player from getting to the majors. Such was the case with Tufts. Six months after he was drafted he was out on a date with a cheerleader the night before Thanksgiving. It was the last football game of the season and the two enjoyed a pep rally and bonfire. After he took her home for the evening, he was on the way home when his car hit a patch of ice and slammed into a pole. His left ankle was badly damaged in the wreck. It wasn't as bad as Humpty Dumpty, but doctors had to put in three pins and fuse some bones to put him back together again. He would require extensive rehabbing. He went to Florida so he could enjoy the warm weather and train all year. Twenty months after being drafted, Tufts finally entered professional baseball. The first baseman didn't have many problems fielding his position, but he couldn't run very fast. "I couldn't run the bases," he explained.

He tried to compensate for his ankle, which resulted in him injuring his left knee, which required surgery in 1976. He made it Double-A before the Indians released him in 1977. "It just wasn't meant to be," he reflected. "It doesn't do any good to dwell on it now."

Baseball was still in his veins though, so he began a career of coaching. Unlike his playing career, he has been successful at other aspects of the game. He coached high school for a couple of years then moved up to Bridgewater State College for a longer spell. The Cape Cod league was next. He also got married and began to raise a family. In 1994, he became a professional again as the Giants hired him as a hitting instructor. Then they made him a manager in their minor league system for three different teams in three seasons.

But just like his promising baseball career, something would change his life again. This time he daughter suffered pulmonary hypertension in a lung and would require a transplant. The Giants turned him into a scout so he could move back to Bridgewater to be close to a children's hospital. There is no cure for the disease, but the two year old was still clinging to life in February 1999. "She was only supposed to live three to five weeks at one point," he said.

The Indians began a four-year stretch in 1976 in which none of their picks became much of anything. In 1976, the Indians first pick was **Tim Glass**, who broke at Double-A. The 1977 first-round choice was even worse as outfielder **Bruce Compton** didn't even get that high. The same fate came to **Phil Lansford** the next year. And in 1979, the Indians picked **Jon Bohnet** as the seventh pick in the draft and all he had was a cup of coffee in the majors.

After a good pick in 1980, the Indians continued picking poorly in the first round. Their 1981 choice was **George Alpert**, who was an outfielder who peaked at Class A. **Mark Snyder**, the first rounder the next year, couldn't top that either. The 1985 first round pick was **Mike Poehl**, a pitcher from the University of Texas. He peaked at Double-A.

The third time was a charm for **Mike Walker** in 1986. It was the third time the pitcher had been drafted. He was selected by Tribe in the second round and this time he signed for $27,000. He was first chosen in the 14th round by Montreal in the 1986 draft after he graduated from Hernando High School, Brooksville, Florida. Then in 1985 after his first year at Seminole Community College, he was picked in the first round of the January Secondary Phase. In 1986, Montreal decided not to pick Walker in the first round of the Regular Draft and instead went with outfielder Kevin Dean, Hogan High School, Vallejo, Calif. The Expos should have stayed with Walker, because Dean never made it past Triple-A.

Threes continued to follow Walker as the Indians called him up three times before they

released him after the 1991 season. It's difficult to understand why though because he had a good season in 1991. His ERA was 2.79 in Double-A and 2.08 with the Indians in five games. He signed with the Tigers for a season before signing again with the Indians, who had him for spring training only in 1993 before releasing him again.

Three was the number of seasons he played with the Iowa Cubs. The Chicago Cubs also called him up once and he pitched most of 1995 with the team.

Cincinnati signed Walker before spring training in 1997 and put him at Triple-A Indianapolis. He experienced one of his best seasons ever as reliever: 9-6, 2.98 ERA in 55 appearances. The Reds failed to call him up though. He was almost as good the following year in setting a record number of appearances (78) for the Indians. But the Reds were not in any pennant race again, so he was not given a call up in September.

He still hopes to get back to the majors before age catches up with him. He celebrated his 32nd birthday in 1998. He has spent more time at Triple-A than he has in the majors.

Best Draft

The Indians have had some key players drafted in 1988, 1989 and 1990, but 1991 seems to be the best of the lot for providing players that have been instrumental in providing championships to the team. **Manny Ramirez** was taken in the first round and he has been a great contributor to the team. **Chad Ogea**, a third-round pick, was a starter on the team for four seasons and compiled a 31-23 record before being traded to the Phillies. Long shot **Albie Lopez**, 20th round gem, was a starter and reliever for the team for five seasons. Others from that class who have made it to the majors, but that the Indians used as trade bait included **Paul Byrd** (4th round), **Pep Harris** (7th round) and **Damian Jackson** (44th round).

Worst Draft

The year 1973 was forgettable in Indians history. Only two players from that draft ever made the majors for a total of nine games. Second-round selection Tommy McMillian from Jacksonville University got a cup of coffee with the Mariners in 1977. Dave Oliver, third round, did about the same with the Tribe in 1977. That was also the year that the Indians picked Tufts in the first round and we know what happened to him.

Where Are They Now?

It's much easier for a draft pick to make his way to the majors with a team that is in the midst of rebuilding effort, because the team is looking more for the future than the present. **Sean Casey** started to dream about going to the majors when he was 12. He didn't get drafted after he graduated from high school. But at the University of Richmond he began to prove himself on the ballfield. "I don't think scouts began to look at me until I was a sophomore," he said. After leading the nation in hitting as a junior in college, scouts began taking an even longer look at the Cape Cod league player. The Cleveland Indians drafted him in the sec-

Sean Casey, an Indians draft pick in 1995 in the second round.

ond round of the 1995 draft. He signed for $223,000.

He soon proved he could hit the ball professionally as he chalked up a .329 average in Class A ball in his first season. He repeated that act the next season at Class A Kingston to earn a promotion to Double-A the next season. He hit even better at Akron (.386-10-66), so the Indians promoted him to Triple-A and finally to the big club in September, where he played in six games.

In 1998, the Indians had Jim Thome at first, which meant Casey had no where to go with the Tribe. So Cleveland did him a favor and dealt him to Cincinnati during spring training for pitcher Dave Burba. Soon after the Reds obtained him, Casey was hit in the eye during batting practice. He had surgery and when he returned to action with the Reds, he hit a paltry .135, so he was sent down to Indianapolis to fully recover from the injury. Had Casey struck out? Not hardly. He soon fully recovered from the injury at the Circle City. After hitting .326 at Indianapolis, the Reds — in the midst of a rebuilding effort — brought him up after the All-Star break to see what he could do at the major-league level. The healed Casey soon proved he could hit there, too. By draft time in 1999, this Casey was leading the league in batting average early in the season. This Casey wasn't striking out.

Chris Chambliss, a first rounder in 1970, was the batting coach for the Yankees in 1998.

The director of player personnel for the San Francisco Giants is none other than **Dick Tidrow**, who was drafted by the Indians in 1967. Tidrow became famous as a setup man for Bruce Sutter. He never pitched for San Francisco, but he was born there.

Rick Cerone, a first-round pick in 1975, became an advance scout for the Yankees after his playing days. Cerone played only 14 games in two seasons with the Indians before being traded to Toronto. He played 18 seasons in the majors.

Gary King, a supplemental-round pick in 1970, was first picked by the Seattle Pilots in 1969 on the same day he graduated from South Bend Clay High School. The Pilots offered him $7,000, but he decided to go to junior college.

Then Cleveland picked him the next January and he signed for a $10,000 bonus. "Baseball was a lot better than college," he said. He played infield for two seasons in the minors. After baseball he went to work as a salesman for Correlated Products in Indianapolis. Now he owns the company. In his off-time, he manages a Brownsburg Little League team. In 1999, he took a team of all-stars to the Little League World Series.

Ones Who Got Away

The Tribe was good at picking players who signed with other teams and turned out to be good major leaguers later.

Joe Niekro was selected in the seventh round in the January draft in 1966, but he passed up the opportunity.

Steve Stone was a long shot pick (16th round) in 1968 out of Kent State and he waited until January the next season to be drafted by the Giants. He turned out to be a good pitcher (107-93 in 11 seasons) for the Chicago teams and the Orioles. Now, he is a broadcaster for Cubs games on WGN-TV.

The Indians selected **Doug Drabek** in the fourth round out of high school. He waited until 1983 before signing with the White Sox, who picked him in the fourth round. He earned the Cy Young Award in 1990 with the Pirates and was still pitching in 1998.

All in the Family

The Indians picked **Mike Glavine**, brother of Braves pitcher Tom, in the 22nd round in 1995 out of Northeastern University. Unlike his brother, Mike was a first baseman who could hit the long ball. He slammed 28 homers in Class A in 1997. The Indians traded him to the Braves in March 1999 for future considerations. Perhaps someday he will be playing alongside his famed brother.

Jaret Wright is the son of former Major League pitcher Clyde Wright, who pitched for 10 seasons in the majors with California, Milwaukee and Texas. Unlike his son, Clyde was a lefthanded pitcher and was 100-111 lifetime.

Tim Drew, a first rounder in 1998, is the brother of J.D. Drew, who was drafted in the

first round by the Cardinals the same year. The drafting of the two brothers made draft history as they are the first siblings taken in the first round of the same draft. The drafting of Tim marked only the second time in the last 15 years and the sixth time in 33 years of the draft that the Indians selected a high school pitcher with their first pick. The last high school pitcher selected by the Tribe in the first round was Wright in 1994.

David Bell became a third-generation major league player when he was called up to the Indians in 1995. He was drafted by the Indians in the seventh round in 1990. He is the son of former Cleveland player Buddy Bell, and grandson of Gus Bell, who played for 15 seasons in the 1950s and '60s. The Indians traded Bell to St. Louis in 1995. The Indians claimed him on waivers in 1997 before trading him to the Mariners for Joey Cora in 1998.

On the Roster

Besides the previously mentioned Nagy, Ramirez and Thome, the Indians had several other players on the roster in 1999 who had been drafted by the team.

The longest shot of the bunch was **Richie Sexson**, a lowly 24th rounder in 1993. He soon

Richie Sexson was drafted by the Indians in the 24th round in 1993. (Photograph by Marty Orr.)

showed he was underrated in the draft. He followed a mediocre rookie league debut, with 14 homers at short-season Columbus. His career took off in 1995 when he led Class A Carolina League in hits, doubles, and RBI, which resulted in his being named as the league's Most Valuable Player. When he got to Triple-A Buffalo in 1997, he exploded for 31 homers to lead the American Association and set a Buffalo franchise record. He was named to the Triple-A All-Star Team as well. The first baseman became a fixture in Cleveland in 1998 and had his first career grand slam against Oakland.

Russell Branyan, a Cleveland draft pick, with the Buffalo Bisons.

Jaret Wright was the first-round pick in 1994 out of high school. He missed two months after having his jaw broken by an errant batting practice swing during the Class A All-Star Game in his third year in the minors. The next year he breezed though Double-A and Triple-A to get a call to the majors halfway through the 1997 season. He charged on to the scene with an 8-3 mark in the regular season and a 3-0 record in the postseason. He cooled off a little his sophomore year going 12-10 with a 4.72 in his first full major league season.

Paul Shuey was the first-round choice in 1992 out of the University of North Carolina. After starting games his first season, he's been a reliever ever since. The right-hander with a forkball has been up and down from the minors to the majors over five seasons. The main reason for the frequent flyer miles has been his inconsistency and minor injuries.

Future Stars?

Russell Branyan, a seventh-round pick in 1994, is following in the footsteps of Richie Sexson and was on track to break Sexson's home run record at Buffalo in 1999. However, he also strikes out a lot and is only a marginal fielder. Branyan has shown some run power ever since he was drafted and hit a career high 40 homers in Class A to be named as an all-star in the South Atlantic League. He was an all-star the next season as well.

The Indians have a large investment in their first-round pick in 1997. **Tim Drew** signed the most lucrative contract in Indians history as he inked a $1.6 million contract. The right-handed starter has made slow progress in the minors so far, but he's plenty young as he was signed out of high school. He may be a 2001 starter for the Indians.

As a 56th-round pick, the Indians weren't risking anything when they selected **David Riske** out of community college in 1996. The relief pitcher saved 33 games at Class A Kinston in 1998, which landed him on the all-star team and earned him the 1998 Bob Feller Award as the best pitcher in the Indians minor league system. By June 1999, he was already at the Triple-A level.

Another 1996 draft pick at Triple-A was **Paul Rigdon**, a sixth-round choice. After missing 1997 with an injury, he was 11-7 at Class-A in 1998. He began 1999 at Double-A and was a perfect 7-0 with a 0.90 ERA to earn a promotion to Triple-A in May.

Jason Rakers, a 25th-round pick in 1995, got a cup of coffee in the majors in 1998 before being optioned to Triple-A Buffalo. The right-handed starter was 8-6 at Buffalo in 1998.

David Miller was the first-round pick in 1995 and moved up to Triple-A in three seasons. The Indians didn't protect him and Philadelphia selected him in the Rule V Draft in 1998, but returned him to the Indians before the season began in 1999. Miller hits for average and not for power, which doesn't make him as desirable as the Indians had hoped for considering his size.

Another outfielder at Triple-A who was a homegrown Indian was **Mark Budzinski**. He was a long shot from the 21st round in 1995. He hits for more homers, but not enough to launch him into the majors just yet.

An even longer shot than Budzinski was **Chan Perry**, another outfielder at Triple-A Buffalo. Perry was a 44th-round pick in the 1994 draft. He does have the home run power among the outfield trio and hit a career high 20 at Double-A in 1997.

The Indians didn't have a first-round pick in 1999, so their first pick was **Will Hartley** in the second round. The catcher out of high school batted .510 his senior season. The speedy catcher stole 111 bases during his high school career.

Their third-round selection in 1999 was **Eric Johnson**, an outfielder from Western Carolina University. He too can steal bases and swiped 46 his senior season. Johnson also played football for the Catamounts and was named all-conference in football.

Detroit Tigers

The draft wasn't very good for the Tigers from the onset. For the first seven years, Detroit didn't pick anyone who turned out to be a notable player. The good players that were selected didn't sign with the Tigers. They went elsewhere. The Tigers selected Andy Messersmith in the first draft, but he decided to wait until the next year and sign with the Angels in the first round of the June secondary draft. The following year Darrell Evans was picked, but he didn't sign either. Detroit selected Ross Grimsley in 1968 in the 8th round, but he also waited a year and was drafted and signed with the Reds.

Not until 1972 did the Tigers draft anyone who would make a significant contribution to the team. Then the Tigers began picking players who finally made in impact in 1984, when the best Tigers team ever won 104 victories and a World Championship. That team had plethora of the team's own draft picks. Nearly half of that team was drafted by Detroit, including Tom Brookens, Marty Castillo, Kirk Gibson, Howard Johnson, Jack Morris, Dan Petry, Lance Parrish, Alan Trammell and Lou Whitaker. Much of that same crew plus a couple of others helped the team finish first again three years later. However, the Tigers haven't finished first since then. In fact, they haven't drafted many players since then that have made an impact on the team and made it a contender like it was in the 1980s. The Tigers have picked some top players that other teams didn't have at the top of their list for whatever reasons. Several of their number ones since 1987 have gone the way of the dinosaurs — extinct. However, there have been some exceptions.

The Tigers' basic draft philosophy is to take the best available player at the time. The team favors pitchers who are big and strong and can throw it hard. When it comes to position players, they are looking for speed more than power.

Detroit will be moving into Comerica Park in 2000 and the park is suppose to favor pitchers more than hitters, which is the opposite from Tiger Stadium which had been around since 1912 and favored power hitting over speed and pitching. Although the stadium had the deepest centerfield in baseball, the short right-field line was a left-handed power hitter's dream. The Tigers are hoping their new park will have the same impact on the team that a new park had on Cleveland, a similar market team.

The Tigers have begun to make some inroads in signing some free agents overseas. They signed their first Japanese player, Masao Kida, in 1998. They have upped their foreign scouting staff and are also evaluating players in Australia, Puerto Rico, Venezuela and other countries. Detroit has about six scouts in each of four regions

Torey Lovullo with the Rochester Red Barons. He was drafted by the Detroit Tigers in the fifth round.

in the United States. They scout high schools and colleges in the spring and they go onto the minors and majors during the summer, so they keep quite busy. The team favors a world draft to put baseball more on an even keel.

Detroit scouts don't always spend a lot of time scouting a player. Joe Cusick saw Mark Fidrych throw one pitch and that was enough for him. However, he heard from other scouts that Fidrych could throw. So the Tigers picked him in the 9th round, 232nd pick in 1974. Fidrych had no scholarship to play at any college. In fact, he was working at a gas station at the time. The Tigers gave him a $3,000 bonus. Fidrych was quite a character. He had moves that earned him the nickname "The Bird." The Bird flew into Detroit in 1976. He had an amazing 19-9 record with a league leading 24 complete games and 2.34 ERA. His success was short-lived due to injuries.

The Tigers had a good draft numberwise in 1998 when they had five of the draft's first 87 selections. They picked 14th, 34th, 57th, 73rd and 87th overall. The 34th pick was compensation for free pitcher Willie Blair signing with Arizona.

Best Draft Picks

When the 1978 draft rolled around, the baseball clubs who were interested in **Kirk Gibson** were sort of hoodwinked by the great athlete. Gibson wanted to play for the Tigers, but Detroit picked 12th in the draft. To discourage the other clubs ahead of Detroit, he told them he was going back and playing football for Michigan State in the fall. Plus, he would be a high pick for the National Football League draft the following year, so teams thought he was going to be a professional football player instead of a baseball player. Teams instantly lost interest except for Detroit. Heck, he had not played college baseball until his junior year, but still opened the eyes of scouts. When he went to a personal tryout in Detroit before the draft, he crushed baseballs into the upper deck like Mark McGwire.

The other teams, like the Yankees and Mariners, must have been certainly surprised when Detroit picked Gibson and signed him a few days later for $200,000. His contract was unusual because it would allow him to play his senior year of football. It read: "Club agrees to grant Player permission to play intercollegiate football at Michigan State University for the 1978 season only, including post-season bowl games if the Player desires to play. The Club excuses the Player from rendering services as a professional baseball player from approximately August 14, 1978, until the completion of the 1978 intercollegiate football season at Michigan State University, including post-season bowl games, if any."

Detroit sent the promising athlete to the Class A Lakeland Tigers, which was managed by Jim Leyland, who was unmerciful on the rookie. The Tigers played good enough to make it into the playoffs, but without Gibson, who went on to MSU for football. Gibson helped the Spartans to a Big Ten Championship and the Rose Bowl. The next season he was good enough at spring training to jump to Triple-A Evansville. Although he hit only .245, Detroit was retooling and promoted him to the majors in September. He was in the right place at the right time.

Gibson went on to an illustrious 17-year career that was highlighted by his play in the World Series. First he helped the Tigers to a World Series victory in 1984 by hitting .333 with two homers and seven RBI. Then in Game One of the 1988 World Series with the Dodgers, the injury-ridden player came off the bench in the ninth inning to hit a home run and lift the team to victory. He will always be known for that shining moment in baseball. It earned him the Most Valuable Player Award. Other players put up better numbers than Gibson that season, but nobody performed in the Series like he did. He served 12 seasons with the Tigers. Gibson didn't put up any Ruthian numbers during his 17-year career and was never named to an All-Star team, but he will go down as one of the best players for Detroit.

Detroit had a couple of draft picks who turned into a great double-play combination that lasted nearly 20 seasons. **Lou Whitaker** and **Alan Trammell** were involved in hundreds of double plays over the span of their stay in Detroit that began in 1977. Whitaker was a fifth round choice in 1975, while Trammell came a year later in the second round. Both were first called up in 1977 and became regulars in 1978. Whitaker garnered three Gold Gloves, while Trammell captured four. Both appeared in four All-Star games. Whitaker's best season came in 1983 when he averaged .320 and picked up his first Gold Glove. Trammell received his first Gold Glove in 1980 and enjoyed his best season in 1987 when he hit .343 with 28 homers, 109 runs scored and 105 RBI.

The Tigers picked **Lance Parrish** in the first round of the 1974 draft as an infielder, but converted him to a catcher in the minors. When he first came up with the Tigers he led the league in passed balls; however, by 1982 he was an All-Star catcher and first-rate hitter. Then he won Gold Gloves at the position three years in a row. After leading the league once more in passed balls in 1988, the Tigers traded him to California. He retired after the 1994 season and ranked third lifetime in homers (320) behind Carlton Fisk and Johnny Bench. Besides the Gold Gloves, he was named to six All-Star teams and earned four Silver Slugger Awards.

Jack Morris, a fifth-round selection in 1976, first came up as a reliever. Converted to a starter in 1979, he recorded a 17-7 record. He became the ace of the staff and was named to his first All-Star Team during the strike-shortened 1981 season. In 1983 he busted the 20-win barrier for the first time. However, 1984 became a better season for him because his 19 wins helped the Tigers to a pennant. Then he was unbeaten in the postseason with a 3-0 record to lead the team to the world championship. Morris pitched 14 seasons with the Tigers before becoming a free agent and signing with the Twins, where he led them to a world championship as well when he recorded two wins in the World Series and was named Series Most Valuable Player. Over his career he was 254-186 and appeared in five All-Star games. He was 7-4 in postseason play.

Dan Petry, a fourth round pick in 1976, was an instrumental starting pitcher on the 1984 and 1987 championship teams. He had one of his best seasons in 1984 when he was 18-8 with a 3.24 ERA. Unfortunately, he picked up the only loss in the World Series. He appeared in the All-Star Game once during 11 seasons with the Tigers. His career ended in 1991 with a 125-104 record.

Howard Johnson was a first-round pick in 1979 and played a couple undistinguished years with the Tigers before being traded to the Mets where he matured into a power hitter. He exploded for 36 homers in 1987 to become as famous as the hotel chain with the same name. HoJo's power ran five years before short circuiting. During that time he led the league once in homers (38 in 1991), hit more than 100 RBI a season and stole more than 23 bases a season. He was also named to two All-Star teams. Then he ran into injuries and his career went south after that.

Travis Fryman was drafted by the Tigers as a first-round sandwich pick in the 1987 draft. The third baseman had his breakout year in the minors in 1989 when he led Double-A Eastern League in doubles and was named to the All-Star Team. After starting the 1990 season at Triple-A, he was soon called up to the Tigers. He became the team's regular third baseman the next season and hit 21 homers in his rookie year. He had no sophomore slump the next season and was named to his first all-star team. He would earn that distinction for four out of the next five seasons. In 1997, he led the American League third basemen in fielding percentage. The Tigers traded him to the Diamondbacks after the 1997 season, but he never played a game there as he was sent on to the Indians a couple of weeks later. He hit a career high 28 homers with the Indians in 1998.

Long Shots

Gabe Kapler became the lowest draft pick in Detroit history to make it to the majors in

Brian Powell, a Tigers draft pick in the second round in 1995.

1998. He was drafted in the 57th round out of Moorpark Junior College in 1995. After a couple of years at Class A, he was promoted to Double-A Jacksonville and became the league MVP there in 1998 as he led the league in homers (25), set a record with 146 RBI and batted .325. That earned him a promotion to the big club on Sept. 20, 1998.

The Tigers selected **John Smoltz** in the 22nd round in 1985 and weren't very impressed by his first two seasons in the minors. He had a 4-10 record and a 5.68 ERA at Double-A Glen Falls when they decided to deal him for more pressing matters — a league championship in 1987. They sent him packing to the Braves for Doyle Alexander. The Tigers never made the World Series that season and probably regret the decision now based on what Smoltz has done in Atlanta. The right-hander struggled his first season with the Braves, but has been a winner ever since. His best performance was a 24-8 record in 1996 when he won the Cy Young Award.

Vern Ruhle was 17th round pick in 1972 and he nearly played that many years in the majors. Ruhle pitched four years with the Tigers before going to Houston, Cleveland and California over 14 years. He turned to coaching after playing and ended up with the Astros as a pitching coach in 1999.

The Tigers picked **Chris Hoiles** in the 19th round in 1986. He was traded to the Orioles with a couple others for Fred Lynn. The Tigers should have kept Hoiles as he has served a decade with Baltimore and has hit for power. He had a career high 29 homers in 1993 when he hit for six homers in six straight games.

Rusty Meacham was a 99–1 shot, which is the odds they list at the track when the horse could be much higher odds, as a 33rd round pick in 1987. But the pitcher worked his way up the ladder with good performances as a starter in the minors. Detroit elevated him to the majors in 1991 then waived him after the season. The Royals claimed him and he went on several seasons with them and one with the Mariners. He spent 1997 and 1998 in Triple-A.

Disappointments

The list of disappointments is long. Of course disappointment is a subjective term, so it depends on what you consider a disappointment. Most major league teams feel that their best pick in the draft should make it to the majors. Most do. And some have an impact. A review of the Tigers' number-one picks reveals that many never it made it to the majors or made an impact there.

Their first-ever pick, **Gene Lamont**, played 87 games at catcher over five seasons with the Tigers — never an impact. However, he went on to become a major league manager with the White Sox.

The next year, the Tigers failed to sign their first pick, **Rick Konik**.

The Tigers didn't get much in 1967 as **Jim Foor** was their first pick in the June regular phase. The lefty had a cup of coffee in the majors.

The following year's pick was worse. **Robert Robinson**, an outfielder out of high school, only got as far as Triple-A. And the 1969 first round pick was a complete flop. **Lenny Baxley**, a first baseman, never got past first base. Then **Terry Mappin**, a first round catcher in 1970, only got to second base (Double-A). It was not until 1971 that a first rounder made an impact with the Tigers. That was Tom Veryzer.

The Tigers had to wait until 1974 before drafting a first-round player who made it to an All-Star Team. First-round selection Lance Parrish made several of them. The next big mistake was a player by the name of **Les Filkins**, who was the third player taken in the 1975 draft. He never made it to the majors.

The Tigers' picking improved in the late 1970s with some good number-one selections. **Ricky Barlow** was the best pick in the June 1981 draft and he became mired in Class A before getting a shot at Triple-A in 1987 before his demise. **Wayne Dotson**, a first rounder in 1983, was dismissed for disciplinary reasons. He never pitched in the majors.

Pitcher **Randy Nosek**, a number-one pick in 1985, was rushed to majors in 1989, hurt his arm and was out of baseball. **Bill Henderson**, a first-round catcher in 1987, quit before he got out of the minors. Also in 1987, Detroit's second selection in the first round was Steve Pegues. He never amounted to anything with the Tigers and the outfielder was waived in 1992. He finally made it to the majors in 1994 and played 100 games in two seasons.

Greg Gohr was the Tigers' first-round pick in 1989 and made his first appearance with the team in 1993. After turning in a "gorrible" record in 1996 (4-8, 7.17 ERA), the Tigers traded him to the Angels for Damon Easley in 1996. The Tigers certainly got the best end of that deal. By 1998 Gohr was out of baseball and Easley was an everyday player.

Another promising first-round pitcher, Mike Drumright, was a disappointing 4-19 with a 6.95 ERA at Triple-A Toledo in 1998. He also had problems with walks and led the International League. Yet another first-round failure was Matt Brunson who was taken in 1993. The Tigers decided he wasn't what they wanted and traded him to the Florida Marlins where he stayed at Class A. He soon became extinct. While the Tigers haven't made some good first-round picks in the 1990s at least they have made some better decisions in trading them before they go sour.

Detroit paid Rick Greene about a half-million dollars after drafting him in the first round in 1992. They made him the right-hander a reliever and Greene got off to a slow start with an ERA around six the first two years. He began to improve in Double-A and had 30 saves in 1996. The Tigers promoted him to Triple-A, but never brought him up before trading him to the Brewers. The Brewers failed to bring him up either and he was granted free agency at the end of 1998. Then he signed with the Reds in 1999 and was still waiting for a chance to pitch in the majors.

A lot of draft picks turn their back on the big money for college first and baseball second, but few ever turn back a bonus once they receive it. Keith Smith ended up doing just that. After leaving the Detroit Tigers the second time around in 1997, he returned the $200,000 the fifth-round draft pick received in 1994 after signing a contract. He played one season in the minors before deciding to return to college and play football for Arizona. Then he returned to the Tigers in 1997 for some extended spring training, but left in June and returned his bonus. He could have just failed and kept the money.

Best Draft

While the country was celebrating its bicentennial, the Tigers also had something to celebrate in 1976. Several of the players taken in the draft that year ended up on the roster of the best Tigers team of recent history, the 1984 World Series champion. Two starting pitchers from that squad were picked in 1976. Dan Petry was taken in the fourth round out of high school and Jack Morris was picked fifth out of college. Also that year Alan Trammel was picked and he ended up as the starting shortstop on that team.

Another good selection in 1976 was Steve Kemp, an outfielder out of USC. Kemp took only a year to make it to the Tigers. He became an All-Star in 1979, which turned out to be his career year. He hit 26 homers that season and batted .318. His career was all downhill after that. He left the Tigers in 1982 for four other teams during his 11 years in the majors. He was with the opposing Yankees during the 1984 championship season.

By 1984, Pat Underwood, the Tigers' first pick in 1976, was no longer in major league baseball. When Pat was drafted his brother, Tom, was already in the majors with Philadelphia. Pat broke into the Tigers' roster in 1979 and contributed for a couple of years before Sparky Anderson decided otherwise at spring training in 1981. "Sparky jacked me over!" he said angrily, recalling his days with the Tigers. He was sent to Evansville where he stayed until the following season. Then the Tigers dealt him to the Reds, but the trade was nullified when the Reds found out he was damaged goods — elbow problems. The Tigers released him and he never pitched in the majors again. Now he is a supervisor for Delco Electronics in his hometown of Kokomo, Indiana.

Worst Draft

The Tigers have never been shut out in the draft. That is they've never had a draft in which no player ever made it to the majors. They came close in 1973 when Bob Adams, a third round pick from UCLA, was the only player to make it. The catcher played 15 games with the Tigers in 1977.

The Tigers also had some other drafts in which they signed several players, but none turned out to be much of anything in the pros. Teams want draft picks who will crack the starting lineup and become significant contributors.

Where Are They Now?

Denny Harriger was drafted in the 18th round out of high school in 1987. "My high school coach wanted me to go on to college, but my parents left it up to me," he explained. He decided that if he would have been drafted in the 25th round or lower that he would sign. Although he's only had a cup of coffee in Detroit in 1998, he doesn't regret the decision because he knows of plenty of pitchers who were worked too hard in college and regretted it later. "If I feel there is something wrong with my arm, they shut me down right away for a couple of days," the right-handed hurler explained. Harriger signed with the Cincinnati Reds and was assigned to Indianapolis in 1999. In a dozen seasons in the minors he has compiled a 92-76 record, but a losing record at the Triple-A level.

Scott Earl got the attention of scouts at Eastern Kentucky University after a 29-game hitting streak. "Six teams called me the day before the draft," he remembered. Detroit took him in the 14th round in the June 1981 draft. "I was kind of disappointed I was drafted in the fourteenth round." He was further disappointed to be offered just $5,000. He wanted twice that. The scout left. But the scout returned and offered $8,000. Earl signed. "Scottie" was beamed up to the Tigers in September 1984 as the Tigers were clinching first place, but he wasn't included on the World Series roster. After that, he was considered a minor league backup for Lou Whitaker at second base. "I was an insurance policy," he explained. Earl played in the minors until 1989 before calling baseball quits. He now lives in Indianapolis with his wife and two daughters, and is an inside sales representative for a steel and aluminum products company.

Chuck Cary's draft experience went sort of like Murphy's Law — if anything can go wrong, it will. He was playing at California High School in San Ramon when he was first approached about playing in the majors. A Toronto scout by

Chuck Cary with the New York Yankees. He was drafted by the Tigers in the second round in 1981. (Photograph courtesy of Chuck Cary.)

the name of Wayne Morgan, who lived on Morgan Street in Morgan, California, asked him, "Do you mind throwing some to your dad?" He did. Afterwards, Morgan said he would like to sign him. Cary already had a full scholarship to the University of California and wanted to become a lawyer. He decided to ask for $100,000. Before he got it out of his mouth, the scout turned away and walked to his car.

Cary didn't get drafted after his senior year and he went off to Berkeley. In his sophomore year he became a great pitcher for California and won a game during the College World Series. That shot the left-hander into first-round territory for the following year's draft. However, he had a poor junior season. "I wasn't getting anyone out," he explained.

By draft time his first round projections had dropped. He was hoping for a second-round selection with the Yankees at a bonus around $80,000. The only two teams he didn't want to play for were the Tigers and Indians. On draft day in June 1981, he was tabbed by the Tigers in the seventh round. His agent told him he would probably be offered about $10,000. Detroit made him one offer that they said it was non-negotiable. It was for $22,500 and Class A ball. There was no money on the table to finish his college. He signed. Cary went off to A ball and got a check for $236 every two weeks. He was in heaven.

Cary worked his way up to the majors and finished his bachelor's degree with a major in political science at the same time. The relief pitcher found his way to the majors by 1985 and hurled for the Tigers for two seasons before going on to the Braves for a couple of seasons. Then he wound up with the Yankees where he was turned into a starter. After 11-22 record in three seasons and injury problems, the Yankees released him. Then he signed a big contract to play in Japan for a season.

When he came back to the States, the White Sox signed him and he had a great spring in 1993. But on the way back to Chicago, he blew out his knee and tore a disc in his back in an exhibition game in Las Vegas. He was on the disabled list most of the season. Then he got to play in the League Championship Series. "It was a nice way to end up," he said from his home in Destin, Florida.

Carey played 13 years of professional baseball and saved a lot of the money he made, so when he retired from the game he sat back for five years to help raise a family. Now he has three young children and is back working as a real estate dealer for resorts all over the United States. "I was a run-of-the-mill big leaguer," he volunteered. "I'm proud of it and happy to have done it."

Ken Szotkiewicz was just a sophomore at Georgia Southern College when he was drafted in the first round in the January Secondary Phase in 1968. He wouldn't be eligible for another year by today's rules. He received over $50,000 for signing, but he doesn't recall the exact amount. "I figured I already had two years of education and I would finish my degree later," he explained.

The shortstop got his shot at the majors with the Tigers in 1970. After 47 games, he man-aged just a .107 batting average with three homers. He was sent back to the minors where he played a few more seasons before tearing up a knee. He was dealt to the Cubs and asked for a big league contract. When he didn't get it, he asked for a release. He didn't get the release, but he left baseball anyway. "If I would have come back, I would have had to do it with the Cubs," he explained. Szotkiewicz is now into sales for a flooring company and lives in Statesboro, Georgia.

The Tigers picked **Bubby Brister** in the fourth round in 1981. In rookie ball he hit a paltry .208 before breaking his hand. He decided to go back to playing football because he had trouble adjusting to the lifestyle of the minors. He was John Elway's backup in 1998 with the Denver Broncos.

Bruce Robbins didn't find much success with the Tigers, but he has on the Internet. Robbins, a 15th round pick in 1977, pitched two seasons with the Tigers before bowing out with back wows. He found more success with a business he began on the Internet that helps people find jobs and businesses find people.

Alan Dunn, a fourth-round pick in 1983, never made it to the majors, but turned to scouting and coaching after playing. He is now with the Cubs' farm system as a pitching coach.

Ones Who Got Away

Besides the previously mentioned Messersmith, Evans and Grimsley, another significant player who was drafted by the Tigers and signed elsewhere was the great "Oz," as he became known. The Tigers selected **Ozzie Smith** in 1976, but he didn't sign and waited until the Cardinals picked him.

A couple of years later, the Tigers picked **Mark Langston** in the 15th round when he finished high school. Langston decided to go to college and later drafted and signed with Seattle.

Like a lot of clubs, the Tigers wasted some picks on players who went to other sports. Detroit signed **Rick Leach**, quarterback with the University of Michigan, who had already been picked in the NFL Draft. Leach decided on football.

All in the Family

Matt Boone, a third-round pick, is the son Bob, a former catcher and manager, and grandson of Ray, a former player and scout. He also has two brothers in the majors: Aaron with Cincinnati and Bret with Atlanta.

Nate Cornejo, a first-round selection in 1998, is the son Mardie Cornejo, who pitched for the New York Mets.

Undrafted Players

Scouts don't get much of a chance to see players in New England for a very long because the season is real short on the East Coast. For that reason, **Ken Hill** from Lynn, Mass., went undrafted after high school and at North Adams State College, although he was undefeated as a pitcher. American Legion coach Dick Champa knew a Tigers scout and called him. The Tigers signed the right-hander. However, Detroit traded him after two seasons. Hill became a solid starter in the majors and signed a two-year deal worth $8.15 million with the Rangers in 1996.

On the Roster

Tony Clark was the veteran draft pick of the Tigers team in 1999. He was drafted in the first round in 1990 by the Tigers out of high school. Clark's baseball career was delayed as he played college basketball. He finally turned his attention full time to baseball in 1994. He got his first call to Detroit in 1995. The following year became his rookie season and he made the most of his debut by hitting 27 homers to finish third in Rookie of the Year Voting. The following season he became the fifth-fastest player in Major League history to reach 50 homers, trailing Mark McGwire, Rudy York, Chuck Klein and Bob Horner. The switch-hitting first baseman hit 32 homers in his sophomore season and another 34 in 1995.

Another power hitting

Tony Clark, drafted by the Tigers. (Photograph by Marty Orr.)

draft pick for the Tigers is **Bobby Higginson**, a 12th rounder in 1992 out of Temple University. His breakout year came in 1994 at Triple-A Toledo when he exploded for 23 homers after hitting less than 10 in each season before then. The next season he was a regular outfielder for the Tigers and has hit double-digit homers every year since. He also has a great arm and tied for second in the American League with 18 outfield assists in 1998.

On the mound, **Justin Thompson** was a first-round draft pick in 1991 out of high school. Injuries beset him early in his career, but he

Kurt Knudsen was a Detroit Tigers draft. (Photograph by Kenny Keiffer.)

rebounded and made the regular rotation in 1997. He became only the second Detroit left-hander to win 15 games in the last 20 years when he was 15-11. The following year his record was the same, but in reverse.

Pitcher **Brian Moehler** was drafted by Detroit in the sixth round in 1993 out of the University of North Carolina–Greensboro. After a 15-6 season at Double-A Jacksonville in 1996 and being named as the Tigers' Minor League Pitcher of the Year, Moehler was promoted to Detroit. In his rookie season, he was second among American League rookie pitchers in wins, strikeouts, and ERA. He made 31 starts in 1998 for the Tigers and went 14-13 with a 3.90 ERA.

Another draft pick pitcher on the staff was **Seth Greisinger**, who was picked by the Tigers in the first round in 1996 out of the University of Virginia. He posted a 9-0 mark in 10 starts for Team USA. He spent one full season in the minors before Detroit promoted him to the big leagues in June 1998. He started 21 games in 1998 and was 6-9 in his first big-league season.

Gabe Kapler with the Detroit Tigers was drafted in the 57th round in 1995. (Photograph by Marty Orr.)

In need of good pitching, the Tigers brought up **Jeff Weaver** on the express elevator. A first-round pick in 1998, the right-hander was recalled from Double-A in mid–April 1999 after just a handful of professional appearances. In five starts in 1998, he was 2-0 with a 1.44 ERA.

The quickest draft pick to make it to the majors from the class of 1998 was **Matt Anderson** of Detroit, a first-round pick from 1997. The late signee from Rice University, who cost the Tigers $2.5 million in bonus money, shot through the Tigers system like a three-stage rocket. The closer picked up 13 saves and two victories in two pit stops in the minors before being called up to the Tigers on June 25. The right-hander showed he was ready for the majors by compiling a 5-1 mark with a 3.27 ERA in 42 appearances with the Tigers the rest of 1998. Anderson is a prime example of a power pitcher that Detroit is searching for in the draft. He has a fastball that consistently hits the 100-mph mark. The Tigers are hoping he is their stopper of their future.

Another player who zipped through the minors was **Robert Fick**, the Tigers' fifth-round pick in 1996. The catcher was an all-star and Most Valuable Player in the Midwest League his second year in the minors after batting .341 and hitting 16 homers. He repeated his all-star performance in 1998 to earn a trip to the majors for good.

Frank Catalanotto, a 10th-round selection in 1992 out of high school, was outstanding in the minors. He hit .325 and was named to the South Atlantic League All-Star Team in 1994 at Class-A Fayetteville. He was an all-star second baseman in the minors, but he wasn't protected by the Tigers and was picked up by the Athletics in the Rule V draft. However, Oakland sent him back during spring training the following season. The Tigers have since found more use for the .300 hitter.

Future Stars?

Dave Borkowski could find himself pitching in the majors at any time because of his winning ways in the minors — 45-22 in four seasons. The 11th round pick in 1995 has made good progress and was promoted to Triple-A in 1999.

Every team is always on the outlook for left-handed pitchers and Detroit feels they have found a good one in **Alan Webb**. The fourth-round pick in 1997 showed good progress and good stuff in his first two years in the minors. Signed out of high school, he shows promise as a starter for the club in the next century.

Nate Cornejo was a sandwich-round selection, 34th overall, in 1998. The fastball pitcher was rated as the top prospect in the state of Kansas and as a senior went 5-1 with a 0.88 ERA, striking out 85 in 42 innings while allowing just 16 hits. "Nate came in as an outstanding athlete and has improved with each year," said Wellington High School head baseball coach Jamie Ybarra. "We had him timed with a 92-mph fastball as a freshman, and this year we had him at 96."

The Tigers' long-shot draft pick who has made good progress is **Javier Cardona**, a 23rd-round draft pick in 1994. The Puerto Rican draft pick was hitting .300 at Double-A and may have a chance to move up the chain if someone ahead of him fails.

The Tigers picked and later signed **Eric Munson**, their first-round pick in 1999. The junior from USC was the first college player selected in the draft. His performance was limited in 1999 due to a broken bone in his right hand. He still clubbed 15 homers on the season and knocked in 41 RBI.

Defensively, Munson committed just one error in 348 total chances for a .997 fielding percentage.

Kansas City Royals

The Royals didn't get much out of the draft when they first began the process in 1968, a year before they began playing in the league. Not until the expansion club started to draft some excellent pitchers did the draft pay off big for the team with a World Championship in 1985. Royals' draft pick pitchers Bret Saberhagen and Danny Jackson contributed much to the effort and so did three drafted fielders — George Brett, Willie Wilson and Buddy Biancalana. The 1980 team that went to the World Series, but lost, was also comprised of half-a-dozen homegrown draft picks, including pitchers Dennis Leonard and Paul Splittorff.

Owner Ewing Kaufmann was a big spender on free agents in the 1980s, which also helped the Royals reach the playoffs. The team's budget was among the top 10 teams for many years although the team was a small-market team. However, the team hasn't been able to outbid other teams for free agents recently and hasn't been in the post-season playoffs since they won the World Series in 1985. Giving away pitcher David Cone in 1987 didn't help matters. He might of made the difference the Royals needed.

The fans are getting restless about the poor showings of the Royals in the 1990s. They protested the Yankees when they came to town to play in 1999. The Royals had nothing to do with the protest. It was the news media. A radio station was responsible. The fans want revenue sharing.

The Royals drafted a lot of pitchers early in their draft history, but their philosophy has changed in recent times. "In general, we're looking for the best athletes," said scouting director Terry Wetzel, who has scouted for the Royals since 1984. They like to draft players who are multi-sport prospects like a Willie Wilson.

The Royals have a good size scouting bureau in the United States with 17 area scouts, a national crosschecker, two regional crosscheckers, 20 part-time scouts and about 200 associate scouts. Overseas, the team has no full-time scouts and concentrates on the Dominican Republic, where they have an academy, and Venezuela. A couple of players on their 40-man roster came from the Dominican. If the draft expanded to cover the world, the team would be hard pressed to fund a large international scouting effort.

The Royals are one of the top teams in baseball in supplying players for major league rosters, according to Wetzel. They also are one

Michael Tucker of the Cincinnati Reds, drafted by the Royals.

ended up 13th all-time in hits with 3,154, 8th all-time in doubles with 634 and 4th all-time in World Series batting average at .373. The lifetime .305 hitter led the American League in batting average and triples three times. Brett was voted the Most Valuable Player in 1980. He also had a rare 20-20-20 (doubles, triples, home runs) season, which has only been accomplished by four other players. The third baseman could also field with the best of them and won a Gold Glove in 1985. He appeared on 13 All-Star teams and led the Royals to the postseason seven times. The Royals retired his uniform number (5) in 1997. Brett's reaction to having a homer disallowed for too much pine tar on his bat will be forever etched in many fan's memories of the prolific hitter. Brett owns all the Royals offensive records except stolen bases.

of the top teams relying on the draft to supply players for their own roster, because they can't afford to spend a lot on money on free agents. They have a hard time spending money on top draft picks. They didn't sign Jeff Austin until February because he wanted what other top picks were getting, which was enough to fund a small country. "The guys around him got so much money," Wetzel commented. The Royals were afraid Austin would do like J.D. Drew did the year before and sit out rather than sign for less.

In 1999, the Royals had two first-round selections and two compensation picks in the draft. Their first seven picks in the draft were right-handed pitchers. The Royals continued to draft more right-handers and ended up taking 22 before it was all said and done. Six lefthanded pitchers were chosen, too.

Best Draft Picks

The best Royals draft pick so far is **George Brett**, who was inducted in the Baseball Hall of Fame in 1999. "Everyone who has ever played this game from Little League on up has a dream," said Brett upon his election. "And that dream is to someday make it to the Hall of Fame." Selected in the second round of the 1971 draft, Brett spent his entire 21-year career with the Royals, a rarity these days with free agency. He was selected in his first go-around because he

The best Royals draft pick so far: George Brett. (Photograph courtesy of the Kansas City Royals.)

The stolen base record is owned by a teammate of Brett's, **Willie Wilson**. He also spent many years on the Royals. The Royals took a big gamble on Wilson when they drafted him in the first round out of high school. Wilson had over 100 college scholarship offers to play football.

But a $90,000 bonus convinced him that baseball was the right way to go. The Royals made the right choice as did Wilson. The outfielder had great speed and led the league in triples five times. His best season came in 1982 when he led the league in average at .332. Wilson played 19 seasons in the majors and appeared on two All-Star teams. He only led the league in stolen bases once — 83 in 1979 — yet his 668 steals lifetime puts him 9th all-time.

The scouts must have been sleeping when **Bret Saberhagen** was evaluated out of high school. He was not drafted until the 19th round in 1982 by the Royals. The righthanded pitcher spent just one season in the minors where he was 16-7. The Royals brought him up after spring training the next season and put him in the regular rotation. The 19 year old was the youngest Royals' player to appear in a game when he pitched in a game on April 4. He struggled the first year, but was 20-6 the next season to lead the Royals to the World Series, where he picked up two victories and was named World Series

Most Valuable Player. "The most memorable team that I played for would be the 1985 Royals, because we won a World Championship," Saberhagen said during an chat on the Internet with the Boston Red Sox. He was rewarded for his performance with a Cy Young Award. He picked up his second Cy Young in 1989 when he was 23-6. He played eight seasons with the Royals before he was traded to the Mets. Saberhagen was named the 1998 Comeback Player of the Year by *The Sporting News* for his remarkable recovery and return from major shoulder surgery.

Mark Gubicza also contributed to the Royals' championship season in 1985. The second-round pick in 1981 was 14-10 during the season and won a game in the League Championship Series. He led the league in starts in 1989. Rotator-cuff surgery in 1994 spelled the end of his career. He pitched 13 seasons for the Royals.

Kevin Appier, a first-round pick in 1987, started off his major league career like a train, slow at first but after it gets going, look out. When he was called up in 1989, he was 1-4 with 9.14 ERA. By the next season, the locomotive was up to full speed as the righthander was 12-8 with a 2.76 ERA. He chugged along each year with a winning record until a losing mark in 1997 because of low run support. In 1998 he underwent right shoulder surgery and ended up on the disabled list most of the season.

One of the Royals' worst trades was **David Cone**, a third-round pick in 1981. After a short trial in 1987 as a reliever, the Royals dealt the hurler to the Mets for a bunch of has-beens in comparison: catcher Ed Hearn, and pitchers Rick Anderson and Mauro Gozzo. Cone made an impact almost immediately when he was 20-3 in 1988 with New York, but he didn't win the Cy Young Award that year despite having the best winning percentage and the lowest ERA. The award finally came

Bret Saberhagen, drafted in the 19th round in 1982 by the Royals. (Photograph courtesy of the Kansas City Royals.)

David Cone, a third-round pick in 1981. (Photograph courtesy of the Kansas City Royals.)

Bo Jackson, one of the best athletes of the century. (Photo courtesy of the Kansas City Royals.)

his way in 1994 when he was back with Kansas City. He started off the season with an 8-1 mark and was named to the All-Star Team. He ended the strike shortened season with a 16-5 record and 2.94 ERA. The Royals again traded him for three mediocre players after the season. Through the 1998 season, Cone had a 166-93 record. The hurler pitched a perfect game for the Yankees in 1999.

Cecil Fielder was another poor trade by the Royals. The fourth-round pick in 1982 was traded to the Blue Jays for Leon Roberts, as the Royals were looking for immediate returns. Roberts wasn't much of an answer to those needs and played part time for the Royals for the next two seasons. Fielder though didn't have an immediate impact in the majors and it wasn't until he went to Japan for a year that he developed into a real home run hitter. When he returned, he went on a four-year tear by averaging 40 home runs and 125 RBI a season. He slacked off after that and by spring training in 1999 with the Blue Jays he looked like a beached whale.

The Royals picked one of the best athletes of the century when they took **Bo Jackson** in the fourth round out of Auburn University. Jack-

son began his baseball career at Double-A and was called up to Kansas City in September. Jackson continued to pursue a football career as well and was drafted by the National Football League. In his rookie season the next year he smashed a club record 22 homers for rookies. He joined the NFL and performed double duty with both professional leagues for four years. "Bo knows" became a popular saying and gave the Royals the notoriety they needed to keep fans interested in a losing team. The Royals released him during spring training in 1991 because he hurt his hip during an NFL game in January. The White Sox took a chance that Bo could still play and signed him. Ironically, he made his comeback with Chicago in a game against the Royals. He underwent hip replacement surgery and everyone thought his baseball career was over. He proved them wrong and returned to play two more seasons of professional baseball.

Tom Gordon, a sixth-round selection in 1986, was the Minor League Player of the Year in 1988 to earn a trip to the majors in September. The following season he was used as both a starter and reliever and finished his rookie season with a 17-9 record and a runner-up for Rookie of the Year honors. The Royals used him strictly as a starter the next year and he showed he was no flash in the pan with a 12-11 mark. For the next two seasons he again filled both roles before the Royals decided on regular rotation duty again in 1994. He became a free agent in 1995 and signed with the Red Sox. In 1998 he was converted to the stopper role and completed 46 saves on the season to win the Rolaids Relief Man Award and put the Red Sox in the playoffs. He earned his first All-Star appearance that season, too. He also set a new Major League record by completing 43 saves in a row.

Long Shots

The Royals probably wish they had protected **Jeff Conine**, a 58th round selection in the 1987 draft, from the expansion draft in 1992. But they could protect only so many players. Florida snatched him up and he turned out to be as durable as Cal Ripken in 1993 when he played in all 162 games. Then he batted a career-high .319 in 1994. His home run total jumped from the teens to 25 in 1995. Then in 1997 he helped the Marlins to the World Championship with his 17 home runs. Soon after the season was over, the Royals got their long shot back when they traded pitcher Blaine Mull for him. With Jeff King at first base, Conine was moved to the outfield in 1998.

The longest shot to make it to the majors with the Royals was **Jose Santiago**, a 70th round pick in 1994. He was promoted in 1997. The right-handed pitcher has been called up twice to the Royals, but he hasn't performed good enough to stay there.

Paul Splittorff was one of the pitchers who pitched well at Arlington Heights High School near Chicago, but not good enough to get noticed by major league team a year before the draft began. However, after three years pitching at Morningside College in Sioux City, Iowa, the newly expansioned Kansas City Royals felt he was ready and selected him in the 22nd round. "It was a strange feeling not having a major

league year yet," he explained. "We didn't have a lot of veteran leadership and I missed that."

Splittorff spent two years in the minors before getting his first call to the majors. In his first start in the majors he gave up a homer to Rick McKinney. "The scoreboard I liked so much as a kid went off," he remembered. In May 1970, he came back to the majors to stay. The lefty played his whole 15-year career with Kansas City, ending with a 166-143 record. Then he became the team's radio announcer.

Dave Howard was a 32nd round pick in 1986 and made it to majors in 1991. The infielder played seven seasons with the Royals before being granted free agency in 1997 and signing with the Cardinals.

Disappointments

The Royals have had their fair share of first-round flops over the years.

The first time the Royals got a first-round pick in 1969, they chose **John Simmons** out of high school. He didn't sign and he never played professional baseball. The next year the Royals had the eighth-pick overall and went with catcher **Rex Goodson** out of high school. He peaked at Double-A. The Royals continued their poor picking for the third year in a row when they selected **Roy Branch**, a high school hurler. He pitched just two games in the majors.

Lew Olson, a first-round pitcher out of high school in 1973, got as far as Triple-A before busting. **Ben Grzybek** didn't even get that far. The first-round pick in 1976 only got to Double-A.

The 1981 first-round choice was an outfielder for a change. The change was not for the better as **John Leeper** out of USC played 19 games in the majors and batted .075.

Tony Clements was a great shortstop in high school, but the first rounder in 1986 could only get as far as Double-A in the majors. That's also as far as **Hugh Walker**, a first round outfielder in 1988, got.

Royals scouts were on hand in 1990 when **Sherrard Clinkscales** of Purdue threw a no-hitter against archrival Indiana. He wasn't good enough to get drafted out of Brebeuf High School in Indianapolis, but his fastball rose to 95 mph by the time he was a junior. The Royals took him 31st overall (supplemental round) and paid him a bonus of $180,000 plus $6,000 a year for schooling. Two years later a rotator cuff injury made him as wild as a cougar, so the Royals released him. The Cubs picked him up. He couldn't find the plate with a seeing-eye dog, and when the strike came in 1994, he decided his baseball days were over. "It was really disappointing to me," he said from his home in Missouri. "I wish I had gotten further." He did, sort of. He became a scout for the Atlanta Braves.

Matt Smith had a football scholarship to Stanford, but the Royals convinced him otherwise when they picked him in the first round in 1994. The Royals hoped he would turn into their next first baseman, but he hit more like a shortstop. He got as far as Double-A and could only manage a .227 batting average. So he moved to the mound in 1998, but Wetzel didn't know if he would make it there either. At age 23, he was beginning his professional career over or his career was just about over, one of the two.

Another first rounder who turned out to be disappointing was **Jeff Granger**. The first-round left-handed pitcher in 1993 didn't show much promise in the majors, so the Royals traded him to Pittsburgh with three other players for Jay Bell and Jeff King. An 18.00 ERA convinced the Pirates he wasn't ready and he was dealt to Texas, who released him. Then he went to the Tigers and an uncertain future.

Doug Blosser, a third-round pick in 1995, was beginning to show progress in the minors by batting .296 in 1997 with Spokane. That's as far as he would get though. He lost control of his Ford Mustang on Jan. 24, 1998, and died in the crash. His brother, Greg Blosser, was a first-round pick by Boston in 1989.

Best Draft

The Royals milk the draft for every drop like it was a Guernsey cow, so they have had a number of good drafts. Probably the best though is 1982 when they picked valuable players in three out of four of the phases. They first picked **Danny Jackson** in the January secondary phase. Then they chose Bret Saberhagen in the June

regular phase. In the June secondary phase they chose Cecil Fielder.

Worst Draft

The year 1977 wasn't very good for the Royals. Their first pick in the June draft was **Mike Jones**. He pitched four seasons with the team and ended his career with an 11-10 record. **Renie Martin** was chosen in the 19th round and his record was 13-19 over three seasons with the Royals. Lastly, **Kelly Heath**, a seventh-round choice, was a one-game wonder in the majors.

Where Are They Now?

Royals players like the organization so much that they have decided to stay in the system after their playing days. Brett is a testimony to that. He is now the vice president of baseball operations for the Royals.

Tom Poquette, a fourth-round selection in 1970, played in three League Championship Series with the Royals and seven years in the majors before turning to managing in the Royals' farm system.

Before beginning his managing career, **Bill Gardner, Jr.,** played in the Kansas City Royals organization for two seasons. His father, Bill Gardner, Sr., managed the Minnesota Twins 1981–85, and the Royals for part of 1987. Junior was a 50th-round draft pick by Royals in the 1987 June draft. He had a successful debut as manager at Class-A Michigan in 1997 as the Battle Cats were 70-67, second in the Western Division.

Another player turned manager is **Jeff Garber**, a 10th rounder in 1988. He made it to Triple-A before turning to managing in the Royals' system.

Yet another manager now is **Kevin Long**. He was indeed a long shot to make it to the majors after being picked in the 31st round in 1989. He never made it to the majors so he turned to managing and was skipper with the Spokane Indians in 1999.

Lester Strode was a fourth-round pick in 1980 and pitched nine seasons in the minors without a major league appearance. He turned to coaching after playing and is the pitching coordinator for the Cubs.

Gary Thurman, a Royals draft choice in 1983, first round, 21st pick.

The Royals signed **Gary Thurman** for his speed. He first impressed them when he was 16 years old at a tryout camp. The high school football player streaked 60 yards in 6.3 seconds — fastest they had ever seen. They began following the promising prospect and were impressed by his performance in the National Sports Festival. He followed that up with a great year at North Central High School, Indianapolis. But the speedy Thurman was highly regarded by colleges for his football abilities. He had intentions of going to Purdue to play football, so he signed a Big Ten Letter of Intent. Then Miami University offered him a baseball scholarship, so he signed a National Letter of Intent to go there. However, the Royals decided to pick him in the first round. He was watching a high school baseball game when he got the news, which excited the youngster. "I never knew much about the draft," he explained. "I thought you went right to the major leagues. That's how naïve I was." When he met with Art Stewart of the Royals, he signed right away for $99,500.

Thurman took until 1991 before be became a regular member of the Royals. He had two full seasons with the team before he was waived in 1993. The Tigers claimed him and he played in Detroit for a season. His career turned south after that and he began a roller coaster ride between the minors and the majors, spending time with the Mariners and Mets before being released in 1998 by the Angels organization. "I told myself that if I ever got released, that would be it," he added. In all, Thurman played three full seasons and parts of six others in the majors or

424 games. He says five-and-a-half seasons. You could say an average performance for a first rounder.

Thurman rejoined the Mariners organization in 1999 as the manager for the Peoria Mariners, a rookie team in Illinois. "That's what I wanted to do," he said.

A player who turned to coaching after playing is **Larry Carter**. He was originally selected in the 10th round by the Royals in 1986. He appeared in six games with the Giants in 1992 before returning to the Royals' organization as a pitching coach.

Joe Szekely, a second rounder in 1982, turned to coaching after playing, too. The catcher never made it to the majors so he turned to coaching. He was the hitting coach for the Spokane Indians in 1999.

Bo knows baseball and he's back. **Bo Jackson**, a Kansas City original draft pick, came back in the spring of 1999 to help Frank Thomas with his hitting after the "Big Hurt" batted some 50 points below his career average in 1998. The coaching must have helped because Thomas was back to his old self in 1999.

Ones Who Got Away

Scott Sanderson was picked in the 11th round out of high school, but he wouldn't sign with the Royals.

The Royals couldn't sign **Ron Hassey** after they picked him in the 22nd round out of the University of Arizona. They drafted him as a third baseman, yet he ended up signing as a catcher the next year with Cleveland.

Hubie Brooks was chosen in the first round of the January Secondary Phase in 1976. He didn't sign until the Mets chose him first the following year.

The Royals took **Frank Viola** in the 16th round in 1978 out of high school. He decided to wait until he had some college completed before he was drafted in the second round by the Twins and signed in 1981.

Another left-hander hurler who wouldn't sign was **Craig Lefferts** in 1979 after the Royals picked him in the seventh round out of college.

Will Clark was chosen in the 4th round

out of high school in 1982, but he waited until the Giants picked him first in the draft.

The following year **Todd Zeile** was drafted as a catcher out of high school. He ended up being drafted in 1986 in the second round by St. Louis and became a third baseman.

"Neon" **Deion Sanders** was chosen in the sixth round of the 1985 draft. He waited until the Yankees picked him in 1988; however, he had dropped all the way to the 30th round.

Undrafted Players

Tom Candiotti was with Independent Victoria in the Northeast League when the Royals discovered him in 1980. They didn't have the righthanded pitcher for long as they lost him the next year to the Brewers in a Rule V draft. Candiotti came up to the majors with the Brewers. After being granted free agency in 1985, he signed with the Indians, where he played in the majors for good. After 15 seasons in the majors, the knuckleballer has a 147-158 record.

Dan Miceli wasn't drafted after graduating from Dr. Phillips High School in Orlando, Florida. Kansas City signed him as a free agent in March 1990. The pure relief pitcher was the Royals' Minor League Player of the Year in 1992 when his ERA was less than 2.00. The Royals traded him to Pittsburgh where he made it to the majors in 1994. Then he was dealt to Detroit and the Padres where he was used as a set-up man.

All in the Family

In 1970 the Royals drafted **Gary Hubbs**, brother of the late Ken Hubbs, a second baseman with the Cubs who died in a plane crash to end his promising baseball career. Gary never got a chance to play in the majors.

The best relative drafted so far in Royals history is **George Brett**. His brother Ken Brett was a pitcher for the Red Sox in 1971 when George was taken in the second round out of high school. The two played together with the Royals in 1980 and 1981 before Ken retired from baseball.

David Landrith, a catcher like his father Hobie, was landed in the 12th round in 1983. Hobie played 14 years in the majors as a catcher. David never played in the majors.

The Royals picked **Brian McRae** in 1985 when his father was still toiling for the team as a designated hitter. Brian has done quite well for himself in the majors and has played more than half of the games and years his father played. Brian will likely never be as good a hitter as his father, but his father has still got a lot to be proud about.

Jeremy Giambi, whose brother Jason plays on the Athletics, was a sixth round pick in 1996.

The Royals picked **Felipe Alou, Jr.,** in the 1998 draft. He is son of Montreal manager Felipe Alou.

On the Roster

The Royals rely heavily on the draft to fill their roster. Going into the 1999 season, they had 16 of their own draft picks on the 40-man roster. A half a dozen of those were pitchers.

Jim Pittsley, a first-round pick in 1992, led the Carolina League with 171 strikeouts for Class A Wilmington in 1994, and was named to the league All-Star Team. But he got off to an auspicious start in the majors. He pitched one game for the Royals in 1995 and promptly suffered an elbow injury which required surgery. That set his career back to the beginning. The righthander worked his way back to the majors in 1997 as a starter. The Royals sent him to the bullpen in 1998 where he made 39 appearances, including two starts. However, his ERA rose to 6.59.

Jose Rosado was drafted by the Royals in the 12th round in 1994. He was called up from the minors in 1996 and made 16 starts, going 8-6 with a 3.21 ERA. The lefthander had losing marks the next two seasons.

Back with the Royals for the third time was **Tim Spehr**, a fifth-round pick of the Royals in 1988. The catcher made his major league debut with the Royals during the 1991 season before being traded to Montreal where he played for four seasons. The Royals purchased his contract from the Red Sox and he returned to play in early 1997 until the Royals released him. He signed with the Braves for a couple of months. Then he went to the Mets. The Royals again signed him in August 1998.

Also back with the Royals after a two-year hiatus was **Joe Randa**, an 11th round pick in

1991. He was a Southern League All-Star in 1993. His first call to the Royals came in 1995, but a batting average below the Mendoza Line sent me packing for the minors again. He finally became a regular in 1996. Then the Royals sent him to the Pirates in a multi-player trade for Jay Bell and Jeff King. He was picked by Arizona in the expansion draft and traded to Detroit where he played in 1998 before going to the Mets for a week on his way back to Kansas City.

Mike Sweeney was drafted by the Royals in the 10th round in 1991. He led the Carolina League with .310 average in 1995, which earned him a call from the Royals at season end. Then he was named to the Texas League All-Star Team in 1996. He split between Triple-A and the majors in 1997 before becoming the Royals' regular receiver in 1998.

Johnny Damon, a first-round sandwich pick in 1992, was an all-star each of his four seasons in the minors before coming up to the majors in 1995. His power hitting has improved each season with the Royals, and he had career highs of 18 homers, 30 doubles, 10 triples, 104 runs scored and 26 stolen bases in 1988.

Future Stars

The Royals are very high on **Jeremy Giambi** and hope he ends up like his brother. The outfielder was an all-star and Rookie of the Year in the Pacific Coast League in 1998 after averaging .372 with 20 homers. The Royals called him up in September 1998.

Another outfielder in the Royals system that got a look-see in September 1998 was **Carlos Beltran**, a second round pick in 1995 out of Puerto Rico. He has all the tools for centerfield and he hit .352 at Double-A.

The Royals were also high on outfielder Mark Quinn, an 11th round pick in 1995. He moved up to Triple-A Omaha in 1999 and was Pacific Coast League Rookie of the Year, as well as a September call from the Royals.

Completing the outfield prospects is **Dermal Brown**, a first-round pick in 1996. The Royals also looked at him in 1998, but he came from Single-A and needs more refinement in the minors.

The Royals picked pitcher **Chad Durbin** in the third round in 1996 out of high school, and he has progressed well in the minors with a good fastball and changeup.

Jeff Austin, a first-round pick in 1998, signed too late in 1998 to play. The righthanded pitcher was drafted in the 10th round out of high school, but he elected to go to Stanford to raise his stock. Austin began his pro career in Class A in 1999. The six-footer has a major league fastball and curveball.

Dan Reichert was a first-round selection in the 1997 draft. The righthander from the University of the Pacific was the seventh pick overall. He was 13-4 with a 2.30 ERA in 20 games as a junior. The starter also led all NCAA Division I pitchers in strikeouts, fanning 169 batters in 133 innings. "He throws in the 90s with a great slider," said Art Stewart, the Royals senior special assistant to the general manager. "He's a pitcher with a high ceiling, and he's a great competitor. He fits the mold we were looking for, which is a pitcher who could get to the majors quickly. His slider is as nasty as you'll find." After two seasons, Reichert had pitched at every level in the Royals farm system and was 9-10 with a 4.98 ERA.

Matt Burch was the first-ever first-round pick of Virginia Commonwealth University when he was selected by Kansas City in 1998. He set a school record with his 122 strikeouts and was second in the league in both ERA and wins. Burch's first season in the minors resulted in a 3-2 record with a 4.79 ERA.

The Royals continued taking pitchers in the first round in 1999 and went with **Kyle Snyder**, a big hurler from North Carolina, as their first selection. Snyder, who hits up to 96 miles per hour, posted a 7-5 mark with a 4.04 ERA and 96 strikeouts in 90 innings in his junior year. "He had a very productive season," said scouting director Terry Wetzel. "We liked the way he pitched in a wooden bat league in Cape Cod. We went with who we thought was the best player at the 7th pick."

They Royals followed Snyder with **Mike MacDougal** from fellow Atlantic Coast Conference rival Wake Forest. MacDougal is a 6-5 right-hander who was selected with the 25th pick. MacDougal owned a 12-2 mark with a 2.42 ERA

and 103 strikeouts in 108 innings during his senior season. He was selected to the All-Atlantic Coast Conference team in 1999. "He's another big guy with an explosive arm," Wetzel said. "He's really come along this year. He's been healthy all year."

The Royals picked **Bryan Bullington** in the 37th round in 1999 out of Madison Consolidated High School Indians. The six-foot-four righthander was 11-0 with a 1.70 ERA in his senior year before the draft. After he was picked, it must have picked him up even more as he led his team to a state championship by pitching a one-hitter in his final game. His fastball, which was hitting in the high 80s in the game, was too much for the high school hitters as he overpowered them. Bullington could have probably gone on to basketball as he was sixth in scoring in the state in basketball. However, he made his intentions clear about baseball by signing early with Ball State University. He wasn't sure whether he was going to sign with the Royals or go on to college. "It all depends on the offer," he said. "I'm looking forward to it."

Bryan Bullington was drafted by the Kansas City Royals in the 37th round in 1999.

Minnesota Twins

A few years before the draft, the Washington Senators moved to Minneapolis to become the Minnesota Twins. The Senators hadn't won a pennant since 1933, so they were looking to the draft to help. The effect of the draft began to show up in 1969 and 1970 when the Twins won division crowns. The draft was even better to the Twins in the late 1980s and early 1990s when some key draft picks helped the team to two world championships. The 1987 World Championship team contained a handful of great draft picks, including Gary Gaetti, Kent Hrbek, Kirby Puckett and Frank Viola. Hrbek and Puckett were on the 1991 championship team as well as Chuck Knoblauch and Scott Erickson. Since 1992 though, the draft hasn't had enough impact on the team to even give it a winning season. The small-market team can't afford to spend money on free agents, so it is now suffering through some hard times.

The Twins used to like to pick big, burly hitters, like Hrbek, who could hit the long ball in the indoor Hubert H. Humphrey Stadium, which was built in 1982 and became known as the "Homerdome." Today, the Twins' draft strategy depends on their position in the draft, according to Mike Radcliff, the head of the scouting department since 1994. He has had to adjust his five-year plan from year to year to be more reactionary to circumstances, such as the number of compensation picks he is getting. The draft has changed drastically because of the compensation round. It was more balanced when teams got one pick per round. Being a small market team, the Twins depend heavily on the draft to give them good talent. "I can't afford to miss in the draft anymore," Radcliff admitted. The Twins' strategy is simple: take the best player available.

The Twins have an average sized scouting staff with 18 area scouts and three regional cross-checkers in the United States. They have no scouts devoted to scouting the minors and majors like some teams, though. The regional

Jayhawk Owens, with the Indianapolis Indians, drafted by the Minnesota Twins. (Photograph by Marty Orr.)

The Twins began a major rebuilding effort in 1999 and by the All-Star break they had already tried out 15 rookies in the majors. They also dealt the aging Rick Aguilera to the Chicago Cubs in favor of getting younger talent.

The Twins showed a lot of interest in catchers in 1999 as their second and third round picks were receivers and they took a total of five. Still half of the Twins' selections were pitchers. And nine picks were outfielders. Seven of the first ten picks were out of high school. Overall, they selected 26 players from high school and 24 players from college.

Best Picks

The Twins thought so much of **Kirby Puckett** that their street address is Puckett Place. Picked in the first round in 1982, Puckett made his debut with the Twins a memorable one as he punched out four hits. It was a great start to an illustrious career that ended a .318 lifetime average, 2,304 hits, 207 home runs, 1,085 RBI and 1,071 runs scored. During the Puckett decade, he led the team in batting average nine of 10 years. He also appeared in 10 All-Star Games, earned six Gold Gloves and led the Twins to two World Championships. His 11th-inning home run won Game Six of the 1991 World Series. Puckett was best at hitting doubles and once tied the major league record of four two-base hits in one game. Off the field, he loved the fans and helped many charities. "He was a class act," said Kevin Trudeau, a former player in the Twins system. "Puck" developed glaucoma, an affliction that usually strikes in older people, in one eye, which led him to prematurely retiring at age 34. "Tomorrow is not promised to any of us," Puckett said at his retirement speech. "Anything can happen to any of us, whether we're reporters or whatever we may be — anything can happen." He should get some consideration for the Hall of Fame when he becomes eligible.

Along with Puckett on those championship teams was long shot draft pick **Kent Hrbek**. The 17th rounder in 1978 also spent his entire career with the Twins. The duo made a great combination as Puckett would get on base and Hrbek would knock him in. Ironically, Hrbek knocked in just one more RBI than Puckett during his

scouts handle those duties as well. "They earn their paychecks," Radcliff commented. "Our guys work harder than anyone else."

After the strike in 1994, the Twins cut back on part-time and associate scouts. Instead, they turned their attention to the international market. They now have three full-time scouts and a few part-time scouts scanning the globe. They have established an academy in Venezuela and are starting one in the Dominican. One scout spends six months in Australia and six months in Canada. And they are looking for players in Asia and Europe. But it is tough for them to compete with richer teams who can offer the same players more money.

The Twins shelled out their largest bonus ever in 1998 when they gave Ryan Mills $2 million. Being a small market team, the Twins would like to see a structured salary by round to stop the yearly inflation that is occurring in baseball. They are also open to the idea of trading draft picks. Draft picks can't be traded until a year after they have signed.

lifetime. He also hit a few more homers, 293 total. The hefty lefty hitter made only one All-Star Team in his rookie season, but he was a fan favorite in Minneapolis. He was just a solid first baseman and designated hitter for many years for the Twins. His only knock was his poor performances in the post season when he averaged less than .200 and hit just three homers in 91 at bats. Injuries took a toll on Hrbek and he retired after the 1994 season.

Another solid player from the 1987 World Championship team was **Gary Gaetti** at third base. The first pick in the June 1979 Secondary Phase made it up to the majors in 1981 and hit a homer in his first at bat. Still in the majors in 1999 with the Cubs, Gaetti played 11 seasons for the Twins. "G-man" could top the 400-homer mark by the time his career is over. He has appeared in two All-Star games.

The best pitcher on the Twins staff during the 1987 championship season was **Frank Viola**, a second-round pick in 1981 from St. Johns University. Viola was the best pitcher on the Twins staff during the 1980s. The Twins wasted no time bringing the talented pitcher up to the majors. He was brought up a year, almost to the date, after he was drafted. "Sweet Music," as he was called, was 17-10 in 1987 and won two games in the World Series to help the Twins to the championship. The following season he won the

Frank Viola, a second-round pick in 1981, with the Indianapolis Indians. (Photograph by Jackie Dowling.)

Cy Young Award after a brilliant 24-7 season. The Twins couldn't afford to keep him, so he was traded to the Yankees for five players, including Rick Aguilera and Kevin Tapani, who would help them win the world title in 1991 as well. Viola retired in 1996 with a 176-160 record.

Another original Twins draft pick on that 1987 squad was **Bert Blyleven**, a third-round pick in 1969. The right-handed pitcher was back with the Twins after stints in Texas, Pittsburgh and Cleveland. After the Twins drafted him, he was rushed to the majors at age 19 in 1970 when Luis Tiant went down. He helped the team to the League Championship Series in his first season. His best year came in 1973 when he won 20 games and led the league with nine shutouts, but being with a losing team didn't help his efforts as he also compiled 17 losses. The Twins decided to trade the consistent performer to Texas in 1976 for four players and cash. It was a bad move, as Blyleven continued to be an effective hurler. During his 22-year career, the pitcher with the big breaking curve won 287

Gary Gaetti with the Chicago Cubs was drafted by the Minnesota Twins as the first pick in the June 1979 Secondary Phase.

games, 22nd all-time, and lost 250 games, ninth all-time. He pitched in two All-Star games and one no-hitter. He is the Twins' all-time leader with 141 complete games, 29 shutouts and 2,035 strikeouts. He became eligible for the Hall of Fame in 1998 and received just 18 percent of the votes.

Chuck Knoblauch, a first-round pick in 1989, arrived to the Twins just in time to help them win a world championship in 1991. In fact, he wound up being named the Rookie of the Year after hitting .281 with 25 stolen bases and a great glove. In the seven seasons he played for the Twins, he led the team in stolen bases each year and set the all-time mark by the time he was traded to the Yankees in 1998. He won a Gold Glove Award the last year he was with the Twins and has been named to four All-Star teams.

The Twins picked **Graig Nettles** in the fourth round of the first draft. He pinch-hit in the League Championship Series in 1969 before the Twins traded him to the Indians for Luis Tiant. When he went to the Yankees a few years later, he began to get the attention he deserved as a power hitter and great fielder. Nettles played 22 years in the majors and slammed 390 homers, but he hasn't been a serious candidate for the Hall of Fame — just a great third baseman.

The Twins dealt **Jesse Orosco** to complete a trade with the Mets in 1979, a year after they drafted him in the second round. The Mets put him to good use as their left-handed stopper and he helped the team to the World Series in 1986.

Jay Bell, a Minnesota Twins draft choice in the first round in 1984.

Orosco has become an ironman on the mound as he has pitched 19 seasons, 1,025 games with 140 saves and a 84-73 record with a 2.97 ERA. He was still throwing in 1999.

Another player that the Twins traded while he was still in the minors was **Jay Bell**, a first-round pick in 1984. Bell has been a consistent performer in the majors during his 13 years in the majors with the Indians, Pirates, Royals and Diamondbacks. He's earned one Gold Glove and has appeared in one All-Star game.

Denny Neagle first came up with the Twins after being drafted in the third round in 1989. The left-hander pitcher was traded to the Pirates for pitcher John Smiley. Neagle pitched well for the Pirates then was dealt to the Braves where he had his best season in 1997 when he was 20-5 with a 2.97 ERA.

Long Shots

Rick Dempsey, a 15th-round pick in 1967, delighted the Twins by being named Most Valuable Player of the New York–Penn League in 1968 in leading catchers in many categories. The Twins called him up three years in a row in September and finally gave him a starting job in 1972, but they weren't happy with his .200 batting average and sent him back to the minors before shipping him out to New York in a trade. He was a backup receiver with the Yankees. Then he was dealt to the Orioles where he came of age. His claim to fame came during the post-season when he batted .400 in the League Championship Series for the Orioles in 1979. He became famous as the World Series Most Valuable Player in 1983 with Baltimore. He played 24 seasons in the majors. Someone thought enough of him to give him a vote for the Hall of Fame in 1998.

The lowest round draft pick to make it with the Twins so far is **Denny Hocking**, a 52nd round pick in 1989. He got three September calls before he became a permanent fixture with the Twins in 1996 as a utility fielder with the team. He is many times a late inning defensive replacement in the outfield.

Eddie Guardado, a reliever with the team since 1993, was a 21st rounder in 1990 signed by scout Kevin Murray. The lefthander was the

Most Valuable Player of his Babe Ruth team in 1985 and Legion team in 1989 before being drafted out of junior college. In the minors, he pitched a no-hitter and was 4-0 with a 1.24 ERA in Double-A before getting his first call to the majors. He was a starter in the minors, but the Twins converted him to a reliever in 1995.

Another long shot who has made it with the Twins recently was **Corey Koskie**, a 26th round pick signed by scout Howard Norsetter from Manitoba, Canada. After a mediocre rookie season, Koskie was selected to Midwest League All-Star Team in 1995 when he clouted 16 homers and batted .310. He's been on a fast track ever since and was called up to the Twins in 1998 after belting 26 homers at Triple-A Salt Lake.

Disappointments

The Twins have had a lot of bad luck with first-round picks over the years.

The bad luck began the draft with a big bombshell as they chose **Eddie Leon** as their first draft choice ever and he didn't sign. Instead, Leon waited until he was drafted by the Indians in 1967. No great loss though as Leon was never much of an impact in the majors. Other number-one picks who didn't sign with the Twins were **Dick Ruthven** in 1972, **Jamie Allen** in 1976, **Tim Belcher** in 1983 and **Jason Varitek** in 1993.

The 1966 first-round pick was also discouraging. **Bob Jones**, a third baseman, only got as far as Single-A. **Alex Rowell**, a first rounder in 1968, didn't do much better as he reached Double-A. The Twins continued the streak of poor number-once picks as **Paul Powell** in 1969 and **Bob Gorinski** in 1970 got little more than a cup of coffee in the majors. The following year first-round shortstop **Dale Soderholm** made it only to Triple-A.

Eddie Bane was a left-handed phenom in college with a 41-4 record. The Twins decided to debut their first-round pick in the majors and a record crowd packed the stadium to see him on July 4, 1973. The short pitcher wasn't good enough for the majors though and made just 44 appearances. **Ted Shipley** was chosen the next year in the first round and the shortstop never got past Double-A.

The next bust came in 1977 when **Paul Croft** was drafted in the first round. The outfielder peaked at Double-A. Even worse was **Kevin Brandt**. The first-round choice in 1979 out of high school only got as far as Class A.

Then there was a trio of first rounders who could only get as far as Triple-A: **Mike Sodders**, a first-round pick in 1981 from ASU; **Jeff Bumgamer**, a first-round right-handed pitcher out of high school selection in 1985; and **Johnny Ard**, a first-round pitcher in 1988.

The Twins released pitcher **Marc Barcelo**, a first-round pick in 1993, in May 1997 after an inflated ERA at Double-A. The Cubs picked him up and tried him at Class A, but he bombed out there as well.

The biggest disappointment in recent times was the loss of **Travis Lee**. The Twins lost the second pick in the draft, because they didn't offer him a proper contract within 15 days, according to Major League Baseball rules. Ratcliff disagreed with the decision. "We could have made a stand," he explained. Instead, Major League Baseball decided to side with the agents and voided the selection. Three other players were also made free agents as a result of the decision. Arizona and Tampa Bay took advantage of the situation and signed Lee and the others.

Best Draft

The Twins have had a lot of good drafts and usually get at least one player each draft that makes an impact on the team. The 1989 draft has produced a lot of good players who have contributed to the Twins as well as other teams. Included in that draft were **Chuck Knoblauch**, **Denny Neagle**, **Scott Erickson**, **Rey Ortiz**, **Marty Cordova**, **Mike Trombley**, **Eddie Guardado**, and **Dennis Hocking**. All of these players came up to the majors with the Twins. **Shawn Gilbert** made it to the majors, too, but with the Mets. The Mets dealt him to the Cardinals in 1998.

Worst Draft

The Twins don't have many poor drafts because they try and squeeze the most out of the draft like juice out of an orange. Probably the poorest draft was 1970, when **Bob Gorinski** and **Mark Wiley** were the only players who made it to the majors and neither was an impact.

Where Are They Now?

Jeff Reboulet, a 10th-round pick in 1986, was first drafted as a shortstop in the 23rd round by Houston in 1985, but he elected to finish his senior year at LSU. "They weren't going to pay me enough money," he explained. "We had a good team coming back." Many times juniors will sign because they lose any leverage when they finish college. He took a chance and it worked out for him. In seven seasons in the minors, he learned to play every position on the field, including pitcher. The experience led him to becoming a valuable utility player with the Twins and now with the Astros. The Ohio-born player now resides in Fishers, Indiana, with his wife and three children. In the off-season he holds a camp for young players. His degree is in business management.

Rick Dempsey became a manager after playing days in 1993 in the Dodgers farm system. In 1999 he was the Dodgers' bullpen coach.

Scott Ullger, an 18th-round pick in June 1977 signed by scout Herb Stein, is now the batting coach with the Twins. The third/first baseman played for the Twins in 1983 and was hitless in first 19 at-bats before singling off Steve Renko for first major league hit and RBI.

Andre David, an eighth-round selection in 1980, hit a home run in his first at bat in the majors off Jack Morris to become the 49th player in the history of the game to accomplish that feat. After two short stints in the majors, he turned to managing in the Royals' farm system.

Graig Nettles is now a scout with the Yankees.

Ones Who Got Away

The Twins have let a lot of good picks slip through their paws over the years probably because they couldn't offer them enough money. Of course quite a few of those players were high school picks who decided to go to college rather than sign. Such was the case with **Steve Garvey**. The Twins chose him out of high school as their number three pick in 1966. Garvey went off to Michigan State University and waited until two years later to get picked by the Dodgers in the first round of the June 1968 Secondary Phase.

Another high school player who went on to fame who didn't sign was **Al Hrabosky**. Minnesota picked him in the 11th round in 1967. The "Mad Hungarian" waited until the Cardinals picked him two years later before signing.

Other high school picks who didn't sign with the Twins included **Rick Burleson** in 1969, **Eric Show** in 1974, **Bret Boone** in 1987 and **Aaron Sele** in 1988.

The Twins also missed a few college picks, too. They selected **Del Unser** as their second pick in the first draft. The Mississippi State player was the son of Al Unser (not the race car driver), who was a scout for Milwaukee and was a former major leaguer. Unser waited until the next year when the Pirates picked him fourth in the January Secondary Phase.

The Twins drafted **Tim Belcher** first in the country in June 1983 out of Mount Vernon Nazarene College and offered him a reported $120,000 bonus. He declined and waited until January 1984 to get a better deal. The Yankees then picked him first in the secondary phase and did just that.

Mark Grace was a 15th round selection by the Twins in the June 1984 draft. The following year, he dropped to the 24th round by the Cubs and signed. Still, Grace may not have got much playing time with the Twins as Hrbek was at first base for a long time.

In 1972, the Twins picked **Dick Ruthven** out of Fresno State University. He waited until the Phillies picked him in the first round of the January 1973 Secondary Phase before signing.

All in the Family

Matt Lawton's brother, Marcus, played in Mets, Angels and Yankees systems, as well as 10 games in the majors. Matt proved that being picked in the 13th round in 1991 was lucky from him. Signed by scout Cal Ermer, Lawton was drafted out of junior college and moved steadily though the minors to get his first call to the majors from Double-A in 1995. He became a regular on team in 1997 replacing Puckett, who was forced to retire. He hasn't filled those big shoes, but he did hit 21 homers in 1998 to make a large contribution.

Javier Valentin's brother, John, first came up with the Boston Red Sox in 1992, a year before he was drafted in the third round. Javier didn't hit above the Mendoza Line in his first full season in the majors, but he showed he can be a backup receiver in the majors. He was the Midwest League All-Star catcher in 1995 at Class-A. He made the jump to the majors from Double-A in 1997.

Undrafted Players

The Twins signed **Mark Portugal** as an undrafted free agent in October 1980. Portugal was not drafted after he graduated from high school where he had played just one season of baseball as a catcher and outfielder. He signed with the Twins a week before his 18th birthday. Portugal worked his way up to the Twins and played with the team until he was traded to the Astros in 1988. He was still pitching a decade later with Boston.

On the Roster

The Twins had more of their own draft picks — more than half — on their roster going into Spring Training in 1999 than any other team in baseball.

The real veteran draft pick on the Twins is **Mike Trombley**, a 14th-round selection in 1989 signed by scout Steve Williams. The pitcher was wild in college as he established an NCAA record in 1989 by hitting 20 batters. He had just a 6-22 record at Duke University, but the Twins felt they could put him under control and they did. He did give up a lot of walks in the minors where he was a starter. The Twins used him in that capacity when they first called him up, but he has been strictly a reliever since 1997. He pitched a more respectable 3.63 ERA in 1998.

Brad Radke, an eighth-round choice in 1991 signed by scout Jeff Schugel, made his major league debut in 1995. The next three seasons he was named as the opening-day starter on the team. In 1998 he was named to the All-Star Team. In 1997 he streaked to 12 consecutive wins, one short of the major league record.

Marty Cordova, a 10th-round pick in 1989 signed by scout Vern Followell, passed up an eighth-round offer by San Diego in 1987 after he completed high school. He was named California League Most Valuable Player in 1992 and made the Twins out of spring training in 1995. His 24 homers in his rookie season led to his selection as the Rookie of the Year. During that season, he homered in five consecutive games to tie a major league record.

Todd Walker, a first-round pick in 1994 signed by scout Marty Esposito, was first drafted by Texas in the 51st round in 1991 after being selected as the Louisiana Baseball Player of the Year. He was likely picked in the 51st round because he was headed to LSU where he made a name for himself. The three-time All-American broke hitting records by Albert Belle and Rafael Palmeiro and led LSU to a College World Series title. He was a member of Team USA in 1993. He averaged over .300 in the minors and was named as the Twins' 1996 Minor League Player of the Year at Triple-A Salt Lake. When he got the call to the majors though in 1997, he had to share duties with other established players and didn't get to play every day, so he couldn't perform up to speed. The Twins traded Chuck Knoblauch to make room for Walker. He responded with a .316 batting average and 12 homers in his first full season in 1998.

Chad Allen, a fourth-round pick in 1996, made the team out of spring training after he collected a team-record 36 hits in the spring. The outfielder made the jump from Double-A after three years in the minors.

Dan Perkins wasn't on the 40-man roster going into spring training, but he came out of camp on the roster of the major league team. Unbeaten in Triple-A the season before, the right-hander was a starter in the minors where his ERA and record went up and down like a yo-yo.

Another pitcher not on the 40-man was **Mike Lincoln**, a 13th round pick in 1996 signed by scout Tom O'Neil, but he made the squad out of spring training, too. The right-hander was an Eastern League all-star in 1998 when he was 15-7 as a starter.

LaTroy Hawkins was drafted in the seventh round in 1991 and signed by scout Dan

Durst. He made his major league debut in 1995, but was sent back down after a poor start (2-3 with an 8.67 ERA). He bounced back and forth from Salt Lake City before securing a spot in the starting rotation in 1997. A high 5.91 ERA and poor run support has led to him having a 16-30 record in the majors though.

Torii Hunter, a first-round choice in 1993 signed by scout Mike Ruth, played a game with the Twins in 1997 and six more in 1998. Before being drafted, he was on the 1992 Junior Olympics Team. His progress has been slow as he hit just .259 in the minors. A knee injury in 1996 slowed him.

Benj Sampson, a sixth-round draft choice out of high school signed by scout Joel Lepel, was a Florida State League all-star in Class A in 1995. The left-handed hurler got a call up to the Twins in 1998 gave up just three runs in 17 innings. His first win came after a nine strikeout performance against Detroit.

Travis Miller was a sandwich pick in 1994 after a stellar career at Kent University. The left-hander moved quickly through the Twins system and debuted in the majors in 1996. He's begun every season since then at Triple-A Salt Lake, but he's been recalled to the Twins every season.

Bob Radlosky went from up and coming to on the roster when he was called up in early 1999. The 22nd round pick from 1993 started off 1999 unbeatable at Triple-A with a 3.69 ERA to get the call in late May.

Future Stars?

Matthew LeCroy, a sandwich pick in 1997, is the Twins catcher of the future. He played for Team USA in the 1996 Summer Olympics. LeCroy was selected to the Class A All-Star Team in 1999.

Doug Mientkiewicz, a fifth-round pick in 1995 signed by scout Brad Weitzel, got his first call to the majors in September 1998. The line-drive hitter is expected to be the starting first baseman for the Twins in the future. He hit .323 in Double-A with 16 homers.

Mark Redman was first drafted in the 41st round by Detroit in 1992 out of high school, but he chose to go the Oklahoma where he was a first team All-American, which skyrocketed his stock as the Twins chose him in the first round in 1995 and scout John Leavitt signed him. In four years in the minors, Redman has yet to achieve any success at the Triple-A level. Then in 1998 he was disabled for a week with a strained lower back.

A. J. Pierzynski was drafted in the third round out of high school and was signed by Brad Weitzel. The catcher has always hit for a good average in the minors (.286 average), which helped him to get a call up in September 1998.

Jacque Jones, a second-round pick in 1996, was named to all-star teams in Single-A and Double-A after hitting 15 homers in 1997 and 21 homers in 1998. The Twins are looking at him as the centerfielder of the future.

The Twins picked **B.J. Garbe** as their first pick in 1999 and signed him within a month. The high school graduate, who was recommended by scout Bill Lohr, batted .500 with five doubles, three triples and six homers during his senior year. He was named the Gatorade 1999 National High School Player of the Year and was offered a scholarship to Stanford University. "The negotiation process was straight forward throughout and was as good as expected," Radcliff said. "We are pleased to get his pro career started early this summer. The more at-bats he gets in his first year will only benefit himself and the Minnesota Twins."

Making good progress in the minors was long shot pitcher **Juan Romero**, a 21st rounder in 1997. He began the season at Double-A with six consecutive saves. Then he was called up to the Twins at the end of the season.

New York Yankees

The draft helped to destroy the dynasty that the Yankees built in baseball for so long. For the 35 years prior to the draft, the Yankees were involved in 22 World Series. Since the draft began in 1965, they have made the trip only six times, which shows how effective the draft was in bringing some parity to the league. However, the New York franchise has since figured out a better formula to rise to the top again in baseball. The formula is a mixture of the draft picks, free agents and foreigners.

Some say the Yankees didn't make it to the final dance a lot since 1972 because of the "George factor." Owner George Steinbrenner, who purchased the team in 1972, at first tried to rely too much on the free-agent market and trading draft picks to build his teams. The result was the team not appearing in the World Series from 1982 to 1995. The recent turnaround in the club is a result of the shipbuilding magnate finally listening to his own staff and using some of the team's own draft picks.

Few of the teams' own picks have risen to fame with the Yankees. Steinbrenner has had the habit of trading away star prospects and spending millions on mediocre talent. All of the good efforts by the scouts went by the wayside because the team would trade the prospects later. Some scouts must have felt like their great picks were all for naught or that they were simply scouting for other teams. The 1978 Championship Team had only a couple of players that were originally drafted by the Yankees, such as pitchers Ron Guidry and Jim Beattie.

A scouting director from another team described the Yankees as a "now" team, which meant the team failed to build a team for the future. Many teams in a pennant race think like that and will trade away future players for the stretch run. That strategy sometimes comes back to bite a team later.

The Yankees have given away 15 compensation picks in 12 years for signing free agents to become one of the highest teams in that category. Former draft pick Carl Everett, now with the Houston Astros, commented, "They don't take care for the young guys there." Everett was

a first-round pick by the Yankees in 1990. New York failed to protect him from the expansion draft in 1992 and the Marlins selected him. The Marlins twice promoted him to the majors, but he failed to impress them, so he was dealt to the Mets where he finally stuck in the majors in 1996. He increasingly improved and, after being traded to the Astros, he batted .296 in 1998 with 15 home runs.

The Bronx Bombers have made some great picks in the draft, such as 19th rounder Don Mattingly, who never once got to a World Series in his 14-year career as he was with the team during that long dry spell. Other players, like Willie McGee, Fred McGriff, Rob Tewksbury and Hal Morris, all turned into good players with other teams. Of course with Mattingly at first base, McGriff and Morris were likely traded because there was no place for them.

The Yankees of the 1990s have shown a little more patience with draft picks and as a result are back in the saddle again. A good example of that is Shane Spencer, who was a 28th round pick in 1990. He developed in the Yankees minor league system and worked his way up to the 1998 championship team, which was his ninth season in the majors.

But the Yankees keep thinking about immediate needs and have recently traded away some prospects to help shore up the lineup. For example, they traded outfielder Brian Buchanan, a first rounder in 1994, and pitcher Eric Milton, a first round pick in 1996, to Minnesota for Chuck Knoblauch in 1998. The second baseman helped the Yankees immediately, while the rookie Milton was 8–14 and wouldn't have helped and Buchanan played in Triple-A, so the trade was good for 1998. Whether the trade will be good later is yet to be seen.

One thing the Yankees don't have to worry about is money to spend on draft picks. Their free spending on draft picks have raised the roof on bonuses in the past. The Yankees were the first team to give a million dollars to a pitcher out of high school. They also aren't afraid to negotiate with any agents. They have a tendency to go after players with high ceilings.

The short right field in Yankee Stadium lends itself to left-handed power hitters. That's one of the reasons why Mickey Mantle and Roger Maris hit so many homers there, just to name a few. The Yankees prefer power in a position player over speed and batting average.

In the scouting department, the scouts span the globe like ABC Sports and have signed some foreigners who have made a great impact on the team in recent times, such as Hideka Irabu from Japan, Mariano Rivera from Panama and prospect pitcher Luis De los Santos from the Dominican. And because the team has a higher budget than all other teams in baseball, it can outbid other teams for a player.

They also have one of the premier farm systems in baseball and stress instruction over winning. Their players think that the Yankees training is the best in baseball. "The development is so much better than other teams," said Casey DeGroote, an 11th round pick in 1998. He qualified that statement by saying he heard other players from other teams making the comparison.

Only once in the history of the draft have the Yankees had the first overall pick in the draft. That came in 1967 after finishing last in the American League the year before. They chose Ron Blomberg because he was Jewish and would draw fans within the city. Blomberg didn't turn out that well and can best be remembered for being the first designated hitter in the American League rather than a star player.

Buck Showalter, a Yankees draft pick.

Best Picks

The Yankees could have signed **Thurman Munson** straight out of high school in 1964, a year before the draft, but they didn't notice him in high school. Yankee scout Harry Hesse first noticed him years later in the Cape Cod League with Kent State University. He was impressed. Munson scored 24 runs and drove in 30 runs in 25 league games. He was named All-American. When the 1968 draft came about, the scouting report was crossed out and replaced by two words: "GET HIM." The Yankees did in the first round. Munson showed he was an excellent choice in his first year in the majors. He won Rookie of the Year honors in 1970. He received 23 out of 24 votes. Munson led the Yanks in hitting that year with a .302 batting average. Six years later he was named Most Valuable Player after batting .302 with 17 homers and 105 RBI in leading the Yankees to the World Series. He became the team's first captain since Lou Gehrig. Munson was still playing baseball when he met his fate in August 1979 in the crash of his twin-engine Cessna. He was 32. The following day the fans filled Yankee Stadium to give him a standing ovation that lasted some eight minutes.

Munson caught probably the best Yankees' drafted pitcher, **Ron Guidry**. The third-round draft pick in 1971 had a marvelous 14-year career, all with the Yankees. In just his second full season in the majors, the Louisiana Lightning left-hander was nearly unbeatable. His 25-3 record with nine shutouts led him to being named for the Cy Young Award that season and helped the Yankees to a world championship. That season he led the league in wins, winning percentage

Brian Johnson with Indianapolis Indians. He was a New York Yankees draft pick.

and ERA with a 1.74. He continued to pitch well for New York and was runner-up for the Cy Young in 1985 when he led the league with 22 wins and winning percentage with .786. He retired in 1988 with a 170-91 record and 5-2 record in postseason play. He appeared in two All-Star Games as well.

Don Mattingly began racking up accolades at an early age. At Evansville Memorial High School, Indiana, he was an all-star defensive back in football and all-conference in basketball. As a junior he led his high school to a state baseball championship in 1978. The following year he took them to the championship again, but his team lost in extra innings. He was honored with the L.V. Phillips Mental Attitude Award. He is considered as the best hitter ever in the Final Four tournament and his name still dots the Indiana High School Record Book. In Indiana he was the best, but with the draft he had to measure up with the rest of the country and scouts didn't give him high enough marks to earn him a higher selection than the 19th round by the Yankees in 1979. The left-handed hitter was well suited for Yankee Stadium. He soon showed the scouts that they had underrated his talent as he batted .349 in rookie ball. He continued to hit over .300 in the minors and was called up to the Yankees halfway through the 1983 campaign. The following season he was named to the All-Star team and won the batting title with a .343 average. It made him the first Yankee lefty to hit over .340 since Lou Gehrig in 1937. Mattingly topped his performance the next season when he hit 35 homers and 145 RBI to earn the Most Valuable Player award. In 1986, the Hoosier set new club records for doubles (53) and hits (238) in a season. Again he was an all-star and won a Gold Glove. During the 1987 campaign, Mattingly streaked to a home run record as he hit 10 homers in an eight-game stretch to tie Dale Long's record streak. He also hit six grand slams during the season for another record. He continued his outstanding play until back problems started to slow him in 1990 and his home-run production began to fall off. Then in 1993 he suffered a muscle stain in his lower left rib cage and was put on the disabled list. He also had wrist problems that had to be corrected with surgery after the season. After 14 years with the Yankees, Mattingly finally saw playoff action in 1995 with the Yankees. However, the Bronx Bombers got shot down by Seattle and he never got to a World Series as a result. It became his last season. A six-time all-star and eight-time Gold Glove winner, he will become eligible for the Hall of Fame in 2000.

In one of the worst trades in Yankees history, **Willie McGee** was dealt to St. Louis for pitcher Bob Sykes. Sykes never pitched again. McGee is still playing. The tall, wiry player was drafted in the secondary phase of the January 1977 draft by the Yankees out of Diablo Valley Junior College. He was an all-star in the Southern League in 1981 after hitting .322, but the Yankees still traded him. McGee has been a consistent performer in his 17 years in the majors, mostly with the Cardinals. His best overall season was 1985, leading the National League with a .353 average, 216 hits, 18 triples, and stealing 56 bases. That performance led him to being named National League Most Valuable Player. He has been named to four All-Star teams and earned three Gold Gloves.

The Yankees didn't do any better in trading **Fred McGriff**. McGriff had just finished rookie ball as an all-star, when the Yankees dealt him along with right-handed pitcher Mike Morgan and outfielder Dave Collins for pitcher Dale Murray and third baseman Tom Dodd. Murray never pitched in the majors and Dodd played eight games with Baltimore. McGriff and Morgan are still playing today. McGriff was first called to the majors with Toronto in 1986 for a couple of games. The next season the Blue Jays made him a regular and he responded with 20 homers and 16 doubles. He's hit 358 home runs since then. The first baseman has been named to four All-Star games. Now he's with Tampa Bay.

Derek Jeter has already made such an impact in New York that he can be considered as one of their best draft picks ever. The Yankees picked the shortstop in the first round in 1992 and he was the first high schooler (sixth overall) taken in the draft. He's been an all-star in professional ball ever since his second year in the minors when he was picked for the South Atlantic League All-Star Team. The following year he was the Most Valuable Player in the Florida State League. In 1995 he was again named to an all-star team at Triple-A. The Yankees first called him up that season. The next season was his first full season and he was named Rookie of the Year after hitting .314 with 10 homers, 25 doubles and 78 RBI. In his first three full seasons in the majors, he broke the Major League record for the most runs scored by a shortstop with 352. In 1999, he was named to his second All-Star Team.

Long Shots

Mattingly's replacement, **Kevin Maas**, was a longer shot than Mattingly. He was picked in the 22nd round in 1986. After hitting 21 homers in 79 games in 1990, the Yankees had hoped he would be their first baseman for the future. But the following season, Maas hit just 23 homers in 148 games. A .205 batting average in 1993 dropped the long shot out of the race for good and his career staggered after that.

Kevin Maas, here with the Indianapolis Indians, was picked in the 22nd round in 1986. (Photograph by Marty Orr.)

The Yankees selected **Shane Spencer** in the 28th round in 1990 out of high school. Many high school players take some time to develop in the minors, and the Yankees showed patience with Spencer. They had to. He spent two seasons in the rookie league and four in Class A before he began to show he had some power behind the plate. He hit 16 homers and batted .300 in 1995 to earn a promotion to Double-A in 1996. At Norwich, he exploded for 29 homers to earn a boost to Triple-A, where he slammed 30 long ones in 1997 to capture the interests of the Yankee ownership. When Chili Davis went on the disabled list early in 1998, Spencer got his shot with the Yankees after nine seasons in the minors. Spencer showed he could hit major league pitching as well by knocking out 10 homers in 67 at bats. It earned him a spot in the playoffs and World Series.

The Yankees picked high school graduate **Brad Ausmus** in the 48th round of the 1987 draft. His chances of ever making it to the majors was longer than a maiden winning the Kentucky Derby. After leading the Carolina League in fielding in 1990, Ausmus started to come around with his hitting the following season to earn him a promotion to Double-A. He moved up to Class AAA Columbus in 1993, but the Yankees didn't protect him from the expansion draft in 1992 and he was picked up by the Rockies. His breakthrough to the majors came the next season when the Rockies traded the Triple-A player in a multi-player trade to the Padres, who needed his services immediately. He was involved again in a big trade to Detroit in 1996. He played half a season there before being dealt to Houston where he played two seasons and signed a three-year deal for more time at the top.

Bob Tewksbury, a 19th-round selection in 1981, has been a reliable starting pitcher for several teams over 13 seasons in the majors. He came up with the Yankees and pitched two seasons in New York before being dealt to the Cubs. Then he was granted free agency and has traveled to St. Louis, Texas, San Diego and Minnesota.

Mike DeJean was a 24th rounder in 1992 out of Livingston University. A reliever all his career, the Rockies purchased his contract from the Yankees in November 1995. Two years later he was promoted to the bigs and pitched well: 5-0 record with a 3.99 ERA. He stuck with the Rockies in 1998 and appeared in 59 games.

Major league teams are always on the lookout for a left-handed pitcher. The Yankees found one in **Andy Pettitte**, a 22nd-round pick out of junior college in 1990. The starter worked his way through the minors with ease, winning in each season. In 1994, the Yankees named him as their Minor League Pitcher of the Year after a 14-4 mark in Double- and Triple-A. The Yankees brought him up in 1995 and he has been a winner in the majors as well. In 1996, he became the first Yankee to win 20 games since Ron Guidry in 1985 when he finished with a 21-8 mark to help the Yankees to a pennant.

Many times Pettitte has pitched to a long shot catcher, **Jorge Posada**. He was picked two rounds after Pettitte the same year. Three times he was an all-star in the minors. He also came up in 1995 and has been there ever since.

Rich Batchelor, a 38th-round pick in 1989, was traded to St. Louis for pitcher Lee Smith in 1993. The reliever has had three strikes at the majors and has struck out at sticking so far. Regardless, he beat the odds just getting where he got.

Doc Medich, who pitched for the Yankees for three full seasons, was a long shot from the 30th round. His best season in the majors came when he was with the Yankees in 1974 when he was 19-15. The Yankees traded him to the Pirates for Willie Randolph, Ken Brett and Doc Ellis. In all, he pitched 11 seasons in the majors with a 124-105 record.

The Yankees are notorious for trading away draft picks before giving them a chance to make it to the top in their own farm system. A recent example of this is **Russ Davis**. The third baseman was selected in the 29th round in 1988. The Yankees dealt him to Seattle in 1995. Two years later Davis showed why he should have been kept in the system. He hit 20 homers in the majors. He repeated that performance in 1998.

Deion Sanders was a 30th-round draft pick of the Yankees in 1988 and began a baseball career before he turned to the National Football League in 1989. Like Bo Jackson before him, "Prime Time" played baseball in the summer and football in the fall. He first came up

Deion Sanders, Cincinnati Reds, drafted by the New York Yankees as a 30th-round pick in 1988. (Photograph courtesy of Marty Orr.)

with the Yankees the same year he played both sports. The Yankees held on to him for another season before releasing him. He played for eight years in the majors. He gave up baseball after the 1997 season to play exclusively for the Dallas Cowboys.

Disappointments

The Yankees did a good job of drafting good first round picks until 1970. That year they chose a pitcher by the name **Dave Cheadle**. He once struck out 49 hitters in a 23-inning summer league game, but he only struck out after only two in two games in the major leagues. However, the top prospect for the New York Yankees was given little opportunity as a major league pitcher.

The Yankees picked Cheadle in the first round and offered him $27,000. "I was insulted as the number 12 in the U.S. and the Yanks' number 1," said the left-handed hurler who had fashioned four no-hitters in his senior year at Asheville High School, North Carolina. He knew that Mike Martin, the fifth pick in the draft, had been offered twice as much by Philadelphia. So Cheadle went on vacation to Myrtle Beach with his senior class and left negotiations to his agent, Bobby Robinson, an attorney and friend of his family who represented him for no fee. The Yankees began upping the offer, but Cheadle didn't begin listening until the figure got up to $60,000. He finally settled for $75,000 plus bonuses for each level achieved and an academic scholarship. He wisely invested in commercial real estate.

For his first two seasons, Cheadle reported late to spring training and left the season early as well to attend the University of North Carolina. He was trying to have the best of both worlds.

Then in 1972 after reporting late to Class A Fort Lauderdale, he experienced losing for the first time in his life. "I didn't handle it well," he now admits. In a fit of frustration, he slammed his pitching hand into the dugout wall and shattered it in seven places. His season was over.

The following season he came back strong. Sometimes he was as wild as an alley cat and other times as accurate as Robin Hood. He once threw back-to-back one-hitters in the International League. He worked his way up to Class AAA Syracuse, yet the Yankees — known for building today instead of tomorrow — had seen enough and traded him to Atlanta for Pat Dobson, a former 20-game winner. The Braves took him straight to the Show.

On Sept. 17 the Braves were in Cincinnati playing the Big Red Machine. The lefty was the only pitcher in the bullpen when the phone rang in the 11th inning with the score tied. The call was for him. He could hardly believe it. He got the side out and the game moved to the 12th inning. Pete Rose led off and Cheadle fanned him on three straight pitches. He walked Johnny Bench, the first drafted player to make it to the Hall of Fame, and was lifted for a righthander, Adrian Devine. Bench eventually scored and Cheadle was tagged for the loss. He had one more appearance with the Braves before the end of the season.

At spring training the next year, Cheadle led the Braves in ERA and wins. The team announced he was coming to the Bigs again, but at 3 a.m. the night before the opener, Braves Manager Eddie Matthews called him to his suite. "He told me they had traded me for catcher Vic Correl, who had no options left," remembered Cheadle, who had options left. He was going back to Triple-A. To make matters worse, his car had already been shipped to Atlanta and he had a furnished apartment waiting for him. Even the hometown newspaper had run a front-page story about him starting the season with the Braves.

Cheadle felt disheartened and humiliated. Manager Clint Courtney had no patience with pitchers without good control, which was one of his problems. "Two straight walks and you were gone. He pulled me in the first inning six or seven times. We grew to despise each other," he explained. That season he went from top prospect to "suspect." The next season wasn't any better so he quit at age 25.

Perhaps the promising lefty was cheated out of a real chance at making it the majors. "If I had won more games, I would have had greater success," he surmised.

Cheadle went on to become a national sales director for a computer firm which fixed Y2K problems associated with the year 2000.

Another football star with the Yankees was **John Elway**, who was drafted in the second round in 1981. He was signed by scout Gary Hughes for $125,000, which was a lot for a second round pick at the time. The Yankees made the mistake of allowing him to retain eligibility to play football at Stanford University. Elway proved himself at Class A Oneonta by batting .318 and throwing out runners at home with a rifle for an arm. After the Baltimore Colts drafted him number one, he forced them to trade him to Denver and the rest is history. The quarterback retired from the NFL in 1999 as one of its best ever.

The Yankees were so high on **Brien Taylor** in 1992 that they gave him an obscene $1.55 million signing bonus, more than double the previous highest bonus. In comparison, Mickey Mantle got $1,400. Besides setting the stage for higher bonuses, the Yankees put a lot of pressure on the high school graduate. His minor league upbringing was going along fine for two seasons. Then he suffered a shoulder injury not from pitching but from a fight in December 1993. He had reconstructive surgery to his 100-mph fast-ball shoulder and sat out 1994. When he returned, he was wilder than a charging rhino. He couldn't find the plate with radar. The result were ERAs that could bring on nose bleeds they were so high: 18.73 in 1996, 14.33 in 1997 and 9.59 in 1998. It proves money can't buy success.

Another Yankees pitcher who has bombed at the box office is **Matt Drews**. Drews pitched well the first two years in the minors. After a slow start in 1995, the Yankees traded him with Ruben Sierra to Detroit for Cecil Fielder. His performance since has been two thumbs down. After a poor 1997 seasons — 8-13 record — he was dealt to the Diamondbacks. In 1998, he posted a 5-17 record and a 6.57 ERA with Class AAA Toledo.

Other first-round round bombs over the years included **Jim McDonald**, **Steve Taylor** and **Jeff Pries**, who all peaked at Triple-A. **Dennis Sherrill** only got a cup of coffee in the majors.

Since compensation began, the Yankees have lost their first-round pick several times as a penalty for signing free agents. In fact, New York didn't pick in the first round for two five-year periods, 1979–1983 and 1985–1989.

Ones Who Got Away

The Yankees picked two players who ended up with the rival Boston Red Sox. **Darrell Evans** was a second-round selection. And **Fred Lynn** was a third-round pick in 1970. Neither signed and waited until the Sox drafted them.

In 1978, **Howard Johnson** was picked in the 23rd round and he ended up playing for the cross-town Mets.

Les Lancaster was a 24th-round selection in 1981. He later signed as a free agent and played with the Cubs.

The New York team wanted to keep **Todd Stottlemyre** in the family with their fifth-round selection out of high school in 1983. However, he decided on college and was drafted in the first round by the Blue Jays in the 1985.

The Yankees have probably signed more National Football League prospects than any other team. Besides the previously mentioned Elway, they picked quarterback **Ken Stabler**. **Bo**

Jackson was their second-round pick in 1982, but he waited a few years to sign with Kansas City.

Where Are They Now?

Rex Hudler, a number-one pick by the Yankees in 1978, finally called it quits on his professional career in July 1998. After being released by the Philadelphia Phillies in mid–June, he signed a Triple-A contract with the Cleveland Indians on July 2. Two weeks later he announced his retirement. "I'm a successful failure because I learned how to deal with failure my whole career and still come away smiling and feeling positive," he told the Associated Press. Hudler signed out of high school and made it to the majors in his seventh professional season. He played for the Yankees, Orioles, Expos, Cardinals, Angels and Phillies, as well as a year in Japan with the Yakult Swallows. The second baseman's best year came in 1996 when he hit .311 with 16 homers for the Angels.

Steve Balboni became a famed slugger with the Royals, but he was drafted by the Yankees in the fourth round in 1978. After his playing career, he became a hitting coach in the Royals' farm system.

Another former player who has turned to baseball management is **Andy Bottin**, a 56th round selection in the 1967 draft. He played in the minors for five seasons and reached Triple-A, but his career was cut short by military service in Vietnam. When he returned he became a policeman in Seattle for 20 years. He retired from the force in 1995 and turned to coaching the Mariners' short-season Class A-Everett.

Jiff Livesey, a 13th round pick in 1988, has turned to coaching, too. The former catcher in the Yankees' minor league system for eight years who couldn't hit a lick — .217 with 16 homers and 102 RBI — is now the hitting coach for the Altoona Curve in the Pittsburgh farm system.

Jim Deshales, a 21st round pick in 1982, turned to broadcasting as an analyst with the Houston Astros after his playing career. He never pitched for the Yankees because he was traded while still in minors. He played for San Diego, Minnesota, San Francisco and Houston. His best season in the majors was 1989 when he compiled a 15-10 mark with Houston. He set a modern-day major league record in 1986 when he fanned the first eight batters he faced in a start against the Dodgers.

Ron Guidry, a third round choice in 1973, is a guest instructor with the Yankees during spring training.

A teammate of Guidry, **Jim Beattie** is now the general manager of the Montreal Expos. The former pitcher was a fourth round pick in 1975.

Back in 1984, the Yankees picked **Kevin Trudeau,** a pitcher at Chabot Junior College, in the sixth round and offered him a $10,000 bonus. Trudeau had signed a letter of intent to go onto a four-year college, so $10,000 wasn't enough. On the last day before the deal would expire, the Yankees sweetened the deal with another $5,000 and money for more college. That was enough to convince to give baseball a try. However, they didn't tell him about the fall instructional league, so his hopes of going to school in the fall were dashed. After a couple of years with the Yankees and not getting very far, he was glad to be traded to the Indians on the last day of spring training. He wasn't there long before being dealt to the Twins. Then it was off to the Angels. He was suddenly being bumped around the minors like a pinball game.

Finally, in 1989 he thought he had his best chance at being called up in September to the Big Leagues. His ERA was under four and he had a winning record. But he was snubbed. "There was some questions as to whether I had an out pitch," he explained. He couldn't understand that because he was getting hitters out in the minors. Heck, he had struck out Bo Jackson twice in one game!

After several years of pitching each summer and then going off to the winter leagues, he developed a dead arm in 1991. He then became a free agent and played ball in Italy to get back into shape. Instead, he became like a tourist and got out of shape. "I had a blast there," he said.

During the strike of 1994, he got a call from Major League teams that he didn't answer. His baseball career was over. Instead, he ended up in Indianapolis where his brother Jack was quarterbacking for the Indianapolis Colts. He now manages an over–30 team in the Men's Adult Baseball League. Now married, he also is a salesman with a medical supplies company in Indianapolis.

Mike Galante, a 62nd round pick in 1966, spent eight seasons in the minors and made it as far as Triple-A Evansville. A member of the Houston organization since 1980, Galante assumed the role of bench coach in 1998.

A 35th round draft pick of the New York Yankees in 1991, **Steve Livesey** played two years in the Yankees' chain before becoming a coach at San Bernardino, an independent team in the California League, in 1993. He spent 1994 and 1995 as a coach for the Yankees' Gulf Coast League team before joining the Devil Rays organization. He is now a coach at Hudson Valley. Steve is the son of Devil Rays' Director of Player Personnel Bill Livesey and the brother of Jeff Livesey, who caught in the Yankees' organization. Steve earned his bachelors' degree from Davidson College.

Undrafted Players

While the Yankees are best known for signing many free agents from foreign countries, the team has also found a few gems looked over by the draft. One was **Jim Leyritz**. He played for the University of Kentucky and impressed none of the scouts except for the Yankees. He was signed in 1985 and became a catcher for the team by 1990. The Yankees later traded him to the Angels. He eventually went to the Padres and played against the New York team in the 1998 World Series.

Another player the Yankees found undrafted was **Marty Janzen**, who had a 1.40 ERA at Gainesville (Fla.) High School. He was signed in 1990, and the Yankees later dealt him to the Blue Jays for David Cone. After two seasons there, the Diamondbacks selected him in the expansion draft.

All in the Family

In the first draft, the Yankees selected **Louis Howell,** son of Homer "Dixie" Howell who played eight seasons for the Pirates, Reds and Dodgers.

The Yankees took **Doug Torborg,** whose

father was then a coach for New York, in the 27th round. And **Mike Dotterer**, the grandson of Yankee scout Dutch, was picked in the 30th round in 1983, too.

The Yankees drafted **Chad Sutter**, son of famed reliever Bruce Sutter. Chad was picked in the 23rd round in 1999. He's a catcher though from Tulane University.

On the Roster

The Yankees only have a handful of picks on their 25-man roster. Besides previously mentioned Derek Jeter, Andy Pettitte, Jorge Posada and Shane Spencer, **Ricky Ledee** was bouncing between Triple-A and the Yankees. Ledee, a long-shot 16th round pick in 1990, finally got a call to the majors in 1998 after nine years in professional ball. He spent three years in rookie ball and another three at Class-A before moving up the ladder. He has power and knocked 21 homers at Triple-A Columbus in 1998.

Mike Jerzembeck, a fifth-round pick in 1993, got his first call to the majors in 1998 and was bombed in three outings and ended up 0-1 with a 12.79 record. In 1999 he landed on the disabled list. Also among the wounded in 1999 was **Darrell Einertson**, an 11th round pitcher drafted in 1995. The right-hander had a mere 1.03 ERA in 1998 at Double-A in 1998 before going down with an injury.

Future Stars

Ryan Bradley was a first-round sandwich pick in 1997 from Arizona State University. The right-handed pitcher zipped through the minors and got a call up to the Yankees in 1998 where he was 2-1 in five games. He was assigned to Triple-A for more seasoning in 1999.

Another draft pick who got brief call to the majors in 1998 was **Jay Tessmer**, a 19th round pick in 1995. The sidewinding stopper had 106 saves in the minors. He was an all-star relief pitcher two seasons and the Florida State League Most Valuable Player in 1996 when he had 35 saves and a 12-4 record in Class A. He too was assigned to Triple-A in 1999.

The Yankees plucked **Randy Choate** in the fifth round in 1997 after he was voted to the

all–ACC team. He helped Florida State to the College World Series with his 13 wins. The left-handed side-armer dominated rookie ball his first season with a 5-0 record. After having problems as a starter in Single-A, the Yankees turned him into a reliever. The result was an immediate turnaround. The transformation was similar to Dennis Eckersley, but from the left side. He skipped Double-A altogether and moved to Columbus in 1999. He should help the Yankees next century.

Coming up the ranks in Class A was **Nick Johnson**, a good hitter with home run power. He set the Class A Tampa record by reaching base safety in 40 consecutive games and he was hitting .334 by mid-season in 1999. That earned him a promotion to Double-A.

Johnson's feats were being outdone by what could the longest shot ever to make it to the majors if he gets that far. **Scott Seabol** was an 88th round pick in 1996 out of West Virginia University. The outfielder/third baseman set a 35-game hitting streak in 1999 with Class A Greensboro and was hitting .339 by mid-season.

Andy Brown didn't have a clue in what round he would drafted, so he made plans to go to the University of Michigan on a scholarship if he wasn't picked high. He figured a bonus of more than $100,000 would likely make up his mind on which way to go on the teeter-totter. "Nobody wants to tell you exactly how you're going to be picked," explained the high school graduate. When the Yankees picked him number one (24th overall) in 1998 and offered him more than a million bucks, the decision was easy. Brown never knew he was a number-one pick because he didn't realize how good he was compared to other high school seniors in the country.

The first baseman/right fielder had good numbers in high school — .470 average with seven homers — and was first team All-State. But it wasn't the numbers that attracted the New York team. It was his potential. "One of the toughest things to find in the draft is power potential," commented Tim Kelly, who scouted Brown for the Yankees. "It was the single biggest tool that stood out. He hits the ball a long way."

Kelly really became interested in Brown when he played for the Indiana Bulls, an independent team that travels all over the United States. Brown said of the Bulls: "That was the best thing I did in my baseball career."

His numbers his first year at Tampa in the Gulf Coast League were .229-3-24. A third of his hits were for extra bases. "My numbers weren't as good as I wanted it to be, but it's not all about numbers. A lot of adjustments need to be made," he evaluated his performance. Then he went to two mini-camps for more training. Brown plans on taking one step at a time and be patient on his route to the majors. "I like what I've seen so far," he commented.

A serious car accident nearly wrecked the baseball career of **Casey DeGroote** before it ever began. On Sept. 29, 1995 — a date etched in his memory — he was the passenger in a car that went awry and landed him in the hospital. He had multiple injuries, including a crushed pelvis

Casey DeGroote, a Yankees draft pick in the 11th round in 1998. (Photo courtesy of Casey De-Groote.)

and fractured hip. He spent eight days in Methodist Hospital in Indianapolis and the next four months in a wheelchair. He was literally held together by screws. But his recovery was nothing short of miraculous as the sophomore at West Vigo High School was determined to play baseball again. The son of an assistant baseball coach at Indiana State University began interesting scouts when he played with the Indiana Bulls between his junior and senior year. "It was unbelievable how many scouts where there," he recalled.

Then in his senior season he exploded for 12 homers and batted .583. That earned the third baseman first team All-State honors and an 11th round selection by the Yankees. DeGroote had a 50 percent scholarship with Auburn University, so the decision was difficult for him. "If I was to go to college, baseball wouldn't be my number one concern," he explained. The Yanks offered him enough money to make up his mind as well as scholarship money for the future, so he signed three weeks later.

His scout said DeGroote would have gone higher in the draft if it hadn't been for the accident. Kelly felt that some teams were turned off because of the injuries, but he liked Casey's attitude and work ethic. "He never missed a baseball game due to the accident," commented Kelly.

The young third baseman who hits from the left side had trouble hitting in the Gulf Coast League with Tampa and managed only a .173 average in rookie ball. He had difficulty adjusting to wooden bats and high-speed pitching. "I just want to do the best I can and improve every year."

Always on the lookout for left-handed pitching, the Yankees picked **Alex Graman** in the third round in 1999. The six-foot-four hurler from Indiana State University was 7-6 in his senior year with a 4.40 ERA, but he shows a lot more potential than the record indicates. With a fastball in the low 90s, a split-finger, curve and changeup, Graman has the necessary pitches to be on a fast track to the majors. "I just want to play," he said the day after he was drafted. He planned to sign rather than going on to his senior year if the money was right.

He wasn't drafted after he graduated from

Southridge High School in his hometown of Huntingburg, Indiana. "I didn't really throw that hard," he explained. "I was skinny in high school." He has since beefed up and added more speed to his fastball to make him more attractive to the pros.

Kansas City/Oakland Athletics

The Athletics are probably the best example of what the first year free-agent draft did for baseball. In the 30 years before the draft began, the Athletics' highest finish was fourth place in the American League, while the franchise was in Philadelphia then Kansas City. In the 30 years after the draft began, the A's have finished first 10 times and made it to the World Series six times, which matched the Yankees in that category. Without the help of the draft, the small-market franchise could have never competed with the Yankees.

When the draft began, the Athletics were still in Kansas City and not playing very well. They were at the bottom of the American League. The team had finished in last place three out of four years as the draft unfolded. The complexion of the team began to change in 1968 as the draft picks of 1965 started to surface in the majors. Then the team finished in second place in 1969, their highest finish since 1932. In 1971 the team started a run of five first-place finishes thanks to some great draft picks. The run finally came to an end and the team sunk back to the bottom. Then owner Charlie O. Finley fired all his scouts in a cost-cutting measure as he was getting ready to sell the team. He went with reports from Major League Baseball Scouting Bureau. The result was predictable. Bureau reports are not meant to provide all information. Teams can't rely 100 percent on the bureau to do their job for them.

Oakland recovered from that downturn and built another small dynasty in the late 1980s with draft picks again. After finishing first again in 1992, the Athletics haven't had a winning season, which shows how much free agency has had an affect on their ability to compete in recent times.

The Athletics rely heavily on the draft to bring new talent to the team, because they can't afford spend big bucks on free agents. Scouting Director Grady Fuson has changed the draft philosophy of the team in the last few years. He doesn't go after the run-and-throw guys like Branch Rickey used to like. He won't pick a run-and-throw player and try to turn him into a hitter. "I believe in instincts and skills, probably more than tools," explained Fuson. He wants to eliminate chance when he makes a decision about a draft pick. "We need to get more bang out of our bucks here."

Being a small-market team, the Athletics don't have as many scouts and crosscheckers as some other teams. "We don't have a large staff," said Fuson. In the United States, the A's have 15 area scouts and two national cross checkers. In Latin America, the A's are concentrating in the Dominican Republic and Venezuela. They are on the ground floor in the Pacific Rim areas.

With four first-round picks in 1997 as a result of compensation, the Athletics were heading toward being a contender again. In 1999, they were in the thick of the wild-card playoff race and surprising the baseball experts with young talent.

Best Picks Ever

Because of the recent impact **Mark Mc-Gwire** has made on sport, the Athletics consider him as their best draft pick ever. "Big Mac" was first selected by the Montreal Expos in the eighth round of the June 1981 free-agent draft after graduating from Damien High School in Claremont, Calif. He decided to attend USC where he hit a Pac-10 Conference record 32 homers in a single season. After his junior year, he was selected by the A's in the first round (10th pick) in 1984. Instead of going directly to professional ball that season, he played on the Olympic Team. He broke into the majors in August 1986 as a third baseman. In his first full season the next year he was named as the Rookie of the Year after hitting a record 49 homers as a rookie. He left Oakland as the Athletics' franchise leader with 363 home runs, 941 RBIs, 563 extra-base hits and a .551 slugging average. The Athletics let the popular hitter go when they decided it was time to rebuild and couldn't afford to pay him free agency money. He went to the Cardinals and hit his record-breaking 70 homers there in 1998. The fan favorite has been named to 10 All-Star teams. He will, without a doubt, be elected to the Hall of Fame, unlike the previous home run leader for a season, Roger Maris.

The A's lucked out in the 1966 draft when the Mets passed on **Reggie Jackson** as the first pick in the draft, supposedly because he was dating a white woman. The Mets took catcher prospect Steve Chilcott, who never made it to the majors. Big mistake. Jackson became "Mr. October" and entered the Hall of Fame on the first vote. A's owner Charles O. Finley offered Jackson $50,000. He wanted $100,000. They finally settled near the middle as Jackson got $75,000 cash, college money and a new maroon Pontiac. Reggie told Finley that he would win him a World Series some day. He did twice. He played 10 seasons for the team and took them to

the playoffs five years in a row in the early 1970s and the World Series. He was named Most Valuable Player in 1973 and was a 12-time All-Star. Jackson led the American League in homers four times in route to hitting 563 career roundtrippers. He earned his famed nickname by hitting 10 homers in the World Series for the A's and Yankees.

A teammate of Jackson was **Sal Bando**, a sixth-round pick in 1965. He received a $30,000 bonus. After three years in the minors, he made the team out of spring training in 1968. By the next season he was team captain and an All-Star. He also hit a career-high 31 homers. Bando helped lead the team to five straight trips to the postseason in the early 1970s. After several battles with management and other players, he played out his option with Oakland and signed with Milwaukee, where he finished out his career. Later, he became the Brewers general manager.

Back in 1967, teams weren't offering much money for a second-round pick. When they took **Vida Blue** as the first player in the second round, 27th overall, owner Finley was thinking more like ten grand, but Blue wanted more. His father

Sal Bando, a sixth-round pick in 1965. (Photo courtesy of the Oakland Athletics.)

Vida Blue, 1967 first pick in the second round. (Photograph courtesy of the Oakland Athletics.)

had died. That left him as the man of the house of five. He needed more. He bargained with the owner until he squeezed $25,000 out of the deal.

It turned out to be a heck of a deal for the A's who Blue would take to the playoffs and World Series for five of the eleven seasons he played there. He was a four-time All-Star during his 17 years in the majors. He also played for six seasons with the Giants. His career ended in 1986 with a 209-161 record and 3.27 ERA.

Had Blue not needed the money when the baseball draft came around, he may have ended up at a big college as a quarterback. "This young fellow is going to be the first big name Negro quarterback," Houston coach Bill Yeomans once said.

When the A's selected **Jose Canseco** in the 15th round in 1982, the Carol City High School in Miami graduate didn't even have a scholarship offer from a junior college, according to Fuson. His twin brother, Ozzie, was actually the better prospect according to one their high school coaches, Mike Dunn. Ozzie was the pitcher of the family; Jose played third. Jose wasn't physically ready for the big game in high school. "I was tall and lanky," he explained at Spring Training in 1999 with the Devil Rays. "I wasn't anywhere near as big as I am right now."

After the A's selected him in the 15th round in 1982, the Cuban born athlete grew in size and began hitting home runs in the minors.

"He hit some bombs in high school," Dunn recalled. "He was good, but he wasn't the best ever."

Jose Canseco with Mike Dunn and son. He was a 15th round pick in 1982 for the Athletics.

Jose became the best ever player in 1988 when he was named American League Most Valuable Player. That season he racked up some big numbers: .307-42-124. He also became a 40-40 man.

"He's deceiving because he's so big that you don't think he can steal bases. He's definitely a fast guy for his size," explained Dunn.

A decade later with Toronto, Jose hit a career high 46 homers. And he began the 1999 season on a tear with Tampa Bay. He went over 400 homers lifetime. "If he had been healthy his whole career, he'd be well over 500 home runs," Dunn explained.

Surprisingly, Jose has only been named to two All-Star teams during his career, but the game is more of a popularity contest as fans do the choosing. He deserves to have been on more with the numbers he has racked up. He wants to reach 500 before retiring, which would secure him a spot in the Hall of Fame.

Meanwhile, Ozzie never turned out as good as his brother. He made it to the majors twice, but wouldn't stick. He had some offers from the Mexican League in early 1999. Ozzie was about to make the Montreal roster a few years before and pulled muscles in his rib cage.

Rickey Henderson, a fourth-round pick in 1976, was back with Oakland for his fourth time in 1998. Considered by many as the greatest leadoff hitter in Major League history, Henderson was still ticking like a Timex in 1999 with the New York Mets. He already owned the Major League record for stolen bases with 1,297 at the end of the 1998 season and was adding more to that in 1999. He became the sixth player in major league history to score 2,000 runs in 1998. Henderson ranks fifth all-time in walks and sixth all-time in runs scored. His best season came in 1990 when he was named Most Valuable Player. That season with Oakland, he racked up 28 homers, 61 RBI and 65 steals, along with a .325 average. He has been named to the All-Star Team 10 times and hit .339 in 14 World Series games. With the numbers he has put up, he's another Hall of Fame contender.

Oakland decided **Mike Morgan**, the first-round pick in 1978, may be ready for the majors after signing him days after the draft. The 18-year-old high school pitching sensation —0.68

ERA in high school — started in three games and lost all three, which earned him a trip to the minors for more experience. Morgan was back the next season, but was ineffective on the mound until he matured more. His best season in the majors came in 1992 when he was 16-8 with the Cubs. The year before he was named to the All-Star Game. His career has stretched over 19 seasons and he was better than ever in 1999 with the Texas Rangers. He won't win any awards for pitching — 121-170 lifetime — but he's been as durable as a Mack Truck on the mound, seldom being injured during his career.

Long Shots

Gene Tenace was a 20th-round pick in 1965. He first got a call to the Athletics in 1969. Then he became the back-up catcher the next

Gene Tenace, Athletics draft pick in 1965 in the 20th round.

four years. When he was moved to first base in 1973, he exploded for 24 homers in 160 games. Then he caught everyone's attention when he hit four homers in the World Series to be the hero and help the A's to a victory. "I got hot at the right time," Tenace reflected. "Timing is everything." He played eight seasons with the team during the glory years. He also appeared in one All-Star Game. In all, he played 15 seasons in the majors and hit 201 homers.

The average for a high school draft pick to reach the majors, if at all, is about five years. **Patrick Bronswell** took twice that! The 25th-round draft pick in 1988 out of high school finally broke into the majors in 1998 at age 27.

The right-hander's professional career was progressing at the right speed until he hit a wall in 1993 with a 7.05 ERA and 3-8 record in Triple-A. That set him back, but he continually improved after that and was 8-5 with a 3.22 with New Orleans in 1997. He was granted free agency and signed a minor league contract with Milwaukee in 1997. When Chad Fox went on the disabled list, Milwaukee brought him to the majors. He ended the season with a 4-1 record and a 4.69 ERA for the Brewers.

Scott Brosius was a 20th-round pick by the A's out of Lindfield College in 1987. He spent two seasons at Single-A and two at Double-A before jumping to Triple-A and the majors in his fifth season. Then he was on a yo-yo trip between Oakland and Tacoma for two more seasons before he could call the majors home for good. He stayed with the A's until he was dealt to the Yankees in late 1997.

The year after Brosius was picked, the A's selected **Darren Lewis** in the 18th round from the University of California. By the end of his third season, he was playing at Oakland. However, there wasn't any room for him there, so he was dealt to Giants for third baseman Ernest Riles. The fine defensive outfielder went onto play five seasons with the Giants before going on the road to the Reds, White Sox, Dodgers and Red Sox.

Steve Connelly, a 24th-round pick in 1995, worked his way up the minors quickly by having an ERA under 4.00 in his relief appearances. After limiting hitters to a .212 average at Triple-A Edmonton, the A's called him up on June 27. The sinker/slider pitcher got a brief appearance with Oakland and will probably be back for more in the future.

Disappointments

As good as Oakland has done in the draft, they had their fair share of players who were picked in the first round on the June draft and didn't work out.

The first disappointing first-round pick for the A's was **Brian Bickerton** in 1968. The left-handed pitcher only got as far as Triple-A.

The Athletics had trouble signing several of their first-round picks. They included **Pete**

Broberg in 1969, **Jerry Honson** in 1974, **Mike Sullivan** in 1976 and **Juan Bustabad** in 1979.

Sugar Bear Daniels had an unusual nickname. The right-handed first-round pitcher never got past Class A after being drafted in 1972. **Craig Harris**, a first rounder in 1972, didn't do much better when he couldn't get any farther than Double-A. **Mike King**, a first-round choice in 1980, did them one step further in getting to Triple-A. That's as far as **Stan Hilton** got. He was the fifth overall pick in the first round in 1983.

A huge disappointment for the Athletics was **Todd Van Poppel** in 1990, particularly because he was the first high school player to get a major league contract. The A's weren't setting any precedent though. Ben McDonald and John Olerud had been signed to major league contracts after they were drafted, too. But they were college kids. Van Poppel was represented by Scott Boras, who wanted a major league contract for the high school pitcher with a great fastball and curveball. Because of Boras' demands,

Todd Van Poppel, a 1990 draft pick by the Athletics. (Photograph courtesy of the Oakland Athletics.)

Van Poppel wasn't drafted until the 14th pick. Since the A's had spent so much on the pitcher, they undoubtedly wanted him up in the majors sooner than other high school prospects. The right-hander was only average in the minors, yet the A's brought him up to the majors to stay in 1994. After an 18-29 record and an ERA around 6.00, the A's waived him in 1996, and he was picked up by the Tigers. After that he was passed around baseball like a hand-me-down coat. He was last seen sitting by his locker at the Pirates' spring training camp as a nonroster invitee in 1999.

He was replaced in the line-up by the A's 18-year-old second-round pick, **Tim Conroy**. Conroy proved he wasn't ready for the majors either. After two starts, he too was shipped to the minors where he suffered an arm injury. Both pitchers found their way back to the majors. Conroy never achieved much success. The left-hander pitched in seven major league seasons and ended with an 18-32 career record.

Don Peters was a first-round choice of the Athletics in 1990 from the College of St. Francis. The right-handed pitcher didn't make it with Oakland due to injuries. The A's cut him loose in 1994 and he signed with the Giants. He retired for a year and a half and then returned to baseball in 1997 with the Arizona Diamondbacks.

The most recent disappointment to the Athletics was **Ariel Prieto**, a first-round draft pick in 1995. The Cuban defector had set himself up for the draft when he came to the United States with a working visa and pitched for an independent team. The A's went with Prieto because they felt the 28-year-old could come straight to the majors and make an impact on the pitching staff and make the team more competitive. He certainly did. He jumped out to a hot start that included a two-hitter. Then he hit a wall. "He got rattled," explained Fuson. "He lost command. He mentally got happy." He was somewhat overcome by the money and the new lifestyle. Prieto was 2-6 in 1995, 6-7 the next season and 6-8 his third year in the majors. The promising pitcher suffered elbow problems and had to have the Tommy John surgery. He was expected to be out of commission until the next century.

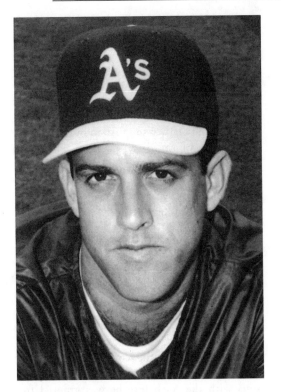

Ariel Prieto, first-round draft pick in 1995. (Photograph courtesy of the Oakland Athletics.)

Best Draft

The last-place finish in 1964 helped the A's get the first first-year free-agent draft pick in history. The team started off draft with a bang. The Kansas City team chose Rick Monday. Finley personally signed him for $104,000. Monday was a sophomore for Arizona State when he was selected. He proved he was worth a number-one pick as he went on to a 19-year career in the majors. He is best remembered for snatching an American flag away from a protester who was trying to burn it in 1976 in Dodger Stadium. Bando and Tenace came out of that first draft, too.

Worst Draft Years

Years? The Athletics had nearly a decade of poor drafts. The 1970s. The dynasty built in the early 1970s with three World Series championships was collapsing.

The A's just about struck out in 1974 when only one player from that year made it to the major leagues. That was **Rick Lysander**, a right-handed pitcher in the 19th round. He pitched in 137 games in the majors. Their first three picks in the June 1974 regular draft failed to sign at all.

After Finley fired all his scouts, the 1979 and 1980 drafts went even worse. The only player who signed in 1979 to make it to the majors was **Bert Bradley**, who pitched just six games there. The only player who made it to the majors from the 1980 draft was **Rich Bordi**, a third-round pitcher from Fresno State University.

Where Are They Now?

Creighton Gubanich was drafted in 1990 and played eight full seasons in the minors before he finally got his calling with the Boston Red Sox early in 1999. Then a split nail put him on the disabled list and he found himself back in Triple-A, where he had played for three years. The high school signee missed his first year in the pros because he signed late. "I had a full scholarship to Texas A&M," he said. But a $60,000 bonus and $20,000 for school convinced him to sign. "College is always going to be there." Gubanich (which he said rhymes with bubonic) spent four years in Class A ball. The A's traded him in 1997 to the Brewers. The free agent signed with the Red Sox in 1998. He hit .291 with 19 homers in 1998, which raised a few eyebrows in Boston.

Sal Bando was part of the A's great teams of the 1970s. Then he signed with the Brewers in 1976 as a free agent. He stayed with the Brewers after his playing days and became the general manager. Now he is the team's senior vice president of baseball operations.

Gene Tenace went into managing and coaching after playing and became the hitting coach for the Pawtucket Red Sox in 1999.

Another player turned manager is **Phil Garner**, a first-round pick in the January secondary phase in 1971. He played four seasons with the A's before going on to a 16-year career in the majors. He turned to managing and has been the Brewers manager since 1991.

Rick Tronerud never made it to the majors as a pitcher, but the 14th round pick in 1972 became a pitching coach with the Athletics and now with the Cubs.

Phil Stephenson, a third-round pick in 1982, played for six major league teams during his career. Then he became a hitting coach in the Royals' farm system.

Keith Atherton was a second-round pick in 1978 and passed up a scholarship with Arizona State University for a bonus of $30,000. "I have no regrets [about signing]," he said from his home in Cobbs Creek, Virginia. The 30th pick in the draft these days is looking at close to a million dollars. The right-handed reliever took six years to get to the majors. He played for the Athletics for four seasons before they did him a favor and traded him to the Twins. Favor, because he was able to play in the World Series in 1987 with Minnesota and earned a ring. "There's a lot of guys who played more than me and never earned a ring," he proudly said. His seven years in the majors ended with the Indians, which was a bad team at the time. "They turned that organization around," he commented. Atherton will be able to draw retirement soon from baseball at age 45. Meanwhile, he's a commercial fisherman in the Chesapeake Bay during the summers.

Ones Who Got Away

The A's wasted a pick for publicity purposes when they chose **Cazzie Russell** out of the University of Michigan with their 522nd pick. The basketball star hadn't played any baseball in college and was destined for the NBA.

The A's chose **Pete Broberg** in the June 1968 draft, but he wouldn't sign because he didn't want to play in the minors. He wanted something in his contract to that effect, but the A's balked at the request. Broberg ended up signing in 1971 with the Senators, who granted him his request.

All in the Family

D.T. Cromer was drafted the same year as his younger brother. He was picked in the 11th round in 1992, while his brother was chosen in the supplemental round by the Blue Jays. Cromer was granted six-year free agency in 1998 and signed with the Reds. The brothers had a reunion in 1999 when the Indianapolis Indians faced the Louisville River Bats.

In 1999, the Athletics drafted **Ryan Ludwick**, brother of Eric Ludwick with the Florida Marlins. Ryan is an outfielder unlike his brother, who is pitcher and was drafted by the Mets in 1993; however, both brothers did have something in common — they were both picked in the second round.

The only father-son first-round tandem in the history of the draft occurred when **Ben Grieve** was picked in 1994. His father, Tom Grieve was Washington's first-round choice in 1966. Tom has worked his way up to Texas Rangers' general manager.

Undrafted Player

The A's scouting director, Dick Bogard, happened on **Mike Bordick** by accident. He was evaluating another player when he spotted Bordick at a Cape Cod League game. The University of Maine player made some good plays that night and impressed the scout enough to get the A's to sign him. The shortstop played seven seasons with the A's before he was granted free agency. Then Bordick signed a three-year $9 million contract with the Orioles.

On the Roster

Jason Giambi, drafted in the second round in 1992, is the veteran draft pick on the team. He showed promise right away in the minors and moved up to the A's by 1995. The outfielder from Long Beach State University has looked at the minors in the rearview mirror ever since. The first full season with the Athletics he pounded out 20 home runs and 40 doubles. He avoided the sophomore jinx in 1997 by nearly repeating those exact numbers. And he was even better in 1998 with 27 dingers and 110 RBI.

A year later in 1993, the A's selected **Scott Speizo** in the sixth round. He took about the same time as Giambi to get to the majors. In 1997 he played his first full season with the Athletics. The rookie hit 14 home runs and batted .243. The second baseman improved on his average in his second year.

The run at good draft picks continued in 1994 when they selected **Ben Grieve**. Ben showed the team that baseball was indeed in his veins.

By 1997 he was playing the outfield with Oakland. In his debut on Sept. 3, he tied a club record with three doubles! He became a permanent fixture with the team after that. In 1998, the rookie right fielder hit 18 homers with 89 RBI.

Then **Ryan Christenson**, drafted in the 10th round in 1995, made it a grand slam of excellent picks when he became the regular centerfielder for the A's in 1998. The outfielder out of Pepperdine University, drove through the A's system in 1997 like it was an expressway. He began at Class A Visalia. Then he went to Class AA Huntsville where he hit .367 and earned a promotion to Triple-A Edmonton. He nearly made the Opening Day roster in 1998. Then he made his debut with the team on April 20.

Another 1995 draft pick, **Mark Bellhorn**, has been called up several times but hasn't stuck. The second round selection from Auburn University spent less than three years in the minors before getting his first opportunity. The third baseman has some power and hit 10 homers at Triple-A in 1998.

Three strikes you're out in baseball. Not so in the draft. For some three times is a charm. Such was the case with **A.J. Hinch**. The Chicago White Sox drafted him in the second round after high school, but he went on to Stanford. After his junior year, Minnesota picked him in the third round and offered him $225,000. Hinch decided the Olympics was more important and snubbed the Twins. He played for Team USA in 1996 and went back to Stanford for his senior year to finish his degree in psychology. The three-time All-American was again taken in the third round in 1996, but this time it was Oakland who made the selection. He was signed soon after the Olympics by A's scout Will Schock. He was offered $75,000, but apparently Oakland didn't properly tender him a contract. Hinch appealed to Major League Baseball to become a free agent. The A's had a change of heart and upped the offer to $125,000, so Hinch signed. The catcher jumped from Class A to Class AAA in 1997 before making it to the A's after spring training in 1998. So far, his major league career has been a charm. The rookie catcher made his major league debut with the A's in 1998 after just one season in the minors.

Eric Chavez was the A's first-round pick in 1996 out of high school and quickly proved himself to get a call up to the majors by September 1998 at age 20. The third baseman throws right, but bats left for both power and average. *Baseball America* named him as the Minor League Player of the Year. He was expected to contend for American League Rookie of the Year honors.

The Athletics pitching staff at the beginning of the 1999 season was comprised of mostly hurlers who came from other teams. They had only a couple of their own draft pick pitchers on the roster.

One of those pitchers was **Tim Kubinski,** a seventh-round pick in 1993. The left-handed pitcher began as a starter, but was slowly converted into a reliever. The Athletics first called him up in 1997, but sent him back to Triple-A for all of 1998. He was called up again in 1999.

Another Oakland original on the roster was **Tim Hudson**, a sixth round pick in 1997. The pitcher from Auburn University made the jump to the majors in 1999 after being at Double-A in 1997.

Future Stars?

Dan Ardoin, a 5th-round selection in 1995, moved up to Triple-A in 1998. The catcher spent 1998 at Double-A Huntsville and hit a career high 16 homers, including three grand slams. He only had a total of 15 homers in his first three seasons in the minors, so he has finally found the range. Teams always like catchers who can hit homers.

The A's had four first-round picks in 1997 and one of the best was **Nathan Haynes**, a speedy centerfielder who shows a lot of promise. Taken out of high school, he moved up to long-season Class A by the end of 1998.

The A's selected right-handed pitcher **Chris Enochs** out of West Virginia with their first pick in the 1997 Free Agent draft. Enochs, 21, was the Big East Pitcher of the Year in 1997. The 6-2, 220 pound Enochs was named as a first team All-American by Collegiate Baseball and second team All-American by *The Sporting News*, *Baseball America* and the National Collegiate Baseball Writers Association. The 11th overall pick in the draft, Enochs was 12-1 with a 3.03 ERA with the Mountaineers.

Another of the 1997 first rounders was left-handed pitcher **Eric DuBose**. He was a two-time All-SEC selection and holds the Mississippi State record with 428 career strikeouts. He posted a 9-4 record and a 4.32 ERA in 1997. After a 6-1 mark in Class A, he moved up to Double-A in 1998 where his ERA was just 2.70. With a fastball in the low 90s and a good breaking pitch, he's headed to the majors on the fast track.

Chad Harville, a second-round pick in 1997, may be short in stature at five-foot-nine, but he throws a fastball in the mid–90s. In two seasons, the right-hander had moved up to Double-A where he recorded eight saves. Then he made two more saves in the Arizona Fall League. The former University of Memphis hurler was promoted to Triple-A in 1999.

The long shot in the system who was progressing well was **Brett Laxton**, a 24th round pick in 1996 out of LSU. The right-handed hurler put together a nine-game winning streak in Double-A that earned him Southern League Pitcher of the Week honors at one point in 1998. It also earned him a promotion to Triple-A, where he pitched in 1999 as well.

The Athletics hope they picked up a couple of good players in the 1998 draft, but it's still too early to tell.

First rounder **Mark Mulder** signed better late than never. He received the highest signing bonus in A's history—$2.9 million. The second choice in 1998 draft did get to pitch in the Arizona Fall League in 1998 and impressed the Athletics enough to start his pro career at Triple-A in 1999. He has a great fastball and changeup.

Second-round pick **Gerald Laird**, a catcher out of high school, was assigned to short-season Class A Southern Oregon for the 1999 season.

Oakland's first pick in 1999 was **Barry Zito**, a left-handed pitcher out of USC. He was expected to move quickly toward the majors.

Seattle Mariners

The expansion club began drafting players in 1977. Back then the team had just five full-time scouts because it couldn't afford to hire more, so it had to rely heavily on the Major League Scouting Bureau. The results weren't very good at first. Seattle was a bottom dweller for more than a decade. The franchise didn't enjoy its first winning season until 1991! Lou Piniella was hired in 1993 and the Mariners began winning with more consistency. Good draft picks in the late 1980s and early 1990s also began to pay dividends. The team won its first division title in 1995 with the help of several of its own excellent picks, particularly Ken Griffey, Jr., and Alex Rodriguez. However, they have traded a few draft picks away before they matured into excellent players, like pitchers Mike Hampton, Shawn Estes and Ron Vallone, and position players Bret Boone, Jason Varitek and Jose Cruz, Jr.

The Mariners strategy is to take the "best available" player when it's their turn to choose. They prefer players with high ceilings, good tools and lots of talent. Scouting director Frank Mattox said there was a fine line between tools

Mike Hampton, 1990 sixth round Seattle Mariners draft pick.

and talents. He admits that some projections don't reach their expectations. He likes to get players in his own backyard if he finds a good one. "There's something to be said for getting local talent in your organization," he said. The team has had some luck finding some good talent locally.

The Mariners have had great luck at picking the right player in the first round, whether they kept them or traded them for more immediate needs. They also have had good success in signing high draft picks in the 1990s. They signed all of their number-one picks since 1991: Shawn Estes in 1991, Ron Villone in 1992, Alex Rodriguez in 1993 and Jason Varitek in 1994, Jose Cruz, Jr., in 1995, Gil Meche in 1996, Ryan Anderson in 1997 and Matt Thornton in 1998. They had some trouble signing Rodriguez because he didn't want to come to Seattle, but he finally signed just before the deadline. Maddox credits the success in the draft to his boss, Roger Jongewaard, the vice president of scouting and player development.

The scouts like to look beyond the athlete's abilities or tools. They look at the player's competitive spirit as well as other factors. "The first thing for us is if we feel the kid wants to play," said Jongewaard. "If he feels he can be in the big leagues in three or four years and is ready to come out instead of going to school. If he feels he's ready to compete physically and mentally, we're interested."

Seattle's scouting department is smaller than most clubs. "We have financial restrictions," explained Maddox. The team has 10 area scouts in the United States and 44 associate scouts. The club has three scouts in Canada. Seattle also has three scouts in the Dominican Republic along with an academy. In Venezuela, it has two scouts and an academy. And let's not forget Panama where they have one scout. They are also looking hard in Korea where they have a scout and an interpreter. Their strategy is to sign younger players before other teams take notice and a bidding war ensues. However, the younger the player the more the risk involved.

Maddox is in favor of an international draft, which would stop the bidding war that is sometimes created overseas for players. The Mariners can't afford to throw millions at foreign prospects like the Yankees did with the $13 million it tossed at Hideki Irabu. The Mariners have signed a few international players who have made it to the majors. Japanese-born Mac Suzuki was signed in 1993 and debuted in the majors in 1996.

Being so close to Canada, the Mariners get to look closely at Canadian players. In the 1999 draft, Seattle picked four Canadians. The team was also big on shortstops although they already have an excellent shortstop in the majors; three shortstops were selected in the first 10 rounds and half a dozen in all. Seattle received compensation for the loss of Mike Timlin to free agency, so they appropriately chose a pitcher. Seattle also chose 26 more pitchers in the draft. "We feel very comfortable with our draft this year," said Mattox about the 1999 draft. "We got a good assortment of position players, as well as pitchers. We feel a bunch of these players have high top ends and we look forward to getting them all in uniforms."

Best Picks

Without a doubt, the best draft pick so far by the Mariners is **Ken Griffey, Jr.**, who was scouted by Tom Mooney. The first player taken in the 1988 draft set some firsts right away as he was the highest draft pick to be the son of a major leaguer and he was the first draft pick to play with his father at the same time. The father-son duo also became the first ever to hit back-

Ken Griffey, Jr., Seattle's best draft pick so far, was chosen in 1988. (Photograph courtesy of the Seattle Mariners.)

to-back homers, which was a very special moment for the family. The younger Griffey became an All-Star in his second year in the majors at age 20 and has been named to the July team ever since. In his first 10 seasons in the majors, he led the American League in home runs three times and has collected 350 homers, which puts him on a pace to possibly break Hank Aaron's career home run record. The Mariners have built their franchise around the talented outfielder and Griffey has become synonymous with Seattle. When he was selected as the Most Valuable Player in 1997, he was only the second first-round draft pick to receive the honor. The other was Jeff Burroughs. Griffey batted .304 with 56 homers and 147 RBI that season. He has been on seven All-Star teams and won nine Gold Gloves in his 10 seasons in the majors. By the end of 1998 he had already accumulated 350 homers and may break 400 before the end of the century. The Mariners dealt Griffey to Cincinnati for prospects for the next century.

Dave Henderson, a first-round pick in 1977, is back with the Mariners again. This time with the broadcasting team. Henderson spent six seasons with Seattle before being traded to Boston where he played for two years. After a stop in San Francisco, he joined the Athletics and was a member of the A's 1989 World Series Championship team. He was named to the All-Star Team in 1991. Henderson clobbered 197 homers during his 14-year career in the majors and batted .324 in 20 World Series games.

Harold Reynolds, a first rounder in the secondary phase in 1980, played a decade with the Mariners and was the starting second baseman for eight seasons. The speedy Reynolds led the American League in stolen bases in 1987 with 60. Then the next season he led the league in triples with 11. The excellent fielder picked up three Gold Gloves with Seattle. He was also named to two All-Star teams during his 12-year career which ended with the California Angels.

Mark Langston was the second-round pick of the Mariners in 1981 and he has become one of the premier pitchers in the American League. By 1984 he was in the majors and making a name for himself by mowing down batters like a weedeater. In his rookie season he was the league strikeout leader and was second in the voting for

Dave Henderson, a first-round pick in 1977 for the Mariners. (Photograph courtesy of the Seattle Mariners.)

Mark Langston was the second-round pick of the Mariners in 1981. (Photograph courtesy of the Seattle Mariners.)

Rookie of the Year honors. A sore elbow soured his sophomore season, but he charged back in 1986 to take the league in K's again. The left-hander jumped out to a 10-6 start in 1987 to earn a trip to the Midsummer Classic where he pitched two innings. He ended the season with 19 victories, the strikeout lead and the first of seven Gold Gloves. The Mariners decided to trade him to Montreal for another good left-handed hurler, Randy Johnson. Langston was the co–Most Valuable Player with Tim Salmon in 1993 with the California Angels after going 16-11 and appearing in his fourth All-Star contest. He went to San Diego in 1998 and didn't help them much in winning the pennant with his 4-6 record in 22 starts.

The Mariners had the first pick in the 1993 draft and chose **Alex Rodriguez**. "Darren Driefort had been incredible that year and it was basically a toss up between us two," said Rodriguez. The Mariners wasted little time getting the shortstop to the majors as they called him up his first year as a professional in 1994. He became a regular in 1996 and slammed 36 homers his first full season in the majors. That performance led him to being named to the All-Star Team the next season. "A-Rod" was named to his second All-Star Game in 1998 en route to a record breaking season as he set the American League record for home runs for a shortstop with 42 dingers. He also became just the third player in major league history with more than 40 HR and 40 SB in one season.

Long Shots

Charles Gipson became the longest shot in Mariners history when the 63rd pick from the 1992 draft was brought up to the team during the 1998 season. He appeared in 44 games in the outfield. The outfielder was at Cypress Junior College when he was drafted.

Todd Haney was a 38th-round pick in 1987 out of the University of Texas, but the Mariners traded him to Detroit in 1991. A year later he made it to the majors with Montreal. After he was granted free agency, the Cubs signed him and tried him at third, but his hitting was erratic. He was granted free agency and signed again with the Mariners, who soon traded

him to the Astros. Then he signed with the Mets.

The Mariners picked **Matt Mantei** in the 25th round in 1991 out of high school and lost him to the Marlins in the Rule V draft in 1994. The Marlins brought the pitcher up the following season. He has spent parts of three seasons with the Marlins as a reliever.

Best Draft

The Mariners picked three good players in the 1981 draft: **Mark Langston**, **Mike Moore** and **Phil Bradley**. Langston had the most success of the three during his six seasons as a starting pitcher with the Mariners. Moore, the first-round choice that year, was a starter, too. He pitched seven seasons for Seattle, but his record wasn't as efficient as Langston. Bradley was an outfielder for the Mariners for five seasons. Bradley's best season came in 1985 when he averaged .300 and slammed 26 homers.

Worst Draft

The only player of consequence that the Mariners picked in 1984 was first-round choice **Bill Swift**, a pitcher out of the University of Maine. He pitched six seasons with the Mariners and had a losing record, but he was a better reliever than starter. His best season was his last in Seattle when he recorded 17 saves with a 1.99 ERA. The following year he was traded to San Francisco where he had the lowest ERA in the National League at 2.08 in 30 starts in 1992. The Mariners signed the free agent for the 1998 season.

Where Are They Now?

James Clifford, a 19th-round pick in 1988 who didn't sign, is now the strength and conditioning coordinator for the Mariners' farm system. Clifford attended the University of Washington rather than signing with Seattle. He didn't play baseball in college until his senior year. Then he signed with the Mariners and spent six seasons in the minors before becoming the strength coordinator.

Another player who decided to turn to

management instead of playing was **Dave Myers**, a 13th-round selection in 1981. He spent eight years in Seattle's farm system, but never made it to the majors. He became a manager instead and has moved steadily up the system to where he is now the skipper with Class AAA Tacoma.

Harold Reynolds turned to broadcasting after baseball and went to work for ESPN. He was a commentator at the 1999 Little League World Series.

Ones Who Got Away

The Mariners selected **Tom Henke** in the 20th round in 1979 out of junior college. He opted for another year of junior college and signed with the Rangers after they drafted him in the fourth round the next year.

Charlie O'Brien was a 21st-round pick by Seattle in 1981 out of Wichita State University. The catcher decided to complete his senior year and sign a year later when the Athletics picked him in the fifth round.

The Mariners picked **Lance Johnson** in the 31st round in 1982 when he was at Triton Junior College. The centerfielder decided to attend the University of South Alabama and sign later with the Cardinals, who picked him in the sixth round.

All in the Family

When **Bret Boone** was drafted in 1990, he was carrying on a long family tradition. His father, Bob, caught a 19-year career in the majors and his grandfather, Ray, had spent 13 years in the big leagues. Then Bret was called up to the Seattle Mariners in 1992, making the Boones a third-generation family in the majors. To add more to the tradition, his brother, Aaron, was drafted in 1994 by Cincinnati and was called up to the Reds in 1997.

Pat Barnes' brother, Larry, played in the minors with the Milwaukee Brewers farm system. He hopes to do better and get to the majors someday. He wasn't picked until the 16th round in 1998 out of high school. "Actually, I anticipated a little higher," he commented. "I didn't have any idea at all that Seattle was going

to pick me. I was shocked." The left-handed hurler hopes to make the short-season A team in 1999. He has a fastball clocked at 91 mph and a good curveball. "I'm still trying to master a changeup."

Sometimes teams will draft the sons of players or managers currently on their rose. **Orlando Martinez**, son of Seattle instructor/scout Marty Martinez, was picked in the 30th round in 1983. Seattle took **Matt Woodward**, whose father is Seattle general manager Woody Woodward, in the 24th round.

On the Roster

Going into the 1999 season, the Mariners had seven of their own draft picks on their 40-man roster and at one time during the off-season they had 11, which says a lot about how much they value the draft.

Gil Meche, a first-round pick in 1996, pitched so well to start the 1999 season, that the Mariners promoted him to the starting staff to become the only Seattle draft pick on the starting staff. After a 3.05 ERA at Double-A New Haven and a 2.08 mark at Triple-A Tacoma, Meche got his chance at the bigs. He was a member of the U.S. Junior Olympic team in 1995 and scouted by Chris Smith. Meche led the entire Mariners' farm system with 168 strikeouts in 1998, which is why the Mariners were so high on him.

Rafael Carmona was a 13th-round choice in 1993. The Puerto Rican was signed by scout Jerry Marik. He began his professional career as a reliever and was an all-star relief pitcher in 1994 when he had 21 saves and compiled an 8-2 record. That propelled him into the majors the next season. He bounced between Triple-A Tacoma and Seattle for two more seasons. Then his career became iffy after he broke his pitching arm in an off-season car accident in 1997. He rehabbed in 1998 and was back in the bullpen with the Mariners in 1999 before being put on the disabled list.

Also picked in 1993 was **Ken Cloude**, a sixth-round choice. He had a full scholarship to the University of Richmond but elected to sign with scout Joe Nigro. Cloude was an all-star pitcher in the minors and was first called up to

Bob Stoddard, a Mariners draft pick. (Photograph courtesy of the Seattle Mariners.)

the Mariners in 1997. He was put in the starting rotation in 1998 and compiled an 8-10 record. In his last win of the season, he struck out 10 White Sox hitters.

Scout Fernando Arguelles signed 36th-round pick **Raul Ibanez** in 1992 and he has not disappointed the scout by making it to the majors in 1996. Ibanez was an all-star catcher in the minors, but he was converted back to an outfielder before his debut in the majors in 1996. He hit for power and average in the minors, but he hasn't showed he can hit major league pitching after three brief appearances with the Mariners. He was back with the Mariners in 1999.

Shane Monahan was a second-round choice in the 1995 draft and signed by scout Don Poplin out of Clemson University where he was a two-time NCAA All-American. He batted .302 in 1997 in Double-A and was named to the Southern League All-Star Team to give his career some adrenaline. The Mariners called him up in mid–1998 and he responded with a .242 average with four homers. "He may stick with the club in 1999," said Mattox.

Brett Hinchliffe, a 16th-round choice out of high school in 1992 scouted by Ken Madeja, made the Mariners out of spring training in 1999. The lanky pitcher at six-foot-five showed he wasn't going to take any guff from anyone when he got into a brawl as a result of hitting someone in a game early in the season. The right-handed starter had been slow to progress through the ranks and didn't make Triple-A until 1998.

Another long shot on the roster is **Brian Fuentes**, a 25th round pick in 1995. The left-handed hurler, who was scouted by Rodney Davis, has been a striking out batters consistently in the minors with a tricky delivery and a variety of speeds.

An even longer shot on the Mariners roster was 63rd rounder **Charles Gipson**. Scout Ken Compton signed him in 1991 out of Cypress College. The versatile fielder played both infield and outfield positions in the minors and finally got a chance to prove himself in the majors after batting .314 in Triple-A in 1997. He must have felt like a yo-yo in 1998 as the Mariners called him up four different times.

Future Stars?

The Mariners have high hopes on **Ryan Anderson**, a 6-foot-10 left-hander reminiscent of Randy Johnson, who the Mariners lost to free agency. He was selected in the first round (19th overall) in 1997 out of high school and scouted by Ken Majeda. He knew he was going to be picked in the first round and let his dad handle the scouts. He also had the advice of the Hendricks Brothers, who he signed with later. He was closemouthed about his draft experience. "There are things no one knows and nobody needs to know," he explained. He pitched against major leaguers for the first time in spring training in 1999 and gave up just one hit in three innings while fanning three. Many fans confused him with the Big Unit. He has some big shoes to fill.

Joel Pineiro is in the same boat with Meche as far as a projection into the majors. The Dominican-born was signed by scout Fernando Arguelles after he was drafted in the 12th round in 1997 from high school. The right-hander also gets batters to strike out a lot. He began to move up the farm system in 1998.

Pitcher **Ryan Franklin** went from long shot to a shot at the majors early in 1999. The Mariners called him up in May 1999 to help the bullpen. The 23rd-round pick in 1993 out of junior college was primarily a starter in the minors and had posted a 44-46 record in six seasons. Options were running out on the right-hander, so Seattle called him up for a try. His best pitching so far occurred in 1997 when he

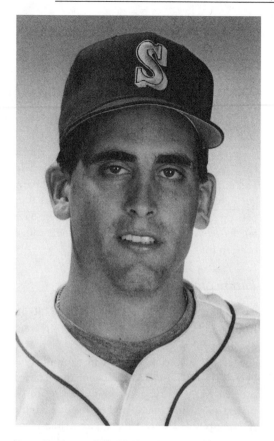

Dave Burba, Seattle draft pick. (Photograph courtesy of the Seattle Mariners.)

threw 14 innings without allowing a hit over three games.

Pitcher **Jordan Zimmerman** also went from long shot to a shot at the majors on the same day as Franklin. The left-hander was a 32nd-round pick in 1994 out of high school, but he didn't start pitching until the 1997 season due to a back injury. The Mariners converted him from starter to reliever at Double-A in 1999 and he responded with a 1.61 ERA before he was called up. Then he was put on the disabled list.

Jermaine Clark is an upcoming second

baseman. The fifth-round pick who was scouted by Larry Harper out of the University of San Francisco hit well over .300 his first two seasons in the minors and was named to the Midwest All-Star squad in 1998. He set the career steals record in college and swiped 40 bases in 1998.

Another Clark is on the horizon as well, but he's not related to Jermaine. **James Clark**, a 19th-round pick in 1997 and signed by scout John McMichen, thought he was going to be picked earlier. He was a draft-and-follow, which means he was picked after graduating from high school and went on to community college instead of baseball right away. In his first season at rookie ball in 1998, he batted .222. "I'm going to short season [Class A]," he said during spring training in 1999. "That's what I tell myself."

"The anticipation of the draft by a player is overwhelming," said **Brian Nelson**, a 39th round selection in 1995. The Edison Community College grad wasn't sure about what he wanted and waited until just before the draft the next year before signing with the Mariners. After two seasons at Class A Everett, he voluntarily retired from baseball. But he was back at spring training in 1999 trying to return to baseball. He has a long, hard road ahead of him.

An even longer shot who has shown progress in the minors is **Jason Regan**, a 51st-round pick in 1996. Scout Chris Smith must have seen power hitting in Regan, because the junior college player has belted 53 homers already in three seasons in the minors. The third baseman also batted .298 in 1998 in Class A and looked to move up to Double-A.

The Mariners selected **Ryan Christianson** in the first round in 1999. The catcher out of high school was hitting .521 with nine doubles, one triple, seven homers and 39 RBI when selected. He was named the Gatorade Circle of Champions High School Baseball Player of the Year for California.

Tampa Bay Devil Rays

The Tampa Bay Devil Rays began drafting players in 1996, two years before they began playing. The following year, the team drafted more players in the expansion draft. By the time the Devil Rays began playing in 1998, only the expansion draft players and free agents were seeing any action. "It usually takes four to five years before the draft has any kind of an impact on an organization," explained general manager Chuck LaMar. "We want to speed the process up but it takes time to sign and develop quality players. It's going to be a few years before the draft is felt here with the Devil Rays."

LaMar feels that Tampa's player development personnel have had an advantage because they had two years to ripen players before the team had to play. "There's one common denominator between any championship organization and that is strong scouting and player development," he said.

One might think that a draft pick with an expansion team would have a better opportunity to make it to the majors, but not necessarily so. The expansion draft and free agency gives an expansion team the opportunity to fill its roster and Triple-A team with veterans or draft picks from other teams, so that it doesn't have to worry about bringing up a regular draft pick before he is really ready physically and mentally to handle the majors.

While their basic strategy is to take the best player available when it's their turn in the draft, the player must also fit the profile the team has established. If he doesn't fit the mode, he's not even considered as draftable. The team does favor athletes and it has signed several players who were headed to college careers as quarterbacks before Tampa Bay intercepted them with bigger bonuses and opportunities.

"We've had the opportunity to set up the program from ground zero," said scouting director Dan Jennings, who came to the Devil Rays in 1995 after a decade of experience in scouting with Cincinnati and Seattle. Before that he played in the Yankees system without ever making it to the majors. He wasn't drafted into baseball, but signed as a undrafted free agent after attending William Carey College. His brother is a scout with Cincinnati.

The team has an average sized scouting department with 15 area scouts and three cross-checkers. Scouts do conduct tryouts after the draft to try and find other players. They are held throughout the United States. The Diamondbacks are looking overseas for talent, too. "We're looking at every market," said Jennings. They have signed players in every market as well, including pitcher Byung-Hyun Kim who played on the South Korea national team. Baseball is still just a game in areas like the Dominican Republic where there isn't a lot of money around and poverty abounds. "The Dominicans don't have all the spoils that Americans do," he said. Too many Americans learn to play baseball on the Nintendo rather than on the field. He said that the problem with American boys is that some have poor work ethics and are generally lazy. There are more opportunities for kids these days. "There's a lack of talent in this country," he commented.

Jennings would only go along with an international draft if it were instituted for all the right reasons. "I'm for it, if you create a level playing surface," he explained.

The Devil Rays do hold tryouts around the country and may have found a gem in 1999. They usually only look at players ages 18–24, but they made an exception with one 35-year-old pitcher. Jim Morris had been drafted by Milwaukee in 1983 and played in the minors until his arm gave out in 1989. After a 10-year hiatus from the sport, Morris tried out for the Rays in June 1999. The scout was so impressed by his 98-mph fastball, that he was signed. He was assigned to Double-A in July, elevated to Triple-A in August and the majors in September.

Best Picks

With only a couple of draft years under its belt, it's difficult to judge who are the best picks in the Tampa Bay system, but two picks have already made it to the majors.

Ryan Rupe, a sixth-round pick in 1998 out of Texas A&M, was the first Devil Ray to be called up to the majors in May 1999. Getting to the majors was probably easier than what he had to overcome in high school. He suffered several injuries from a car accident in high school to return to the mound and pitch well enough to get drafted. That's an accomplishment in itself. He was put on the fast track after going 7-1 in 1998 in Class A with two teams. He was pitching in Double-A Orlando when he got his opportunity in the majors.

The second Devil Ray draft pick to surface in the majors was **Mickey Callaway**, a seventh-round choice out of the University of Mississippi in 1996. Also a pitcher, Callaway was 4-1 at Triple-A Durham when he had his contract purchased. He did quite well in the minors putting together a 32-20 record in three-and-a-half seasons. The righthander started and won his first game in the majors by defeating Montreal on June 12 in six innings of work.

Expansion Draft Picks

The first expansion draft pick to see action for the Devil Rays was **Tony Saunders**. The left-handed pitcher made his debut with the Marlins in 1997, but he wasn't protected from the draft. Tampa Bay put him right to work in 1998 as a starter. His 6-15 record in 1998 was due more to lack of run support than poor ERA (4.12). Saunders was a nondrafted free agent, originally.

Randy Winn got drafted by the Marlins in the third round in 1995 before he was drafted by the Devil Rays in the expansion draft in 1997. Winn felt it was a win-win situation because the Devil Rays gave him a chance to play in the majors. "There was no guarantee with the Marlins that I would have been there," he commented.

At Santa Clara University, Winn was a two-sport player and scouts thought of him as more of a basketball prospect. "I kind of snuck up on people," he said. He wasn't drafted out of San Ramon High School. He was first told he would be drafted in the low rounds, but as he got better and better in his junior year his stock got better and better. He told scouts that he would sign if he was picked in the first five rounds. His father helped him research the draft. College players are not allowed to sign with an agent until after they leave college.

Another pitcher to make it to the majors with Devil Rays after being drafted was **Mike Duval**. Originally drafted in the 19th round by the Marlins in 1995 out of junior college, the lefthanded pitcher was promoted to the majors in September 1998 for a cup of coffee. He found himself back with the Durham Bulls to begin the 1999 season.

Aaron Ledsma was drafted by the Mets in the second round in 1990. He was in junior college and knew he was going to be in the top five, but he was surprised to be taken in the second round. He wasn't aware of the high bonuses for

baseball, so he was taken aghast by the offer and signed right away. "I never really thought about playing baseball," he said. He just wanted baseball to give him a scholarship. He was heading toward being a trainer, not a player.

He went through a culture shock when he got into minors because he hadn't been out of California much. "Oh, oh, what did I get myself into," he said. He wound up in Tennessee, but he responded well and was the Appalachian League all-star shortstop in his first professional season.

He broke into the majors with the Mets at third base when somebody got hurt in 1995. Then he was traded to the Angels. He became a free agent in 1996 and signed with the Orioles where he got into the playoffs. Then the Devil Rays drafted him. "I thought I was going to be part of their [Baltimore's] future," he explained.

Now he's a utility fielder for the Devil Rays. At Baltimore he played second base, but he's adjusted well. "We're the unsung heroes. You don't really hear about us much. But we're extremely important to a baseball team."

His most shining moment wasn't his first game like most. He was with the Orioles when he first got to play in front of his father, a former boxer. "I think playing in that game was a real emotional moment for me. It put a smile on my face," he explained. His dad never pushed him in baseball, but he was very supportive. His older brother helped pushed him and he was always played with older boys which gave him a level of confidence which helped him later in life.

The Devil Rays and the press were high on **Bubba Trammell** at spring training in 1999, but he failed to impress enough people to be put on the roster and was assigned to Triple-A. Detroit failed to protect the power hitter, who they drafted in the 11th round in 1994 out of the University of Tennessee. Trammell got a call from Detroit in 1997 and he wasn't very impressive with a .228 average. The Devil Rays called him up in 1998 and he fared a little better as he hit .286 and 12 homers.

Terrell Wade was left unprotected by the Atlanta Braves after he had elbow and shoulder surgery in 1997. The Devil Rays took him with the idea that it would not be until 1999 before

Bubba Trammel with the Durham Bulls, called up by the Devil Rays in 1998.

the lefthander would be fully recovered. The big, bulky hurler strained an oblique muscle on his right side early in the 1999 season. He debuted with the Braves in 1995 and pitched three seasons with them before being drafted. In 1998, he had appeared in two games for the Devil Rays. He was assigned to the Durham Bulls to begin the 1999 season. Originally, he was a nondrafted free agent out of high school.

The Braves also left **Bobby Smith** unprotected in the expansion draft and he was gobbled up as well. Smith played the whole first season with the Devil Rays, but found himself being sent back down to Triple-A in May 1999 when he couldn't hit his weight. He was hitting .154 with two homers in 29 games.

The Devil Rays drafted **Rich Butler** off the Blue Jays. He had received his first call up with Toronto in September 1997. The Devil Rays brought up the outfielder in 1998 out of spring training, but he hit only .226 and was sent back

to Triple-A. He injured an Achilles tendon in spring training in 1999 and was assigned to the Durham Bulls on April 18. The local Toronto boy was originally signed by the Blue Jays in 1990 as a nondrafted free agent.

Steve Cox came from Athletics in the draft. The first baseman had risen to Triple-A before the draft and the Devil Rays have kept him there. He was originally picked in the fifth round by the A's in the 1992 draft. Cox began the 1999 season with the Durham Bulls and had amassed 12 homers by early June.

All in the Family

Jared Sandberg, nephew of Ryne Sandberg, who played with Cubs, was picked in the 16th round in 1996. He began his career by being named the Most Valuable Player of the Appalachian League in 1997.

On the Roster

John Flaherty was a long shot to make the majors when he was first picked by the Red Sox

John Flaherty, drafted by the Red Sox in 1988 in the 25th round.

Rich Butler with the Durham Bulls came to the Devil Rays in 1998.

in 1988 in the 25th round, but he was a lower pick. "I was very disappointed [about the draft]," Flaherty explained. "I was told that I was going to go anywhere from the third to the sixth round." However, Boston scout Phil Rosie told him not to get discouraged because he was the first catcher taken in that year's draft. And because Boston and a number of teams in the New York area were where he was from, he decided to sign and give professional baseball a try.

Flaherty's ability to catch and throw moved him quickly through the system as he leapfrogged from Single-A to Triple-A. Then he made it to the majors in 1992. "That 25th round doesn't seem to stand on your back anymore," he commented. He developed late physically.

"When the career's over, I'll be able to look myself in the mirror and say I did the best I could. Fortunate enough for me, I got some breaks. The Red Sox gave me the opportunity. I was just happy to get an opportunity."

The Cardinals picked **Aaron Holbert** in the first round in 1990. He was in his high school library when he received the call. "I had a reporter with me the whole day," he recalled. He

Aaron Holbert with the Durham Bulls signed with the Devil Rays in 1998.

thought he was going to be drafted by Seattle as the sixth selection, but the Mariners took Marc Newfield. Holbert received a September call-up in 1996 to get a cup of coffee in the majors. The free agent signed with the Devil Rays in November 1998 and was assigned to the Durham Bulls in 1999. The shortstop was hitting .306 by draft time in 1999 with Durham. The Bulls let him finish a blowout on the mound against Syra-

cuse and he allowed eight more runs. Instead of losing 14–2, the Bulls lost 22–2.

Another shortstop with the Durham Bulls was **Chris Martin**, a second-round choice of the Expos in 1990 out of Pepperdine University. He was drafted by the Yankees as a junior in 1989 in the 26th round, but he chose to finish his degree in philosophy and raise his stock, which he did. He entered the 1999 season without serving a day in the majors yet. Martin would like to see draft picks become free agents after four seasons instead of six so teams can't "hide them in the minors for years" like he was by Montreal.

Future Stars?

A long shot who has overcome the odds is **Dan Wheeler**, a 34th round pick in 1996. The draft-and-follow pitcher signed in 1997 after his sophomore year at Central Arizona Junior College. A 3.00 ERA at Class A Hudson Valley moved him up to Charleston the next season. Then in 1999, he was simply outstanding at Double-A and was promoted to Triple-A Durham. He said he got there on the strength of his fastball, which was clocked in the low 90s. He also has a good changeup and great control.

Bobby Seay was drafted June 4, 1996, by the White Sox. By June 19 he had not received a contract. He said he got it in the mail about a week after the deadline.

The offer was for $855,000. He was in Cuba when he heard he was granted free agency by Major League baseball. Then he got a $3 million offer from the Devil Rays. Injuries, appendicitis and a perforation of his colon have hampered his progress in the minors. In his first two seasons in the minors he was 4-11, but he said his performance improved in the fall 1998 instructional league.

Travis Harper was first drafted by the Mets first in the 14th round in 1994, but he decided to go on to James Madison University. He was then drafted by Boston in 1997, but had his contract voided because of elbow problems. Tampa Bay decided to gamble on the elbow and signed him in 1998. He responded with a 6-2 record and a 1.92 ERA in short season A ball.

Alex Sanchez got to the draft via a raft. The member of the Cuban Junior National

Travis Harper was drafted by the Red Sox in the third round in 1997. Tampa Bay signed him in 1998.

Team came to the United States aboard raft in 1994 and had to spend 16 months in a refugee camp in Guantanamo Bay in Cuba before being allowed in the country. When he did arrive, he attended Miami-Dade Wolfson Junior College and became eligible for the first-year player draft. Tampa Bay picked him in the fifth round in 1996.

The Devil Rays had the first pick in the 1999 draft and chose **Josh Hamilton**, an outfielder out of high school. Terms were not revealed but LaMar said that the left-handed hitting outfielder would receive the highest signing bonus in the history of the draft. Press reports

later had that amount at $3.65 million. They signed him three days after the draft, so they undoubtedly had been negotiating with him for awhile, which was permissible. "It's a unique situation to get a top draft pick signed that quickly," LaMar said. "I think it speaks well of the family but also of the trust we built up with them. We knew where we wanted to get and Josh knew where he wanted to get. So, we cut right to the chase. We got a contract done and everybody is happy."

The Rays have been watching Hamilton for some time now. Hamilton hit .529 his senior year with a school record 13 home runs and 35 RBI in just 25 games. He also showed a patient eye at the plate, walking 26 times while striking out on just seven occasions. Hamilton, who stands six-foot-four and weighs 205 pounds, was sent to Rookie Ball at Princeton in the Appalachian League. "There is no timetable as to when we have to have him in a Devil Rays uniform," LaMar said.

Jennings really liked Hamilton's makeup and character. "He's an old-fashioned baseball player." That's probably why the Rays didn't have trouble signing him. Those types of players are more interested in playing than they are in the money. They figure the pot is at the end of the rainbow and not the beginning.

Washington Senators/Texas Rangers

When the franchise began drafting in 1965, it was located in Washington, D.C. The Senators were the doormat of the American League and had lost at least 100 games every season since it began in 1961. The Senators finally withdrew from the nation's capitol in 1971 and moved to Arlington, Texas, where it became the Texas Rangers, so named for the famed marshals of the old west. By the early 1970s, the draft was beginning to help the struggling franchise. The team finished second in 1974 and began turning in winning records after that. However, it was not until the 1990s that the Rangers won a pennant.

In the history of the draft, the Rangers haven't fared all that well. They really haven't had any picks that have been seriously been con-

sidered for the Hall of Fame. Jeff Burroughs, Jim Sundberg and Roy Smalley were excellent players, but received only one write-in vote each. However, the Rangers have made some better selections in more recent times and perhaps one of those players will become Hall of Fame material in the future.

If anything, the team has had some draft picks who have done better managing the game than playing it. The Senators picked Tom Grieve in the first round of the 1966 draft. The outfielder played nine undistinguished seasons in the majors. He's done better as an administrator as he became the general manager of the team in 1985. Mike Hargrove, who went on to manage the Cleveland Indians, was picked by the Rangers

Jim Riggleman (left), manager of the Chicago Cubs, and Ed Lynch, general manager of the Cubs. Lynch was drafted by the Texas Rangers.

in the 25th round in 1972. And Ed Lynch, who became the general manager for the Cubs, was a 22nd round selection in 1977.

The Rangers' philosophy is to take skilled baseball players who are agile athletes and have a good attitude. "A number of things go into the recipe," explained Chuck McMichael, who has been the scouting director for the last three drafts. McMichael came from the Kansas City scouting system where he was a crosschecker.

The Rangers have an average-size scouting staff stateside—16 area scouts, 10 part-time scouts and three national crosscheckers. "We're really committed to the amateur draft," McMichael said. Maybe so, but the team has become more of a "now" team and traded away many of their draft pick prospects for veteran players. They've also dipped into the free agent market to get some quality players instead of waiting for players to ripen in their own system.

Internationally, they have a large staff in comparison to most teams. A dozen scouts cover the globe for Texas. "We've taken a quantum leap on the international side," explained McMichael. "We are going beyond the traditional areas." Those areas include Germany and southern Europe. If the draft ever goes international, Texas will be ready. The Rangers have been good in the past getting players from foreign markets as evidenced by the signing of Pudge Rodriguez and Juan Gonzalez from Puerto Rico before the draft took place on the island.

The Rangers view the draft as an investment into the future. The Rangers try to avoid

any disappointments, but those do come anyway. "Doug Melvin [general manager] breeds brutal honesty. We don't overevaluate anyone," added McMichael. He had lots of praise for his predecessor, Sandy Johnson, who took some heat for not having some number-one picks who never made it to the majors. "A director can only be as good has his scouts and crosscheckers."

The Ballpark in Arlington is tailor-made for left-handed power, so the Rangers have been picking some players in the late 1990s to fit that mold. Their first two picks in 1998 were left-handed power hitters. And they signed free agent Rafael Palmeiro, a left-handed power hitter in 1999.

The Rangers' player development philosophy is one step forward, one step back, if necessary. In other words, if a player is not doing well at a level, he is sent back a level until he proves himself before coming back to that level instead of just sitting at that level until he improves.

In 1999, the Rangers didn't get a true first-round pick because they signed Palmeiro. Their first pick wasn't until the compensation round when they received the 38th choice overall as compensation for Todd Stottlemyre. They also received compensation pick for losing free agent Will Clark. That didn't seem to bother McMichael, who thought the draft was rather "thin" anyway.

Best Picks

Jeff Burroughs was the first choice in the nation in 1969 and the Senators gave him an $88,000 bonus. He lived up to the top billing by being named the Most Valuable Player in the American League in 1974 after hitting 25 homers and leading the league in RBI with 118 to take Texas to a second-place finish. That him earned a trip to the All-Star Game. The Rangers decided to trade him in 1975 for five players and cash. He continued to deliver for the Braves and hit a career high 41 homers in 1977. He completed a 16-year career as a designated hitter in Toronto. He hit 240 homers over his career.

Another first-round choice of the Rangers was **Jim Sundberg** in 1973. The catcher turned out to be the best defensive receiver in the American League during his tenure and one of the best in the century. Unfortunately, he was only an average hitter. The star catcher at the University of Iowa was first drafted by the Oakland A's then the Rangers a second time before he finally signed. He played just a year and a half in the minors before becoming the Rangers' regular receiver in 1974. He began picking up Gold Gloves in 1976, but his bat lagged behind until he came up with a .291 average in 1977. The following year he was named to the All-Star Team, a feat he would accomplish just once more over his career. However, he ended up with six Gold Gloves and established an American League fielding percentage record of .995 in 1979. A Don Aase fastball nearly ended his career in 1979, but the resilient Sundberg recovered. He played a decade for the Rangers before being traded to Milwaukee. He returned to Texas for the 1989 season, his last.

Still another first-round pick with the Rangers who has turned out well was **Kevin Brown** in 1986. He was a durable member of the Rangers' starting rotation for six seasons, pitching over 200 innings three times. In his rookie year of 1989 he led American League rookie pitchers with 3.35 ERA and seven complete games. His best overall season came in 1993 when he led the American League with 21 wins and 265.2 innings. After he left the Rangers, he pitched for the Orioles for a season before signing with the Marlins. In 1996 he was runner-up for the Cy Young as he was 17-11 and led the National League with a 1.89 ERA. The next season he helped the Florida franchise to the world championship with his 16-8 mark. Then he went to San Diego where he was 18-7 to help the Padres reach the World Series. The right-handed hurler became the highest paid player in the game in 1998 when he signed a big contract with the Los Angeles Dodgers.

Another good pitcher out of the Texas organization was **Dave Righetti**. The Rangers drafted him in the first round in 1977, but traded him a year later in a multi-player deal with the Yankees that brought Sparky Lyle to the Rangers. The left-hander was a starter for New York for several years until the Yankees found out he was better as a stopper. He led American League relievers in wins in 1985 with 12. Then he set the pace the following year with 46 saves. He played

16 seasons in the majors and ended up with 252 saves. He never once played for Texas.

Dean Palmer put a lot of balls in the bleachers during his stay at Texas. The third-round pick in 1986 first showed his power in the minors when he was a Texas League All-Star and led the league with 25 homers. In his rookie season of 1991 he hit below the Medoza Line, but 15 homers was second among American League rookies. It was easy for him to improve on that performance and he did just that. His home run total rose to 33 in 1993. And his average improved to .336 by 1995, but injuries limited him to just 36 games. He enjoyed his best season of his career for the Rangers in 1996, hitting .280 with 98 runs, 38 homers, and 107 RBI in 154 games. He was traded halfway through the 1997 campaign to Kansas City. In 1998, Palmer recorded the best power numbers in Royals history, slamming 34 HR and 119 RBI. The third baseman was named to the Silver Slugger team that season.

Long Shots

Mike Hargrove was the 527th player picked in the draft in 1972. Two years later he jumped from Class A to the Rangers and became the American League Rookie of the Year in 1974. That led him to being named to the All-Star Team the next season. The 25th round selection spent his first five of his 12 years in the major leagues with the Rangers. Then he went on to San Diego and Cleveland. At Cleveland, he was named as the Tribe's Man of the Year twice. The .290 lifetime hitter once had a 23-game hitting streak with the Indians. He was solid player, but has turned into an even better manager of the Indians. He took the team to four straight American Central Division titles, two American League titles and two World Series appearances.

The Rangers didn't select **Kenny Rogers** until the 39th round in 1982 out of high school. Rogers bounced between Single-A and Double-A in his seven seasons in the minors. Seven turned out to be his lucky number, as he leaped over Triple-A and got his calling on the Opening Day roster in 1989. He spent his first four seasons with the Rangers in the bullpen and picked up 28 saves. He was turned into a starter in 1993 and responded with a 16-10 mark. The Georgian by birth put his name in the record book on July 28, 1994, by throwing a perfect game in a 4–0 victory over the Angels. It was the first perfect game by an American League left-hander. He became a free agent in 1995 and signed with the Yankees. In his career at Texas, he had the highest career winning percentage (.579) in Rangers history. He also ranked among the club's all-time leaders in games (2nd), wins (4th), walks (5th) innings (6th), strikeouts (7th) and saves (tied for 7th). In 10 years in the majors, he has accumulated a 104-74 record. Not bad for a 39th-round selection.

Another recent long shot that the Rangers have picked up in the draft was **Robb Nen**. They chose the high school graduate in the 32nd round in 1987. They are probably wishing they held on to the reliever who has become one of the best stoppers in the game. However, when Nen was in the Rangers farm system, he had elbow and shoulder problems that hindered his development. The Rangers gave him a try in 1993, but he didn't show much so he was traded to the Florida Marlins for pitcher Chris Carpenter. Maybe it was the Florida sun or something in the water, but Nen turned his troubled career around the following season and began saving games for the young Marlins. He became their stopper in 1995 and responded with 23 saves. Then in 1997 he helped lead Florida to the League Championship Series where he picked up two saves. That led to the World Series and two more saves, which helped the Marlins to a World Championship. Nen became the Marlins career saves leader and helped the team to its first World Series. Soon after the Series, the Marlins traded Nen to the Giants for three pitching prospects. He had a career high 40 saves for San Francisco in 1998.

After **Jeff Frye** was named first team NAIA All-America and Oklahoma Intercollegiate Conference player of the year as a senior at Oklahoma State University, the Rangers selected him in the 30th round in 1988. The infielder progressed normally through the farm system with a solid bat and good fielding skills. The Rangers called him up in 1992 after he hit .300 at Triple-A Oklahoma City. After sitting out a season due to injury in 1993, he rebounded the following

season. The Rangers granted him free agency in 1995. He signed with the Tigers, who released him during spring training in 1996. He signed briefly with the Rangers again in 1996, but stayed at Triple-A and was released. He signed with the Red Sox, who turned him into their second baseman for a couple of seasons.

Walt Terrell was a 33rd round choice in 1980, but he was traded to the Mets before he ever came up to the majors in 1982. He pitched 11 seasons in the majors, but never with the Rangers.

Disappointments

The biggest state in the continental U.S. has had some big disappointments over the years. The first was first-round disaster catcher **John Jones**. The 1967 first rounder couldn't get past first base. The next year the Senators chose **Donnie Castle**, who got a cup of coffee in the majors. After that it was **Charles Maxwell** in 1970. The first-round infielder made it to Triple-A before leaving baseball. Then **Roger Quiroga** was drafted in the first round in 1971. The right-handed hurler peaked at Class A.

The Rangers' most heralded draft pick and biggest disappointment in Rangers' history has to be **David Clyde**. The native Texan had a 95-mph fastball that was nearly untouchable. In his senior year at Houston's Westchester High School he was 18-0! In high school the left-hander was

David Clyde of the Texas Rangers. (Photograph courtesy of David Clyde.)

53-13 with a 0.65 ERA. And he struck out a record 843 batters in 475 innings! The struggling franchise chose him as the first player taken in the draft and reported that he received the highest bonus ever paid to an 18 year old. Reports said the bonus was over $100,000. In fact, Clyde reports that he received a $65,000 bonus. He didn't have an agent advising him at the time.

Because the Rangers needed immediate help on the roster and in the stands, Clyde was sent directly to the majors. Three weeks after being drafted he was on the mound for the Rangers. Surrounded by a lot of hoopla, Clyde pitched in his first major league game on June 27 before a sellout crowd, the first in Rangers history since moving to Texas from Washington in 1971. Clyde won his spectacular debut, but his career went downhill after that fantastic start. He saved the franchise that year, but bringing him up so quickly sacrificed a long career. He became the sacrificial lamb.

Clyde now agrees that going straight to the majors hurt his career because of "lack of instruction at the major league level." The next season his new manager, Billy Martin, wanted him shipped back to the minors. When the Rangers refused, Martin put the young hurler on the bench for a month. Clyde ended up with a losing record for the second year in a row. The Rangers finally sent him to the minors in 1975. The left-hander suffered shoulder problems and had surgery resulting in him missing much of 1976. He was traded to Cleveland where he continued to struggle for two seasons. He was taken back by the Rangers, who released him in spring training. His hometown Astros gave him a shot, but he failed in the minors and never made it back to the majors. Now he owns his own lumber yard in Tomball, Texas.

In 1975, the Rangers picked **Jim Gideon**, whose hometown was in Houston and he had attended Texas University. The local favorite got to pitch one game in the majors. The following year the Rangers picked Billy Simpson and the outfielder only got to Class A. That's as far as **David Hibner** got, too. He was the first-round pick in 1977. **Tim Maki**, a first-round pitcher from 1980, met the same fate.

The Rangers picked **Dan Smith** in the first round in 1990. The left-handed hurler was not very impressive in the minors. At Triple-A Oklahoma City in 1991 he was 4-17 with a 4.42 ERA. He improved the next season at Double-A, so the Rangers gave him a try in the majors that season. In four games, he was 0-3 with a 5.02 ERA. He was sent back to the minors for more seasoning. His next appearance in the majors came in 1994 and he was 1-2 with a 4.30 ERA in 13 games in relief. Then he was injured and was out all of 1995. After a disappointing return at Triple-A in 1997 when he was 3-14, the Rangers let the loser go. His professional career record was 31-55. The Rangers released him after the 1997 season.

Some Who Didn't Sign

The Senators picked **Dick Tidrow** in the first draft when he graduated from high school. He decided not to sign.

Chris Speier was selected by the Washington team in 1968, but he passed on the pick and went on to a long career with the Giants.

The Senators drafted **Bruce Sutter** in 1970. He passed up the opportunity and came up with the Cubs. He became famous for throwing a split-finger fastball and earning 300 saves. He was put on the ballot for the Hall of Fame in 1994, but he hasn't mustered any serious consideration.

Another reliever who didn't sign when drafted by Texas in 1974 was **Tim Stoddard**. "Big Foot," as he was known, signed a year later with the White Sox. He also became a stopper and played for the Cubs. He appeared in 485 games during his 13-year career.

All in the Family

The Senators picked **Joe Coleman, Jr.**, in the first round in the first draft. He was the son of Joe Coleman, who pitched for the Athletics, Orioles and Tigers in the 1940s and '50s. Junior went on to top his dad as he pitched for the Senators for six years and 15 years in the majors.

In 1970, the Senators selected **Steve Greenberg**, the son of Hall of Famer Hank Greenberg, who made his fame with the Tigers and played in four World Series. By 1972, the young Greenberg made it up to Triple-A Denver. A scout said he would probably make it to the majors if he could hit the breaking ball. He never did figure out how to hit a curveball, so he never made it to the majors.

Robb Nen is the son of former Major Leaguer Dick Nen, who was a first baseman in the 1960s for three teams. His father appeared in 367 games, so his son still needs a couple of seasons to catch his dad in that category.

The Rangers' first pick in 1993 was **Mike Bell**, the son of Tigers manager Buddy, and grandson of Gus, a former big leaguer. He was traded to the Angels in 1997. By the end of 1998 he had progressed to Triple-A. So he will be a third-generation player if he makes it to the majors.

Where Are They Now?

Texas picked a homegrown favorite for their number one pick in 1975: **Jim Gideon** of Houston who compiled a 17-0 mark and helped pitch Texas to the College World Series title. The 17th selection received a signing bonus of $50,000 and $7,500 for college. Texas even gave him a one start that season in the majors, but he proved ineffective in his only start, giving up a home run and seven hits in five and two-thirds innings. Two years later he underwent shoulder surgery, which ended his quest back to the majors. He was still pitching in 1998 though. This time he competed in the Nike World Masters and pitched his team to a Silver Medal. He is now a health insurance broker.

Pete Hartmann was drafted by the Rangers in the 9th round. He went to the Brewers before deciding to try Taiwan in 1998 after not making it to the majors. It was a profitable trip for the left-handed pitcher as his salary was much better than Triple-A, but a little lower than the minimum in the majors. However, he's not likely to do it again. "The language barrier is tough," he explained. "The league is run by the Mafia. Everyone is on the take." The season is also much longer—March 1 to Oct. 31. But teams only played three games a week, so the schedule wasn't as intense as American baseball. He got bored with being there, because it is only an island and there's no place to go. After his year there, he returned to sign a contract with

Baltimore and was assigned to Triple-A Rochester. "It was an experience." One that he will never forget.

Mike Cubbage was first drafted by the Senators in the sixth round in June 1968 out of high school. "They liked me," he commented while watching hitters in the batting cage during spring training in 1999. Washington offered

Mike Cubbage of the Houston Astros, first drafted by the Senators in the sixth round in 1968.

the Lane High School, Charlottesville, Virginia., graduate $10,000, but he decided to go on to college. After his junior year at the University of Virginia, he gave the Senators permission to draft him again and they did. He has been in baseball ever since: First, as a Ranger for parts of three seasons and player for eight seasons in the majors then as a hitting instructor and manager with the Mets organization and now coach for the Houston Astros.

Another player who turned to coaching is **Dick Such**, an eighth-round pick in the January 1966 Secondary Phase. Such is now the pitching coach for Minnesota. Such won just one game in the majors for the Senators in 1970.

Steve "Doc" Watson, a fourth-round choice in 1981, has also turned to coaching. He played one season in the Rangers' system and four in

Cincinnati, but never got to the majors. He became a pitching coach after that with the Pirates and is now with the Class A Hickory Crawdads.

Another former Rangers draft pick with the Pirates organization is **Curtis Wilkerson**, a fourth-round choice in 1980. Wilkerson spent six seasons with the Rangers during his 11-year major league career. He became a hitting coach for a season before managing the Williamsport Crosscutters, a rookie team of the Pirates.

Darrin Garner, a first-round pick in the 1985 June Secondary phase, also turned to baseball management after an unsuccessful attempt at getting to the majors as a player. Garner played six seasons in the Rangers' minor league system before becoming a coach. He turned to managing in 1997 and took over the skippering at Class-A Lancaster in 1999.

Mike Jirschele was a fifth-round choice in 1977. He played for nine seasons in the Ranger system, but never made it to the majors once. He turned to managing and coaching in the Royals systems after his playing career ended.

A year later the Senators picked **Rick Stelmaszek** in the 11th round in June. He is now the bullpen coach for the Twins. Stelmaszek was signed by Jack Sheehan, the same scout who signed Rick's father many years before. He played three seasons in the majors with the Senators, Angels and Cubs.

Undrafted Players

Danny Darwin wasn't drafted when he attended Grayson County Junior College, so the Rangers signed him. Darwin spent just three-and-half seasons in the minors before becoming a starter or reliever for the Rangers. In his first full season, Darwin was 13-4 as a reliever. He was still pitching in 1998 at age 42.

On the Roster

The Rangers had only few of their own draft picks on the team and a few more on the 40-man roster going into the 1999 season.

Rick Helling boomeranged back to the Rangers in August 1997 just in time for a shining performance in 1998. The first round pick in 1992 performed well in the minors as he was

named to the Texas League All-Star Game in 1993 and was the American Association Pitcher of the Year for Oklahoma City in 1996 after going 12-4, but the Rangers decided to trade him to Florida in September rather than call him up themselves. The Marlins used him as a reliever for a year before trading him back to the Rangers. Texas made him a starter in 1998 and he responded by winning 20 games. He became only the third 20-game winner in Rangers history and set the Rangers' record for highest winning percentage (.741)

The long shot on the Rangers roster was **Danny Patterson**, a 47th-round pick in 1989 out of Cerritos Junior College. His progress in the minors was hampered by an elbow injury in 1994. After posting a 1.68 ERA with 10 saves for Triple-A Oklahoma City in 1996, he was called up to the majors. The next season he tied the major league lead with 10 relief wins. The reliever made 56 appearances and earned two saves in 1998.

Rusty Greer has been in the Rangers organization since 1990 when he was drafted in the 10th round out of University of Montevallo. He broke out with a .291 average and 15 homers at

Steve Larkin with the Cincinnati Reds. He was drafted by the Rangers. (Photograph by Marty Orr.)

Double-A Tulsa in 1993. The following season he led Major League rookies with a .314 average in 1994 and finished third in Rookie of the Year voting. Greer hit .332 in 1996, fifth in the American League, and he was second in the league in doubles and third in RBI. The following season he became only the second hitter in Texas history to hit more than .320 two years in a row. He continued his fine hitting in 1998 and made just three errors.

Ryan Glynn, a fourth-round pick in 1995 out of Virginia Military Institute, was given a call in May 1999 when Esteban Loaiza went on the disabled list. Glynn had moved steadily up the Rangers farm system and was getting better and better. Then the right-hander moved up to Triple-A in 1999 and proved himself early to get the call. He completed his degree while in the minors, which is something a lot of players have a hard time finding time to do.

Jonathon Johnson, a first-round pick from 1995, got his first call to the majors in 1998 with the Rangers for one appearance, which was not promising, so he was sent back to Triple-A in 1999 for more experience.

Kelly Dransfeldt, a fourth-round pick in 1996, got his opportunity at the Bigs early in the 1999 season when Royce Clayton went on the disabled list. The University of Michigan shortstop caught the attention of the Rangers after he was named to the Florida State League All-Star Team in 1998 when he batted .322 and knocked out 27 homers.

Another 1999 arrival to the majors was **Mike Venafro**. The left-handed hurler, a 29th-round pick in 1995, got called up in April 1999 when John Burkett went on the disabled list. Venafro was an all-star in the minors his first season when he went 9-1. The reliever had been a stopper in the minors.

Future Stars?

When Texas drafted **R.A. Dickey** in the first round (18th pick overall) in 1996, they thought they were getting a pitcher with a great arm. They were about to offer him a contract worth $800,000 when they found out he was missing an ulnar collateral ligament in his pitching arm. Their offer dropped ten-fold. Dickey

Scott Eyre with the Charlotte Knights, a Texas Rangers draft pick.

still signed for $75,000. The lack of the ligament hasn't hurt Dickey as he had 33 saves with Class A Charlotte in 1998. He was promoted to Triple-A in 1999.

Another Triple-A pitcher who was drafted by the Rangers was **Brandon Knight**. The 14th-round pick from 1995 has had his ups and downs in the minors. After a 6-6 performance at Double-A in 1998, he was 0-7 in Triple-A with a 9.74 ERA. In 1999, he was adjusting better at Triple-A.

The Rangers picked **Corey Lee** in the first round in 1996 and the left-hander advanced to Double-A by 1998. He was 26-18 through his first three seasons in the minors and was winning in 1999 at Charlotte again. If the Rangers need a lefty, he's probably ready and he's a winner to boot.

Shawn Gallagher, a fifth-round pick in 1995, finally broke out to a great season in 1998 when he hit 26 homers at Class A Charlotte to earn Most Valuable Player in the Florida State League. That earned him a promotion to Double-A.

Right behind Gallagher at Class A Charlotte was **Carlos Pena**, the first-round pick in 1998. Pena showed some promise right away by shooting up to long-season Class A in his first professional season. He continued to develop at Class A Charlotte in 1999 and led the team in homers.

A long shot who has made it to Triple-A was **Mike Zywica**, a 24th-round pick from 1996 and the last player listed in the player encyclopedia. He had a breakthrough season in 1998 when he was named to the Florida State League

All-Star team after batting .381. The high average elevated him to Double-A.

The Texas Rangers selected a pair of right-handed pitchers with their first two selections in the 1999. With the 38th overall selection in the draft, the Rangers picked right-handed pitcher **Colby Lewis** from Bakersfield College. Lewis, who is six-foot-five, was 4-5 with a 2.86 ERA in 12 games, striking out 108 batters in 88 innings at Bakersfield.

With the 47th overall pick in the draft, Texas selected right-handed pitcher **David Mead** from Soddy Daisy High School, Tennessee, which is located near Chattanooga.

He too is the same height as Lewis and was 2-3, 3.56 with 61 strikeouts in 41 innings this spring.

The Rangers made it three right-handed pitchers in a row when they selected right-handed pitcher **Nick Regilio** from Jacksonville University in Jacksonville, Florida. The 72nd overall pick in the draft was 7-2, 4.58 with 66 strikeouts in 72.2 innings.

Toronto Blue Jays

Toronto began drafting players the first year of its existence, which put the team well behind the power curve. Previous expansion clubs started drafting a year before they began playing. Nowadays, expansion teams begin two years before they begin playing. As a result of getting a late start on the draft, the Blue Jays got a late start on winning. The team was like a bottom feeding carp for seven seasons. Under manager Bobby Cox, the Blue Jays worked their way up to first place in 1985, thanks in part to the draft. However, the Jays were edged out by the Royals in the playoffs. That team included such draft picks as Jesse Barfield and Lloyd Moseby.

Then Jimy Williams took over as the manager. He kept the club winning, but failed to get them to the series. Cito Gaston became the manager and finally got the Blue Jays to the World Series. The Blue Jays beat the Atlanta Braves to win the World Series in 1992. The Series squad had some of the best Blue Jay draft picks in its history: pitchers Jimmy Key, Todd Stottlemyre, Mike Timlin and David Wells. Original draft pick hitters included Derek Bell, John Olerud and Pat Borders.

The Blue Jays had losing seasons during the mid–'90s, but turned that around in 1998 when they had a run at the wild-card spot. Some of the draft picks the team made earlier in the decade were beginning to have an impact on the team like Shawn Green. "It shows that our drafts have worked and they're coming into their own right now," said manager Tim Johnson at spring training in 1999. Two weeks later he was fired for lying about going to the Vietnam War when he was in the Marine Corps during the 1960s.

Toronto has a large scouting staff with 23 area scouts, 30 associate scouts and three regional supervisors in the United States. In Canada, the team has 14 area scouts and 11 associate

John Olerud was drafted by the Blue Jays in the third round in 1989. (Photograph by Kenny Keiffer.)

scouts. Tim Wilken is the scouting director. The staff was reorganized in 1998 with Wayne Morgan taking over international scouting, where the team has scouts in Australia, Brazil, Dominican Republic, the Netherlands, Panama and Venezuela. The team searches out some of the local talent by holding tryouts for teens all across Ontario, which also serves as good public relations for the team. The team held clinics for the fourth consecutive year in Rome and Vienna to continue to development of baseball on an international basis.

The Blue Jays had a foreign flavor to their 1999 draft as the team drafted three Puerto Ricans and five Canadians. Most of the players drafted were pitchers (34), but the first two picks in the draft were third basemen. Seven of the first 10 picks were from high school. After that, Toronto concentrated more on college players.

Best Picks

Jesse Barfield was a ninth round selection in Toronto's first draft in 1977. He was first called to the majors in 1981 and was the Jays Rookie of the Year in 1982 after hitting 18 homers in his debut. He set an American League record in 1985 with extra-base hits in 11 consecutive games and helped the Blue Jays to the League Championship Series that season. Barfield was named to the All-Star Team in 1986 when he led the league with 40 home runs. The outfielder had a great arm and led the league in outfield assists four times. He also garnered a couple Gold Gloves. He went to the Yankees in 1989 for four seasons then Japan for a year before retiring from baseball due to injuries. He turned to coaching and is now the Seattle Mariners hitting coach.

In the same draft class as Moseby was another outfielder, **Dave Stieb**. He wasn't an outfielder for long as the Blue Jays converted him to a pitcher, which turned out to be a great move. After getting called up in 1979, he soon became the ace of the starting staff. Stieb continued to improve every season and he led the league in innings pitched and complete games in 1982. Unfortunately, he sometimes didn't get the run support and never reached the 20-win plateau during his 14 seasons with the Blue Jays.

He led the league in ERA at 2.48 in 1985, but could only manage a 14-13 record. Despite the lack of wins, he was recognized as one of the best pitchers in the American League and was named to six All-Star teams. Stieb seemed snake bit during a couple of performances during his career. He had a no-hitter going into the ninth inning once and gave up a homer. Even worse than that, he retired 26 consecutive Yankees before giving up a hit to lose his bid at a perfect game. In the postseason, he was a disappointing 1-3. His 174 winning games with the Blue Jays is a franchise record though.

The Blue Jays brought **David Wells** back into their fold in 1999 in a trade with the Yankees that sent Roger Clemens packing. Wells was a second round pick by the Jays in 1982, so he was the oldest Blue Jay veteran on the team. The lefthander became the 14th pitcher in major league history to record a perfect game in 1998, but the Rocket outdid him in the Cy Young Award voting. The southpaw was 18-4 with the Bronx Bombers in 1998 to help the Yankees on their way to a World Championship. He also appeared in his second All-Star Game in 1998. Wells agreed to a two-year contract extension in 1999, assuring he will be with the Jays until 2002.

One of the key pitchers on the staff for nearly a decade was **Jimmy Key**, a third round pick in 1982. The lefthander was in the minors for two seasons before becoming a regular. He was strictly a reliever his first season, but the Jays found a spot in the rotation the following year and he responded with a 14-6 record. He was a starter after that until his last season in 1998 with the Orioles. His best season with the Jays came in 1987 when he was 17-8. He was granted free agency in 1992 and he signed with the Yankees. He was named to four All-Star teams during his career. His career record was 186-117.

Going into the 1999 season, **Pat Hentgen** was one of the longtime homegrown veterans on the team being drafted back in 1986 by the team. The right-handed hurler first broke into the majors in 1991 and became the ace of the staff in 1993 when he broke the club record with 11 wins by the All-Star break and he was named to the All-Star Team as well. On the year, he was 19-9. He won the Cy Young Award in 1996 when he was 20-10 on the year with a 3.22 ERA. It didn't mean much as the team suffered a losing season. The award led him to being named to the All-Star Team the next year for the third time.

Long Shots

Toronto has done a good job drafting pitchers in the lower rounds who have made it to the majors. Pitchers, especially lefties, have a good shot of making the majors regardless of when they are taken in the draft.

Lefty **Richardo Jordan** was a lowly 37th round pick in the 1990 draft. He spent three seasons at Class A until he moved up the ladder to the majors. The reliever failed to impress Toronto in his call-up to the majors in 1995, so he was traded to the Phillies. Then he went to the New York Mets and Cincinnati.

The Blue Jays look all over Canada for players of course. They found **Steve Sinclair** at Kwantien College in British Columbia. and drafted him in the 28th round in 1991. Sinclair was slow to develop in the minors, spending three seasons in the rookie ball. Then he spent another three seasons in Class A. After lowering his ERA, the reliever jumped to Triple-A and then Toronto in two seasons. He appeared in 24 games in 1998 for the Jays.

Another 28th round pitcher to rise to the top was **Darren Hall**. Drafted in 1986 out of Dallas Baptist University, Hall took baby steps through the minors and by the end of his sixth year was only at Double-A. He was granted free agency and re-signed with Toronto. The strategy finally paid off in 1994 when he was elevated to the majors with the Blue Jays. The reliever was granted free agency again in 1995 and signed with the Dodgers.

The third 28th round wonder was **Woody Williams**. The right-hander came from the University of Houston and spent six seasons in the minors before being promoted to the majors. He was a starter and long reliever for six seasons for the Blue Jays before being dealt to the Padres for Joey Hamilton.

Another long-shot pitcher picked by the Blue Jays was **Aaron Small** in the 22nd round in 1989. After climbing up to the majors in six

Chris Stynes, Cincinnati Reds, drafted by the Blue Jays. (Photograph by Marty Orr.)

seasons, Toronto decided to trade him to the Marlins for a player to be named later. Small pitched one season with Florida before going to the A's and pitching three seasons there.

Besides pitchers, a few other long shots have made it to the majors. **Tom Quinlan** was a 27th round pick in 1986. The Blue Jays called him up twice, but he failed to hit his weight, so he was let go. The free agent has since signed with four other teams. He has yet to stick in the majors. The third baseman has some clout as he has slammed 156 home runs in the minors.

The lowest Toronto draft pick to make it to the majors so far was **Travis Baptist**, who was picked in the 45th round. Blue Jays scout Andy Pienovi found him at Hillsboro High School in Oregon. Baptist had played baseball, basketball and football and was twice named to the All-State team in baseball among other accolades. The Jays failed to protect the left-handed pitcher from the Rule V draft and he was picked up by the Twins in 1996. In 1998 he finally came of age as he was selected starting pitcher for the Pacific Coast League in the Class AAA All-Star game. Soon after that game, the Twins brought him up to the majors.

Disappointments

The Blue Jays received the next to last pick in the first round in its first draft in 1977 and chose Tom Goffena. The shortstop out of high school didn't get past first base. The same result occurred to **Jay Schroeder**, a first-round catcher in 1979.

Then **Garry Harris**, the second overall pick in 1980, couldn't do much better as the shortstop peaked at Double-A. The next shortstop the Jays picked in the first round was **Augie Schmidt** and he never got past Triple-A. He too was the second overall pick in the draft.

In 1983, the Jays picked **Matt Stark**. The catcher managed a cup of coffee in the majors.

After not having a first-round pick in 1984, Toronto chose **Greg David** in the first round the following year. The outfielder got as far as Double-A, which was also as far as **Earl Sanders**, a pitcher picked first in 1986.

Toronto also picked a pitcher the next year in the first round. **Alex Sanchez** pitched just four games in the majors.

Best Draft

The year 1982 turned out to be an excellent draft as the Blue Jays got three starters out of the group. Plus, the three came from the toughest positions to find: left-handed pitchers and catchers. Pitchers **David Wells** and **Jimmy Key**, both lefties, were picked second and third in the regular phase of the June draft. Wells was out of high school, but Key came from college. Catcher **Pat Borders** was drafted as a third baseman or outfielder, but he turned to catching to make it to the majors.

Worst Draft

The year 1980 was worth nothing to the Blue Jays as far as someone reaching the majors. Nobody did.

Where Are They Now?

In the better-late-than-never category, **Webster Garrison** may be the draft pick who played the most years in the minors before mak-ing it to the majors. The Blue Jays picked him in the second round in 1984 out of high school. He played 13 seasons in the minors before finally getting his chance with Oakland at the end of the 1996 season. He turned to being a player/coach for the Athletics' Double-A Midland in 1999, so he could still see some action if need be.

Todd Stevenson, a first-round pick in 1992, retired from playing after the 1998 season became a coach in the Cardinals' minor league system. The Cardinals first drafted him in the sixth round in 1989, but he decided to attend ASU. He's the cousin of former major leaguer Ron LeFlore.

Ones Who Got Away

The Blue Jays selected **Oddibe McDowell** out of Miami–Dade North Community College, but he waited to sign with Texas a couple of years later.

Dwight Smith was a third round pick in the January regular phase in 1984. He waited until the Cubs picked him first in the draft.

Toronto picked **Jim Abbott** after he completed high school. Abbott went on to college and the Olympics before coming to the Big Leagues.

Danny Ainge was a 15th round pick in Toronto's first draft in 1977. After three mediocre seasons with the Blue Jays, he defected to the Boston Celtics where he turned out to be a much better professional basketball guard.

All in the Family

Brandon Cromer is younger than his brother, but he was drafted higher the same year that his brother, D.T. Cromer, was picked. Brandon was a compensation first round pick in 1992, while his brother was an 11th round pick by the Athletics. The Blue Jays never gave him a chance to get to the majors and traded him to the Pirates in 1996. "I probably didn't deserve it," he admitted. He was granted free agency in 1998 and signed with the Brewers. The brothers had a reunion in 1999 when the Louisville River Bats faced the Indianapolis Indians, D.T.'s team.

Undrafted Players

Rob Ducey wasn't drafted out of Seminole Community College, although he was eligible, so the Blue Jays signed the Canadian-born outfielder as a free agent. He took just four years to get to the majors and played parts of six seasons with the Jays before he was traded to the Angels. Toronto drafted a couple of Canadian players in 1999.

On the Roster

More so than a lot of teams, the Blue Jays roster is jammed packed with its own draft picks as the team doesn't have the funds necessary to jump into the free agent pool much. Toronto would much rather develop talent than have to buy it.

Chris Carpenter, a first-round choice in 1993, became a regular on the starting staff in 1998 and went 12-7 with a 4.37 ERA. He made his major league debut in May 1997, but was sent back to Syracuse to develop a little more. His minor league career was less than shining with a 23-33 record, but he has pitched better in the majors.

Anthony Sanders, a seventh-round selection in 1992 got his first call up in April 1999 when Dave Hollins was put on the disabled list. The outfielder was an all-star twice in the minors and has home run power as evidenced by his 26 homers in 1997. Getting to the majors was probably easier than personal tragedy he went through after his wife died in a skiing accident in 1996.

Brandon Cromer, a Blue Jays draftee, now with the Louisville River Bats.

Shawn Green, a first round, 16th pick in 1991 for the Blue Jays.

Shawn Green, a first rounder in 1991, went from platoon player to starting right field in 1998. He responded by becoming Toronto's first player to hit 30 homers and steal 30 bases. He also knocked in 100 RBI. In 1999, he was named to his first All-Star Team after batting .326 with 24 home runs and 68 RBI before the break.

Shannon Stewart, a baseball, football and track star out of Miami, was the Jays first-round choice in 1992. "I didn't know much about Toronto," he admitted. He got his first call up to the Blue Jays in 1995 and finally became a regular in 1998. He lit up the base paths in 1998 with 51 steals on the season. The outfielder was big on speed, but a little short on power at the beginning of his professional career. His first major league homer came off Ken Hill in 1998. "It took me a long time to hit and I finally did it," he explained. "It was like a relief. I finally broke the ice." He broke the ice another 11 times in 1998.

Billy Koch, a first-round pick in 1996, was a starter for two seasons in the minors, but the right-hander hurler with a three-digit fastball was converted to a stopper in early 1999 and found himself saving games for the Jays. The fourth-overall pick in the 1996 draft came out of Clemson University. He was also a member of Team USA in the 1996 Olympics.

Should Koch need help in the stopper role, long shot **Steve Sinclair** was being primed from the left side at Triple-A in 1999. The 28th-round choice from 1991 spent seven years in the minors before making a jump from Class A to Triple-A in 1997. The Jays brought him up in 1998 for half a season. Then he was sent back to Syracuse in 1999 to develop more.

Roy Halladay, also a number-one pick from 1996, got off to a great start in the minors as he was named to Florida State League All-Star Team. The right-hander showed he was ready for the big leagues at the end of the 1998 season as he took a no-hitter down to the last batter in the season finale in Toronto to impress everyone. "Halladay is going to be one of the better young pitchers in baseball some day," said manager Tim Johnson. The Jays made him part of their staff in 1999 and he was used both as a starter and reliever.

On the surface **Alex Gonzalez** was a long shot at making the big leagues being selected in the 14th round in 1991. But a scratch of that surface revealed a whole different story. "I had a good feeling I was going to be drafted, but I didn't know what round." And it really did matter that he as taken in the 14th round, because the Blue Jays paid him second-round money. He signed for $145,000. "After I signed, Toronto said they were going to treat me like a second round pick," he explained. The Blue Jays pushed him through the system in 1994. Sure enough, he made the club after Spring Training, which he considers his best moment so far in baseball.

Future Stars

Casey Blake is on the fast track to the majors at the rate he is going. The third baseman spent less than a half a season at Double-A in 1998 after being named a Florida State League all-star and hitting .350 with 11 homers. Blake was elevated to Triple-A in 1999 with just three years in the minors. He batted .372 at Double-A Knoxville! Blake was drafted three times before he finally decided to sign on the dotted line. The Philadelphia Phillies first drafted him in 1992 in the 11th round after he graduated from high school. He decided to go on to Wichita State University instead. Then the New York Yankees picked him in the 45th round after his junior year. He decided to finish school. After he graduated, the Blue Jays picked him in the seventh round. "They were very fair to me," he commented. He had no leverage, but they gave him a nice bonus anyway.

John Bell was also drafted three times. In 1996, he was picked in the fifth round by the Blue Jays and signed. "I was expecting to go a little higher, but I had injuries near the end of the season," he said. He was first drafted by the Cardinals in the 12th round in 1994. In 1995, he was picked in the sixth round by the Orioles.

"The reason I didn't sign with the Cardinals and Baltimore is I wanted to get some college underneath my belt before I signed," he explained. "I just wanted a sense of security knowing I had school behind me." His goal in 1999 was to get to Triple-A or the majors by the end of the year.

Bell began his pro career as a starter and was turned into a reliever in 1998. "I feel more aggressive coming out of the pen. Every organization needs a good setup man." If baseball doesn't work out for Bell, he could always head security for a major league team. He has a bachelor's degree with a major in criminal justice.

Joe Lawrence was playing shortstop at age 14 with the American Legion when scouts first took notice of him. Then he went to many different showcases in his junior and senior year in high school. He had a scholarship offer to play at LSU, but a first round selection by Toronto and a large bonus changed his mind. "There are pluses and minuses to signing early," he explained. "I got drafted and signed a month later to be able to play in rookie ball." The Blue Jays showed Lawrence they were very high on him by putting him on the 40-man roster in 1998. This gave him insurance, a pay raise and assurances. The shortstop hit .301 at Class A Dunedin in 1998 and was promoted to Double-A in 1999.

The Blue Jays are high on **Tom Davey**, a fifth-round pick in 1994. He started out as an outfielder at Henry Ford Community College in Michigan, but wound us as a pitcher. His stock for the draft rose quite a bit when he got exposure at the Junior College World Series. Davey completed a two-year degree, and Toronto gave him money to finish a bachelor's degree. He's been so busy with baseball that he hasn't been able to go back to college. He'd like to stay in baseball even after he's done playing, but that could be a long time from now if he continues to progress at the rate he is going. "I'll either be in Syracuse closing or I have a shot at making the club as a reliever," he said during spring training in 1999. He got part of his wish and moved up to Syracuse in 1999.

Tom Evans got a shot at playing first base in spring training in 1999. He was a fourth round pick in 1992. "I had no idea what round I was going in," he said about his draft experience. He was a pitcher and first baseman, and many teams looked at him as a pitcher, but Toronto pegged him for third base. He was first called up in September 1997 when Ed Sprague

Ed Sprague was drafted by the Blue Jays.

went down with an injury. Then he went down with an injury two weeks later. He was called up again in September 1998 and didn't get a hit in 10 at bats. If Evans doesn't stick in the majors at first, he could always go back to being a pitcher.

The Jays selected **Felipe Lopez** with their first pick in 1998. The eighth overall pick in the draft out of high school batted .375 his first professional season at Class-A and he fields shortstop with ease.

The Hispanic trend continued in 1999 as the Jays picked **Alex Rios** from Puerto Rico as their first choice. The six-foot-five third baseman was rated as the best prospect from the island. It marked the third year in a row that the Blue Jays had drafted a high school player in the first round.

The Blue Jays finally signed three draft-and-follow players — all right-handed pitchers — just prior to the 1999 draft. **Ryan Houston** was drafted in the 31st round in 1998 and spent the year at Pensacola Junior College. **Cameron Reimers** was chosen in the 35th round in 1998 and went to the College of Southern Idaho before signing. **Aaron Dean** was the 38th round pick and went to Sacramento City College for a year of more seasoning.

AMERICAN LEAGUE

Arizona Diamondbacks

The Arizona Diamondbacks began picking players in the free-agent draft in 1996, two seasons before they began playing in 1998. This meant the fruits of their labor wouldn't ripen for four or five seasons if they let nature take its course. To allow that to happen, Arizona owner Jerry Colangelo made some big moves at the end of the 1998 season. After seeing his new baseball team end up in last place in the National League West with a 65-97 record — 33 games out of first place — Colangelo decided he needed to do something about the situation to make the team more competitive before the new century. He went to the free agent market and spent about $100 million on players. The gamble paid off and his team was headed to a division championship in 1999.

The largest acquisition literally was the Big Unit — Randy Johnson. Several teams were after

his talents after Houston let him go after helping the Astros to the playoffs, but not the World Series. The Diamondbacks spent $52.4 million on Johnson for a four-year deal. They also picked up Todd Stottlemyre, Armando Reynoso, Greg Swindell and Greg Colbrunn on the open market.

"It really allows us to put guys like Brad Penny, John Patterson and Nick Bierbrodt on the schedule they should be on — pitch Double-A this year and Triple-A next year," Colangelo explained at a press conference. "It allows us to put guys on the time frame they should be on." The money spent on free agents was to make the team a winner right away and took the pressure off of player development.

"It does resist the urge to bring up a draft pick too soon," Arizona scouting director Don Mitchell further clarified. He knows the danger

Rob Ryan, an Arizona draft pick in 1996, 26th round.

of bringing up a player before he is ready. He recalls some of the failures, such as Todd Van Poppel, that resulted when players were brought up too soon. He doesn't want the same situation to occur in Arizona.

The team leans more toward drafting high school players because they turn out better, according to Mitchell. "When you crunch the numbers, a lot of quality players come from high school," he explained. "We like to take players early in the draft that will make a difference at the Major League level." Nearly 50 percent of Arizona's picks came from high school in 1998. Another 20 percent came from junior colleges.

The Diamondbacks also like to pick players who have more than just the necessary tools. "Makeup is a big part of it — the intangibles," said Scott Jaster, an Arizona scout in the Midwest. "To find those tool players with quality attitude. We don't like bad boys in the dessert."

Arizona has stockpiled a lot of pitchers the first three years. More than 50 percent of the players in the 1998 draft were pitchers. However, the team hasn't purposely taken more pitchers. It has just turned out that way. "Our scouts have done a good job with pitchers," Mitchell mentioned.

Arizona took advantage of a bad situation in 1996 to try and get ahead of other teams. When Major League Baseball declared four draft picks free agents because they weren't offered proper contracts within the 15-day deadline, the Diamondbacks signed Travis Lee and John Patterson. Mitchell called both scouting directors to tell them how he was glad to get the players, but sad

that the system had declared them free agents on a loophole. He thought Major League Baseball should have told the players that they could either negotiate with the team that drafted them or wait until the next draft. Being declared free agents was like giving a kid a Cadillac for graduating from high school instead of a Chevy. Both players got millions more as a result of the faux pas.

"We took a tremendous amount of heat from everybody in baseball," said Mitchell. His team was publicly criticized and some told it to his face. Many said it would ruin the draft. It didn't. The draft survived. Players the following year didn't get as much as those players who found a way around the draft.

While the scouting department has only been around a few years, it has more than 100 years of experience. Kendall Carter is Mitchell's right-hand man and the national coordinator. Mitchell also has several assistants helping him in headquarters. The United States is divided into three area crosscheckers: East, Midwest and West. They check the work of 17 full-time area scouts and 10 part-time scouts. And there are 150 bird dog scouts. Internationally, scouts are located in the Dominican Republic, Latin America, Puerto Rico, Panama, Mexico, Venezuela, Australia, Italy, Japan and Korea.

In Arizona's first draft, it picked 62 players, which was a few more than most teams selected. Exactly half of those picks were pitchers, eight of which were lefthanders. The next most favorite position taken was catchers, as Arizona took a dozen of those. Going for youth vs. experience, the Diamondbacks took 29 players out of high school.

Arizona continued the pattern it began in 1996 by drafting a lot of high school players and pitchers. The Diamondback drafted 29 players from high school and 29 pitchers, but not all the pitchers were from high school. After that, they selected just about an equal amount from each position and some players who could pitch or field.

By the end of 1998, the Diamondbacks had signed more than 60 percent of the players they had drafted, which was higher than most teams. That says a lot for the scouting bureau about insuring signability before drafting. Their first pick wasn't until the third round. They signed all of their first 10 picks except for Brendan Fuller, a right-handed pitcher from Clearwater High School, Florida. Before the draft, Fuller said he would sign for $75,000. Arizona drafted him and his agent, Paul Fernandez, told him not to sign for less than $125,000, according to Mitchell. So the team didn't sign him and he went on to the University of South Florida.

Overall, the Diamondbacks drafted 25 pitchers, 10 infielders, seven outfielders and six catchers in the 1999 draft. Eighteen selections were high-school products, 12 from four-year colleges and eight played at the junior-college level. The Diamondbacks selected four Arizona players: Corey Myers from Phoenix Desert Vista High School, first round; Derek Forbes of South Mountain Community College, 37th round; Jared Liebeck of Glendale's Mountain Ridge High School, 45th round; and Keith Schuttler of Agua Fria High School in Avondale, 48th round. The Diamondbacks received a sandwich choice between the first and second rounds as partial compensation for the free-agent signing of Devon White by Dodgers. Then they lost their own selections in rounds two through five as compensation for free-agent signings of Randy Johnson (second round, Astros), Greg Swindell (third round, Red Sox), Todd Stottlemyre (fourth round, Rangers) and Steve Finley (fifth round, Padres).

Future Stars?

The first pick of the Diamondbacks in 1998 was 18-year-old **Nick Bierbrodt**. The 6-foot-5, 190-pound left-handed pitcher from Long Beach, Calif., had signed a national letter of intent to play for Arizona State University. As a junior, Bierbrodt was 7-2 and had a 0.85 ERA and 82 strikeouts. In his senior year at Robert A. Millikan High School, Bierbrodt was 4-4 and had a 2.63 ERA in 61 innings, striking out 86 and walking 53.

Bierbrodt has progressed as expected. His ERA is just 3.13 in three years in the minors as a starter. He was named an all-star in his first professional season at the Arizona Fall League when his ERA was a mere 1.66 in eight starts. Bierbrodt was promoted to Double-A in 1999.

The first round pick in 1997 was **Jack Cust**, an outfielder out of high school. He hit for average and power in the rookie league and was named to the all-star team in 1998. The Diamondbacks hope to turn the ex–first baseman into a left fielder and power hitter. He was placed at long season Class A in 1999.

Brad Penny was a fifth round pick in 1996 and his progress in the minors has been as shiny as a silver dollar. The right-hander boasts a 26-12 record with a 2.79 ERA in his first three seasons. He struck out 207 in 164 innings in 1998 at Class A High Desert. Penny was promoted to Double-A in 1999.

The Diamondbacks selected **Mark Osborne** in the third round in the first draft. The catcher out of high school has shown some power in Class A, but needs more work with the bat before he can move to the next level. He started 1999 at long-season Class A High Desert where he had some trouble in 1997.

The Diamondbacks chose **J.D. Closser** in the fifth round in 1998 after he led his Alexandria High School to an Indiana State Championship. A .542 average in his senior year helped him earn an early round selection. "It didn't matter to me where I got drafted," the catcher explained. "I have to prove myself."

Arizona picked him because he had good tools, but just as important his intangible parts shined. "He came straight from the heart," his scout Scott Jaster, a 10-year minor league player himself, explained. "He's committed. He'll bust his rear end."

Closser did just that in Rookie Ball. He put up some good numbers: .313-4-21 with 13 doubles to boot, which earned him a six-game promotion to Class A South Bend before the end of the season. Then he batted over .400 in the Fall Instructional League. He wants to be like Ivan Rodriguez one day. "I want to be a starting catcher in four or five years in the majors," he said.

Joining Closser at South Bend as well was another good pick in 1998 pick —**Andrew Good**, a right-handed pitcher out of high school. Good was picked in the eighth round and began in rookie ball before getting a couple of appearances at South Bend.

When **Jeff Pass** was a sophomore in high

Jeff Pass was drafted by Arizona in the seventh round in 1998. (Photograph courtesy of Steve Pass.)

school, he could throw a fastball at 89 mph, but he was passed over by the high school varsity coach. He finally made the varsity squad the next year and Major League baseball scouts wondered what rock he had been hiding under. They were certainly impressed with the six-foot-one left-hander who also had a good curveball and change-up.

Pass continued to impress the scouts when he joined the Indiana Bulls, an independent team which travels all over the United States. Over the winter, he showed off more at the Hoosier Diamond Winter Camp. What really vaulted him into the top ten rounds in the draft was his senior year. His fastball climbed to 93 mph and he mowed down hitters like a lawn-mower. He set a school record for strikeouts with 17 during a no-hitter. He also tossed a one-hit-ter and averaged two strikeouts an inning his se-nior season. He was named to the first team All-State. "Awards have never thrilled him," his father, Steve, explained. "He's a low-key kid."

Arizona was one of the first teams to scout Pass and ended up drafting him in the seventh

round. Jaster called him a "bantam rooster" type of player with a good arm, a lot of heart and confidence.

Pass refused to give a figure on his bonus. "I thought the money was fair for the round," he said. Had he been taken too low or not offered enough money, he would have opted for college as he had a scholarship to South Alabama.

He went off to Rookie Ball with the Tuc-son Diamondbacks and was elevated to Class A South Bend in his first season. "I thought for my first year I did pretty good," he commented. He was used mainly in a relief role. Then he was sent to the Fall Instructional League for further training. His goal is to get to the majors in the next four years.

Corey Myers earned the distinction of being the highest drafted Arizona high school player in the history of the draft when the Diamondbacks picked him in 1999. The 18-year-old shortstop from Phoenix Desert Vista High School was Ari-zona's high school player of the year, hitting .560 and setting single-season state records with 70 hits, 22 home runs and 77 RBI. "There are a lot of players, and I've been involved in drafting some and signing some that had tremendous natural ability, but they either didn't know how to play the game or they didn't have quality makeup or approach to the game," Mitchell said. "This guy has both of those, no doubt!"

Arizona got the 31st overall pick in the 1998 draft thanks to the Dodgers giving it up for compensation for signing Devon White. The Diamondbacks picked **Casey Daigle**, a pitcher from Tulane University. " We feel he has great potential and he steadily got better during the course of the year," Mitchell said.

The Diamondbacks took another pitcher in the second round when they chose **Jeremy Ward.** "He's a power guy, a big strong body that we've seen throw 91-92 mph with an above av-erage curveball. He started and he relieved for Long Beach State University. We're going to help him with a changeup and we feel he has a chance to be a good starter."

Long Shots

One of the long-shot draft picks who has progressed up the minor league ladder is **Erik**

Erik Sabel was drafted by the Diamondbacks in the 42nd round in 1996.

Jason Conti was a 32nd round pick in the first draft and he has made it to Triple-A, too. After hitting .315, 15 homers and 31 doubles at Double-A, he earned a promotion to Tucson in 1999. The twice all-star in the minors may get a September call-up in 1999.

Another long shot who is doing well is **Jackie Rexrode**, a 17th round pick in 1996. The second baseman is a leadoff prospect and has hit for a .309 average so far in the minors. The high school graduated from Class A ball and made the next step in 1999.

Expansion Draft Picks

Edwin Diaz was the first player taken by the Diamondbacks in the expansion draft. Originally, he was a Texas Rangers second-round pick in 1993. The second baseman was given a peek at the majors in 1998 for three games. Unfortunately, he didn't pick up his first hit in the majors. He was back at Triple-A to gain more experience in 1999.

The Yankees didn't protect **Ben Ford** from the expansion draft in November 1997, so the Diamondbacks selected the pitcher, a 20th round free-agent draft pick in 1994. He had been in the Yankees system for three-and-a-half seasons before moving up to Double-A. The big right-handed reliever responded well to the change in climate and upgraded to Triple-A Tucson. Arizona recalled him on Aug. 20, 1998, and he finished the season with the team.

Sabel, a 42nd rounder in 1996. The Diamondback were able to lure him away from his senior year at Tennessee Tech for $2,500 and school money for his last year. "I didn't know if I was going to get another opportunity," Sabel explained why he signed as a junior. "I took it and I don't regret it at all." The right-handed hurler began at Lethbridge his first year and moved up to Class A High Desert in 1997. He began the 1998 season at High Desert. The Diamondbacks tried him at Triple-A Tucson, but he was shelled as a reliever. He ended the season at Double-A Tulsa, where he was undefeated (7-0). In three seasons in the minors the sinkerballer has a 20-16 record with a 4.45 ERA. In the off-season he teaches kids the fundamentals of baseball and keeps in shape himself at Round Trippers Baseball Academy in Carmel, Indiana. He hopes to get a shot at the majors in 1999.

Milwaukee/Atlanta Braves

When the draft began, the Braves were still in Milwaukee, but that didn't last but one year as the franchise moved to Atlanta. Scouting director Paul Snyder has seen the rise and fall and rise again of the Atlanta Braves since starting with the organization in 1957 as a player. The success the Braves had when he first got there was replaced by a long dry spell reminiscent of the Dust Bowl of the 1930s partly because the scouting staff was reduced to ruin. The staff of 22 scouts dwindled to five and the Braves sank like the *Titanic*. The team soon found out it could

not rely fully on the Major League Scouting Bureau to do the job. When the team recovered financially thanks to tycoon Ted Turner, the scouting staff was rebuilt and the result was a competitive team for the 1990s. Instead of trying to trade for players so much, the team has rebuilt itself using a combination of factors: picking talented high school players with good tools, scouting other parts of the world, looking at players in independent baseball and signing free agents who fit the team's mold.

The team began drafting high school players

in the 1980s who showed a lot of potential and had the right personality ingredients to bake the Braves' cake. "That's been the backbone of our success," explained Snyder. He would rather get a player straight out of high school than from college, so the player can be molded into the Braves' system at the earliest age. He compared it to raising a family. "Do you want to raise them or do you want some nanny to raise them? There's some great college players, too — don't get me wrong."

"College players have three more years of bad habits to break," added former long-time Atlanta scout Bob Turzilli. One bad habit was the use of aluminum bats, which don't help scouts get a true picture of a hitter. He also would tell high school hurlers that if they signed they might be pitching in the majors by the time they were 22. If they went to college, they wouldn't pitch in the majors until they were 24.

Of course the Braves have missed on some high school players because there is a certain amount of risk involved, but the upside is the player may turn into an All-Star sometime in the future. "You can't win the lottery, if you don't buy a ticket," Snyder commented.

Another thing the Braves look for in players is competitive spirit, mental toughness and dedication. They have traded for players who show that type of personality and the talent to boot. The Braves also like to give its players every chance to develop, which some teams fail to do. "We have more patience and give players more opportunity," added Atlanta scout Sherrard Clinkscales. "We don't want to deter anyone."

One of the problems that teams have with drafting college pitchers is that the team doesn't really know what they're getting until a year after the draft, according to Clinkscales. Atlanta likes to rest its newly drafted pitchers the first fall because they have already pitched in the spring and summer and need a rest.

The Braves have one of the largest stateside scouting departments with 23 regional scouts. In addition, the department has three regional crosscheckers and a national checker. The Braves also still believe in holding open tryouts all over the country for players that weren't drafted and may have been missed.

The Braves' lean toward high school play-

Damon Hollins, a fourth round draft pick in 1992 for the Braves. (Photograph by Marty Orr.)

ers was evident in the 1998 draft as 26 of their 49 picks came from high school. Nearly 50 percent of their choices were pitchers. By the end of the year, the team had signed about 50 percent of their draft picks. A few of their high school choices decided to go on to college and sign at a later time. That's the biggest risk associated with choosing high school players.

Atlanta didn't get a pick in the 1999 draft until the second round, 82nd overall. They lost their first-round pick to compensation for signing outfielder Brian Jordan as a free agent. Two teams have seven picks before the Braves get to pick for the first time. However, that didn't seem to bother Snyder.

Best Picks

When the Braves selected **Dale Murphy** in the first round of the 1974 draft, the press said he would be the next Johnny Bench. Murphy had a gun for an arm and hit .400 in high school.

The Phillies were interested in him as well and their scouts rated him as a good hitter but that he wouldn't develop as a power hitter. Both sources were wrong of course. Murphy breezed through the Braves minor league system in three seasons and found himself in the majors. But his arm began misfiring and he was sent back to the minors. The befuddled Murphy nearly quit baseball as a result. The Braves convinced him to come back and switched him to first base and later to the outfield. It was the best decision they made, because Murphy was about the only bright spot on a team that wasn't very good at the time. The fans would come to see him and not necessarily the Braves. He played for 15 seasons with the Braves and appeared in seven All-Star games during that time. In all, he played for 18 seasons in the majors, hit 398 home runs, won back-to-back MVP awards and five straight Gold Gloves. He retired in 1993 and many hope he is someday inducted into the Baseball Hall of Fame. Murphy is now the Mission President for the Church of Latter-Day Saints in Boston. He is serving there until July 2000.

Bob Horner earned the top spot in the draft in 1978 by setting the NCAA record for home runs with 56. The Braves signed him with a bonus of $175,000 and decided to send him directly to the majors, which turned out to be the right opening move as he homered in his first game and went on to Rookie of the Year honors. Horner and Dale Murphy made a great one-two punch in the Braves lineup and the home run duo helped the Braves to a first place finish in 1982; however, the team was swept in the League Championship Series. Injuries and salary squabbles with the Braves finally led him to sign with a Japanese team for a season. When he returned to the States, he signed with the Cardinals but retired after 60 games.

Ralph Garr was one of the fastest players in Braves history and he was nicknamed the Roadrunner for it. Drafted in the third round in 1967, he led the Texas League in stolen bases with 32 in his first professional season. He got his first call up to the Braves in 1968. Then in 1970 at Richmond he led the International League with a .329 average and 63 stolen bases. The second baseman was converted to an outfielder to take advantage of his speed. He became a regular

outfielder with the Braves in 1971. His career year with Atlanta came in 1974 when he led the National League in batting with .353, hits with 214 and triples with 17. His performance earned him a spot on the All-Star Team. He also led the league in triples the next season as well. He was traded to the White Sox and finished his career with the Angels with a lifetime .306 average. After his playing days, he returned to the Braves as a baserunning and batting instructor.

Tom Glavine slid to the second round in the draft only because teams thought he was going to opt for hockey instead of baseball. The Los Angeles Kings had drafted Glavine in the fourth round. Teams that showed the most interest in the left-handed hurler — Brewers, Red Sox and Blue Jays — undoubtedly now regret not taking him in the first round. He had thrown a perfect game in American Legion ball. And he had some no-hitters. He was a strikeout artist. Good fastball. When the Braves called, Glavine's father was speaking for his son. The Braves offered $60,000. His father's response, "I guess Tommy will be going to school." The Braves upped the offer to $80,000. Offer accepted. He soon showed he was worth the money as he was an All-Star at Double-A before being elevated to the majors in 1987. Glavine is the winningest left-handed pitcher in baseball over the last ten years, with 151 victories (1989–1998). He has twice had been honored with a Cy Young Award. His first came in 1991 when he was 20-11 and led the team to a first-place finish, its first in a decade. His second came in 1998 when he was 20-6. He was named World Series MVP in 1995 when he won two games to lead the Braves to victory over Cleveland. He's been named to five All-Star games. Glavine can hit the ball as well and won the Silver Slugger Award in 1996 with a .289 batting average.

Chipper Jones was the first player picked in the draft in 1990 because the Braves finished with the worst record in the National League in 1989. Jones has shown he was the right player to pick as he has been a solid performer. He hit over .300 in the minors and was named to the Triple-A All-Star team in 1993. His promotion to the majors was delayed a year when he injured a knee in spring training and missed all of 1994. Next year was his rookie year in the majors and he made the most of it by being named Rookie of the Year after hitting 23 homers. The following season he became the first Braves player since Dale Murphy to hit .300, hit 30 homers, and drive in and score 100 runs. He continued with similar numbers his next two seasons. He was named to All-Star teams in 1996 and 1997. He had a career .371 average in 10 League Championship Series games and .286 in 12 World Series games.

David Justice was a fourth round pick by the Braves in 1985 out of Thomas More College. Justice showed he could hit for power right away as he pounded out 10 in his rookie year in the minors. He made steady progress in the minors and was first called up in 1989. The following season was his rookie season and he made the most of it. His 28 homers and 78 RBI in 127 games earned him Rookie of the Year honors. He was named to All-Star teams in 1993 and 1994. Justice slammed a career hit 40 homers and 120 RBI in 1993. He began having shoulder problems in 1995 and dislocated his right shoulder in 1996. The Braves decided to trade him to Cleveland, where he recovered from his injuries and was named to the All-Star Team in 1997.

Ron Gant may have played more years for the Braves had he not broken his leg during a

Ron Gant of the Cincinnati Reds. He was drafted by the Braves. (Photograph by Marty Orr.)

dirt bike accident in the off season in 1994. The Braves decided to release him after the accident. He recovered from the broken leg, but all his numbers went down after it, so the Braves may have made the right decision after all. After he was drafted, he developed slowly in the minors until he broke out with 26 home runs in 1986. That turned him into an all-star in the minors and moved him toward the majors quickly. Atlanta first called him up in 1987 and he earned a permanent spot in 1990. That year he became a 30-30 man (homers-stolen bases). The following season he hit 32 homers to help the Braves to first place. Then he was named to the All-Star Team in 1992. When he came back to baseball in 1995, he signed with the Reds and was named to the All-Star Team again. The Reds couldn't afford him and traded him to the Cardinals. In 1998, he was traded to the Phillies. He has hit five homers in 31 career League Championship Series games.

Eights were wild with **Mark Wohlers**. He was picked in the eighth round in 1988, spent eight seasons with the Braves and recorded eight saves in his last year with Atlanta. Wohlers began his professional pitching career as a starter, but was soon converted to a reliever because he had a fastball that could hit triple digits on the radar gun. He started saving games in his third season in the minors. After saving 32 games in 1991, the Braves promoted him to the majors. Sure enough, he recorded a save in his debut. He was used in middle relief until 1995 when he became the team's closer. That year he posted 25 saves in helping the Braves to the World Series, where he picked up two saves in helping them to the championship. The following season he set a franchise record with 39 saves, which was fourth best in the league. Then mysteriously in 1998, he lost control of his fastball and was shipped back to the minors. The Braves let him go and he signed with the Reds in 1999, but he couldn't find the plate with radar. One of his best games with the Braves was when he threw two innings in a combined no-hitter with Kent Mercker and Alejandro Pena on Sept. 11, 1991.

Another Atlanta original who has ended up in Cincinnati is **Steve Avery**, a first round choice in 1988. The left-handed hurler ran through the minors like a jack rabbit. His ERA was a minus-

Steve Avery, third pick by the Atlanta Braves in the first round draft in 1998. (Photograph by Marty Orr.)

cule 1.50 in 10 starts at rookie to earn him a 7-1 record. The following season, he stepped up two levels. And after 13 starts at Triple-A in 1990, he became a member of the Braves starting rotation; however, he was slow out of the gate with a 3-11 record and 5.64 ERA. He filed that season under inexperience and put it behind him. The next year he was 18-8 and helped the Braves to first place. He was named to the National League All-Star Team in 1993 after a hot start. He finished the season with a 18-6 record and became the youngest pitcher in Atlanta history to record 50 wins. After losing records in 1995 and 1996, the Braves let him go. He signed a free agent contract with Boston. After a couple of seasons there, he went to the Reds where he was helping them with a resurgency in 1999. Avery was particularly effective in League Championship Series for Atlanta as he had a career 4-1 record in 11 starts.

Ryan Klesko, a sixth round pick in 1989, moved through the minors quickly after being named an all-star three times. He first landed in Atlanta in 1992, but he couldn't muster a hit in 14 at-bats. The following year he was called up and showed he could hit major league pitching with his .353 average in 22 games. That assured his promotion to the majors for good. His best year so far came in 1995 when he averaged .310 and hit three home runs in the World Series against Cleveland. He led the team in roundtrippers the following season with 34. He was moved to first base in 1999 after Andres Galarraga went down.

Ryan Klesko, sixth round pick in 1989. (Photograph by Marty Orr.)

Jeff Blauser was a first round pick in the secondary phase of the June 1984 draft. The shortstop led the Carolina League in total chances in 1986 and was a consistent performer in the minors. He got his first call to the majors in 1987 and became a regular in 1989. His best season occurred in 1993 as he played in 161 games, hit .305 with 15 homers and set the Braves franchise record with 110 runs scored. Blauser also hit two homers in the League Championship Series. His next best season with the Braves was his last when he hit .308 with 17 homers. In all, he played 11 seasons for Atlanta. Injuries plagued him much of his career. He slumped to .219 hitting for the Cubs in 1998 and was used sparingly in 1999.

Long Shots

Dusty Baker turned a long shot into a long career as he played for 19 years in the majors. He was a baseball, basketball, football and track star in high school. Drafted in the 26th round in 1967, the outfielder was first called up to the Braves in his second year in the pros. He became a regular in the outfield in 1972 and played four more seasons with Atlanta before being traded to the Dodgers where he matured as a hitter. He hit a career high 30 homers in 1977 with Los Angeles to help the team to the World Series. He played in three series with the Dodgers.

Glenn Hubbard was just a 20th round pick in 1975, but he worked his way up to become the Braves' regular second baseman for a decade. The defensive specialist led the National League in double plays three times and assists twice. His best season came in 1983 when he hit .263 with 12 homers and 70 RBI to earn a spot on the All-Star Team. After 10 years in Atlanta, he went to Oakland as a free agent and got to play in the World Series for the Athletics.

The Braves selected **Brett Butler** in the draft as a favor to his college coach. Butler had been passed over by the draft after his junior year at Oklahoma State. His coach, Doc Purham, felt Butler was one of the best players he had ever coached and deserved a chance at the majors. So he convinced Atlanta scouting to consider him. The Braves selected him in the 23rd round. Bob Mavis offered him $1,000. Butler wanted $5,000. "Your being drafted at all was a favor to your coach," Mavis told him. Teams had shied away from Butler because he was too small. They feared balls would bound over the five-foot-ten outfielder on artificial turf. He certainly proved

them wrong and went on to a successful career. He played his first three seasons in the majors with the Braves and led the league in triples in 1983. He did that feat three more times with the other teams — Indians, Giants, Dodgers and Mets. He was picked for the All-Star Team as well in 1991. So much for his short stature.

Mark Lemke was a lowly 27th round pick in 1983, but he soon showed he was better than that. In his second year in the minors, he was named to the Gulf Coast All-Star Team. He was also named as an all-star in Double- and Triple-A before earning a permanent position in the majors in 1990. He played second base for a decade with the Braves and was a member of four World Series teams. He was granted free agency after the 1997 season and signed with Boston. He batted barely above his weight (.187) in 1998 in just 31 games before suffering any injury which put him out the rest of the season. When nobody would sign him in 1999, he signed with the New Jersey Jackals of the Northern League and took up knuckleball pitching and coaching.

Disappointments

Disappointments were common to Atlanta early on in the draft. The Braves' first ever choice in the draft, with the team still in Milwaukee, was a first baseman named **Dick Grant** out of high school. He only got as far as Double-A.

The Braves made a great choice — **Tom Seaver** — in the second draft in January 1966. However, Commissioner William Eckert nullified the contract because it violated the rules, even though the NCAA declared him ineligible about the same time. Eckert made Seaver available to any other team if they matched the Braves' offer. Three teams expressed interest. The Mets won a drawing and signed Seaver for $50,000. Tom became "Tom Terrific" as he turned out to be one of the best modern-day pitchers. In 20 seasons he compiled a 311-205 record, was named to 12 All-Star teams, appeared in two World Series, threw one no-hitters, led the league in ERA three times, won three Cy Young awards and was elected to the Hall of Fame in 1992. He is 16th all-time in wins and 4th all-time in strikeouts.

The Braves struck out again in the 1967 draft as they picked outfielder **Andrew Findlay**, who got as far as Double-A. The next year they picked outfielder **Curtis Moore** who did only a little better and got to Triple-A. The Braves made it three years in a row with a bust as they chose **Gene Holbert** in 1969. The catcher peaked at Double-A. The streak continued the following year when pitcher **Ron Broaddus** didn't get past Class A.

After a great pick in 1974 (Dale Murphy), the Braves picked **Donald Young** and the catcher stopped at Class A.

Tim Cole was the fourth pick in the country for Atlanta in 1977. Atlanta scout Bob Turzilli thought he'd certainly make it to the majors some day and gave him high marks. He was highly regarded by other teams, too. Cole never made it out of A Ball. His problem was that he couldn't handle losing. He had been a great pitcher in school and won all the time, so for him losing was something he hadn't experienced and he couldn't handle it, according to Turzilli. "You don't know what's inside their head," the now retired scout explained.

The worst fiasco in the 20-plus years that Snyder has been the scouting director at Atlanta was **Jay Roberts**, a first-round pick in 1981. That draft had very few players that his scouts thought had much talent. Roberts had been an all-state athlete at basketball, football and track. He hadn't played baseball in high school, but he had played American Legion baseball. He had a scholarship to the University of Washington, but gave it up for the bonus. Roberts played four seasons and didn't progress past Class A. His final average was below the Mendoza Line. After baseball, he went to Washington to play football. Later in life, he got mixed up in a rape charge and died in a car wreck, according to the scouting director.

Drew Denson got a cup of coffee in the majors. The 1984 first rounder was an outfielder and first baseman and played just 16 games in the majors.

The most recent disappointment was **Jamie Arnold**, a first rounder in 1992 out of high school. He didn't reach Triple-A until 1998. A starter most of his career, Arnold had compiled a 32-44 record in the minors with a 4.55 ERA.

The Braves decided to let him become a free agent in October 1998 and he signed a month later with the Dodgers. After a 1-0 start with a 1.29 ERA at Triple-A, the Dodgers called him up on April 20, 1999, when the Dodger reassigned Rick Wilkins.

Best Draft

The year 1978 was a great one for the Braves in the draft as the first four players drafted in June were signed, sealed and delivered to the majors. Powerhouse **Bob Horner** was the first player taken. The next best was **Steve Bedrosian**, who was the third pick in the draft. "He was physically abused or should I say overused in college," said Turzilli, who scouted him. "Bed Rock," as he became known, had pitched for the University of New Haven. Bedrosian pitched five seasons for the Braves and went onto the Phillies where he won a Cy Young Award in 1987 when he saved 40 games on the season. Others who made it to the majors from the draft included **Gerald Perry**, **Jose Alvarez**, **Rich Behenna** and **Matt Sinatro**.

Worst Draft

Nineteen eighty-one. It's an easy choice because nobody that the Braves picked ever made it to the majors. Roberts was the first pick and he peaked at Class A. The Braves gave up their second choice to the Mets as compensation for free agent Claudell Washington. And they gave up the third choice as compensation for free agent Gaylord Perry.

Where Are They Now?

Dusty Baker played only a year with the Giants during his 19-year career, but he ended up as their manager. The two-time Manager of the Year entered his sixth season with the Giants in 1999.

Roe Skidmore was a sophomore at Millikan University when the Braves decided to pick him in the 47th round in June 1966, the second year of the draft. Nowadays, four-year college players aren't eligible until they are juniors. Scout Al Unser offered him $2,500 and he signed immediately. "Little did he know I would have paid them," he explained from his home in Decatur, Illinois.

The way his career began, he should have known he was going to have a hard time of it. His first night in professional baseball was spent in an airport waiting for a flight the next day.

Skidmore was traded to the Cubs and was called up in September 1969, but never saw any action as the Cubs were trying to win the pennant. The following season he was called up again in September and this time got to pinch hit once. He made it count and got a single in his only major league at bat. In all, he played 12 professional seasons before quitting and becoming a financial advisor. Skidmore is married and has five children.

Atlanta scout Bob Turzilli eyed **Dan Morogiello** when he was pitching at Seton Hall University. The Braves picked the left hander in the 3rd round in 1976 and gave the 51st pick in the draft an $18,000 bonus and $10,000 in incentives.

He made his way up the minor league ladder until he got stuck at Triple-A. "I was there when they [the Braves] were the worst team in baseball," he explained. "You would think they would have given me a chance, but Ted Turner would rather sign free agents then bring his own up."

Instead of getting a chance with the Braves, he was traded to the Cardinals, which meant he wouldn't get the $7,500 incentive bonus had he been called up to the Braves for 90 days. He was in the Cardinals organization when they won the World Series in 1982, but he was at Triple-A.

Then he was dealt to the Orioles in 1983, who finally gave him a chance in the majors. The reliever responded well in 22 appearances for the Orioles and posted a 2.39 ERA. Baltimore won the World Series that year and this time he was on the team, but he never threw a pitch in the series.

Morogiello was traded to Detroit the following season and sure enough the Tigers won the Series, but he was stuck in the minors. "I had the possibility of winning three rings, but I only got one," he said.

After 10 years in professional baseball with one season in the majors, he left the game and

Dan Morogiello was picked in the third round in 1976. (Photograph courtesy of Dan Morogiello.)

almost became a policeman. But Turzilli gave him a better offer. Go to work for him at Tri-State Brick in New York as a salesman. Morogiello has been there ever since and lives in Whitehouse, New Jersey.

Rick Matula was the 315th player taken in the 1976 draft by the Braves and he received a paltry $2,400 in bonus money. But that's better than what Montreal offered him in 1972, which was nothing, he recalled. The Expos drafted him out of high school in the 11th round, he thought. "I wasn't ready for it," he said about the Expos offer. Instead, he went off to college at Sam Houston State College and waited until he was drafted again before making baseball his life for awhile.

Matula worked his way up to the majors in 1979 with the Braves, who weren't very competitive at the time. "We weren't exactly a powerhouse," he said frankly and coughed liked he had a cold. He struggled with two losing records over two seasons as a result.

After spring training in 1981, he was sent down to Triple-A. He was called up later and appeared in five games before the player's strike hit. "That's one time I wish I had stayed down," he admitted. His performance was poor. Atlanta released him and he signed with Detroit, but he never was able to get back to the show again.

Now the former hurler manages a soft drink company in Wharton, Texas.

Brad Ripplemeyer was named coach for the Charleston RiverDogs just prior to the start of 1997 spring training replacing Howard Johnson who accepted a tryout with the New York Mets. Ripplemeyer, 27, was a catcher in the Atlanta Braves organization for the past six seasons after being selected by the Braves in the ninth round of the 1991 amateur draft. That year he hit a career best .358 at Idaho Falls. The next season he hammered a personal best 19 home runs at Class A Durham. Ripplemeyer's father, Ray, is currently the pitching coach for the New York Mets' AAA affiliate at Norfolk.

Ones That Got Away

The Braves picked **Randy Johnson** in the fourth round 1983 after he finished high school, but the Big Unit went on to college and was drafted by Montreal. The following year they picked **Jay Buhner**, who was in community college. He didn't sign either.

A few years later they picked **Steve Finley** and **Ben McDonald** in the same draft. They both didn't sign.

Jason Schmidt was an eighth-round pick in 1991, a pitcher out of high school. He was first called up with the Braves in 1995. He was a winner his first game in the majors, when he shut out the Cubs for eight innings. "I remember when the game was over and walking out on

Jason Schmidt, Pirates player, drafted by the Braves in the eighth round in 1991.

the field and they got CONGRATULA-TIONS JASON up on the scoreboard and all these fireworks going off," he remembered. He played another season with Atlanta before they traded him to Pirates to complete a trade for Denny Neagle.

Undrafted Players

Kerry Lightenberg was a 1989 graduate of Park Cottage Grove High School, where he was All-Conference in baseball, but he wasn't drafted. He began playing in the Independent leagues and was signed by the Mariners as a replacement player in 1995, but he hurt his shoulder after five days and returned to independent baseball.

His attempt to get into the majors might have been over, but his manager was former Braves catcher Greg Olson. The Southern Minny Stars manager called his former team and scouts came out to see Lightenberg. He impressed them enough to land a minor league contract. Olson sold the pitcher to his former team in 1996 for six dozen balls and two dozen bats. Lightenberg became the Braves stopper in 1998.

Because he was a replacement player, the players association won't let him join. "At the time, I didn't know what I was doing," he said in a newspaper interview in August 1998. The reliever suffered a partial tear of a ligament in 1999 and went under the knife.

The Braves also signed undrafted free agent **Adam Butler** from an independent team — the Florence Flame in 1995.

Probably the best undrafted free agent find by the Braves was **Paul Assenmacher**. Scouts weren't impressed by the lefty from Aquinas College because he didn't light up the radar gun. He was not drafted after graduating. But Braves scout Tony Stiel saw something different — a great curveball. The Braves signed him to a contract for a mere $3,000. The Braves switched him from a starter to a reliever and he pitched four seasons for the team before being dealt to the Cubs. By 1998, Assenmacher had appeared in 800 games — only the 22nd pitcher to reach that milestone. At that time he was pitching for Cleveland.

All in the Family

The Braves booked **Oscar Brown** out of USC in the 1966 June secondary draft. His brother, Ollie, was playing with the Giants at the time. Oscar made it to Atlanta in 1969 and played 160 games over five seasons, while his brother, also an outfielder, played a little longer.

The following year the Braves chose **Omar Lown**, the son of former Cubs/White Sox pitcher Turk Lown. Omar was a hurler, too, but he never made it to the big leagues.

The Braves drafted **Mike Yastrzemski**, son of Carl, in the January 1984 secondary draft. He had awful big shoes to fill and he never made it to the majors.

On the Roster

Besides the previously mentioned Glavine, Jones and Klesko, the Braves had several pitchers on the roster to start the 1999 season.

Kevin McGlinchy, a fifth round pick in 1995, made the club out of spring training in 1999. After only six games at Double-A, the right-hander who was a starter in the minors was given the call. He had pitched in Puerto Rico over the winter and showed improvement.

Long shot pick **Derrin Ebert**, an 18th rounder from 1994, was recalled when Mike Remlinger went on the disabled list. The left-hander pitched a full year at each level in making his way to the top.

John Rocker was an 18th rounder, too. Drafted in 1993 out of Mercer University, the lefthander was impressive in the minors. He was used primarily as a starter in the minors and threw a no-hitter in 1996. After starting the 1998 season with Triple-A Richmond, where he was 1-1 with a 1.42 ERA in 19 innings, he made his major league debut on May 5. The Braves began using him as a closer in 1999.

Another pitcher from the draft of 1993 was **Kevin Millwood**. The 11th round pick was a steady performer in the minors and emerged as the fifth starter for the Braves in 1997. He showed last was not least in his first full season in 1998 as he posted a 17-8 record and was named to the All-Star Game. He became the first pitcher in Atlanta history to record as many

as 13 strikeouts in a game without issuing a walk.

Future Stars

George Lombard turned down a football scholarship just to sign with the Braves. He was picked in the second round in 1994 and got a September 1998 call up, but was assigned to Triple-A in 1999 when the Braves signed Brian Jordan. He could become a regular by 2000. The athletic outfielder has power, runs well and has improved command of the strike zone. He was an all-star in 1998 in the Southern League when he hit .308 with 22 homers and 35 steals.

The Braves would like **Micah Bowie** to be the eighth wonder of the team. The left-handed pitcher was an eighth round pick in 1993. He has an above-average fastball and throws his curve, slider and change for strikes, which earned him an 11-6 record and 3.48 ERA, with 160 strikeouts in 163 innings in Double-A in 1998. A major sleeper, Bowie began 1999 in Triple-A, but could be recalled quickly if the Braves need a pitcher.

A.J. Zapp was the first round pick in 1996 out of high school and hoped to get to the

A.J. Zapp, pictured with his girlfriend, was the first round pick by the Braves in 1996.

majors by the turn of the century. All 30 teams contacted the hot first base prospect. "I tried to stay away from the money part and tell them that if I was drafted in the first round, I would sign," he explained. Zapp had already committed to Notre Dame in the fall. "I had something to fall back on, so I had some bargaining power."

Atlanta picked him because of his bat speed and work ethic, according to Atlanta Braves scout Jim Martz, who was responsible for giving Zapp such high marks. The Hoosier signed for $650,000 cash plus other incentives. He signed because he felt he would have a "head start" on those players who went to college.

In his first season in the Rookie League, he felt the pressure of being a first-round pick. "All eyes are on you once you step into the clubhouse," he said. The pressure got to him and he failed to hit his weight, so he needed the head start as it turned out. If he hadn't been a number-one pick, his baseball career may have ended right there, but the Braves had invested too much to let him go.

The following season he hit .338 at Danville in the Rookie League. He avoided turmoil in the clubhouse, which resulted in one player's expulsion from the team.

He earned a promotion to Class A Macon in 1998. The lefthander was the starting first baseman until he fractured a finger and missed two months of the season after surgery. Then right after he returned, he sustained strained ligaments in his left elbow, which kept him out of the line-up for the remainder of the season.

The injuries have set Zapp back, like missing a grade in school. "He has lost a whole year," said Martz. "He still has youth on his side."

Marcus Giles could be one of the longest shots to make it to the Braves if he continues to hit over .300 and pounds homers in the minors. The 53rd round pick in 1996 clobbered Class A pitching in 1998 when he hit 37 homers, 108

RBI and batted .329, which earned him South Atlantic League most valuable player honors. At five-foot-eight, he has amazing power. He's not a defensive specialist at second base, but his bat is unbelievable.

The Braves are hoping **Jason Marquis**, a sandwich pick in 1996 out of high school, turns into one of their marquee pitchers someday. The right-handed pitcher has a fastball in the mid-'90s and had two solid seasons before suffering a 2-12 record in long season Class A in 1998. If he continues having trouble in a starting role, the Braves will likely turn him into a reliever.

Another pitcher making good progress is long shot **Richard Dishman**. A 23rd round pick in 1997, the right-hander has started and relieved in the minors with good results at either role. In 1999, he was moved up to Double-A as a starter.

Wes Helms, a 10th round pick in 1994 out of high school, was an all-star in his second season in the minors at Macon. The third baseman hits for power and the Braves called him up in September 1998. If he continues to make progress, look for Atlanta to bring him up and find him a spot somewhere.

Mark DeRosa was a quarterback at the University of Pennsylvania when the Braves drafted him in the seventh round in 1996. The shortstop has hit .266 in the minors and the Braves gave him a September call-up in 1998. Then they assigned him to Triple-A in 1999, so the Braves have put him on a fast track to the majors.

The Atlanta Braves selected right-handed pitcher **Matt Butler** out of high school as their first pick in the second round in 1999. The 19 year old was 13-3 with a 1.48 ERA and 178 strikeouts in 92 innings as a senior. He allowed 43 hits and had 59 walks. The 6-2, 190-pounder was 40-8, including 13-0 as a junior, during his high school career.

Chicago Cubs

The Cubs began the draft much like how they've done the last 50 years — discouraging. It was not until 1969, that the Cubs picked a first rounder who wasn't a disappointment or complete failure. The Cubs haven't had a lot of success with the draft, but then again they haven't had a lot of success since the draft began. Their League Championship team of 1984 was made

Ozzie Timmons, with the Indianapolis Indians, was drafted by the Chicago Cubs. (Photograph by Marty Orr.)

up of a lot of draft picks that weren't their own. About the only player of significance that came from the Cubs system was Lee Smith. They had traded first rounder Joe Carter for Rick Sutcliffe in a multi-player deal. It turned out to be a great trade for the Cubs as the "Red Baron" went 16-1 the rest of the season and helped the Cubs to first place.

Their own draft efforts showed up more in their other playoff teams in 1989 and 1998. The '89 squad had several Cubs' draft picks: Greg Maddux, Shawon Dunston, Mark Grace, Dwight Smith and Rick Wrona. Grace was the only Cubs player from the 1989 team to be on the 1998 wild card team, which included Rookie of the Year Kerry Wood. The 1998 team also included Kevin Tapani, who the Cubs selected in the 1985 draft. However, Tapani didn't sign and waited until the next year to sign with Oakland after being selected in the second round.

The basic philosophy of the team is to take the best available player. "We try to get the best available player out of the draft," said general manager Ed Lynch. "In a lot of ways the draft is a gamble." And the Cubs so far have been losing at the game in comparison with other franchises.

The Cubs traded away some of their future in 1999 when they dealt Jason Ryan and Kyle Lohse to get closer Rick Aguilera from Minnesota when Rob Beck went on the disabled list in late May. Ryan was a ninth round pick in 1994 and had a 31-41 record with a 4.27 ERA in five years in the minors, but he was had begun 1999 with a 5-0 record with a 1.41 ERA. Lohse was a 29th round pick in 1996 and was 15-10 in the two seasons with a 3.17 ERA. Aguilera didn't prove very effective and pennant hopes soon melted in the hot sun.

Scouting director **Jim Hendry** has drafted heavily for pitching as evidenced by Wood and other recent picks of the Cubs. The scouting staff consists of 19 area scouts and three regional supervisors or crosscheckers. Internationally, the Cubs effort has come mostly in the Caribbean. They have signed players from Columbia, the Dominican Republic, Panama and Venezuela.

The Cubs have given up on hosting open tryouts for players who were not drafted. They will, however, hold a personal tryout for someone that draws their interest.

Best Picks

One of the best Cubs picks came in the first draft. The Cubs selected University of Illinois pitcher **Ken Holtzman** in the fourth round. He pitched in the minors for a short time before the bottom-dwelling Cubs called up the 20-year-old phenom in his first season. The following year, Holtzman posted an 11-16 record for the last-place Chicago northside team. He was unbeatable in 1967. He went 9-0 in a season shortened by military service. In 1969, with the Cubs in the pennant hunt, the right-hander pitched his first no-hitter. Then in 1971, the Cubs traded him for the first-ever first-year free-agent draft pick, Rick Monday. Holtzman returned to the Cubs in 1978 and played there until his retirement.

The Cubs selected **Burt Hooton** in the first round of the June secondary phase in 1971 and brought him to Chicago for a game with the Cubs before he was sent to the minors. However, he was back the next season. His performance for the Cubs went downhill and after a losing record four seasons in a row he was dealt to Los Angeles. He fared much better with the Dodgers where he was an All-Star one season. The knuckleballer ended up with a career mark of 151-136.

Greg Maddux was just a second round pick in 1984 out of high school. He soon showed he probably deserved first-round consideration as he was an all-star in the Appalachian League in his rookie year. He continued his all-star ways in the minors, but struggled when he was first called up to the Cubs as he recorded two losing seasons in a row. He found the winning formula in 1988 and helped lead the Cubs to first place in 1989. Maddux won his first Cy Young Award in 1992 with the Cubs when he was 20-11 with a 2.18 ERA. He became a free agent and decided to go to Atlanta where he has led the Braves to postseason play each season. He dominated the Cy Young Award the next three seasons. Maddux is a complete player as he has also won nine Gold Gloves awards and can hit. He has appeared in three All-Star games. About his only downfall has been lackluster performances in the

Greg Maddux, with the Atlanta Braves, was a second round pick by the Cubs in 1984. (Photograph by Marty Orr.)

postseason. He picked up two losses in the League Championship Series in 1997 with led to the Braves' demise. He is 2-2 in two World Series.

While we are on the subject of pitchers, the best reliever in Cubs history was also a draft pick. **Lee Smith**, a second round pick in 1975, retired in 1998 with more saves than any pitcher in the history of the game. He saved 478 games over his 18-year career, eight with the Cubs. Smith also ranks first in Cubs history in relief appearances with 452 and saves with 180. He also holds the National League record for the most saves in a season with 47, which was achieved in 1992 with the Cardinals. He saved 33 games and won nine in 1984 to became an integral part of the Cubs' winning the Eastern Division title. He also picked up a save in Game 2 of the League Championship Series, but lost in Game 4. The Cubs made a poor decision when they traded him to the Red Sox for pitchers Al Nipper and Calvin Schiraldi. Smith continued his saving ways for another nine seasons, while Nipper and Schiraldi couldn't manage a winning season. The trade ranks second to the Lou Brock blunder a year before the draft began.

Enough about pitchers. The Cubs made some great draft picks in the 1980s that helped them toward first-place finishes. **Shawon Dunston** was the Cubs' number one pick in the June 1982 regular draft. Scout Gary Nichels signed him for a reported $135,000 bonus. He was an all-star for his first three years in the minors then the Cubs called him up. The shortstop with a rifle arm became an asset on the field, in the dugout and in the stands where his favorite fans kept track of his batting average with the "Shawn-O-Meter." Dunston ran into back injury problems for a couple of seasons before the Cubs rejected his offers to stay. He went to the Giants before coming back to the Cubs again for a season. In all, he was with the Cubs during parts of 12 seasons. He appeared in one All-Star Game and helped the Cubs to the League Championship Series in 1989. In 1999 he was with St. Louis. "I still don't know why they took me over Dwight Gooden," he said.

Mark Grace has turned into one of the best pure hitters in baseball. Spider Jorgensen must have looked into a crystal ball when he scouted Grace because the Cubs waited until the 24th

Mark Grace, a Cubs 24th round choice in 1985.
(Photograph by Marty Orr.)

they chose **Kerry Wood** in the first round of the 1995 draft. Wood was an all–American and Texas 5-A Player of the Year at Grand Prairie High School. After scout Bill Capps signed him, the young pitcher quickly moved up the Cubs farm system as he struck out more than a batter per inning with his big league fastball. Wood debuted on April 12, 1998, against Montreal and earned his first loss. Three weeks later he mowed down 20 Houston Astros to tie a major league record owned by Roger Clemens for most strikeouts in a game. He became an overnight success. He continued to dominate hitters and outdueled ex–Cub Greg Maddux in a victory in July over Atlanta. He set the Cubs' 20th century single-season rookie strikeout record August 31 against Cincinnati. Elbow troubles sidelined him in September and he had only a brief appearance in the playoffs. However, he became the first Cub to reach the 200-mark since Ferguson Jenkins in 1971. He ended the year with a 13-6 mark, 3.40 ERA. Unfortunately, Wood's fame may have been short-lived as he suffered elbow problems and had to undergo Tommy John surgery in the spring of 1999. He was expected to return to action in the next century.

The Cubs chose **Rafael Palmeiro** in the first round in 1985 and called him up the next season after he batted .306 in Double-A and was picked for the all-star team. He became a regular outfielder on the team the next season. The Cubs dealt him the next season in a multi-player trade. The result was a first-place finish in 1989 for the Cubs, but they lost the services of a player who has gotten better and better each year. In the 1990s, the left-handed power hitter became one of the best home run hitters and RBI leaders in the league. By 1998, he had hit 318 homers, won two Gold Gloves in the outfield and appeared in two All-Star games, which was better than a lot of outfielders the Cubs have had until Sammy Sosa showed up.

Another great outfielder the Cubs traded before he turned into a superstar was **Joe Carter**, a first-round pick in 1981 who was signed by scout Buck O'Neil. Carter also was dealt in a multi-player trade which turned out to be an immediate return as the Cubs got Rick Sutcliffe, who was 16-1 the rest of the 1984 season and helped the Cubs to a first-place finish. Carter

round in 1985 to pick him. Grace proved right away he was better than a 500-to-1 shot to make it to the majors. He was an all-star both seasons he spent in the minors before getting the call to Chicago in his third professional season. He batted .296 his rookie year then helped lead the Cubs to the League Championship Series in 1989 with a .314 average. Ten years later he helped the team again to a wild-card berth. The lifetime .310 hitter has won four Gold Glove awards and been named to three All-Star games. The Cubs exercised an option on him for the 1999 season because of his consistency. Grace entered the 1999 campaign ranking in the Cubs' Top 10 in nine major offensive categories.

The Cubs concentration on pitchers in the first round over the years finally paid off when took a couple of seasons before he became a home-run power hitter and RBI machine. By the time he retired after the 1998 season, he had accumulated 396 homers and 10 seasons with more than 100 RBI. He was named to five All-Star teams.

Long Shots

Rick Wilkens wasn't chosen until the 23rd round in 1986 out of Florida Community College. He gained the attention of the organization right away when he was picked as an all-star in his rookie season at Class A Geneva. He moved up the minors steadily until getting a call midway through the 1991 season. He had his career year in 1993 when he batted .303 with 30 homers. Then the bottom dropped out and he was traded to Houston after dipping below the Mendoza Line two years later. He has since had many problems trying to hit major league pitching again and has bounced back and forth from the minors to the majors with several teams.

Odds are about 10,000 to 1 that a 74th round pick will make it to the majors, but **Jason Maxwell** beat those odds in 1998. The infielder earned a September call-up in 1998 after hitting .298 with 15 homers at Class AAA Iowa. He pinch-hit in his first game on Sept. 1 and struck out. But later in the month he hit a home run. He may fit in as a utility player in the future as he also played shortstop during his five full seasons in the minors. He has the versatility for such a role. The Middle Tennessee State player has certainly done better than many others drafted before him.

Disappointments

The list of Cubs' disappointments is longer than most teams. The Cubs have not had great success with number-one draft picks except for a couple that were previously mentioned.

The Cubs' very first draft pick in 1965, pitcher **Rick James**, threw just three games in the majors. The following year the Cubs picked another pitcher first—**Dean Burk**. The right-hander peaked at Triple-A.

In fact, the failures with first picks continued for awhile. The second pick in the 1967 draft was **Terry Hughes**. The shortstop played just two games with the Cubs and 54 in the majors.

The next number one was **Ralph Rickey**. The outfielder only made it to Triple-A.

In 1971 the Cubs chose pitcher **Jeff Wehmeier** out of high school. The right-hander never made it above Class A. Nor did the next pitcher the next year, **Brian Vernoy**.

After a couple of good picks, the Cubs chose **Brian Rosinski** in the first round from nearby Evanston High School and he got as far as Triple-A.

First rounder **Herm Segelke** in 1976 got only a cup of coffee in the majors. The right-handed pitcher earned an ERA of 8.31 in three games.

The Cubs picked **Mike Sember** in the second round of the 1976 draft out of Tulsa University to become an infielder for their future. Sember had played only one year of baseball at Bishop Noll Institute, a Catholic high school in Hammond, Ind. He was the starting quarterback on the football team, a starting point guard on the basketball team and became the starting shortstop on the senior baseball team after not playing the sport in four years. He was named as the most valuable athlete in the school.

The excellent athlete wanted to play more than one sport in college, but he found that difficult. "Back then it was tough to find a university that would let you play two sports," he recalled from his home in Boca Raton, Florida. He went to Tulsa University on a football scholarship. He tried out for the baseball team, but didn't make the cut. However, the baseball coach called him back later to play as a utility player.

After his senior year, the Cubs picked him and signed him for $40,000. He was assigned to Double-A. By 1977 he had advanced to the 40-man roster. When Mick Kelleher broke a finger in August, Sember got his calling from the Cubs. He appeared in a few games the rest of the season.

The following year he didn't get a call up until September. "What happened is that the Cubs' whole starting infield, outfield and catcher came from somewhere else," he explained. "The only thing we had that was home grown was the pitching staff. All the guys that were having good minor league development had nowhere to go."

Sember was waived by the Cubs and he was picked up by the Blue Jays. After being assigned to Triple-A and not seeing much action, he retired. The Cubs were probably more of a disappointment to him than vice versa. He wasn't given much of a chance.

Bill Hayes, a first round catcher from Indiana State in 1978, also got a cup of java.

Then in 1983 the Cubs spent their first round pick on **Jackie Davidson**. The right-handed hurler never made it past Triple-A.

Jerome Walton, a second round pick in the January 1986 regular phase, started off great as he was an all-star twice in the minors and the Rookie of the Year in 1989 when he came up with the Cubs. Two years later his batting average sunk to .219 and he became a disappointment with Chicago. His average sank to .127 the next season, so he was let go at the end of the season. Walton became a free agent and signed with the Angels and went back to the minors to find his stroke. He found it and became a productive centerfielder again with several other teams.

The Cubs chose **Ty Griffin** in the first round in 1988. He peaked at Double-A.

The Cubs thought they had a good draft in 1989 when they picked **Earl Cunningham** in the first round. Cunningham was a power hitter who set a state record with 34 homers in high school. At Wrigley Field he wouldn't have any problem clearing the ivy. After five years in the minors, the Cubs gave up on the prospect after he showed he was better at striking out than hitting home runs in the minors. He hit below the Mendoza Line at Class A Peoria in 1993 to earn a release from the Cubs. He tried with three other organizations and never made it with them either.

Then the following year the Cubs drafted left-handed picking prospect **Lance Dickson** in the first round. The Cubs decided to call him up that same year and he failed miserably. After that season, he never made it back to the majors.

The Cubs hoped **Kevin Orie** would be their third baseman of the future when they drafted him in the first round in 1993. After he was drafted, he was astounded by the signing process. "Negotiations were a little more than I thought would happen," he explained. "Basi-

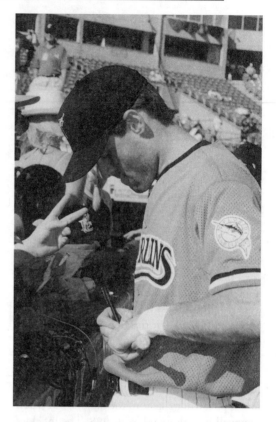

First round draft choice in 1993, Kevin Orie, shown here with the Marlins.

cally, they pick you and then they come in your house and tell you how bad you are. That was surprising." His dad handled negotiations. The Indiana University student had some leverage in the signing process because he was a junior.

Orie got off to a slow start and played three years at Single-A before climbing the ladder. Then he skyrocketed through Double-A and Triple-A in one season. He earned a starting spot out of spring training in 1997 and played decently, but didn't put up the numbers the Cubs were looking for at third. After a miserable start in 1998 by hitting below his weight, the Cubs dealt him to the Marlins, where he recovered.

At spring training in 1999 he had more than baseball on his mind. Coming off the field after a game against Houston, a fellow player told him that girls were waiting for them after they got cleaned up — shades of *Bull Durham*. Baseball wasn't the only thing on his mind.

Best Draft

Some good players from top to bottom were produced in 1985. The top pick was **Rafael Palmeiro**, who has had an outstanding career with other teams. The bottom pick was **Mark Grace** in the 24th round. The others included **Doug Dascenzo** and **Rick Wrona**. Dascenzo played outfield with the Cubs for five seasons during his seven years in the majors. Wrona was a backup catcher for the Cubs for three seasons before going to three other teams over a six-year career.

Worst Draft

The year 1990 was a real downer. Three players from that class made the majors, but none had any success. **Lance Dickson** was a failure; **Ryan Hawblitzel** was shipped out; and **Pedro Valdes** couldn't hit major league pitching and was released.

All in the Family

Hanging out with those players more interested in off-the-field activities was one of the reasons **Jim Boudreau**, son of the famed Cleveland All-Star shortstop Lou Boudreau, listed for not making it to the majors. Boudreau was taken in the 22nd round of the 1982 draft as a pitcher out of Arizona State University. The Cubs gave him a $2,500 bonus. Jim feels his father didn't play a significant part in his draft other than drawing a little more attention his way. He was completely opposite from his dad. His dad was an infielder and right-handed hitter. Jim was a left-handed pitcher and didn't have to worry about hitting.

Another reason Jim said for his not making it to the majors was his off-season workouts. He admits now he should have increased his velocity to achieve new pitches. "I was a finesse pitcher and depended on control as opposed to velocity," he explained.

Now a recruiting manager for the Lante Corporation, a computer consulting company in Chicago, he is amazed by the amount of money that is currently being offered to draftees. "It used to be an honor and the money was sec-

Jim Boudreau, drafted by the Cubs in the 22nd round in 1982. (Photograph courtesy of Jim Boudreau.)

ondary when drafted," he commented. "You have unproved players basing what they want on the amount of money the person ahead and behind them got to sign. It's not what is used to be. It's all about money now."

When the Cubs picked **Greg Maddux** in 1984, his brother was at Double-A ball with the Phillies. Yet 1986 became both of their rookie seasons in the majors and they ended up facing each other once to mark the first time that rookie brother pitchers had ever opposed each other in the majors.

The Cubs picked **Dave Amaro**, son of Cubs coach Ruben, as their 24th pick in June 1984. He failed to make the majors though.

There are many players in the history of the game that have played only one game in the majors. After the 1998 season, **Justin Speier** could include himself in that category, but the 55th rounder for the Cubs hopes it doesn't stop there. The son of former Cubs shortstop Chris Speier pitched in relief in one game in May 1998 before getting sent back to Triple-A Iowa, where he picked up 12 saves on the season.

Where Are They Now?

Derrick May, a number one pick in 1986, played five seasons with the Cubs before he went on the road like some rock band. He ended up playing in Milwaukee, Houston, Philadelphia and Montreal before landing on the Rochester Red Wings, the Triple-A affiliate of the Orioles, in 1999. The lifetime .271 hitter with 48 homers in 771 at bats never turned out to be the power hitter the Cubs had hoped for so he was let go.

Derrick May with the Rochester Red Wings; he was a number one draft pick in 1986 for Chicago.

Damon Farmar, a second round pick in the June 1982 secondary phase, became a hitting coach in the Cubs farm system after playing with the Cubs, Oakland, Baltimore, California and Cincinnati organizations.

Also turning to coaching was **Stan Kyles**, a fourth-round selection in 1979 after graduating from Chicago's Wendell Phillips High School. He became a pitching coach in the Cubs' farm system after pitching for 11 seasons in the minors.

Die-hard Cub fans remember the Evers-to-Tinker-to-Chance double-play combination early in the 20th century. The Cubs may have been thinking about that when they drafted **Bill Evers**, no relation to the famed Johnny Evers, in the sixth round of the June 1976 Secondary

Phase. This Evers was a first baseman though and played four years in the minors before turning to coaching instead of playing. He has coached with the Cubs, Yankees and Giants.

Also with the Devil Rays is former player **Billy Hatcher**, a sixth round pick in 1981, is now the first base coach with the Devil Rays. Hatcher played 12 seasons with seven clubs.

Billy Hatcher, a Chicago Cubs sixth round pick in 1981.

Steve Roadcap, an 18th round pick in 1982, played five minor league seasons as a catcher. He turned to managing after playing and has been manager in the Cubs farm system ever since 1988. He took over the reigns of Class A-Wisconsin in 1999.

Another player turned manager is **Dan Rohn**, a fourth round pick in 1977. Rohn had a brief career in the majors with the Cubs and Indians before turning to managing. Now he is the manager with the Class AA–New Haven in the Mariners' system.

Jim Tracy, a fourth-round pick in 1977, played a couple of seasons with the Cubs before going Japan to play. When he returned to the

States he went into coaching and managing. Now he is coaching with the Dodgers.

Gary Scott, a second round pick in 1989, couldn't prove himself at third base in two seasons and was traded on the day of the 1992 expansion draft. It was not entirely all his fault as the Cubs didn't give him much seasoning in the minors, but they needed somebody at third base. After playing in the minors in four organizations and failing to get back to the majors, Scott called it quits. Now he sells real estate in South Carolina.

Some Who Didn't Sign

The Cubs have had several good players slip through their hands and sign with other teams later. In the first draft, the Cubs picked **Darrell Evans** in the 13th round. He went on to a 21-year career in the majors with other teams.

Ken Forsch was a fourth round selection in the June Secondary Phase draft in 1967. The pitcher went to Houston instead and spent 16 seasons in the majors.

The Cubs picked **Terry Francona** in the 2nd round of the 1977 draft, but he didn't sign.

Tom Henke could have worn a Cubs uniform had he signed when drafted in the first round of the January Secondary Phase of the 1980 draft. He waited until June when Texas drafted him before signing. He made a name for himself north of the border in Toronto.

The Cubs selected **Jeff King** in the 23rd round in 1983 when he graduated from high school. King went to the University of Arkansas and waited until Pittsburgh picked him in the first round in 1986.

The Cubs first had **Kevin Tapani** in their grips in 1985 when they picked him in the ninth round. He didn't sign then, so the Cubs traded for him later and he ended up on the 1998 wild-card team.

The Cubs wasted a pick in the January 1985 draft when they took **Gary Geiger**, son of a 12-year player with the same name. Geiger never signed.

Undrafted Players

The Cubs spotted **Dave Pavlas** in an amateur league while he was enrolled in graduate school and signed him to a contract in 1984. The pitcher wasn't drafted out of high school or at Rice University. The right-handed hurler worked his way up to the Cubs in 1990 with little success. He ended up in the Mexican League for a couple of seasons before returning to American baseball during the 1995 strike. He pitched in a couple of replacement games and was labeled a "scab," although he had only signed a minor league contract with the Yankees. Later in the season, he was called up to the Yankees. Team captain Don Mattingly objected to the pitcher and told reporters, "Basically, I'm going to treat him like a scab, to tell you the truth." Pavlas went over to Japan in 1997. He has also played in Italy and Taiwan.

On the Roster

The Cubs started 1999 with a baker's dozen of their own draft picks on their roster, which was about average among major league teams. The roster included only a few players who were never drafted, such as Jeremi Gonzalez of Venezuela.

Steve Trachsel was selected by the Cubs in the eighth round in 1991 out of Long Beach State University and scouted by Gene Handley. He progressed quickly through the minors and was pitching with the Cubs by the end of 1993. He became a regular starter in 1994. His career has been good and bad. He has followed every losing season with a winning season. Fortunately for the Cubs, Trachsel had his best year in 1998 when he went 15-8 to help the Cubs to a wild card playoff berth. He has also contributed with the bat and has become one of the best hitting pitchers in the National League.

Another Cubs original on the pitching staff was **Terry Adams**. The fourth round pick in 1991 out of high school, who was scouted by Jeff Kahn, began his career as a starter, but didn't begin to get better until he was used as a closer in the minors. The Cubs put him in that role in 1997 when Mel Rojas was unproductive and he responded with 18 saves. Yet the Cubs went out and got Rob Beck, a more proven performer. Adams did appear in 63 games during 1998 to contribute much to the relief staff.

Robin Jennings was on the verge of

becoming a regular on the team in 1999, but suffered an injury to prevent that from happening. Scout Joe Housey found the outfielder at Manatee Junior College and he was drafted not until the 33rd round in 1991. He had been drafted in the 30th round the year before by Baltimore. He was an all-star twice in the minors before getting a call from the Cubs in 1996. He also got a call the next year, but injuries held back his progress in 1998.

Kyle Farnsworth, a 47th round pick in 1994 scouted by Preston Douglas, also got the call to the Cubs in 1999 when the club was hit with pitching injuries early in the season. He was 13-11 in Double-A and Triple-A in 1998. The tall right-hander has a fastball in the mid-'90s and fools batters with a split-fingered fastball as well. The Cubs put him in the starting rotation and he responded well.

Rich Barker was another pitcher who got an early call from the Cubs in April 1999. The 33rd round draft pick in 1994, who was signed by scout Ed Ford, had worked his way up to Triple-A by 1998 as a reliever. He had 16 saves in Double-A in 1998.

A 40th round selection to get a call up in 1999 when injuries put Cubs outfielders on the disabled list was **Bo Porter**, who was scouted by Ed Ford out of high school. A star defensive back at the University of Iowa, this Bo knows baseball better and picked it over football. Porter was mired in Class A for four seasons until making his move up the ladder after being named an all-star in 1997 in the Florida State League. He had five homers in the month of April 1999 to earn the promotion.

Future Stars?

If the Cubs need a left-handed hurler soon, they may turn to **Brian McNichol**, a second round pick in 1995 scouted by Billy Swoope. He got off to a slow start by being on the disabled list in his second year in the minors. He moved up to Triple-A in 1998 after a 12-9 record in Double-A.

Pat Cline may be the next Cubs catcher to come up from the minors. Selected by Cubs in the 6th round of the 1993 draft and scouted by Joe Housey, Cline got off to a slow start as he

missed his second pro season because of wrist surgery. He rebounded from it to make the Florida State League All-Star team in 1996. He has worked his way up to Triple-A and has sufficient skills to break into the majors soon.

Chad Meyers was an all-American in his junior year at Creighton University to attract scouts and get selected by the Cubs in the fifth round in 1996. He was an all-star in the Midwest League to earn a promotion to Double-A. The speedy second baseman batted .290 and stole 60 bases in 1998. He could be a leadoff hitter for the Cubs once he gets to the majors because of his speed and lack of power.

Another catching prospect who is several years away is **Jeff Goldbach**, a second round pick in 1998. The Princeton High School graduate was highly recruited and talked to all 30 teams. "I was surprised they [the Cubs] picked me," he said. He signed two weeks later for a bonus of $440,000.

Scout Scott May became interested in Goldbach in his sophomore year. Interest turned to passion after he led the state in homers in his junior year. Then he led the Indiana Bulls 17-year-old squad to a national championship and was named Most Valuable Player. He was also first team All-State and first team All-American in his senior year.

Goldbach put up some good numbers in his rookie season: .272-4-25 along with 11 doubles. And he hit around .300 in the Fall Instructional League. "My goal is to take a level a year and get there [to the majors] as soon as possible," he commented.

One of the toughest first-round picks to sign in 1998 was **Corey Patterson**, the third pick overall. It took the Chicago Cubs and more than three months after the draft to sign the high school outfielder. Patterson reportedly signed for $2.89 million. He astounded scout Oneri Fleita by hitting .528 with 22 home runs and 61 RBI in leading his team to a state title. He signed too late to play in 1998. He began 1999 in Class A.

Ben Christensen had the highest winning percentage (.955) in Wichita State history, which is one of the reasons the Cubs drafted him in the first round in 1999. He amassed a 21-1 record during his three seasons there. He was scouted by Mark Servais. "We think Ben is an outstanding prospect," said Jim Hendry, the Cubs' director of player development and scouting. "He comes from a great program, and we were very pleased that a player of his talent was available to us when it was our time to choose."

The Cubs picked controversial pitcher **Ryan Christenson** as its first pick in the 1999 draft. Christenson was suspended by the Missouri Val-ley Conference for the remainer of the 1999 season after hitting Anthony Molina in the face with a warm-up pitch. Molina was 24 feet away from home plate when Christenson took aim and beaned him. The pitcher said he was only doing what his coach ordered and was only trying to hit him in the waist. Instead, he shattered his eye and ended Molina's baseball career.

Cincinnati Reds

Cincinnati got off to a fast start with the draft system as the team picked the right players from the beginning and produced the Big Red Machine of the 1970s. Many of the players from those championship teams can trace their roots to the first few drafts. Among those was the first draft pick to be inducted into the Baseball Hall of Fame — Johnny Bench.

After winning six pennants in the 1970s, the club couldn't get above second place in the next decade. Then the team's scouting department became confused with the influx of conflicting reports from the Major League Scouting Bureau. The result was poor draft choices and a funk in the 1980s. The Reds scouts went their own way and began to find some talent on their own. The Reds rebounded in the 1990s to win three pennants and a World Series championship despite being a small market team. However, the team has not fared well since 1995.

The Reds strategy was to take the best player available, regardless of position. That's what the team did in 1996, 1997 and 1998. Those number-one picks were sluggers, not pitchers. After that, the Reds concentrated on pitching. In the 1998 draft, 15 of the first 25 were pitchers.

However, that philosophy is changing now that the Reds will have a new stadium in 2002. Cinergy Field, a circular city-owned stadium built in the 1970s, will be replaced by a stadium just for baseball. The Reds used to rely on speed because of the Astroturf, but the new field will be a natural surface, explained scouting director DeJon Watson. And because right field will be shorter, the Reds are now looking for lefthanded power hitters and left-handed pitchers.

Historically, the Reds have been more inclined to draft high school picks to get young talent into their system early. Watson has continued that tradition. "You have to be aggressive and go after the younger kids," Watson explained. The Reds have also gone after players with speed in order to react better to the fast field that they play on.

Watson, who has been with the Reds for two years, knows a lot about the draft from a personal viewpoint. He was drafted himself in 1985 by the Kansas City Royals in the third round. "So I know what they're going through," he said frankly.

Marge Schott's tightness for money is now history as she has been forced out of the decision making process by Major League Baseball. She used to anger some players during her regime for being too tight. Eric Davis was once forced to pay for plane fare, which made him a little angry. However, other players had great respect for her. For example, former Reds player Jon Nunnally liked her because she was straight-shooter and "told it like it was." You knew where you stood with her.

The tightness on the money was put to the wayside in 1999 when the Reds spent millions to get free agent Greg Vaughn from the San Diego Padres. The home-run hitter turned the Reds into a competitor again early in the 1999 season.

The Reds hate to lose players who run out of options, so they give their draft picks every chance possible. They also don't like to put someone on the waiver wire and would rather trade with another team.

The Reds are investing more in international scouting as well. They opened a new academy in the Dominican in 1998. It has five fields, dorms, and classrooms to teach English and other amenities for the foreign players. The Reds opened an academy in Venezuela in 1999 and now have 20 players under contract there. The team has a presence in Panama, too, as it has signed nine players there. They are also interested in players from Aruba, Columbia and Nicaragua. In the Pacific Rim area, they have looked for talent in places like Thailand. "You have to be aggressive and go after the younger kids," said Watson. The Reds would be ready for an international draft if one were held, but Watson refused to answer questions on changes to the draft.

Watson uses the draft-and-follow rule and has signed several players to follow for future needs. In the 1999 draft, he signed left-handed pitcher Matt Lynch out of high school in the 46th round. Lynch had a fastball in the low 90s and a good-breaking curveball. Another draft-and-follow was 39th round pick Josh Andrade, a right-handed pitcher with a fastball in the low 90s, too. The same was true of Scott Hindman, a left-handed hurler in the 48th round. He was going on to Princeton University.

The Reds do a good job of signing their draft picks. The average is around 50 percent, but Cincinnati signed more than 65 percent of its draft picks in 1998 and were well on their way to doing the same in 1999.

The Reds are still very high on open tryout camps. They host camps throughout the country that their area scouts conduct to look at players who may have slipped through the cracks somehow. However, the number of youngsters that come to these tryouts has been dwindling every year.

An unusually cool day descended on Indianapolis on June 15, 1999. It was the type of day that reminded one of Minnesota instead of a city in the heartland of the country where temperatures exceeded 90 degrees just a week before. The sun as well as David Jennings greeted about 100 youngsters who had gathered at Victory Field, the home of the Indianapolis Indians, in the hopes of getting noticed by Jennings. The eight-year scout had never once signed a prospect straight out of a tryout, but there was always hope. None of these kids knew that fact and even if they did, they would still try to buck the odds. Maybe one out of a thousand is signed to a major league contract on the spot. Jeff

Treadway was signed by the Reds scout at a tryout very much like the one Jennings would hold on the crisp day.

The Cincinnati scout ran the players through their paces. A 60-yard dash gave the scout an indication of their speed. Then he viewed the throwing and fielding abilities. Did anyone have a gun for an arm? Did they field like Ozzie Smith? After a couple of hours of evaluations, it was time to test the pitchers out on the batters. Mike Anderson who had just graduated from Chesterton High School lit up the radar gun with his 87-mph fastball and got Jennings' attention. The right-handed hurler was just 2-5 on the season with an ERA somewhere between 2 and 3. He didn't know. "I had a terrible infield behind me," he explained. A teammate of his agreed with the analysis. Scouts didn't find their way to little Chesterton, so he went unnoticed. That's why he came to the tryout. He had tried out for the Pirates the year before when he was a junior, but they didn't draft him.

"I'd give it [baseball] one year," Jennings told the youngster. The six-foot lad could get stronger and bigger over that year and increase his fastball to 90. Then he'd get noticed more. The Reds were looking for hard throwers, like most teams. If a pitcher sent the gun above 90, then he stood a chance of getting signed immediately, if not sooner.

Another lefthander sent the radar gun up to 87 during the tryout, but he had about as much control as Mark Wohlers, who the Reds were hoping to harness as well. He hit a batter who brushed it off and stood in there again like some major leaguer. They didn't need a project. They needed a pitcher.

Few hitters did much against the mediocre pitching of the day. Mediocre in comparison with Major League pitching that is. One player did display some power by hitting a homer in left field. Nobody cheered. The crowd of 50 onlookers, mostly wives, girlfriends or parents, just sat there like crows on a telephone wire. There would be no cheers in Mudville this day. Casey has struck out.

"There's a couple of young guys that I'll keep up with," Jennings said. He'd love to sign someone at a tryout camp, but he's yet to do that.

Jennings never played baseball professionally, but he does love the game though and that counted for a lot. His brother, Dan, was the scouting director for the Tampa Bay Devil Rays, so perhaps scouting ran in their bloodline.

Best Picks

The Reds had the right idea about the draft in its first year. They picked **Johnny Bench** in the second round. He became the first draft pick to enter the Baseball Hall of Fame. Bench, who was part Choctaw Indian, was a great player at several positions at Anadarko High School in Binger, Okla. He compiled a 16-1 record as a pitcher. But the Reds wanted him on the other side of the plate. He was so good in the minors that he bypassed Double-A altogether going from Class A Peninsula to Triple-A Buffalo. A broken thumb stopped him from getting a September call-up. The following season he slammed 23 home runs at Buffalo and was named Minor League Player of the Year. This time Cincinnati called him up for the final month of the season. In his first full season in the majors, he was named Rookie of the Year. In 1970 he became the youngest player in the National League to be named Most Valuable Player. He helped Cincinnati become the Big Red Machine in the 1970s as he twice led the league in home runs and three times in RBI. He was named to the All-Star Team a total of 14 times out of his 17 years in the majors. The catcher was a great fielder as well and won nine Gold Gloves in a row. In all, he hit 389 lifetime homers, the most

Johnny Bench (right) and Ken Griffey, both drafted by the Reds. (Photograph by Marty Orr.)

by any catcher in the history of the game. He also set single season standards for catcher with 45 homers and 148 RBI. He was named to the Hall of Fame in 1989.

Another player who was taken in the first draft and served a long time was **Hal McRae**. Cincinnati's sixth pick played 23 years of pro baseball with 19 seasons in the majors with the Reds and Royals. McRae made his debut with the Reds in 1968 and was there to stay in 1970. He appeared in two World Series with the Reds in 1970 and 1972. After being traded with Wayne Simpson for Roger Nelson and Richie Scheinblum in 1972, McRae came of age and began putting up numbers that landed him on the All-Star Team three times. He appeared twice more in the World Series with the Royals. By the time his career was over, he had hit over .300 six times, including a career high .332 in 1976, which was one percentage point behind league leader and teammate George Brett. He hit .400 in 17 World Series games. Hal's son, Brian, followed his footsteps and was playing for the Mets in 1999. Meanwhile, Hal was the hitting instructor for the Philadelphia Phillies.

The first-round choice in the June 1996 draft was **Gary Nolan**. The Reds wasted no time with the high school player and put him in the pitching rotation the next season at age 18. He showed he could handle the promotion and was 14-8 his first season. At the end of the season he won a game in the League Championship Series, but lost one in the World Series. His best season for the Reds came in 1972 when he was 15-5 to lead the league in winning percentage. He appeared in four World Series for the Big Red Machine before going to the California Angels in 1977, his last season in the majors. His career mark was 110-70.

After the Reds grabbed **Don Gullett** as their first choice in the June 1969 draft they wasted little time bringing him up. He pitched just 11 games in the minors before jumping to the majors as a 19-year-old rookie in 1970. And it didn't take him long to make his mark on the team and the league. He led the National League the next season in winning percentage (.727) with a 16-6 record. In fact, over a four-year span from 1973 to 1976, Gullett posted a combined record of 61-26 (.701 winning percentage). He appeared in four World Series for the Big Red Machine before becoming a free agent after the 1976 season and signing with the Yankees, where he appeared in two World Series. A rotator cuff injury ended his career prematurely in 1978. Gullett finished his career with a 109-50 record and a 3.11 ERA. His .686 career winning percentage is third best in modern big league history for pitchers with at least 100 victories. Later, he returned to the Reds as a pitching coach.

Barry Larkin may just be the next drafted Reds player to be named to the Baseball Hall of Fame if he continues his brilliant career. After being drafted in the first round in 1985 out of the University of Michigan, he began at Double-A. Then he was promoted to Triple-A the next season and hit .329 with 10 homers to earn a call to the Reds, where he has been ever since. By the next season, he was being named to the All-Star Team and has been on 10 teams since then. Then he began winning Gold Gloves in 1994 and has earned three so far. Larkin hit .353 in the 1990 World Series to help the Reds sweep Oakland. He has hit .317 in 10 League Championship Series games in his Reds career. In 1995, he was named Most Valuable Player as he hit .319 with 15 homers, 51 stolen bases, and a Gold Glove. He followed that with a career high 33 homers the next season. In his career, he has 315 steals in 372 attempts, one of the highest success rates in baseball history (.847).

Eights were wild when it came to **Eric Davis**. He was an eighth-round pick in 1980 and spent eight years with the Reds the first time he was with the team. The speedy outfielder played parts of two seasons with the team before he became a permanent fixture in 1986. He streaked to 80 stolen bases his first year and clubbed 27 homers. The following year he won the first of three successive Gold Gloves playing centerfield and swiped about 50 bases while hitting a career-high 37 home runs. He was also named to his first All-Star Team. Injuries began to curtail his playing time, so the Reds let him become a free agent and he signed with the Dodgers. He was traded to Detroit where a herniated disc in his back nearly put him out of baseball. He took a year off before coming back to the majors again with the Reds. Then he

signed with Orioles. During the 1997 season he was diagnosed with colon cancer. He had surgery to remove the cancer and took three months off. In 1998 he played with the Orioles again and was named as the American League Comeback Player of the Year.

Paul O'Neill, a fourth-round draft pick in 1981, was about to become a regular member of the Reds when he was injured and set back. He finally became a mainstay with Cincinnati in 1988. He helped the Reds tremendously in the League Championship Series in 1990 when he hit .471. The following season he hit a career high 28 homers and was named to his first All-Star Game. When he slumped to a .246 batting average in 1992, the Reds dealt him to the Yankees for Roberto Kelly. O'Neill rebounded to a .311 average the next season in New York and he has broke .300 every year since. Then he ballooned to .359 in 1994 to win the batting title and another spot on an All-Star Team. In 1998, he was named to his fifth All-Star Team and had a career-high 17-game hitting streak on his way to a .317 average with 24 homers and a career high 116 RBI.

Scout Gene Bennett noticed **Chris Sabo** when he broke a collarbone in a collision with a catcher at home plate in 1981. Two years later the Reds drafted him in the second round and Bennett signed him. Sabo proved he was a good choice as he became the National League Rookie of the Year in 1988. In the 1990 World Series, he hit .563 to help the team to the championship. Reds manager Pete Rose loved him because he reminded him of himself. The reckless style of Sabo proved his downfall, however. His career ended in 1996 in Cincinnati after trips to Baltimore, Chicago and St. Louis.

Long Shots

Back in 1969, the Reds selected **Ken Griffey** in the 29th round because of his arm and speed. He had received a college scholarship offer to play football, but the Reds were offering him $500 a month to play baseball. That was a lot of money to him at the time. He needed a lot of work to become a successful baseball player. With time, he developed into a solid hitter. A scout made the observation in 1973 that Griffey had the ability to play in majors but was a year or two away. He proved that scout wrong by sticking in the majors in 1973. He became part of the Big Red Machine and ended up playing 19 seasons in the majors. And he passed those baseball genes on to his son, who is turning out to be a better player than his dad.

Jerry Spradlin was a 19th round pick in 1988 out of junior college. The reliever came up with the Reds in 1993. After a dismal performance in 1994 — 10.13 ERA in six games — he was put on waivers and claimed by the Marlins. A year later he was granted free agency and signed with the Reds, who released him in 1996. He signed on with the Phillies and played two seasons for Philadelphia before being traded to the Indians.

Disappointments

The Reds didn't have its first first-round disappointment until 1968 when it picked **Tim Grant** out of high school. The right-hander couldn't get beyond Class A.

While the Big Red Machine was racing to championships in the 1970s, the team wasn't getting much out of its first round picks during that same time. **Gene Polczynski** was the first choice in 1970. The shortstop got as far as Double-A. Shortstop **Mike Miley** refused to sign after he was picked in the first round the next year. The following year the Reds picked pitcher **Larry Payne**, who peaked at Triple-A. **Charles Kessler** made it three bad years in a row when he failed to go beyond Double-A. The streak continued when the Reds chose **Steve Reed** in the first round in 1974. The right-handed pitcher made it up to Triple-A. First round outfielder **Tony Moretto** kept the string of poor choices going the next year as he could only get to Double-A. **Mark King** could only pitch his way to Class A after being selected in the first round in 1976 to keep the streak intact. The last poor pick in the string was **Tad Venger**, a third baseman. He also peaked at Class A. The last first-round pick in the 1970s was **Mike Sullivan** and the pitcher only reached Double-A. Of course many of those first-round selections came at the end of the round because the Reds were winning championships or finishing high.

The Reds received two first-round picks in 1982 and neither made it to the majors. Both picks were pitchers: **Scott Jones** and **Billy Hawley**.

Pat Pacillo, a first round pitcher in 1984, got a cup of coffee in the majors.

The Reds chose **Scott Bryant** as a pitcher or outfielder in 1989 and he peaked at Triple-A.

The Reds picked **Chad Mottola** in the first round (5th overall) out of the University of Central Florida. The outfielder started out strong hitting homers in the minors and being named as an all-star, but his call-up to the majors in 1996 was less than exciting. He hit .215 in 35 games with three homers in 79 at bats. The Reds traded him to the Rangers for a player to be named later. Mottola has yet to find his way back to the majors, but he's still young.

The Reds had high hopes for **Johnny Oliver**, the 25th player taken overall in the 1996 draft. The first-round outfielder from Lehman High School, Pa., hasn't displayed major league talent so far. In his first season he failed to hit his weight (.206) at Class A Princeton. The following season he tore a hamstring after six games and was out the rest of the year. He showed little improvement in 1998 as he hit .224 at Class A Charleston; however, he did slam 11 home runs. He still has a way to go to get to the majors. He still has a shot at the majors, but so far he's been disappointing.

Best Draft

One of the Reds' best drafts was the very first. **Bernie Carbo** was the team's initial pick in the draft. The outfielder was part of the 1970 championship Reds team. Carbo went to the Red Sox and took some wrath out on his old team by hitting two pinch hit homers when the Sox faced the Reds in the 1975 World Series. However, the Reds won in the end. He played for 12 seasons in the majors with three teams. The second pick was even better, **Johnny Bench**, who turned out to be the first draft pick to reach the Baseball Hall of Fame. The sixth pick in the first draft was **Hal McRae**, who played for the Reds for four seasons before he was dealt to the Royals. Kansas City made him a designated hitter and he responded with a career .290 batting average over 19 seasons.

Worst Draft

Nineteen seventy-three was without any doubt the worst draft year by the Reds because nobody picked made it to the majors. The Reds picked **Gary Lucas** in January and again in June, but he didn't sign. **Jay Howell** was selected in the 14th round out of high school and he elected to go to college instead of signing. The Reds decided on high school seniors the first seven rounds and none turned into anything major.

Where Are They Now?

The Reds players like the organization so much that many of them have stuck around to coach with the team.

Tom Hume was the Reds' first selection in the secondary phase of the 1972 January draft. He pitched 11 major league seasons, compiling a 57-71 record with a 3.85 ERA. As a Red, Hume became a stopper and saved 88 games. In 1980 he appeared in a career-high 78 games, while being selected as the co-winner of the *Sporting News* Fireman-of-the-Year. He appeared in one All-Star game. In 1999, he was the bench coach with Cincinnati.

Another former draft pick and now coach with the Reds is **Ron Oester**, a ninth round pick in 1974. Oester played his whole 13-year career with the Reds at second base and shortstop. He was part of the championship team in 1990.

Don Gullett is the pitching coach for the Reds. He had the task of trying to put Mark Wohlers under control in 1999. Gullet was the first-round pick in 1969.

Tom Foley, a seventh-round pick in 1977, has become the director of minor league operations for the Tampa Bay Devil Rays. Foley played three seasons with the Reds.

Tom Lawless never played for the Mets, but he is now a coach with the Norfolk Tides, New York's Triple-A affiliate. Lawless never played for the Reds, but he was drafted by them in the 17th round in 1978.

The Reds spend a lot of time in their own backyard and found **Eddie Milner** in Central State University in Wilberforce, Ohio. Cincinnati selected the Columbus, Ohio, born player in the 21st round in 1976. The outfielder got the first call to Cincinnati in 1980 for a couple of games. He broke into the regular roster in 1982 and batted .268 that season. The speedster laced 23 doubles the next season and swiped a career-high 41 bases. The consistent performer went to the Giants in 1987 for a season and got to play in the League Championship Series. Then he boomeranged back to the Reds the next year, which was his last in the majors. In nine seasons in the majors, he played in 804 games and averaged .253. After baseball, Milner settled down in Cincinnati and became a financial analyst.

The Reds drafted **Skeeter Barnes** in the 16th round of the 1978 draft. He became a utility player for the Reds, Expos, Cardinals and Tigers. He finished up his playing career in 1992 and has stayed in baseball as a coach for the Tigers' organization.

Dave Miley was a second round pick in 1980 out of high school. He had a scholarship offer from the University of Florida, but his bonus, which he wouldn't reveal, helped in deciding otherwise. "I wanted to play professional ball," he explained. He never made it to the majors, but he's made it to Triple-A as a manager for the Indianapolis Indians.

Milt Hill, a 28th round pick in 1987, played parts of four seasons in the majors with the Reds, Braves and Mariners. He pitched in 350 minor league games. Now he's a coach with the Devil Rays.

Other ex–Reds now coaching with the Devil Rays are **Steve Henderson**, a 1974 draft pick, and **Greg Riddock**, a third-round selection in 1967. Henderson's major league career spanned a dozen seasons with five different teams, but he never played on the Reds. Riddock was a minor league manager with the Reds for eight seasons. He never played in the majors.

Nardi Contreras, a 12th-round pick of the Reds in 1969, played one season in the majors for the White Sox, where he is now the pitching coach.

Ones Who Got Away

The Reds tried twice to get **Chris Chambliss**. They first drafted him in 1967 when he was at Mira Costa Junior College. He didn't sign. Then in the secondary phase of the January 1968 the Reds picked him second. He didn't sign. The Indians got the jump on the Reds the following year and picked Chambliss in the first round of the January draft. This time he signed.

The Reds chose **Bob Dernier** in 1977 in the 12th round of the January 1977 regular phase out of community college. He didn't sign. Dernier had his best years with the Chicago Cubs.

Otis Nixon was picked the next year in the 21st round and he passed on the offer. Nixon went on to play for the Atlanta Braves and other teams as an outfielder.

Randy Myers was selected by Cincinnati in the third round of the January 1982 draft, but he didn't sign. The Reds finally got him under their fold by trading for the lefty with the Mets, who drafted him in the first round in June 1982.

Dan Dumoulin didn't sign when he was drafted in the 19th round in 1972. The Reds offered him $2,000, but he had quit school to get married and he was already working in an auto assembly plant. Instead, he waited until a tryout camp in 1974. Ironically, the Reds offered him the same amount as before to sign. This time he did sign. "Dummy," as he was nicknamed by an announcer who couldn't pronounce his last name, finally got his shot at the majors in 1977. In his first major league appearance, he struck out two batters before he was lifted by Manager Sparky Anderson. "Sparky wasn't big on giving younger kids a chance," Dumoulin said. The fireballer ran into arm problems, which ended his career a couple of years later in the minors.

Undrafted Players

Bobby Ayala was not drafted after finishing Rio Mesa High School in Oxnard, Calif. The Reds signed him in July 1988. Five years later he was pitching for the Reds and did so for two seasons before being traded to the Mariners, where he has been a reliever for five seasons.

All in the Family

The Reds drafted **Jose Tartabull, Jr.**, whose father played nine seasons in the majors, in January 1985 as their last pick. He didn't sign.

The Reds already had one Boone on the team, Bret, so they drafted **Aaron Boone** in the third round in 1994. The third generation ballplayer — father Bob and grandfather Ray both played — said his bonus was $115,000 and $30,000 more toward finishing his degree in communications from USC. The third baseman worked his way up the minors quickly and joined his brother in 1997 with the Reds after he hitting 22 homers in Indianapolis. The brothers played together for the Reds in 1998 before Bret was traded to the Braves. Aaron batted .282 in his rookie season, but he hasn't put up the power numbers in the majors that he displayed in the minors.

Alex LeFlore, a sixth-round pick in 1999, is son of Ron LeFlore, who played nine seasons with Detroit, Montreal and the Chicago White Sox. "He's a left-handed hitter with above average power," said DeJon Watson. His father was a right-handed hitter.

Bryan Erstad is the brother of Darin Erstad, who plays for the Angels. Bryan was the Reds' 42nd round pick in 1999.

On the Roster

The Reds had less than 10 of their own draft picks on their 40-man roster to begin 1999 season. Larkin led the group in experience as a veteran of 13 seasons in Cincinnati.

Scott Sullivan was drafted out of Auburn in 1993. After going undefeated at rookie ball, he leaped over Class A altogether and was placed at Double-A. He was a starter and reliever early in his professional career, but was moved to the bullpen permanently when he moved up to Triple-A Indianapolis. He was first called up in 1995, but 1997 was his rookie year in the majors and he led all rookie relief pitchers in strikeouts and innings pitched. The next year he led all major league relievers with 102 innings on the mound as a long and middle reliever.

Brett Tomko was picked two years later than Sullivan and made an even quicker route to the majors as 1997 became his rookie year as well. But Tomko is strictly a starter. The right-hander began pro career with 1.84 ERA in nine games for Class A Charleston in 1995. He spent 1996 at Double-A and 10 games at Triple-A Indianapolis before being called up to the Reds. He

Bret Tomko of the Indianapolis Indians was drafted by the Reds. (Photograph by Marty Orr.)

Pokey Reese was drafted by the Reds in the first round in 1991. (Photograph by Marty Orr.)

was 11-7 his first season in the majors to lead National League rookie pitchers in winning percentage. He had tougher luck in his sophomore season going 13-12 in 34 starts. Then after a slow start in 1999, he was sent back to Indianapolis, but that wasn't for long as he was called back up to the surging Reds.

The Reds drafted **Eddie Taubensee** in the sixth round in 1986 out of high school. The catcher was slow to develop with the bat and was still at Class A after five seasons, so the Reds didn't protect him from the Rule V draft and he was picked up by the Athletics. Then the Indians claimed him on waivers and later traded him to Houston where he began to develop as a hitter. Houston then traded him back to the Reds for a couple of pitchers. Since then he's been a consistent contributor to the Reds.

Scott Williamson, a ninth round pick in 1997, joined the pitching staff out of spring training as a non-roster invitee. The Pioneer League All-Star in his first pro season, he moved up to Triple-A in 1999. The right-hander had a 2.70 ERA in spring training to advance him to the majors. He turned into the team's stopper in 1999.

Pokey Reese was drafted as a shortstop in the first round in 1991 out of high school. He was rated as the best defensive shortstop at each level he played at, but his hitting lagged behind. With Larkin at short, the Reds decided to turn him into a second baseman and called him up in 1997.

Backing up Reese at Triple-A is the Reds' former second baseman, **Jeff Branson**. The second round pick in 1988 played six seasons with Cincinnati before being traded to Cleveland in a multi-player trade. Then he was granted free agency and came back to the Reds organization for the 1999 season.

Jason La Rue was put on the fast track to the majors after hitting .365 in Double-A in 1998. The fifth round pick from 1995 out of Dallas Baptist University was a South Atlantic League all-star catcher in 1997 to raise the eyebrows of the Reds player development. When Brian Johnson went down with an injury early in 1999, La Rue got his first call to the majors.

Mike Frank of the Indianapolis Indians, a seventh rounder by the Cincinnati Reds in 1997.

Jason La Rue with the Indianapolis Indians was drafted by the Cincinnati Reds as a fifth round pick in 1995. (Photograph by Marty Orr.)

Future Stars?

Mike Frank, a seventh-round selection in 1997, became the quickest player from that draft to make it to the majors. And he was surprised to get a call so quickly to the majors. During mid-season in 1998, he figured the first taste he'd get in the majors would be September at the earliest, not in July when it occurred. Frank was one of those players that was so good at baseball that he could be drafted as a pitcher or fielder. "I actually thought I was going to be drafted as a pitcher," he explained. He was 11-0 as a pitcher at Santa Clara University during his senior year. However, the Reds didn't see it that way. He was told he could always pitch. They instead drafted him as an outfielder because he was such a good hitter, too. He signed for $40,000. The Reds may have made the right decision and certainly got their money's worth right away. Frank hit a whopping .375 in Rookie League at Billings in 1997 and was named a Pioneer League All-Star. The next season he shot up through the system

like a missile. After spring training, he began at Double-A Chattanooga and hit .325 with 12 homers in two months' time. He was promoted to Indianapolis, where he hit .341 in 22 games. Cincinnati was in a rebuilding mode for the year so Frank was in the right place at the right time. He played in 28 games before he suffered an injury and was sent back down to Double-A. He began the 1999 season back with Indianapolis. If Frank doesn't get back to the majors as an outfielder, he can always turn to pitching again as several players have done before him.

If it wasn't for the draft, **Jason Williams** would likely be a construction manager right now working on some building in Baton Rouge, Louisiana. After being selected by Cincinnati in the 16th round of the 1996 draft, the fifth-year senior at LSU decided baseball was the route to go even though he was only being offered $4,000. Then he made the Olympic Team that summer, becoming the lowest draft pick to make the team. But not being the best has never stopped Williams. He was used to hearing that he was too short (5-foot-8), too slow or didn't have enough power. "I heard that every year," he explained with a Cajun accent. That never stopped him though. "I have to work harder than some people who have the talent."

His hard work resulted in him being the best hitter on the Olympic Team with a .417 batting average. "I played the game hard and was out to win," he said. In the pros, he has come up like quick-rising bread. In 1997, his first season in the minors, he hit .324 in Single-A Burlington to earn a promotion to Double-A Chattanooga halfway through the season, where he hit .310, resulting in a promotion to Triple-A Indianapolis for the 1998 season. The second baseman performed well at second base for the Indians and hit .266 on the year. The hard worker looks to be headed to the majors some day despite his previous critics.

Adam Dunn, a second round pick in 1998, told the Reds he was done with playing football for the University of Texas during spring training in 1999, so the Reds promised him a call-up to the majors by Sept. 1, 1999. He batted .533 with 16 homers and 32 RBI in 74 at-bats during his senior season in high school. Considered by many as one of the best athletes among high school players in the draft, Dunn had tremendous power and speed, and had stolen 71 bases in 71 attempts combined in his final two years of high school ball. The outfielder hit .288 in 1998 with Billings in the rookie league.

The third round pick was **Greg Porter**, who batted .464 with 13 doubles, two triples, six homers, 31 RBI and 33 runs scored in his senior year of high school. He was a first-team all-district performer in baseball, football and basketball, and named the *Dallas Morning News'* "Male Athlete of the Year."

First-round pick **Brandon Larson** has a long way to go before he gets to the majors, too, after hitting .221 at Class A Burlington in 1998. The 14th pick overall in the 1997 draft was begun at Double-A after he signed in 1997, but he was sent back down for the 1998 season. The Reds took him because of two tools: power and speed. Needless to say, he hasn't shown much of either, yet. He may very well end up as a disappointment instead of a future star.

Being drafted four times before signing is unusual these days now that the draft is just once a year. One such player is **Justin Atchley**. The left-handed pitcher was first drafted in 1991 by San Diego after he graduated from high school. "I came from a small town and my social skills weren't ready," he explained as his reason for not signing. He was from Sedro Woolley, Washington.

He went on to junior college and was drafted after his freshman year by the Atlanta Braves. He decided to transfer to Texas A&M and, after his junior season, he was selected by the Dodgers. "The offer was very good," he said. It wasn't enough for him to sign though. After his senior year, the Reds picked him in the 12th round. This time he signed. Although he had lost all the leverage he had when he was a junior, he still got a "decent" bonus. Atchley got off to an unbeatable start his rookie season with a 10-0 mark to be named to the Pioneer League All-Star Team. He moved up to Double-A in 1997, but was out all of 1998 due to a shoulder injury. By mid–1999, he found himself at Triple-A Indianapolis.

After beginning college with a 1-8 record in his freshman year, **Dustin Robinson** was likely thinking more about basketball than baseball. But in 1996 the 6-foot-5 turned that record inside out as he posted a 13-3 record and led Oklahoma Baptist University to their second NAIA World Series. He also was voted Sooner Athletic Conference and Great Plains Region Tournament MVP. Robinson was also named an All-America honorable mention for his efforts. Robinson likely moved down in the draft when he finished his college career with a 9-6 record and a 3.79 ERA. The Reds chose him in the 12th round in the 1997 draft. In 1998 he was 5-10 with a 4.47 ERA with Class A Charleston. He may have to rebound like he did in his sophomore year if he is to go further with the Reds.

The Reds had high hopes for **Travis Dawkins**, the second-round pick in 1997. "Gookie," who was signed by Steve Kring, led all Reds minor league players with 37 steals. The shortstop debuted in the majors in 1999 when Barry Larkin was injured. He also helped Team USA to a silver medal in the Pan Am Games. Dawkins may have to wait a while longer before becoming a regular in the majors, at least until Larkin retires.

The Reds picked **Austin Kearns**, a high

school graduate and recipient of Kentucky's 1998 "Mr. Baseball" award, in the first round in 1998. Kearns was considered by most as one of the best overall power-hitting prospects among high school players. He began his senior season by collecting 20 hits in his first 27 at-bats and finished the regular season hitting .577 with 11 homers and 43 RBI. A member of Team USA's national junior team in 1997, Kearns hit .478 with 5 homers and 14 RBI and then helped guide Team USA to a bronze medal finish in the World Junior Championships by batting .615 with 8 hits, 2 doubles and 3 RBI. "We felt Austin was the best player available at our selection," said Watson. "We are all very excited to add the best power-hitting high school prospect in this year's draft to our organization, not to mention the fact that he is a local talent." In the rookie league his first season, he hit .315 at Billings.

Rob Dibble, a Cincinnati Reds draft pick. (Photograph by Marty Orr.)

Colorado Rockies

The Rockies have yet to see an all-star blossom from the first-year free-agent draft, although some players are finally making an impact with the team, such as Todd Helton. Colorado began picking players in 1992, a year before they began playing. They have had better results with the expansion draft.

In that first draft, the team concentrated on right-handed pitchers with their first four picks. In fact, 10 of their first 15 picks were pitchers. By 1999, none of the pitchers had made an impact at the major league level. The best player of that lot turned out to be Craig Counsell, who was later traded to Florida for pitcher Mark Hutton. Counsell became a regular player in the Sunshine State.

The 1993 draft produced right-handed pitcher Jamey Wright, who has become a regular starter with the team, but he hasn't been a winner. The following year the Rockies lost their second, third and fourth round picks for signing free agents Ellis Burks, Walt Weiss and Howard Johnson. The result was a winning team the following season that made it to the playoffs as a wild card. Colorado became the quickest expansion team to get into the postseason. How-

ever, the success was short-lived and Colorado must now rely on the draft to bring them better results to be more competitive.

The Rockies' draft philosophy has been to draft the best player available when it comes to their turn in the draft, according to Pat Daugherty, vice president of scouting. Daugherty has headed the scouting department from the team's inception. He came from Montreal where he had been managing and scouting for 20 years. Daugherty and his staff looks at the "best to worst" in each position. Needs are not considered. He wouldn't mind having five great catchers in the minors, because the team could always trade some to fill other needs in the majors.

The best available first-round player in seven of the first eight years has been a pitcher from the Rockies' perspective. With a launching platform as a stadium, the Rockies are a little more conscious of the need for good pitching.

The Rockies scouts have looked very closely at a player's signability before the draft is conducted. The team still has some trouble signing players though because the players want more money or thought they should have been drafted higher. "They [the players] got you by the ass, pardon the expression," Daugherty explained. "We haven't drafted a kid who didn't think they should have gone higher. It's a monster we've created."

The Rockies scouting department is made up of 18 area scouts, three regional crosscheckers and two national crosscheckers. The Rockies don't hold open tryouts for players. Overseas, the team has an academy in Venezuela and a team in Dominican Republic summer league. They also have a scout in Panama. Besides the Caribbean area, the team has recently begun looking at players in the Pacific Rim.

Best Picks

Todd Helton, the first-round pick in 1995, was the reason the Rockies could let high-priced free-agent Andres Galarraga sign somewhere else. Helton was an all-star twice while coming up in the minors. He showed he could hit for power in 1997 when he launched 16 homers at Triple-A Colorado Springs. In 1998, his rookie year with the Rockies, he didn't disappoint the fans with his performance. In one game he hit the game-winning homer in the ninth inning. Then he batted for the cycle that same week to earn the National League Player of the Week. He finished the season hitting .315 with 25 homers and 97 RBI to earn runner up for Rookie of the Year. His biggest thrill so far: "Hitting a home run in my first game," he said during an Internet chat. "That, and just to be asked to come back after my first year."

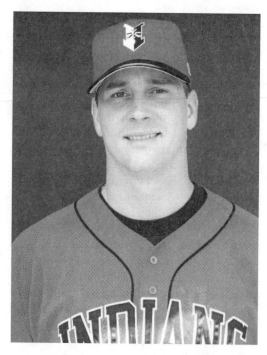

Mark Thompson of the Indianapolis Indians, drafted by the Colorado Rockies. (Photograph by Marty Orr.)

Mark Thompson, a second-round pick in the Rockies' first draft, became the first Rockies draft pick to make it to the majors in 1994. Scout Ty Coslow spotted him at the University of Kentucky. He signed the same day he was drafted. "I was anxious and I wanted to play," he commented. His bonus was $110,000. He also was the first Rockies winning pitcher at Coors Field in 1995 when he pitched one inning of relief and picked up the win.

Thompson played five seasons with the Rockies before Colorado let him go to free agency in 1998 after his six years ran out. Thompson signed with the Cincinnati Reds and was assigned to Indianapolis. He had a tough time in 1998 after coming off of shoulder surgery. "Hopefully, I'm on my way back to the big leagues," he said in July 1999 after earning his first win of the season.

Craig Counsell was drafted in the 11th round in 1992 after his senior year in college. Since he was a senior, he was told to sign or forget it. There wasn't any negotiation. "I'm probably not the typical scout's dream," Counsell said. "I don't have the tools and things." Counsell

Todd Helton, first-round pick in 1995 for the Colorado Rockies.

signed and figured he'd make money later. He did. He got a cup of coffee with Colorado before he was traded to Florida for pitcher Mark Hutton. The Marlins put him to work there and he earned a World Series ring in 1997. After another season with the Marlins, he was traded to the Dodgers.

Long Shots

One of the long shots from the 1992 draft was 28th round pick **Mark Strittmatter**. The catcher out of Virginia Commonwealth University beat the odds in 1998 by getting a call from the Rockies after six years and five months in the minors. Strittmatter toiled at Triple-A at nearby Colorado Springs and got the call after hitting .276 with six home runs during the 1998 season. He played in just four games and had no hits in four at bats during his first month in the majors.

Another long shot from that first draft who has made it to the majors was **Angel Echevarria**, a 17th round pick. He showed steady progression in the minors until he broke out with 21 homers in 1995 at Double-A to get named to the Eastern League All-Star Team. That led to him getting his first call to the majors in 1996. He also got brief stints with the Rockies in 1997 and 1998.

Disappointments

The first high-school pitcher to be drafted in the 1994 June amateur draft was **Doug Million** and he nearly received an amount equal to his name. The Colorado Rockies took him as their seventh pick in the first round and signed him for $905,000. The young pitcher looked very promising to the Rockies. He had earned national high school player of the year honors after going 12-2 with a 1.21 ERA and 149 strikeouts in 87 innings in his senior year at Sarasota High in Florida. However, Million had one health problem — asthma. The disease had long been an impediment to his conditioning. Million was impressive in his first professional season. He went 5-3 with a 2.34 ERA for Bend in the rookie league. His asthma continued to cause him problems with his conditioning. Million's 1997 season was a disappointment from the outset. He went 0-5 with a 9.23 ERA for Double-A New Haven before being demoted to Salem. He finished 5-9 with a 5.12 ERA for the Avalanche. During an injury rehabilitation in Salem, Million was at a restaurant when he suffered a severe asthma attack. Teammate Jason Romine called 911. Million's pulse stopped in the ambulance on the way to the hospital. When he arrived at the hospital, doctors worked on him for 45 minutes without any success.

The promising pitcher was dead at 21.

"This is an extremely difficult time for myself and the entire Rockies' family," said Bob Genhard, Rockies' executive vice president and general manager. "Doug was a terrific young man who we had very high hopes for, and all of our heartfelt sorrow goes out to his family in Sarasota and teammates throughout the system. It is so unfair to have life snuffed out of a 21-year old body and he will be greatly missed by all of us."

"Life is not fair, and he just got cheated," his father, Dave, told a newspaper.

The Rockies needed **David Nied** when they took him first overall in the first round of the expansion draft. The Braves pitcher was 3-0 with a 1.17 ERA in a September call-up. He started the first game in Rockies history and won three of his first four starts. Then everything began to unravel like a bad marriage. He lost five games in a row. A torn elbow ligament put him on the disabled list until September. The following year he suffered more elbow problems. His career ended after the 1996 season with a 17-18 record.

Expansion Round Picks

Vinny Castilla has turned out to be Colorado's best expansion draft pick. Castilla was becoming a star in the Mexican League when his contract was purchased by Atlanta in 1990. He was progressing slowly in the Braves system and was called up to Atlanta for a dozen games in 1992. The Braves decided not to protect him from the expansion draft and the Rockies grabbed him up. The Rockies used him as a utility fielder at first until he had his breakout season in 1995 when he hit 32 homers and was named to his first All-Star Game. Since then he has 40 or more home runs each season in the high Colorado air. His 170 home runs is second best in Rockies history and the best all-time among Mexican-born players. Castilla is just the seventh National League player ever to collect 40 or more home runs in three consecutive season. He was again named to the All-Star Team in 1998.

Kevin Ritz was taken in the second round in the 1992 Expansion Draft. Originally drafted by Detroit in 1985, Ritz had compiled a 6-18 record pitching for the Tigers, so he wasn't protected when the draft came about. He missed the entire 1993 season due to elbow surgery. He returned a new pitcher and became a winning pitcher in Colorado. Ritz missed most of the 1998 season due to shoulder surgery. His best season so far came in 1996 when he was 17-11 in 35 starts. That performance made him the Opening Day starter in 1997, but a torn right labrum ended his season early.

Curtis Leskanic was a third round selection in the 1992 expansion draft. Originally drafted by the Indians in the 8th round in 1989, the pitcher from LSU had been traded to the Twins in 1992 while still in the minors. The Rockies put him to work right away when they called him up from the minors in its first season. He was used as a starter and reliever at first, but was turned into strictly a reliever in 1995, his first full season in the majors. He picked up 10 saves that season in helping the team to the playoffs. In his six seasons with the Rockies, he has posted a 25-18 record with 20 saves.

Where Are They Now?

John Burke, Colorado's first-ever pick in the first-year free agent draft, was granted free agency after the 1998 season and signed with the Cleveland Indians. In his seven years in the Rockies organization, he appeared in just 28 games with a 6.75 ERA and a 4-6 record.

All in the Family

Edgard Clemente, a 10th round pick in 1993, is the nephew of the famous Roberto Clemente. His name was originally Edgard Velazquez.

On the Roster

The Rockies had few of their own on their roster going into the 1999 season. Players from the first couple of drafts were beginning to arrive in the majors.

David Lee went from up and coming in Double-A to the Rockies early in 1999 when he got the call up to the majors. The right-handed pitcher was drafted in the 23rd round in 1995 out of Mercyhurst College. Strictly a reliever in the minors, he had recorded 65 saves and his ERA was just 1.04 in 1999 before getting the call.

Also on the 40-man roster was **Edgard Clemente**, a 10th round pick in 1993. The outfielder from Puerto Rico had his breakout season in the minors in 1995 when he was named to the Carolina League All-Star Team. Clemente moved up to Triple-A in 1997 and got a call up to the Rockies in 1998 after slamming 22 homers at Colorado Springs.

Future Stars

Derrick Gibson has shown that 13 is a lucky number after all. The 13th round draft pick in 1993 worked his way to the majors by leaving a trail of home runs in his path in the minors. His 32 dingers in Class A in 1995 earned him a promotion to Double-A. His 23 homers there in 1996 jumped him up to Triple-A Colorado Springs. The Rockies finally called him up in 1998 at the end of the season after he hit 14 homers with a .292 average.

Mike Kusiewicz is on the verge of breaking into the majors. The eighth round pick in 1994 out of high school pitched very successfully in 1998 at Double-A as he was 14-7 with a 2.32 ERA and was named to the Eastern League All-Star Team.

Ben Petrick, a second round pick in 1995, was an all-star catcher his first season in professional ball at Class A Asheville. He continued to be an all-star the next season at Salem when he slammed 15 homers. The catcher is speedy, too. He stole 30 bases in 1997. He has been compared to a young Craig Biggio. He was promoted to Triple-A in 1999.

Josh Kalinowski was a long shot in the 33rd round in 1996 and didn't begin his professional career until the next season. The left-handed pitcher showed he was underrated and was 12-10 at Class A in 1998.

Chad Liter was surprised he was even picked in the 37th round in the 1999 draft. "I look as myself as a sleeper," said the Madison Consolidated High School, Indiana, senior. Liter admitted that scouts were at his school looking at pitcher Bryan Bullington, who was drafted in the same round by the Royals. The Colorado scout also became interested in Liter and he was invited to a tryout camp. He was the fastest player at the tryout.

Chad Liter was picked in the 37th round in the 1999 draft by the Colorado Rockies.

The speedy left-handed hitter performed well whenever the scouts were around and hit nearly .500 his senior year with 13 homers. In his last high school game, which came after the draft, he hit two triples in Victory Field in Indianapolis to lead his school to a state championship. The Rockies are looking at Liter as a draft-and-follow player as he is going to attend Wabash Valley Community College to develop more first before getting a better offer. The six-foot-two outfielder hopes to put on 20 more pounds and get stronger with some weight training.

Jason Jennings, a pitcher from Baylor University, was the first round pick in 1999 from Baylor University. The 21 year old fashioned a brilliant career at Baylor with a 27-10 career record to date, including a 13-1 mark in 1999 with a 2.27 ERA in 20 games. Named by "Collegiate Baseball" as the 1999 National Player of the Year, he has walked just 45, while fanning 170 in 142.2 innings and posted three shutouts. In addition to being named the National Player of the Year, Jennings also earned Big XII Player of the Year honors, consensus All-America status and was named the Outstanding Player on the Big XII All-Tournament Team. The 6-2, 235-pound right-hander is also an outstanding hitter, as he currently leads the Bears with a .382 average adding 16 homers and 63 RBI in 50 games. A junior sociology major from Mesquite, Texas, Jennings also excelled in the classroom, as he was named to the 1999 Academic All-America First Team as a pitcher.

Florida Marlins

The Florida Marlins began drafting in 1992 and by 1997 they were the World Champions due to free agency not the draft. Only a couple of their draft picks were on that championship team. It normally takes about a decade before the draft has a real impact on an expansion team. The Marlins didn't want to wait that long. Owner H. Wayne Huizenga went out on a limb and spent millions on free-agent market to drum up the necessary team to win his division and the World Series. Soon after the series he cleared house of the free agents and reduced the team salary to $10 million. As a result the team finished last in 1998 and was competing with Montreal for last place again in 1999.

Now that the Marlins are under new ownership, a rebuilding process has begun in the farm system after much of the team's talent was drained off. The Marlins want a new stadium with a retractable roof to prevent rain delays. The new stadium would raise revenue in order to meet the high salaries of players today. The team has told the public that it could not commit to a $20 million payroll playing at Pro Players Stadium and it wants $60 million for players in order to compete with other teams.

The scouting director is Al Avila, a former catcher in the Dodgers organization for two seasons. Avila was the director of Latin American operations for the Marlins and has been in the

Billy McMillion with the Rochester Red Barons, an 8th round draft pick in 1993 for the Florida Marlins.

scouting department since its inception. He took over the position from Orrin Freeman. Avila heads an average scouting staff of 16 area scouts, three regional crosscheckers and two national crosscheckers. The scouts do hold open tryouts around the country for those players who weren't drafted. The team also has international scouting interests in Latin American and the Pacific Rim.

A few of Florida's draft picks are now starting to pay some dividends for the team, but it will still be some time before the team rebuilds from the bottom up.

Best Picks

The Marlins made the most of their first draft as their first-ever draft pick was catcher **Charles Johnson**. The following season he led the Midwest League with 94 RBI and was named to the All-Star Team. Then he led Eastern League with 28 homers in 1994. He became the team's first drafted player to play in the majors when he appeared in his first game in Pro Player Stadium on May 6, 1994. Facing Curt Schilling for the first time, he hit a homer in his second at-bat and went two-for-three in the game. In his rookie season, he earned a Gold Glove, an unusual accomplishment for a rookie. He has proven that was no fluke as he has picked up four more Gold Gloves, the most by a catcher since Johnny Bench. His defensive skills and clutch hitting helped the Marlins to the World Championship in 1997. He hit .357 in the World Series. The Marlins traded him to the Dodgers after the series.

Another gem in Florida's short draft history is outfielder **Mark Kotsay**. He played for Cal-State Fullerton's National Championship team in 1995 and was selected as the most outstanding player in the College World Series after he hit two historic grand slams. Picked in the first round in 1996, Kotsay became the first in his class to make it to the majors when he was called up in 1997 from Double-A. In 1998, the outfielder spent the whole season with the Marlins batting .279 and hitting 11 homers. As a result he was named on several rookie all-star teams.

Charles Johnson was a first round, 28th pick in the 1992 draft for the Marlins. (Photograph courtesy of the Florida Marlins.)

Mark Kotsay, 1996 first round pick for the Marlins. (Photograph courtesy of the Florida Marlins.)

Long Shots

The lowest draft selection to make it to the majors so far is **Dave Berg**. He was picked in the 38th round in 1993. After five seasons in the minors, the 28-year-old University of Miami infielder played the entire 1998 season with the Marlins as a utility infielder and batted .313 in 81 contests.

Another long shot who made his way to the majors was **Andy Larkin**. The right-handed starting pitcher got a guest appearance in 1996. Then in 1998 the struggling Marlins gave him more of a shot as he pitched in 17 games. However, he would need to improve on the 3-8

Andy Larkin was a 1992 25th round pick for the Marlins. (Photograph courtesy of the Florida Marlins.)

Josh Booty, first round pick in 1994 for the Marlins. (Photograph courtesy of the Florida Marlins.)

Expansion Round Picks

The only Expansion Round pick to survive until the 1997 World Series was **Jeff Conine**, who the Marlins picked in the first round from Kansas City. Conine was originally a 58th round pick in 1987 out of UCLA. He had a couple of trips to Kansas City where he didn't prove himself, averaging .250 with no homers in 37 games. He also was hampered by injuries in the minors, which probably had something to do with the Royals not protecting him. When he got to Florida, the climate was more to his liking and

record with a 9.64 ERA to stick like super glue in the majors.

Disappointments

The Marlins gave **Josh Booty** the boot in 1999 after he failed to hit for average in the minors or majors. The first-round pick in 1994 out of high school was given a $1.6 million bonus. The third baseman had plenty of power, but struck out too much. The Marlins gave him three tries in the majors and he struck out there as well. He played 13 games in the majors, which turned out to be an unlucky number for the prospect.

his average shot up to the .300 mark and he was hitting homers with regularity. In 1994 his average shot up to .319. The next season he hit 25 homers and 105 RBI. At the All-Star Game in 1995 he was named as Most Valuable Player after a game-winning homer in his first at bat. His numbers dipped in 1997, which probably led to him being traded back to his original team. In 1999 he was in Baltimore.

The Marlins got **Trevor Hoffman** in the expansion draft from Cincinnati. He played half a season for Florida before he was traded to San Diego for Gary Sheffield, who helped the team in winning the World Championship in 1997. The Padres turned Hoffman into a stopper and he has been in that role ever since.

Carl Everett was only at Class A with the Yankees when the Marlins picked him in the second round. They saw more in him then New York and gave him a chance. The rise to the majors was so quick he must have gotten the bends. He had trouble with major league pitching. The answer was a trade to the Mets. He was then dealt to Houston where he rose his batting average to .298 and he powered 15 homers. After an injury in 1999, Everett was hitting the ball like Mark McGwire.

On the Roster

By the end of the 1998, the Marlins had just a handful of players on their roster who they had originally drafted.

Todd Dunwoody was picked in the seventh round out of high school in 1993. School and grades were a priority of his, which made his decision tough. He was more prepared to go to college than to go to professional baseball. "I got to skip school and wait on the phone call," he said about the day he was drafted. It took him until July 1 that summer to make up his mind and sign with the Marlins. His breakout year in the minors came in 1995 when the outfielder was named to the All-Star Team. He earned all-star berths the next two seasons as well when he hit 24 and 23 homers. That launched him into the majors at the right time. He helped the Marlins the last month of the championship season. He didn't get to play in the World Series though, but he earned a ring.

The Marlins picked **Brian Meadows** in the third round in 1994. The right-handed pitcher went undefeated his rookie season in the minors with a 3-0 record and 1.95 ERA. He came down to earth after that season and worked steadily until Florida put him in the starting rotation in 1998, his rookie year in the majors. He was 11-13 in 31 starts.

Also from the class of 1994 was **Rob Stanifer**, a 12th-round pick. He too is a right-handed hurler, but a reliever instead of a starter. After a 21-14 record in the minors, the Marlins first called him up in 1997 for about half a season. He saw a bit more action in 1998 with Florida.

Ryan Jackson was a seventh-round selection in 1994. The first baseman was named to the Midwest League All-Star team as an outfielder in 1995. After averaging over .300 in the minors, the Marlins first called him up in 1998 where he didn't fare as well when he hit just .250.

Future Stars?

The Marlins didn't let **Brent Billingsley** pitch much in Triple-A in 1999 before promoting him to the majors as a reliever despite him being 0-4 with a 5.82 ERA on the season. The much needed lefthander was drafted in the fifth round in 1996 out of Cal State Fullerton. He led the Eastern League in strikeouts in 1998 and had a fine ERA of 3.74, but didn't get much help which resulted in a 6-11 record. In 1997 at Class A Kane County, he was the Marlins' pitcher of the year.

Nate Rolison was selected in the second round in 1995 out of high school and he has worked his way up to Double-A by slamming out homers and hitting for average at first base. He may be ready for the majors early in the next century.

Also moving up to Double-A was another 1995 pick, **Michael Tejera**. The former member of the Cuban Junior Team who defected to the United States was a sixth round pick. The left-handed pitcher was 9-5 with a 4.11 ERA at Double-A and began 1999 with an 8-1 record.

The Marlins are trying to find a spot for **John Roskos**, a second round pick in 1993. They drafted him as a catcher and he moved steadily up through the minors. Then he was moved to first base and the outfield. In 1997 he stroked 24 homers at Double-A to earn a promotion to Triple-A. He got his first call to the majors in 1998, but began the 1999 season in the outfield at Triple-A Calgary.

The Marlins selected right-handed pitcher **Josh Beckett** with the second overall pick in the first round of the 1999 draft. The high school senior posted a 10-1 record with a 0.46 ERA in his senior year with 155 strikeouts. He had been named the Texas 5-A High School Player of the Year in each of the past two seasons. "Beckett is a much more advanced than most pitchers coming out of high school," said Executive Vice President and General Manager Dave Dombrowski. "He has two dominant pitches, a fastball and a curve ball, and has been working on a slider and a change-up."

Houston Astros

Houston tried to get the most out of the draft in 1965 when it picked the most players — 72 — that year. The expansion team of 1962 needed more prospects to dig its way out of the last-place hole it was mired in. The draft certainly helped the franchise and by 1972 it was a contender, but some poor trades of players and some draft picks, like John Mayberry, prevented the team from reaching first in the 1970s. Not until 1980 did the franchise finish first. The team has since finished first five times in its history, but it has yet to get to the World Series. None

of those squads had even a handful of original draft picks. "We're a contending team," explained Tim Purpura, assistant general manager. "Contending teams will sometimes have to trade players that they have drafted and signed. Our one and only goal is to win a world championship."

The draft has been good to Houston in some respects in recent times. Several Houston draft picks helped the team to the playoffs in 1998. "I think we've had some good drafts and some bad drafts," Purpura said. "Some of those middle-tier guys haven't worked out the way we wanted them to."

The 1999 squad didn't have a proliferation of Houston draft picks either, but any help it got of their own choosing was greatly appreciated. The team was playing its last season in the Astrodome and hopes where high that it would play in the Series there before moving to the Ballpark at Union Station in 2000.

The Astros showed they were high on draft pick Scott Elarton. They could have traded him to the Blue Jays for Roger Clemens, but they decided not to. The budget was part of the reason because they would have had to put out a lot more money for Clemens to keep him. The middle-market team only has so much money. The Astros failed to sign some of their players in previous drafts due to monetary considerations. "We didn't have what we could sign them for, " said Purpura. "We don't have the money the Yankees have."

The Astros draft strategy is simple: take the best talent available when it's their turn to pick. "There's no way to predict what you're going to need in six years," explained Pat Murphy, assistant scouting director. "You can't draft for need."

Best available is a player that has the tools and a good attitude. "I look at the makeup of the kid," said part-time scout Joe Bogar, the son of Astros player Tim Bogar. Joe likes to look at how a player carries himself. He doesn't particularly like hot shots. When he's not scouting for the Astros, he's a director of marketing and sales in Indianapolis. Tim was drafted by the Mets before Joe became a part-time scout for the Mets, Expos and now Astros. The Astros have 19 other area scouts throughout the United States, three crosscheckers and one national crosschecker.

The Astros have two separate departments to scout players. One department takes care of searching the minors and majors for talent; whereas, the other handles high school and college players. In this manner, they don't miss scouting the minors and majors early in the season when the school kids are playing. The department has also concentrated on international efforts. "Over the past several years we have put a lot of energy into our Venezuela program, which are non-drafted players," said Purpura.

The team has also put a lot of effort into the Dominican Republic lately.

When the draft comes every year, upper management only gets involved in the first five picks. After that, the scouts have the control. "It's left to their creativity to find the rest," commented Purpura.

The Astros also give draft picks every chance to make the club. "This organization concentrates on the top pick and everybody else," said Joe Milulik, an instructor in the minor league system. "Houston has done good with drafting a lot of pitchers with good arms. Larry Dierker [the manager] has been strong about pitching and defense."

Best Picks

J.R. Richard, a first-round choice in June 1969, had more than 100 scholarship offers in high school where he was a star in football, basketball and baseball. A bonus of $100,000 convinced him to pass up all the offers. The six-foot-eight power pitcher with an 100-mph fastball zipped through the minors and got a September call-up in 1971. He struck out 15 in his first start! In 1978 he recorded 300 strikeouts, the first modern pitcher to hit that mark. He performed the feat the next season as well. He was almost unhittable in 1980 when disaster struck. He had a stroke. His entire left side was paralyzed. After two years of therapy, he tried to come back to baseball. He still had some zip in his fastball, but his control was gone and he couldn't field. His baseball career was over. Lifetime he was 107-71.

Glenn Davis, a first round pick in the January secondary phase in 1981, got a call to the majors in 1984 and was there to stay. In his rookie season, he slammed 20 home runs and was under consideration for Rookie of the Year honors. He came closer to an award the next season when he slammed 31 dingers and was second in the voting for MVP. The two-time All-Star helped the Astros to the National League Championship Series in 1986 and hit one homer during the playoffs. He played for Houston for seven seasons before finishing out his career with Baltimore.

Dave Smith, an eighth round choice in

1976, began saving games for Houston in 1980. He helped the Astros reach the National League Championship Series twice during his 11-year stay with the team. The right-handed reliever was picked for one All-Star game during his 13-year career. His 199 saves with the Astros is a team record.

The Astros picked **John Mayberry** as their No. 1 choice in June 1967 out of high school. After playing a little over 100 games for Houston in four seasons, he was traded to Kansas City. The Astros should have waited, because "Big John" soon came of age and began driving in more than 100 runs a season. His best seasons aided the Royals to two American League West titles. However, he didn't produce in the playoffs. The Royals sold him to Toronto in 1978 where he continued to hit homers and drive in runs. He ended his career with the Yankees with a total of 255 home runs. He also appeared in two All-Star games.

Craig Biggio was the first non-pitcher of the 1987 draft class to reach the majors when his contract was purchased by the Astros on June 26, 1988. By 1998 he had been named to the National League All-Star team for the seventh time in his career and for the fifth consecutive season. He also had picked up his fourth consecutive Rawlings Gold Glove Award as the best defensive player at his position. Biggio finished 1998 with a club record 51 doubles and a career-best 50 stolen bases. His name appears prominently in team records and his career is far from over.

Ken Caminiti, a third-round pick in 1984, jumped from Double-A to the majors in July 1987 after hitting 15 homers and averaging .325 in the Southern League. Like a fine wine, the third baseman got better with time, but the Astros decided to trade him to the Padres in 1994 before he matured completely. The wine became ready in 1996 as Caminiti batted .326 with 40 homers and 130 RBI to earn the Most Valuable Player award. Injuries plagued him the next two seasons. After helping the Padres to a World Series in 1998, he boomeranged back to the Astros as a free agent. The third baseman has been a defensive gem as well, earning three Gold Gloves. He's also been on the National League All-Star team three times so far.

Long Shots

The longest shot who has done the best with the Astros was **Eric Anthony,** a 34th round pick in 1986. The player from a local high school ascended to the majors in four years by being named to league all-star teams in the minors. After hitting 29 homers in 1988 in Single-A and 28 in Double-A, the Astros brought him up to the majors in 1989. He finally stuck in the majors in 1992. He's never lived up to the home run power he displayed in the minors, but his numbers were good enough for the majors. In 1998 he signed a contract in Japan.

Teams are always looking for good southpaw pitchers and the Astros found one in **Alvin Morman,** a 39th round pick in the 1991 draft out of Wingate (N.C.) College. He put up some good numbers as a reliever and starter in the minors, and Houston promoted him to the majors in 1996. He relieved in 53 games. The following season he was traded to the Indians for pitcher Jose Cabrera. Then he went on to the Giants and Royals.

The Astros made a heck of a selection when they chose **Darryl Kile** in the 30th round of the 1987 draft. Kile broke into the Astros' pitching rotation by 1991. After a fast start in 1993, he was selected as the lone representative for the team at the All-Star Game. Then on Sept. 8, he tossed a no-hitter against the Mets. After a couple of off years, he again dominated hitters and gained 19 wins in 1997, which tied him with Greg Maddux and Shawn Estes for the second best total in the league. He became a free agent in October 1997 and signed with the Rockies.

Another long shot pitcher to make it to the majors with the Astros was **Donnie Wall,** a 20th round pick in 1989 from the University of Southwestern Louisiana. The right-hander slowly progress through the minors until 1992. Then he went from Class A to Class AAA in one season. Houston called him up in 1995 and he played parts of three seasons with Houston until being waived. He ended up with San Diego in 1998, which landed him in the World Series.

Jim Dougherty was drafted in the 26th round by Houston in 1990. He had graduated from the University of North Carolina. He had no leverage. Basically, he decided not to go to baseball, but he changed his mind and called Houston. "I didn't want to work yet," he said laughingly. He asked to be released because he didn't want to be caught in the logjam the team had caused by bringing in trades and free agents for a pennant push. Houston had missed the playoffs by a game. Ironically, his best moment in baseball was in a losing effort. In 1998 he pitched in Yankee Stadium on opening day. "I grew up in New York and was a Yankee fan," he commented. He was with Oakland at the time. "I didn't really get the opportunity that I thought I should get." He was a six-year free agent. "Dodge," as he is called, is married and is a physical therapist. His degree is in psychology, but he doesn't think he will go into that. He'd like to be a coach in professional ball once he's done playing the game.

Whoever said 13 was unlucky wasn't from Italy, where 13 is supposed to be considered lucky. **Ray Montgomery** considered himself lucky to be drafted in the 13th round and still make it to the majors. "My wife's Italian and she tells me that's good luck in Italy," he explained. It took him seven seasons before he got his shot with Houston. He got a July 1996 call-up when someone got hurt and then the next season broke camp with the team. However, he didn't hit good enough to stick in the majors that season and was sent back down to Triple-A, where he spent most of 1998 as well. He was then granted free agency in October 1998 and signed a minor league contract with the Pirates. He didn't know when he was going to go in the draft. Scouts tell you anything. "I don't know why?" Houston was the only team he didn't talk to. "I was very surprised." Some other teams told him they were going to select him. He was a junior at Fordham. He let it be known that he would go for his senior year. He got a $35,000 package. When he started with Houston, their budget was only $20 million. Now its $55 million. His major was in finance. He will go to Triple-A if he doesn't make the squad.

Ken Forsch, an 18th round choice in June 1968 out of Oregon State University, entered the majors in 1970. He was a starter at first, but the Astros made him a reliever and the results were better. His famed forkball baffled batters and he was named to the All-Star team in 1976, a year

in which he had 19 saves. In 1979 he became a starter again and threw a no-hitter against the Braves on April 7, 1979. During his stint with the Astros, he appeared in the National League Championships Series twice. Then he was sent to the Angels to finish out his career with a 114-113 record. His brother Bob also pitched in the majors.

The Astros should have probably kept **Kenny Lofton,** a 17th round pick in 1988. The speedy centerfielder was traded after a poor showing with the Astros in 1991. Houston got Willie Blair, who pitched for one season with the team, and Eddie Taubensee, who was traded three years later. Since Lofton was traded he has been a premier player with the Indians and Braves, averaging .311 and stealing bases like few others. He has earned four Gold Gloves over his career. Lofton has appeared on three All-Star teams.

Kenny Lofton, drafted by the Astros in 1988, a 17th round pick. (Photograph by Marty Orr.)

Julio Lugo, a 43rd round pick in 1994, spent the regular season at Class A Kissimmee where he hit .303 with seven home runs and 62 RBI in 128 games. He led the Florida State League with 14 triples and tied for fifth with 51 stolen bases. His 223 total bases established a Cobras' single-season record, while his 45 multiple-hit games led the club. He still has a way to go.

Disappointments

The Astros have been very good at picking players in the first round of the June regular draft over the years. Most all of them have made it to the majors. Of course there are some exceptions.

The biggest disappointment in Houston history has to be **Floyd Bannister.** The Astros had the first pick in the nation in June 1976 and picked the 1976 College Player of the Year who led the nation in strikeouts his final two years at Arizona State. After some bitter draft negotiations that lasted more than a month, he signed and went to rookie level where he was brilliant. However, the lefthander was not so shiny the next season in the majors as he registered an 8-9 mark in 24 starts. His performance was even worse in 1978 as he was 3-9 with a 4.83 ERA. A disgusted Houston club traded him to Seattle for Craig Reynolds. It was a great trade as Reynolds played 11 years for the Astros at shortstop, while Bannister was a loser. Not until he went to the White Sox as a free agent in 1983 did he begin to become a winner in the majors and helped the Sox to a division championship. In all, he pitched 15 seasons in the majors and retired with a losing record—134-142.

The Astro also had similar bad luck in picking the first overall player in the draft in 1992. They chose **Phil Nevin** out of Cal State Fullerton. Nevin played at Triple-A for three seasons before he got a call to the majors, where he couldn't hit his weight. He became the player to be named later in that season's trade with Detroit. He was then dealt to Anaheim in 1997. He led American League catchers in passed balls in 1998 with 20.

The Astros said never to **Tom Nevers,** a first-round pick (21st overall) in 1990 out of high school. Nevers never got past Double-A with Houston, so he was traded in 1995 to the Brewers for Derrick May. He later became a free agent

and signed with the Cardinals, Angels and Reds. He never made it to the majors with either of those teams.

Jimmy Gonzalez was a sandwich pick in 1991 out of high school. As a catcher, he was a much needed commodity. He developed slowly and by the time he had six years in the minors, he was only in Double-A, so the Astros let him become a free agent. He signed with the Padres and moved up to Triple-A in 1998.

Branden Berg was a third round pick in 1997 was released. "He just never turned into the player we had hoped he would. He had limited mobility at first," said Perpura.

Best Draft

A great year for the Astros was 1976 as eight drafted players eventually made their way to the majors. **Floyd Bannister** was the first round pick in the regular phase of the June draft. He pitched a couple of seasons with Houston before going on to a 15-year pitching career in the majors. **Dave Smith** was also in that class and he pitched 11 years with the Astros.

Worst Draft

In 1980, the only two players drafted made it to the majors. Houston had lost its first two choices to compensation for signing free agents Nolan Ryan and Joe Morgan. **Jeff Calhoun,** a third-round pick in the regular June draft, and **Jeff Heathcock,** a first round pick in the June secondary phase, were both relievers who made it to the Astros, but neither made much of an impact.

Ones Who Got Away

The Astros picked **Ken Landreaux** out of high school in 1973, but he didn't sign. He waited until the Angels made him a first-round pick in 1976 out of Arizona State University. Landreaux went on to a 11-year career in the majors.

Where Are They Now?

Jeff Juden, a number one pick in 1989, signed a minor league free agent contract with

Jeff Juden, a number one pick in 1989 for the Houston Astros.

the Yankees in January 1999 and found himself back in Triple-A pitching for the Columbus Clippers. The power pitcher first came up with Houston in 1991. The Astros traded him the next season to Philadelphia for Mitch Williams. He is now with his eighth team in as many years.

Joe Mikulik is back with the Houston organization after spending some time with Cleveland. He was drafted and signed by the Astros in January regular phase in 1984 out of San Jacinto Junior College, Texas. "The winter draft was pretty good for options," he explained. "If you got drafted in the winter, you could play college ball in the spring and get drafted again in June. It gave you more options." Because he

had options to go on to more college, he had leverage and got a bonus of $40,000. The winter draft was done away with a couple of years after he was picked. Mikulik played and managed in the minors for 15 years. The Astros brought him back in 1998 as baserunning and outfield coach for the minor leagues.

Also back with the Astros as coach is **John Massarelli.** He was drafted in the eighth round in 1987 and played in the Astros organization for seven seasons. After playing a year in Taiwan, he turned to coaching with the Astros.

Mark Bailey also decided to come back to his original team to coach after his playing career ended. The sixth round pick of the 1982 draft was part of the club's National League West championship team in 1986. He played five seasons with the Astros and finished his career with the Giants.

And **Jim Pankovits** is back with the Astros, too. The fourth round pick in 1976 with Houston played six seasons in the organization before being traded to San Diego. He came back to Houston and made his major league debut with the club in 1984. The infielder then went on to play with Pittsburgh, Los Angeles and Boston. After playing he turned to managing and was leading the Jackson minor league team in 1998.

Another former Astro who turned to coaching was **Mike Easler,** a sixth round pick in 1969. "The Hit Man" played with the Astros from 1973 to 1975 before going on to four other teams during a 14-year career in the majors. He turned to being a hitting coach and was with the Red Sox in 1998.

Still another former Astros draft pick turned to coaching is **John McLaren.** Selected by Houston in the seventh round of the 1970 June draft, he homered in his first professional game. He never played in the majors, but turned to scouting, managing and coaching. He was with Seattle in 1998 as a bench coach.

Bill Doran, a sixth round pick, is now coaching with the Cincinnati Reds. Doran played nine seasons with the Astros before going to the Reds for the remainder of his 11-year career. The solid second baseman helped Houston reach the League Championship Series in 1986.

Cliff Johnson, a fifth round pick in 1966,

Joe Mikulik was drafted by the Astros in 1984.

went into farming after playing and is now re-tired. He played seven seasons with the Astros during his 15-year career.

All in the Family

Houston had high hopes for **Robbie Wine,** whose father, Bobby, had played for Philadelphia and was coaching for them then. The catcher from Oklahoma State made it to the Astros in 1986, but played just 23 games in two seasons.

Mel Stottlemyre, Jr., son of Yankee pitcher Mel, was drafted and signed in the January 1985 Secondary Phase. The pitcher never made it to the majors like his dad and later his brother, Todd.

On the Roster

Houston doesn't have a lot of their own draft picks on the roster, because they have traded away many future major leagues for more experienced players to help the team out now.

Billy Wagner, a first round pick in 1993, was a starter in the minors, but was put in the bullpen for the majors. The Astros soon discovered he was more effective as the team's stopper. Then in 1998 the lefty with the triple-digit fastball helped Houston to the playoffs with 30 saves during the season. Only Doug Jones in 1992 (36) and Dave Smith in 1986 (33) have had better totals in a Houston uniform. The Astros signed him to a three-year contract in 1999. "Billy Wagner is an extraordinary talent," General manager Gerry Hunsicker said. "I believe a contract of this length for a player with two-plus years of major league service is unprecedented in our organization. I'm also hard pressed to think of many other players in his situation to have earned this type of agreement."

Shane Reynolds was a third-round pick out of the University of Texas in 1989 and became a key member of the first-place Astros in 1998 when he turned in a 19-8 performance on the mound. The right-hander has been a 30-plus game starter for Houston for five seasons. His record with Houston through the 1998 season was 63-47. His best season came in 1998 when he compiled a 19-8 mark to help Houston to a first-place finish. He is signed through 2002 with a club option for 2003.

The Astros took **Scott Elarton** in the first round out of Lamar (Colo.) High School in 1994. His progress was slow at first. He spent his first three seasons in Single-A. After a 12-7 mark and 2.92 ERA at Class A Kissimmee, the right-hander was finally promoted to Double-A in 1997. He took less than a season to prove himself there and ended up in Triple-A by the end of the season. The Astros brought him up on June 20, 1998, and he appeared in 28 games the rest of the season with Houston, finishing the season with a 3.32 ERA as a reliever. However, he was expected to be a starter for the club in 1999. Team officials were very high on his performance and wouldn't consider him in a trade for Roger Clemens.

Tony McKnight, a first-round pick in 1995 who was recommended by scout Chuck Edmondson, has been disappointing so far, but the Astros put him on the 40-man roster to protect him and give him more time. Chosen out of Arkansas High School in Texarkana, Ark., McKnight could have gone to just about any college with a full scholarship. Instead, he chose pro ball. "You can always go to school," he explained. McKnight was overused in high school — in one game he threw over 200 pitches — which led to him having an elbow problems in his first seasons in the minors. He saw limited action his first two seasons due to the elbow injury. Not until 1998 did he have his first full season in the minors. Then he had back spasms, but he worked his way past that. "The last half of the season, I pitched really well," he said. He feels being put on the 40-man roster as a real positive step in his professional career.

Tony McKnight was a first round pick in 1995 for the Astros.

Chris Holt, a third-round pick in 1992, didn't think he'd ever get drafted when he played baseball at Navarro Junior College. "I played the infield and I wasn't going anywhere. I just started pitching in my sophomore year in college. It all happened in a matter of about six months," he commented. Scouts Ben Galante and Ralph Bratton signed him. Holt got a September call-up in 1996. Then he made the squad out of spring training the next year. Getting to the playoffs in 1997 was his biggest thrill so far. Holt was competing for a spot in the Expos' regular rotation at spring training in 1999 after coming off shoulder surgery, which kept him from pitching with Houston in 1998.

Another draft pick hoping to stick with the Astros in 1999 was **Russ Johnson,** a first-round pick in 1994. The shortstop was surprised to be picked by Houston, because he hadn't heard anything from them. "I just waiting for a spot," he said optimistically at spring training in 1999.

Russ Johnson was a first round pick in 1994 by Houston.

"You've got to wait your turn. That's just part of the game." Johnson has been called up twice and got his first major league hit off Atlanta pitcher Tom Glavine. Then he hit his first homer off Pedro Martinez. "Those are two feathers in my cap so far."

He works hard and gives the game 100 percent every day, so he feels will be eventually rewarded. They say good things come to those who wait. His patience was rewarded in 1999 when Houston called him up in May.

Future Stars

Wade Miller, a 20th round pick in 1996, has made good progress and was a perfect 5-0 with a 2.32 ERA in 10 starts for Double-A Jackson in 1998. In 62.0 innings, he walked only 27 batters while striking out 48. His season ended early after he suffered scarring of a tendon in his index finger, which required surgery.

At Triple-A was **Brian Sikorski,** a fourth-round choice in 1995. The right-handed pitcher has steadily climbed up the ladder as a starter and was called up to Houston in September 1998, but did not appear in a game.

Lance Berkman was selected 16th overall in the first round of the 1997 draft. The switch hitter was named 1997 National Player of the Year by National Collegiate Baseball and Western Athletic Conference Player of the Year. Berkman was also the national leader in home runs (41) and RBI (134), which were both Rice and WAC records. His home-run total was the third-best single-season total in NCAA history, while his RBI total is second only behind Pete Incaviglia's record 148. "Lance clearly has a chance to be an impact player in the major leagues," said Astros General Manager Gerry Hunsicker when he was signed. "Not since the signing of Glenn Davis in 1980 has this organization signed a player with this much offensive potential." In two seasons in the minors the outfielder moved up to Triple-A and was named as a Texas League all-star. He hit 30 homers in 1998.

Brad Lidge, the club's number-one pick in the 1998, was named 1998 Big East Conference Pitcher of the Year. He was a member of the 1997 USA Baseball trials, too. The hard-throwing righty had a fastball clocked in the high 90s. "He's raw, but he's got a good arm," Purpura said. Lidge was first selected by the San Francisco Giants in the 45th round of the 1995 draft while still in high school at Cherry Creek.

The Astros picked **Jay Perez** in the second round out of high school. Perez, who was selected as the 55th pick, batted .596 with eight home runs and 28 RBI in 1999. "Jay has the potential to be a very good hitter," said scouting director David Lakey. "He has good hands and a decent arm. We feel like he could become a solid catcher."

Another second-round selection was right-handed pitcher **Travis Anderson** from the University of Washington. The 6-4, 225-pound Anderson, who was the 80th pick, was a three-year letter winner at Washington. He started 13 games and made one relief appearance during his junior campaign. He was 2-2 over 50.0 in-nings. "Travis is a power pitcher with a lot of durability," Lakey said. "He is a strong pitcher who throws in the low 90s. I can foresee him being able to throw a lot of innings. He is another player we feel very fortunate to land where we were."

Houston's first pick in 1999 was **Michael Rosamond** out of the University of Mississippi where he hit .310 with 18 homers. "Where we drafted [42nd overall], we were fortunate to get him," said Lakey. "He comes from a good, solid program with great competition."

Los Angeles Dodgers

The Dodgers have believed in the farm and draft systems for a long time and will continue that thinking in the future. The best evidence of that is their knack for picking players who become instant successes and are named rookie of the year. The team began that tradition long before the draft when it was still based in Brooklyn. In the first year of the award, Jackie Robinson won the award despite playing out of position and having to put up with racial slurs and death threats. The first draft pick to be bestowed the honor was Ted Sizemore in 1969. Then the team went through a 10-year drought before **Rick Sutcliffe** was honored in 1979. The number-one draft choice of 1974 went 17-10 in his rookie season to earn the award. The following season another draft pick, **Steve Howe**, picked up 17 saves, which led to his selection for the award. The team went through another dry spell until sixth-round pick **Eric Karros**, a first baseman, hit 20 home runs in 1992 to win the award. He was followed the next year by **Mike Piazza**, an unbelievable 62nd round pick, who slammed out 35 homers and 112 RBI in his first season. The next Dodger draft choice to win the honor was **Todd Hollandsworth**, an outfielder who batted .291 and hit 12 homers in his debut in 1996. Hollandsworth was a third-round pick in 1991. In all, the Dodgers have won the Rookie of the Year more than twice as many times as other teams.

Another indication that the Dodgers have profited from the draft is their record since 1970, when the draft began taking effect on teams. The Dodgers have finished in first place nine times in 30 years and played in five World Series. Those teams were laced with a combination of good draft picks and free agents. Tommy Lasorda was the manager for all those teams except one, which was managed by Walter Alston.

During the first decade of the draft, the Dodgers concentrated on picking high school players with their first pick, but in more recent times they have focused on college players. They also have concentrated on players with a lot of speed to steal bases and cover the field better.

A changing of the guard in Los Angeles resulted in the Dodgers cleaning house in the scouting staff in 1998. The new staff went into 1999 with a new attitude. Ed Creech came over from the Mets to lead the staff and Kevin Slater came from the Orioles to be his assistant. The new directors revamped the entire system with a new grading system and very aggressive approach to scouting. ""We're looking forward to this year (1999)," said an excited Slater. "We won't leave any stone unturned."

The new staff favors athletes with high ceilings, in other words, lots of potential. They want players who will be stars in the future. They hope to carry on a long tradition of getting players who become rookies of the year. Everything has become computerized, too, and new radar guns ordered. The Dodgers are going to look at the minors and other professional leagues more closely than in the past by doubling evaluations and crosschecking more. Los Angeles still believes in tryouts and its scouts hold open tryouts around the country and publish that information on their website.

The Dodgers have two national crosscheckers, three regional supervisors and 17 full-time scouts in the United States. They have an academy in the Dominican Republic and four full-time scouts internationally. Of course, the Dodgers have had some good Mexican players, such as Fernando Valenzuela, who was also a Rookie of the Year. They are very active in Asia and signed their first Taiwanese player in late 1998. According to a report in *The Boston Globe* in May 1999, the Dodgers illegally tried to recruit Cuban minor league players. The newspaper claimed the Dodgers held secret tryouts and arranged for the escapes of first baseman Juan Carlos Diaz and outfielder Jose Perez, who have asked the commissioner's office to declare them free agents on grounds they were signed illegally. Teams are prohibited from scouting in Cuba. Also, helping a Cuban player to escape to the United States would violate the trade embargo.

Best Draft Picks

Draft picks **Ron Cey, Steve Garvey, Davey Lopes** and **Bill Russell** played the infield together for a nine incredible seasons during the 1970s and early 1980s—something that will unlikely be done again with free agency the way it is. The quartet helped the Dodgers to four National League pennants and a World Series victory in 1981. Garvey, who anchored first base, led the team in hitting five of these years and RBI in seven of the nine years. Cey led the team in on-base percentage four of those years, and homers and RBI for a couple of seasons. Lopes led the team in stolen bases during that span. And Russell specialized in bunting, stealing and hitting behind runners.

Garvey, a first-round pick in the June 1968 secondary phase, had his best season in 1974 when he was named the Most Valuable Player. He earned four Gold Gloves and appeared in 10 All-Star games during his 19-year career, 14 with the Dodgers. However, "Mr. Clean" has not been a serious contender for the Hall of Fame.

Cey, who was picked two rounds after Gar-

vey, appeared in six All-Star contests during his 17 years in the majors, a dozen with the Dodgers. "The Penguin," who got that name for his peculiar way of running, hit more homers (316) than Garvey during his career

Lopes, another 1968 pick, was the gazelle on the team, but he could hit for power as well and hit 26 leadoff homers during his 16 years in the majors, ten with the Dodgers. The leadoff hitter appeared in four All-Star games during his career and won a Gold Glove once. He stole 557 bases during his career, including a stretch of 38 consecutive stolen base successes.

Russell's blood turned Dodger blue as he played his whole 18-year career with Los Angeles as well as coaching and managing the team after that. However, he couldn't fill Tommy Lasorda's shoes.

Bill Buckner, a second-round pick in 1968, could have been a wide receiver in the National Football League, but he chose baseball and made his first appearance with the Dodgers in 1969. He became a regular with the Dodgers by 1971 in the outfield and first base. The fleet-footed Buckner stole a career-high 31 bases in 1974. The following season he injured his left ankle and lost his speed, which relegated him to first base. With Garvey on the team, the Dodgers traded him to Cubs where he won the National League batting title in 1980 with a .324 average. Then he went to the Red Sox where he made an error that would put him on every highlight film. He allowed a ball to slip through his legs to allow the winning run to score and rob the Sox of a World Series.

Another Dodger who ended up in a Cub uniform was **Rick Sutcliffe**, a first-round pick in 1974. The young Sutcliffe was 17-10 with the Dodgers in 1979, but slumped to 3-9 in 1980, so he was traded to Cleveland for a couple of seasons before going to the Cubs at the beginning of 1984. The Windy City turned his career around as he earned a Cy Young in helping the Cubs to the League Championship Series with his remarkable 16-1 record. Sutcliffe again helped the Cubs to the LCS in 1989. He retired after the 1994 season with a 171-139 record after 18 years in the majors.

Charlie Hough, an eighth-round pick in 1966, was signed as an infielder and pitcher but

Manager Tommy Lasorda liked him more as a pitcher. Three years later he hurt his pitching arm in Triple-A, so Dodgers scout Gordie Holt showed him how to throw a knuckleball. That did the trick and Hough was on his way to becoming another Hoyt Wilhelm. He pitched for seven full seasons with the Dodgers before being traded to the Texas Rangers. After stints with the White Sox and Marlins, Hough was forced to retired in 1994. The oldest player in professional sports is the only pitcher in the history of the game to pitch 400 starts and 400 relief appearances. He finished with a 216-216 record.

The Dodgers traded away **John Wetteland** before he became a great closer. After Los Angeles drafted him in the second round of the 1985 January secondary phase, they made him a starter in the minors. Then he was converted into a reliever in 1990 before they traded him to the Reds, who shipped him to Montreal a month later. The Expos used him as their stopper and he responded with 37 saves in his first season with Montreal. He set the high mark for saves at Montreal with 43 saves in 1993 before being traded to the Yankees. He posted all four saves in 1996 World Series against Atlanta to bring the championship back to New York. He became a free agent in 1997 and signed with the Rangers. Through 1998, Wetteland had become one of the best relievers in the game and had been named to three All-Star games.

Long Shots

The Dodgers are famous for picking long shots and getting them to the majors, which speaks a lot for their farm system and training programs. Several great players were originally long shots with the Dodgers.

The odds of a 62nd round draft pick making it to the majors and being one of the best players in the majors is like winning the lottery, which is something like seven million-to-one. **Mike Piazza** beat those odds and has earned more in baseball than any lottery player. He would have never been drafted had it not been for his godfather, Lasorda, long-time skipper of the Dodgers and now vice president.

When Piazza was a youngster, Lasorda would use him as a batboy for the Dodgers

Mike Piazza was drafted by the Dodgers as a 62nd round pick. (Photograph by Marty Orr.)

whenever the team was near his home to play the Phillies. The youngster got his taste of professional baseball and wanted to play for the Dodgers some day. He concentrated on baseball at Phoenixville Area High School in suburban Philadelphia and became a good hitter.

The Dodgers' manager asked five scouts from five different organizations to check him out. They did. "All five scouts said he can't do anything," said Lasorda.

After going undrafted in 1987, Piazza enrolled at the University of Miami, but he wasn't getting much playing time there, so Lasorda got him into Miami–Dade North Community College where he played everyday.

Before the 1988 draft, Lasorda asked the organization, "Do you think I have a favor coming?" He only wanted him drafted and he didn't care what round. The Dodgers honored the request by drafting him as their last pick — the 1,390th pick of the draft.

Lasorda had Piazza come out to show the scouting director what he had. After the tryout the director said he wouldn't sign Piazza if he was a first baseman. Lasorda asked the director if he would sign him if he was a catcher and the director said he would. "Sign him. He's a catcher," Lasorda told him. Piazza wasn't a catcher. He signed for $15,000.

Lasorda sent him to the Dodgers' baseball

academy in the Dominican Republic to transform the first baseman into a catcher. Piazza was the first American player at the academy. He didn't know Spanish. The players there didn't know English. But Piazza had a tremendous desire to become a Dodger some day and he worked hard.

In his first two seasons in Class A, he was a little above average in hitting. Then his third year at Single-A was his breakout year when he pounded 29 homers. This earned him a promotion to Double-A where he hit .371 to get him another promotion to Triple-A and finally the Dodgers in 1992.

In his rookie season in 1993, he removed any doubt about his ability to play in the majors as he put up great numbers — .318-35-112 — to earn Rookie of the Year selection. He continued to put up big numbers and was runner-up for MVP voting two years in a row.

In Lasorda's last game as manager of the team, Piazza made the departure a memorable one as he hit a homer in the ninth to win the game. The All-Star catcher was traded twice in 1998 and ended up with the New York Mets. If he continues his success, he will end up as the best hitting catcher ever and the second drafted catcher to make it to the famed hall. Johnny Bench was the first.

Doyle Alexander was a distant 44th-round draft pick in the 1968 draft and reached the majors in 1971 with the Dodgers. That was his only season with the Dodgers, but he went on to a 19-year career in the majors with eight different teams and finished with a 194-174 record. He was named to one All-Star team and appeared in one World Series. Probably his best season came in 1987 when he was traded to the Tigers and went 9-0 the rest of the season to help Detroit win the pennant. On three different occasions he won 17 games in a season.

Orel Hershiser was a 17th-round choice out of Bowling Green State University in 1979. The righthander pitched mainly in relief in the minors and climbed up to the Dodgers in five seasons. The Dodgers found out he was better as a starter. Then in 1985 he was nearly unbeatable with a 19-3 mark on the season. However, he didn't win the Cy Young Award until 1988 when he went 23-8 and won one game in the

playoffs and two games in the World Series to give the Dodgers a world championship. Then he threw 59 consecutive scoreless innings during one stretch to break former Dodger Don Drysdale's record. After a dozen years with the Dodgers, he became a free agent and signed with the Indians. Then he went on to the Giants.

Dave Stewart played a couple of years with the Dodgers, but didn't mature as a starting pitcher until he was sent back where he came from. Stewart was born in Oakland, went to school in Oakland and probably should have been drafted by Oakland, but the Dodgers picked him in the 16th round in 1975 out of an Oakland high school right under the noses of the Athletics scouting staff. The Dodgers couldn't decide what he was best at — starter or reliever. He was good at both, but not enough to persuade the Dodgers to keep him, so he was traded for a more secure pitcher in Rick Honeycutt. Honeycutt was a better pitcher while he was in Los Angeles than Stewart was as a reliever with the Rangers and Phillies. Ironically, both pitchers ended up in Oakland about the same time and Stewart became a starter and Honeycutt became a reliever. Stewart started a string of 20-win seasons and was a candidate for the Cy Young four years running. He helped the Athletics win the shaky 1989 World Series with two wins. It was shaky because that was the year the earthquake hit San Francisco and delayed the series for 10 days. The 16th-round pick wrapped up his 16-year career in Oakland in 1995 with a 158-129 record. He was sweet 16.

Another Dodgers long shot to make it big was **Eric Young**, a 43rd round pick in the 1989 draft. The outfielder from Rutgers University showed he could hit and moved up quickly through the Dodgers' system, but as a second baseman. In his fourth year in the minors, Young cracked into the Dodgers' lineup. However, the Dodgers lost him in the expansion draft to the Colorado Rockies in 1993. The Dodgers wanted him back though and traded Pedro Astacio to the Rockies for him in 1997.

Another 43rd rounder to make it to the majors was **Mike James** in 1987. He was traded to the Angels in 1993 for outfielder Reggie Williams before he ever got to the majors. California finally promoted him in 1995 and the right-handed reliever has performed well in the majors ever since.

The Dodgers have had their share of good outfielders, which made **Garey Ingram's** job even harder for a 44th round pick in 1989. He was called up to the Dodgers three different seasons, but never stayed there for long. He was granted free agency in 1998 and signed with the Red Sox.

Todd Williams, a 54th round choice in 1990, pitched his way to the majors in 1995 with Los Angeles. However, he was traded to the Athletics before the end of the season. Williams again got a call up with the Reds in 1998.

Ten years after being drafted, 35th round **Hector Ortiz** finally had his dream come true as a September call-up in 1998 with Kansas City. The Puerto Rican born catcher was selected by the Dodgers. After gaining free agency in 1994, he signed with the Cubs, who took his as far as Triple-A. Then he signed with the Royals in 1997. The weak hitter—.227 career average—makes up for his lack of hitting by being a good defensive catcher.

Disappointments

As good as the Dodgers have done in the draft, their were a few rotten apples in the bushel.

The Dodgers got off to a poor start in the first draft when they chose **John Wyatt**, a shortstop out of high school in the first round. Wyatt never got higher than Single-A.

The year 1968 was a great draft year for the Dodgers, but the first-round pick, **Bobby Valentine**, never materialized as a player for the Dodgers. Injuries derailed his major league career before it ever began. He was hit by a pitch which fractured his cheekbone while he was in Triple-A. Then he broke his nose. The Dodgers traded him to California in 1972 and he broke his right left leg when he ran into a wall in April 1973. After his playing career, he became more famous as the manager of the Texas Rangers.

The Dodgers chose catcher **Terry McDermott** as a first-round choice in 1969. He only ended up playing nine games for the Dodgers in 1972.

Another first-round catching bomb was

Bobby Valentine was a first round pick in 1968 for the Dodgers. (Photograph by Marty Orr.)

Ted Farr in 1973. He only got as far as Triple-A with the Dodgers before bowing out in 1977.

Lefthanded pitchers always have a good chance at making it to the majors. Such was not for the story for two lefthanded first-round pitchers in 1983 and 1984. **Eric Sonberg** and **Dennis Livingston** were both drafted out of college and both made it only as far as Triple-A.

The Dodgers were high on righthanded pitcher **Jim Haller**, a first-round pick in 1970. The high school prospect got as far as Triple-A. Other first-round pitchers who never got to the majors include **Bill Bene**, in 1988, and **Dan Opperman**, in 1987.

Billy Ashley is one of the Dodgers' latest disappointments, but he feels the team never really gave him much of an opportunity. The first-round pick from 1988 was called up six times with the Dodgers and managed just a .233 average and 28 homers with the team in 632 games. He was an all-star, player of the year and most valuable player in the minors, but never produced in the majors. He signed with the Devil Rays in 1999 and hoped to do better.

Best Draft

In 1968 the Dodgers picked several players who would later take them or other teams on to World Series fame. In the January draft, L.A. picked up **Davey Lopes**. Then in June regular draft, they acquired **Bill Buckner**, **Tom Paciorek** and **Doyle Alexander**. **Steve Garvey** and **Ron Cey** were chosen in the June secondary phase.

Worst Draft

The 1986 draft was nearly a waste as only one player, **Mike Munoz**, made it to the majors and he wasn't much of an impact with the Dodgers.

Where Are They Now?

Signing a major league contract after high school or going on to college can be a difficult decision for a player. It wasn't for **Paul Konerko**. He told the Dodgers: "Look guys, I'm going to sign. Let's get this over so I can play." After being picked 13th in the first round by the

Paul Konerko, first round, 13th pick in the 1994 draft.

Dodgers, the Chaparral High School, Arizona, graduate signed 10 days later for $830,000.

In three years time, he moved from Single-A to Triple-A. Konerko doesn't regret not going to college. "If I had gone to college, I would have been drafted last June," he said in 1998 with the Indianapolis Indians. "I'd probably in Double-A right now. I've already been in Triple-A two years. I've always thought, you can't get called up from college." He is partially right there. Only a few players have gone directly from college to the pros.

Konerko was first called up by the Dodgers in September 1997, but he only played in six games — not enough to display his talents. He had knocked out 37 homers in the light air of Albuquerque that season, which earned him Minor League Player of the Year honors.

The following season the Dodgers were in desperate need of relief pitching, so they traded him and another player to Cincinnati for Jeff Shaw. Konerko felt he had "poor timing" being with the Dodgers, who had Eric Karros at first and Bobby Bonilla and Todd Zeile at third. With Cincinnati, he had a better shot at getting established in the majors. He again showed he was ready for the majors as he hit .327 at Indianapolis before the Reds called him up in September. The Reds decided there wasn't any room for him there, so they dealt him to the White Sox, where he has found a home at first base.

Jim Riggleman began his professional career in 1974 after being selected by the Los Angeles Dodgers in the 4th round of the June draft. He played in the minors for eight seasons in the

Jim Riggleman (left), manager of the Chicago Cubs, and Ed Lynch, general manager of the Cubs. Riggleman was drafted by the Dodgers in the 4th round in 1974.

Los Angeles (1974–1976) and St. Louis (1976–1981) farm systems. He finally made it to the majors as a manager with the Padres for two seasons. Then he went to the Cubs and took them to the playoffs in 1998.

Another player who stayed in baseball after playing is **Tracy Woodson**, a third-round pick in 1984. He played three years with the Dodgers and was a member of the 1988 World Championship team. He also played a couple of years with the Cardinals. After his playing days ended, he became a manager in the Pirates organization with the Class A Hickory Crawdads.

After his playing days, **Rick Sutcliffe** turned to broadcasting. He became a baseball pitching analyst for ESPN.

Rick Sutcliffe, drafted as a first-round pick in 1974 by the Los Angeles Dodgers. (Photograph courtesy of Jackie Dowling.)

When the Dodgers picked **Kevin Dotson** in the 12th round of the June 1983 draft, they selected him as a catcher. "I never caught until I was drafted, so that's kind of ironic," said Dotson. His tool was a good arm, so the Dodgers thought they could turn the infielder at Memphis State University into a receiver. He received a "small" bonus for signing. He played rookie ball at Lethbridge in Alberta, Canada. At spring training the next season, he was released because the Dodgers had traded for a couple of receivers. He was crushed. He looked to other teams, but rosters were full. His professional baseball career was over. At least he had his degree in business management. Now a district manager for an office supply company in Indianapolis, he still plays baseball in the Men's Adult Baseball League.

Ones Who Got Away

The Dodgers drafted **Tom Seaver** in the first draft, but didn't offer him a contract. He then was drafted by the Braves the following January; however, the Mets ended up getting him after a draft mixup.

The Dodgers picked **Mike Garrett**, a running back in the Super Bowl with the Kansas City Chiefs, in the 35th round in 1970. Garrett said he was playing out his option with the Chiefs and would turn to baseball. He became the oldest player selected at 26. But Garrett decided he was better off staying in football and never signed.

Undrafted Players

Ron Kittle was not drafted after he graduated from high school, so he went to work in a steel plant, toiling up to 14 hours a day as an iron worker. "I was cleaning my boots one day and I saw this paper below my feet that said the Dodgers were holding a tryout camp," the Gary, Indiana, native said. "My dad said I had to go. He took me to the tryout. That's where I put on a hitting display." The barrage of home runs earned him a $5,000 contract from the Dodgers.

Not long after his professional career started, it nearly ended in Class A ball. "I slid across home plate and the catcher landed on me," he explained. He suffered crushed vertebrae in his neck. After the season, he had spinal fusion surgery. The Dodgers released him. A couple of years later he was given a second chance by the White Sox. He went on to a 10-year professional career, hitting 176 home runs.

All in the Family

In 1969 the Dodgers drafted **Gary Erskine**, son of Carl, a great pitcher from the 1950s when the team was still in Brooklyn. The high school pitcher and outfielder never signed. He is now a vice president of a bank in Anderson, where his father was the president at one time.

Ricky Bell, a third round pick in 1997, is

the son of former Tigers manager and player Buddy Bell. Like father, like son, he's a third baseman.

Chris Latham's father, William Sledge, played in Philadelphia's system in the mid–'60s. Latham, an 11th round pick in 1991 signed by scout Gail Henley, was traded to the Twins in 1995 where he made it to the majors in 1997.

When the Dodgers picked **Chris Gwynn** in the first round in 1985, they were undoubtedly hoping good hitting was in the genes. Tony, who played down the road in San Diego, was turning out to be just about the best hitter around baseball. Chris made it to the majors and spent seven seasons with the Dodgers, but he wasn't a facsimile of his brother.

The Dodgers drafted twins in 1990. They selected **Mike** and **Mark Mimbs** in the 24th and 25th round, respectively. The Mimbs were both lefthanded hurlers out of Mercer University. The Dodgers released Mike in 1993 and let Mark become a free agent at the end of the 1996 season without ever calling the twins to the majors. Mike later signed with the Phillies and made it to the majors with Philadelphia. Mark was 9-2 with a 2.08 ERA for Triple-A Norfolk when he was released by the Mets in 1998.

On the Roster

Eric Karros is one of the veteran draft picks on the team as he was picked in the sixth round in 1988 out of UCLA. The first baseman laid waste to minor league pitching during his four seasons there as he batted .329 and was the Dodgers' Minor League Player of the Year in 1991. He hasn't lived up to that average in the majors, but he's made up for it with more homers and RBI. He had three seasons in a row where he hit more than 30 homers and 100 RBI for the Dodgers. Ironically, his first major league homer didn't come until his 72nd at-bat in Wrigley Field. He's hit 176 more since then in eight seasons.

Todd Hollandsworth was certainly worth a third-round pick by the Dodgers in 1991. The high school pick breezed through the minors and was one of the youngest players in Triple-A Albuquerque at age 21, where he hit .285 with 19 homers and 15 steals in 1994. His rookie season

with the Dodgers was in 1996 and he made the most of it by hitting .291 with 12 homers, 26 doubles and 21 steals to earn National League Rookie of the Year honors. Injuries have since limited him to 160 games in two seasons. A healthier body could bring him back to form.

Darren Dreifort was drafted by the Dodgers in the first round in 1993 out of Wichita State University, where he was Golden Spikes Award Winner as the nation's top amateur player in 1993. The Dodgers brought him straight to the majors as a reliever after signing him. His start in the majors was less than spectacular. Dreifort struggled to a 0-5 record with a 6.21 ERA, but he did have six saves. Then he missed all of 1995 due to elbow surgery. He split the next two seasons between Triple-A and the Dodgers. Then in 1998, the Dodgers threw him into the starting rotation. He ended the season with an 8-12 record.

Onan Masaoka, a third-round pick in 1995 out of a Hawaiian high school, made the Dodgers line-up out of spring training in 1999. A 0.69 ERA during spring training convinced the Dodgers the left-hander was ready. The native Hawaiian made the jump from Double-A where he was used primarily as a starter.

A long shot on the Dodgers' roster is **Jeff Kubenka**, a 38th-round draft pick in 1996. A reliever his whole professional career with the Dodgers, the lefthander got his first September call to the majors in 1998. The Dodgers liked that performance, so they called him up again in 1999. He may soon become a permanent fixture.

Mike Piazza's departure from Los Angeles opened the door for other catchers in the minors. Like Piazza, who was a 62nd rounder, **Paul LoDuca** was long shot, too — 25th round pick in the 1993 draft. The cousin of former Mets star Lee Mazzilli hit .308 at Albuquerque to earn his way to the majors in five years and three months. He got his first call to the majors in 1998.

Future stars?

Glenn Davis was the first-round pick back in the 1997 draft out of Vanderbilt University. The power hitting prospect showed he could knock it over the fences in his sophomore season in the minors as he hit 26 homers at Single-A and Double-A. He's versatile enough to play first base or the outfield, so his chances at getting to the majors soon are increasingly good. Ironically, he has the same name and plays the same position as the previous Glenn Davis in the majors who played with the Astros and Orioles. That Davis hit 190 homers in 10 seasons. If he lives up to that, the Dodgers would be more than pleased.

Another power hitting prospect coming up through the rank and file is **Nick Leach**. The fifth-round pick out of high school in 1996 is a first baseman, too. However, he's a step behind Davis. Leach was named an all-star in the Northwest League in 1997 after hitting .313 there with seven homers, 18 doubles and 47 RBI.

The 1996 first-round selection **Damian Rolls** has shown pop in his bat, too. The third baseman has had double-digit homer seasons ever since he entered pro ball after high school.

A long shot in the 22nd round in 1994, **Adam Riggs** got a booster shot to his career when he was an all-star and most valuable player in the California League in 1995 where he hit .362 with 24 homers and 106 RBI. Thoughts of Ryne Sandberg must have danced in the heads of Dodgers executives after that. Sandberg had been a long shot as well and ended up at second base like Riggs. Riggs got a brief call up in 1997 and was not impressive, but he is still doing good at Triple-A, so he was just a step away.

"When the Dodgers called, I was shocked," said **Eric Riggs**, a fourth-round selection in 1998. He's no relation to Adam. "I didn't know my dad had talked to them." He only knew the Cubs were trying to get a hold of him the day before the draft. Perhaps the Dodgers got the jump on the Cubs, because Riggs thought he wasn't going to be drafted that early.

Some negotiations take days, weeks or months, but the Central Florida University junior didn't care to dicker. "I wasn't going to

Ted Lilly with the Ottawa Lynx, a Dodgers draft pick.

waste any time," he explained. He signed in about an hour for six figures and was sent to Class A Vero Beach in the Florida State League.

Riggs was not drafted when he graduated from Brownsburg High School in Indiana because he had a scholarship to play basketball. That lasted a year before he switched to baseball as a sophomore at Central Florida. After hitting .394 his junior year, the shortstop became primed for the draft. Teams liked his speed, agility and switch-hitting capabilities. At one stretch in college, he went 11-for-11 hitting from both sides!

His first year with the Dodgers was a productive one. He put up some fair numbers in Class A—.248-3-17 with three triples—and went on to Fall Instructional League for more intense practice. In the off season, he preaches what he practices at the Brownsburg Baseball Academy to other youngsters.

By 2001, Riggs' odyssey just might end up with the Dodgers. You never know.

Jason Repko was the Dodgers' first pick in the 1999 draft. The shortstop batted .581 with 18 home runs, 47 RBI and 14 stolen bases in 21 games during his senior season in high school. The Dodgers signed him not too long after the draft.

Milwaukee Brewers

The Milwaukee Brewers began drafting players in 1968 as the Seattle Pilots, which played one season in Seattle before moving to Milwaukee after the Braves' departure to Atlanta. It took about a dozen years before the draft started to have a great impact on the team. Then the Brewers won a division title, but fell short in the World Series.

The 1982 World Series team, which lost in seven games to St. Louis, had a handful of draft picks, which were all starters on the team: Paul Molitor, Robin Yount, Gorman Thomas, Jim Gantner and Moose Haas. The team came close again in 1992 when it finished second in its division. Since then, the team hasn't had a winning record. The franchise was moved over to the National League Central Division in a realignment of the leagues in 1998, which didn't seem to help matters.

The scouting department is led by Ken Califano, who supervises a large staff of 22 area scouts in the United States and five crosscheckers. The Brewers have an average size international staff with scouts in the Dominican Republic, Venezuela and Australia. Milwaukee doesn't believe much in open tryouts and held just four, all in Wisconsin, in 1999.

The Brewers have had a lot of luck or skill in choosing number-one picks who have made it to the majors and contributed significantly to the team. That's what any team wants nowadays because of the money they are paying the top picks.

Except for a few shining stars, many of the Brewers' other draft picks have been lackluster. This may be due to the team's concentration on proven college talent versus high school potential. The Brewers have gone with college almost exclusively in the first round in recent drafts. However, that philosophy seems to be changing as the team's first five picks in 1999 were out of high school.

The small market team can't afford a lot of free agents, so it must rely on the draft to bring it talent. Milwaukee's new park, Miller Park, which opens in 2001, will help in raising additional revenue for the team, which will help in its effort to compete with richer franchises. The team also made some administrative changes in August 1999 when manager Phil Garner was fired and general manager Sal Bando was moved to another position.

The Brewers likely need to be rebuilt from the farm system up before they can become competitive again and the draft, of course, is one of the best ways to do that for this or any small-budget team.

Best Picks

Robin Yount was the first Brewers draft pick to enter the Baseball Hall of Fame. The team didn't wait until his induction in 1999 to retire his number "19" in ceremonies in 1994. The first-round pick in 1973 became the regular shortstop for the team at age 18 the following season. He amassed some great statistics during his 20-year career, all with the Brewers. "The Kid" won the Most Valuable Player Award in 1982 and 1989 at different positions. Twice he led the league in doubles and triples. He is the only player to have at least 200 hits against every team he has played against. He became the 17th player in baseball history to record 3,000 career hits when he accomplished the feat on September 9, 1992, against the Cleveland Indians at County Stadium. Yount was named to just three All-Star games during his career, but that might be because of where he was playing and not how he played. His only Gold Glove came in 1982 for his play at shortstop. That year he hit .331 with 29 homers and 114 RBI to lead his team to its only World Series appearance.

The next Brewers draft pick likely to be named to Cooperstown is **Paul Molitor**. Molitor had his uniform number "4" retired on June 11, 1999, in a special pre-game ceremony at County Stadium. When the Brewers picked him in the first round (third overall) in the 1977 draft, scout Dee Fondy signed him for $80,000. Molitor was originally drafted by the Cardinals in the 28th round in 1974, but he passed it up to attend the University of Minnesota where he was all-conference twice. He had been picked in the 28th round out of high school, so he had improved his standing quite a bit after playing at the University of Minnesota. After a season at Class A Burlington, he made the opening-day roster in 1978. He played the next 15 seasons in Milwaukee before becoming a free agent and moving on to the Blue Jays. The seven-time all-star retired in 1998 after 21 seasons and a career .306 batting average. He is only the fifth player all-time with more that 3,000 hits and 500 stolen bases. In one game he stole second, third and home! He also was part of that 1982 World Series team.

Another member of that 1982 team was **Jim Gantner**, a 12th-round pick in 1974. His defensive skills at second base, especially with the double play, prompted the Brewers to move Paul Molitor to the outfield. Gantner played his whole 17-year career with the Brewers. He never made the All-Star Team or led the league in anything; he was just a solid ballplayer who contributed to his team for a long time and the Brewers consider him as their best-ever second baseman. They named him to their 20th anniversary team.

Another member of that 1982 team and the 20th anniversary team was **Gorman Thomas**, a first-round pick in 1969 by the Pilots. The home run leader in 1982 couldn't manage any dingers in the series though and hit less than his weight. While Thomas led the American League in home runs twice, he also led the league in strikeouts twice. His slammed 268 lifetime home runs and struck out 1,339 times. He ranks as one of the best home run hitters and with the lowest average of .225 lifetime. However, he was a fan favorite in Milwaukee.

Dan Plesac, a first-round pick in 1983, became a savior for the Brewers when he arrived in 1986. The left-handed reliever was 10-7 with 14 saves in his rookie year. In his sophomore year, he was named to the All-Star team on his way to earning 23 saves. By 1989, he became the first Brewers pitcher to accumulate 100 saves. He became the first Brewers pitcher ever to be chosen to three straight All-Star games. The Brewers turned to another stopper in 1991, which changed his role to part-time starter and reliever. He was traded to Cubs in 1993. He was still on the mound in 1999.

Dan Plesac, a first round pick in 1983 for the Milwaukee Brewers.

So was **Doug Jones**. The third round pick in January 1978 broke Plesac's record amount of saves with 36 in 1997. He also converted a club record 25 consecutive save opportunities. Jones' baseball passport is just about full as he has pitched for seven different teams in 15 seasons in the majors, including four with Milwaukee. The finesse pitcher had recorded 291 saves by the end of 1998.

Darrell Porter, a first-round pick in 1970, was a bright star with the cellar dwelling expansion Brewers and was named to his first All-Star team in 1974. He was traded to the Royals in 1977 after hitting a lowly .208 the year before. It was one of the Brewers' worst trades as Porter rebounded to be a productive hitter again. He helped the Royals to the playoffs in three out of four seasons. In 1980 he was named to his fourth All-Star team. He appeared in three World Series during his 17-year career. Ironically, he was named World Series Most Valuable Player with the Cardinals in their defeat of his former team.

B.J. Surhoff, another first-round pick, became a solid outfielder for the Brewers for nine seasons. He reached a couple of career milestones in 1995 playing in his 1,000th game in a Brewers uniform and picking up his 1,000th hit as a Brewer. After become a free agent the first time in 1994, he re-signed with the Brewers. However, the next time free agency came up he signed with the Orioles, where he has developed into a home run hitter. He hit a career high 22 homers with Baltimore in 1998.

Gary Sheffield, the first-round choice in 1986, could have been a superstar with the Brewers, but his attitude toward some of the players and fans ended up being his downfall in Milwaukee. After he was shipped out to the Padres in 1991, the club's record improved as well as the atmosphere in the clubhouse. He became an all-star in the National League and the youngest player to win the batting title in 1992 in 30 years. He made a serious bid for the Triple Crown that season and was third in MVP voting. Sheffield helped the Marlins to the World Series in 1997 then went to the Dodgers. He's been on the All-Star team three times, too.

Greg Vaughn left off where Sheffield began and became the superstar for the Brewers in the

Greg Vaughn of the Cincinnati Reds was drafted in the first round in 1986 by the Brewers. (Photograph by Marty Orr.)

1990s. Like Sheffield, he too was drafted in the first round in 1986, but in the secondary draft. And like Sheffield, he was an all-star in the minors and quickly made his way to the Brewers in 1989. He became a power source for the Brew Crew knocking out an average of more than 20 homers a season. He was named to the All-Star Team in 1993. Then injuries limited his play the next two seasons and the Brewers traded him in 1996 before his price tag became too high for them to afford.

Vaughn had a brownout in 1997 with the Padres when he batted only .216; however, he rebounded the next season with 50 homers — the 10th National League player to accomplish that feat — to help the Padres to a World Series appearance. He was also named to his third All-Star team. The Padres unloaded the high salary player to the Reds after the series. In 1999, he made Cincinnati a contender again with his long clouts.

Long Shots

The Brewers aren't big on long shots for some odd reason. Very few players beyond the 10th round have made it to the majors with the Brew Crew. Maybe that's a problem. They just haven't had a Ryne Sandberg, Don Mattingly or Mike Piazza surface as a superstar yet.

Two long shots from the 1972 draft made it to the majors. **Bob Sheldon**, the 22nd round pick, played three undistinguished seasons with the Brewers. **Joe Erardi** was the 24th round pick and he got a cup of coffee with Seattle in 1977.

Anthony Iapoce could be the next long shot to get a shot at the majors. Drafted in the 33rd round in 1994 out of Lamar University, the speedy centerfielder stole a career high 35 bases and batted .314 at Double-A in 1998. That earned him a promotion to Triple-A in 1999.

Disappointments

The Brewers have had their fair share of disappointments over the years.

Milwaukee's first first-round frustration was **Tom Bianco**, a shortstop out of high school. He made it for a cup of coffee as he couldn't hit major league pitching — .176 batting average in 18 games. Another first-round coffee drinker was **Butch Edge**, a right-handed pitcher taken in 1974.

Danny Thomas, a first-round selection in 1972, was headed to stardom after winning the triple crown in the Eastern League in 1976 while coming up to the majors. He got called up briefly to the Brewers twice. Physically, he was ready for the big leagues, but mentally he fell short. He suffered from depression and hung himself in a jail cell in 1980.

In 1975, the Brewers picked **Rich O'Keefe**, a left-hander hurler, and he could do no better than Triple-A.

The Brewers couldn't convince first-round pick **Bill Bordley** to sign a contract. No big loss as the lefty pitched just eight games in the majors.

Nick Hernandez, a catcher out of high school, was the first-round choice in 1978 and he couldn't get past first base. Hernandez rhymes with Fernandez. The Brewers didn't have much luck with **Alex Fernandez** when they picked him first in 1988. He decided to go to community college and signed a year later with the White Sox.

Pat Listach, a fifth-round pick in 1988, was Rookie of the Year in 1992 when he hit .290 for the club. His fame was fleeting though as his batting average fell, his foot speed dropped and with it his career in baseball. He sunk back into the minors after hitting below the Mendoza Line with Houston in 1997. The Reds gave him a try at spring training in 1999 before releasing him.

Milwaukee didn't get a choice in the first round in 1979 or 1990.

The Brewers picked **Jim Morris** in the first round of the January Secondary Phase in 1983. The lefthander only got as far as Class A and retired in 1989 with arm problems and numerous surgeries. However, he wasn't done. He finished his degree, became a head baseball coach and taught chemistry and physics at Reagan County High School, Texas. In 1999, he promised his baseball team that if they made it to the state tournament then he would try out for pro ball. They made it. He kept his promise and went to a tryout camp for the Devil Rays. The 35-year-old lit up the radar gun at 98 mph! The Rays signed him. After extended spring training, he was assigned him to Double-A Orlando. After three appearances there, his ERA was just 1.80, so he was elevated to Triple-A Durham just one step away from making the majors. In September, he was called up to the majors to become the oldest draft pick ever to make it to the majors at age 35. What a comeback!

Jim Morris (left) with the Durham Bulls. He was drafted by Milwaukee in 1983.

The latest failure is pitcher **Tyrone Hill**, a first-round pick in 1991 out of high school. Injuries knocked him out of action for a season and he didn't pitch much in the minors after that, so the Brewers released him. The Angels signed him for a season before letting him become a free agent in 1998.

Best Draft

The Brewers had eight players make it to the majors from the 1983 draft, including five pitchers. Lefthanded hurler **Dan Plesac** was the best of the lot followed by righthanded pitcher **Jeff Parrett**.

Worst Draft

The Brewers first draft as the Pilots was forgettable. Nobody from that draft made any significance to the team. **Bill Parsons**, **Tom Kelly** and **Wilbur Howard** were the players drafted.

Where Are They Now?

Troy O'Leary was selected in the 13th round in 1987 out of high school and was given two brief stints with the Brewers before being claimed on waivers by the Red Sox in 1995. Boston made him a regular in the outfield the next season and he batted .308 with 10 homers. He has been a regular ever since. "I have no regrets for Milwaukee," he wrote during a chat on the internet. "I still love the fellas there, but it's probably the best thing that ever happened to me."

Minnesota Twins manager **Tom Kelly** was the Seattle Pilots' fifth round pick in June 1968. Kelly was released by the Brewers and signed with the Twins as a free agent in 1971. He played one season with the Twins in 1975 before turning to managing. He has been the Twins manager since 1986 and has led the team to two World Championships.

Charlie Montoyo begins his first season in the managing ranks and first year in the Devil Rays organization. Montoyo spent 10 years as an infielder in the Milwaukee Brewers, Montreal Expos, and Philadelphia Phillies organizations and played all four infield positions and the outfield during his career. His lone Major League experience came when he spent 27 days with the Expos in September of the 1993 season. He had a game-winning double in his first at bat in the majors on September 7 vs. Colorado. He was a sixth round draft choice of the Brewers in the June 1987 amateur draft. In 1988, he drew 156 walks in 134 games for Stockton in the Class A California League. Charlie also spent 10 seasons playing winter ball in Puerto Rico. Montoyo attended San Jose De Anza Junior College in San Jose, Calif., and Louisiana Tech University in Ruston, La. He and his wife, Dana, reside in Port St. Lucie, Fla.

Rick Kranitz, a fourth rounder in the 1979 June draft, pitched in the Brewers' organization for five years before being traded to the Cubs in 1984. He soon became a pitching coach and has been at each level in the Cubs' system ever since.

The Brewers drafted **Jeff Kinder** in 1987 and he spent four seasons in the minors before calling it quits. Now he's a fireman in Richmond, Indiana.

Ones That Got Away

The Brewers drafted big **Bob Stoddard** in 1976 out of high school, but he didn't sign.

Tim Teufel and **Kevin McReynolds** were picked in 1978, but they waited to sign with other teams and ended up with the Mets together.

Don Slaught was chosen in the 20th round in 1979. He waited until the following year when he was drafted in the seventh round by the Royals.

Tom Pagnozzi was a 24th-round choice in 1982, but he didn't sign. He waited until the Cardinals picked him in the eighth round the following year.

Bobby Thigpen was chosen in the seventh round in 1983 out of a community college. Instead of signing then, he attended Mississippi State University and signed two years later with the White Sox.

The Brewers drafted **Nomar Garciaparra** in the fifth round when he graduated from high school in 1991. He grappled with the decision, but decided to go to Georgia Tech. Boston made a better offer to the shortstop and picked him in the first round in 1994.

On the Roster

Nearly half the 1999 team was originally drafted by the Brewers, which shows how much the team relies on the draft.

Cal Eldred was originally selected by the Mets in the 26th round in 1986, but he chose to attend the University of Iowa. The choice was a wise one because Milwaukee chose him in the first round (17th overall) in 1989. His first call to the Brewers came in 1991 and he became a regular with the club the following season. His performance that first season was nothing short of great with an 11-2 record in 14 starts with a 1.79 ERA, including 10 straight wins. American league batters have become more accustomed to the righthander after that and he has been nearly a .500 pitcher since. The starter had more difficulty in 1998 and was just 4-8 in 23 starts. Then elbow injury in late July put him out the rest of the season.

Jeff Cirillo was selected by Milwaukee in the 11th round in 1991. In his first season in the minors he was an all-star in the rookie league. That earned him a promotion the next season and helped him get to the majors more quickly than most. He was first called up to the Brewers in 1994 and became their regular third baseman. He reached his full potential in 1996 when he

Jeff Cirillo was selected by Milwaukee in the 11th round in 1991.

batted .325 with 15 homers and 46 doubles, which tied Yount for the most doubles in Brewers' history. In 1998 he was named to his first All-Star game.

Scott Karl, a sixth-round pick in 1992, was an all-star twice in the minors to put him on the fast track to the majors. He became a regular on the team in 1995. The lefthanded starter's best season was his sophomore year in the majors when he was 13-9 with the Brewers. He was bothered by a strained ligament in his left hand in 1998.

Mark Loretta was selected by Milwaukee in the seventh round in 1993. A .336 batting average in Class A skyrocketed him to Double A the next season where he was named to the Texas League All-Star team. Two seasons later he was named to the American Association All-Star team, which prompted the Brewers to call him up. He filled a utility infielder role in 1997.

Jeff D'Amico has had his share of injuries since being drafted in the first round in 1993. He sat out his first season due to a weakness in his shoulder. The righthander made up for lost time by zipping through the minors and being called up halfway through his second season in the professional ranks. D'Amico led the Brewers to a 4-2 win over the Cubs in the Brewers' first interleague game in 1997. He pitched for two seasons before problems forced him out in 1998 and the beginning of 1999.

Steve Woodard was a fifth-round choice in 1994 out of high school. He owned the rookie league in his first season when he was 8-0 as a starter. He slowed down a little in Class A the next two seasons, but then became an all-star pitcher and Most Valuable Player in Double-A with a 14-3 performance. He was first called to the majors in 1997. He made his major league debut in game one of a July 28, 1997, doubleheader with Toronto at County Stadium. Woodard picked up his first win by tossing eight innings of one-hit ball and striking out 12 batters. He outdueled Roger Clemens and tied the American League record for most strikeouts in a major league debut since Elmer Myers of the Philadelphia Athletics in 1915. He became a regular on the staff in 1998 and was 10-12 in his rookie year.

Brian Banks, a second-round selection in

Geoff Jenkins, a first round draft pick in 1995 for Milwaukee.

1993 out of BYU, was a Texas League all-star in 1995 in Double-A when he hit .308 with 10 triples and 12 homers. The speedy outfielder can also steal bases. He has been up and down with Milwaukee for three seasons since 1996.

The first-round choice in 1995 was **Geoff Jenkins** from USC. The outfielder went through three levels his first year. After batting .330 in Triple-A in 1998, the Brewers called him up where his average dropped nearly 100 points like the stock market on a bad day. Jenkins became the first Brewers player ever to homer in his first big league game. He belted a solo homer off of San Francisco's Orel Hershiser at 3Com Park on April 24. Jenkins joined Chuck Tanner (1955) as the only players in Milwaukee baseball history to homer in their first game.

Ron Belliard, a eighth-round pick in 1994, was named to two all-star teams on his quick romp through the minors in five seasons to get his first call to the majors in 1998. The Brewers made him their regular second baseman in 1999. Belliard can hit for average and power.

Bobby Hughes was a second-round pick out of USC in 1992. The Brewers began the catcher in rookie ball and he made progress every year. After batting .310 in Triple-A in 1997, the Brewers elevated him to the majors for the 1998 season.

Future stars?

Scott Krause, drafted in the tenth round in 1994, has been on three all-star teams in the minors and looks to move up to the Brewers in 1999 sometime. He pounded out 26 homers in Triple-A in 1998.

Kevin Barker was a third-round pick in 1996 out of Virginia Tech. He moved up to Triple-A in 1998, a year in which he hit 28 homers and 110 RBI between two clubs. He was considered as one of the best power hitters in the organization. And with John Jaha gone, the first base job in the majors was more open to his moving up if someone can't hack it in the majors.

Kyle Peterson was shagging balls out in the field during batting practice at the College World Series with Stanford University when he found out he had been drafted in the first round. It came as no surprise, though. "I had talked to them that morning and they said I would be picked in the first round," the righthanded pitcher explained. The Brewers made him no offer before the draft and waited until he was done with the World Series before negotiating

Kyle Peterson with the Louisville River Bats was drafted by the Brewers in 1997, a first round 13th pick.

with him. He had an advisor and signed at the end of July. the Brewers immediately put him on the fast track to the majors as he went from Single-A to Triple-A in 1998. Peterson's best game in the pros is a shutout against Rochester.

While Peterson is on the fast track, **Chad Green**, the Brewers's first-round pick in 1996, was on a slower track. He had only moved up to Double-A by the end of 1998 after batting .344 in Single-A.

Pitcher **Doug Johnston**, a ninth-round choice in 1996, was 19-5 in the minors in his first three seasons in the minors. If he continues that progress, it will put him in the majors by 2001.

That may well be the case for **Kelly Wunsch**, a first-round pick from 1993 out of Texas A&M. The southpaw pitcher was going along fine then was out all of 1996 due to injury, which set him back. He has rebounded from injury and was moved up to Triple-A for awhile in 1998. But Milwaukee sent him back to Double-A in 1999. He could just end up in the disappointment column.

It's too early to tell if **J.M. Gold**, the first-round pick in 1998, will be worth his weight in that precious metal. He passed the first step of rookie ball in 1998 and was moved up to Class A in 1999.

And Milwaukee's first rounder in 1999 was also a pitcher, **Ben Sheets**, out of Northeast Louisiana University. "Ben has got three legitimate major league pitches," said Califano. "His fastball is in the mid–90s and his curveball and change-up are of major league caliber. He compares to a stronger version of David Cone."

Montreal Expos

It's no wonder that the Expos have never been in the World Series if you analyze their drafts since 1968 when they were first thrown into the mix. Many of their first-round picks never made it to the majors or made an impact there. And being a small market team, they were forced to trade off the real good picks to other teams because they couldn't afford to meet their salary demands once they reached free agency. The team has finished first twice and both times

during strike seasons. In 1981, the Expos won the second half of the season and the Division Series against Philadelphia to earn a trip to the League Championship Series, which they lost to the Dodgers. That squad contained many Montreal originals, including Gary Carter, Warren Cromartie, Andre Dawson, Terry Francona, Bill Gullickson, Tim Raines, Steve Rogers, Tim Wallach and Jerry White. The Expos squad was in first place when the players ended the 1994 season in August with no playoffs or World Series.

Generally, the Expos have drafted some talented players over the years, but their problem has been holding on to them. They have pulled the trigger a little early on several players because they couldn't afford to pay them a high bonus. They sent Randy Johnson to the Mariners for a couple of has beens before he developed into the pitcher he is today. Cliff Floyd was also traded before he came of age. The Expos wasted their top pick in 1982 in order to sign free agent catcher Tim Blackwell, a 29-year-old poor hitter. Blackwell played in just 29 games as a backup to Gary Carter over two seasons. Another wasted pick was John Patterson, a first rounder in 1996. The pitching prospect was declared a free agent on a technicality. The team failed to mail his contract offer within the 15 days required.

The compensation rules that were implemented with the draft after free agency have helped the team get something for players they lose. For example, in 1990, Montreal had 10 picks in the first two rounds after losing Hubie Brooks, Mark Langston, Pascual Perez and Bryn Smith, and failing to sign 1989 first-round pick Charles Johnson. Shane Andrews and Rondell White were among the 10 chosen.

The Expos have lost some of their top picks because they have failed to sign them due to budgetary restrictions. "Signability is not a factor in the first round," explained Scott Engler from Montreal's baseball operations. "It is sometimes an issue." Montreal's philosophy is to take the best available, according to Engler.

The Expos have drafted mainly high school players as their first pick over the last 20 years of the draft. Their emphasis has been on raw athletic skills over ability to help the team in the short run. They have also been reluctant to rush any players through their system too quickly. This strategy is based on some bitter experiences, such as Balor Moore in their first draft in 1969. They rushed him to the majors and the result was disparaging. Montreal's latest strategy is to sign the younger player to a long-term contract before he becomes a superstar and wants more later when free agency comes about.

Another Montreal strategy is to trade vet-

Brian Barnes with the Indianapolis Indians was drafted by the Montreal Expos. (Photograph by Jackie Dowling.)

erans for good young draft picks made by other teams. They employed that tactic in 1998 when they picked up some draft picks from the Dodgers, Rockies and Red Sox. Look for more of that in the future unless profit sharing comes about. One strategy that the Expos have employed a few times is to sign the younger player to a long-term contract before they become a free agent. They did that with Rondell White when they signed him to a four-year deal in 1996.

Montreal's scouting director is Jim Fleming, who took the position in 1997. He began as an area scout in the organization in 1990 and moved up to supervisor and crosschecker before becoming director. Fleming's background was in college coaching and not professional playing. He leads a scouting staff that is smaller than most teams because of the team's budget. The team has 15 area scouts in the United States and two crosscheckers. The Expos also keep an eye on independent teams for players. Mike Lansing was taken in the 1990 draft by the Miami Miracle,

Gabe White with Cincinnati was drafted by the Montreal Expos. (Photograph by Marty Orr.)

an independent team. He played two seasons there and was seen by Expo manager Felipe Alou, which led him to be signed by the Expos in 1991. Lansing became one of the few infielders to make the jump from Double-A to the majors. He played four seasons with the Expos before being dealt to the Rockies for three players. He agreed to a $23.25 million contract with Colorado.

With the hiring of manager Felipe Alou in 1992, the team's emphasis has been more toward players from his neck of the woods. The team's 40-man roster to begin the 1999 campaign contained eight players from the Dominican Republic, two from Venezuela and one each from Columbia, Panama and Puerto Rico. Montreal had only one player from Canada on its roster as well as one Aussie player. The roster is also one of the youngest in baseball. The Expos try to sign young players. "We're so young at all levels," said Engler.

The Expos are hoping their youth movement will bring them a championship caliber team at the same time that their new downtown ballpark will open in 2001. The smaller LaBatt Park will be an open-air natural grass field to

35,000 Canadian baseball fans. The ballpark may help revitalize a franchise that nearly moved.

Best Picks

Gary Carter was a versatile athlete in high school and excelled in baseball, basketball and football. The quarterback signed a letter of intent play football at UCLA, but the Expos were able to lure him to baseball after drafting him in the third round in 1972. In the minors, he continued to show his versatility by playing first, third, the outfield and catcher. He was called up to the Expos as an outfielder in September 1974. In his rookie year, he was named to his first All-Star Team and was runner-up for Rookie of the Year. He moved behind the plate in 1977 and took over where Johnny Bench left off. He spent a decade with the team and ranks among the top four in nine major offensive categories. He was also a great defensive catcher and earned three Gold Gloves. Twice he was selected as the Expos Player of the Year. He was also named to four All-Star teams during that time. And he was named to five Silver Slugger teams. In all, he played 19 seasons in the majors and played in three League Championship Series and one World Series with the Mets. He was named to 10 All-Star teams during his career. Montreal retired his number "8" jersey in 1993. He became the team's television commentator. He has received a lot of votes for the Hall of Fame, but not enough to be named.

Another former Expos player who will likely be considered as a serious candidate for the Hall of Fame is **Andre Dawson**, an 11th-round selection in 1975. He was Rookie of the Year in 1977 with the Expos after he hit 19 home runs. He was also Player of the Year for the Expos twice. He was named to the All-Star Team twice with the Expos, too. He became a free agent in 1987 and signed with the Cubs. He exploded with 49 homers in his first season with the Cubs as Wrigley Field was more to his liking. His performance was rewarded with the Most Valuable Player Award. He helped the Cubs to a first-place finish, but he couldn't help the team in the playoffs, hitting just .105. In all, he played on nine All-Star teams, earned six

Andre Dawson, a Montreal Expos 11th round selection in 1975.

best season in the majors came in 1991 when he was with Detroit as he led the American League with 20 victories.

Tim Wallach was added to the Expos Hall of Fame in 1998. The first-round pick in 1979 was twice Player of the Year for the Expos. He was named to three All-Star teams, earned three Gold Gloves and two Silver Slugger Awards. Wallach's best year in an Expo uniform came in 1987 when he lead the league in doubles with 42 and knocked in a club record 123 RBI. Wallach was traded to the Dodgers in 1993 and his 17-year career came to an end in 1996.

Gold Gloves and three Silver Slugger Awards. He ended up with 438 career home runs. He was named to the Expos Hall of Fame in 1997, and his number "10" was retired.

Steve Rogers was a first-round pick in the June 1971 Secondary Phase out of the University of Tulsa. He spent two years in the minors before becoming a starter with the Expos in 1973. His 10-5 record and 1.54 ERA resulted in him being named Rookie Pitcher of the Year. He went into a sophomore slump and led the league in losses with 22 the following season. And he has a miserable 7-17 record to lead the league in losses again in 1976, but it wasn't all his fault. He rebounded to become a productive pitcher. In 1981, he helped Montreal to the playoffs and picked up two wins in the Division Series to send Montreal into the LCS. Rogers put up some big numbers with the Expos in his 13 years with the team. He still leads the team in several areas: most victories (158), complete games (129) and shutouts (37). He was named to the Expos Hall of Fame.

Another Expos Hall of Fame pitcher is **Bill Gullickson**, a first-round pick in 1977. He came up to Montreal in 1980 and was named Rookie Pitcher of the Year after putting together a 10-5 record. He picked up a victory in the 1981 Division Series, but suffered two losses in the LCS. The Expos traded him in 1985 to the Reds. His

Tim Raines isn't in the Expos Hall of Fame yet because he's still playing after 21 years in the majors. He was a fifth-round draft choice in 1977 and got his first call up to the majors in 1979 as a pinch runner. Two years later as a rookie he batted .304 and led the league in stolen bases with 71 to help the Expos finish first in the West. He was runner-up for Rookie of the Year honors. The next three seasons he led the league in stolen bases. In 1986, he led the league in hitting with a career high .334 average. He was three-time Player of the Year for the Expos before he went on to the White Sox in 1991. Now with the Yankees, "Rock" continues to steal bases and contribute. He ranks fifth all-time in stolen bases. He still holds the Expos record for most runs scored in a season (133).

Montreal traded **Randy Johnson** to Seattle long before he became the dominant pitcher he has become in the 1990s. The Expos drafted him in the second round in 1985 out of USC. The "Big Unit" was prone to control problems early in his career and led the Florida State League in walks. Once he got his walk total down to less than a 100 a season, he became the pitcher he is today. He played parts of two seasons with Montreal for a record of 3-4 before the Expos dealt him to Seattle for Mark Langston and Mike Campbell in 1989. Johnson's breakout year came in 1993 when he went 19-8 with Seattle. Johnson

Randy Johnson, drafted by the Expos in the second round in 1985. (Photograph by Marty Orr.)

won the Cy Young two years later when he posted an 18-2 mark with the Mariners. Since leaving the Expos he has appeared in five All-Star games.

Long Shots

The longest shot to ever make it to the majors with the Expos was **Tony Scott**, a 71st round pick in 1969, the second year of the draft for the team. The outfielder got a couple of September call-ups in the early 1970s before playing 92 games in 1975 with Montreal. Then he went to St. Louis and Houston where he succeeded as a starter for those clubs. In all, he played 991 games in the majors over 11 years.

Only a few drafted players have successfully made the transition from fielding to pitching over the years. **Kevin Foster** was originally drafted by the Expos as an infielder in the 29th round. After three seasons in the minors, he was hitting a paltry .215. He decided to switch gears and go to the mound to try and make the majors. The move was for the best. After a couple of trades he landed with Philadelphia and was called up in 1992. He crash landed his first time up. Then he went to the Cubs where he finally succeeded as a pitcher in the majors.

Left-handed pitchers get more chances to make it than right-handers. **Billy Brewer** was a 28th round pick in 1990 with Montreal; however, the Expos lost him to the Royals as a result of a Rule V draft in December 1992. The Royals needed his services more and gave him a reg-

ular spot in relief in 1993. He was with Kansas City for three seasons before being traded to Los Angeles. Then he began earning frequent flyer miles as he went to New York, Cincinnati, Oakland and Philadelphia. With the Phillies he has an astronomical ERA of 108.00! That's because he only pitched in two games in 1998.

Curt Schmidt was a 41st-round pick in 1992. He made it to the majors in 1995, but his performance was lackluster. By 1998 he was out of baseball.

Sometimes it takes a long shot longer to get to the majors than a higher pick, because the player has to prove himself more. **Darrin Winston** was an 18th-round pick in 1988 and became a relief pitcher in the minors. Montreal finally gave up on him in 1994 and he was granted free agency. Winston signed with the Pirates, who placed him at Triple-A. Then the left-hander sat out the 1996 season to be with his family. He was signed by the Mets, but released in spring training in 1997. The Phillies were looking for a lefty so signed him seven days later. He pitched good enough to finally get his call to the majors at age 31.

Disappointments

The biggest disappointment in Montreal history has to be **Pete Incaviglia**. The best hitter in college history didn't want to be drafted by Montreal, but the Expos took a chance on him anyway in the first round in 1985. Incaviglia refused to sign with the Expos until they agreed to trade him to a team he wanted. Montreal signed him to a major league contract and traded him to the Rangers for minor league pitcher Bob Sebra and infielder Jim Anderson. However, the loss wasn't all that bad as the only thing "Inky" ever led the league in was strikeouts during his career. He didn't win any Gold Gloves, either. He ended an 11-year career with a .247 batting average and 206 homers.

While the Expos had trouble signing "Inky," Montreal never did sign **Condredge Holloway**, a first-round pick (fourth overall) in 1971. He decided to go to college and play football instead. The quarterback found the doors to the NFL closed to black quarterbacks, so he went north to the Canadian Football League to play. He made his debut with Ottawa Rough Riders in 1975 and became a star in the northern professional football league.

Balor Moore was a promising left-handed pitcher from Smithville, Texas. The Expos made him their first pick in the draft in 1969. He was dominating in the low minors and rushed to the Expos the next year in May. The result was an 0-2 record with a 7.20 ERA in six games. He wasn't ready. He was sent back to the minors for more seasoning. In 1972, he was give more of an opportunity and responded better with a 9-9 mark. But that would be his best season with Montreal. He was let go and he signed with the Angels and later traded to the Blue Jays. His career ended in 1980 with a 28-48 mark.

Ron Sorey, a first-round pick in 1974, was an fleet-footed outfielder who couldn't hit for average and struck out 137 times in 1975. The Expos released him in 1976. He never made it to the majors. The following year the Expos picked **Art Miles**, a first-round second baseman. The low-average hitter with no power failed to establish himself in Class A and was released.

Glen Franklin, a first-round pick in 1978, was a bust. The hitter with speed was drafted as a shortstop, but he didn't have a position in the field. He made it as far as Double-A before he was released.

Darren Dilks was a promising left-handed first-round hurler in 1981. The college pitcher was immediately assigned to Double-A. He had difficulty striking out players and never made it to the majors. After ERAs in the sixes, he was released.

While **Kevin Dean**, a number-one choice in 1986, moved up the ladder toward the majors, his average declined. The Expos traded him and two other minor leaguers for Zane Smith. He never played in the majors.

Montreal decided on drafting a Canadian player in the first round in 1988. **Dave Wainhouse** has been a winner in the minors, but a bust in the majors. He has had tries as a reliever with four teams with no success.

Hiram Bocachica, a first-round choice from Puerto Rico in 1994, had little success in the minors and was tried at shortstop, second base and the outfield before the Expos gave up on him and traded him to the Dodgers.

Several first-round picks the Expos have had over the years were lost to injury. **Bobbie Goodman**, a catcher picked in 1972, suffered a very serious knee injury the year after he was picked and was never the same afterward. Another catcher fatality due to injuries was **Bob Caffrey**, a first-round pick in 1984. The U.S. Olympic team player had a rash of injuries in 1986 and didn't hit above .242 after that. He was released in 1988. **B.J. Wallace**, the third overall pick in 1992, suffered an arm injury in the minors and never made it to the majors. **Cliff Floyd**, a first-round choice in 1991, was an all-star player in the minors where he hit 26 home runs at Double-A, which led to his call up in 1993. But the home runs eluded him in the majors. Then he shattered his left wrist in a freak injury at first base in May 1995 that nearly ended his career. The Expos decided then to trade him to the Marlins for pitcher Dustin Hermanson. He finally figured out major league pitching in 1998 as he broke out with a .282 average and 22 homers.

Best Draft

The 1985 draft was a real winner for getting players who lasted a long time in the majors, not so much with the Expos. **Randy Johnson** was the second pick in the draft and has turned into one of the most powerful pitchers in the game. **Mark Gardner**, the eighth round pick, has worked up to a opening day starter for San Francisco in 1999. The first pick was **Pete Incaviglia**, who turned into an excellent choice for somebody else.

Worst Draft

No players from the Expos' first draft in 1968 ever made it to the major leagues.

Where Are They Now?

The Expos gambled on taking **Delino De-Shields**, who was a basketball player for Villanova, in the first round in 1987. Montreal must have figured that DeShields was too short for the NBA at six-foot-one. But he was just right for infield duty and he played shortstop in the minors. He improved at every level and was converted to second base. The move was a smart one and he became the opening-day second baseman in 1990. He kept the job until a trade to the Dodgers for Pedro Martinez after the 1993 season.

Norm Charlton was drafted by the Expos in the first round in 1984, but Montreal traded him two years later for a player to be named later to the Reds for Wayne Krenchicki. The first rounder hadn't showed much in the minors at the time as he was 8-14 with a 4.58 ERA in two seasons. Surprisingly, the southpaw regained his form and the Reds were a bit more patient with the prospect. Then they turned him into a reliever and he became one of the "Nasty Boys" with the Reds world championship team in 1990. He has since been a productive pitcher and has recorded 95 saves over his career. He joined the Tampa Bay Devil Rays staff in 1999.

Terry Francona would have likely turned out to be a great player if it hadn't been for his bad knees. Drafted first by the Expos in June 1980, he shot through the farm system quickly with a .350 batting average to earn a promotion to the majors in August 1981. The following season he was hitting .321 before his first knee injury. Then he was hitting a career-best .346 in 1984 before hurting the other knee. He became a frequent flyer after leaving the Expos with stops in Chicago, Cincinnati, Cleveland and Milwaukee before ending his professional career as a pitcher for Louisville in 1991. He turned to managing after playing and was the Phillies manager in 1999.

A roommate of Francona at the University of Arizona, **Brad Mills**, was also picked by the Expos a year earlier. The 17th round pick played four seasons with Montreal during his eight-year pro career. Now he's joined Francona at Philadelphia as the first base coach.

Another ex–Expo draft pick, **Bobby Ramos**, has stayed in baseball after his playing career. The seventh-round selection in the June 1974 draft played parts of five seasons with Expos, primarily as a back-up to perennial All-Star catcher

Gary Carter. He managed for some years with the Houston Astros organization after his playing career.

Wallace Johnson and **Bryan Little** are now coaches with the White Sox. Johnson was originally selected by Montreal in the sixth round of the June 1979 draft and played 10 seasons with the Expos. Little was a ninth-round pick in 1980 and was an infielder with the Expos for three seasons.

Jerry White, a 14th-round pick in 1970 signed by scout Al Ronning, is now the first base coach for the Minnesota Twins.

Manny Mota, the first player taken in Montreal's expansion draft, is a coach with the Los Angeles Dodgers.

Ones Who Got Away

Montreal wasted a first-round pick in 1971 when they chose **Condredge Holloway**. He chose college football over baseball and became a successful quarterback in the Canadian Football League.

The Expos also drafted **Mark McGwire** in the 8th round in 1981 out of high school, but he ended up waiting until Oakland picked him in the first round. Other players that the Expos signed out of high school, but wouldn't sign include: **Roy Smalley, Jeff Reardon, Hubie Brooks, Billy Hatcher, Chris Sabo, Jeff Brantley** and **Charles Johnson**. The Expos ended up trading with the Mets to get Reardon, who later became a stopper for the team for six seasons. In fact, he led the National League in saves in 1985 with Montreal.

Undrafted Free Agent

After not being drafted out of the University of Arizona, **Casey Candaele** signed as with the Expos in 1982 as a free agent. "They probably didn't think I was good enough," he figured. The scouts may not have realized he was the son of Helen Callaghan, who played five seasons in the All-American Girls Professional Baseball League in the 1940s. "She was a better player than me," he explained. The five-foot-nine outfielder showed scouts he could indeed play the game and worked his way up to the majors in four seasons. By 1999, he had played parts of nine seasons in the majors at many positions and was a non-roster invitee at the Houston Astros spring training camp. After he's done playing, he is considering staying in baseball in some capacity.

All in the Family

In 1984 the Expos drafted a couple of favorite sons. One was **Jeff Cisco**, son of their coach Galen, who was a catcher out of Winthrop College. The other, **Jose Alou**, was the son of Felipe, who would manage the team someday. Jose didn't sign.

Montreal chose **Terry Francona**, son of Tito, in the compensation round of the 1980 draft. Terry came up to the Expos a year he was drafted and played for a decade in the majors. Like his father, the son played outfield and first base. They ended up with nearly identical batting averages, too. However, Tito had more power and hit nearly 10 times the amount of homers as his son.

Razor Shines was drafted by the Expos. (Photograph courtesy of the Indianapolis Indians.)

The Expos were a real family affair after Felipe Alou took over as manager of the team in 1992. His son, Moises, was already playing in the outfield and his nephew, Mel Rojas, was called up from Indianapolis to pitch for the team. His other son, Felipe, was drafted by the Royals in 1998.

The Expos drafted **Cletis Boyer**, son of the famed Clete Boyer who played with the Yankees in the 1960s, in the seventh round in 1999. Cletis is a shortstop, which is a position his father sometimes played. His uncle, Ken, played for the Cardinals.

On the Roster

Rondell White was signed by Ed Creech out of high school in the first round as compensation when the Expos lost Randy Johnson. An all-star player in the minors, he has turned into a solid starting outfielder for the Expos. Injuries hurt his progress when he first came to the majors. When he is healthy, he can be productive at any spot in the batting order and has hit as many as 28 home runs in a season. His best game in the majors came in 1994 when he was four-for-five and knocked in all seven runs for his team in single-handedly beating the Dodgers.

Shane Andrews, a first-round pick in 1990, was a shortstop and pitcher in high school with great power when Manny Estrada scouted him. It took Andrews awhile in the minors to overcome striking out too much and making too many errors. He finally broke into the majors in 1995 and again was slow to respond as he hit just .214. He improved the next season to .227 and pounded out 19 homers. A shoulder nerve injury in 1997 abbreviated his season. But in 1998 he broke out to a .238 average and 25 homers.

With Andrews at third and Chris Widger at catcher, the Expos will have to figure out what to do with **Michael Barrett**, a first-round pick in 1995. Drafted as a shortstop and scouted by Hank Sargent, the Expos switched him to catching in 1995. By the following season he was named to the South Atlantic League All-Star game as a receiver. The following season he was named to the all-star team in the Eastern League, where he hit .320 with 29 homers and

32 doubles. This prompted his call up to Montreal in September from Double-A.

Another jumper from Double-A in 1998 was **Jeremy Powell**, a fourth-round pick from 1994, who was signed by John Hughes. The right-handed starter was named to the Florida State League All-Star Game in 1997. Powell was 9-7 at Harrisburg in 1998 with a 3.01 ERA before the call. He got roughed up a bit in Montreal, going 1-5 with a 7.92 ERA. The big right-hander may need more seasoning before he earns a permanent spot in the majors.

Trace Coquillette was a 10th-round pick in 1993 signed by scout Hughes. The infielder has developed into a prospect at second base, but could also fill the roll of utility infielder with his background. He has hit more for average than power in the minors.

Brad Fullmer became Montreal's first baseman in 1998. Signed by Scott Stanley, the second round pick in 1993 didn't play in the minors until 1995 because he signed in September 1993 and was on the disabled list in 1994. Fullmer made up for lost time though by breezing through the farm system in three seasons as he got a September call in 1997. In his debut, he became the second Expo to hit a home run in his first at-bat in the majors.

J.D. Smart, a fourth-round choice in 1995, made the Expos out of spring training in 1999. The right-handed starter recorded 30 wins in four years in the minors with a 3.25 ERA. Known for his control, Smart walked just one batter in every four innings in the minors. He was scouted by Dennis Cardoza.

Another pitcher who is a Montreal original is **Mike Thurman**. Selected by the Expos in the sandwich round of the June 1994 draft as compensation for Dennis Martinez, he was signed by Dave Malpass as a junior out of Oregon State University. In 1996 he was selected to the Florida State League All-Star Team. The Expos first called him up in September 1997 and July 1998.

Jose Vidro, a sixth-round pick in 1992, was first called up in 1997. The Puerto Rican second baseman was called up again in 1998, but hit only .220 with the Expos.

Another not too successful player in 1998 was **Javier Vazquez**, a fifth-round pick in 1994. The right-handed pitcher was 5-15 with Montreal in his first season with the club. The Puerto Rican player was signed by Fred Ferriera and Juan Loyola.

The longest shot on the roster was **Bob Henley**. The 26th rounder from 1991 finally got his call in 1998 after being named Eastern League all-star catcher in 1997. He was the backup receiver to Widger in his first season in the majors.

Another long shot was **Tim Young**, a 19th-round choice in 1996. The left-handed reliever was brought up in 1998.

Future Stars?

Milton Bradley, not be confused with the company who makes games, improved in 1998 enough to be considered a prospect again. The switch-hitting outfielder has some power and good speed on the bases as evidenced by his 11 homers and 30 steals in Class A.

Another outfielder on the rise is long shot **Chris Stowers**, a 17th-round pick in 1996. He hit 17 homers in Double-A in 1998 and went 100 games without an error to raise some eyebrows. Scout Hank Sargent signed him after he completed his senior year at the University of Georgia.

Keith Evans, an eighth round pick in 1996, pitched his way up to Double-A in 1998. The large right-hander has a good fastball, but needs to improve on his other pitches.

The Expos first-round pick in 1997 was pitcher **Donnie Bridges**. The high school hurler had 8-1 record, an 0.49 ERA, to go with 96 strikeouts in only 57 innings of work. The 23rd pick overall received a $850,000 bonus. After two seasons in the minors, the Expos moved him up to long-season Class A Jupiter.

The Expos drafted and signed first-round draft pick **Josh Girdley** in 1999. The 18-year-old left-handed pitcher from Jasper, Texas, was Montreal's sixth overall pick in this year's draft. The six-foot-four hurler finished the season 8-2, 0.34 ERA in 17 games, 11 starts. He struck out 178 batters in 82.2 innings of work including 29 in a 10-inning game on April 6. Girdley's 93 mph fastball held opposing batters to an .097 batting average while firing nine complete games and seven shutouts.

New York Mets

The New York Mets began playing in 1962 and were terrible their first seven years, finishing last in the National League five of those seasons. By the time the draft rolled around in 1965, the team needed CPR, which is what the draft provided. New York had the first, second, third or fourth pick the first seven years of the draft because of their poor performances. The Mets drafted a couple of famous football players in the early years of the draft for publicity purposes. In the January 1967, they selected Arnie Chonko, an Ohio State linebacker, and Ken Stabler who went on to a long career in the National Football League. Then in 1969, the Miracle Mets surprised everyone by winning the pennant and the World Series. That Series team had a few draft picks, including pitchers Nolan Ryan, who picked up a save, and Tom Seaver, who earned one of the victories over Baltimore. Seaver was not drafted by the Mets, but he was acquired by them after he was declared a free agent in a draft faux pas. In 1970, the Mets got the last pick in the first round for the first time.

Since 1969, the Mets have finished first three more times and the draft was instrumental in bringing the necessary players to win a championship. The world championship team that beat the Red Sox in seven games in 1986 had several original draft picks that helped the team, including Rick Aguilera, Wally Backman, Dwight Gooden, Lee Mazzilli, Roger McDowell, Darryl Strawberry and Mookie Wilson.

Lately, the Mets are becoming a lot like their neighbors in the American League and are trading their future for players who can help them now. For example, they traded two first rounders and a third rounder in 1998 to the Florida Marlins for Mike Piazza. One of those players was Preston Wilson, a first-round pick in 1992. He was on the verge of a breakout season in the majors and did so in 1999. The other two picks were left-handed pitchers Geoff Goetz, a first round pick in 1997, and Ed Yarnall, a third round pick in 1996. Just before the trade deadline in 1999, the Mets traded Terrence Long, a first-round pick in 1994, for veteran pitcher Kenny Rogers. The strategy was working in 1999

as the team was competing for first place with the Braves. But the team was likely mortgaging its future with its short-term loans. The Mets lost their first-round pick in 1999 to the Chicago White Sox when they signed type-A free agent Robin Ventura during the off-season.

The Mets like to "pick and choose" to help fill deficiencies in their farm system, according to a former scout. For example, one year the word was put out to look for good catchers, but most of the time they were looking for good pitchers, like most teams. They wanted pitchers who had "live" arms and good velocity. The Mets also started giving psychological tests in the 1980s to players. One player who took the test dropped from second round to a much later round as a result of the test. That same player was taken in the first round by a team who didn't test the individual. Turns out the player never made it to the majors, so the test was right on. Some other teams use psychological tests as well, but not all will admit it.

The Mets have a good size scouting staff with 19 area scouts, three regional crosscheckers and a national crosschecker. Like many teams, they have an academy in the Dominican and concentrate on Latin American players. They also have scouts looking in other parts of the globe and signing players from the far east, such as Masato Yoshii, who played in the Japanese major leagues. They have signed Korean players as well, such as Jae Seo, a right-handed pitcher.

Good scouting has sometimes paid off for the Mets. For example, Mets scout Phil Favia found out that Tim Bogar was really a junior for draft eligibility purposes when he was a sophomore at Eastern Illinois University. The infielder had changed majors and didn't have enough credits to be considered a junior by the school. But for baseball purposes he was a junior. The Mets took notice of Bogar when he played in the NBC World Series and hit a homer off of Mike Hartke. At Eastern Illinois, he had batted .408 and hit 17 homers to earn All-Conference honors in 1987.

Tim Bogar, drafted by the New York Mets in the ninth round in 1987.

Best Picks

The first Mets draft pick to be named to the National Baseball Hall of Fame was **Nolan Ryan**, a lowly 12th round pick in the first draft. The Mets scouted Ryan in high school where he was 20-4. When the general manager of the Mets, Bing Devine, showed up to see him, he pitched the worst game of the season. He was losing 3-1 when the GM left. That's probably why Ryan ended up to be the 295th player taken in the first draft. He still received a $20,000 signing bonus. Ryan became a regular Mets pitcher in 1968. In the 1969 World Series, he earned a save in one of the Mets' victories. It was the only World Series he got to pitch in during his long career. He never really materialized as a true pitcher until he was with the California Angels though. Then he began to lead the league in strikeouts. In his 27 years in professional baseball, he was named to seven All-Star teams, led the league in strikeouts 11 times and ERA twice. He never earned a Cy Young Award, but was considered for it several times. In 1998, he was

named on the first ballot — six votes shy of unanimous — to the Baseball Hall of Fame.

Darryl Strawberry was one of the reasons why the Mets became a championship team in the 1980s. He became the heart of the Mets batting order. As the first player taken in the 1980 draft, he commanded a $200,000 bonus and was signed by scout Roger Jongewaard. The high school player was the Most Valuable Player in the Texas League after clotting 34 homers. After a pit stop in Triple-A, the Mets brought him up the majors in 1983. He slammed 26 homers that season to be named Rookie Player of the Year. His 27 homers helped the team with the pennant in 1986 and he hit three postseason homers. He became a free agent after the 1990 season and signed with the Dodgers. He helped the Yankees to championships in 1996 and 1998. Strawberry's career came in doubt following colon cancer surgery in October 1998. He was hoping to play with the Yankees in 1999, but he was suspended for drug use. In his career, he has been named to six All-Star games.

Dwight Gooden, scouted by Carlos Pascual and drafted by the Mets in the first round of the 1982 June draft, was another great pick by the Mets. He led the Class A Carolina League with 19 wins, 2.50 ERA, and 300 strikeouts in 1983 to earn a starting job with the Mets in 1984. In his rookie year, he led the league in strikeouts to establish a rookie record. His 17-9 mark that season earned him Rookie of the Year honors. He topped that performance the next season by leading the league in strikeouts again and compiling a 24-4 mark to become the youngest player ever to win the Cy Young Award. He also become the youngest pitcher in the modern era to win 20 games. He helped the Mets win the pennant the next season with a 17-6 mark, but earned three losses in post-season play. When the Mets got to the League Championship Series in 1988, he was more effective but failed to get any decision in two starts as the Mets lost a close series to the Dodgers. On June 19, 1989, Gooden won 100th Major League game, becoming the third-youngest player to win 100 games in the modern era, behind Noodles Hahn and Bob Feller. His pitching career started heading south when he started having shoulder problems in 1989. He experienced his first losing season in 1992 when he was 10-13. He was granted free agency in October 1994. Then he was suspended for the entire 1995 season for violations of Major League Baseball's drug use policy. He returned from the suspension to sign a free agent contract with the Yankees. He threw a no-hitter, May 14, 1996, against Seattle. He signed with Cleveland in 1998. Gooden has appeared in four All-Star games during his career, all while he was with the Mets.

Another pitcher with those championship teams was **Rick Aguilera**, who was selected by the Mets in the third round of the June 1983. He was a starter back then. He was first called up to the team in 1985 and posted a 10-7 record, which turned out to be his record for the following year as well. The Mets used him out of the bullpen in postseason play. He earned a victory in the 1986 World Series. The Mets traded him along with four other pitchers to the Twins for Frank Viola in 1989. He became the stopper on the Twins the next season and filled that role for nine seasons. He helped the Twins to the world championship in 1991 when he recorded 42 saves in the regular season and two in the World Series. He holds the Twins' all-time save record. He has also been named to two All-Star teams. The Twins traded him to the Cubs in 1999.

Yet another star from those championship years was **Randy Myers**, a first-round pick (ninth overall) of the June 1982 secondary phase. He was a starter in the minors, but the Mets moved him to the bullpen when they first called him up in 1985. In his first full year with the Mets in 1988, he was nearly unhittable. His 1.72 ERA was one of the best in the league and he recorded 26 saves with a 7-3 record. He also earned two victories in the League Championships Series in 1988. The Mets decided to trade him after the 1989 season to the Reds for John Franco in an exchange of stoppers. Since leaving the Mets, he's appeared on three All-Star teams. Myers has been a stopper for the Reds, Cubs, Orioles, Blue Jays and twice with the Padres, his current team.

Another member of the 1988 Mets team was **Gregg Jefferies**, a first-round pick in 1985. He hit .333 in the 1988 LCS. The high school pick spent four seasons in the minors and was an all-star three of those years. He was named

Minor League Player of the Year in 1987. He played five seasons with the Mets and led the league in doubles in 1990 when he hit 40 of them. The Mets traded him to the Royals after the 1991 season. His best years in the majors came when he was with the Cardinals in 1993 and 1994 when he .325 and .342, respectively, and was named to All-Star games those years. He suffered a broken thumb in 1996 and his career hasn't been the same since with the Phillies and Angels.

Long Shots

The Mets picked a long shot in their very first draft —**Steve Renko**. The University of Kansas first baseman and pitcher was not picked until the 24th round.

Thirteen is unlucky for some, but it turned out to be lucky for **Lenny Dykstra**. But it wasn't luck that got him to the majors. He was a hard worker. The 13th rounder in 1981 out of high school made it to the majors with the Mets in 1985. The outfielder was a clutch hitter and shined in the LCS and World Series for the Mets in 1986 when he hit three homers and averaged .300. In the 1988 LCS he averaged .429 with three doubles and a homer. The Mets traded him to the Phillies in 1989. The next season he had his best season when he averaged .325 and led the National League with 192 hits. Injuries began to take their toll on him the year after

Tim Foli, a New York Mets draft pick.

that. He ended up playing 12 seasons in the majors. He made two appearances in the Midsummer Classic.

Ricky Otero was a long, long shot to make it to the majors as a 45th round pick in 1990. But the Puerto Rican outfielder could hit for average in the minors and worked his way up to the Mets in 1995. He could hit major league pitching at first, so the Mets dealt him to the Phillies, where he did much better. Now he's with the Orioles.

The Mets waited until the 31st round in 1989 to pick **Dave Telgheder** out of the University of Massachusetts. The right-handed starter took five seasons to get to the majors and has had an up-and-down career since with the Mets, A's and Indians.

Disappointments

Alan Zinter was a first-round pick (24th overall) in 1989 out of the University of Arizona. The catcher's progress as a hitter was slow at first. He could hit the long ball, but he struggled with his average in Double-A, so the Mets dealt him to the Tigers in 1994 for Rico Brogna. Zinter moved up to Triple-A and continued to hit homers. By the end of the 1998 season he had accumulated 164 long balls in the minors. At a spring training game in 1999 with the Cubs, he pounded out three straight homers, which looked more like a Sammy Sosa performance. "I did that once before in the Arizona Fall League in 1994," he said after the game. The great spring training didn't lead him to the majors because the Cubs signed veteran free agent Benito Santiago.

Vincente Rosario, an eighth-round draft pick out of New York's George Washington High School in 1977, was suspended for the rest of the 1998 season after he and four other Mets players were arrested for gang-raping a 17-year-old girl.

Best Draft

Nineteen eighty-two produced a bumper crop of pitchers for the Mets. **Dwight Gooden** and **Randy Myers** were first-round picks that year and both turned into superstars. Both were still pitching in 1999. **Roger McDowell** was a stopper for the Mets and saved 159 games during his 13-year career. Wes Gardner was a 22nd round pick and pitched a couple of seasons for the Mets during his eight-year career. **Floyd Youmans** pitched six years in the majors, but none with the Mets.

Worst Draft

The year 1970 was one for the Mets to forget. Only three of the players they chose in the four drafts ended up in the majors and none was an impact player. The Mets gambled on high school players the first two picks of the June Regular Phase and neither signed. No loss because they never played in the majors either.

Where Are They Now?

Brian Daubach was a 17th-round draft pick by the Mets in 1990 and he steadily improved, but with John Olerud solidly at first base for the Mets, there was no room for him, so he was let go to free agency. The Marlins signed him and he burst through in 1996 with 22 homers at Triple-A. He topped that in 1998 with 35 dingers. Florida gave him a call up to the majors in September, but then released him after the season for some odd reason. Boston promptly signed the left-handed hitter to replace Mo Vaughn at first base. Daubach has responded at Boston by being a legitimate contender for rookie of the year after nine seasons in the minors. "At the time I got released by the Marlins, I was really disappointed," he said in chat room session on the Internet in 1999. "In the end everything's worked out better than I could have expected."

Scott Sauerback graduated from Miami University in Ohio before the Mets picked him in the 23rd round in 1994. "It's just nice to know somebody wants you," he commented. "I signed for a thousand dollars and a plane ticket." He actually thought the Twins were going to pick him because they had called the first day of the draft and said they were going to select him first the next day. They never called.

He really wanted to be drafted by the Reds because he grew up in Cincinnati. Because of his low draft status, he was a roster fill in rookie ball. "When they got their butt kicked in the first five innings, I went in there for them. I had to work hard to get where I am today," he said from spring training camp with the Pirates. The Pirates picked him up as a Rule V draft in December 1998, which may have been his ticket to the majors. The Pirates had to put him on the 25-man roster to start the season or he would be shipped back to the Mets. That was not likely because the Pirates purchased his contract for $50,000 and would hate to lose that.

Lindsay Gulin was picked in the 16th round in 1995 out of high school and was still looking to advance to Double-A in 1999. The left-handed hurler wanted to try his hand at baseball before going to college and bonus money convinced him of that. He showed some success in the minors, but the Mets traded him to Seattle for catcher Rick Wilkins in May 1998. At spring training in 1999, he was still hoping to get to the majors some day. "As long as you keep getting people out, you have a job," he explained.

The Mets picked **Mike Jorgensen** in the fourth round in the 1966 June draft. His major league career spanned 18 years, ending in 1985 with the Cardinals. He was hired as a minor league instructor by the Cardinals and has worked his way up to becoming the director of player development.

When Gil Hodges was managing the Mets back in 1971, the Mets drafted his son, who had played at C.W. Post College. Junior never followed in his father's footsteps.

Ron Gardenhire, a sixth-round pick in June 1979, is now the third base coach for the Minnesota Twins. Born in Butzback, Germany, he played five seasons for the Mets in the early 1980s.

Another former player who turned to coaching is **Dwight Bernard**, a second-round pick in 1974 out of Belloit College. He is now the pitching coach for Louisville River Bats, a Triple-A affiliate of the Brewers, another team Bernard pitched for in the majors.

Scott Little, a seventh-round pick in 1984, also stayed in baseball after playing. He spent four seasons in the minors before going to Pittsburgh where he made his debut in 1989. After his cup of coffee in the bigs, he turned to man-

aging in the Pirates' farm system. Now he is the manager of the Pirates' Class A Lynchburg Hillcats.

All in the Family

Being the son of a major league player may help in getting drafted or earn a higher selection, but it doesn't assure the player will ever get to the majors. "It doesn't help you get to the big leagues just because your dad is who he is and his name," said **Todd Hundley**, a second-round pick by the Mets in 1987.

Todd Hundley, a second round pick by the Mets in 1987.

Hundley followed in his father's footsteps, who also was a catcher for 14 seasons in the majors, mostly with the Cubs. The Mets had scouted him all the way through high school and liked what they saw. "I wanted to be drafted by the Mets that year because they won the World Series in 1986," Hundley admitted. Todd may someday exceed his father's accomplishments in the majors. Like his father, he's been an All-Star. As of 1998, he had played nine seasons in the majors and has already exceeded his father in career home runs and RBI. One thing his father never did was play any other position but catcher. The Mets tried moving Hundley to the outfield upon his return from an injury in 1998, because they had obtained Mike Piazza in his absence. After Hundley looked like a lost soul in the outfield, the Mets used him as a pinch hitter late in the season. Then he was dealt to the Dodgers in favor of Piazza.

When **Scott Jaster** finished high school, his focus was on college. But being the son of a major leaguer weighed heavily on his mind and he developed a burning desire to follow in the footsteps of his father. Unlike his father, a pitcher who spent seven seasons with Atlanta, Montreal and St. Louis, Scott was an outfielder. None of the teams his dad played for picked him in the draft. Instead, the New York Mets selected the junior college player in the second round of the Winter Draft. "They gave me enough to buy a new car and put an equal amount in the bank," he said about his bonus. He also received scholarship money to finish his college.

Year by year he got better and better, but the corner outfielder wasn't putting up enough numbers to satisfy the major league teams. Then he broke his wrist, which finally ended his dream after 10 years. "I'd still be out there playing if not for the injury," he explained. However, his efforts didn't go without some reward. He became a scout for the Arizona Diamondbacks after his playing career ended, so he's had some measure of success in baseball. At least he can try to help others with their dream.

Benny Agbayani, Norfolk Tides, drafted by the Mets.

Ones Who Got Away

The Mets picked **Ron Cey** in the 19th round in the 1996 June draft out of high school, but he didn't sign until the Dodgers picked him years later.

Burt Hooton was a fifth-round pick in 1968 out of high school, but he waited until the Cubs picked him to sign.

The Mets drafted **Bud Black** in the second round in 1977 when he was in Lower Columbia Junior College, Washington. Black declined though. He decided to get more college under his belt and went to San Diego State University. Then he was drafted in the 17th round in 1979 by Seattle.

Mark Davis was the Mets' 22nd choice in 1978 out of high school but he didn't sign. The pitcher went to junior college for two years and was drafted in 1979 by Philadelphia, who signed him.

Roger Clemens would have been in New York City sooner than 1999 had he signed when the Mets picked him in the 12th round in 1981. However, Clemens waited until the Red Sox took him in the first round in 1983.

Rafael Palmeiro was picked by the Mets in 1982 in the 8th round out of high school. He waited until the Cubs picked him.

The Mets took **Matt Williams** in the 27th round in 1983 after he graduated from high school. Williams waited for a better offer from San Francisco.

John Wetteland could have signed with the Mets after high school when he was picked in the 12th round of the 1984 draft, but he didn't.

John Olerud, Jr., didn't sign with the Mets when he was chosen in the 27th round in 1986. Instead, he waited until 1989 when Toronto picked him third and he went directly to the majors.

Undrafted Players

The first non-drafted free agent approved by the Mets' Joe McIlvaine was none other than one of the best ever signed by the team —**Kevin Mitchell**. The former gang member was passed over by draft probably because he came from the

Brook Fordyce with the Cincinnati Reds, drafted by the Mets. (Photograph by Marty Orr.)

rough section of San Diego. "I've been shot three times," he once said in an interview. He was signed after a tryout with the Mets in November 1980.

Mitchell progressed normally through the minors and reached the majors in 1984. After a couple of seasons with the Mets, he was dealt to the Padres in a multi-player trade, which gave the New York team Kevin McReynolds. The Padres kept him only half a season and traded him to the Giants. Mitchell matured with the Giants and was named the National League's MVP after clouting 47 homers that season and leading the team to the World Series. Mitchell was named to the All-Star Team in 1989 and 1990. Mitchell went from gang to riches when he signed a $3.5 million contract with the Mariners. He failed to live up to the money and Seattle dealt him to the Reds.

Another undrafted Mets choice that has gone far in the majors is **Heathcliff Slocumb**. The pitcher from John Bowne High School in Flushing was passed over by the draft in 1984. Mets scout Mike Becker saw him play there and put him on his Long Island Mets team. Whenever other scouts came around, Becker let Slocumb ride the bench. The Mets scout finally

signed Slocumb to a $5,000 contract in July 1984. He was left unprotected in 1986, and the Cubs took him in the Rule V draft. The reliever worked his way up to a $2,975,000 contract with the Red Sox in 1997.

All in the Family

The Mets drafted Carrington Fisk, nephew of famed catcher Carlton Fisk, in the 39th round in 1999. This Fisk is a pitcher, though, out of high school.

On the Roster

The Mets don't have many of their own draft picks on their 40-man roster going into 1999 because they have traded most of them away to get veterans, a trend they began a few years ago.

Bobby Jones was a compensation pick (36th pick overall) in 1991 after a brilliant college career. He was selected College Pitcher of the Year after going 16-2 with a 1.88 ERA at Fresno State University. In a way, he was following in the footsteps of Tom Seaver, because he attended the same high school as Seaver, Fresno High School, was on the same team and was a winner. In his six seasons with the Mets, he was 60-47 and his 15 victories in 1997 was the most by a Mets pitcher since Frank Viola's 20 wins in 1990. He signed a three-year contract with the Mets in 1998. He was named to the All-Star Team in 1997 as well.

The long shot hurler on the roster was **Jason Isringhausen**, a 44th-round pick in 1991. The right-hander got better and better in the minors. After a 9-1 record with a 1.55 ERA in Triple-A Norfolk, he earned a trip to the majors. And he was super in his first season as he compiled a 9-2 record in 14 starts in 1995. He endured a sophomore slump the next season as his ERA ballooned to 4.77 and his record was 6-14. Injuries and surgery took him out of action for the 1998 season, but he was back to form in 1999.

With Piazza on the disabled list, **Vance Wilson** also got his chance to catch his first game in the majors in 1999. The 44th rounder was a draft-and-follow from 1993 and has turned into a good defensive catcher. His visit to the majors was just a couple of weeks before he was sent back to Triple-A.

Sometimes injuries set back the best players from making it to the majors sooner than predicted. Such was the case with **Jay Payton**, a first-round supplemental pick in 1994. The excellent hitter was headed to the majors when elbow problems resulted in a couple of surgeries and a year and half setback. But Payton finally got a September 1998 call up where he hit .318 in 15 games as an outfielder. He can also play first, but John Olreud is currently stationed there. The Mets called him up again in 1999 when their outfield was beset by injuries.

Future Stars

Terrence Long, the Mets' first-round pick in 1994, took a long time to develop at Class A — three seasons — but the slow cooking paid off as he hit .297 at Double-A with 16 homers to earn a promotion to the Mets in April 1999 before settling down to Triple-A for the season. He's a left-handed hitter with some power and speed.

Grant Roberts, an 11th-round pick in 1995, was dazzling his first couple of years in the minors. His record was 22-5 with an ERA of 2.20 after his first three seasons in professional ball. But elbow problems and surgery set him back in 1998 and tarnished his progress with a losing mark, 4-5 with a 4.23 ERA. The Mets assigned him to Double-A Binghamton in 1999.

Another Mets drafted pitcher at Double-A was **Kenny Pumphrey**, a fourth-round pick in 1994. His 10-6 record at St. Lucie earned the right-hander a spot on the Florida State League All-Star Team.

Another player at Double-A in 1999 was **Jason Tyner**, the first-round pick in 1998. The Texas A&M outfielder batted .301 his rookie year at Class A. The speedy outfielder is a singles hitter and could be a leadoff man eventually in the majors.

A long shot making progress in the minors is **Dicky Gonzalez**, a 16th round pick in 1996 out of Puerto Rico. After three seasons in the minors, he was 21-16 with a 3.61 ERA. He was assigned to Class A St. Lucie in 1999.

The New York Mets selected left-handed pitcher **Neal Musser** with their first pick (73rd overall) in 1999. The high school senior posted a 7-1 record with a 1.40 ERA during the regular season. "Neal has a solid delivery and has command of three pitches, a fastball, curveball and change-up, and can throw all three for strikes," said Gary LaRocque, Met amateur scouting director. "He had great command with great mound presence."

With their second selection, which was in the third round (84th overall), the Mets chose right-handed pitcher **Jake Joseph** from Cosumnes River Junior College. Joseph was a Compensation C Pick from the Arizona Diamondbacks for signing free agent Armando Reynoso. Joseph was 11-3 with one save and a 1.64 ERA in 1999 in college. Joseph was selected Pitcher of the Year in the Bay Valley Conference and was also an All-American selection.

Philadelphia Phillies

The draft helped the Phillies to seven first-place finishes and three World Series in 35 years compared to the one pennant and a World Series in the 35 years before the draft. Draft picks Greg Luzinski and Mike Schmidt powered the team to four division titles and a World Series victory in 1980. That team also included Philadelphia picks Warren Brusstar, Larry Christenson, Keith Moreland, Dick Ruthven, Lonnie Smith, Dickie Thon and Bob Walk. Three years later the team was back in the Series with Schmidt as the leader on the roster. Schmidt was also a member of the 1993 World Series team, which included draft picks Darren Daulton and Mickey Morandini. Since 1993, the Phillies have been a losing ballclub.

The Phillies also became big losers when they failed to sign first-round choice J.D. Drew in 1997. Drew's agent, Scott Boras, wanted a guaranteed package of over $10 million, which included a $5 million signing bonus. And he wanted a major league contract for his player. Up until then, the largest signing bonus had been $2 million. Philadelphia couldn't afford the high price and countered with an offer that included a $2.6 million signing bonus, a four-year major league contract and $6 million in incentives to sign for four years. And the Phillies upped that offer in 11th hour negotiations, but Boras still wouldn't budge.

"There is a structure in place in baseball, first the draft, then arbitration and then free agency," said Phillies General Manager Ed Wade. "We approached it in a professional manner trying to get a drafted player signed. They tried to create change in the structure. I'm disappointed because J.D. would have helped advance our cause of building with young players. He could have been on a fast track to the majors with us. He has unique tools and the unique ability to get to the majors soon. We offered him a unique contract and it didn't work."

Drew was redrafted in the first round the following year by St. Louis. When he came to Philadelphia the next season as an outfielder for the Cardinals, the Philadelphia fans greeted him with harassing signs and a shower of batteries, resulting in a near forfeit of the game.

The Phillies have concentrated on pitching with their first pick a majority of times in the 35 years of the draft, but they haven't succeeded much in landing the big one yet. Many of the pitchers were high school prospects who for one reason or another failed to get to the majors. Injury was just part of the reason. "There's a higher risk for every organization with high school pitchers," scouting director Mike Arbuckle explained. "However, many of the top pitchers in baseball today were high school drafts and I think the potential return warrants a higher risk."

The Phillies philosophy is to take the best available player. "We take the philosophy that we want the best players based on ability rather than pure signability," Arbuckle said after the 1999 draft. In the 1999 draft, Philadelphia was looking for good catchers and shortstops though.

Personality profiles are used on prospective players, but the prime factor is the evaluation made by the area scouts who will have seen the player several times. The scouts are also looking for players that fit the Philadelphia profile.

Willie Greene, a first-round, 18th pick for the Philadelphia Phillies in 1989.

"We have made the commitment to bring young talent into the organization and build a strong foundation and we have followed through with a significant expenditure in last year's draft and we anticipate similar success this year," said Arbuckle.

In 1981 the Phillies had a huge scouting staff by today's standards with 28 full-timers, 60 part-timers and 200 bird dog scouts. Of course, the team had just won the World Series and was riding high. Today, they have an average scouting staff with 15 area scouts and three regional supervisors. Outside the United States, the Phillies have just a couple of scouts. Like most teams, they have concentrated their efforts in the Caribbean and Pacific Rim. The Phillies have had a full squad in the Dominican Republic summer league since 1996. Brian Harris, a second baseman in the Phillies farm system, sees the Phillies as more of an American team with a few foreign players.

Best Picks

Greg Luzinski and **Mike Schmidt** combined for 503 homers during nine years together with the Phillies, which is the sixth best for teammates in National League history. Luzinski was a first-round pick in 1968, while Schmidt was picked in the second round in 1971.

Schmidt was voted by the fans as the best Phillie to ever play the game. The media agreed with that assessment when 97 percent of them voted him into the Baseball Hall of Fame in 1995. Ten times he won the Gold Glove at third base and was named to the All-Star Game. Eight times he led the league in home runs. Four times he led the league in RBI. Three times he was named the National League Most Valuable Player. On the downside, he led the league in strikeouts four times. His 578 homers lifetime ranked him seventh all-time. His 1,883 K's ranked him third all-time. His best season with the long ball came in 1980 when the Phillies needed him the most. He homered in the next to last game of the season to lead the team to the playoffs and World Series. He batted .381 to win Series MVP honors and lead the Phillies to their only world title in franchise history.

Luzinski was just 17 when he signed and he first got called up to the majors before he was old enough to vote. By 1972, he became a regular outfielder with the team. "The Bull" earned the nickname for his exploits with the bat. In the outfield, he was more like a bull in a glass store. The cleanup hitter slugged more than 100 homers during the three-year run with the National League East flag from 1976 through 1978. His best year came in 1977 when he had career highs with a .309 batting average, 39 homers, 99 runs, 130 RBI, .594 slugging percentage and, unfortunately, 140 strikeouts. After hitting 35 homers in 1978, Luzinski suffered some brownouts with the power and was shipped to the White Sox for cash after a poor showing in the 1980 World Series. He was named to four All-Star teams during his 15 years in the majors. He hit a total of 307 home runs during his career and ended with one of the highest strikeout percentages.

Another Phillies draft pick who can make a bid for the Hall of Fame is **Ryne Sandberg**, a 20th-round pick in 1978 out of high school. But Sandberg didn't become famous with the Phillies. After being named to the Eastern League All-Star team, he was called up to the majors and played 13 games for the Phillies. Then he was a thrown-in with the trade of Larry Bowa to the Cubs for Ivan DeJesus. Cubs General Manager Dallas Green, who had come from the Phillies organization, insisted on Sandberg and the Phillies obliged. The trade will go down in Phillies history as one of their worst as Sandberg turned into a superstar. The Cubs moved the third baseman to second and he promptly rewrote the record book. Sandberg became famous during a nationally televised game when he

Ryne Sandberg, a 20th round pick in 1978 for the Phillies. (Photograph by Kenny Keiffer.)

hit two homers off Bruce Sutter to lead the Cubs to victory in 1984. He also led the Cubs to win the National League East, their first crown since 1945. That season he was named Most Valuable Player. Sandberg again led the team to the League Championship Series in 1989. He surprised everyone when he retired in mid-season of 1994. He had nine Rawlings Gold Glove awards to his credit and had been named to 10 All-Star teams. But he returned to baseball in 1996 for two more seasons, which allowed him to break the all-time record for homers by a second baseman with his 282 round trippers. His streak of 123 consecutive errorless games set a major league record for second basemen.

Another Phillies long shot to become a great player is **Darren Daulton**, a 25th round pick out of high school in 1980. The catcher was a three-time all-star with the Phillies and helped the team to a World Series appearance in 1993. "Dutch" was a hard hitting left-handed batter who punched out 197 doubles and 137 homers during his 14 seasons with the Phillies. He also earned a Silver Slugger award in 1992. While he couldn't get a World Series ring with Philadelphia, he earned one with the Florida Marlins in 1997, his last season in the majors.

Dick Ruthven was drafted in January 1973 and made his major league debut on April 17 with the Phillies after getting a reported $80,000 bonus. A 10-3 pitcher in college with Fresno State, he was 6-9 in his first season in the majors. He wasn't a winning pitcher until his sixth season in the majors. Then he came of age and was more effective with the Phillies his second time around with the team. He was named to the All-Star team in 1981 after a 17-10 mark the year before in helping the Phillies to the World Series. He ended up his 14-year career with the Cubs and a lifetime 123-127 record.

Another Phillies draft pick who helped the team to the World Series in 1993 was **Mickey Morandini**, a fifth-round pick in 1988. The Indiana University shortstop was a member of the 1988 U.S. Olympic baseball team. After two years in the minors, Morandini took over second base for the Phillies. He committed just two errors in 103 games from June 1, 1993, to June 1, 1994. In 1995, he was named to the All-Star Team. The Phillies traded him to the Cubs in 1998 for Doug Glanville.

Larry Hisle, a second-round pick in 1965, became a solid player, but not for the Phillies. The powerful swinger was considered for rookie of the year honors in 1969 after clouting 20 homers. Then he was bit by the sophomore bug when he managed half that total and only averaged .205. That prompted the Phillies to send him back to the minors and trade him to the Dodgers. He ended up with the Twins and finally developed into a consistent power hitter. He became a designated hitter. His best season came with the Brewers when he hit 34 home runs and knocked in 115 RBI to finish third in most valuable player voting. After playing, he turned to coaching.

Scott Rolen is bringing back memories of Mike Schmidt at third base. He was drafted in the second round after several teams passed on him because they thought he was going to play basketball in college. After being named to the Eastern League All-Star Team in 1996, Rolen got his first call to the majors that same season. The following year he was named Rookie of the Year after hitting 21 homers and 92 RBI. He avoided the sophomore jinx by becoming even better. He outdid all his freshman stats when he batted .290 with 45 doubles, 31 homers and 110 RBI. And he won a Gold Glove at third base. He has a long way to go to surpass Schmidt, but his performance so far has been remarkable.

The Phillies signed **Mark Davis** in the first round of the January 1979 Secondary Phase out of junior college. The left-handed pitcher was signed by scout Eddie Bochman. He got two short tries with Philadelphia before he was traded to the Giants where he learned to lose a lot. He posted a 5-17 record in 1984! He then went to San Diego and the Padres converted him to their stopper. He saved 28 games in 1988. The following season he was nearly unhittable and saved a league leading 44 games to win the Cy Young Award. Davis played 12 seasons in the majors.

Long Shots

One of the more recent long shots to crack the Phillies lineup is **Bobby Estalella**, a 23rd rounder in 1992 from Miami-Dade Community College. He was first called up to the Phillies in 1996. Then after hitting 17 homers at Scranton, he returned to the Phillies in 1998 as the back-up catcher for Mike Lieberthal. However, a shoulder injury hobbled him for the beginning of the 1999 season. Estalella has raw power that could lead to a lot of homers if he can hit major league pitching as well as he did in the minors.

Bobby Estalella with the Rochester Red Barons was drafted by the Phillies in 1992 in the 23 round.

A year after Estalella was drafted, **Kevin Sefcik** was selected by the Phillies in the 33rd round. He wasn't sure that he wasn't going to get drafted at all after completing his senior year at St. Xavier College in Chicago. "I was a little more smaller in size and stature," explained the five-foot-ten, 180-pound outfielder. "They probably thought I was going to be one of those guys that would just fill in somewhere, but I turned out a little bit better than what they anticipated." Sefcik ran into a little trouble in his first season because he was behind a first rounder, but he showed he could hit for average and led all short-season Phillies in average (.299). He moved up to Double-A then. He first got a call to the Phillies at the end of his third season in professional ball. He finally cracked the lineup for good with the Phillies in 1997. In his first full season with Philadelphia in 1998, he batted .314 in 104 contests.

Dave Doster felt he was fortunate just to get drafted. "For me, it didn't matter when I got called as long as I got called to play," explained the Indiana State University graduate. He patiently waited by the phone and got a call late the second day of the draft. The Phillies had picked in the 27th round. "It was a big thing to finally be over and be with somebody." He received a $1,000 bonus, but more importantly a chance to play.

The baby-faced player from New Haven, Indiana, didn't get drafted as a junior because he thinks his coach told scouts that his players wouldn't sign. "Supposedly that happened before, but I don't know if that's the truth or not," he commented. Teams don't want to waste a draft pick on someone who isn't going to sign.

The second baseman worked hard in the minors and learned to play all infield positions. "People told me I couldn't make it. I'm a very determined person when someone says I can't do it," he explained as his reason for making it up to the majors. He was called up to the Phillies twice in 1996 and played in 39 games, hitting a solid .267. He played 1997 and 1998 with Class AAA Scranton waiting for another call that didn't come, but he has accepted his role as a backup player.

Toby Borland was a 27th-round pick in 1987 and worked his way up until he reached the majors in 1994. He spent two full seasons with the Phillies before being traded to the Mets in 1996. The Phillies signed him again in March 1998, but didn't keep him and he was granted free agency in July and signed with the Marlins.

Bob Scanlan, a 25th-round pick in 1984, was traded to the Cubs before he ever made it to the majors. The Cubs dealt two relievers, Chuck McElroy and Mitch Williams, for the starter and brought him up from Triple-A quickly. The Cubs moved him more into a relief role and he

picked up 14 saves in 1992. Then he was traded to the Brewers and his career has been up and down since.

Greg McCarthy went the same route as Scanlan. The 36th rounder in 1987 was dealt to Seattle before he ever made it to the majors in 1996. He spent another season there before his career ended.

Left-handed pitchers are always given consideration regardless of when they were drafted. The Phillies took **Matt Whisenant** in the 18th round in 1989, but traded him in 1990 for more immediate needs. The southpaw finally made it to the majors with the Marlins in 1997.

A long shot still hoping to make it to the majors with the Phillies was **Tony Fiore**. Originally an outfielder in his younger days, he graduated in 1989 from Holy Cross High School, but went undrafted. Then a couple of years later he went to Triton College and was a walk-on with the baseball team. "I only pitched 16 or 17 innings in college," he explained.

He tried out with Cincinnati and they told him they were going to take him as their last pick, but Philadelphia stepped in and grabbed him in the 28th round of the 1992 draft. "The Phillies called me and surprised me." He had thrown to the Phillies scout and must of impressed him. He really learned how to pitch in the minors and worked his way up to Triple-A by 1996. His best season in the minors came in 1997 when he was 11-8 on the season with a 3.35 ERA. He hadn't made it to the Phillies by the end of the 1998 season, but he was a non-roster invitee at the 1999 spring training camp. The six-year free agent hopes to crack the Phillies' starting rotation in 1999.

One of the long shots the Phillies signed in 1998 for a grand was **Roger Rodeheaver**, a 36th-round pick. The Indiana University graduate had an offer from the Secret Service, but he decided to give baseball a try before having to work for a living. After a month at Class A Batavia, he was beginning to wonder if he should have gone to the Secret Service. "I started out 1 for 26, .038," he explained. "I was trying to press a lot. I was trying to do things I couldn't do." It was the low point and he began to wonder if he could play at that level. His parents and his coaches convinced him otherwise. He recovered and began hitting again. Then he got hurt. He sprained his wrist sliding into second base. That ended his season early and he wasn't able to go to the Fall Instructional League. He recovered in the off-season and hopes to make a comeback. His goal is to work his way up the system to see where it takes him. "I just want a chance," he said. If he doesn't make it, the Secret Service is still waiting for him.

Disappointments

Besides J.D. Drew, the biggest disappointments in the Phillies organization have been pitchers. All of the pitchers who were ever drafted first by the Phillies have been unsuccessful. None of them has ever turned out to be a superstar or made much of an impact on the team. All the great pitchers on the Phillies since 1965 were either free agents or draft picks with other teams.

The first pitching blunder was **Mike Biko**, a first rounder out of high school in 1966. The right-hander never got past Single-A. Another pitching bomb was **Mike Martin** out of high school in 1970. The first round lefty could only get as far as Triple-A. The same held true for **Sam Welborn**, a first-round right-handed pitcher in 1975. In 1977 the Phillies picked pitcher **Scott Munninghoff** out of high school as their first pick. He pitched a total of four games with the Phillies in 1980 before nose diving. **Rip Rollins** was a first baseman/pitcher picked out of high school in the first round in 1978. He never made it past Single-A. Pitcher **Johnny Abrego** was taken out of high school in the first round in 1981. He held out for awhile and the Phillies upped his signing bonus to $70,000 before he finally signed. They didn't get any return on their investment. He got a cup of coffee with the Cubs in 1985 before bombing out. **Brad Brink**, a first-round pick (7th overall) in 1986, pitched for USC. He made it for one trial with the Phillies in 1992 and lost four games.

One of the most recent disappointments was not a pitcher. **Jeff Jackson**, a first-round pick in 1989, never got higher than Double-A with the Phillies before he was taken in the Rule V Draft in 1994 by Seattle. The Mariners took a look at the outfielder and released him after

spring training the next season. The Cubs picked up the local favorite from Simeon High School in Chicago, but released him the next spring. After that he went to the Independent leagues.

The Phillies picked **Ricky Williams** in the eighth round in 1995 out of high school before he turned into an outstanding running back for the University of Texas. Williams' progress was not as spectacular in baseball as in college football. He barely kept his head above the Mendoza Line his first three years in the minors then finally showed some progress in 1998. After he won the Heisman, the Phillies didn't protect him from the Rule V Draft and he was picked up by Montreal in December 1998. The next day his contract was purchased by Texas. Williams was picked fifth in the NFL draft by the New Orleans Saints in early 1999 and has put baseball in his rearview mirror. He signed an eight-year contract to play football. Just as well, because he was still a long way from making it in baseball. The Rangers could have picked him up just for publicity purposes, which is what teams did early in draft history.

Best Draft

The Phillies had several good years of drafts in which they picked up some decent players, but the 1974 draft produced a couple of players who appeared on the 1980 World Championship team. **Warren Brusstar** was a fourth-round pick in January, and **Lonnie Smith** was a first-round pick in June that year. Second-round selection **Kevin Saucier** played three seasons for Philadelphia. And **Jim Morrison** played a couple of years with the Phillies before going on to a dozen years in the majors.

Worst Draft

The only player from the 1967 draft to make it to the majors was **Scott Reid**, an outfielder from Arizona State University. He made no impact with the team.

Where Are They Now?

Mike Jackson, a second-round pick in 1984, began his pitching career with the Phillies as a starter the first two seasons in the minors before being converted to a reliever. The right-hander has become better through the years as one of the best stoppers in the American League. In 1998, he recorded 40 saves with the Cleveland Indians.

John Vukovich, who was originally drafted by the Phillies in 1966, is now the Phillies' third base coach. After playing 16 years, he took up coaching first with the Cubs then with managing and coaching with the Phillies.

Dave Brundage, a fourth-round selection in 1986, has turned to coaching. After playing in the minors as an outfielder and pitcher, Brundage became a player/coach with the Mariners. Now he is a coach with the Mariners' Class AAA-Tacoma team.

Ones Who Got Away

The Phillies' very first-ever draft pick, **Mike Adamson**, didn't sign in 1965. He went to USC and signed two years later with the Orioles. No matter, he wasn't very good anyway and pitched just 11 games in the majors in three seasons.

The Phillies drafted **Chuck Knoblauch** in the 18th round of the 1986 draft out of high school. Instead of signing, he attended Texas A&M University and waited until after his junior year to sign with the Twins, who picked him in the first round. The second baseman became the Rookie of the Year in 1991 and won a Gold Glove in 1997.

All in the Family

In the first draft, the Phillies drafted **Del Wilber, Jr.**, the son of Del Wilber, a catcher for Philadelphia in 1951 and 1952. Wilbur played eight years in the majors and became a manager for the Rangers in 1973 for one game, but Junior never got to the Big Leagues.

Mike Maddux was a fifth-round pick in 1982, two years before his younger brother, Greg, was drafted by the Cubs. In his rookie season, he ended up facing his brother to mark the first time that rookie brother pitchers had ever opposed each other. The Phillies released Mike in 1989 and he became a journeyman pitcher with many clubs.

Where Are They Now?

Mike Murphy, a sixth-round pick of the Philadelphia Phillies in 1990, received a telegram in the mail notifying him that he was drafted. "I had a 103 fever that day," he recalled. He was drafted out of high school. He was drafted twice more in Rule V minor league drafts by the Blue Jays then the Indians. In 1999, he was with the Rochester Red Wings still looking to get a shot at the majors. The outfielder has a lifetime .273 average in the minors. He was an all-star in the Florida State League in 1996.

The Phillies drafted **Bob Walk** in the third round in 1976 and brought him up as a starter in 1980. He posted a decent 11-7 record and was the starting pitcher in Game One of the World Series that year. The Phillies traded him anyway to Atlanta for Gary Matthews. He was just average with the Braves. Then he signed with the Pirates and became a much better starting pitcher the remainder of his career. He finished up his 14-year career with a 105-81 record in 1993. Now he is the color analyst for the Pirates broadcast team.

Undrafted Players

Scott Service wasn't drafted by his home-town Reds after he completed high school in Cincinnati, so he signed a free agent contract with the Phillies. The Phillies tried him once in the majors in 1988 before letting him go. His hometown Reds finally picked him up on waivers. Then they traded him only to pick him up again after the Giants released him. In all, he pitched as a long reliever in parts of seven seasons in the majors.

The Phillies signed **Andy Ashby** as a free agent in 1986. He went undrafted after playing at Crowder Junior College. Ashby was slow to progress and stayed at Class A for four seasons before earning a promotion in 1990. After going 2-8 with the Phillies in 1992, he was left unprotected and Colorado picked him up in the expansion draft. Then he went to the Padres and helped the team to a pennant in 1998.

Phillies scouts found **Ricky Bottalico** at Central Connecticut State University and signed him to a contract in 1991. The right-handed hurler moved up to the majors by 1994 and became the team's stopper in 1996 with 34 saves in two consecutive seasons before losing the job. The Phillies traded him to the Cardinals in 1998.

Bob Bowser was six-foot-seven, 240 pounds and a junior in college. He had a fastball clocked in the low 90s. He also had a curveball, slider and changeup. He was 11-0. He was all-conference and all-region, but his coach didn't put him up for All-American consideration. With numbers like that most scouts would be drooling. But Bowser never got drafted in 1995. The Braves had scouted him heavily and told his parents that they would be calling the first day of the draft. The call never came.

Bowser thinks he was "blackballed" by his baseball coach, Mike Moyzis at St. Joseph's College. His coach wanted him to stay another year, but Bowser was more interested in going pro. He admits he wasn't a very good student. "I don't know how I passed all my classes," he explained. "I didn't show up for class half the time."

Bowser knows how he passed a coaching class in the summer to become eligible to pitch in his junior year. His coach taught the class. "He gave me a book and told me to show up with a five-page paper. I never showed up with anything," the Indianapolis resident said. He received an "A" in the course and became eligible for the baseball team. The NCAA may categorize that as giving fraudulent academic credit, if it were true. Another no-no the coach supposedly did was give his players money to buy dinner or have some fun, according to Bowser. This too could be a violation of NCAA rules for giving extra benefits.

After not getting drafted, the hurler tried out with the Cubs, Reds and the Phillies, before Philadelphia signed him to a $1,000 minor league contract. He played rookie ball and hurt his arm. The Phillies offered to repair his rotator cuff injury and give him another try the following spring, but he chose to quit baseball. "I saw that it was all political," he commented. "I didn't want to spend five years in the minor leagues."

Now he plays ball in the Men's Adult Baseball League and owns a construction company.

His coach felt differently about the situation. "If he thinks this staff had anything to do with him not being drafted, he's wrong," Moyzis said in a telephone interview in 1999. Bowser's work ethic was at the "bottom of the list," according to the college coach. "He needs to look in the mirror."

"He had it in for me," countered Bowser. "I was the first [in his college] to get a pro contract." Bowser said the work ethic stemmed from him not lifting weights or running extra laps as ordered by the coach.

Moyzis said he continues to promote his players today, which he did with Bowser. "Other than that, I have no comment," he said and hung up.

On the Roster

The Phillies rely heavily on the draft to fill their roster. Going into Spring Training in 1999, the team carried 19 of their own draft picks on the roster. Six of those players were originally first-round picks, so the Phillies like to hang on to their handpicked players.

The two draft picks on the roster with the most time with Philadelphia were both catchers: **Mike Lieberthal**, a first-round pick in 1990, and **Gary Bennett**, an 11th round pick the same year. Also on the roster was another catcher: **Bobby Estalella**, a 23rd-round choice in 1992.

Gary Bennett, an 11th round pick in 1990 for the Phillies.

The Phillies have yet to produce a great pitcher from their own draft ranks, but they have high hopes on **Carlton Loewer**, a first-round choice in 1994. The right-hander won the Paul Owens Award for the best Phillies pitcher in the minors in 1998. He was called up to the majors in 1998 and was 7-8 with a 6.09 ERA. The Phillies would like him to turn out like another pitcher they had with a similar-but-backwards name, Steve Carlton.

Marlon Anderson was a junior at South Alabama when scouts became interested in him in 1995. "I probably talked to about 20 teams," he explained at spring training in 1999. "A lot of

Marlon Anderson, a Phillies second round pick in 1995.

teams that thought they were going to get me didn't get a chance because the Phillies took me." Philadelphia picked him in the second round. The Prattville, Alabama, native has climbed steadily through the Phillies farm system and in 1998 charged into Class AAA Scranton where he hit .306 with 32 doubles, 16 homers and 86 RBI. He set club records for hits (176), runs (104), singles (114), triples (14), extra-base hits (62) and total bases (284). He only needed to improve on his defensive abilities at second base to become a regular in the majors. He was named International League Rookie of the Year and also received the Paul Owens Award for being the best player in the Phillies minor league system. The Phillies recalled him on Sept. 8, 1988, and he became the first Phillies player ever to hit a pinch-hit homer in his first major league plate appearance. It came in Philadelphia. He will likely hit a lot more to come in the future.

Seven is a lucky number in craps, but not necessarily in baseball. **Matt Beech** was chosen in the 7th round in 1994 and pitched well in the minors, but he hasn't had much luck in the majors. First called up in 1996, the left-handed

starter was 8-22 after three seasons with the Phillies. And he began 1999 on the disabled list.

Wayne Gomes, a first-round choice in 1993, became a regular relief pitcher on the Phillies in 1998. The right-hander was a workhorse for the team as he appeared in 71 games. He was 9-6 with a 4.24 ERA.

Tyler Green, a first rounder in 1991, has had his share of injuries that has affected his performance in the pros. He first had shoulder problems in 1992 in the minors. Then he missed the entire 1996 season to shoulder surgery. In 1998 Green was on the disabled list due to swelling in his elbow. The right-hander started the 1999 season recovering from elbow and shoulder surgeries.

Another 1991 choice who pitches for the Phillies is **Mike Grace**, a 10th rounder. He was first called up in 1995 and was 7-2 in 1996 before running into shoulder problems. He spent the next two seasons between the minors and majors.

Wendell Magee, a 12th-round choice in 1994, has been up with the Phillies three times and hasn't stuck yet. Will it be three strikes you're out for the outfielder or will he finally stick soon in 1999?

Another 12th-round pick on the roster who hasn't stuck yet was **Jon Zuber**, another outfielder who was drafted in 1992. He has hit just .250 in two tries with the Phillies.

Future Stars?

After losing their number-one pick in 1997, the Phillies are hoping the **Pat Burrell**, the first player taken in the 1998 draft, will heal the wound left by J.D. Drew's refusal to sign. "I'm very excited to be part of the Phillies organization," he said after the draft. "I'm looking forward to getting my feet wet in pro ball." Burrell still cost the Phils a lot of money — a reported $3.15 million bonus. The Phils started the collegiate star from the Miami Hurricanes at Class A Clearwater where he hit .303 with seven homers and 30 RBI in just 132 at-bats. The Phils have moved the third baseman to first because Scott Rolen, another number-one pick, is at third. If he lives up to his bonus, he should be called up to the Phils by the end of 1999, if not sooner.

Because the Phillies couldn't sign Drew, they were given a supplemental pick in 1998 and they chose **Eric Valent**, an outfielder from UCLA. Valent broke the Pac-10 home run records. The left-handed hitter showed he could hit with the wooden bat as he knocked out 13 homers in Class A.

Brad Baisley, a second-round selection in 1998, threw his first professional shutout, 3-0, over the Asheville Tourists in early June 1999 to earn Minor League Player of the week honors. The 6-foot-9 right-hander allowed three hits, walking one and striking out six. His season record up to that point was 5-5 with a 2.32 ERA for 13 starts at Piedmont.

The other Player of the Week early in June was **Reggie Taylor**, a first-round pick in 1999. He hit .500 (12-24) in six games with three homers and seven RBI. He raised his season average to .283.

Teams are always after a good left-handed pitcher, so Philadelphia drafted **Randy Wolf** in the second round in 1997. In two seasons, the Pepperdine University pitcher had progressed up to Triple-A. Then he did well in the Arizona Fall League in 1998 giving up just 29 hits in 33 innings and striking out 37. The Phillies called him up early in 1999 to replace an injured Carlton Loewer.

Another rising hopeful in the Phillies system is **Ryan Brannan**, a fourth-round pick in 1996 out of Long Beach State University. With a fastball in the high 90s, the right-hander could be a stopper some day for the Phillies. However, he sometimes has trouble harnessing that speeder. Brannan progressed up to Triple-A in 1998, but was rocked and sent back to Double-A. He was still working on a stronger second pitch at the end of 1998.

David Coggin, a supplemental-round pick in 1995, could have gone to a major college as a quarterback prospect but he chose baseball. The Phillies are hoping he made the right decision. Coggin has an excellent fastball and curve, but he hasn't come up with the right formula yet.

The next long shot to make the Phillies may just be **Matt Guiliano**, a 20th-round pick in 1994 out of Iona College. The shortstop has some pop in the bat as he hit 12 homers in 1998

at Double-A Reading. The Phillies moved him up to Triple-A in 1999.

Brian Harris was first picked in the 45th round by Pittsburgh after graduating from high school. He was offered $5,000 and scholarship money, but he chose college instead. After his senior year, the Phillies picked him in the 3rd round and offered the fifth-year senior $25,000.

Brian Harris, eighth round pick for the Philadelphia Phillies in 1997.

He didn't haggle and signed right away. "I didn't want to start my professional career with a mark on me that said this guy didn't want to play and just wanted more money," explained Harris. "I was of senior age, which is why I didn't get more." He was one semester away from completing a degree in sports management.

Harris hit .311 at Class A Batavia his first season. Then in 1998 he progressed up to Double-A Reading by the end of the season. He had 29 extra-base hits in 1998, including five homers. He hoped to start at Double-A in 1999 and move up to Triple-A by the end of the season. Then he wants to make the 40-man roster in 2000 with a call up to the majors by September 2000.

Brett Myers, an 18-year-old right-handed pitcher out of high school, was the Phillies' first-round selection in 1999. The 12th overall pick had an 8-2 record and 0.80 ERA in his senior year. In 78 innings, he allowed 25 hits, walked 34 and struck out 131. "He's a big, strong kid who has the potential to be a power pitcher on the major league level," said scouting director Mike Arbuckle after making the selection. "He's an excellent competitor and very confident. His curve ball has the makings of being a power pitch, too. Arbuckle compared him to Curt Schilling, which is probably why the Phillies were so high on him. The Phillies had seven different scouts look at the hurler. His fastball hit a high of 96 mph on the gun and was consistently in the low 90s.

Pittsburgh Pirates

In the 35 years before the draft, the Pirates won the pennant and World Series only once. That was in 1960 when Danny Murtaugh was the manager. Murtaugh returned to the team in 1970 and again took the team to the top, but this time with the help of the draft. In the 35 years since the draft began, the Pirates finished first nine times and won two World Series championships. The draft helped to contribute to that tremendous swing.

The 1971 World Championship team had a handful of draft picks that contributed: Dave Cash, Gene Clines, Richie Hebner, Milt May and Bob Moose. The 1979 World Championship team also had a handful of original draft picks, including John Candelaria, Bruce Kison, Steve Nicosia, Ed Ott and Dave Parker.

The team slumped in the 1980s without a championship, but it rebounded in the early 1990s thanks to some great picks in the draft and free-agent acquisitions. The Pirates did make it to the League Championship Series three years in a row thanks to some of its own draft picks: Barry Bonds, Jeff King, Stan Belinda, John Smiley, Tim Wakefield and John Wehner.

Because Pittsburgh is a small-market team, it must rely on the draft more than the large-market teams. The team couldn't bid high enough to keep the services of Bonds when he became a free agent. And they have had to trade other players before they turn free agents or all they get is a compensation pick in the draft the next year.

Mickey White, who was hired as the new scouting director in November 1998, hopes to revive the struggling franchise, which hasn't made the playoffs since 1993. He was very successful as the scouting director for the Cleveland Indians in 1991 and 1992 when 18 players he signed made it to the majors and turned that franchise into a winner in the 1990s. He hoped to do the same miracle work with Pittsburgh, which is a much smaller market team. "I've al-

ways looked at the draft as a futures commodity broker," explained White. In other words, he's looking for talent and hopes to get the best players for the team. Pittsburgh's philosophy is to take the best player available. The Pirates also like young players with a lot of speed. Pittsburgh has now drafted a high school player as their first choice in six of the last eight years.

The scouting staff is a little smaller than most teams because of the budget, so it has to "outhustle" other teams to get an advantage. In the United States, the Pirates have four regional coordinators, 15 full-time area scouts, 10 part-time scouts and about 25 associate scouts. The Pirates have baseball academies in the Dominican and Venezuela. The Pirates also have a working agreement with the Mexico City Red Devils, a Triple-A team in the Mexican League. The Pirates probably have more Mexican players in their farm system than any other team in baseball. The team doesn't scout much of the rest of the globe.

The Pirates have a brighter future ahead of them because they will be getting a new ballpark. They are hoping that PNC Park does for the team what a new stadium did for Cleveland.

Best Picks

Barry Bonds will be the first Pirates draft pick to reach the Hall of Fame five years after he retires. The first-round draft pick out of Arizona State University from 1985 secured that spot when he earned his third Most Valuable Player award in 1993 after leading the league with 38 homers and 123 RBI. He became the only player to win three MVP awards in a four-season period. His first MVP award came in 1990 after he clouted 33 homers and 114 RBI to lead the Pirates to the League Championship Series. Two years later he earned his second MVP award to again power the Pirates to the LCS. Bonds does a lot of talking with his glove as well and had earned eight Gold Gloves. He's also been on the All-Star Team seven times so far. The Pirates haven't been the same since his departure in 1992 when he became a free agent and signed with San Francisco. Bonds surpassed the 400 home-run mark in 1998 and has even more stolen bases during his career. He was the first player in Major League history to hit 350 home runs and steal 350 bases.

The first Pirates draft pick to earn a MVP award was **Dave Parker**. Parker was just a 14th-round pick in 1970 probably because of a knee injury while playing football at his Cincinnati high school. He led the league in slugging average (.541) his first full season in the majors in 1975 after hitting 25 homers, 10 triples and 35 doubles. Two seasons later he earned the MVP award when he led the league with a .338 batting average, 215 hits and 44 doubles. He also won the first of his three Gold Gloves that season. He played 11 seasons with Pittsburgh before going to Cincinnati where he led the league in 1985 with 42 doubles and 125 RBI. Over his 19-years in the majors he hit 339 homers. He was named to six Midsummer Classics during his days.

Dave Parker, 14th round pick in 1970 for the Pittsburgh Pirates. (Photograph courtesy of the Pittsburgh Pirates.)

John Candelaria, second round pick in 1972 for the Pirates. (Photograph courtesy of the Pittsburgh Pirates.)

John Candelaria, a second-round pick in 1972, pitched a decade for the Pirates and had only one losing season during that period. His best season with the team came in 1977 when he was 20-5 to lead the league in winning percentage with .800. He also led the league in ERA and was considered for a Cy Young Award. "Candy Man" also picked up one of the wins in the 1979 World Series. After he left Pittsburgh in 1985, he pitched for seven teams in nine years. He retired in 1993 with a 177-122 record.

Richie Hebner was a first-round choice of the Pirates in 1966 and became a real asset in the early 1970s when the team won five pennants and a World Series. Hebner was the starting third baseman for eight seasons with the Pirates before becoming a free agent and signing with the Phillies. After stints with the Yankees and Tigers, he returned to Pittsburgh in a utility role for a couple of seasons. He compiled 203 home runs during his 18-year career. Then he turned to managing and coaching. He is now the hitting coach for the Nashville Sounds in the Pirates' farm system.

Willie Randolph was a seventh-round pick with the Pirates in 1972 and was called up to the Pirates in 1975. Pittsburgh decided to trade him to the Yankees and he made a name for himself there. The slick fielding shortstop played 13 seasons for the Yankees and 18 years in the majors. He appeared on five All-Star teams.

Baseball is like a religion with some families. It was like that in the King family. "My dad played professional ball a little bit," said **Jeff King**. His father played minor league ball in the Philadelphia Phillies organization in the 1950s. "I had two brothers that played, too. It [baseball] was part of the family."

King didn't start playing organized baseball until he was nine. He soon found out he could play well and advanced from Little League to Babe Ruth to high school ball. The Chicago Cubs first drafted him in 1982 in the 23rd round. He decided to attend the University of Arkansas and led the team to a third-place finish in the College World Series as he averaged .369 during the season with 17 home runs. His outstanding performance as a Razorback earned him the *Sporting News* College Player of the Year honor. This led to him being drafted in the first round in 1986 by the Pirates. King played eight seasons with the Pirates at third base. He was moved to first base and his best season was his last when he hit 30 homers. The Pirates dealt him to Kansas City Royals where he had two more good seasons before he decided to retire halfway through the 1999 season due to back problems.

Long Shots

Long shots get a long look from the Pirates. Being a small-market team, the Pirates squeeze as much out of their players as possible and give its draft picks all the rope they need to make it to the majors regardless of what position they were drafted.

Vance Law was at BYU when the Pirates selected him in the 39th round of the 1978 draft. After two years with the Pirates, he went on to an 11-year career in the majors.

Drafted in the 20th round in 1990 by Pittsburgh, **Mark Johnson** picked a career in baseball over Wall Street. As of 1998, he

Vance Law, selected in the 39th round in 1978. (Photograph courtesy of the Pittsburgh Pirates.)

wasn't in the majors, but he didn't regret the decision. Johnson was first drafted by the Pirates in the 42nd round in 1989 when he was a junior at Dartmouth College and a star in the Cape Cod League, but he didn't sign. "It was a difficult decision because it puts you a year behind," he remembered. "But I was looking to finish my education."

The following year he was graduated with a degree in psychology. He also was the school's second best passer in football. But he decided on baseball and signed for $3,000 with the Pirates after being picked in the 20th round. He went off to Class A Welland and played two years at that level. Then he played a couple of years at Class AA before getting Pittsburgh's attention

by being named the Southern League MVP for hitting 23 homers on the year.

A home run was also his first hit in the majors, when Pittsburgh brought him up at the beginning of the 1995 season. However, he hit only .208 with the club, so he was sent back to Triple A after he had logged 79 games with the Pirates. The following season he played the whole season with the Pirates and hit .274 with 13 home runs in 127 games.

After hitting poorly in 1997, he was sent back to the minors again and the Pirates waived him at the end of the season. Cincinnati claimed Johnson and he was assigned to the Indianapolis Indians, where he played outfield. Early in the season he hoped to make an impact and get called up with the Reds. "Realistically, I think I have a shot to get back in the major leagues," he explained. "If I didn't see the opportunity to get back or I didn't feel I was good enough to get back, I would move on." He stayed the whole season and hit .300 with 22 home runs, but the Reds failed to call him up in September. After the season was over, he signed with Seattle.

The Pirates selected **Kevin Polcovich** in the 30th round in 1992 out of the University of Florida. The shortstop started at Double-A, but was demoted to Class A after hitting .171. He stayed there for a couple of seasons before moving back to Double-A. After hitting .306 at Triple-A Calgary, the Pirates called him up in 1997 and he hit .273 the rest of the season. But he had trouble in 1998 trying to get above the Mendoza Line and ended up with a .189 average, which jeopardizes his staying in the majors.

Adrian Brown, a 48th round choice in 1992 out of high school, slowly worked his way up the minors until he was called up in 1997, but he couldn't hit above .200 either. However, the next season he improved his hitting at the major league level and played in 41 games.

The Pirates found a solid left-handed starter when they drafted **Steve Cooke** in the 35th round in the 1989 draft. He took just three seasons to make it to the majors for good. Then he started for the Pirates for a couple of sessions before suffering bursitis in his pitching shoulder. He recovered to start again for the Pirates before being released and going on to Cincinnati and Tampa Bay.

Another lefty long shot was **Rick Honey-cutt**, a 17th round pick in 1977. Drafted as a pitcher/first baseman out of the University of Tennessee, he was traded to Seattle before the Pirates could evaluate his talents as a pitcher. Honeycutt played on eight different major league teams in 11 years and ended his career with a 109-143 record.

Still another left-handed long shot was **Chris Peters**, a 37th-round selection in 1993 out of Indiana University. Peters was first promoted to the Pirates club in 1996 and found a spot in the rotation in 1998.

Some players only get one chance at the majors and must show their mettle or they may never get back. Such may have been the case for **Chance Sanford** in 1998. The 27th round pick out of San Jacinto North Junior College in 1992 received a chance when Freddy Garcia was sent back down to the minors on April 30. His poor performance in the majors — .143 batting average in 14 games — may have been his last chance at the majors. Then again, maybe not. Low draft picks don't get many chances at making the majors and better make the best of any chance they get.

Best Draft

Pittsburgh usually gets several draft picks each year that eventually make it to the majors. And many years there are several that make an impact. Pittsburgh drafted several players in 1966 that made an impact on the team. The first pick was **Richie Hebner**, who made contributions for many years. **Dave Cash** and **Gene Clines** each played five seasons for the Pirates before going elsewhere for more playing time.

Worst Draft

The Pirates haven't had that many lean years in the draft, but 1968 was a real bummer. Only one player from that draft ever made it to the majors and **Tom Dettore** wasn't an impact player.

Disappointments

Pittsburgh's first ever draft pick was **Doug Dickerson**, an outfielder out of high school. He couldn't get past Class A. Neither could the first pick of the 1967 draft, **Joe Grigas**, who was also an outfielder.

Then the Pirates turned to picking pitchers in the first round and suffered two successive disappointments in 1969–1970. **Bob May** and **John Bedard** never made it to the majors.

In 1972, the Pirates picked catcher **Dwayne Peltier** in the first round and the backstop only got as far as Double-A.

The Pirates were disappointed in 1976 with pitcher **Jim Parke**, who never got past first base as he peaked at Class A. **Anthony Nicely**, the first pick the next year, and **Gerry Aubin** the year after that couldn't do any better.

In 1983, the Pirates selected outfielder **Ron DeLucchi**, who couldn't make it past Class A. **Kevin Andersh**, the first pick in the 1984 draft, didn't do much better as he only made it up to Double-A.

Mark Merchant was the second player drafted in 1987, so the Pirates gave him every chance to develop, but the high school outfielder never got higher than Triple-A in 11 seasons in the minors. **Austin Manahan**, the first rounder in 1988, couldn't do that good.

The latest disappointment for the Pirates is **Jon Farrell**, a catcher/outfielder picked in 1991. He only got as far as Double-A.

Where Are They Now?

Tim Wakefield was first drafted as a first baseman by the Pirates in 1988. After showing he couldn't him professional pitching, he turned to pitching and developed the knuckleball as his best pitch. Wakefield was unhittable his first year in the majors in 1992 when he was 8-1 with a 2.15 ERA. He lost his stuff the next season and was sent back to the minors where he struggled as well. The Pirates released him and Boston picked him up almost immediately. Again, he was great his first year as American Leaguers couldn't hit him and he compiled a 16-8 record with a 2.95 ERA. He hasn't done as well since with the Red Sox.

Another Pirate pitcher gone elsewhere is **Stan Belinda**, a 10th-round pick in 1986, who played five seasons with the Pirates before he had to pack his bags after being traded to Kansas

City. Belinda then became a free agent and went to Boston and Cincinnati. In 1998 he contracted multiple sclerosis, a disease that attacks the body's nerve endings. He told a reporter in 1999 that he didn't want to be remembered for that though. Pirates fans will likely remember him more for helping the team to the League Championship Series in 1992 then giving up the series ending run to the Braves in the ninth inning.

Gene Clines, a sixth-round choice in 1966, joined the San Francisco coaching staff in 1997. He played 10 seasons in the big leagues including five with the Pirates. He took part in three League Championship Series with the Pirates and was part of the World Championship team in 1971. His best year as a player came with the Pirates in 1972 when he averaged .334.

Another former Pirates player on the Giants' coaching staff is **Ron Wotus**, a 16th round draft pick in 1979. Wotus played pro ball for 11 seasons, including parts of two seasons with the Pirates in 1983 and 1984. After playing he turned to managing in the Giants' farm system.

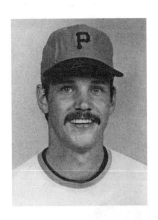

Richie Zisk, a third-round pick in 1967, became a hitting coach in the Cubs' farm system, although he never played for the team during his 13-year career. Zisk played in the National League Championship Series with Pittsburgh in 1974 and 1975.

Another former draft pick turned hitting coach is **Mitchell Page**. Drafted by Pittsburgh in the third round in 1973, he ended his career by playing 1984 with the team. He became the Cardinals minor league hitting coordinator in 1999.

Willie Randolph also turned to coaching after playing and was stationed at third base in 1998 with the Yankees.

Ken Macha is now the bench coach for the

Richie Zisk, third round pick in 1967 for the Pirates. (Photograph courtesy of the Pittsburgh Pirates.)

Oakland Athletics. He played professionally for 14 seasons in the Pittsburgh, Montreal and Toronto organizations. He was originally drafted by the Pirates in the sixth round of the 1972 June draft and played portions of the 1974, '77 and '78 seasons with Pittsburgh.

Chris Estep was a 12th round pick in 1988 out of the University of Kentucky and received a $35,000 bonus. He never made it to the bigs, but he has created a big academy in Carmel, Indiana. Chris began the Round Tripper Baseball Academy in 1992 after making his way to Triple-A. "Pittsburgh couldn't figure out what to do with me," he explained. "I was a project." Looking back on the draft now, he wishes he would have finished his degree first before going on to professional baseball.

Ones Who Got Away

The Pirates lost a couple of picks to cross-state rival Philadelphia. The Pirates selected **Mickey Morandini** in the seventh round of the 1987 draft. At the time, he was a junior at Indiana University. The second baseman elected to stay another year and finish his degree before signing with the Phillies in the fifth round of the 1988 draft. Morandini has been in the majors nine seasons with the Phillies and Cubs.

The Pirates picked **John Kruk** in the third round in the January 1981 draft when he was at Allegany Community College, Pa. Kruk made a name for himself with Philadelphia, too.

Lance Johnson was also chosen by the Pirates in 1981 in the third round in the January phase. He decided to go on to college and was drafted three years later in the sixth round by St. Louis. Although he's never played for the Cardinals, he's been in the majors since 1987.

Undrafted Players

Back in 1981, general manager Sid Thrift was impressed by one of his son's teammates on the U.S. amateur team in Europe. "I couldn't believe that he hadn't been drafted," he said. The player was **Bobby Bonilla**. A few years later the Pirates lost Bonilla in the Rule V draft to the White Sox, but traded for him in 1996 for right-handed pitcher Jose DeLeon. The Pirates enjoyed

Bonilla for six seasons until he was granted free agency. The Mets signed him to a five-year contract for $29 million, the richest at the time. In November 1996, the Marlins signed him to a $23.5 million four-year contract. The six-time All-Star helped lead Florida to a World Series title in 1997. After 13 years in the majors, he has 273 home runs.

The Pirates actually found a left-handed pitcher who wasn't drafted. Pittsburgh signed **Jason Christiansen** in 1991 after he wasn't drafted. He had played at Cameron University. The reliever worked his way up to the majors in 1995 after four years in the minors. He's been there ever since.

All in the Family

The Pirates drafted **Mark Pettit** in June 1971. His father, Paul, was a pitcher with the Pirates in 1951 and 1953. Mark never made it to the majors.

Harding Peterson announced that his own son, **Eric Peterson**, had been selected by the Pirates in the seventh round. However, Eric didn't sign.

Barry Bonds and his father, Bobby, have more home runs, RBI, and stolen bases than any other father-son combination in the Major Leagues. Bobby played 14 years on the majors and clouted 332 homers, 1,024 RBI and 461 steals. His son has since passed those marks with the exception of stolen bases in 13 seasons.

On the Roster

Going into the 1999 season, the Pirates had eleven of their own picks on the 40-man roster. Six of the players were rookies and five were long shots (beyond 10th round), so the roster looked more like the line-up for a maiden thoroughbred race than a major league team. Only one Pirates' first rounder, **Chad Hermanson**, was on the roster.

Roy Smith scouted Hermanson at Green Valley High School in Nevada where he was the High School Player-of-the-Year. The outfielder has been on the fast track to the majors after being named the short-season Player of the Year in 1995. Then he was an all-star the next season.

In 1998 he slammed out 28 homers at Triple-A Nashville, but he also struck out 152 times.

Also at Nashville in 1998 was **Jimmy Anderson**, a ninth-round pick in 1994. The left-handed pitcher was scouted by Steve Fleming at Western Branch High School, Virginia. He was all-city and all-state all four years in baseball. The starter made great progress until he got to Triple-A where his ERA has been above 5.00 in two seasons.

Another lefty on the roster was **Kevin Pickford**, a second rounder in 1993 scouted by Jim Nelson out of high school. He was primarily a starter until the Pirates tried him out of the bullpen in Double-A in 1997. He had a rough time just being a reliever and his ERA jumped to 7.36. He moved up to Triple-A in 1998 and was 11-2 on the season with a 3.66 ERA.

Alex Hernandez, a fourth rounder from 1995, was signed by Jose Luna when he graduated from Pedro Albizo Campos High School in Puerto Rico. Hernandez has made steady progress since being drafted with his power, speed and fielding. He moved up to Double-A in 1998 and became Carolina's centerfielder. He led the club in triples with seven on the season.

Going into his junior year at Clemson, **Kris Benson** was projected in the first round, so he

Kris Benson was drafted by Pittsburgh in the first round in 1996.

went about getting an agent to represent him for the draft. He couldn't sign a contract because he was still in college and would lose his eligibility. His family interviewed nine agencies and narrowed that field to three with the help of a questionnaire. "It was a long process," he said.

After finishing the season with a 14-2 record, the strikeout artist's value rose to the top by Pittsburgh standards and they chose him first in the country. Being a member of Team USA, he went off to the Olympics instead of going to pro baseball. He went undefeated during the 31-game pre–Olympic tour and won twice in the Olympics before losing to Japan. With the Olympics out of the way, his agency helped him secure a big bonus package. "They definitely got me the money I was expected to get," he explained.

In his first two seasons in the minors, he had compiled a 16-17 record and had progressed up to Triple-A. To give him more experience, the Pirates brought him to its spring training camp as a non-roster invitee in 1999, because they didn't have to put him on the 40-man roster yet. At spring training in 1999, he was hopeful he could break into the majors by June or a September call-up. His wishes came quicker than that as the Pirates called him up on April 9 when Pat Meares was placed on the disabled list.

Brian O'Connor received a lot of promises from different teams before he heard from the Pirates in the 11th round in 1995. One scout told him he was going to be drafted anywhere from round three to five and what he might get offered. Milwaukee called him in the fifth round, but didn't take him. Then he got called by the Cubs in the 10th round, but didn't take him either. "You really can't listen to the scouts and what they say," he explained. "I guest it's their job to come in and pump up the family. It's better if they didn't do that." Pittsburgh scout Steve Demeter was honest with him, however. O'-Connor had signed a letter of intent with a junior college, but he wanted to get drafted after completing high school. He told scouts he would sign. After he was drafted, he was used as a reliever for awhile until he was made a starter again. He led the New York–Penn League in losses (10) in 1996, but he improved after that. After a promotion to Double-A in 1998, the Pirates added

him to the 40-man roster in November. He was hoping to move up to Triple-A in 1999.

Long shot **Adrian Brown**, who was scouted by Boyd Odom and picked in the 48th round in 1992, climbed his way to the majors by getting better each year. The outfielder got his first call to the majors in 1997, but got sent back down after hitting below the Mendoza Line. He came back in 1998 and was much better by batting .283 in about the same amount of games.

Jason Phillips, a 14th-round pick in 1992, made the Pirates out of spring training in 1999 after seven seasons in the minors. Always a starter in the minors, he made his debut as a reliever.

The four veteran draft picks on the roster for the Pirates were **Kevin Young**, a seventh-round choice in 1990, **Keith Osik**, a 24th-round pick the same year, and **Chris Peters**, a 37th-round pick in 1993, and **Tony Womack**, their all-star second baseman who was drafted in the 7th round in 1991. However, Womack was traded to Arizona during spring training in 1999.

Young, who was scouted by Bob Rossi, was first called up to the majors in 1992. After he slumped to .205 in 1994 and .232 in 1995, the Pirates released him. Kansas City signed him to a minor league contract and he worked his way back to the majors with them in 1996. The Royals released him at the end of the season and the Pirates signed him again. This time he found the right formula and led the team in homers and RBI despite being out 35 games with a thumb injury. He threw a tirade in the clubhouse after returning from the disabled list. In 1998 he again led the team in homers and RBI. That performance led the Pirates to sign him to a four-year deal worth $24 million.

Osik, another Rossi prospect, played all nine positions in a game with LSU before he was drafted. That versatility has helped get where he is today as a backup catcher and utility fielder. He showed steady progress in the minors until exploding for a .336 average in 1995 with Calgary, which helped him earn his promotion to the majors.

Peters attended Indiana University and was scouted by Bill Bryk. The lefty had trouble sizing up the competition his first two seasons then he got much better and the Pirates called him up in 1996. He was strictly a reliever in 1997 before starting 21 contests in 1998. He even had a five-game hitting streak.

Future Stars

Bronson Arroyo was selected in the third round in 1995 out of high school and was scouted by Scott Lovekamp. The right-handed hurler was an all-star in the Carolina League in 1997 when he was 12-4 as a starter. He was troubled by an injury in 1998, but should be fully recovered to do better in Double-A in 1999.

The Pirates selected outfielder **J.J. Davis** in the first round in 1997. Davis batted .527 with seven doubles, one triple, eight home runs and 28 RBI as a senior in high school. Davis signed rather than going to USC or Oregon State, who offered him scholarships. "He has the combination of power, make-up and instincts that we feel give him the best chance to be a franchise-type player with the Pittsburgh Pirates," said White. Davis was assigned to long-season Class A Hickory in 1999 and was beginning to hit for power.

Another 1997 pick was **Kory DeHaan**, who was scouted by Grant Brittain at Morningside College. He broke Augusta's single-season franchise record of .313 set by Moises Alou when he batted .314. He also led the league in doubles with 39 on his way to being named the South Atlantic League All-Star Team. DeHaan was assigned to Class A Lynchburg in 1999.

A long shot from the class of 1997 was **Kevin Haverbusch**. Scout Steve Fleming discovered Haverbusch at the University of Maryland and the Pirates selected him in the 20th round in 1997. The pick was better late than never and has turned out great for the Pirates. Haverbusch was the Most Valuable Player and all-star in the New York–Penn League his first year after batting .311. He bettered his average the following season and was named an all-star again. The third baseman likes to line drive the ball and has displayed some power along with the average.

Garrett Long, a second-round pick in 1991, has been a little short on power in the minors for a first baseman and outfielder, but his average

Moises Alou with the Indianapolis Indians, drafted by the Pittsburgh Pirates. (Photograph by Jackie Dowling.)

improved in 1998 in Double-A. Tom Barnard scouted him at Yale University and the Pirates drafted in him the second round in 1995. He was a non-roster invitee at spring training in 1998. He began 1999 at Double-A.

The first pick in 1998 was **Clint Johnston**, a left-handed hurler who was 15th overall. He went 2-0 with one save and a 2.66 ERA in 16 relief appearances as a junior at Vanderbilt University. If he doesn't work out as a pitcher, the Pirates could always turned him into a first baseman or outfielder. At Vanderbilt he batted .424 with 16 doubles, 19 home runs and 74 RBI in 53 games. After a 3-3 start and 2.75 ERA in 1998 at Augusta, the Pirates assigned him to Class A Hickory.

The Pirates selected right-handed pitcher **Bobby Bradley** in the first round in 1999. He went 12-1 with a 0.38 ERA, 156 strikeouts and 13 walks in 92 innings as a senior in high school. The team signed him a month later and assigned him to Bradenton in the Gulf Coast League.

St. Louis Cardinals

When the draft began in 1965, the Cardinals already had some great players with the likes of Bob Gibson, Lou Brock, Curt Flood and Dick Groat, to name a few. The team continued to be competitive with the help of the draft and finished first three times in the 1980s with some valuable draft picks. The draft didn't help the Cardinals that much when they got to the 1982 World Series other than providing them fuel for trading. Only two players of any consequence — Bob Forsch and Keith Hernandez — had been drafted by St. Louis. However, the 1985 and 1987 World Series squads were well represented by the Cardinals' own draft picks. Besides Forsch, Todd Worrell and Terry Pendleton were on both of those teams. The 1996 playoff team was comprised of a handful of Cardinals draft picks, too, including Alan Benes, Tom Pagnozzi, Dmitri Young and T.J. Matthews.

The team used be one that relied on excellent pitching and speed over power, but they have waivered on that in recent times. Getting Mark McGwire was a real move to power. St. Louis is also usually conservative with their first-round picks and take proven college talent rather than unproven, more risky high school players. For example, in 1998 they drafted J.D. Drew, a proven professional player, rather than a high school or college prospect. Drew had played a year in the independent Northern League after refusing to sign a contract with the Philadelphia Phillies. The Cardinals knew it would take a big contract to sign him, but they also knew he would be less of a gamble than somebody out of high school.

The scouting staff is an average size department with 15 area scouts and three cross-checkers in the United States. Internationally, the Cardinals' main concentration is in the Caribbean. They have signed plenty of players from the Dominican Republic and Venezuela, but nowhere else. John Mozeliak took over as the scouting director in 1999.

The Cardinals have been bitten by the injury bug with their first-round picks in the 1990s. Adam Benes, Donovan Osborne and Matt Morris all missed a full season due to injury. Osborne, a first-round pick in 1990, missed all of 1994. Benes, the 1993 pick, was out all of 1998 and much of 1999. And Morris, a 1995 first rounder, was scheduled to miss all of 1999.

In recent times, the Cardinals have given their draft picks every chance to develop in the farm system and a shot at the majors.

Best Picks

Ted Simmons was a football star in high school, but the Cardinals lured him away from that sport when they picked him in the first round in 1967 and gave him a $50,000 signing bonus. He soon proved himself in the minors with the bat as he led the California League with a .331 average and was named Most Valuable Player. He became the Cardinals' backup catcher in 1970 and regular receiver the following season. Being a solid switch-hitter led to the Cardinals using him 90 percent of the time behind the plate, although he led the league in passed

Andy Van Slyke with the Pittsburgh Pirates was drafted as a number one pick in 1979 by the St. Louis Cardinals. (Photograph by Marty Orr.)

balls three times. He was a clutch hitter and twice belted pinch-hit homers during his 21-year career, a decade of which was with the Cardinals. He was selected to eight All-Star teams during his career.

A year after Simmons came **Bob Forsch**, a 25th-round pick in 1968 out of high school. It took him to 1974 to make it to the majors, but once he did he became a consistent starter for the Cardinals for 14 seasons. He ranks third in Cardinal history in innings pitched and wins. His best season came in 1977 when he was 20-7. He won 15 in helping the Cardinals to the pennant in 1982 and picked up a shutout in the League Championship Series; however, he lost two games in the World Series, but the Cardinals won it in seven games. He pitched two no-hitters during his 16-year career. He was also a good hitter and twice won Silver Slugger awards as the best hitting pitcher.

Garry Templeton, a first-round pick in 1974, was up to the majors by 1976 and the following year turned the sophomore jinx into the best year of his career. The switch-hitting speedy shortstop led the league in triples and finished second in average at .322. His performance led to him being selected for the All-Star Team. He led the league in triples the next two seasons. When he was named as an alternate to the All-Star Game, he refused to go. That was the beginning of the end for him in St. Louis. Then he gave the finger to a fan in 1981 and the Cardinals decided to trade the trouble maker for an even better defensive shortstop — Ozzie Smith. With the Padres, Templeton was never as good as he was in St. Louis, but good enough to make the All-Star Team again in 1985.

Keith Hernandez was lucky he was drafted at all after quitting the baseball team during his senior year in a dispute with his coach at Capuchino High School in Millbrae, California. But his tools were so good, the Cardinals couldn't pass him up and selected him in the 42nd round in 1971. He was so good, in fact, he reached Class AAA in his first season. Then he won the American Association batting title in 1974. By 1975 he was the Cardinals' regular first baseman. He really reached his prime in 1979 when he won the National League batting title with a .344 average. He helped the Cardinals

win the World Series in 1982 with a team-leading eight RBI performance. The next season he was traded to the Mets. And two years later he admitted to cocaine use when testifying in a Pittsburgh drug trial. He was named to five All-Star teams during his 17 years in the majors and won the same amount of Gold Gloves.

Terry Pendleton was a seventh-round choice in 1982 and it turned out to be a lucky number for him. He soon proved himself in the minors and was called up to the Cardinals in 1984. In his first Major League game, he went three-for-five. His great defense at third helped the Cardinals to the World Series in 1985 and 1987. He picked up his first of three Gold Gloves in 1987. It was not until he became a free agent and signed with the Braves that his bat started to do more of the talking than his glove. The switch hitter helped Atlanta to the World Series in 1991 with his .319 average, which led him to be named Most Valuable Player. He retired in 1998 after 15 years in the majors. He appeared in one All-Star Game. He played in four World Series, but never picked up a ring.

The Cardinals called up **Todd Worrell**, a first-round pick in 1982, in August 1985 to help them with the stretch run and he did just that by saving five games and winning three others. He won the sixth and final game of the League Championships Series against the Dodgers to propel the Cardinals into the Series where he earned a save in Game 1 and tied a Series record by fanning six in a row. However, he picked up a loss during the Cardinals' demise in the Series. The following season he mowed down batters like a machine gun. He saved 36 games to establish a major league rookie record and be named as the Rookie of the Year. He was the Cardinals' savior for the next three seasons until elbow problems sidelined him for two seasons. He returned in 1991 but not as the same pitcher that he had been. Then he went to the Dodgers for five seasons and became a stopper again for them. He was his old self by 1995 when he saved 32 games. His career ended in 1997 with 256 saves.

Tom Pagnozzi, an eighth-round pick in 1983, was named to three all-star teams in the minors to earn a utility role with the Cardinals in 1988. He became the team's regular receiver

Steve Montgomery was drafted by the Cardinals in the third round in 1992.

in 1990. He earned three Gold Gloves in the next four seasons and improved with the bat as well. After a dozen seasons with the Cardinals, he was released in August 1998 after hitting just .219.

For a 10th round pick, **Vince Coleman** was quite a steal as he turned out to be a Rookie of the Year in 1986. He was also a great basestealer for the Cardinals. He was signed by Marty Maier. Unfortunately, Coleman will go down in history as the player who threw a powerful firecracker into a group of fans in a Dodger Stadium parking lot, which led to his unpopular demise.

Long Shots

Ken Reitz was a 31st-round choice in 1969 and he turned out to be quite a defensive specialist at the third base as he won a Gold Glove in 1975. In 1980 he set the National League record by committing only eight errors at third base. Eight of his 11 seasons were spent in St. Louis and he led third basemen in fielding percentage six of nine seasons. His best season with the bat came in 1977 when he clouted 17 homers; otherwise, he was just an average hitter. He was named to one All-Star Team.

The Cardinals didn't pick **John Denny** until the 29th round in 1970. The right-hander had great control and an unhittable curve ball which led him to becoming a starter with the team by 1975. Two years later he led the league starters with a 2.52 ERA, but only finished with an 11-9 record. After an 8-11 season in 1979, the

Cardinals traded him to the Indians. Then a couple of years later he helped the Phillies to a pennant with a 19-6 mark to earn him a Cy Young Award. He went on to the Reds and retired in 1986.

Another member of the draft class of 1970 who was a long shot was **Bake McBride**, a 37th-round pick. McBride, whose father played for the Kansas City Monarchs, was called up in 1973 and hit .300 for the Cardinals for the next five seasons before being dealt to the Phillies in a five-player trade. His career in the majors lasted 11 seasons.

Disappointments

The Cardinals received the last pick in the first round of the first draft, so the cream of the crop was already gone. They chose **Joe DiFabio**, a right-handed pitcher from Delta State. He only got as far as Triple-A.

A couple of years later in 1968, St. Louis had the next to last pick in the first round. The result was a player, **James Hairston**, who peaked at Single-A. That was the same result for the first pick the next June as **Charles Minott** couldn't pitch his way past Class A. The string of poor picks in the first round continued for the next two years with **Jim Browning** peaking at Double-A and **Ed Kurpiel** going as far as Triple-A.

The 1972 and 1973 first-round selections both made it to the majors, but their performance was disappointing to say the least. **Dan Larson**, a right-handed hurler, pitched 78 games in the majors with a resulting 10-25 record. And **Joe Edelen**'s ERA was 6.75 in 27 appearances. Hardly anything to write home about. Then in 1975 the Cardinals chose another pitcher, **David Johnson**. The lefthander peaked at Double-A.

After a couple of good years, the Cardinals picked **Robert Hicks** first in 1978. The first baseman couldn't get to Triple-A. **Don Collins** made it to Triple-A, but that's as far as the first rounder from 1980 could go.

One out of two is how the Cardinals ended up in 1988. They had two first-round picks and one of those made it to the majors. The one who didn't was **Brad DuVall** out of Virginia Tech. He only made it to Class A.

The following year the Cardinals picked

Paul Coleman instead of Frank Thomas, who was the next player taken. Coleman peaked at Double-A and Thomas has turned into one of the best hitters of the 1990s.

Major league teams are always on the outlook for catchers and the Cardinals thought they had a good one when they picked **Dan Cholowsky** in the compensation round in 1991. The 39th pick in the draft didn't put up the numbers with the bat, so the Cardinals released him in May 1996. He was signed by the Cubs, but couldn't manage a .200 average at Triple-A. The Rockies purchased his contract from the Cubs in July 1997. He was then granted free agency in October 1998.

The latest disappointment to the Cardinals is first round pick **Tom McKinnon** from 1991. The high school pick couldn't hack it as a pitcher or outfielder with the Cardinals and was released in March 1996. The Devil Rays signed him for a season, but he wasn't good enough there either.

Where Are They Now?

Two Cardinals moved upstairs to the broadcast booth after their playing days were over. **Al Hrabosky** worked as a sportscaster for a local TV station during his playing days, so the transition to broadcasting Cardinal games after playing was about as smooth as an ice for the "Mad Hungarian." After **Ozzie Smith** ended is career in 1996, he also moved to color commentating the Cardinal games and joined the *This Week in Baseball* staff.

With Cincinnati in a rebuilding mode in 1998, 42nd-round pick **Keith Glauber** got a shot at the majors. Originally drafted by St. Louis from Montclair State (N.J.) University, the Reds picked him up in the 1997 Rule V draft. The starter turned reliever turned starter turned reliever again pitched at Single-A for three seasons as a reliever before moving up the ladder. In 1998, he was a starter at Double-A and Triple-A. Then he relieved in three games during his September call-up. The Reds kept him on the 40-man roster to start 1999.

Terry Kennedy, the Cardinals' first-round pick (sixth overall) in the 1977 June, is now with the Cubs as the manager of their Triple-A Iowa Cubs. Kennedy spent 14 seasons in the majors

Keith Glauber with the Indianapolis Indians, drafted by the St. Louis Cardinals in 1997. (Photograph by Marty Orr.)

from 1978 to 1991 with St. Louis, San Diego, Baltimore and San Francisco. He participated in four All-Star games and two World Series.

The Cardinals took **John Rickert Dempsey** in the 12th round of the June 1989 draft hoping he'd turn out like his father, Rick Dempsey. Both were catchers. Rick was still in baseball at the time with the Los Angeles Dodgers. He had been in baseball for 24 seasons with six different teams, but not once with the Cardinals. The younger Dempsey played for five seasons and failed to make much process in the minors. He was at Class A Wilmington in 1994 when a log jam occurred at catcher. The Cardinals wanted to make a pitcher out of him. He decided to retire and finish his college degree at Villanova. Now he works at a brokerage house in Los Angeles.

John Tamargo, a sixth-round choice in 1973, managed the New Orleans Zephyrs to the Triple-A World Series title in 1998, beating Buffalo in the best-of-five series three games to one. The former catcher played three seasons for the Cardinals during his five years in the majors.

Larry Oman, a 31st rounder in 1987, is the Battle Cats' pitching coach for 1998, after serving in that same role with Lowell last year and the Gulf Coast Rookie team in 1995–96.

David Bialas spent his entire minor league career in the Cardinals' organization after being drafted by the club in the fourth round of the 1972 June amateur draft. Dave is in his fifth season as the Cubs' bullpen coach. He was a manager in the St. Louis Cardinals' organization for 11 seasons. The former outfielder spent parts of four seasons at the Triple-A level.

Dan Radison, a 10th-round selection in the 1972 June draft, caught three seasons in the Cardinals' minor league system. He is now a first base coach with the Cubs.

Another 10th rounder who turned to coaching is Marc Hill, who was drafted in 1970. Hill is the roving catching instructor for the Pittsburgh Pirates. His major league career spanned 14 years with four different teams, including the Cardinals. His father played for the St. Louis Browns in the 1940s.

Also in the Pirates' organization is Bobby Meacham, a first-round player in 1981. He played six seasons in the majors with the Yankees. Then he began a coaching career with the Royals. Now he is the roving infield instructor for Pittsburgh.

Gene Roof, a 12th-round pick in 1976, turned to managing after playing and was the manager for the Toledo Mudhens in 1999. He played three years in the majors with the Cardinals and Detroit. After playing he turned to coaching in 1986. Then he became a manager for the Mudhens in 1997.

The Cardinals drafted Rick Langford twice, but was never able to sign him. That was in 1971 and 1972 when he was attending Manatee Junior College. They basically offered to pay for the rest of his college, so he decided the offer wasn't worth it. When he completed college, he signed a free agent contract with the Pirates. After his playing days, he tried coaching. "I didn't enjoy the coaching aspect back then," he explained. Then in 1995 he got a call from Jeff Burroughs to help him with a new team in the Western League. Langford was ready then and has been a pitching coach ever since. Now he's with the Syracuse Skychiefs of the Toronto Blue Jays.

Mark Williams, a St. Louis Cardinals draft pick.

After a long pitching career with the Cardinals, Pirates, Dodgers and White Sox, Jerry Reuss went to work as a baseball announcer for ESPN. Reuss was a second-round pick in 1969 and signed a bonus for $30,000. He won over 200 games during his career, but never had 20 or more wins in any season.

Jeff Shireman was a long shot to make it to the majors when he was drafted in the 23rd round in 1988 by the Cardinals. He played seven seasons in the minors before turning to managing. He took the helm of New Jersey in 1999.

Another long shot turning to managing was Brian Rupp, a 43rd round pick in 1992. He played for seven seasons in the minors before turning to managing the Peoria farm club of the Cardinals in 1999.

Ones Who Got Away

The Cardinals drafted Bucky Dent and Bill Madlock out of high school in 1969, but both players decided not to sign and go to college.

Paul Molitor was a 28th-round selection in the 1974 draft when he finished high school. Three years later he was drafted by the Brewers in the first round. Molitor went on to play 21 seasons in the American League and is headed to the Hall of Fame after a long, illustrious career.

The Cardinals also lost Dan Plesac to the Brewers. St. Louis picked him in the second round in 1980, but it wasn't good enough for him to sign out of high school and he went on to North Carolina State University. The Brewers chose him in the first round in 1983. The left-handed reliever was still pitching in 1999.

The Cardinals picked **Gary Gaetti** in the fourth round of the January 1978 draft. He didn't sign, went to college and got drafted by the Twins. The Cardinals finally got Gaetti after he became a free agent. He then played three seasons with St. Louis before being released in 1998.

Rob Dibble was picked in the 11th round in June 1982 out of high school. He waited for Cincinnati to draft him the following year in the first round of the June Secondary Phase.

The Cardinals picked **Todd Stottlemyre**, a pitcher like his dad Mel, in the first round of the January 1985 Secondary Phase. He didn't sign and waited until Toronto drafted him in June that year. The Cardinals traded four players to Oakland to obtain him in 1996. He pitched three seasons with the Cardinals before he was dealt to Texas.

Best Draft

The Cardinals had three first-round picks in the 1991 draft thanks to compensation for free agents it lost. St. Louis chose **Dmitri Young**,

Dmitri Young, 1991 fourth pick in the first round for the Cardinals.

Allen Watson and **Brian Barber**, who all made it to the majors with the Cardinals. Also in that draft were **John Mabry**, **John Frascatore** and **Mike Busby**. When it comes to the number of

players making it to the majors from a single-year draft, it was the best.

Worst Draft

The Cardinals got off to a poor start the first year of the draft as only **Harry Parker**, a pitcher drafted in the fourth round, played for the big club.

In 1978 the Cardinals signed just one player who eventually found the yellow brick road to the majors. That was **George Bjorkman**, who played only 29 games in the majors.

All in the Family

When the Cardinals drafted **Alan Benes** in the first round in 1993, his brother, Andy, was pitching in San Diego. In 1996, the Benes brothers were pitching side-by-side on the starting staff and combined for 31 wins to help the Cardinals to the playoffs. The two pitched together again for the Cardinals in 1997 before an injury to Alan and free agency to Andy split the brothers up.

Although **Kirk Bullinger** wasn't picked until the 32nd round by the Cardinals, he had more incentive than other pitchers. His brother, Jim, was already a pitcher in the majors, so he had something to prove. It took Kirk about the same amount of time, six seasons in the minors, to make it to the majors like his brother. Ironically, by the time Kirk was elevated to Montreal in September 1998, his brother was no longer pitching in the majors. His brother last pitched in the majors in 1997 for the Expos and ended his seven seasons in the majors with a 34-40 mark. Jim was a starter, while Kirk is a reliever. Kirk relieved in eight games in September 1998 and won one with a 9.00 ERA. Now the questions will be whether or not he will be a better pitcher than his brother.

Bob Forsch and his brother Ken are the only brothers to each pitch a no-hitter in the majors. Ken was drafted by Houston in the 18th round in June 1968.

On the Roster

The veteran on the roster was **Ray Lankford**, a third-round pick in the 1987 draft. He charged through the minors, leading in triples twice and being named Texas League Most Valuable Player. In his rookie season, he led the National League in triples. The following season he led the Cardinals in most offensive categories. He has been a consistent performer since and continues to provide power to the Cardinal lineup.

J.D. Drew breezed through the minors after a signing with the Cardinals, although his call to the majors may have been in his contract. He hit .328 at Double-A and .316 at Triple-A before he joined the Cardinals in August. Then he hit .417 in 14 games with St. Louis. 1999 became his rookie season with the Cardinals.

Time was running out on **Joe McEwing** when he finally found his stroke in Double-A in 1998. The 28th-round pick from the 1992 draft finally began hitting for average and batted .354 to earn a promotion to Triple-A where he continued with the hot bat, which earned him a promotion to the majors in September. He was hitting the ball so well that the Cardinals released veteran Carlos Baerga in favor of the young hitter. He took the starting spot at second in 1999 and hasn't looked back at the minors since.

Mike Busby, a 14th-round pick out of high school in 1991, slowly worked his way through the minor league system first as a starter then as a reliever. He became a regular in the bullpen in 1998, but suffered a strained right elbow and was on the disabled list half the season.

Eli Marrero was selected in the third round in 1993 after John DiPuglia saw the Cuban-born catcher at Coral Gables High School. His breakout year in the minors came in 1996 when he was named to the Texas League All-Star team after hitting 19 home runs. Another 20 dingers the next year led the Cardinals to first call him up in 1997. He was back with the Cardinals again in 1998 for much of the season.

Future Stars?

The Cardinals picked **Adam Kennedy** in the first round in 1997 after he led the nation in hits for two consecutive seasons. He was an All-American for California State. "We feel he was the best pure hitter in the draft and we look for-

ward to watching Adam develop into a Major League ballplayer," said Cardinals vice president and general manager Walt Jocketty after signing him. The shortstop has turned into a .300 hitter in the minors and climbed to Triple-A.

Another shortstop right behind Kennedy at Double-A is **Brent Butler**, a third-round pick in 1996 out of high school. The Cardinals think so much of him that they made him a non-roster invitee at the 1999 spring training camp. He shows a bit more power than Kennedy with the bat.

Matt DeWitt was also a non-roster invitee at the 1999 camp. The 10th round right-handed hurler has gradually improved his ERA since he was drafted in 1995. He moved up to Double-A for the 1999 season.

Chris Haas was a supplemental pick in 1995 for Gregg Jefferies signing with the Phillies. Scout Tom McCormack signed him out high school. The third baseman earned his way to Triple-A Memphis in 1999 after clouting 20 homers at Arkansas.

A long shot doing good in the Cardinals system is **Keith McDonald**, a catcher who was picked in the 24th round in 1994. Scout Chuck Fick spotted him at Pepperdine University.

The Cardinals gave **Rick Ankiel** a $2.5 million signing bonus, a record until they drafted Drew the following year. The left-handed pitching sensation with the 95-mph fastball was 11-1, 0.47 ERA, in high school before the draft. Many scouts thought of him as first rounder, but he wasn't picked until the 72nd spot because he was being advised by agent Scott Boras, who many teams thought wanted too much money for the prospect. Ankiel proved his worth his first season in the pros as he was 12-6 with a 2.63 ERA in Class A to earn him Cardinals' Minor League Pitcher of the Year Award. He ranked first in strikeouts among all minor league pitchers in 1998, fanning 222 in 161 innings pitched. He was promoted to Triple-A Memphis in 1999.

The next player chosen after Ankiel was **Chad Hutchinson**, another pitcher. He was drafted in the first round out of high school by Atlanta in 1995, but he chose to attend Stanford University for three years before turning back to baseball. He could have chosen professional football as he threw 20 touchdowns in two seasons with Stanford and was named Most Valuable Player of the 1996 Sun Bowl. After pitching in Class A and Triple-A in 1998, he was put at Double-A in 1999.

Sixth-round pick **Josh Teekel** was disappointed when he heard he was drafted in the sixth round in 1999. The right-handed pitcher out of Belaire High School in Greenwell Springs, La., had been told all along that he would likely be picked as high as the sandwich round and no lower than the third round. *Baseball America* had him rated the 35th best high school player in the nation, upped him to 20th best high school player in the nation a month before the draft then dropped him off the list of top 100 players just before the draft. Scouting directors say they don't look at the lists that are published, but many times the publication is right on the money.

The right-handed pitcher had a fastball clocked at 92 mph. The six-foot-five, 195-pound hurler also throws a curve, split-finger fastball and changeup. He was 11-3 in his senior year with 12 complete games. He struck out 150 batters. "A lot of people say I look like Shane Reynolds," he said.

As the first day of the draft progressed, he received a call from a scout not about his choice in the draft, but to make him an offer and he had 15 seconds to accept it. He did, but the scout called back two minutes later saying he couldn't get that amount, so the team didn't draft him in the fourth round. The move was against the rules. Teams are not supposed to make offers prior to drafting a player. That's supposed to come afterwards. The next day the scout called back to apologize. "There's a lot of stuff under the table," Teekle explained. He refused to name the team, saving it some embarrassment.

"We're in a mourning state," his mother, Donna, said the weekend after the draft. "It was a real numbing experience."

Teekel was scouted by Scott Nichols, who did a lot of apologizing after the draft as well. The best high school player in Louisiana was thinking more about going on to LSU then signing immediately after the draft. "At least I was drafted," he said. He can't understand his drop to the sixth round because his advisor never said anything about not signing, bonuses or rounds.

One of the long shots picked in the 1999 draft was **Matthew Vincent**, a left-handed pitcher out of Lindsey Wilson College. He compiled a 12-2 record in his junior year with a 2.32 ERA and was named as an NAIA second team All-American. His fastball has been clocked up to 91 and he has a good slider as well as a straight change and overhand curveball.

Three times may be a charm for the Floyd Knobs, Indiana, country boy. The Mariners picked him in the 25th round as a draft-and-follow player out of high school because he needed some work on his game. He went on to junior college and the Yankees picked him the following year in the 29th round as a draft-and-follow as well.

Vincent began pitching at age eight and never really thought about being a professional baseball player. "You just believe in yourself and faith in God," he said.

San Diego Padres

The Padres began drafting players in 1968, a year before the team began playing. In its first draft, the Padres chose just 16 players in the June regular phase, about half of what most teams drafted that year. San Diego kept that trend up for a long time. This strategy is the reason the team hasn't had many long shots reach the majors because they haven't drafted many long shots. Still, the franchise has produced two World Series teams in the 30 years it has played.

The draft was partially responsible for the Padres getting to the World Series in 1984, which they lost to Detroit in five games. A handful of draft picks were key components on that club, including Tony Gwynn, Tim Flannery, Andy Hawkins and Eric Show. Also on that team was Bruce Botchy, who would later manage the club to another World Series in 1998.

Botchy was hired in 1995 by new ownership that had inherited a team with the worst record

Dave Hollins with the Angels, drafted by the San Diego Padres.

in the majors during the strike-shortened 1994 season. The first move of the "new" Padres was a blockbuster 12-player trade with Houston that brought Ken Caminiti and Steve Finley, plus four others, in exchange for Derek Bell and five others as well as the firing of Jim Riggleman. Both Caminiti and Finley won Rawlings Gold Glove Awards in 1995 and both had career-best years on offense which helped the Padres improve to third place.

Then in 1996, the Padres hired general manager Kevin Towers, who obtained Wally Joyner, Rickey Henderson and Bob Tewksbury to complement the leadership of Finley, Caminiti and Tony Gwynn. The result was a ballclub that made the playoffs in 1996 with Padres' draft picks: Gwynn, Joey Hamilton, Scott Sanders and Tim Worrell.

In the drive for more immediate success, the Padres ended up trading some of their draft prospects for players that could help them right away. Players like Homer Bush, Matt Mieske and Rich Loiselle were all traded while they were coming up in the minors, so they ended up in the majors with another team.

As a result of trading their own draft prospects, they ended up with only two of their own draft picks who were major contributors to the 1998 World Series team that lost to the Yankees. After the series, the team unloaded some of that talent and as a result was headed back to the cellar in 1999 with few of their own draft picks on the squad.

The Padres were compensated in the 1999 draft with three picks in the "sandwich" round. The compensation picks may help them rebuild

for the future. The 1999 team was left with a lot of leftovers from the 1998 team or players they had picked up in trades. Original draft picks on the team were about as scarce as water in the desert.

Over the years the Padres traded away some of their best picks before they had time to develop, which is like drinking wine before it's time. Probably the team's worst decision was sending Ozzie Smith to the Cardinals. They also traded Mitch Williams when he was still in the minors. Then in 1993, owner Tom Werner cut the budget, which prompted some more trades and the club plummeted to the cellar. Several draft picks were given the opportunity to show their talents on that club and they failed miserably. In fact, for some it was the only season they ever played in the majors. For example, Darrell Sherman and Kevin Higgins, who were drafted in 1989, batted .222 and .221, respectively.

The Padres have an average size scouting staff with 16 area scouts, including such familiar names as Joe Botchy, Rich Brodi and Chris Gwynn, and three crosscheckers. The Padres usually hold one tryout a year in their own stadium; otherwise, they rely on reports from the Major League Scouting Bureau.

The Padres will likely have to rebuild so they can be ready for a new stadium, which will open in April 2002. It will house the new San Diego Padres Hall of Fame.

Best Picks

One of the first players named to the Padres Hall of Fame when it began in 1999 was **Randy Jones,** a fifth-round pick in 1972. The pitcher rebounded from a National League worst 22 losses in 1974 to a best 22 wins in 1976 to earn a Cy Young Award with the Padres, who finished a dismal fifth that season. Jones was the first Padres player to win a coveted award and earned tremendous popularity among Padres fans, a relationship that remains strong. He remains the club leader in innings pitched (1,765.0), starts (253), complete games (71) and shutouts (18). He was an All-Star in 1975 and 1976, establishing a unique rapport with Padres fans, who gave him a standing ovation as he approached the mound for every start. After those glorious years, his career when downhill and he was traded to the Mets. Jones remains an active ambassador for Padres baseball in the community, making dozens of appearances annually and running his popular Randy Jones Ballpark Barbecue at Qualcomm Stadium.

Undoubtedly, **Tony Gwynn** will be named to the Padres' Hall of Fame as well as the Baseball Hall of Fame when he retires. When he gets to Cooperstown, he will join Honus Wagner as only player in history to win eight National League batting titles. His last title came in 1997 when he hit .372 for his fourth straight title. His .394 average was the highest by a National League player since Bill Terry hit .401 in 1930. In 1999 he was named to his 15th All-Star Team and broke the 3,000-hit mark later in the season, becoming the 22nd player to reach that feat. "I can't tell you how proud I am to put on this Padres uniform, and the fans of San Diego are a big reason why," Gwynn said the day after breaking 3,000. "There's no question, they're a big reason why I'm still here."

He had a .339 lifetime average entering the 1999 season. Gwynn was also a good defensive player and picked up five Gold Gloves during his career. He helped the Padres reach the World Series twice.

Another Padres pick headed to both Halls of Fame is **Dave Winfield**, a first round choice in 1973. The University of Minnesota product was drafted by pro football, basketball and baseball. He signed with the Padres and went directly to the majors. He debuted on June 19 against Houston. Winfield played eight seasons with the Padres before becoming a free agent in 1980 and signing with the Yankees. During his 22 years in the majors, Winfield won six Gold Glove awards, appeared on 12 All-Star teams, played in 2,973 games and hit 465 homers.

Another nominee for the Padres' Hall of Fame was **Eric Show**, an 18th round draft pick. He was one of the pitchers who helped the Padres to the World Series in 1984. He logged 10 seasons as a starter for the Padres. Show turned to drugs after baseball and wound up dead at a California drug rehabilitation center in 1994.

The Padres took one of their best draft picks — **Ozzie Smith** — and made him one of their worst trades. Smith was dealt to the Car-

Tony Gwynn was a Padres draft choice. (Photograph by Marty Orr.)

dinals for Garry Templeton after he was the runner up for Rookie of the Year honors. The "Oz" became the National League leader in games at shortstop. He picked up 13 straight Gold Glove awards and appeared in 14 All-Star games.

The Padres had the first pick in the 1988 free-agent draft and selected pitcher **Andy Benes**, a junior at the University of Evansville. Benes was a pre-med student at the time, so he had a good paying job ahead of him if he stayed in school. The Padres changed his mind by offering him a $235,000 bonus. Three weeks later he signed. "It was a tough decision," recalled Benes. "If I hadn't gone number one, I probably wouldn't have signed." A year later he was in the majors. In all, he spent six and a half seasons with the Padres, who dealt him to the Mariners before he became a free agent at the end of 1995. He signed with the Cardinals for two seasons until they screwed up his contract and he was given free agency again. This time he signed with Arizona.

Kevin McReynolds, a first-round pick in 1981, was the first player with the Padres to be named Minor League Player of the Year in 1983 when he hit .377, 32 homers and 116 RBI. The following season he helped the Padres to postseason play in 1984 and made a difference in the League Championship Series when he hit a three-run homer in Game to to give the Padres the win. He broke a bone in his left hand in

Andy Benes was drafted by the Padres as the first pick in the first round in 1988. (Photograph by Marty Orr.)

Game 4, so he wasn't able to play in the World Series. He was traded in 1986 to the Mets. In 12 seasons McReynolds hit 211 homers with three different teams.

Andy Hawkins, a first-round pick in 1978, helped the Padres finish first in 1984 and won the only World Series game for the Padres. He experienced his best season the next year with an 18-8 mark. Injuries to his throwing hand and shoulder contributed to his downfall after that with the Padres. In 1989 he became a free agent and signed with the Yankees. He hurled a no-hitter against the White Sox the next year, but lost the game because of unearned runs after an error.

John Kruk, a third-round pick in the June 1981 Secondary Phase, averaged .300 in 10 seasons in the majors and appeared in two All-Star games. He broke in with the Padres in 1986 and became a clutch hitter with the club. After slumping below the Mendoza Line in 1989, the Padres traded him to Philadelphia for Chris James. Bad

move as Kruk rebounded to a .331 average the rest of the year, and James managed just .264. James got worse while Kruk improved and helped Philadelphia to the World Series in 1993.

Another bad move the Padres made came with **Mitch Williams**, an eighth-round pick in 1982. He was dealt to Texas for Randy Asadoor in April 1985. Asadoor played a total of 15 games in 1986 with the Padres. Williams became a reliever who helped the Cubs to the League Championship Series in 1989 with his 36 saves. Nicknamed "Wild Thing" for his wild pitches, the left-handed reliever was named to one All-Star Game during his career which spanned 11 seasons with six teams. He saved 192 games during that span.

The Padres let **Mike Caldwell** slip away, too. The 11th-round pick in 1971 pitched his way to a 13-25 record in three seasons with San Diego to earn a trade to the Giants where he turned in a 14-5 record the next year. He slumped after that until he went to Milwaukee and registered a 22-9 record with a league leading 23 complete games in 1978.

Long Shots

The Padres have had a lot of pitchers in latter draft rounds make it to the majors.

The first long shot hurler was **Gary Lucas**, a 19th-round pick in 1976 from Chapman College. The lefthander made it to the majors in 1980 and was with the Padres for four seasons before going to Montreal and California for four more years.

Another pitcher who had an even longer major league career than Show was **Bob Patterson**, 21st round in 1982. He came up through the Padres system and was called up in 1985, but he had a dismal 24.75 ERA in three games. The Padres traded him to the Pirates for Marvell Wynne the next season. Patterson improved and was in the majors to stay in 1989. The reliever then went on to the Rangers, Angels and Cubs. By 1998, he had appeared in 559 games.

One more pitcher still in the majors in 1999 was **Tim Worrell**, a 20th-round pick by the Padres in 1989. The right-handed starter worked his way up to the Padres in four seasons and has been in the bigs ever since. He pitched five

Gabe Alvarez with the Toledo Mud Hens, drafted by the San Diego Padres. (Photograph by Marty Orr.)

seasons with San Diego until being traded to Detroit.

Pitcher **Lance Painter** was a 25th-round selection in 1990. The southpaw pitcher was picked up in the expansion draft by Colorado and came up with Denver in 1993. He was later claimed on waivers by St. Louis.

Still another long shot pitcher for the Padres was **Rich Loiselle**, a 38th-round pick in 1991. Loiselle worked his way up to Triple-A before the Padres traded him with Jeff Tabaka to the Astros for Phil Plantier in 1995. A year later he was dealt to the Pirates for Danny Darwin. The Pirates made him their stopper in 1997 and he picked up 29 saves.

He gained another 19 saves the following season.

All in the Family

The Giants picked **Greg Sparks**, whose father, Joe, was a coach with the Reds, as a first baseman from Mesa Community College. Greg signed but never made it to the majors though.

Gary Matthews, Jr., son of the 16-year player by the same name, was a 13th-round se-

lection in 1993. He was added to the 40-man roster in 1998. Matthews entered the 1999 season as the best defensive outfielder in the Padres organization. He spent the 1998 season with the Double-A Mobile Bay Bears, establishing career-highs in average (.307), slugging percentage (.480), and on-base percentage. Matthews will likely roam the outfield soon for the Padres like his father did with several major league teams. Wrist injuries slowed his progress in the minors.

The Padres drafted **Chris Prieto**, a 24th rounder in 1993. Chris has a twin brother, Rick, who is an outfielder in the Padres organization. His brother was drafted in the 28th round by the Indians and later signed as a free agent contract with the Padres. Both played together at Triple-A in 1998, but Rick got sent back down to Double A in 1999.

Sean Burroughs fell into the same steps as his father when he was drafted by the Padres in the first round in 1998. Burroughs father, Jeff, was also a first-round selection with the Washington Senators back in 1969. In fact, both came out of the same high school, Long Beach Wilson High. The big difference was the amount of their bonus. Jeff signed for $88,000, while Sean received a signing bonus of $2.1 million. The left-handed hitter, who was scouted by Padres area scout Tim McWilliam, batted .507 with five home runs, 29 RBI and nine stolen bases in 1998 as a high school senior. "Sean has enjoyed tremendous success everywhere he has played, and we are confident that will carry into his professional career," said Padres General Manager Kevin Towers. "We thought he was one of the best players available in the draft. He is a polished high school hitter with great bloodlines. Sean's got a terrific arm, a great bat and a lot of intangibles. He is a joy to watch, and I can't wait to see him in a Padres uniform."

Disappointments

Mike Ivie was touted as the best high school catcher in years when the Padres chose him as the first player of the 1970 draft. Ironically, the receiver developed a phobia to throwing the ball back to the pitcher. So much so, he had to be moved to first base. After complaining that he had to share first-base duties with Gene Tenace, the Padres traded the temperamental player. Instead of a gem, he was more like poison ivy.

The Padres had the second pick in the draft in 1971 and chose **Jay Franklin** out of high school. The right-handed pitcher pitched just three games in the majors.

The following year, the Padres had the first pick and chose **Dave Roberts** from the University of Oregon. The Padres rewarded the infielder with a pass directly to the majors. He played in a 100 games his first season and hit .244. Then he improved to .286-21-64 in his sophomore season. But back injury problems sent him down to .167 the next season and he never recovered from that crevasse.

After six seasons with San Diego, Roberts went to the Rangers for a couple of years, then Houston and finally with Philadelphia. His career average was well below average—.239 with 49 career homers.

In 1975 the Padres picked second in the June draft and took left-handed pitcher **Mike Lentz**. The high school hurler only got as far as Double-A.

The Padres first pick in 1977, **Brian Greer**, played in just five major league games. **Joe Lansford**, a first rounder in 1979, didn't fare much better. The first baseman played in 25 games in the majors. The next year's first round pick was **Jeff Pyburn**, who peaked at Triple-A.

Left-handed pitcher **Ray Hayward** was the first choice in 1981 and he contributed just 19 games in the majors. **Kevin Garner**, a first-round pick in 1987, was a pitcher and outfield but never made the majors at either position. He got as far as Triple-A.

Selecting a player out of high school is always more risky for a team. The Padres took a risk when they selected **Robbie Beckett** in the first round in 1990. Beckett had lots of problems with control in Class A ball as he walked about as many players as he struck out. In 1991, he was 2-14 at Charleston. He was switched to a reliever role in 1994, but not with much success. The Padres finally let him go in 1996 and he was claimed on waivers by the Marlins in spring training. A month later he was claimed on waivers by the Rockies. Colorado has twice given him a shot at the majors and he has a nosebleed ERA of 11.57 in seven games.

Where Are They Now?

To find what happened to **Kevin Towers**, one only has to look higher in the organization. The Padres' general manager was a first-round draft choice in 1982 with the Padres. The BYU pitcher made it as high as Triple-A before arm operations ended his career.

Steve Smith, a 24th-round pick in 1976, played seven seasons in the Padres' farm system and got as far as Triple-A as a player. He turned to managing after playing in the San Diego farm system. Then he went to the Mariners system where he finally the majors, but as a coach.

Ones Who Got Away

Doug DeCinces was an 18th-round selection in 1969 out of Los Angeles Pierce Junior College. He waited until two years later to sign with the Orioles, who picked him in the third round of the January secondary phase.

The Padres drafted **Harold Reynolds** out of high school; however, he went on to college and was signed by the White Sox.

Best Draft

The Padres got an outfield of major leaguers in the 1981 draft. McReynolds, Gwynn and Kruk were all picked in 1981. Gwynn made quite a name for himself in San Diego where he spent his whole career and was still playing there in 1999. McReynolds made a mark with the Mets, while Kruk became famous with the Phillies.

Worst Draft

At a time when the Padres needed players during their first season in the majors, they only got one who eventually made the team. **Randy Elliott** was the first round pick and he ended up playing just 114 games in the majors. Nobody else from that draft made it to the majors with San Diego.

On the Roster

The Padres had just half a dozen of their own products on their roster going into the 1999 season. They traded some of their own draft picks in 1998 for the stretch run. Then after the

A.J. Sager with the Indianapolis Indians, drafted by the San Diego Padres.

World Series they unloaded a few players who were free agents as a budget cutting measure.

The senior citizen draft pick on the Padres roster was **Gwynn**, who was drafted way back in June 1981 out of San Diego State University.

Another veteran was **Ed Vosberg**, who was drafted by the Padres in the third round in June 1982. He was back with the Padres after spending time with eight other teams and a trip to Italy. The left-handed hurler was first drafted by St. Louis in 1979 and Toronto in January 1982. He has had 83 appearances with the Padres. He sat out 1998 with shoulder tendinitis.

Matthew Clement, a third-round pick in 1993, was the Padres Minor League Pitcher of the Year in 1997. That led him to a call-up to the majors in 1998 where he was 2-0 in four appearances. He began the 1999 season with the Padres in the starting rotation.

Future Stars

The Padres have several of their own draft picks at Triple-A Las Vegas who could get called to the majors at any time.

Greg LaRocca, a 10th-round pick in 1994, exhibited defensive versatility and an explosive bat at Triple-A Vegas in 1998. He recorded a career-high .493 slugging percentage and equaled his single-season high for home runs with eight. On July 1, 1998, versus Nashville, he became the fifth player in Stars history to hit for the cycle. He went 4-for-5 with 3 RBIs. LaRocca's career took off after being named an all-star in Class A in 1995.

Another 1994 draft pick at Triple-A was **Shane Dennis**, a seventh rounder out of Wichita State University, where he compiled a 29-11 record, and a 3.33 ERA in four seasons for the Shockers. He spent the last two years in Japan in exchange for rights to Hideki Irabu, which the Padres traded to the Yankees. He was the Padres 1996 Minor League Player of the Year after compiling a 9-1 record and 2.27 ERA at Double-A Memphis. In Japan, he pitched for the Chiba Lotte Marines of the Japanese Pacific League in 1997, going 0-3 with a 5.45 ERA. Then in 1998, he pitched in the Japanese minor league where he went 3-6 with a 4.90 ERA.

Another Padres pitcher at Triple-A was **Bryan Wolff**, an 18th-round selection in 1993. He split the 1998 season with the Double-A Mobile, and the Stars. He made 33 appearances (14 starts) with the BayBears, recording a 9-3 record with 2.29 ERA. His 2.29 ERA was the second best in the Padres organization, and his 142 strikeouts was the fourth best. He led the Southern League with a 2.29 ERA.

Another long shot hurler at Triple-A was **Brendan Sullivan**, a 26th rounder from 1996. He split the 1998 season between the Single-A Rancho Cucamonga and Double-A Mobile. He posted 21 saves in 1998 to send him to the next level.

The longest shot of the Triple-A group was **Dusty Allen**, who was drafted in the 30th round in 1995 out of Stanford University. He was moving through the minors on the strength of double-digit homers every season. In Double-A Mobile, he also won the first-ever Community Relations Award for the BayBears.

The Padres picked **Ben Davis** in the first round in 1995 out of prep school and he became an all-star in the rookie league his first season. By 1998 he had moved up to Double-A and was named an all-star there, too. The Padres called the catcher up for a game in 1998. He has great defensive skills and hits with power.

Junior Herndon, a ninth-round pick out of high school, has progressed well in the minors and looks to be a starter with the Padres in the future. The right-handed pitcher has good command of his pitches.

Kevin Nicholson was the first Canadian ever drafted in the first round. The Padres picked the shortstop in 1997 out of Stetson University. His defensive skills were fine, but he slumped with the bat in Double-A and needs to cut down on strikeouts if he wants to progress.

Kevin Burford, a 15th-round choice in 1997 by the Padres, lit up rookie ball like a comet by batting .389 which led him to being named Most Valuable Player for the Arizona League.

He settled down to .258 in Single-A in 1998, but the outfielder has the tools to make the majors.

The best looking long shot that the Padres picked in the 47th round is **Wilbert Nieves**. The catcher has played solidly behind the plate in both capacities.

The Padres soon came to terms after the draft with their first-round picks in 1999. They signed **Vince Faison**, an outfielder out of high school, **Gerik Baxter**, a high school hurler, and Omar Ortiz, another pitcher out of the University of Texas–Pan American. "Anytime you can get draft choices — particularly first-round picks — signed this quickly it's a plus for everybody," said scouting director Brad Sloan. "It is a tribute to our scouts, these young men and their families."

San Francisco Giants

The Giants, who moved from New York in 1958, had a good team as the draft unfolded. The team needed the draft a lot less than other teams as it finished second five years in a row after the draft began. The Giants climbed to first in 1971 and the draft provided a handful of players to that squad: Jim Barr, Ron Bryant, Al Gallagher, Dave Kingman and Chris Speier. However, the team lost to the Pirates in the League Championship Series.

San Francisco nosedived immediately after that season and stayed in a funk until the late 1980s. Manager Roger Craig brought the team back to prominence with the help of some draft picks. The 1987 first-place team that lost to the Cardinals in a hard fought seven-game LCS contained a trio of good Giants draft picks: Will Clark, Chili Davis and Robby Thompson. Clark and Thompson were still around two years later when the Giants got swept in the earthquake interrupted World Series. That team also had a couple of other Giants originals: Jeff Brantley, Atlee Hammaker, Kirt Manwaring and Matt Williams.

Unlike the previous first-place teams, the 1997 squad, which came in first and got swept in the Division Series by the Florida Marlins, lacked any of their own draft picks. A combination of poor picks and trades had left the team with draft picks from other teams and free agents.

In the history of the draft, the Giants have never had the first pick in the regular June draft. In a way this statistic could be considered fortunate. It shows they've never had the worst record in the National League when it was the league's turn to pick first in the draft. Also, none of the Giants draft picks have ever gone straight to the majors. They've all had to earn their way to the top.

The Giants have changed quite a bit since the departure of Al Rosen, according to Chris Lampe, a part owner of the San Jose Giants. "The new ownership knows more about the draft than Rosen did," he commented. Lampe has seen many of the pitching prospects recently taken in the draft and likes what he sees. Many were established pitchers in college, so they are already proven prospects. Under Rosen, his Class A team was never competitive. "They'd call good players up in mid-season and give us crap," he explained. Now his team is making the playoffs instead of finishing last.

The Giants' basic philosophy is to draft "big, strong athletic kids with high ceilings." The Giants also prefer college players over high

Jeff Brantley with the Cincinnati Reds, drafted by the San Francisco Giants. (Photograph by Marty Orr.)

school, unless they think the player is on the express train to the majors. Plus, college players tend to be more mature and are less risky in the end because of their proven talent. In the latter rounds, they consider signability as a key factor. They don't want to waste a pick on someone they can't sign. They also look more for pitching now. "You can't have enough pitching," a Giants spokesman said. With Dick Tidrow, a former pitcher, as vice president of player development, you know pitching is high on the want list.

Continuing to place a high priority on pitching as an organization, the Giants selected promising young arms with each of their first four picks in 1999. "In line with our recent draft history, we placed added emphasis on pitching again this year," said Dick Tidrow, the Giants' vice president, player personnel. Six of the first seven players in the 1999 draft and 21 of the first 24 picks were from college.

Since General Manager Brian Sabean joined the organization in 1993, San Francisco has selected a pitcher as its top choice in five of the past seven drafts. Under Sabean and Tidrow, the Giants' minor league system owns a 118-92

overall record (.562) which is the third best organizational mark in baseball behind Toronto and Cincinnati.

Over the history of the draft, the Giants have been good at picking players, but poor at picking pitchers as evidenced by the best picks. Their philosophy of taking big, strong players produced quite a few big home run hitters, although they traded away a few before their prime.

Best Picks

Ironically, two of the best draft picks the Giants made both had the same last name, but were not related. They were **Jack Clark** and **Will Clark**.

Jack was the first of the Clarks to come along. He was drafted in the 13th round in 1973 and signed for $10,000. He was drafted as a pitcher and outfielder because he was 11-3 as a pitcher and hit .517 in his senior year of high school. Because of his power, the Giants decided he'd make a better outfielder. He was first called up to the Giants in 1975 and by 1978 he was an all-star. He hit 25 homers that season. He played a decade with San Francisco until he got into a dispute with the front office, which sent him packing to St. Louis. He helped the Cardinal get to the World Series after hitting a game-winning homer in the League Championships Series. Two seasons later he had his career year with the bat when he hit 35 homers, 106 RBI and led the league in slugging percentage. He became a free agent in 1988 and signed with the Yankees. He continued to hit homers, but also lead the league in strikeouts. After 18 years, he was released by Montreal and his career ended in 1993 with 340 lifetime homers. He appeared in four All-Star games.

Will kind of took over where Jack left off. His first season in the majors came two years after Jack had departed. He hit 11 homers his first season to earn some votes as Rookie of the Year. He soared past the sophomore slump the next year to hit 35 homers to make fans forget about the first Clark and helped the Giants get to the playoffs. "Will the Thrill" continued to woe fans and led the league in RBI with 109 and walks with 100 in his third season. In 1989 he led the league in runs scored to help the Giants get all the way to the World Series, before the A's and an earthquake destroyed their hopes. In 1991 he earned a Gold Glove at first base. After eight seasons with the Giants, he became a free agent and signed with the Rangers. He was named to five All-Star teams during those eight years with the Giants. He signed with the Orioles for the 1999 season.

Gary Matthews was drafted in the first round in 1968 out of high school. By 1972 he was playing with the Giants and spent five seasons with the club. "Sarge," a nickname he picked up from Pete Rose for his leadership, played 16 years in the majors with five different clubs. Following his playing career he worked in private industry and broadcasting before beginning a coaching career in 1995 with the Cubs. Now the batting coach with Toronto, he can show players how he hit 319 doubles, 51 triples and 234 homer runs over his career.

In college, **Dave Kingman** started off like Babe Ruth with great pitching and mammoth home runs. Because he could hit the long ball, pitching became secondary after he was drafted by the Giants in the first round in the June 1970 Secondary Phase. By July the next season he was playing with San Francisco and hitting homers. His 17 homers in 41 games helped the Giants to the pennant in 1971. Kingman had a great arm, but fielded poorly. The Giants tried him at first, third and the outfield without much success at either. He played four seasons with the Giants before requesting a trade. The Giants sold him to the Mets. In 1977, he played for four teams before landing in Chicago the next season. He

found Wrigley Field to his liking and hit 48 homers in 1979 to lead the league, but he also led the league in strikeouts with 131. He went back to the Mets again and led the league in homers (37) and strikeouts (156) in 1982. Finally, he found himself in Oakland where he was much better suited as a designated hitter. He hit 442 homers over his career and struck out 1,816 times, fifth all-time. He twice was named to the All-Star Team in the National League. His home run total is the most by any player who has not made it to the Hall of Fame.

Matt Williams, the third overall pick in the 1986 draft out of UNLV, played a decade for the Giants. The third baseman had trouble with Major League pitching when he first got called to the majors in 1987. His first full season came in 1990 and he pounded out 33 homers and drove in a career-high, league-leading 122 RBI on his way to his first All-Star appearance. The following season he earned his first Gold Glove. In 1994 he was on a pace to break the home-run mark when the season was ended by the strike. His 43 homers led the league and he made another All-Star appearance. He hit a career high .336 in 1995, but injuries limited him to 76 games. The Giants traded him in 1997 to Cleveland where he played for a season before going to Arizona. During his career so far, he has been named to five All-Star games, and won four Gold Gloves and Silver Slugger awards. In 1999 he topped the 300-homer mark.

What was a good draft pick turned out to be a bad trade when it came to **George Foster**. The Giants picked Foster in the third round in January 1968. They called up him up three times then traded him in 1971 for Frank Duffy and Vern Geishert. Duffy bombed out right away with the Giants hitting just .179, so he was dealt to Cleveland. Geishert never pitched for the Giants. Foster went on to an 18-year career that featured 348 home runs. He became the fuel for the Big Red Machine in Cincinnati. Foster led the National League in RBI three years in a row and homers two consecutive years. He was named Most Valuable Player in 1978. He was named to five All-Star teams. Three gold gloves.

Robby Thompson was a first-round pick in the June 1983 Secondary Phase. Three years later he made the jump from Class AA to the

Matt Williams, a San Francisco Giants first round choice in 1986.

George Foster with the Cincinnati Reds. He was drafted by the Giants in the third round in 1968. (Photograph by Marty Orr.)

Giants' starting lineup and was second in the voting for Rookie of the Year after leading the team in hits and runs scored. Thompson became a consistent fielder at second base and hitter for the Giants. His best season came in 1993 when he hit .312, which included a 21-game hitting streak, 19 homers and a team record 65 RBI for a second baseman. He was again named to the All-Star team. He played his entire 11-year career with the Giants.

One of the best draft picks turned reliever for the Giants was **Jeff Brantley**, a sixth round pick in the 1985 draft. Brantley was a starter in the minors, but the Giants brought him up in 1988 as a reliever. The following season he appeared in 59 games and ended with a 7-1 mark. The right-hander was turned into a stopper in 1990, saved 19 games and appeared in the All-Star Game, which he lost. The Giants used him in several roles in 1993 before he became a free agent. The Reds made him a stopper again and he earned 44 saves in 1996 to become the National League Rolaids Relief winner. The Reds traded him to the Cardinals for Dmitri Young,

where he spent one season before going to Philadelphia and suffering injury problems.

Long Shots

The lowest round selection to make it the majors with the Giants is **Ken Grundt**, who was a 53rd rounder in 1991. The Giants released the left-handed hurler in 1993. Grundt was signed by the Sioux Falls of the independent Northern League the next season. The Rockies then signed him in 1995 for a season. Colorado tried him at each minor league level before releasing him. The Red Sox called him up for a game in 1996 and two more in 1997. Boston released him and the Marlins picked him up for awhile before letting him go as well.

Dennis Cook was an 18th-round pick back in 1985. The left-handed pitcher moved quickly through the minors and was first called up in 1988. Cook was traded to the Phillies the next season. He was a starter at the beginning of his career, but was turned into a long reliever while with Cleveland. He became a frequent flyer in the majors traveling to nine teams in 11 seasons. He made 73 appearances with the Mets in 1998.

Catchers, regardless of where they were picked, have a shot at making it to the majors. **Steve Decker** was a 21st-round pick in 1988 and first made it to the majors with the Giants in 1990. After three seasons with the Giants, the Marlins picked him in the 1992 expansion draft. After the Marlins released him in 1995, the Giants signed him again for a season before letting him go.

Randy Bockus was drafted as an outfielder in the 34th round in 1982, but he made it to the majors in 1986 as a pitcher. The relief pitcher played three seasons for the Giants and one for the Tigers.

Disappointments

The Giants scouting staff did a good job of reading palms the first years of the draft as they choose players in the first round who would eventually make it to the majors. It was not until a decade after the draft began before the Giants picked a first-round player in the June regular draft who didn't make it to the majors. That was

Terry Lee, a second baseman out of high school. He only made it to Triple-A. That began a trend which lasted for the next four years. **Ted Barnicle**, a left-handed pitcher from Jacksonville State, **Mike Kuecker**, a shortstop out of high school, and **Craig Landis**, another shortstop, all peaked at Class AAA. Then in 1978 the Giants picked **Bob Cummings**, a catcher from high school. He only managed to get to Double-A.

Jessie Reid was the top pick in 1980. The first baseman managed two cups of coffee in the majors. In other words, he lasted eight games over two seasons with the Giants. Another first baseman who only got a taste of the majors was **Steve Stanicek**, a first rounder in 1982.

The Giants didn't have a first-round pick in 1983. Then they picked **Alan Cockrell** in the first round the following year. The outfielder from the University of Tennessee reached Triple-A.

The Giants picked **Adam Hyzdu** in the first round in 1990 out of high school. After the outfielder failed to perform at Double-A in 1993, the Giants failed to protect him from the Rule V draft and lost him to the Reds. The Reds kept him for a couple of seasons and let him go. The free agent signed with Boston and hit 23 homers at Triple-A in 1997, but it wasn't good enough to get him a call to the majors. He then signed with the Diamondbacks, but played at Triple-A in 1998.

Eric Christopherson was another first-round pick of the Giants in 1990. The Giants didn't protect the 19th overall selection later and he was picked up in the Rule V draft by Seattle. However, the Mariners didn't find him much use and returned him to the Giants. After not making it to the majors with the Giants, he was granted free agency. He was signed by the Astros, Rangers, Mets and finally traded to the White Sox. After nine seasons in the minors, he was still waiting for his call in the majors at Triple-A Charlotte.

One of the most recent disappointments is **Calvin Murray**, an outfielder. The Indians picked Murray in the first round in 1989. He didn't sign. Murray went on to the University of Texas. The Giants picked him in the first round (seventh pick overall) three years later. After six minor league seasons, Murray had yet to prove

Jeff Urban was drafted by the Giants in the first round as the 41st pick in 1998. (Photograph courtesy of Jolene McMeans.)

he could hit at Triple-A. He managed only a .233 average with Fresno in 1998, but he was showing improvement as the 1999 season evolved.

Best Draft

The Giants had all four of its first-round picks in 1970 make it to the majors with the club. Those picks were **Randy Moffitt, Billy Speier, John D'Acquisto** and **Dave Kingman**. Moffitt was picked first in the January regular draft. The reliever played 10 seasons for the Giants and 12 in the majors. He ended with 534 appearances and 96 saves. Speier was the first pick in the January secondary draft. The shortstop played his first seven seasons in the majors with the Giants before going onto a 19-year career that included selection to three All-Star games. D'Acquisto was the first player taken in the June regular draft. He started for four years with the Giants. The righthanded hurler was converted to a reliever and spent 10 seasons in the majors. He pitched in 266 games. Kingman was the first pick in the June secondary draft and he spent four seasons with the Giants.

Worst Drafts

The year 1976 was a great one for the country as the United States celebrated the Bicentennial. The Giants had nothing to celebrate about 1976. Only two of their draft picks — **Dennis Littlejohn** and **Jeff Stember** — made it to the majors and pitched in a total of 79 games. Hardly worth the effort.

Even worse was 1980. Their number-one pick — **Jessie Reid** — turned out to be a disappointment as he played in just eight games in the majors. The other two picks who made it to the majors — **Alan Fowlkes** and **Mark Dempsey** — played a total of 26 games. In all, the Giants got 34 games total out of the draft.

The Giants made some good picks in 1982, but they didn't sign. High school players **Barry Bonds** and **Pete Incaviglia** failed to sign and went to college instead. The Giants finally got Bonds in the end; however, they had to wait until he was done with Pirates, who drafted him first. Incaviglia was drafted later by Montreal.

All in the Family

The Giants took **Hal Jeffcoat, Jr.,** in the first draft hoping he'd keep on a family tradition. His father played the Cubs and Reds in the 1940s and '50s, and his uncle, George, played for Brooklyn and Boston in the 1930s and '40s. But Junior wasn't able to do so.

In January 1984 the Giants drafted **Jose Alou**, son of Felipe, who played for the Giants, but he failed to sign.

Where Are They Now?

Steve Stone turned to broadcasting after playing and was the color man for Harry Caray in Chicago. He was just an average pitcher when he threw for the Giants then he had one super season with the Orioles in 1980. After a 25-7 record he won the Cy Young Award. That same season he was picked for the All-Star Game.

Steve Hosey, a first-round pick in 1989, played 10 seasons in the pros, which included 24 games with the Giants. Afterward, he turned to coaching in the Royals' farm system.

Dave Heaverlo, who was drafted in the

Steve Stone was drafted by the San Francisco Giants.

1973 January Secondary Phase, played for the Giants, Athletics and Mariners. He now hosts a radio show and provides color commentary for televised University of Washington games.

Craig Colbert begins his first year as a full-time coach for Las Vegas after spending the previous two years as a player/coach. Colbert, a catcher, has played professional baseball since 1986, including 72 major league games as a member of the San Francisco Giants.

On the Roster

The Giants had 11 of their own draft picks on their 40-man roster going into spring training in 1999.

The veteran of that group was **Charlie Hayes**. The Giants originally drafted him in the fourth round in 1983. After breaking into the majors with the club in 1988, he was traded to the Phillies the following season. The third baseman was shuffled around like luggage at an airport with stops in New York twice, Colorado, Philadelphia again and Pittsburgh before a return flight to San Francisco in late 1997. When a fan asked him about coming back to the Giants, he responded: "When I first got traded, I thought I was a failure. But getting traded actually helped me get to the Major Leagues. There wasn't a spot for me here at the time so the Giants gave me the opportunity to play with another team and get to the majors faster. That same year I went up to the majors and never went back since. I started out here and hopefully I'll end up here."

Sharing third with Hayes is **Bill Mueller**,

a 15th-round pick in 1993. "I didn't decide that I really wanted to do baseball until my senior year in high school," Mueller said. "I decided I could possibly get a scholarship and that's when I really poured my heart into it and went on to play college baseball and get drafted."

Yet another long shot on the roster to break into the majors with the Giants was **Marvin Bernard**. The Giants claim Bernard is their best ever long shot to make it to the majors and be successful. The outfielder was selected in the 50th round in 1992. After a year of adjustment in A ball, Bernard progressed one level a year and received a September call-up in 1995. The Nicaragua-born player, who came to the United States when he was 12, hit .322 in 1998 to become a regular fixture in the Giants outfield. The Giants re-signed the free agent to a two-year contract late in 1998. "If it was up to me, I would stay here for the rest of my career," Bernard said.

Also on the roster was **Doug Mirabelli**, a fifth-round selection in 1992, a catcher who had yet to become a regular at the major-league level. He's been called up three times, but was stationed at Triple-A again in 1999 until Scott Servais got put on the disabled list midway through the season then he was back with the big club.

The only Giants original on the starting pitching staff was **Russ Ortiz**, a fourth-round pick in 1995. The righthander began his pro career as a stopper, but he was converted to a starter in Double-A. He made the adjustment and the Giants out of spring training in 1998. In 1999, he became the ace of the staff and was leading the team in ERA and wins midway through the season.

Future Stars?

The Giants were probably hoping that **Steve Soderstrom**, a first-round selection in 1993, would be a starting pitcher on the staff by now. They gave him a call-up in 1996 and he won two games, but with a 5.27 ERA. He was sent back to Triple-A where he remained. Halfway through the 1999 season he went from prospect to disappointment with a 0-4 record and 11.70 ERA.

The Giants are hoping more recent pitching picks do better than Soderstrom. The Giants spent a team record $1.875 million on **Jason Grilli** in 1997. He was the fourth overall pick that year. His first season in 1998 he was named to the Texas League All-Star Team despite a losing record on the season. He moved up to Triple-A and was stationed there in 1999. He was doing much better than Soderstrom.

A long-shot draft pick who has come around to do well is **Robbie Crabtree**, a 21st round pick in 1996. He too was at Triple-A. The righthanded relief pitcher was nearly unhittable in 1998 at Single- and Double-A to earn a promotion to Fresno, but he's not doing as well there.

Scout Glenn Tufts thinks **Josh Santos**, 4th round 1998, and **Doug Clark**, 6th round, both have a real good chance of making it to the majors some day. Santos got off to a great start in the Northwest League by posting a 4-1 record with Salem-Keizer. Clark was on the same team and batted .336. Another outfielder on the team, **Jeff Allen**, slammed 11 home runs. Allen was selected in the 15th round of the 1998 draft.

Joe Nathan was drafted as a shortstop in the sixth round in 1995, but the Giants liked him better as a pitcher. He wasn't thrilled with their decision and decided not to play the 1996 season, which put him on the restricted list. The decision turned out to be a good one as the righthander pitched well enough in the minors to get a promotion to the majors in April 1999. In his debut, he pitched seven shutout innings to earn a victory.

The most the Giants spent on a player in the 1998 was $975,000 for **Tony Torcato**, a third baseman from high school. The first rounder passed his initial test at Class A short-season in 1998 and was assigned to long-season Class A Bakersfield in 1999.

Kurt Ainsworth was the first-round pick of the Giants in 1999. He has posted a 13-5 record and a 3.04 ERA at LSU. Ainsworth rebounded from 1997 elbow surgery to lead the Southeastern Conference in strikeouts (91) and starts (11). Overall in 1999, the Baton Rouge, La., product fanned 152 batters and walked 44 in 124.1 innings, limiting the opposition to 101 hits and a .216 batting average against. "Our scouts were impressed with his command and assortment of pitches, which include a sinking fastball, curveball and change," said Dick Tidrow, the Giants' vice president, player personnel.

The Giants selected another pitcher, **Jerome Williams** from Waipahu High School in Hawaii, with its second pick, which was in the sandwich round. The six-foot-four hurler was 8-3 in his senior season with two saves, while striking out 140 and issuing 14 walks in 13 games. The highlight of his senior year came when he tossed a 10-strikeout no-hitter and clubbed three home runs. With a fastball that tops out at 95 mph, Williams once struck out 20 batters in a nine-inning game.

Pitcher **John Thomas** from Righetti High School in Santa Maria, California, was the second-round choice in 1999. Thomas, a member of last year's Junior USA Team, has reeled off a 22-1 record over his last two years.

San Francisco then chose Wisconsin-Oshkosh pitcher **Jack Taschner** with its own second-round pick. He went 7-0 with a 1.51 ERA to guide his college to the Wisconsin Intercollegiate Athletic Conference title.

One of the players the Giants drafted in 1999 was a sophomore at Ball State University. **Jayson Hickman** was eligible for the draft because he would turn 21 before his senior season began, which was a new rule. He thinks that many teams didn't realize he was even eligible for the draft. "A scout from the Tampa Bay Devil Rays didn't know a week before the draft," he explained. "I didn't know I was going to get drafted." He didn't know he was eligible for the draft until the season began. The Giants picked him as a draft-and-follow in the 42nd round and didn't offer him a bonus, but they wanted him to fill in the blanks on the contract they sent him. He was already playing summer ball in the Coastal Plain League when he heard about being drafted. So they told him that would get back with him on contract negotiations before he started his junior year at the Muncie, Indiana, school.

Hickman had an unusually high ERA—8.70—but that was because he pitched in a game where the wind was blowing out like it does at Wrigley Field sometimes. He pitched just 24 innings during his sophomore year mostly in relief. He would rather be a starter. "I think that's made it kind of difficult for me. It's tough to go from one to another," he said. But with a fastball in the low 90s, he's got the speed that the majors wants and his fastball is a live one. He also throws a slider and circle change. He's even been compared to Sandy Koufax.

After a few weeks in the Carolinas, he was pitching very well and scouts from other teams showed a lot of interest in the prospect. "It would have been to my advantage not to have been draft," he commented. He wasn't sure he would sign with the Giants and may wait to go back into the draft pool again after his junior year.

Appendix: Players Drafted

Under each franchise named in the appendix, listed are players who were drafted and signed by the respective team and later made it to the Major Leagues. The first year a player played the majors is indicated along with the team and how many years played with that team and in the majors. The Appendix is organized by league, current team name as of 1999, and year.

AMERICAN LEAGUE

Anaheim Angels

1965

June — Regular Phase

1— Jim Spencer, 1b; B: Hanover, PA; Andover HS, Glen Burnie, MD; 1968 CAL (6) (15)

5 — Joe Henderson, 3b-rf; B: Lake Comorand, MS; Edison HS, Fresno, CA; 1974 CHW (1) (3)

6 — Clyde Wright, of-lhp; B: Jefferson City, TN; Carson-Newman College; 1966 CAL (8) (10)

7 — Marty Pattin, rhp; B: Charleston, IL; Eastern Illinois University; 1968 CAL (1) (13)

Class A (San Jose and Quad Cities) selections:

16 — Jarvis Tatum, of; B: Fresno, CA; Edison HS, CA; 1968 CAL (3) (3)

21— Doug Griffin, 2b; B: South Gate, CA; El Monte HS, La Puente, CA; 1970 CAL (1) (8)

1966

January — Regular Phase

2 — Vern Geishert, rhp; B: Madison, WI; University of Wisconsin; 1969 CAL (1) (1)

June — Regular Phase

17 — Bruce Christensen, ss; B: Madison, WI; Chatsworth HS, Canoga Park, CA; 1971 CAL (1) (1)

18 — Randy Brown, c; B: Leesburg, FL; Florida State University; 1969 CAL (2) (2)

35 — Steve Hovley, of; B: Ventura, CA; Stanford University; 1969 SEA (1) (5)

June — Secondary Phase

1— Andy Messersmith, rhp; B: Toms River, NJ; University of California; 1968 CAL (5) (12)

2 — Ken Tatum, rhp; B: Alexandria, LA; Mississippi State University; 1969 CAL (2) (6)

1967

January — Secondary Phase

Major League selection:

1— Tom Murphy, rhp; B: Cleveland, OH; Ohio University; 1968 CAL (5) (12)

5 — Dave LaRoche, lhp; B: Colorado Springs, CO; No school; 1970 CAL (2) (14)

June — Secondary Phase

1— Greg Washburn, rhp, B: Coal City, IL; Lewis University; 1969 CAL (1) (1)

June — Regular Phase

Major League selection:

1— Lloyd Allen, rhp; B: Merced, CA; Selma (CA) HS; 1969 (5) (7)

7 — Tom Bradley, rhp; B: Asheville, NC; University of Maryland; 1969 CAL (2) (7)

10 — Harvey Shank, rhp; B: Toronto, ON, Canada; Stanford University; 1970 CAL (1) (1)

1969

June — Regular Phase

4 — Rudy Meoli, ss; B; Troy, N.Y.; Royal Oak HS, Covina, CA; 1971 CAL (4) (6)

25 — Andy Hassler, lhp; B: Texas City, TX; Palo Verde HS, Phoenix, AZ; 1971 CAL (5) (14)

1970

January — Regular Phase

2 — Morris Nettles, of; B: Los Angeles, CA; Venice (CA) HS; 1974 CAL (2) (2)

January — Secondary Phase

1— John Doherty, of; Woburn, MA; No school; 1974 CAL (2) (2)

June — Regular Phase

1— Paul Dade, 3b-of; B: Seattle, WA; Nathan Hale HS, Seattle, WA; 1975 CAL (2) (6)

2 — Dan Briggs, lhp-of; B: Scotia, CA; Sonoma (CA) HS; 1975 CAL (3) (7)

5 — John Balaz, of; B: Toronto, ON, Canada; San Diego CC; 1974 CAL (2) (2)

7 — Dick Lange, rhp; B: Harbor Beach, MI; Central Michigan University; 1972 CAL (4) (4)

8 — Doug Howard, 1b; B: Salt Lake City, UT ; BYU; 1972 CAL (3) (5)

24 — Sid Monge, lhp; B: Agua Prieta, Mexico; Brawley (CA) HS; 1975 CAL (3) (10)

1971

January — Secondary Phase
1 — Bob Allietta, c; B: New Bedford, MA; No school; 1975 CAL (1) (1)

8 — Jerry Remy, 2b; B: Fall River, MA; Roger Williams College; 1975 CAL (4) (10)

June — Regular Phase
1 — Frank Tanana, lhp; B; Detroit, MI; Catholic Central HS, Detroit, MI; 1973 CAL (8) (20)

2 — Ron Jackson, 3b; B: Birmingham, AL; Wenonah HS, Birmingham, AL; 1975 CAL (7) (10)

3 — Billy Smith, ss; B: Hodge, AL; John Jay HS, San Antonio, TX; 1975 CAL (2) (6)

1972

January — Regular Phase
1 — Tom Donohue, of; B: Mineola, NY; Nassau CC, NY; 1979 CAL (2) (2)

June — Regular Phase
1 — Dave Chalk, 3b; B: Del Rio, TX; University of Texas; 1973 CAL (6) (10)

2 — Bruce Bochte, 1b-of; B: Pasadena, CA; Santa Clara University; 1973 CAL (4) (12)

4 — Dave Machemer, ss; B: St. Joseph, MO; Central Michigan University; 1978 CAL (1) (2)

June — Secondary Phase
1 — Dave Collins, 1b-of; B: Rapid City, SD; Mesa CC, AZ; 1975 CAL (2) (16)

1973

January — Secondary Phase
2 — Mike Overy, rhp; B: Clinton, IL; Olivet College; 1976 CAL (1) (1)

June — Regular Phase
3 — Pat Kelly, c; B: Santa Maria, CA; Santa Maria HS, CA; 1980 TOR (1) (1)

1974

June — Regular Phase
1 — Mike Miley, ss; B: Yazoo City, MS; LSU; 1975 CAL (2) (2)

3 — Rance Mulliniks, ss; Tulare, CA; Monache HS, Woodville, CA; 1977 CAL (3) (16)

4 — Thad Bosley, of; B: Oceanside, CA; Oceanside (CA) HS; 1977 CAL (1) (14)

5 — Stan Cliburn, c; B: Jackson, MI; Forrest Hill (MI) HS; 1980 CAL (1) (1)

6 — Gary Wheelock, rhp; B: Bakersville, CA; UC Irvine; 1976 CAL (1) (3)

7 — Ralph Botting, lhp; B: Houlton, MA; Burbank HS, CA; 1979 CAL (2) (2)

12 — John Verhoeven, rhp; B: Long Beach, CA; University of LaVerne; 1976 CAL (2) (4)

June — Secondary Phase
Class A (Davenport) selections:
1 — John Caneira, rhp; B: Waterburn, CT; Eastern Connecticut State University; 1977 CAL (2) (2)

1975

January — Regular Phase
Major League selection:
1 — Willie Aikens, 1b; B: Seneca, CA; South Carolina State College; 1977 CAL (2) (8)

2 — Jim Dorsey, rhp; B: Oak Park, IL; Los Angeles Valley JC; 1980 CAL (1) (3)

January — Secondary Phase
1 — Gil Kubski, 3b; B: Longview, TX; Cal State Northridge; 1980 CAL (1) (1)

5 — Bobby Clark, ss; B: Sacramento, CA; Riverside CC, CA; 1979 CAL (5) (7)

June — Regular Phase
1 — Danny Goodwin, c; B: St. Louis, MO; Southern University; 1975 CAL (3) (7)

2 — Jim Anderson, ss; B: Los Angeles, CA; Kennedy HS, Granada Hills, CA; 1978 CAL (2) (6)

3 — Carney Lansford, ss; B: San Jose, CA; Wilcox HS, Santa Clara, CA; 1978 CAL (3) (15)

4 — Floyd Rayford, c; B: Memphis, TN; Manual Arts HS, Los Angeles, CA; 1980 BAL (6) (7)

9 — John Flannery, ss; B: Long Beach, CA, Lakewood HS, CA; 1977 CHW (1) (1)

10 — Paul Hartzell, rhp; B: Bloomsburg, PA; Lehigh University; 1976 CAL (3) (6)

19 — Steve Eddy, rhp; B: Sterling, IL; United Township HS, Moline, IL; 1979 CAL (1) (1)

1976

January — Regular Phase
4 — Mark Brouhard, c; B: Burbank, CA; Los Angeles Pierce JC; 1980 MIL (6) (6)

5 — Keith Comstock, lhp; B: San Francisco, CA; Canada JC, CA; 1984 MIN (1) (6)

June — Regular Phase
1 — Ken Landreaux, of; B: Los Angeles, CA; Arizona State University; 1977 CAL (2) (11)

2 — Bob Ferris, rhp; B: Arlington, VA; University of Maryland; 1979 CAL (2) (2)

7 — Chuck Porter, rhp; B: Baltimore, MD; Clemson University; 1981 MIL (5) (5)

12 — Mike Bishop, 3b; B: Santa Maria, CA; Righetti HS, Santa Maria, CA; 1983 NYM (1) (1)

17 — Ken Schrom, rhp; B: Grangeville, ID; University of Idaho; 1980 TOR (2) (7)

29 — John Harris, 1b; B: Portland, OR; Lubbock Christian College; 1979 CAL (3) (3)

June — Secondary Phase

2 — Dan Boone, lhp; B: Long Beach, CA; Cal State Fullerton; 1981 SDP (2) (3)

1977

January — Regular Phase

1 — Alan Wiggins, inf; B: Los Angeles, CA; Pasadena CC, CA; 1981 SDP (5) (7)

3 — Daryl Sconiers, 1b; B: San Bernardino, CA; Orange Coast JC, CA; 1981 CAL (5) (5)

June — Regular Phase

1 — Richard Dotson, rhp; B: Cincinnati, OH; Anderson HS, Cincinnati, OH; 1979 CHW (9) (12)

4 — Brian Harper, c; B: Los Angeles, CA; San Pedro HS, Rolling Hills, CA; 1979 CAL (2) (16)

5 — Ricky Steirer, rhp; B: Baltimore, MD; University of Maryland Baltimore County; 1982 CAL (3) (3)

8 — Brad Havens, lhp; B: Highland Park, MI; Kimball HS, Royal Oak, MI; 1981 MIN (3) (8)

June — Secondary Phase

1 — Mike Walters, rhp; B: St. Louis, MO; Chaffey JC, CA; 1983 MIN (2) (2)

1978

June — Regular Phase

Major League selection:

1 — Tom Brunansky, of; B: Covina, CA; West Covina HS, CA; 1981 CAL (1) (14)

3 — Dave Engle, 3b; B: San Diego, CA; University of Southern California; 1981 MIN (5) (9)

4 — Mike Witt, rhp; Fullerton, CA; Servite HS, Buena Park, CA; 1981 CAL (10) (12)

14 — Dan Whitmer, c; Redlands, CA; Cal State Fullerton; 1980 CAL (1) (2)

1979

January — Regular Phase

6 — Gary Pettis, of; B: Oakland, CA; Laney JC, CA; 1982 CAL (6) (11)

June — Regular Phase

5 — Pat Keedy, 2b; B: Birmingham, AL; Auburn University; 1985 CAL (1) (3)

9 — Darrell Miller, c; B: Washington, DC; Cal Poly Pomona; 1984 CAL (5) (5)

1980

June — Regular Phase

1 — Dennis Rasmussen, lhp; B: Los Angeles, CA; Creighton University; 1983 SDP (5) (12) (from Astros for Nolan Ryan)

7 — Mike Brown, of; B: San Francisco, CA; San Jose State University; 1983 CAL (4) (5)

June — Secondary Phase

1 — Bill Mooneyham, rhp; B: Livermore, CA; Merced JC, CA; 1986 OAK (1) (1)

1981

January — Secondary Phase

1 — Ron Romanick, rhp; B: Burley, ID; ASU; 1984 CAL (3) (3)

June — Regular Phase

1 — Dick Schofield, ss; B: Springfield, IL; Griffin HS, Springfield, IL; 1983 CAL (10) (14)

6 — Devon White, 3b; B: Kingston, Jamaica; Park West HS, Manhattan, NY; 1985 CAL (6) (14)

10 — Sap Randall, 1b; B: Mobile, AL; Grambling State University; 1988 CHW (1) (1)

20 — Craig Gerber, ss; B: Chicago, IL; Cal Poly San Luis Obispo; 1985 CAL (1) (1)

1982

June — Regular Phase

1 — Bob Kipper, lhp; B: Aurora, IL; Central Catholic HS, Aurora, IL; 1985 CAL (1) (8)

3 — Tony Mack, rhp; B: Lexington, KY; Lamar University; 1985 CAL (1) (1)

4 — Kirk McCaskill, rhp; B: Kapuskasing, Ontario; University of Vermont; 1985 CAL (7) (12)

9 — Mark McLemore, ss; B: San Diego, CA; Morse HS, San Diego, CA; 1986 CAL (5) (13)

1983

June — Regular Phase

3 — Wally Joyner, 1b; B: Atlanta, GA; Brigham Young University; 1986 CAL (6) (13) (from Yankees for Don Baylor)

4 — Pat Clements, lhp; B: McCloud, CA; UCLA; 1985 CAL (1) (8)

16 — Ray Chadwick, rhp; Durham, NC; Winston-Salem State University; 1986 CAL (1) (1)

1984

January — Regular Phase

2 — Doug Jennings, 1b-of; B: Atlanta, GA; Brevard CC, FL; 1988 OAK (4) (5)

June — Regular Phase

1 — Erik Pappas, c; B: Chicago, IL; Mt. Carmel HS, Chicago, IL; 1991 CHI (1) (3)

3 — Sherman Corbett, lhp; B: New Braunfels, TX; Texas A&M University; 1988 CAL (3) (3)

4 — Kent Anderson, ss; B: Florence, SC; University of South Carolina; 1989 CAL (2) (2)

17 — Dante Bichette, of; B: W. Palm Beach, FL; Palm Beach JC, FL; 1988 CAL (3) (11)

1985

January — Second Phase

1 — Chuck Finley, lhp; B: Monroe, LA; West Monroe, LA; 1986 CAL (11) (13)

June — Regular Phase

1 — Willie Fraser, rhp; B: New York, NY; Concordia College, NY; 1986 CAL (5) (6)

1 — Mike Cook, rhp; B: Charleston, SC; University of

South Carolina; 1986 CAL (3) (5) (from Orioles for Fred Lynn)

5— Bobby Rose, ss; B: Covina, CA; San Dimas HS, Glendora, CA; 1989 CAL (4) (4)

14—Jeff Manto, 1b; B: Bristol, PA; Temple University; 1990 CLE (2) (7)

15—Frank DiMichele, lhp; B: Philadelphia, PA; Philadelphia CC; 1988 CAL (1) (1)

1986

June— Regular Phase

1— Roberto Hernandez, rhp; B: Santurce, PR; University of South Carolina–Aiken; 1991 CHW (7) (8)

1— Lee Stevens, 1b; B: Kansas City, MO; Lawrence (KS) HS; 1990 CAL (3) (6)

1— Mike Fetters, rhp; B: Van Nuys, CA; Pepperdine University; 1989 CAL (3) (10) (from Orioles for Juan Beniquez)

4— Paul Sorrento, of; B: Sommerville, MA; Florida State University; 1989 MIN (3) (10)

June— Secondary Phase

1— Alan Mills, rhp; B: Lakeland, FL; Polk CC, FL; 1990 NYY (2) (9)

1987

1— John Orton, c; B: Santa Cruz, CA; Cal Poly San Luis Obispo; 1989 CAL (5) (5)

1— David Holdridge, rhp; B: Wayne, MI; Ocean View HS, Huntington Beach, CA; 1998 SEA (1) (1)

2— Kevin Flora, of; B: Fontana, CA; Bonita HS, LaVerne, CA; 1991 CAL (2) (2)

4— Mark Holzemer, lhp; B: Littleton, CO; Seminole, JC, OK; 1993 CAL (3) (5)

11— Ruben Amaro, of; B: Philadelphia, PA; Stanford University; 1991 CAL (1) (8)

1988

1—Jim Abbott, lhp; B: Flint, MI; University of Michigan, 1989 CAL (5) (9)

4— J.R. Phillips, 1b; B: West Covina, CA; Bishop Amat HS, La Puente, CA; 1993 SFG (4) (6)

6— Gary DiSarcina, ss; B: Malden, MA; University of Massachusetts; 1989 CAL (8) (10)

7—Jim Edmonds, of; B: Fullerton, CA; Diamond Bar (CA) HS; 1993 CAL (6) (6)

11— Scott Lewis, rhp; B: Grants Pass, OR; UNLV; 1990 CAL (5) (5)

30— Damion Easley, ss-2b; B: New York, NY; Long Beach CC; 1992 CAL (5) (7)

1989

1— Kyle Abbott, lhp; B: Newburyport, MA; Long Beach University; 1991 CAL (2) (4)

2— Joe Grahe, rhp; B: West Palm Beach, FL; University of Miami; 1990 CAL (5) (6)

3— Tim Salmon, of; B: Long Beach, CA; Grand Canyon College; 1992 CAL (5) (5)

4— Erik Bennett, rhp; B: Yreka, CA; Cal State Sacramento; 1995 CAL (1) (2)

45— Chad Curtis, of; B: Marion, IN; Grand Canyon University; 1992 CAL (3) (7)

1990

2— Phil Leftwich, rhp; B: Lynchburg, VA; Radford University; 1993 CAL (3) (3)

4— Garrett Anderson, of; B: Kennedy HS, Granada Hills, CA; 1994 CAL (5) (5)

6— Troy Percival, rhp; B: Riverside, CA; UC Riverside; 1995 CAL (4) (4)

18— Mark Dalesandro, c; B: Chicago, IL ; University of Illinois; 1994 CAL (2) (2)

20— P.J. Forbes, 2b; B: Pittsburg, KS; Wichita State University; 1998 BAL (1) (1)

21— Ken Edenfield, rhp; B: Jessup, GA; Western Kentucky University; 1995 CAL (2) (2)

50— Anthony Chavez, rhp; San Jose State University; 1997 ANA (1) (1)

1991

1— Eduardo Perez, 1b; B: Cincinnati, OH; FSU; 1993 CAL (3) (6)

1— Jorge Fabregas, c; B: Miami, FL; University of Miami; 1994 CAL (3) (5) (supplemental pick for Chili Davis)

2— Chris Prichett, 1b; B: Merced, CA; UCLA; 1996 CAL (1) (1)

7— Chris Turner, c; B: Bowling Green, KY; Western Kentucky University; 1993 CAL (5) (6)

9— Mark Sweeney, of; B: Framingham, MA; University of Maine; 1995 STL (3) (4)

17— Shad Williams, rhp; B: Fresno, CA; Fresno CC; 1996 CAL (2) (2)

33— Orlando Palmeiro, of; B: Hoboken, NJ; University of Miami; 1995 CAL (4) (4)

1992

1— Jeff Schmidt, rhp; B: Northfield, MN; University of Minnesota; 1996 CAL (1) (1) 5 — Paxton Briley

6— Bill Simas, rhp; B: Hanford, CA; Fresno CC; 1995 CWS (4) (4)

13— John Snyder, rhp; B: Southfield, MI; Westlake HS, Westlake Village, CA; 1992 CHW (1) (1)

1993

2 — Ryan Hancock, rhp; B: Santa Clara, CA; BYU; 1996 CAL (1) (1)

3 — Matt Perisho, lhp; B: Burlington, IA; McClintock HS, Tempe, AZ; 1993 ANA (1) (2)

4— Andrew Lorraine, lhp; B: Los Angeles, CA; Stanford University; 1998 SEA (1) (1)

7— George Arias, 3b; B: Tuscon, Ariz.; University of Arizona; 1996 CAL (2) (3)

12— Todd Greene, of; B: Augusta, GA; Georgia Southern University; 1996 CAL (2) (2)

1994

6 — Jason Dickson, rhp; B: London, ON, Canada; Northeastern, OK; 1996 CAL (1) (3)

17 — Mike Holtz, lhp; B: Arlington, VA; Clemson University; 1996 CAL (3) (3)

1995

1 — Darin Erstad, of; B: Jamestown, ND; University of Nebraska; 1996 CAL (3) (3)

2 — Jarrod Washburn, lhp; B: La Crosse, WI; University of Wisconsin–Oshkosh; 1998 ANA (1) (1)

5 — Justin Baughman, ss; B: Mountain View, CA; Lewis & Clark College; 1998 ANA (1) (1)

1997

1 — Troy Glaus, 3b; B: Tarzana, CA; UCLA; 1998 ANA (1) (1)

Baltimore Orioles

1965

June — Regular Phase

3 — Frank Tepedino, 1b; B: Brooklyn, NY; Wingate HS, Brooklyn, NY; 1967 NYM (5) (8)

6 — Bill Dillman, rhp; B: Trenton, NJ; Wake Forest University; 1967 BAL (1) (2)

21 — Charlie Sands, c; B: Newport News, VA; Newport News (VA) HS; 1967 NYY (1) (6)

1966

June — Regular Phase

11 — Terry Crowley, 1b-of; B: Staten Island, NY; Long Island University; 1969 BAL (12) (15)

1967

January — Secondary Phase

1 — Johnny Oates, c; B: Sylva, NC; Virginia Tech; 1970 BAL (2) (11)

3 — John Montague, rhp; B: Newport News, VA; no school; 1973 MON (3) (7)

June — Regular Phase

1 — Bobby Grich, ss; B: Muskegon, MI; Wilson HS, Long Beach, CA; 1970 BAL (7) (17)

2 — Don Baylor, of; B: Austin, TX; Austin (TX) HS; 1970 BAL (6) (19)

5 — David Johnson, rhp; B: Abilene, TX; Cooper HS, Abilene, TX; 1974 BAL (2)(4)

June — Secondary Phase

1 — Mike Adamson, rhp; B: San Diego, CA; USC; 1967 BAL (3)(3)

1968

January — Regular Phase

1 — Tom Walker, rhp; B: Tampa, FL; Brevard CC, FL; 1972 MON (3) (6)

June — Regular Phase

1 — Junior Kennedy, ss; B: Fort Gibson, OK; Arvin (CA) HS; 1974 CIN (7) (7)

4 — Jesse Jefferson, rhp; B: Midlothian, VA; Carver HS, Midlothian, VA; 1973 BAL (3) (9)

5 — Ronald Dunn, 2b; B: Oklahoma City, OK; Hoover HS, Fresno, CA; 1974 CHC (2) (2)

11 — Al Bumbry, of; B: Fredericksburg, VA; Virginia State University; 1972 BAL (13) (14)

21 — Rich Coggins, of; B: Indianapolis, IN; Garey HS, Pomona, CA; 1972 BAL (3) (5)

1969

June — Regular Phase

1 — Don Hood; B: Florence, SC; Southside HS, Florence, SC; 1973 BAL (2) (10)

6 — David Skaggs, c; B: Santa Monica, CA; North Torrance HS, Lawndale, CA; 1977 BAL (3) (4)

June — Secondary Phase

1 — Wayne Garland, rhp; B: Nashville, TN; Gulf Coast CC, FL; 1973 BAL (4) (9)

1970

January — Secondary Phase

1 — Mike Reinbach, of; B: San Diego, CA; UCLA; 1974 BAL (1) (1)

2 — Jim Fuller, 1b; B: Bethesda, MD; San Diego Mesa JC; 1973 BAL (2) (3)

3 — Doug DeCinces, 3b; B: Burbank, CA; Los Angeles Pierce JC; 1973 BAL (9) (15)

June — Regular Phase

9 — Tim Nordbrook, ss; B: Baltimore, MD; Loyola College, MD; 1974 BAL (3) (6)

10 — Rob Andrews, of; B: Santa Monica, CA; South Torrance HS, CA; 1975 HOU (2) (5)

12 — Herb Hutson, rhp; B: Savannah, GA; Georgia Southern College; 1974 CHC (1) (1)

1971

June — Regular Phase

1 — Randy Stein, rhp; B: Pomona, CA; Ganesha HS, Pomona, CA; 1978 MIL (1) (4)

3 — Kiko Garcia, ss; B: Martinez, CA; Ygnacio Valley HS, Walnut Creek, CA; 1976 BAL (5) (10)

June — Secondary Phase Delayed

1 — Paul Mitchell, rhp; B: Worchester, MA; Old Dominion University; 1975 BAL (1) (6)

1972

June — Regular Phase

11 — Bobby Brown, of-3b; B: Norfolk, VA; Northampton HS, Eastville, VA; 1979 TOR (1) (7)

20 — Mike Willis, lhp; B: Oklahoma City, OK; Vanderbilt University; 1977 TOR (5) (5)

22 — Willie Royster, c; B: Clarksville, VA.; Springarn HS, Washington DC; 1981 BAL (1) (1)

1973

January — Secondary Phase

2 — John Flinn, rhp; B: Merced, CA; Los Angeles Valley JC; 1978 BAL (3) (4)

3 — Gil Rondon, rhp; B: Bronx, NY; New York, NY; 1976 HOU (1) (2)

June — Regular Phase

1 — Mike Parrott, rhp; B: Oxnard, CA; Camarillo HS, CA; 1977 BAL (1) (5)

3 — Eddie Murray, c-1b; B: Los Angeles, CA; Locke HS, Los Angeles, CA; 1977 BAL (13) (20)

7 — Mike Flanagan, lhp; B: Manchester, NH; University of Massachusetts; 1975 BAL (15) (18)

1974

June — Regular Phase

1 — Rich Dauer, ss-2b; B: San Bernardino, CA; USC; 1976 BAL (10)

4 — Mike Darr, rhp; B: Pomona, CA; Norco (CA) HS; 1977 TOR (1) (1)

5 — Randy Miller, rhp; B: Oxnard, CA; University of California–San Diego; 1977 BAL (1) (2)

June — Secondary Phase

4 — Tom Chism, of; B: Chester, PA; Brandywine JC, DE; 1979 BAL (1) (1)

1975

June — Regular Phase

1 — Dave Ford, rhp-of; B: Cleveland, OH; Lincoln West HS, Cleveland, OH; 1978 BAL (4) (4)

3 — Steve Lake, c; B: Inglewood, CA; Lennox HS, CA; 1983 CHC (5) (11)

6 — Darry Cias, c; B: New York, NY; Kennedy HS, Granada Hills, CA; 1983 OAK (1) (1)

30 — Chris Smith, c; B: Torrance, CA; Bishop Montgomery HS, Hermosa Beach, CA; 1981 MON (2) (3)

June — Secondary Phase

3 — Jeff Rineer, lhp; B: Lancaster, CA; Franklin Marshall College; 1979 BAL (1) (1)

1976

January — Regular Phase

2 — Mark Corey, of; B: Tucumcari, NM; Central Arizona JC; 1979 BAL (3) (3)

January — Secondary Phase

1 — Wayne Krenchicki, ss; B: Trenton, NJ; University of Miami; 1979 BAL (3) (8)

June — Regular Phase

1 — Dallas Williams, of; B: Brooklyn, NY; Abraham Lincoln HS, Brooklyn, NY; 1981 BAL (1) (2)

6 — Jim Smith, ss; B: Santa Monica, CA; Cal State Long Beach; 1982 PIT (1) (1)

1977

January — Regular Phase

1 — John Shelby, ss; B: Lexington, KY; Columbia State CC, TN; 1981 BAL (7) (11)

June — Regular Phase

1 — Drungo Hazewood, c-of; B: Mobile, AL; Sacramento HS, CA; 1980 BAL (1) (1)

9 — Mark Smith, rhp; B: Arlington, VA; American University; 1983 OAK (1) (1)

1978

June — Regular Phase

2 — Larry Sheets, of; B: Staunton, VA; Lee HS, Staunton, VA; 1984 BAL (6) (8) (from Mets for Elliott Maddox)

2 — Cal Ripken, 3b; B: Haure De Grace, MD; Aberdeen HS, MD; 1981 BAL (18) (18)

3 — Bob Bonner, ss; B: Uvalde, TX; Texas A&M University; 1980 BAL (4) (4)

6 — Mike Boddicker, rhp; B: Cedar Rapids, IA; University of Iowa; 1980 BAL (9) (14)

7 — Don Welchel, rhp; B: Atlanta, TX; Sam Houston State University; 1982 BAL (2) (2)

1979

June — Regular Phase

5 — Allan Ramirez, rhp; B: Victoria, TX; Rice University; 1983 BAL (1) (1)

7 — Storm Davis, rhp; B: Dallas, TX; University Christian HS, Jacksonville, FL; 1982 BAL (6) (13)

26 — Bill Swaggerty, rhp; B: Sanford, FL; Stetson University; 1983 BAL (4) (4)

1980

January — Secondary Phase

1 — Mike Young, of; B: Oakland, CA; Chabot JC, CA; 1982 BAL (6) (8)

June — Regular Phase

2 — Al Pardo, c; B: Oviedo, Spain; Jefferson HS, Tampa, FL; 1985 BAL (2) (4)

3 — Ken Dixon, rhp; B: Monroe, VA; Amherst County HS, Monroe, VA; 1984 BAL (4) (4)

4 — Carl Nichols, c-ss; B: Los Angeles, CA; Compton HS, CA; 1986 BAL (3) (6)

6 — Mark Brown, rhp; B: Bellows Falls, VT; University of Massachusetts; 1984 BAL (1) (2)

15 — Ricky Jones, ss; B: Tupilo, MS; West Georgia College; 1986 BAL (1) (1)

1981

June — Regular Phase

10 — Tony Arnold, rhp; B: El Paso, TX; University of Texas; 1986 BAL (2) (2)

12 — Jeff Schaefer, 2b; B: Pacthogue, NY; University of Maryland; 1989 CHW (1) (5)

1982

January — Secondary Phase
4 — Mike Blowers, 3b, Tacoma CC

June — Regular Phase
3 — John Habyan, rhp; B: Bayshore, NY; St. John Baptist HS, Brentwood, NY; 1985 BAL (4) (11)
5 — Ken Gerhart, of; B: Charleston, SC; Middle Tennessee State University; 1986 BAL (3) (3)
9 — Eric Bell, lhp; B: Modesto, CA; Beyer HS, Modesto, CA; 1985 BAL (3) (6)
11— Billy Ripken, rhp-ss; B: Haure De Grace, MD; Aberdeen HS, MD; 1987 BAL (7) (12)
21— Jim Traber, 1b; B: Columbus, OH; Oklahoma State University; 1984 BAL (4) (4)

1983

June — Secondary Phase
2 — Bob Milacki, rhp; B: Trenton, NJ; Yavapai JC, AZ; 1988 BAL (5) (8)

1985

June — Regular Phase
4 — Brian Dubois, lhp; B: Joliet, IL; Reed Custer HS, Briarwood, IL; 1989 DET (2) (2)
7 — Jeff Ballard, lhp; B: Billings, MT; Stanford University; 1987 BAL (5) (7)
9 — Pete Stanicek, 2b; B: Harvey, IL; Stanford University; 1987 BAL (2) (2)

June — Secondary Phase
1— Craig Worthington, 3b; B: Los Angeles, CA; Cerritos JC, CA; 1988 BAL (4) (7)

1986

June — Regular Phase
9 — Blaine Beatty, lhp; B: Victoria, TX; Baylor University; 1989 NYM (2) (2)
14 — Gordie Dillard, lhp; B: Salinas, CA; Oklahoma State University; 1988 BAL (1) (2)

1987

1— Pete Harnisch, rhp; B: Commack, NY; Fordham University; 1988 BAL (3) (11)
13 — Steve Finley, of; B: Paducah, KY; Southern Illinois University; 1989 BAL (2) (10)
18 — David Segui, 1b; B: Kansas City, MO; Louisana Tech University; 1990 BAL (4) (9)

1988

1— Gregg Olson, rhp; B: Scribner, NE; Auburn University; 1988 BAL (6) (11)
1— Ricky Gutierrez, ss; B: Miami, FL; American HS, Hialeah, FL; 1993 SDP (2) (6)
2 — Arthur Rhodes, lhp-of; B: Waco, TX; La Vega HS, Waco, TX; 1991 BAL (8) (8)

12 — Pete Rose Jr., 3b; B: Cincinnati, OH; Oak Hills HS, Cincinnati, OH; 1997 CIN (1)

1989

1— Ben McDonald, rhp; B: Baton Rouge, LA; LSU; 1989 BAL (8) (8)
12 — Brad Pennington, lhp; B: Salem, IN; Vincennes University JC, IN; 1993 BAL (3) (5)
13 — Mike Oquist, rhp; B: LaJuna, CO; University of Arkansas; 1993 BAL (3) (6)
17 — Greg Zaun, c; B: Glendale, CA; St. Francis HS, Glendale, CA; 1995 BAL (2) (4)
36 — Keith Kessinger, ss; B: Forrest City, AR; University of Mississippi; 1993 CIN (1) (1)

1990

1— Mike Mussina, rhp; B: Williamsport, PA; Stanford University; 1991 BAL (9) (9)
2 — Erik Schullstrom, rhp; B: San Diego, CA; Fresno State University; 1994 MIN (2) (2)
5 — Bobby Chouinard, rhp; B: Manila, Philippines; Forest Grove (OR) HS; 1996 OAK (1) (2)
10 — Damon Buford, 2b-of; B: Baltimore, MD; USC; 1993 BAL (3) (6)
33 — James Dedrick, rhp; B: Los Angeles, CA; USC; 1995 BAL (1) (1)

1991

1— Mark Smith, of; B: Charlotte, NC; USC; 1994 BAL (2) (3)
3 — Alex Ochoa, of; B: Miami Lakes, FL; Miami Lakes HS, Hialeah, FL; 1995 NYM (3) (3)
4 — Vaughn Eshelman, lhp; B: Philadelpha, PA; University of Houston; 1995 BOS (3) (3)
7 — Jimmy Haynes, rhp; B: LaGrange, GA; Troup County HS, LaGrange, GA; 1995 BAL (2) (3)
12 — Curtis Goodwin, of; B: Oakland, CA; San Leandro (CA) HS; 1995 BAL (1) (4)
23 — Rick Krivda, lhp; B; McKeesport, PA; California University, PA; 1995 BAL (3) (3)

1992

1— Jeffrey Hammonds, of; B: Scotch Plains, NJ; Stanford University; 1993 BAL (6) (6)
2 — Brian Sackinsky, rhp; B: Pittsburgh, PA; Stanford University; 1996 BAL (1) (1)
5 — Scott Kingenbeck, rhp; B: Cincinnati, OH; Ohio State University; 1994 BAL (2) (3)

1993

14 — Kimera Bartee, of: Omaha, NE; Creighton University; 1996 DET (3) (3)
19 — Rocky Coppinger, rhp; B: El Paso, TX; Coronado HS, El Paso, TX; 1996 BAL (3) (3)

1994

2 — Tommy Davis, 3b; B: Mobile, AL; University of Southern Mississippi; 1999 BAL (1) (1)

9 — Chris Fussell, rhp; B: Oregon, OH; Clay HS, Oregon, OH; 1998 BAL (1) (1)

1995

10 — David Dellucci, of; B: Baton Rouge, LA; University of Mississippi; 1997 BAL (1) (2)

1996

33 — Ryan Minor, 3b; B: Canton, OH; University of Oklahoma; 1998 BAL (1) (1)

1997

11 — Jerry Hairston Jr., inf; B: Des Moines, IA; Southern Illinois; 1998 BAL (1) (1)

Boston Red Sox

1965

June — Regular Phase

1 — Billy Conigliaro, of; B: Revere, MA; Swampscott (MA) HS; 1969 BOS (3) (5)

3 — Ken Poulsen, 3b; B: Van Nuys, CA; Birmingham HS, Van Nuys, CA; 1967 BOS (1) (1)

5 — Amos Otis, ss; B: Mobile, AL; Williamson HS, Mobile, AL; 1967 NYM (2) (17)

7 — Jim Hutto, 3b-rhp; B: Norfolk, VA; Pensacola (FL) HS; 1970 PHI (1) (2)

18 — Ray Jarvis, rhp; B: Providence, RI; Hope HS, Providence, RI; 1969 BOS (2) (2)

1966

January — Regular Phase

2 — Mark Schaeffer, lhp; B: Santa Monica, CA; Cleveland HS, Canoga Park, CA; 1972 SDP (1) (1)

January — Secondary Phase

1 — Dick Baney, rhp; B: Fullerton, CA; Anaheim HS, CA; 1969 SEA (1) (3)

June — Regular Phase

1 — Ken Brett, lhp-of; B: Brooklyn, NY; El Segundo HS, CA; 1967 BOS (4) (14)

6 — Mike Nagy, rhp; B: Bronx, NY; St. Helena HS, Bronx, NY; 1969 BOS (4) (6)

16 — Ed Phillips, rhp; B: Ardmore, OK; Colby College; 1970 BOS (1) (1)

June — Secondary Phase

3 — Dick Mills, rhp; B: Boston, MA; Parsons College; 1970 BOS (1) (1)

1967

January — Regular Phase

1 — Carlton Fisk, c; B: Bellows Falls, VT; no school; 1969 BOS (11) (24)

2 — Don Newhauser, rhp; B: Miami, FL; Broward CC, FL; 1972 BOS (3) (3)

Other Class AAA (Toronto) selections:

June — Regular Phase

1 — Mike Garman, rhp; B: Caldwell ID; Caldwell CC, ID; 1969 BOS (4) (9)

1968

June — Regular Phase

3 — Lynn McGlothen, rhp; B: Monroe, LA; Grambling HS, Simsboro, LA; 1972 BOS (2) (12)

6 — Cecil Cooper, 1b; B: Brenham, TX; Brenham (TX) HS; 1971 BOS (6) (17)

11 — Ben Oglivie, inf-of; B: Colon, Panama; Roosevelt HS, Bronx, NY; 1971 BOS (6) (17)

22 — Bill Lee, lhp; B: Burbank, CA; USC; 1969 BOS (10) (14)

June — Secondary Phase

1 — John Curtis, lhp; B: Newton, MA; Clemson University; 1970 BOS (4) (16)

1969

June — Regular Phase

2 — Rick Miller, of; B: Grand Rapids, MI; Michigan State University; 1971 BOS (12) (13)

3 — Buddy Hunter, inf; B: Omaha, NE; Pershing College; 1971 BOS (3) (3)

4 — Jim Wright, rhp; B: Reed City, MI; Coopersville (MI) HS; 1978 BOS (2) (2)

5 — Dwight Evans, 3b-of; B: Santa Monica, CA; Charsworth HS, Northridge, CA; 1972 BOS (19) (20)

7 — Steve Barr, lhp; B: St. Louis, MO; Carson HS, Torrance, CA; 1974 BOS (2) (3)

1970

January — Secondary Phase

1 — Rick Burleson, ss; Lynwood, CA; Warren HS, South Gate, CA; 1974 BOS (7) (13)

June — Regular Phase

13 — Tim Blackwell, 3b-c; B: San Diego, CA; Crawford HS, San Diego, CA; 1974 BOS (2) (11)

June — Secondary Phase

1 — John LaRose, lhp; B: Pawtucket, RI; Cumberland HS, RI; 1978 BOS (1) (1)

1971

June — Regular Phase

1 — Jim Rice, of; B: Anderson, SC; Hannah HS, Anderson, SC; 1974 BOS (15) (15)

9 — Bill Moran, rhp; B: Portsmouth, VA; Louisburg JC, NC; 1974 CHW (1) (1)

25 — Mark Bomback, rhp; B: Portsmouth, VA; Durfee HS, Fall River, MA; 1978 MIL (1) (4)

26 — Jack Baker, 1b; B: Birmingham, AL; Auburn University; 1976 BOS (2) (2)

June — Secondary Phase Delayed
1— Jim Burton, lhp; B: Royal Oak, MI; University of Michigan; 1975 BOS (2) (2)

1972

June — Regular Phase
2 — Steve Dillard, ss; B: Memphis, TN; University of Mississippi; 1975 BOS (3) (8)

6 — Don Aase, rhp; B: Orange, CA; Savanna HS, Anaheim, CA; 1977 BOS (1) (13)

10 — Andy Merchant, c; B: Mobile, AL; Auburn University; 1975 BOS (2) (2)

15 — Ernie Whitt, c; B: Detroit, MI; Macomb CC, MI; 1976 BOS (1) (15)

1973

June — Regular Phase
1— Ted Cox, ss; B: Oklahoma, OK; Midwest City HS, OK; 197 BOS (1) (5)

2 — Fred Lynn, of; B: Chicago, IL; USC; 1974 BOS (7) (17)

5 — Rick Jones, lhp; B: Jacksonville, FL; Forrest HS, Jacksonville, FL; 1976 BOS (1) (3)

8 — Butch Hobson, 3b; B: Tuscaloosa, AL; University of Alabama; 1975 BOS (6) (8)

1974

January — Regular Phase
1— Chuck Rainey, rhp; B: San Diego, CA; San Diego Mesa JC; 1979 BOS (4) (6)

January — Secondary Phase
1— Bob Stanley, rhp; B: Portland, MA; Kearny HS, NJ; 1977 BOS (13) (13)

2 — Steven Burke, rhp, B: Stockton, CA; Merritt JC, CA; 1977 SEA (2) (2)

June — Regular Phase
7 — Sam Bowen, 2b; B: Brunswick, GA; Valdosta State College; 1977 BOS (3) (3)

9 — Joel Finch, rhp; B: South Bend, IN; Washington HS, South Bend, IN; 1979 BOS (1) (1)

1975

June — Regular Phase
2 — Dave Schmidt, c; B: Mesa, AZ; Mission Viejo HS, CA; 1981 BOS (1) (1)

3 — Ed Jurak, ss; B: Los Angeles, CA; San Pedro HS, CA; 1982 BOS (4) (6)

10 — Dave Stapleton, 2b; B: Fairhope, AL; University of South Alabama; 1980 BOS (7) (7)

22 — Mike O'Berry, c; B: Birmingham, AL; University of South Alabama; 1979 BOS (1) (7)

23 — Mike Paxton, rhp-inf; B: Memphis, TN; Memphis State University; 1977 BOS (1) (4)

1976

January — Regular Phase
2 — Dennis Burtt, rhp; B: San Diego, CA; Santa Ana JC, CA; 1985 MIN (2) (2)

January — Secondary Phase
3 — John Tudor, lhp; B: Schenectady, NY; Georgia Southern College; 1979 BOS (5) (12)

June — Regular Phase
1— Bruce Hurst, lhp; B: St. George, UT; Dixie HS, St. George, UT; 1980 BOS (9) (15)

2 — Glenn Hoffman, ss; B: Orange, CA; Savanna HS, Anaheim, CA; 1980 BOS (8) (9)

5 — Mike Smithson, rhp; B: Centerville, TN; University of Tennessee; 1982 TX (2) (8)

7 — Wade Boggs, ss; B: Omaha, NE; Plant HS, Tampa, FL; 1982 BOS (11) (17)

9 — Gary Allenson, c; B: Culver City, CA; ASU; 1979 BOS (6) (7)

12 — Reid Nichols, 2b; B: Ocala, FL; Forest HS, Ocala, FL; 1980 BOS (6) (8)

22 — Chico Walker, 2b; B: Jackson, MS; Tilden Tech HS, Chicago, IL; 1980 BOS (4) (11)

1977

June — Regular Phase
2 — Bobby Sprowl, lhp; B: Sandusky, OH; University of Alabama; 1978 BOS (1) (4)

8 — Roger LaFrancois, c; B: Norwich, CT; University of Oklahoma; 1982 BOS (1) 91)

10 — Steve Shields, rhp; B: Gadsden, AL; Hokes Bluff HS, Gadsden, AL; 1985 ATL (2) (5)

25 — Pete Ladd, rhp; B: Portland, ME; University of Massachusetts; 1979 HOU (1) (6)

26 — Lee Graham, of; B: Summerfield, FL; Lake Weir HS, Belleview, FL; 1983 BOS (1) (1)

1978

January — Secondary Phase
1— Brian Denman, lb-rhp; B: Minneapolis, MN; Richfield, MN; 1982 BOS (1) (1)

June — Regular Phase
13 — John Lickert, c; B: Pittsburgh, PA; Langley HS, Pittsburgh, PA; 1981 BOS (1) (1)

1979

June — Regular Phase
2 — Marc Sullivan, c; B: Quincy, MA; University of Florida; 1982 BOS (5) (5)

7 — Tom McCarthy, rhp; B: Lundstahl, West Germany; Plymouth Carver HS, MA; 1985 BOS (1) (3)

June — Secondary Phase
1— Marty Barrett, 2b; B: Arcadia, CA; ASU; 1982 BOS (9) (11)

1980

June — Regular Phase
2 — Mike Brown, rhp; B: Camden Co., NJ; Clemson University; 1982 BOS (5) (7)

6 — Pat Dodson, 1b; B: Santa Monica, CA; UCLA; 1986 BOS (3) (3)

8 — Al Nipper, rhp; B: San Diego, CA; Northeast Missouri State University; 1983 BOS (5) (7)

16 — Oil Can Boyd, rhp; B: Meridian, MS; Jackson State University; 1982 BOS (8) (11)

20 — Tom Bolton, lhp; B: Nashville, TN; Antioch HS, Brentwood, TN; 1987 BOS (6) (8)

1981

January — Regular Phase

1 — Danny Sheaffer, c; B: Jacksonville, FL; Harrisburg Area CC, PA; 1987 BOS (1) (6)

June — Regular Phase

1 — Steve Lyons, ss-of; B: Tacoma, WA; Oregon State University; 1985 BOS (5) (9)

3 — Rob Woodward, rhp; B: New Haven, CT; Lebanon (NH) HS; 1985 BOS (4) (4)

4 — Todd Benzinger, 1b; B: Dayton, KY; New Richmond HS, Cincinnati, OH; 1987 BOS (2) (9)

June — Secondary Phase

1 — Steve Ellsworth, rhp; B: Chicago, IL; Cal State Northridge; 1988 BOS (1) (1)

1982

January — Regular Phase

1 — Mike Rochford, lhp; B: Methuen, MA; Santa Fe CC, FL; 1988 BOS (3) (3)

4 — Charles Mitchell, rhp; B: Dixion, TN; Columbia State CC, TN; 1984 BOS (2) (2)

June — Regular Phase

1 — Sam Horn, 1b; B: Dallas, TX; Morse HS, San Diego, CA; 1987 BOS (3) (8)

2 — Kevin Romine, of; B: Exeter, NH; ASU; 1985 BOS (7) (7)

3 — Mike Greenwell, 3b; B: Lewisville, KY; North Fort Myers HS, FL; 1985 BOS (12) (12)

8 — Jeff Sellers, rhp; B: Compton, CA; Paramount HS, Long Beach, CA; 1985 BOS (4) (4)

1983

January — Regular Phase

1 — Ellis Burks, of; B: Vicksburg, MI; Ranger JC, TX; 1987 BOS (6) (12)

June — Regular Phase

1 — Roger Clemens, rhp; B: Dayton, OH; University of Texas; 1984 BOS (13) (15)

2 — Mike Brumley, ss, B: Oklahoma City, OK; University of Texas; 1987 CHC (1) (8)

7 — John Mitchell, rhp; B: Dixion, TN; Overton HS, Nashville, TN; 1986 NYM (4) (5)

1984

January — Secondary Phase

3 — John Leister, rhp; B: San Antonio, TX; Michigan State University; 1987 BOS (2) (2)

June — Regular Phase

1 — John Marzano, c; B: Philadelphia, PA; Temple University; 1987 BOS (6) (8)

7 — Steve Curry, rhp; B: Winter Park, FL; Manatee JC, FL; 1988 BOS (1) (1)

8 — Jody Reed, ss; B: Tampa, FL; FSU; 1987 BOS (6) (10)

13 — Zachary Crouch, lhp; B: Folsum, CA; Cordova HS, Sacramento, CA; 1988 BOS (1) (1)

1985

June — Regular Phase

6 — Todd Pratt, c; B: Bellevue, NE; Hilltop HS, Chula Vista, CA; 1992 PHI (3) (6)

10 — Brady Anderson, of; B: Silver Spring, MD; University of California; 1988 BOS (1) (11)

June — Secondary Phase

1 — Eric Hetzel, rhp; B: Crowley, LA; LSU; 1989 BOS (2) (2)

1986

January — Regular Phase

2 — Curt Schilling, rhp; B: Anchorage, AK; Yavapai JC; AZ; 1988 BAL (3) (11)

June — Regular Phase

3 — Scott Cooper, 3b; B: St. Louis, MO; Pattonville HS, St. Louis, MO; 1990 BOS (5) (7)

1987

1 — Reggie Harris, rhp; B: Waynesboro, VA; Waynesboro (VA) HS; 1990 (2) (5)

11 — Phil Plantier, of; B: Manchester, NH; Poway (CA) HS; 1990 BOS (3) (8)

1988

5 — John Valentin, 3b; B: Mineola, NY; Seton Hall University; 1992 BOS (7) (7)

8 — Tim Naehring, 3b; B: Cincinnati, OH; Miami University, OH; 1990 BOS (8) (8)

25 — John Flaherty, c; B: Bronx, NY; George Washington University; 1992 BOS (3) (7)

1989

1 — Greg Blosser, of; B: Bradenton, Fla.; Sarasota (FL) HS; 1993 (2) (2)

1 — Mo Vaughn, 1b; B: Norwalk, CT; Seton Hall University; 1991 BOS (9) (9)

3 — Eric Wedge, c; B: Fort Wayne, IN; Wichita State University; 1991 BOS (3) (4)

4 — Jeff Bagwell, 3b; B: Boston, MA; University of Hartford; 1991 HOU (8) (8)

6 — Paul Quantrill, rhp; B: London, ON, Canada; University of Wisconsin; 1992 BOS (3) (7)

10 — Greg Hansell, rhp; B: Bellflower, CA; Kennedy HS, La Palma, CA; 1995 LAD (1) (3)

1990

2 — Frank Rodriguez, rhp; B: Brooklyn, NY; Howard JC, TX; 1995 BOS (1) (4)

3 — Walt McKeel, c, B: Wilson, NC; Greene Central HS, Snow Hill, NC; 1996 BOS (2) (2)
4 — James Baldwin, rhp; B: Southern Pines, NC; Pinecrest HS, Southern Pines, NC; 1995 CHW (4) (4)
5 — Ray Durham, 2b; B: Charlotte, NC; Harding HS, Charlotte, NC; 1995 CHW (4) (4)
6 — Gar Finnvold, rhp, B: Boynton Beach, FL; FSU; 1994 BOS (1) (1)

1991

1 — Aaron Sele, rhp; B: Golden Valley, MN; Washington State University; 1993 BOS (5) (6)
1 — Scott Hatteberg, c; B: Salem, OR; Washington State University; 1991 BOS (4) (4)
8 — Luis Ortiz, 1b; B: Santo Domingo, DR; Union University, TN; 1993 BOS (2) (4)
10 — Tony Rodriguez, ss; B: Rio Piedras, PR; University of Charleston, WV; 1996 BOS (1) (1)
15 — Cory Bailey, rhp; B: Herrin, IL; Southeastern Illinois JC; 1993 BOS (2) (6)
17 — Tim VanEgmond, rhp; B: Sharpsburg, GA; Jacksonville State University; 1994 BOS (2) (3)
18 — Ron Mahay, of; B: Crestwood, IL; South Suburban JC, IL; 1995 BOS (1) (1)
21 — Joel Bennett, rhp; B: Binghamton, N.Y.; East Stroudsburg (PA) University; 1998 BAL (1) (1)

1992

5 — Steve Rodriguez, 2b; B: Las Vegas, NV; Pepperdine University; 1995 BOS (1) (1)
13 — Bill Selby, 3b; B: Monroeville, AL; University of Southern Mississippi; 1996 BOS (1) (1)
27 — Joe Hudson, rhp; B: Philadelphia; West Virginia University; 1995 BOS (3) (4)

1993

1 — Trot Nixon, of; B: Durham, NC; New Hanover HS, Wilmington NC; 1996 BOS (2) (2)
2 — Jeff Suppan, rhp; B: Oklahoma City, OK; Crespi HS, Encino, CA; 1995 BOS (3) (4)
3 — Ryan McGuire, 1b; B: Bellflower, CA: UCLA; 1997 MON (2) (2)
25 — Shayne Bennett, rhp; B: Adelaide, Australia; JC of Du Page, IL; 1997 MON (2) (2)

1994

1 — Nomar Garciaparra, ss; B: Whittier, CA; Georgia Tech; 1996 BOS (3)(3)
3 — Brian Rose, rhp; B: New Bedford, MA; South Dartmouth (MA) HS; 1997 BOS (2) (2)
5 — Brian Barkley, lhp; B: Conroe, TX; NC State University; 1998 BOS (1) (1)
11 — Donnie Sadler, Gholson, TX; Valley Mills (TX) HS; 1998 BOS (1) (1)
13 — Carl Pavano, rhp; B: New Britain, CT; Southington (CT) HS; 1998 MON (1) (1)

18 — Michael Coleman, of; B: Nashville, TN: Stratford HS, Nashville, TN; 1997 BOS (1) (1)

Chicago White Sox

1965

June — Regular Phase
4 — Fred Rath, rhp; B: Little Rock, AR; Baylor University; 1968 CHW (2) (2)
10 — Ron Lolich, 3b-of; Central Catholic HS, Portland, OR; 1971 CHW (1) (3)
21 — Paul Edmondson, rhp; B: Kansas City, KS; Cal State Northridge; 1969 CHW (1) (1)
31 — Danny Lazar, lhp; B: East Chicago, IN; Indiana State University; 1968 CHW (2) (2)

1966

June — Regular Phase
1 — Carlos May, of; B: Birmingham, AL; Parker HS, Birmingham, AL; 1968 CHW (9) (11)
3 — Jim Magnuson, lhp; B: Marinette, WI; University of Wisconsin–Oshkosh; 1970 CHW (2) (3)
5 — Ken Frailing, lhp; B: Marion, WI; Marion HS, WI; 1972 CHW (2) (5)
16 — Charles Brinkman, c; B: Cincinnati, OH; Ohio State University; 1969 CHW (6) (7)
37 — Art Kusnyer, c; B: Akron, OH; Kent State University; 1970 CHW (4) (6)

1967

January — Secondary Phase
1 — Bob Spence, 1b; B: San Diego, CA; Santa Clara University; 1969 CHW (3) (3)

June — Regular Phase
6 — Dennis O'Toole, rhp; B: Chicago, IL; De LaSalle HS, Chicago, IL; 1969 CHW (5) (5)

1968

June — Regular Phase
1 — Rich McKinney, ss-3b; B: Piqua, OH; Ohio University; 1970 CHW (2) (7)
2 — Hugh Yancy, ss; B: Sarasota, FL; Sarasota (FL) HS; 1972 CHW (3) (3)
3 — Lamar Johnson, c; B: Bessemer, FL; Wenonah HS, Birmingham, AL; 1974 CHW (8) (9)
14 — Rich Moloney, rhp; B: Brookline, MA; Brookline HS, MA; 1970 CHW (1) (1)
16 — Stan Perzanowski, rhp; B: East Chicago, IN; Morton HS, Hammond, IN; 1971 CHW (2) (5)

June — Secondary Phase
1 — Bart Johnson, rhp; B: Torrance, CA; no school; 1969 CHW (8) (8)
2 — Ken Hottman, of; B: Stockton, CA; Sacramento CC, CA; 1971 CHW (1) (1)
3 — Daniel Neumeier, rhp; B: Shawano, WI;

University of Wisconsin, Oshkosh, WI; 1972 CHW (1) (1)

1969

June — Regular Phase

7 — Bruce Kimm, c; B: Cedar Rapids, IA; Norway HS, IA; 1976 DET (2) (4)

19 — Glenn Redmon, 3b; B: Detroit, MI; University of Michigan; 1974 SFG (1) (1)

June — Secondary Phase

3 — Rich Hinton, lhp; B: Tucson, AZ; University of Arizona; 1971 CHW (4) (6)

1970

June — Regular Phase

1 — Lee Richard, ss; B: Lafayette, LA; Southern University; 1971 CHW (4) (5)

2 — Terry Forster, lhp; B: Sioux Falls, SD; Santana (CA) HS; 1971 CHW (5) (15)

3 — Jerry Hairston, inf; B: Birmingham, AL; Gardendale HS, Birmingham, AL; 1973 CHW (14) (14)

6 — Jim Geddes, rhp; B: Columbus, OH; Ohio State University; 1972 CHW (2) (2)

9 — Rich Gossage, rhp; B: Colorado Springs, CO; Wasson HS, Colorado Springs, CO; 1972 CHW (5) (22)

20 — Bruce Miller, ss; B: Fort Wayne, IN; Indiana University; 1973 SFG (4) (4)

June — Secondary Phase

1 — Bucky Dent, 3b; B: Savannah, GA; Miami–Dade North CC; 1973 CHW (4) (12)

1971

January — Secondary Phase

1 — Samuel Ewing, 1b; B: Lewisburg, TN; University of Tennessee; 1973 CHW (2) (4)

June — Regular Phase

2 — Bill Sharp, of; B: Lima, OH; Ohio State University; 1973 CHW (3) (5)

17 — Jeff Holly, lhp; B: San Pedro, CA; Aviation HS, Redondo Beach, CA; 1977 MIN (3) (3)

June — Secondary Phase

1 — Pete Varney, c-1b; B: Roxbury, MA; Harvard University; 1973 CHW (4) (5)

1972

June — Regular Phase

6 — George Enright, c; B: New Britain, CT; Hialeah HS, FL; 1976 CHW (1) (1)

16 — Nyis Nyman, of; B: Pomona, CA; Rancho Cordova HS, CA; 1982 CHW (2) (2)

1973

June — Regular Phase

1 — Steve Swisher, c; B: Parkersburg, WV; Ohio State University; 1974 CHW (4) (9)

2 — Jim Otten, rhp; B: Lewistown, MT; ASU; 1974 CHW (3) (5)

3 — Ken Kravec, lhp; B: Cleveland, OH; Ashland College; 1975 CHW (8) (8)

18 — Mike Squires, 1b; B: Kalamazoo, MI; Western Michigan University; 1975 CHW (10) (10)

1974

January — Regular Phase

1 — Kevin Bell, 3b; B: Los Angeles, CA; Mt. San Antonio JC, CA; 1976 CHW (5) (6)

June — Regular Phase

1 — Larry Monroe, rhp; B: Detroit, MI; Forest View HS, Mt. Prospect, IL; 1976 CHW (1) (1)

2 — Jack Kucek, rhp; B: Warren, OH; Miami University, OH; 1974 CHW (6) (7)

3 — Pete Vuckovich, rhp; B: Johnstown, PA; Clarion University; 1975 CHW (2) (11)

18 — Dave Frost, rhp; B: Long Beach, CA; Stanford University; 1977 CHW (1) (6)

1975

January — Secondary Phase

2 — Tim Stoddard, rhp; B: East Chicago, IN; North Carolina State University; 1975 CHW (1) (14)

June — Regular Phase

1 — Chris Knapp, rhp; B: Cherry Point, NC; Central Michigan University; 1975 CHW (3) (6)

17 — Marv Foley, c; B: Standford, KY; University of Kentucky; 1978 CHW (4) (5)

1976

January — Regular Phase

6 — Fred Howard, rhp; B: Portland, MA; Miami–Dade South CC; 1979 CHW (1) (1)

January — Secondary Phase

1 — Leo Sutherland, of; B: Santiago, Cuba; Golden West JC, CA; 1980 CHW (2) (2)

2 — Rich Wortham, lhp; B: Odessa, TX; University of Texas; 1978 CHW (3) (4)

6 — Harry Chappas, ss; B: Mt. Ranier, MD; Miami–Dade North CC; 1978 CHW (3) (3)

June — Regular Phase

1 — Steve Trout, lhp; B: Detroit, MI; Thornwood HS, South Holland, IL; 1978 CHW (5) (12)

2 — Mike Colbern, c; B: Santa Monica, CA; ASU; 1978 CHW (2) (2)

8 — Lorenzo Gray, ss; B: Mound Bayou, MI; Lynwood HS, CA; 1982 CHW (2) (2)

1977

January — Regular Phase

8 — Mark Esser, lhp; B: Erie, PA; Miami–Dade North CC; 1979 CHW (1) (1)

June — Regular Phase

1 — Harold Baines, 1b; B: Easton, MD; St. Michaels HS, MD; 1980 CHW (10) (17)

2 — Rich Barnes, lhp; B: Palm Beach, FL; Lake Worth HS, FL; 1982 CHW (1) (2)

6 — Rod Allen, of; B: Los Angeles, CA; Santa Monica HS, CA; 1983 SEA (1) (2)

11— Rusty Kuntz, of; B: Orange, CA; Cal State Stanisiaus; 1979 CHW (5) (6)

19 — Dewey Robinson, rhp; B: Evanston, IL; Southern Illinois University; 1979 CHW (3) (3)

20— Ross Baumgarten, lhp; B: Highland, IL; University of Florida; 1978 CHW (4) (5)

1978

June — Regular Phase
2 — Britt Burns, lhp; B: Houston, TX; Huffman HS, Birmingham, AL; 1978 CHW (8) (8)

1979

January — Regular Phase
3 — Randy Johnson, lb; B: Miami, FL; Miami–Dade South CC; 1980 CHW (1) (2)

June — Regular Phase
1— Rick Seiheimer, c; B: Brenham, TX; Brenham (TZ) HS; 1980 CHW (1) (1)

3 — Frank Mullins, ss; B: Oakland, CA; Santa Clara University; 1980 CHW (1) (3)

June — Secondary Phase
1— Bob Fallon, lhp; B: Bronx, NY; Miami–Dade North CC; 1984 CHW (2) (2)

1980

January — Regular Phase
3 — Jim Siwy, rhp; B: Central Falls, RI; University of Rhode Island; 1982 CHW (2) (2)

January — Secondary Phase
1— Tim Hulett, 2b; B: Springfield, IL; Miami–Dade North CC; 1983 CHW (5) (12)

June — Regular Phase
1— Cecil Espy, of; B: San Diego, CA; Point Loma HS, San Diego, CA; 1983 LAD (1) (8)

1981

June — Regular Phase
1— Daryl Boston, lhp; B: Cincinnati, OH; Woodward HS, Cincinnati, OH; 1984 CHW (7) (12)

4 — Craig Smajstria, ss; B: Houston, TX; Pearland HS, TX; 1988 HOU (1) (1)

8 — Wade Rowdon, ss; B: Riverhead, NY; Stetson University; 1984 CIN (3) (5)

13 — Al Jones, rhp; B: Charleston, MI; Alcorn State University; 1983 CHW (3) (3)

1982

January — Regular Phase
4 — John Cangelosi, of; B: Brooklyn, NY; Miami–Dade North CC; 1988 PIT (1) (1)

June — Regular Phase
1— Ron Karkovice, c; B: Union, NJ; Boone HS, Orlando, FL; 1986 CHW (9) (9)

3 — Kenny Williams, of; B: Berkeley, CA; Mt. Pleasant HS, San Jose, CA; 1986 CHW (3) (6)

7 — Mike Trujillo, rhp; B: Denver, CO; University of Northern Colorado; 1985 BOS (2) (6)

June — Secondary Phase
1— Joel McKeon, lhp; B: Covington, KY; Miami–Dade North CC; 1986 CHW (2) (2)

1983

June — Regular Phase
1— Joel Davis, rhp; B: Jacksonville, FL; Sandalwood HS, Jacksonville, FL; 1985 CHW (4) (4)

1— Russ Morman, 1b; B: Independence, MO; Wichita State University; 1986 CHW (3) (8)

4 — Bruce Tanner, rhp; B: New Castle, PA; FSU; 1985 CHW (1) (1)

11— Doug Drabek, rhp; B: Victoria, TX; University of Houston; 1986 NYY (1) (13)

1984

June — Regular Phase
5 — Adam Peterson, rhp, Timpview HS, Provo, Utah, 1987 CHW (4) (5)

1985

January — Regular Phase
3 — Tony Scruggs, of; B: Riverside, CA; Mt. San Antonio (CA) JC, 1991 TEX (1) (1)

June — Regular Phase
2 — Jose Mota, 2b; B: Santo Domingo, DR; Cal State Fullerton; 1991 SDN (1) (2)

4 — Bobby Thigpen, rhp; B: Tallahassee, FL; Mississippi State University, 1986 CHW (8) (9)

6 — John Pawlowski, rhp; B: Johnson City, NY; Clemson University, 1987 CHW (2) (2)

10 — Wayne Edwards, lhp; B: Burbank, CA; Azusa Pacific University, 1989 CHW (3) (3)

17 — Tom Drees, lhp; B: Des Moines, IA; Creighton University, 1991 CHW (1) (1)

19 — Randy Velarde, ss; B: Midland, TX; Lubbock Christian College; 1987 NYY (9) (12)

23 — Donn Pall, rhp; B: Chicago, IL; University of Illinois; 1988 CHW (6) (11)

1986

June — Regular Phase
3 — Scott Radinsky, lhp; B: Glendale, CA; Simi Valley (CA) HS, 1990 CHW (4) (9)

7 — Matt Merullo, c; B: Winchester, MA; University of North Carolina, 1989 CHW (4) (6)

12 — Mark Davis, of; B; San Diego, CA; Stanford University, 1991 CAL (1) (1)

1987

1— Jack McDowell, rhp; B: Van Nuys, CA; Stanford University; 1987 CHW (7) (11)

2 — Brent Knackert, rhp; B: Los Angeles, CA; Ocean View HS, Huntington Beach, CA, 1990 SEA (1) (2)

5 — Dan Rohrmeier, 3b; B: Cincinnati, OH; St. Thomas University, FL; 1997 SEA (1) (1)

6 — Jerry Kutzier, rhp; B: Waukegan, WI; William Penn College, 1990 CHW (1) (1)

10 — Rob Lukachyk, ss, B: Jersey City, NJ; Brookdale (NJ) CC, 1996 MON (1) (1)

12 — Buddy Groom, lhp; B: Dallas, TX; University of Mary Hardin–Baylor; 1992 DET (4) (7)

13 — Dwayne Hosey, of; B: Sharon, PA; Altadena, CA; 1995 BOS (2) (2)

1988

1— Robin Ventura, 3b; B: Santa Maria, CA; Oklahoma State University, 1989 CHW (10) (10)

3 — Stacy Jones, rhp; B: Gadsden, AL; Auburn University; 1991 BAL (1) (2)

4 — Johnny Ruffin, rhp; B: Butler, AL; Choctaw County HS, Butler, AL. 1993 CIN (4)(4)

10— John Hudek, rhp; B: Tampa, FL; Florida Southern College; 1994 HOU (5) (6)

42 — Derek Lee, inf-of; B: Chicago, IL; University of South Florida;1993 MIN (1) (1)

1989

1— Frank Thomas, 1b; B: Columbus, GA; Auburn University, 1990 CHW (9) (9)

19 — Brian Keyser, rhp; B: Pensacola, FL; Stanford University, 1995 CHW (2) (2)

32 — Joe Borowski, rhp; B: Bayonne, NJ; Marist HS, Bayonne, NJ; 1995 BAL (1) (3)

1990

1— Alex Fernandez, rhp; B: Miami Beach, FL; Miami–Dade South CC; 1990 CHW (7) (9)

2 — Bob Wickman, rhp; B: Green Bay, WI; University of Wisconsin–Whitewater; 1992 NYY (5) (7)

3 — Robert Ellis, rhp; B: Baton Rouge, LA; Panola JC, TX; 1996 CAL (1) (1)

4 — James Baldwin, rhp; B: Southern Pines, NC; Pinecrest HS, Southern Pines, NC; 1995 CHW (4) (4)

5 — Ray Durham, 2b; B: Charlotte, NC; Harding HS, Charlotte, NC; 1995 CHW (4) (4)

12 — Jimmy Hurst, of; B: Druid City, AL; Three Rivers JC, MO; 1997 DET (1) (1)

13 — Rod Bolton, rhp; B: Chattanooga, TN; University of Kentucky; 1993 CHW (2) (2)

36 — Jason Bere, rhp; B: Cambridge, MA; Middlesex (MA) CC; 1993 CHW (5) (5)

1991

1— Scott Ruffcorn, rhp; B: New Braufels, TX; Baylor University; 1993 CHW (4) (5)

2 — Larry Thomas, lhp; B: Miami, FL; University of Miami; 1995 CHW (3) (3)

3 — Mike Robertson, 1b; B: Norwich, CT; USC; 1996 CHW (1) (3)

4 — Brian Boehringer, rhp; B: St. Louis, MO; UNLV; 1995 NYY (3) (4)

11— Alan Levine, rhp; B: Park Ridge, IL; Southern Illinois University; 1996 CHW (2) (3)

12 — Doug Brady, 2b; B: Jacksonville, IL; Liberty University; 1995 CHW (1) (1)

18 — Mike Cameron, of; B: La Grange, GA; La Grange (GA) HS; CHW (4) (4)

31— Mike Bertotti, lhp; B: Jersey City, NJ; Iona College; 1995 CHW (3) (3)

1992

6 — Chris Snopek, ss; B: Cynthiana, KY; University of Mississippi; 1995 CHW (4) (4)

13 — Craig Wilson, 2b; B: Chicago, IL; Kansas State University; 1998 CHW (1) (1)

32 — Chris Tremie, c; B: Houston, TX; University of Houston; 1995 CHW (1) (2)

1993

2 — Greg Norton, 1b; B: San Lendro, CA; University of Oklahoma; 1996 CHW (3) (3)

11— Tom Fordham, lhp; B: San Diego, CA; Grossmont (CA) JC; 1997 CHW (2) (2)

15 — Mike Sirotka, lhp; B: Chicago, IL; LSU; 1995 CHW (4) (4)

48 — Mario Valdez, 1b; B: Hialeah, FL; Miami–Dade North CC; 1997 CHW (1) (1)

1994

1— Mark Johnson, c; B: Wheat Ridge, CO; Warner Robins (GA) HS; 1998 CHW (1) (1)

1— Chris Clemons, rhp; B; Baytown, TX; Texas A&M University; 1994 CHW (1) (1)

3 — Carlos Castillo, rhp; B: Boston, MA; Southwest HS, Miami, FL; 1997 CHW (2) (2)

4 — Jeff Abbott, of, B: Atlanta, GA; University of Kentucky; 1997 CHW (2) (2)

1996

13 — Chad Bradford, rhp; B: Jackson, MS; University of Southern Mississippi; 1998 CHW (1) (1)

1997

1— Jim Parque, lhp; B: Norwalk, CA; UCLA; 1998 CHW (1) (1)

Cleveland Indians

1965

June — Regular Phase

1— Ray Fosse, c; B: Marion, IL; Marion HS, IL; 1967 CLE (6) (12)

9 — Vic Albury, 1b-lhp; B: Key West, FL; Key West (FL) HS; 1973 MIN (4) (4)

1966

January — Regular Phase

1— Ted Ford, of-ss; B: Vineland, NJ; Richland, NJ; 1970 CLE (3) (4)

4 — Phil Hennigan, rhp; B: Jasper, TX; Sam Houston State University; 1969 CLE (4) (5)

June — Regular Phase

14 — Russ Nagelson, 1b; B: Jasper, TX; Ohio State University; 1969 CLE (4) (5)

27 — Billy Harris, ss-2b; B: Hamlet, NC; University of North Carolina;1968 CLE (1) (2)

June — Secondary Phase

4 — Bert Gramly, rhp; B: Dallas, TX; Texas Christian University, TX; 1968 CLE (1) (1)

1967

January — Secondary Phase

4 — Dick Tidrow, rhp; B: San Francisco, CA; Chabot; 1972 CLE (3) (13)

June — Regular Phase

1— Jack Heidemann, ss; B: Brenham, TX; Brenham HS, TX; 1969 CLE (5) (8)

2 — Mark Ballinger, rhp; B: Glendale, CA; Thousand Oaks HS, Newbury Park, CA; 1971 CLE (1) (1)

5 — Ed Farmer, rhp; B: Evergreen Park, IL; St. Rita HS, Chicago, IL; 1971 CLE (3) (11)

9 — Vic Correll, c; B: Washington DC; Georgia Southern College; 1972 BOS (1) (8)

20— Mike Paul, lhp; B: Detroit, MI; University of Arizona; 1968 CLE (4) (8)

34 — Jack Brohamer, ss; B: Maywood, CA; Huntington Beach HS, CA; 1972 CLE (5) (9)

June — Secondary Phase

2 — Eddie Leon, ss; B: Tucson, AZ; University of Arizona; 1968 CLE (5) (8)

3 — Lou Camilli, 3b; B: El Paso, TX; Texas A&M University; 1969 CLE (4) (4)

1968

January — Secondary Phase

3 — Rick Sawyer, rhp; B: Bakersfield, CA; Bakersfield JC; 1974 NYY (2) (4)

June — Regular Phase

3 — Bob Kaiser, lhp; B: Cincinnati, OH; Weber HS, Ogden, UT; 1971 CLE (1) (1)

9 — Larry Doby Johnson, c; B: Cleveland, OH; East Tech HS, Cleveland; 1972 CLE (2) (5)

11— Vince Colbert, rhp; B: Washington DC; East Carolina University; 1970 CLE (3) (3)

12 — Charles Machemehl, rhp; B: Brenham, TX; Texas Christian University; 1971 CLE (1) (1)

18 — John Lowenstein, ss; B: Wolf Point, MT; University of California Riverside; 1970 CLE (8) (16)

June — Secondary Phase

1— Rick Austin, lhp; B: Seattle, WA; Washington State University; 1970 CLE (2) (4)

1969

June — Regular Phase

3 — Alan Ashby, c; B: Long Beach, CA; San Pedro HS, CA; 1973 CLE (4) (17)

8 — Rob Belloir, ss; B: Heidelberg, Germany; Mercer University; 1975 ATL (4) (4)

16 — Buddy Bell, ss; B: Pittsburgh, PA; Moeller HS, Cincinnati, OH; 1972 CLE (7) (18)

June — Secondary Phase

1— Rich Hand, rhp; B: Bellevue, WA; University of Puget Sound; 1970 CLE (2) (5)

1970

January — Regular Phase

1— Chris Chambliss, 1b; B: Dayton, OH; UCLA; 1971 CLE (4) (17)

June — Regular Phase

Major League selection:

1— Steve Dunning, rhp; B: Denver, CO; Stanford University; 1970 CLE (4) (7)

5 — Tommy Smith, of; B: Albemarce, NC; North Carolina State University; 1973 CLE (4) (5)

10 — Dennis Kinney, lhp; B: Toledo, OH; Bedford HS, Temperance, MI; 1978 CLE (1) (6)

26 — Jeff Newman, c-1b; B: Fort Worth, TX; Texas Christian University; 1976 OAK (7) (9)

1971

January — Secondary Phase

5 — Jim Norris, of; B: Brooklyn, NY; University of Maryland; 1977 CLE (3) (4)

June — Regular Phase

3 — Wayne Cage, lhp-1b; B: Monroe, LA; Ruston HS, Choudrant, LA; 1978 CLE (2) (2)

7 — Larry Andersen, rhp; B: Portland, OR; Interlake HS, Bellevue, WA; 1975 CLE (3) (17)

1972

January — Regular Phase

1— Eric Raich, rhp; B: Detroit, MI; USC; 1975 CLE (2) (2)

January — Secondary Phase

1— Duane Kuiper, ss; B; Racine, WI; Southern Illinois University; 1974 CLE (8) (12)

June — Regular Phase

1— Rick Manning, ss; B: Niagara Falls, NY; LaSalle HS, Niagara Falls, NY; 1975 CLE (9) (13)

3 — Dennis Eckersley, rhp; B: Oak, CA; Washington Union HS, Freemont, CA; 1975 CLE (3) (24)

1973

June — Regular Phase
2 — Tommy McMillan, inf; B: Richmond, VA; Jackson University, 1977 SEA (1) (1)
3 — Dave Oliver, inf; B: Stockton, CA; Cal Poly San Luis Obispo; 1977 CLE (1)(1)

1974

June — Regular Phase
1 — Tom Brennan, rhp; B: Chicago, IL; Lewis University; 1981 CLE (3) (5)
18 — Orlando Gonzalez, 1b; B: Havana, Cuba; University of Miami, FL; 1976 CLE (1) (2)

June — Secondary Phase
2 — Sandy Wihtol, rhp; B: Palo Alto, CA; DeAnza JC, CA; 1979 CLE (3) (3)

1975

June — Regular Phase
1 — Rick Cerone, c; B: Newark, NJ; Seton Hall University; 1975 CLE (2) (18)
10 — Dave Schuler, lhp; B: Farmingham, MA; University of New Haven; 1979 CLE (2) (3)

1976

January — Secondary Phase
1 — Garry Hancock, of; B: Tampa, FL; University of South Carolina; 1984 OAK (1) (1)

June — Regular Phase
18 — Ron Hassey, c; B: Tuscon, AZ; University of Arizona; 1978 CLE (7) (14)

1977

June — Regular Phase
6 — Eric Wilkins, rhp; B: St. Louis, MO; Washington State Unversity; 1979 (1) (1)
14 — Kevin Rhomberg, 3b; B: Dubuque, IA; College of St. Francis, IL; 1982 CLE (3) (3)
15 — Jerry Dybzinski, ss; B: Cleveland, OH; Cleveland State University; 1980 CLE (3) (6)

1978

June — Regular Phase
2 — Chris Bando, c; B: Cleveland, OH; ASU; 1981 CLE (8) (10)

1979

June — Regular Phase
1 — Jon Bohnet, lhp; Pasadena, CA; Hogan HS, Vallejo, CA; 1982 CLE (1) (1)
7 — Von Hayes, inf; B: Stockton, CA; St. Mary's College, CA; 1981 CLE (2) (12)

31 — Larry White, rhp; B: San Fernando, CA; San Francisco State University; 1983 LAD (2) (2)

1980

June — Regular Phase
1 — Kelly Gruber, ss; B: Houston, TX; Westlake HS, Austin, TX; 1984 TOR (9) (10)
6 — Rich Thompson, rhp; B: New York, NY; Amherst College; 1985 CLE (1) (3)
13 — Mike Jeffcoat, lhp; B: Pine Bluff, AK; Louisiana Tech University; 1983 CLE (2) (10)
29 — Jack Fimple, ss-3b; Darby, PA; Humboldt State University; 1983 LAD (3) (4)

June — Secondary Phase
1 — Dave Gallagher, of; Trenton, NJ; Mercer County (NJ) CC; 1987 CLE (1) (9)

1981

June — Regular Phase
2 — Neal Heaton, lhp; Holtsville, NY; University of Miami (FL); 1982 CLE (5) (12)
7 — Dwight Taylor, of; Los Angeles, CA; University of Arizona; 1986 KCR (1) (1)

1982

June — Regular Phase
2 — Jim Wilson, 1b; B: Corvallis, OR; Oregon State University; 1985 CLE (1) (2)
13 — Jeff Barkley, rhp; B: Hickory, NC; The Citadel; 1984 CLE (2) (2)

1983

June — Regular Phase
1 — Dave Clark, of; B: Tupelo, MS; Jackson State University; 1986 CLE (4) (14)
2 — Andy Allanson, c; B: Richmond, VA; University of Richmond; 1986 CLE (4) (8)

1984

June — Regular Phase
1 — Cory Snyder, ss; B: Inglewood, CA; BYU; 1986 CLE (5) (10)
2 — John Farrell, rhp; B: Monmouth Beach, NJ; Oklahoma State University; 1987 CLE (4) (8)

June — Secondary Phase
1 — Mark Higgins, 1b; B: Miami, FL; University of New Orleans, LA; 1989 CLE (1) (1)

1985

June — Regular Phase
4 — Scott Jordan, of; B: Waco, TX; Georgia Tech; 1988 (1) (1)
5 — Rod Nichols, rhp; B: Burlington, IA; University of New Mexico; 1988 CLE (5) (6)

9 — Luis Medina, 1b; B: Santa Monica, CA; ASU; 1988 CLE (3) (3)

1986

January — Regular Phase
1— Jeff Shaw, rhp; B: Washington Court House, OH; Cuyahoga (OH) CC; 1990 CLE (3) (10)
2 — Mike Walker, rhp; B: Chicago, IL; Seminole CC, FL; 1988 CLE (3) (3)

June — Regular Phase
1— Greg Swindell, lhp; B: Fort Worth, TX; University of Texas; 1986 CLE (8) (14)
2 — Kevin Wicander, lhp; B: Fort Dodge, IA; Grand Canyon College; 1989 CLE (4) (5)
3 — Joe Skalski, rhp; B: Burnham, IL; St. Xavier College; 1989 CLE (1) (1)
4 — Rudy Seanez, rhp; B: Brawley, CA; Brawley (CA) HS; 1989 CLE (3) (7)
7 — Tommy Hinzo, 2b; B: San Diego, CA; University of Arizona; 1987 CLE (2) (2)
11— Tom Lampkin, c; B: Cincinnati, OH; University of Portland; 1988 CLE (1) (5)

June — Secondary Phase
1— Jim Bruske, of; B: East St. Louis, IL; Loyola Marymount University; 1995 LAD (3) (3)

1987

2 — Joey (Albert) Belle, of; B: Shreveport., LA; LSU; 1989 CLE (8) (11)
5 — Tom Kramer, rhp; B: Cincinnati, OH; Logan JC, IL; 1991 CLE (2) (2)
16 — Steve Olin, rhp; B: Portland, OR; Portland State University; 1989 (4) (4)
25 — Beau Allred, of; B: Mesa, AZ; Lamar University; 1989 CLE (3) (3)

1988

1— Mark Lewis, ss; B: Hamilton, OH; Hamilton (OH) HS; 1991 CLE (4) (8)
1— Charles Nagy, rhp; B: Bridgeport, CN; University of Cincinnati; 1990 CLE (9) (9)
7 — Greg McMichael, rhp; B: Knoxville, TN; University of Tennessee; 1998 ATL (4) (6)

1989

3 — Jerry DiPoto, lhp; B: Jersey City, NJ; Virginia Commonwealth University; 1993 CLE (2) (6)
4 — Jesse Levis, c; B: Philadelphia, PA; University of North Carolina; 1992 CLE (4) (7)
5 — Alan Embree, lhp; B: Vancouver, WA; Prairie HS, Vancouver, WA; 1992 CLE (3) (6)
8 — Curtis Leskanic, rhp; B: Homestead, FL; LSU; 1993 COL (6) (6)
11— Kelly Stinnett, c; B: Lawton, OK; Seminole JC, OK; 1994 NYM (2) (5)
13 — James Thome, ss; B: Peoria, IL; Illinois Central JC; 1991 CLE (8) (8)

17 — Brian Giles, of; B: El Cajon, CA; Granite Hills HS, El Cajon, CA; 1995 CLE (4) (4)
25 — Robert Person, ss-of; B: Lowell, MA; Seminole (OK) JC; 1995 NYM (2) (4)
31— Bill Wertz, rhp; B: Cleveland, OH; Ohio State University; 1993 CLE (2) (2)

1990

1— Tim Costo, ss; B: Melrose Park, IL; University of Iowa; 1992 CIN (2) (2)
2 — Darrell Whitmore, of; B: Front Royal, VA; West Virginia University; 1993 FLA (3) (3)
3 — Jason Hardtke, ss; B: Milwaukee, WI; Leland HS, San Jose, CA; 1996 NYY (2) (3)
7 — David Bell, 3b; B: Cincinnati, OH; Moeller HS, Cincinnati, OH; 1995 CLE (4) (4)
17 — Dave Mlicki, rhp; B: Cleveland, OH; Oklahoma State University; 1992 (2) (6)
18 — Steve Gajkowski, rhp; B: Seattle, WA; Bellevue (WA) CC; 1998 SEA (1) (1)
51— Carlos Crawford, rhp; B: Charlotte, NC; Montreat-Anderson (NC) JC; 1996 PHI (1) (1)

1991

1— Manny Ramirez, 3b-of; B: Santo Domingo, DR; George Washington HS, NY; 1993 (6) (6)
2 — Herbert Perry, 3b; B: Mayo, FL; University of Florida; 1994 CLE (3) (3)
3 — Chad Ogea, rhp; B: Lake Charles, LA; LSU; 1994 CLE (5) (5)
4 — Paul Byrd, rhp; B: Louisville, KY; LSU, 1995 NYM (2) (4)
7 — Pep Harris, rhp; B: Lancaster, SC; Lancaster (SC) HS; 1996 CAL (3) (3)
20— Albie Lopez, rhp; B: Mesa, AZ; Mesa (AZ) CC; 1993 CLE (6) (6)
44 — Damian Jackson, ss; B: Los Angeles, CA; Ygnacio Valley HS, Concord, CA; 1996 CLE (2) (3)

1992

1— Paul Shuey, rhp; B: Lima, OH; UNC; 1994 CLE (5) (5)
3 — Jon Nunnally, of; B: Pelham, NC; Miami–Dade CC South, FL; 1995 KC (3) (4)
12 — Mitch Meluskey, c; B: Yakima, WA; Eisenhower HS, Yakima, WA; 1998 HOU (1) (1)

1993

8 — Steve Kline, lhp; B: Sunbury, PA; West Virginia, University; 1993 CLE (1) (2)
15 — Roland Delamaza, rhp; B: Granada Hills, CA; Cal State Sacramento; 1997 KCR (1) (1)
24 — Rickie Sexson, 1b; B: Portland, OR; Prairie HS, Brush Prairie, WA; 1997 CLE (2) (2)

1994

1— Jaret Wright, rhp; B: Anaheim, CA; Katella HS, Anaheim, CA; 1997 CLE (2) (2)

4 — Danny Graves; rhp; B: Saigon, Vietnam; Univesity of Miami; 1996 CLE (2) (3)

7 — Russell Branyan, 3b; B: Warner Robins, GA; Strafford Academy, Warner Robins, GA; 1998 CLE (1) (1)

30— Bruce Aven, of; B: Orange, Texas; Lamar University; 1997 CLE (1) (1)

1995

2 — Sean Casey, 1b; B: Willingboro, NJ; University of Richmond; 1997 CLE (1) (2)

14 — Scott Winchester, rhp; B: Midland, MI; Clemson University; 1997 CIN (2) (2)

25 — Jason Rakers, rhp; B: Pittsburgh, PA; New Mexico State University; 1998 CLE (1) (1)

Detroit Tigers

1965

June — Regular Phase

1— Gene Lamont, c; B: Rockford, IL; Hiawatha HS, Kirland, IL; 1970 DET (5) (5)

10— Gary Taylor, rhp; B: Detroit, MI; Central Michigan University; 1969 DET (1) (1)

37 — Bill Butler, lhp; B: Hyattsville, MD; Herndon (VA) HS; 1969 KCA (3) (7)

1966

January — Regular Phase

4 — Jon Warden, lhp; B: Columbus, OH; Harrisburg (OH) HS; 1968 DET (1) (1)

June — Regular Phase

4 — Leslie Cain, lhp; B: San Luis Obispo, CA; El Cerrito (CA) HS; 1968 DET (4) (4)

June — Secondary Phase

2 — Robert Reed, rhp; B: Boston, MA; University of Michigan; 1969 DET (2) (2)

1967

January — Secondary Phase

1— Mike Adams, ss; Cincinnati, OH; Fullerton JC, CA; 1972 MIN (2) (5)

June — Regular Phase

1— Jim Foor, lhp; B: St Louis, MO; McClure HS, Ferguson, MO; 1971 DET (2) (3)

5 — Paul Jata, c; B: Queens, NY; Long Island City (NY) HS; 1972 DET (1) (1)

6 — Dennis Saunders, rhp; B: Alhambra, CA; Pioneer HS, Whittier, CA; 1970 DET (1) (1)

15 — Isiah Blessitt, of; B: Detroit, MI; Hamtramck (MI) HS; 1972 DET (1) (1)

36 — Gary Ignasiak, lhp; B: Mt. Clemens, MI; St. Mary's HS, Anchorville, MI; 1973 DET (1) (1)

1968

January — Regular Phase

7 — Bill Slayback, rhp; B: Hollywood, CA; Glendale JC, CA; 1972 DET (3) (3)

January — Secondary Phase

1— Kenneth Szotkiewicz, ss; B: Willmington, DE; Geogria Southern College; 1970 DET (1) (1)

2 — Chuck Scrivener, ss; Alexandria, VA; CC of Baltimore; 1975 DET (3) (3)

June — Regular Phase

2 — Bob Molinaro, of; B: Newark, NJ; Essex Catholic HS, Newark, NJ; 1975 DET (3) (8)

10— Marvin Lane, of; B: Sandersville, GA; Pershing HS, Detroit, MI; 1971 DET (5) (5)

18 — Bob Strampe, rhp; B: Janesville, WI; Janesville (WI) HS; 1972 DET (1) (1)

June — Secondary Phase

1— Elliott Maddox, inf-of; B: East Orange, NJ; University of Michigan; 1970 DET (1) (11)

1969

June — Regular Phase

3 — Bill Gilbreth, lhp; B: Abilene, TX; Abilene Christian University; 1971 DET (2) (3)

6 — Lerrin LaGrow, rhp; B: Portland, ME; ASU; 1979 HOU (1) (6)

1970

June — Regular Phase

8 — John Knox, 2b; Newark, NJ; Bowling Green State University; 1972 DET (4) (4)

9 — Phil Mankowski, 3b; Buffalo, NY; Bishop Turner HS, Cheektowaga, NY; 1976 DET (4) (7)

10— Fernando Arroyo, rhp; B: Sacramento, CA; Burbank HS, Sacramento, CA; 1975 DET (4) (8)

21— Fred Holdsworth, rhp; B: Detroit, MI; Northville (MI) HS; 1972 DET (3) (7)

June — Secondary Phase

1— Chuck Seelbach, rhp; B: Lakewood, OH; Dartmouth College; 1971 DET (4) (4)

1971

June — Regular Phase

1— Tom Veryzer, ss; B; Port Jefferson, NY; Islip (NY) HS; 1973 DET (5) (11)

2 — Dennis DeBarr, lhp; B: Cheyenne, WY; Kennedy HS, Fremont, CA; 1977 TOR (1) (1)

7 — Gene Pentz, rhp; Johnstown, PA; Johnston (PA) HS; 1975 DET (1) (4)

13 — Gary Christenson, lhp; B: Mineola, NY; New Hyde Park (NY) Memorial HS; 1979 KCA (2) (2)

June — Secondary Phase

2 — Danny Fife, rhp; B: Harrisburg, IL; University of Michigan; 1973 MIN (2) (2)

3 — Ron Cash, ss; B: Atlanta, GA; FSU; 1973 DET (2) (2)

1972

January — Regular Phase

2 — Dan Gonzales, of; B: Whittier, CA; Fullerton (CA) JC; 1979 DET (2) (2)

6 — Art James, of; B: Detroit, MI; Macomb (MI) CC; 1975 Det (1) (1)

June — Regular Phase

1— Jerry Manuel, ss; B: Hahira, GA; Rancho Cordova (CA) HS; 1975 DET (2) (5)

4 — Dan Meyer, 2b; B: Hamilton, OH; Santa Ana JC, CA; 1974 DET (3) (11)

10— Leon Roberts, of; B: Vicksburg, MI; University of Michigan; 1974 DET (2) (11)

16 — Dave Lemanczyk, rhp; B: Syracuse, NY; Hartwick College; 1973 DET (4) (7)

17 — Vern Ruhl, rhp; Midland, MI; Olivet College; 1974 DET (4) (13)

19 — Mark Wagner, ss; B: Conneault, OH; Harbor HS, Ashtabula, OH; 1976 DET (5) (9)

27 — George Cappuzzello, lhp; B: Youngstown, OH; Ursuline Catholic HS, Girard, OH; 1981 DET (1) (2)

1973

June — Regular Phase

3 — Bob Adams, 3b; B: Pittsburgh, PA; UCLA; 1977 DET (1) (1)

1974

June — Regular Phase

1— Lance Parrish, inf; B: McKeesport, PA; Walnut HS, Diamond Bar, CA; 1977 DET (10) (19)

10— Mark Fidrych, rhp; B: Northboro, MA; Worcester Academy HS, Northboro, MA; 1976 DET (5) (5)

19 — Bob Sykes, lhp; B: Neptune, NY; Miami–Dade North CC; 1977 DET (2) (5)

1975

January — Regular Phase

1— Tom Brookens, ss; B: Chambersburg, PA; Mansfield University; 1979 DET (10) (12)

January — Secondary Phase

1— Dave Tobik, rhp; B: Euclid, OH; Ohio University; 1978 DET (5) (8)

4 — Dave Rozema, rhp; B: Grand Rapids, MI; Grand Rapids JC; 1977 DET (8) (1)

June — Regular Phase

4 — Jason Thompson, lhp-1b; B: Hollywood, CA; Cal State Northridge; 1976 DET (5) (11)

5 — Lou Whitaker, 3b; B: Brooklyn, NY; Martinsville (VA) HS; 1977 DET (19) (19)

1976

January — Regular Phase

1— Steve Kemp, of; B: San Angelo, TZ; USC; 1977 DET (5) (11)

June — Regular Phase

1— Pat Underwood, lhp; B: Kokomo, IN; Kokomo (IN) HS; 1978 DET (5) (5)

2 — Alan Trammell, ss; B: Garden Grove, CA; Kearny HS, San Diego, CA; 1977 DET (20 (20)

4 — Dan Petry, rhp; B: Palo Alto, CA; El Dorado HS, Placentia, CA; 1979 DET (9) (13)

5 — Jack Morris, rhp; B: St Paul, MN; BYU; 1977 DET (14) (18)

8 — Glenn Gulliver, ss; B: Detroit, MI; Eastern Michigan University; 1982 BAL (2) (2)

16 — Roger Weaver, rhp; B: Amsterdam, NY; SUNY-Oneonta; 1980 DET (1) (1)

23 — Kip Young, rhp; B: Georgetown, OH; Bowling Green State University; 1978 DET (2) (2)

June — Secondary Phase

1— Dave Stegman, of; B: Inglewood, CA; University of Arizona; 1978 DET (3) (6)

1977

January — Secondary Phase

1— Mike Chris, lb; B: Santa Monica, CA; West Los Angeles JC; 1979 DET (1) (3)

June — Regular Phase

3 — Darrell Brown, of; B: Oklahoma City, OK; Cal State; 1981 DET (1) (3)

7 — Ricky Peters, of; B: Lynwood, CA; ASU; 1979 DET (3) (5)

14 — Bruce Robbins, lhp; B: Portland, IN; Blackford HS, Dunkirk, IN; 1979 DET (2) (2)

1978

January — Regular Phase

1— Chris Codiroli, rhp; B: Oxnard, CA; San Jose CC, CA; 1982 OAK (6) (8)

June — Regular Phase

1— Kirk Gibson, of; B: Pontiac, MI; Michigan State University; 1979 DET (12) (17)

4 — Jerry Ujdur, rhp; B: Duluth, MN; University of Minnesota; 1980 DET (4) (5)

5 — Marty Castillo, 3b; B: Long Beach, CA; Chapman College; 1981 DET (5) (5)

7 — Bruce Fields, of; B: Cleveland, OH; Everett HS, Lansing, MI; 1986 DET (1) (3)

16 — Dave Rucker, lhp; B: San Bernardino, CA; University of LaVerne; 1981 DET (3) (7)

27 — John Martin, lhp; B: Wyandotte, MI; Eastern Michigan University; 1980 STL (4) (5)

1979

January — Secondary Phase

1— Howard Johnson, 3b; B: Clearwater, FL; St. Petersburg JC, 1982 DET (3) (14)

June — Regular Phase

1— Rick Leach, of; B: Ann Arbor, MI; University of Michigan; 1981 DET (3) (10)

12 — Mike Warren, rhp; B: Inglewood, CA; Fullerton HS, Garden Grove, CA; 1983 OAK (3) (3)

1980

January — Regular Phase
1— Mike Laga, 1b; B: Ridgewood, NJ; Bergen CC; 1982 DET (5) (9)

June — Regular Phase
1— Glenn Wilson, 3b; B: Baytown, TX; San Houston State University, TX; 1982 DET (2) (12)
10— Chuck Hensley, lhp; B: Tulare, CA; University of California; 1986 SFG (1) (1)
11— Dwight Lowry, c; B: Lumberton, NC; University of North Carolina; 1984 DET (3) (4)
30— Ron Mathis, rhp; B: Kansas City, MO; University of Missouri; 1985 HOU (2) (2)

1981

January — Secondary Phase
1— Bob Melvin, c; B: Palo Alto, CA; Canada JC, CA; 1985 DET (1) (10)

June — Regular Phase
2 — Nelson Simmons, of; B: Washington, DC; Madison HS, San Diego, CA; 1984 DET (2) (3)
6 — Bryan Kelly, rhp; B: Silver Spring, MD; University of Alabama; 1986 DET (2) (2)
7 — Chuck Cary, lhp; B: Whittier, CA; University of California; 1985 DET (2) (8)
14 — Scotty Earl, 2b; B: Seymour, IN; Eastern Kentucky University; 1984 DET (1) (1)

June — Secondary Phase
1— Randy O'Neal, rhp; B: Asland, KY; University of Florida; 1984 DET (3) (7)

1982

June — Regular Phase
1— Rich Monteleone, rhp; B: Tampa, FL; Tampa (FL) Catholic HS; 1987 SEA (1) (10)
3 — Colin Ward, lhp; B: Los Angeles, CA; UCLA; 1985 SFG (1) (1)
6 — Chris Pittaro, ss; B: Trenton, NJ; University of North Carolina; 1985 DET (1) (3)
9 — Doug Baker, ss; B: Fullerton, CA; ASU; 1984 DET (4) (7)
30— Don Heinkel, rhp; B: Racine, WI; Wichita State University; 1988 DET (1) (2)
31— Don Gordon, rhp; B: New York, NY; University of South Carolina; 1986 TOR (2) (3)

1983

June — Regular Phase
3 — Jeff M. Robinson, rhp; B: Ventura, CA; Azusa Pacific University; 1987 DET (4) (6)
9 — Jim Walewander, 2b; B: Chicago, IL; Iowa State University; 1987 DET (2) (4)
23 — Carl Willis, rhp; B: Danville, VA; University of North Carolina, Wilmington; 1984 DET (1) (9)

1984

June — Regular Phase
4 — Mike Henneman, rhp; B: St. Charles, MO; Oklahoma State University; 1987 DET (9) (10)

1985

June — Regular Phase
1— Randy Nosek, rhp; B: Omaha, NE; Chillicothe (MO) HS; 1989 DET (2) (2)
3 — Steve Searcy, lhp; B: Knoxville, TN; University of Tennessee; 1988 DET (4) (5)
6 — Scott Lusader, of; B: Chicago, IL; University of Florida; 1987 DET (4) (5)
7 — Doug Strange, 2b; B: Greenville, SC; North Carolina State University; 1989 DET (1) (9)
15 — Mark Lee, lhp; B: Williston, ND; Florida International University; 1988 KCR (1) (4)
22 — John Smoltz, rhp; B: Warren, MI; Waverly HS, Lansing, MI; 1988 ATL (11) (11)

June — Secondary Phase
4 — Kevin Ritz, rhp; B: Eatontown, NJ; Indian Hills CC; 1989 DET (4) (9)

1986

June — Regular Phase
2 — Milt Cuyler, of; B: Macon, GA; Southwest Macon (GA) HS; 1990 DET (6) (8)
4 — Billy Bean, of; B: Santa Ana, CA; Loyola Marymount University; 1987 DET (3) (6)
19 — Chris Hoiles, c; B: Bowling Green, OH; Eastern Michigan University; 1989 BAL (10) (10)

1987

1— Steve Pegues, of; B: Pontotoc, MS; Pontotoc (MS) HS; 1994 CIN (1) (2)
1— Travis Fryman, 3b; B: Lexington, KY; Tate HS, Gonzalez, FL; 1990 DET (8) (9)
2 — Rob Richie, of; B: Reno, NV; University of Nevada–Reno; 1989 DET (1) (1)
5 — Torey Lovullo, 2b; B: Santa Monica, CA; UCLA; 1988 DET (2) (7)
21— Mike Schwabe, rhp; B: Fort Dodge, IA; ASU; 1989 DET (2) (2)
33 — Rusty Meacham, rhp; B: Stuart, FL; Indian River CC, FL; 1991 DET (1) (6)

1988

1— Rico Brogna, 1b-lhp; B: Turner Falls, MA; Watertown (CN) HS; 1992 DET (1) (6)
2 — Scott Livingstone, 3b; B; Dallas, TX; Texas A&M University; 1998 DET (4) (8)
9 — Kurt Knudsen, rhp; B: Arlington Heights, IL; University of Miami; 1992 DET (3) (3)
15 — David Haas, rhp; B: Independence, MO; Wichita State University; 1991 DET (3) (3)
17 — Rich Rowland, c; B: Cloverdale, CA; Mendocino CC, CA; 1990 DET (3) (5)

1989

1— Greg Gohr, rhp; Santa Clara, CA; Santa Clara University; 1993 DET (4) (4)

8 — John DeSilva, rhp; B: Fort Bragg, CA; BYU; 1993 DET (1) (2)

28— Ivan Cruz, 1b; B: Fajardo, PR; Jacksonville University; 1997 NYY (1) (1)

1990

1— Tony Clark, of; B: Newton, KS; Christian HS, El Cajon, CA; 1995 DET (4) (4)

5 — Shannon Withem, rhp; B: Ann Arbor, MI; Willow Run HS, Ypsilanti, MI; 1998 TOR (1) (1)

14— Ben Blomdahl, rhp; B: Long Beach, CA; Riverside (CA) CC; 1995 DET (1) (1)

1991

1— Justin Thompson, lhp; B: San Antonio, TX; Klein Oak HS, Spring, TX; 1996 DET (3) (3)

1— Trever Miller, lhp; B: Louisville, KY; Trinity HS, Louisville, KY; 1996 DET (1) (2)

3 — Brian Edmondson, rhp; B: Fontana, CA; Norte Vista HS, Riverside, CA; 1998 ATL (1) (1)

4— Sean Bergman, rhp; B: Joliet, IL; Southern Illinois University; 1993 DET (3) (6)

9— Clint Sodowsky, rhp; B: Ponca City, OK; Connors State JC, OK; 1995 DET (2) (4)

15— Phil Stidham, rhp; B: Tulsa, OK; University of Arkansas; 1991 DET (1) (1)

30— Kevin Morgan, ss; B: Lafayette, LA; Southeastern Louisiana University; 1997 NYM (1) (1)

1992

3 — Chris Gomez, ss; B: Los Angeles, CA; Long Beach State University; 1993 DET (4) (6)

7— Pat Ahearne, rhp; B: San Francisco, CA; Pepperdine University; 1995 DET (1) (1)

10— Frank Catalanotto, 2b; B: Smithtown, NY; Smithtown (NY) HS; 1997 DET (2) (2)

11— Sean Whiteside, lhp; B: Lakeland, FL; UNC Charlotte; 1995 DET (1) (1)

12— Bob Higginson, of; B: Philadelphia, PA; Temple University; 1995 DET (4) (4)

20— Brian Maxcy, rhp; B: Amory, MS; University of Mississippi; 1995 DET (2) (2)

1993

6 — Brian Moehler, rhp; B: Rockingham, NC; UNC Greensboro; 1996 DET (3) (3)

12— Bryan Corey, rhp; B: Thousand Oaks, CA; Pierce JC; 1998 ARZ (1) (1)

13— Eddie Gaillard, rhp; B: Camden, NJ; Florida Southern College; 1997 DET (1) (2)

1994

11— Bubba Trammell, of; B: Knoxville, TN; University of Tennessee; 1997 DET (1) (2)

15— Daryl Ward, of; B: Lynwood, CA; Rancho Santiago JC, CA; 1998 HOU (1) (1)

1995

2 — Brian Powell, rhp; B: Bainbridge, GA; University of Georgia; 1998 DET (1) (1)

57 — Gabe Kapler, of; B: Hollywood, CA; Moorpark (CA) JC; 1998 DET (1) (1)

1996

1— Seth Greisinger, rhp; B: Kansas City, KS; University of Virginia; 1998 DET (1)

5 — Robert Fick, c; B: Torrance, CA; Cal State Northridge; 1998 DET (1) (1)

1997

1— Matt Anderson, rhp; B: Louisville, KY; Rice University; 1998 DET (1) (1)

Kansas City Royals

1968

June — Regular Phase

7 — Lance Clemons, lhp; B: Philadelphia, PA; West Chester University; 1971 KCR (1) (3)

9 — Monty Montgomery, rhp; B: Albemarle, NC; Pfeiffer College; 1971 KCR (2) (2)

25 — Paul Splittorff, lhp; B: Evansville, IN; Morningside College; 1970 KCR (15) (15)

1969

June — Regular Phase

4 — Al Autry, rhp; B: Modesto, CA; Grace Davis HS, Modesto, CA; 1976 ATL (1) (1)

5 — Keith Marshall, of; B: San Francisco, CA; Loara HS, Anaheim, CA; 1973 KCR (1) (1)

16 — Jim York, rhp; B: Maywood, CA; UCLA; 1970 KCR (2) (7)

47 — Frank Ortenzio, of; B: Fresno, CA; San Joaquin Memorial HS, Fresno, CA; 1973 KCR (1) (1)

75 — Al Cowens, ss; B: Los Angeles, CA; Centennial HS, Los Angeles, CA; 1974 KCR (6) (13)

June — Secondary Phase

3 — Doug Bird, rhp; B: Corona, CA; Mt. San Antonio JC, CA; 1973 KCR (6) (11)

1970

January — Regular Phase

3 — Greg Minton, rhp; B: Lubbock, TX; San Diego Mesa JC; 1975 SFG (13) (16)

January — Secondary Phase

3 — Jim Wohlford, ss; B: Visalia, CA; College of the Sequoias, CA; 1972 KCR (5) (15)

June — Regular Phase

4 — Tom Poquette, of; B: Eau Claire, WI; Memorial HS, Eau Claire, WI; 1973 KCR (5) (7)

1971

January — Regular Phase

1 — John Wathan, c; B: Cedar Rapids, IA; University of San Diego; 1976 KCR (10) (10)

June — Regular Phase

1 — Roy Branch, rhp; B: St. Louis, MO; Beaumont HS, St. Louis, MO; 1979 SEA (1) (1)

2 — George Brett, ss; B: Glendale, WV; El Segundo (CA) HS; 1973 KCR (21) (21)

4 — Joe Zdeb, 3b; B: Compton, IL; Maine South HS, Park Ridge, IL; 1977 KCR (3) (3)

12 — Mark Littell, rhp; B: Cape Girardeau, MO; Gideon HS, MO; 1973 KCR (4) (9)

June — Secondary Phase Delayed

2 — Steve Busby, rhp; B: Burbank, CA; USC; 1972 KCR (8) (8)

June — Secondary Phase Active

2 — Steve Staggs, inf; B: Anchorage, AK; Cerritos JC, CA; 1977 TOR (1) (2)

1972

June — Regular Phase

1 — Jamie Quirk, ss; B: Whittier, CA; St Paul HS, Whittier, CA; 1975 KCR (11) (18)

2 — Dennis Leonard, rhp; B: Brooklyn, NY; Iona College; 1974 KCR (12) (12)

11 — Rodney Scott, 3b; B: Indianapolis, IN; Arlington HS, Indianapolis; 1975 KCR (1) (8)

16 — George Throop, rhp; B: Pasadena, CA; Cal State Long Beach, CA; 1975 KCR (4) (14)

1973

June — Regular Phase

3 — Ruppert Jones; B: Dallas, TX; Berkeley HS, CA; 1976 KCR (11) (12)

June — Secondary Phase

3 — Bob McClure, lhp; B: Oakland, CA; College of San Mateo, CA; 1975 KCR (2) (19)

1974

January — Regular Phase

1 — Mark Souza, lhp; B: Redwood City, CA; College of San Mateo, CA; 1980 OAK (1) (1)

6 — Bobby Castillo, rhp; B: Los Angeles, CA; Los Angeles Valley JC; 1977 LAD (5) (9)

June — Regular Phase

1 — Willie Wilson, of; B: Montgomery, AL; Summit HS, NJ; 1976 KCR (15) (19)

1975

June — Regular Phase

1 — Clint Hurdle, of; B: Big Rapids, MI; Merritt Island HS, FL; 1977 KCR (5) (10)

5 — Rich Gale, rhp; B: Littleton, NH; University of New Hampshire; 1978 KCR (4) (7)

11 — Danny Garcia, of; B: Brooklyn, NY; Baruch College; 1981 KCR (1) (1)

14 — Randy McGilberry, rhp; B: Mobile, AL; Louisiana Tech; 1977 KCR (2) (2)

1976

January — Secondary Phase

3 — Bill Paschall, rhp; B: Norfolk, VA; University of North Carolina; 1978 KCR (3) (3)

June — Regular Phase

6 — Jim Gaudet, c; B: New Orleans, LA; Tulane University; 1978 KCR (2) (2)

15 — Ken Phelps, of; B: Seattle, WA; ASU; 1980 KCR (2) (11)

1977

June — Regular Phase

1 — Mike Jones, lhp; B: Penfield, NY; Sutherland HS, Pittsford, NY; 1980 KCR (4) (4)

7 — Kelly Heath, ss; B: Plattsburgh, NY; Louisburg, JC, NC; 1982 KCR (1) (1)

19 — Renie Martin, rhp; B: Dover, DE; University of Richmond; 1979 KCR (3) (6)

1978

June — Regular Phase

1 — Buddy Biancalana, ss; B: Larkspur, CA; Redwood HS, Greenbrae, CA; 1982 KCR (6) (6)

2 — Darryl Motley, of; B: Muskogee, OK; Grant HS, Portland, OR; 1981 KCR (5) (6)

3 — Mark Royal, lhp; B: Henryetta, OK; Dewar HS, OK; 1982 KCR (1) (6)

8 — Jeff Cornell, rhp; B: Kansas City, MO; University of Mississippi; 1984 SFG (1) (1)

24 — Ron Johnson, 1b; B: Long Beach, CA; Fresno State University; 1982 KCR (2) (3)

June — Secondary Phase

1 — Craig Chamberlain, rhp; B: Hollywood, CA; University of Arizona; 1979 KCR (2) (2)

2 — Bill Laskey, rhp; B: Toledo, OH; Kent State University; 1982 SFG (5) (6)

1979

January — Regular Phase

1 — Mike Brewer, rhp; B: Shreveport, LA; Foothill JC, CA; 1986 KCR (1) (1)

January — Secondary Phase

1 — Jeff Schattinger, rhp; B: Fresno, CA; USC; 1981 KCR (1) (1)

June — Regular Phase

1— Atlee Hammaker, lhp; B: Carmel, CA; East Tennessee State University; 1981 KCR (1) (12)

3 — Pat Sheridan, of; B: Ann Arbor, MI; Eastern Michigan University; 1981 KCR (4) (9)

25 — Jeff Twitty, lhp; B: Lancaster, SC; University of South Carolina; 1980 KCR (1) (1)

1980

June — Regular Phase

1— Frank Wills, rhp; B: New Orleans, LA; Tulane University; 1983 KCR (2) (9)

6 — Rondin Johnson, 2b; B: Bremerton, WA; University of Washington; 1986 KCR (1) (1)

7 — Don Slaught, c; B: Long Beach, CA; UCLA; 1982 KCR (3) (15)

8 — Cliff Pastornicky, ss; B: Seattle, WA; BYU; 1983 KCR (1) (1)

12 — Butch Davis, of; B: Martin County, NC; East Carolina University; 1983 KCR (2) (8)

17 — Tom Romano, of; B: Syracuse, NY; Coastal Carolina College; 1987 MON (1) (1)

June — Secondary Phase

1— Keith Creel, rhp; B: Dallas, TX; University of Texas; 1982 KCR (2) (4)

1981

January — Regular Phase

10 — Bill Pecota, 3b; B: Redwood City, CA; DeAnza JC, CA; 1986 KCR (6) (9)

June — Regular Phase

1— Dave Leeper, of; B: Santa Ana, CA; USC; 1984 KCR (2) (2)

2 — Mark Gubicza, rhp; B: Philadelphia, PA; Penn Charter HS, Philadelphia, PA; 1984 KCR (14) (14)

2 — Tony Ferreira, lhp; B: Quincy, MA; North HS, Riverside, CA; 1985 KCR (1) (1)

3 — Dave Cone, rhp; B: Kansas City, MO; Rockhurst HS, Kansas City, MO; 1986 KCR (3) (13)

7 — John Davis, rhp; B: Chicago, IL; Centennial HS, Pueblo, CO; 1987 KCR (1) (4)

1982

January — Secondary Phase

1— Danny Jackson, lhp; B: San Antonio, TX; Trinidad State JC, CO; 1983 KCR (5) (14)

June — Regular Phase

1— John Morris, of; B: Bellmore, NY; Seton Hall University; 1986 STL (5) (7)

9 — Israel Sanchez, lhp; B: Falcon Lasuias, Cuba; Von Steuben HS, IL; 1988 KCR (2) (2)

19 — Bret Saberhagen, ss; B: Chicago Heights, IL; Cleveland HS, Northridge, CA; 1984 KCR (8) (14)

June — Secondary Phase

4 — Cecil Fielder, 1b; B: Los Angeles, CA; La Puente, CA; 1985 (4) (11)

1983

June — Regular Phase

1— Gary Thurman, of; B: Indianapolis, IN; North Central HS, Indianapolis, IN; 1987 KCR (6) (8)

11— Kevin Seitzer, 3b; B: Springfield, IL; Eastern Illinois University; 1986 KCR (6) (11)

14 — Tom Edens, rhp; B: Ontario, OR; Lewis-Clark State College; 1987 KCR (1) (7)

23 — Jeff Schulz, of; B: Evansville, IN; Indiana State University, Evansville, IN; 1989 KCR (2) (3)

1984

June — Regular Phase

1— Scott Bankhead, rhp; B: Raleigh, NC; University of North Carolina; 1986 KCR (1) (10)

2 — Luis de los Santos, 3b-c; B: San Cristobal, OR; Newtown HS, Elmhurst, NY; 1988 KCR (2) (3)

1985

June — Regular Phase

1— Brian McRae, ss; B: Avon Park, FL; Manatee HS, Blue Springs, FL; 1990 KCR (5) (9)

4 — Mike Macfarlane, c; B: Stockton, CA; Santa Clara University; 1987 KCR (12) (12)

1986

January — Secondary Phase

1— Sean Berry, inf; B: Santa Monica, CA; UCLA; 1990 KCR (2) (9)

June — Regular Phase

4 — Bo Jackson, of; B: Bessamer, AL; Auburn University; 1986 KCR (5) (8)

6 — Tom Gordon, rhp; B: Sebring, FL; Avon Park (FL) HS; 1988 KCR (8) (11)

16 — Greg Hibbard, lhp; B: New Orleans, LA; University of Alabama; 1989 CHW (4) (6)

32 — Dave Howard, of; B: Sarasota, FL; Manatee JC, FL; 1991 KCR (7) (8)

June — Secondary Phase

2 — Mike Butcher, rhp; B: Davenport, IA; Northeastern Oklahoma A&M JC; 1992 CAL (4) (4)

1987

1— Kevin Appier, rhp; B: Lancaster, CA; Antelope Valley JC, CA; 1989 KCR (10) (10)

2 — Terry Shumpert, 2b; B: Paducah, KY; University of Kentucky; 1990 KCR (5) (9)

3 — Stu Cole, ss; B: Charlotte, NC; University of North Carolina–Charlotte; 1990 KCR (1) (1)

58 — Jeff Conine, 3b-1b; B: Tacoma, WA; UCLA; 1990 (2) (8)

1988

2 — Bob Hamelin, 1b; B: Elizabeth, NJ; Rancho Santiago JC, CA; 1993 KCR (4) (6)

14 — Victor Cole, rhp; B: St. Petersburg, Russia; 1992 PIT (1) (1)
16 — Kerwin Moore, of; B: Detroit, MI; Martin Luther King HS, Detroit, MI; 1996 OAK (1) (1)

1989

1— Brent Mayne, c; B: Loma Linda, CA; Cal State Fullerton; 1990 KCR (6) (9)
8 — Mart Karchner, rhp; B: Berwick, PA; Bloomsburg State University, PA; 1995 CHW (4) (4)
1990
8 — Phil Hiatt, 3b; B: Pensacola, FL; Louisiana Tech; 1992 KCR (2) (3)
30 — Brian Bevil, rhp; B: Houston, TX; Angelina (Texas) JC; 1996 KCR (3) (3)

1991

1— Joe Vitello; B: Cambridge, MA; University of Alabama, 1995 KCR (3) (3)
2 — Ryan Long, of; B: Houston, TX; Dobie HS, Pasadena, TX; 1997 KCR (1) (1)
5 — Shane Halter, ss; B: La Plata, MD; Francis Marion College, SC; 1997 KCR (2) (2)
6 — Mike Bovee, rhp; B: Mira Mesa (CA) HS; 1997 ANA (1) (1)
10— Michael Sweeney, c; B: Framingham, MA; Ontario (CA) HS; 1995 KCR (3) (3)
12 — Mike Fyhrie, rhp; B: Long Beach, CA; UCLA; 1996 NYM (1) (1)
13 — Rod Myers, of; B: Conroe, TX; Conroe (TX) HS; 1996 KCR (2) (3)
25 — Les Norman, of; B: Warren, MI; College of St. Francis, IL; 1995 KCR (2) (2)

1992

1— Michael Tucker, ss; B: South Boston, VA; Longwood College; 1995 KCR (2) (4)
1— Johnny Damon, of; B: Fort Riley, KS; Dr. Phillips HS, Orlando, FL; 1995 KCR (4) (4)
2 — Jon Lieber, rhp; B: Council Bluffs, IA; University of South Alabama; 1994 PIT (5) (5)
3 — Chris Eddy, lhp; B: Dallas, TX; Texas Christian University; 1995 OAK (1) (1)
9 — Bart Evans, rhp; B: Springfield, MO; Southwest Missouri State University; 1998 KCR (1) (1)
15 — Mel Bunch, rhp; B: Texarkana, TX; Texarkana (TX) JC; 1995 KCR (1) (1)

1993

1— Jeff Granger, lhp; B: San Pedro, CA; Texas A&M University; 1993 KCR (1) (4)
37 — Sal Fasano, c; B: Chicago, IL; University of Evansville; 1996 KCR (3) (3)

1994

2 — Jed Hansen, 2b; B: Tacoma, WA; Standford University; 1997 KCR (2) (2)
3 — Jamie Bluma, rhp; B: Beaufort, SC; Wichita State University; 1996 KCR (1) (1)
5 — Tim Byrdak, lhp; B: Oak Lawn, IL; Rice University; 1998 KCR (1) (1)

1995

2 — Carlos Beltran, of; B: Manati, P.R.; Manati (P.R.) HS; 1998 KCR (1) (1)

1996

1— Dermal Brown, of; B: Bronx, NY; Varlboro (NY) Central HS; 1998 KCR (1) (1)
6 — Jeremy Giambi, of; B: San Jose, CA; Cal State Fullerton; 1998 KCR (1) (1)

Minnesota Twins

1965

June — Regular Phase
4 — Graig Nettles, 3b; B: San Diego, CA; San Diego State University; 1967 MIN (3) (22)
8 — Ron Keller, rhp; B: Indianapolis, IN; Indiana University; 1966 MIN (2) (2)
44 — Bob Gebhard, rhp; B: Lamberton, MN; University of Iowa; 1971 MIN (2) (3)

1966

January — Regular Phase
3 — Tom Hall, lhp; B: Thomasville, NC; Riverside, CA; 1968 MIN (4) (10)

June — Regular Phase
10 — Steve Braun, ss-2b; B: Trenton, NJ; Hopewell Valley HS, Titusville, NJ; 1971 MIN (6) (15)

June — Secondary Phase
1 — Buzz Stephen, rhp; B: Porterville, CA; Fresno State University; 1968 MIN (1) (1)

1967

June — Regular Phase
1 — Steve Brye, 3b; B: Alameda, CA; Elizabeth HS, Oakland, CA; 1968 MIN (8) (9)
5 — Dave Goltz, rhp; B: Pelican Rapids, MN; Rothsay HS, MN; 1972 MIN (8) (13)
13 — Steve Luebber, rhp; B: Clinton, MO; Joplin HS, MO; 1971 MIN (3) (5)
15 — Rick Dempsey, c; B: Fayetteville, TN; Crespi HS, Simi Valley, CA; 1969 MIN (4) (24)
24 — Jim O'Bradovich, 2b; B: Ft. Campbell, KY; Fort Knox HS, KY; 1978 HOU (1) (1)

June — Secondary Phase
2 — Dan Monzon, ss; B: Bronx, NY; Buena Vista College; 1972 MIN (2) (2)

5 — Mike Sadek, c; B: Minneapolis, MN; University of Minnesota; 1973 SFG (8) (8)

9 — Peter Hamm, rhp; B: Buffalo, NY; Stanford University; 1970 MIN (2) (2)

1968

January — Secondary Phase
1— Eric Soderholm, inf; B: Cortland, NY; South Georgia JC; 1971 MIN (5) (10)

June — Regular Phase
4 — Jim Nettles, of; B: San Diego, CA; San Diego State University; 1970 MIN (3) (6)

18 — Jerry Terrell, 2b; B: Waseca, MN; Mankato State University; 1973 MIN (5) (8)

June — Secondary Phase
1— Danny Thompson, ss; B: Wichita, KA; Oklahoma State University; 1970 MIN (7) (8)

1969

June — Regular Phase
1— Paul Ray Powell, of; B: San Angelo, TX; ASU; 1971 MIN (1) (3)

3 — Bert Blyleven, rhp; B: Zeist, Holland; Santiago, HS, Garden Grove, CA; 1970 MIN (11) (22)

33 — Jim Hughes, rhp; B: Los Angeles, CA; St. Bernard's HS, Los Angeles, CA; 1974 MIN (4) (4)

1970

June — Regular Phase
1— Bob Gorinski, ss; B: Latrobe, PA; Mt. Pleasant HS, Calumet, PA; 1977 MIN (1) (1)

2 — Mark Wiley, rhp; B: National City, CA; La Mesa, CA; 1975 MIN (1) (3)

1971

June — Regular Phase
7 — Dave Edwards, c; B: Los Angeles, CA; Jefferson HS, Los Angeles, CA; 1978 MIN (3) (5)

13 — Rob Wilfong, 2b; B: Pasadena, CA; Northview HS, Covina, CA; 1977 MIN (6) (12)

June — Secondary Phase Delayed
1— Glenn Borgmann, c-1b; B: Paterson, NJ; University of South Alabama; 1972 MIN (8) (9)

1972

June — Regular Phase
3 — Willie Norwood, of; B: Green County, AL; University of LaVerne; 1977 MIN (4) (4)

7 — Randy Bass, 1b; B: Lawton, OK; Lawton HS, OK; 1977 MIN (1) (7)

26 — Lyman Bostock, of; B: Birmingham, AL; Cal State Northridge; 1975 MIN (3) (4)

June — Secondary Phase
2 — Alvis Woods, 1b; B: Oakland, CA; Laney JC; 1977 TOR (6) (7)

1973

June — Regular Phase
1— Eddie Bane, lhp; B: Chicago, IL; ASU; 1973 MIN (3) (3)

7 — Luis Gomez, ss; B: Guadalajara, Mexico; UCLA; 1974 MIN (1) (8)

9 — Larry Wolfe, ss; B: Melbourne, FL; Sacramento CC, CA; 1977 MIN (2) (4)

1974

January — Secondary Phase
1— Jerry Garvin, lhp; B: Oakland, CA; Merced JC, CA; 1977 TOR (6) (6)

June — Regular Phase
2 — Butch Wynegar, c; B: York, PA; Red Lion HS, York, PA; 1976 MIN (7) (13)

14 — Terry Bulling, c; B: Lynwood, CA; Cal State Los Angeles; 1977 MIN (1) (4)

1975

June — Regular Phase
1— Rick Sofield, ss; B: Cheyenne, WY; Morristown HS, NJ; 1979 MIN (3) (3)

5 — Dan Graham, c; B: Ray, AZ; University of La-Verne; 1979 MIN (1) (3)

June — Secondary Phase
1— Hosken Powell, of; B: Selma, AL; Chipola JC, FL; 1978 MIN (4) (6)

1976

January — Regular Phase
1— Bob Veselic, rhp; B: Pittsburg, PA; Mt. San Antonio JC, CA; 1980 MIN (2) (2)

7 — Kevin Stanfield, lhp; B: Huron, SD; San Bernardino Valley JC, CA; 1979 MIN (1) (1)

January — Secondary Phase
1— Pete Redfern, rhp; B: Glendale, CA; USC; 1976 MIN (7) (7)

June — Regular Phase
2 — Terry Felton, rhp; B: Texarkana, AR; Baker (LA) HS; 1979 MIN (4) (4)

3 — John Castino, 3b; B: Evanston, IL; Rollins College; 1979 MIN (6) (6)

16 — Mark Funderburk, of; B: Charlotte, NC; Louisburg JC, NC; 1981 MIN (2) (2)

1977

June — Regular Phase
3 — Roger Erickson, rhp; B: Springfield, IL; University of New Orleans; 1978 MIN (5) (7)

9 — Darrell Jackson, lhp; B: Los Angeles, CA; ASU; 1978 MIN (5) (5)

18 — Scott Ullger, ss; B: New York, NY; St. John's University; 1983 MIN (1) (1)

1978

January — Regular Phase
2 — Jesse Orosco, lhp; B: Santa Barbara, CA; Santa Barbara CC, CA; 1979 NYM (8) (19)

June — Regular Phase
1 — Lenny Faedo, ss; B: Tampa, FL; Jefferson HS, Tampa, FL; 1980 MIN (5) (5)
17 — Kent Hrbek, 1b; B: Minneapolis, MN; Kennedy HS, Bloomington, MN; 1981 MIN (14) (14)

1979

January — Regular Phase
5 — Eddie Hodge, lhp; B: Bellflower, CA; Cerritos JC, CA; 1984 MIN (1) (1)

June — Regular Phase
2 — Randy Bush, of; B: Dover, DE; University of New Orleans; 1982 MIN (12) (12)
3 — Tim Laudner, c; B: Mason City, IA; University of Missouri; 1981 MIN (9) (9)
10 — Mike Kinnunen, lhp; B: Seattle, WA; Washington State University; 1980 MIN (1) (3)

June — Secondary Phase
1 — Gary Gaetti, 3b; B: Centralia, IL; Northwest Missouri State University; 1979 MIN (10) (18)

1980

June — Regular Phase
1 — Jeff Reed, c; B: Joliet, IL; Joliet (IL) West HS; 1984 MIN (3) (15)
2 — Jim Weaver, of; B: Kingston, NY; FSU; 1985 DET (1) (3)
2 — Tim Teufel, 2b; B: Greenwich, CN; Clemson University; 1983 MIN (3) (11)
3 — Scott Madison, c; B: Pensacola, FL; Vanderbilt University; 1985 DET (2) (5)
4 — Rob Booker, ss; B: Los Angeles, CA; University of California; 1987 STL (3) (5)
8 — Andre David, of; B: Hollywood, CA; Cal State Fullergon; 1984 MIN (2) (2)
16 — Jim Eisenreich, of; B: St. Cloud, MN; St. Cloud State University; 1982 MIN (3) (15)
26 — Rich Yett, rhp; B: Pomona, CA; Don Lugo HS, Chino, CA; 1985 MIN (2) (6)

1981

June — Regular Phase
2 — Frank Viola, lhp; B: Hempstead, NY; St. John's University; 1982 MIN (8) (15)
3 — Curt Wardle, lhp; B: Downey, CA; University of California, Riverside, CA; 1984 MIN (2) (3)
5 — Dave Meier, ss; B: Helena, MO; Stanford University; 1984 MIN (2) (4)
9 — Steve Lombardozzi, ss; B: Malden, MA; University of Florida; 1985 MIN (4) (6)

1982

January — Regular Phase
1 — Kirby Puckett, of; B: Chicago, IL; Triton JC, IL; 1984 MIN (12) (12)

June — Regular Phase
1 — Bryan Oelkers, lhp; B: Zaragoza, Spain; Wichita State University; 1983 MIN (1) (2)
2 — Allan Anderson, lhp; B: Lancaster, OH; Lancaster HS, OH; 1986 MIN (6) (6)
11 — Mark Davidson, of; B: Knoxville, TN; Clemson University; 1986 MIN (3) (6)
19 — Marty Pevey, c; B: Savannah, GA; Georgia Southern College; 1986 MON (1) (1)

1984

June — Regular Phase
1 — Jay Bell, ss; B: Elgin, AFB, FL; Gonzalez Tate HS, Pensacola, FL; 1986 CLE (3) (13)
20 — Gene Larkin, 3b-1b; B: Flushing, NY; Columbia University; 1987 MIN (7) (7)

1985

June — Regular Phase
3 — Paul Abbott, rhp, B: Van Nuys, CA; Sunny Hills HS, Fullerton, CA; 1990 MIN (3) (5)
21 — Lenny Webster, c; B: New Orleans, LA; Grambling State University; 1989 MIN (5) (10)

1986

January — Regular Phase
1 — Jarvis Brown, of; B; Waukegan, IL; Triton JC, IL; 1991 MIN (2) (5)
4 — Mike Dyer, rhp; B: Upland, CA; Citrus JC, CA; 1989 MIN (1) (2)

June — Regular Phase
10 — Jeff Reboulet, ss; B: Dayton, OH; LSU; 1992 MIN (5) (7)
13 — Scott Leius, 3b; B: Yonkers, NY; Concordia College, NY; 1990 MIN (6) (8)

1987

1 — Willie Banks, rhp; B: Jersey City, NJ; St. Anthony's HS, Jersey City, NJ; 1991 (2) (7)
2 — Terry Jorgensen, of; B: Kenwaunee, WI; University of Wisconsin, Oshkosh, WI; 1989 MIN (3) (3)
6 — Larry Casian, lhp; B: Lynwood, CA; Cal State Fullerton; 1990 MIN (5) (9)
7 — Mark Guthrie, lhp; B: Buffalo, NY; LSU; 1989 MIN (6) (10)
17 — Chip Hale, 2b; B: San Jose, CA; University of Arizona; 1989 MIN (6) (6)

1988

2 — Alan Newman, lhp; B: La Habra, CA; Fullerton Junior College, CA; 1999 TAM (1) (1)

4 — Steve Dunn, 1b; B: Champaign, IL; Robinson HS, Fairfax, VA; 1994 MIN (2) (2)

6 — Pat Mahomes, rhp; B: Bryan, TX; Lindale (TX) HS; 1992 MIN (4) (6)

9 — Doug Simons, lhp; B: Bakersfield, CA; Pepperdine University; 1991 NYM (1) (2)

11— J.T. Bruett, of; B: Milwaukee, WI; University of Minnesota; 1992 MIN (2) (2)

1989

1— Chuck Knoblauch, ss; B: Houston, TX; Texas A&M University; 1991 MIN (7) (8)

3 — Denny Neagle, lhp; B: Gambrills, MD; University of Minnesota; 1991 MIN (1) (8)

4 — Scott Erickson, rhp; B: Long Beach, CA; University of Arizona; 1990 MIN (6) (9)

10 — Marty Cordova, 3b; B: Las Vegas, NV; Orange Coast (CA) JC; 1995 MIN (4) (4)

12 — Shawn Gilbert, 3b; B: Camden, NJ; Fresno State University; 1997 NYM (2) (2)

14 — Mike Trombley, rhp; B: Springfield, MA; Duke University; 1993 MIN (6) (6)

52 — Dennis Hocking, inf; B: Torrance, CA; El Camino CC, Torrance, CA; 1993 MIN (6) (6)

1990

1— Todd Ritchie, rhp; B: Portsmouth, VA; Duncanville (TX) HS; 1997 MIN (2) (2)

1— Midre Cummings, of; B: St. Croix, Virgin Islands; Edison HS, Miami, FL; 1993 PIT (5) (6)

2 — Jayhawk Owens, c; B: Cincinnati, OH; Middle Tennessee State University; 1993 COL (4) (4)

3 — Rich Becker, of; B: Aurora, IL; Aurora (IL) West HS; 1993 MIN (5) (6)

5 — Brent Brede, of; B: New Baden, IL; Wesclin HS, Trenton, IL; 1996 MIN (2) (3)

12 — Pat Meares, ss; B: Salina, KS; Wichita State University; 1993 MIN (6) (6)

20— Damian Miller, c; B: La Crosse, WI; Viterbo College, WI; 1997 MIN (1) (2)

21— Eddie Guardado, lhp; B: Stockton, CA; San Joaquin Delta JC, CC; 1993 MIN (6) (6)

41— Brian Raabe, 2b; B: New Ulm, MN; University of Minnesota; 1995 MIN (2) (3)

1991

1— Dave McCarty, of; B: Houston, TX; Stanford University, CA; 1993 MIN (3) (6)

1— Scott Stahoviak, 1b; B: Waukegan, IL; Creighton University; 1993 MIN (5) (5)

2 — Mike Durant, c; B: Columbus, OH; Ohio State University; 1996 MIN (1) (1)

7 — LaTroy Hawkins, p; B: Gary, IN; Gary (IN) West Side High School, 1995 MIN (4) (4)

8 — Brad Radke, rhp; B: Eau Claire, WI; Jesuit High School, Tampa, FL; 1995 MIN (4) (4)

13 — Matthew Lawton, of; B: Gulfport, MS; Harrison Central (MS) HS; 1995 MIN (4) (4)

1992

1— Dan Serafini, lhp; B: San Francisco; Serra HS, San Mateo, CA; 1996 MIN (3) (3)

14 — Dan Naulty, rhp; B: Los Angeles, CA; Cal State Fullerton; 1996 MIN (3)(3)

23 — Scott Watkins, lhp; B: Tulsa, OK; Oklahoma State University; 1992 MIN (1) (1)

1993

1— Torii Hunter, of; B: Pine Bluff, AR; Pine Bluff (AR) HS; 1997 MIN (2) (2) (from Reds for John Smiley)

3 — Javier Valentin, c; B: Manati, PR; Fernando Callejo HS, Manati, PR; 1997 MIN (2) (2)

6 — Benj Sampson, lhp; B: Des Moines, IA; Ankeny (IA) HS; 1998 MIN (1) (1)

14 — Ryan Radmanovich, of; B: Calgary, ON, Canada; Pepperdine University; 1998 SEA (1) (1)

21— Shane Bowers, rhp; B: Glendora, CA; Loyola Marymount University; 1997 MIN (1) (1)

1994

1— Todd Walker, 2b; B: Bakersfield, CA; LSU; 1996 MIN (3) (3)

1— Travis Miller, lhp; B: Dayton, OH; Kent University; 1996 MIN (3) (3)

3 — Anthony Pierzynski, c; B: Bride Hampton, NY; Dr. Phillips (FL) High School; 1998 MIN (1) (1)

26 — Cory Koskie, 3b; B: Sorrey, British Columbia, Canada; Springfield Collegiate High School, Oakbank, Manitoba, Canada; 1998 MIN (1) (1)

1995

5 — Douglas Mientkiewicz, 1b; B: Toledo, OH; FSU; 1998 MIN (1) (1)

1996

1— Travis Lee, 1b; B: San Diego, CA; San Diego State State University; 1998 ARZ (1) (1)

New York Yankees

1965

June — Regular Phase
1— Bill Burbach, rhp; B: Diceyville, WI; Wahlert HS, Dickeyville, WI; 1969 NYY (3) (3)

4 — Stan Bahnsen, rhp; B: Council Bluffs, Iowa; University of Nebraska; 1966 NYY (5) (15)

17 — Mickey Scott, lhp; B: Welimar, Germany; Newburg Free Academy, NY; 1972 BAL (2) (5)

34 — Tom Shopay, of; B: Bristol, CT; Dean JC, MA; 1967 NYY (2) (7)

1966

June — Regular Phase
1— Jim Lyttle, of; B: Hamilton, OH; FSU; 1969 NYY (3) (8)

2 — Gary Timberlake, lhp; B: Laconia. IN; Meade County HS, Bradenburg, KY; 1969 SEA (1) (1)

7 — Steve Kline, rhp; B: Wenatchee, WA; Lake Chelan HS, WA; 1970 NYY (5) (6)

18 — Joseph Pactwa, lhp-of; B: Hammond, IN; North Thornton HS, Calumet, IL; 1975 CAL (1) (1)

54 — Rusty Torres, of; B: Aquadilla, PR; New York Vocational HS, Jamaica, NY; 1971 NYY (2) (9)

1967

January — Secondary Phase

3 — Terry Ley, lhp; B: Portland, OR; Clark JC, WA; 1971 NYY (1) (1)

June — Regular Phase

1 — Ron Blomberg, 1b; B: Atlanta, GA; Druid Hills HS, Atlanta, GA; 1969 NYY (7) (8)

4 — Larry Gowell, rhp; B: Lewiston, MA; Edward Little HS, Auburn, ME; 1972 NYY (1) (1)

28 — Loyd Colson, rhp; B: Wellington, TX; Bacone JC, OK; 1970 NYY (1) (1)

67 — Roger Hambright, rhp; B: Sunnyside, WA; Columbia River HS, Vancouver, WA; 1971 NYY (1) (1)

June — Secondary Phase

2 — Frank Baker, ss; B: Meridian, MS; University of Southern Mississippi; 1970 NYY (2) (4)

1968

June — Regular Phase

1 — Thuman Munson, c; B: Akron, OH; D: Canton, OH; Kent State University; 1969 NYY (11) (11)

5 — George Zeber, ss; B: Ellwood City, PA; Loara HS, Anaheim, CA; 1977 NYY (2) (2)

7 — Wayne Nordhagen, of; B: Thief River Falls, MN; Treasure Valley CC, OR; 1976 CHW (7) (8)

1969

June — Regular Phase

1 — Charlie Spikes, 3b-of; B: Bogalusa, LA; Central Memorial HS, Bogalusa, LA; 1972 NYY (1) (9)

10 — Ken Crosby, rhp; B: New Denver, BC, Canada; BYU; 1975 CHC (2) (2)

1970

June — Regular Phase

1 — Dave Cheadle, lhp; B: Greenboro, NC; Asheville HS, NC; 1973 ATL (1) (1)

7 — Don DeMola, rhp; B: Glencove, NY; Commack South HS, NY; 1974 MON (2) (2)

30 — Doc Medich, rhp; B: Aliquippa PA; University of Pittsburgh, PA; 1972 NYY (4) (11)

1971

June — Regular Phase

1 — Terry Whitfield, of; B: Blythe, CA; Palo Verde HS, Blythe, CA; 1974 NYY (3) (10)

3 — Ron Guidry, lhp; B: Lafayette, LA; University of Southwest Louisiana, LA; 1975 NYY (14) (14)

5 — Larry Murray, of-inf; B: Chicago, IL; Phillips HS, Chicago, IL; 1974 NYY (3) (6)

June — Secondary Phase Delayed

1 — Mike Pazik, lhp; B: Lynn, MA; Holy Cross College; 1975 MIN (3) (3)

1972

January — Secondary Phase

1 — Rick Anderson, rhp; B: Inglewood, CA; Los Angeles Valley JC, CA; 1979 NYY (1) (2)

June — Regular Phase

1 — Scott McGregor, lhp; B: Inglewood, CA; El Segundo HS, CA; 1976 BAL (13) (13)

2 — Ken Clay, rhp; B: Lynchburg, VA; EC Glass HS, Lynchburg, VA; 1977 NYY (3) (5)

4 — Mickey Klutts, ss; B: Montebello, CA; El Rancho HS, Pico Rivera, CA; 1976 NYY (3) (8)

5 — Darryl Jones, ss; B: Meadville, PA; Westminster College, PA; 1979 NYY (1) (1)

21 — Bob Kammeyer, rhp; B: Kansas City, MO; Stanford University; 1978 NYY (2) (2)

1973

June — Regular Phase

2 — Mike Heath, ss; B: Tampa, FL; Hillsborough HS, Tampa, FL; 1978 NYY (1) (14)

4 — Kerry Dineen, of; B: Englewood, NJ; University of San Diego, CA; 1975 NYY (2) (3)

5 — LaMarr Hoyt, rhp; B: Columbia, SC; Keenan HS, Columbia, SC; 1979 CHW (6) (8)

8 — Garth Iorg, ss; B: Eureka, CA; Arcata HS, CA; 1977 PHI (1) (10)

1974

June — Regular Phase

1 — Dennis Sherrill, ss; B: Miami, FL; South Miami HS, FL; 1978 NYY (2) (2)

2 — Dave Bergman, 1b-of; B: Evanston, IL; Illinois State University, IL; 1975 NYY (2) (17)

6 — Jerry Narron, c; B: Goldsboro, NC; Goldsboro HS, NC; 1979 NYY (1) (8)

19 — Dennis Werth, c-1b; B: Lincoln, IL; Southern Illinois University, Edwardsville, IL; 1979 NYY (3) (4)

1975

4 — Jim Beattie, rhp; B: Hampton, VA; Dartmouth College; 1978 NYY (2) (9)

5 — Willie Upshaw, 1b; B: Blanco, TX; Blanco HS, TX; 1978 TOR (9) (10)

7 — Mike Fischlin, ss; B: Sacramento, CA; Cosumnes River JC, CA; 1977 HOU (3) NYY (1) (10)

1 — Gil Patterson, of-rhp; B: Philadelphia, PA; Miami–Dade South CC; 1977 NYY (1) (1)

2 — Randy Niemann, lhp; B: Scotia, CA; College of the Redwoods; 1979 HOU (2) NYY (2) (8)

1976

June — Regular Phase

1— Pat Tabler, of; B: Hamilton, OH; McNicholas HS, Cincinnati, OH; 1981 CHC (2) (13)

4 — Ted Wilborn, of; B: Waco, TX; McClatchy HS, Sacramento, CA; 1979 TOR (1) NYY (1) (2)

June — Secondary Phase

1— Roger Slagle, rhp; B: Wicheta, KS; University of Kansas, KS; 1979 NYY (1) (1)

1977

January — Secondary Phase

1— Willie McGee, of; B: San Francisco, CA; Diablo Valley JC, CA; 1982 STL (9) (17)

June — Regular Phase

3 — Joe Lefebvre, of; B: Concord, NH; Eckerd College; 1980 NYY (1) (6)

4 — Roger Holt, ss; B: Daytona Beach, FL; University of Florida, FL; 1980 NYY (1) (1)

21— Chris Welsh, lhp; B: Wilmington, DE; University of South Florida, FL; 1981 SDP (3) (5)

1978

June — Regular Phase

1— Rex Hudler, ss; B: Tempe, AZ; Bullard HS, Fresno, CA; 1984 NYY (2) (9)

1— Matt Winters, of; B: Buffalo, NY; Williamsville HS, NY; 1989 KCR (1) (1)

2 — Steve Balboni, 1b; B: Brockton, MA; Eckerd College; 1981 NYY (5) (11)

4 — Tim Lollar, lhp-1b; B: Poplar Bluff, MO; University of Arkansas, AK; 1980 NYY (1) (7)

6 — Andy McGaffigan, rhp; B: West Palm Beach, FL; Florida Southern College, FL; 1981 (1) (13)

16 — Brian Dayette, 3b; B: New London, CT; St. Leo College; 1983 NYY (2) (5)

17 — Don Cooper, rhp; B: New York, NY; New York Tech; 1981 MIN (2) NYY (1) (4)

1979

June — Regular Phase

3 — Fred Toliver, rhp; B: Natchez, MS; San Gorgonio HS, San Bernardino, CA;1984 CIN (1) (8)

5 — Greg Gagne, ss; B: Fall River, MA; Somerset HS, MA; 1983 MIN (10) (15)

6 — Stefan Wever, rhp; B: Marburg, West Germany; UC Santa Barbara; 1982 NYY (1) (1)

9 — Pete Filson, lhp; B: Darby, PA; Temple University; 1982 MIN (5) NYY (1) (7)

15 — Keith Smith, ss; B: Los Angeles, CA; Canyon HS, Canyon Country, CA; 1984 NYY (2) (2)

19 — Don Mattingly, 1b; B: Evansville, IN; Reitz Memorial HS, Evansville, IN; 1982 NYY (14) (14)

June — Secondary Phase

1— Otis Nixon, 3b; B: Columbus County, NC; Louisburg JC, NJ; 1983 NYY (1) (16)

1980

January — Secondary Phase

1— Tom Dodd, of; B: Portland, OR; University of Oregon, OR; 1986 BAL (1) (1)

June — Regular Phase

15 — Clay Christiansen, rhp; B: Wichita, KS; University of Kansas, KS; 1984 NYY (1) (1)

1981

June — Regular Phase

3 — Scott Bradley, c; B: Glenridge, NJ; University of North Carolina, NC; 1984 NYY (2) (9)

3 — Phil Lombardi, c; B: Abilene, TX; Kennedy HS, Granada Hills, CA; 1986 NYY (3) (3)

4 — Eric Plunk, rhp; B: Wilmington, CA; Bellflower HS, CA; 1986 OAK (3) NY (3) (13)

6 — Mike Pagliarulo, 3b; B: Medford, MA; University of Miami, FL; 1984 NYY (6) (11)

9 — Fred McGriff, 1b; B: Tampa, FL; Jefferson HS, Tampa, FL; 1986 TOR (5) (13)

19 — Rob Tewksbury, rhp; B: Concord, NH; St Leo College; 1986 NYY (2) (13)

20 — Logan Easley, rhp; B: Salt Lake City, UT; College of Southern Idaho; 1987 PIT (2) (2)

1982

June — Regular Phase

2 — Tim Birtsas, lhp; B: Pontiac, MI; Michigan State University, MI; 1985 OAK (2) (5)

3 — Dan Pasqua, of; B: Yonkers, NY; William Paterson College; 1985 NYY (3) (10)

21— Jim Deshales, lhp; B: Massena, NY; LeMoyne College; 1984 NYY (1) (12)

25 — Jim Corsi, rhp; B: Newton, MA; St. Leo College; 1988 OAK (4) (7)

26 — Tom Barrett, 2b; B: San Fernando, CA; University of Arizona, AZ; 1988 PHI (2) (3)

27 — Pete Dalena, 1b; B: Fresno, CA; Fresno State University; 1989 CLE (1) (1)

40 — Mike York, rhp; B: Oak Park, IL; Argo Community HS, Chicago, IL; 1990 PIT (1) (2)

1983

January — Regular Phase

2 — Ozzie Canseco, rhp; B: Havana, Cuba; Miami Dade South CC; 1990 OAK (1) (3)

June — Regular Phase

15 — Steve Frey, lhp; B: Meadowbrook, PA; Bucks County CC, PA; 1989 MON (3) (8)

June — Secondary Phase

1— Brad Arnsberg, rhp; B: Seattle, WA; Merced JC, CA; 1986 NYY (2) (6)

2 — Bill Fulton, rhp; B: Pittsburgh, PA; Pensacola JC, FL; 1987 NYY (1) (1)

1984

January—Secondary Phase
1—Tim Belcher, rhp; B: Mount Gilead, OH; Mt. Vernon Nazarene College; 1987 LAD (5) (12)

June—Regular Phase
2—Keith Miller, of; B: Dallas, TX; Oral Roberts University; 1988 PHI (2) (2)
3—Al Leiter, lhp; B: Toms River, NJ; Central Regional HS, Pine Beach, NJ; 1987 NYY (4) (12)
24—Bob Davidson, rhp; B: Brad Kurznach, West Germany; East Carolina University; 1989 NYY (1) (1)

1985

June—Regular Phase
3—Ken Patterson, lhp; B: Costa Mesa, CA; Baylor University; 1988 CHW (6) (7)
6—Shane Turner, ss; B: Los Angeles, CA; Cal State Fullerton; 1988 PHI (1) (3)

1986

January—Regular Phase
2—Dean Wilkins, rhp; B: Blue Island, IL; San Diego Mesa JC, CA; 1989 CHC (2) (3)
13—Matt Gruver

June—Regular Phase
4—Steve Rosenberg, lhp; B: Brooklyn, NY; University of Florida, FL; 1988 CHW (3) (4)
8—Hal Morris, 1b; B: Fort Rucker, AL; University of Michigan, MI; 1988 NYY (2) (11)
12—Andy Stankiewicz, 2b; B: Inglewood, CA; Pepperdine University; 1992 NYM (1) (7)
14—Scott Kamieniecki, rhp; B: Mount Clemens, MI; University of Michigan; 1991 NYY (6) (8)
18—Turner Ward, of; B: Orlando, FL; University of South Alabama; 1990 CLE (2) (9)
22—Kevin Maas, 1b; B: Castro Valley, CA; University of California; 1990 NYY (4) (5)

1987

7—Dave Eiland, rhp; B: Dade City, FL; University of South Florida, FL; 1988 NYY (5) (8)
14—Gerald Williams, of; B: New Orleans, LA; Grambling State University; 1992 NYY (5) (7)
48—Brad Ausmus, c; B: New Haven, CT; Cheshire HS, CT; 1993 SDP (4) (6)

1988

9—Pat Kelly, 2b; B: Philadelphia, PA; West Chester University, PA; 1991 NYY (7) (8)
10—Ken Greer, rhp; B: Boston, MA; University of Massachusetts; 1993 NYM (1) (1)
15—Bobby Munoz, rhp; B: Rio Piedras, PR; Palm Beach JC, FL; 1993 NYY (1) (6)
29—Russ Davis, ss; B; Birmingham, AL; Shelton State JC, AL; 1994 NYY (2) (5)

30—Deion Sanders, of; B: Fort Myers, FL; FSU; 1989 NYY (2) (7)

1989

2—Andy Fox, 3b; B: Sacramento, CA; Christian Brothers HS, Sacramento, CA; 1996 NYY (2) (3)
5—J.T. Snow, 1b; B: Long Beach, CA; University of Arizona; 1992 NYY (1) (7)
7—Russ Springer, rhp; B: Alexandria, LA; LSU; 1992 NYY (1) (7)
9—Sterling Hitchcock, lhp; B: Fayetteville, NC; Armwood HS, Seffner, FL; 1992 NYY (4) (7)
16—Brian Johnson, c; B: Oakland, CA; Stanford University; 1994 SDP (3) (5)
44—Mike Figga, c; B: Tampa, FL; Central Florida CC; 1997 NYY (2) (2)

1990

1—Carl Everett, of; B: Tampa, FL; Hillsborough HS, Tampa; 1993 FLA (2) (6)
2—Robert Eenhoorn, ss; B: Rotterdam, Netherlands; Davidson College; 1994 NYY (3) (5)
4—Kirt Ojala, lhp; B: Kalamazoo, MI; University of Michigan; 1997 FLA (2) (2)
16—Ricky Ledee, of; B: Ponce, PR; 1998 NYY (1) (1)
20—Kevin Jordan, 1b; B: San Francisco, CA; University of Nebraska; 1995 PHI (4) (4)
22—Andy Pettitte, lhp; B: Baton Rouge, LA; San Jacinto JC, TX; 1995 NYY (4) (4)
24—Jorge Posada, c; B: Santurce, PR; Calhoun CC, AL; 1995 NYY (4) (4)
25—Matt Dunbar, lhp; B: Tallahassee, FL; Florida State University; 1995 FLA (1) (1)
28—Shane Spencer, of; B: Key West, FL; Granite Hills HS, El Cajon, CA; 1998 NYY (1) (1)

1991

5—Lyle Mouton, of; B: Lafayette, LA; LSU; 1995 CWS (3) (4)
9—Kenith Garagozzo, lhp; B: Camden, NJ; University of Delaware; 1994 MIN (1) (1)

1992

1—Derek Jeter, ss; B: Pequannock, NY; Kalamazoo (MI) Central HS; 1995 NYY (4) (4)
4—Mike Buddie, rhp; B: Berea, OH; Forest University; 1998 NYY (1) (1)
8—Matt Luke, of; B: Long Beach, CA; University of California; 1996 NYM (1) (2)
9—Ryan Karp, lhp; B: Los Angeles, CA; University of Miami; 1995 PHI (2) (2)
24—Mike DeJean, rhp; B: Baton Rouge, LA; Livingston (AL) University; 1997 COL (2) (2)

1993

5—Mike Jerzembeck, rhp; B: Queens, NY; University of North Carolina; 1998 NYY (1) (1)

17 — Frank Langford, rhp; B: Atlanta, GA; University of Virginia; 1998 LAD (1) (1)

1994

20 — Ben Ford, rhp; B: Cedar Rapids, IA; Indian Hills (IA) CC; 1998 ARZ (1) (1)

1995

19 — Jay Tessmer, rhp; B: Meadville, PA; University of Miami; 1998 NYY (1) (1)

20 — Mike Lowell, 3b; B: San Juan, PR; Florida International University; 1998 NYY (1) (1)

1996

1 — Eric Milton, lhp; B: State College, PA; University of Maryland; 1998 MIN (1) (1)

1997

1 — Ryan Bradley, rhp; B; Covina, CA; ASU; 1998 NYY (1) (1)

Kansas City/Oakland Athletics

1965

June — Regular Phase

1 — Rick Monday, of; B: Batesville, AR; ASU; 1966 KCA (6) (19)

2 — Joe Keough, 1b; B: Pamona, CA; Mt. San Antonio JC, Pomona, CA; 1968 OAK (1) (6)

4 — Peter Koegel, of-1b; B: Mineola, NY; Seaford HS, Seaford, NY; 1970 MIL (3) (3)

6 — Sal Bando, 3b; B: Warrensville, OH; ASU; 1966 KCA (11) (16)

10 — George Lauzerique, rhp; B: Havana, Cuba; George Washington HS, New York, NY; 1967 KCA (3) (4)

15 — Bob Brooks, of; B: Los Angeles, CA; Los Angeles Harbor JC, Harbor City, CA; 1969 OAK (3) (4)

20 — Gene Tenace, ss; Valley HS, Lucasville, OH; 1969 OAK (8) (15)

1966

June — Regular Phase

1 — Reggie Jackson, of; B: Wyncote, PA; ASU; 1967 KCA (10) (20)

5 — Dave Hamilton, lhp; B: Edmonds, WA; Edmonds HS; 1972 OAK (6) (9)

1967

January — Secondary Phase

5 — Jim Panther, rhp, B: Burlington, IA; Southern Illinois University; 1971 OAK (1) (3)

June — Regular Phase

2 — Vida Blue, lhp, B: Mansfield, LA; DeSoto HS, Mansfield, LA; 1969 OAK (9) (17)

June — Secondary Phase

4 — Warren Bogle, lhp, B: Passiac, NJ; University of Miami, FL; 1968 OAK (1) (1)

7 — Darrell Evans, 3b; B: Pasadena, CA; Pasadena CC, CA, 1969 ATL (9) (21)

1968

January — Regular Phase

1 — George Hendrick, of, B: Los Angeles, CA; Fremont HS, Los Angeles, CA; 1971 OAK (2) (18)

2 — Reggie Sanders, of, B: Birmingham, AL; Venice HS, CA; 1974 DET (1) (1)

June — Regular Phase

26 — John Strohmayer, rhp, B: Belle Fourche, SD; University of Pacific; 1970 MON (4) (5)

1969

June — Regular Phase

1 — Don Stanhouse, rhp-ss, B: DuQuinn, IL; DuQion HS, IL; 1972 TEX (3) (10)

2 — Tommy Sandt, ss, B: Brooklyn, NY; Pacifica HS, Garden Grove, CA; 1975 OAK (2) (2)

3 — Steve Lawson, lhp, B: Oakland, CA; San Lorenzo HS, San Leandro, CA; 1971 TEX (1) (1)

8 — Glenn Abbott, rhp, B: Little Rock, AK; North Little Rock HS, AK; 1973 OAK (4) (11)

19 — Charles Chant, ss, B: Bell, CA; Narbonne HS, Harbor City, CA; 1975 OAK (1) (2)

1970

January — Secondary Phase

1 — Vic Harris, ss, B: Los Angeles, CA; Los Angeles Valley JC, CA; 1972 TEX (2) (8)

June — Regular Phase

1 — Dan Ford, of; B: Los Angeles, CA; Fremont HS, Los Angeles, CA; 1975 MIN (4) (11)

1971

January — Secondary Phase

1 — Phil Garner, inf, B: Jefferson City, TN; University of Tennessee; 1973 OAK (4) (16)

1972

January — Regular Phase

10 — Bob Lacey, lhp; B: San Jose, CA; Central Arizona JC, Tucson, AZ; 1977 OAK (4) (7)

June — Regular Phase

1 — Chet Lemon, ss; B: Jackson, MS; Fremont HS, Los Angeles, CA; 1975 CHW (7) (16)

12 — Chris Batton, rhp; B: Los Angeles, CA; St. Bernard's HS, Los Angeles, CA; 1976 OAK (1) (1)

1973

January—Regular Phase
1— Mike Norris, rhp; B: San Francisco, CA; Yorba Linda, CA; 1975 OAK (9) (16)

June—Regular Phase
1— Randy Scarbery, rhp; B: Fresno, CA; University of California, Fresno, CA; 1979 CHW (2) (2)
7 — Matt Keough, 3b-rhp; B: Ponoma, CA; Corona Del Mar HS, Ponoma, CA; 1977 OAK (7) (10)
8 — Derek Bryant, of; B: Lexington, KY; University of Kentucky; 1979 OAK (1) (1)
9 — Wayne Gross, 1b; B: Riverside, CA; Cal Poly Pomona, Riverside, CA; 1976 OAK (9) (11)
15 — Dwayne Murphy, of; B: Merced, CA; Antelope Valley HS, Lancaster, CA; 1978 OAK (10) (12)

June—Secondary Phase
1— Craig Mitchell, rhp; B: Santa Rosa, CA, Spokane Falls CC, WA; 1975 OAK (3) (3)

1974

June—Regular Phase
19 — Rick Lysander, rhp; B: Huntington Park, CA; Cal State, Los Angeles, CA; 1980 OAK (1) (4)

1975

January—Secondary Phase
1— Rob Picciolo, inf; B: Santa Monica, CA; Pepperdine University, Santa Monica, CA; 1977 OAK (6) (9)

June—Regular Phase
1— Bruce Robinson, c; B: LaJolla, CA; Stanford University; 1978 OAK (1) (4)

June—Secondary Phase
1— Denny Walling, of; B: Neptune, NJ; Clemson University; 1975 OAK (2) (18)

1976

June—Regular Phase
4 — Rickey Henderson, of; B: Chicago, IL; Technical HS, Oakland, CA; 1979 OAK (13) (20)
11— Robert Moore, rhp; J.F. Kennedy HS, Sepuveida, CA; 1985 SFG (1)

June—Secondary Phase
1— Ernie Camacho, rhp; B: Salinas, CA; Hartnell CC, CA; 1980 OAK (1) (10)

1977

June—Regular Phase
3 — Mike Davis, of; B: San Diego, CA; Hoover HS, San Diego, CA; 1980 OAK (8) (10)
6 — Dave Beard, rhp; B: Atlanta, GA; Sequoyah HS, Chamblee, GA; 1980 OAK (4) (7)
13 — Jeff Jones, rhp; B: Detroit, MI; Bowling Green State University; 1980 OAK (5) (5)
25 — Shooty Babitt, inf; B Oakland, CA; Berkeley HS, Berkeley, CA; 1981 OAK (1) (1)

1978

June—Regular Phase
1— Mike Morgan, rhp; B: Tulare, CA; Valley HS, Las Vegas, NV; 1978 OAK (2) (12)
1— Tim Conroy, lhp; B: McKeesport, PA; Gateway HS, Monroeville, PA; 1978 OAK (5) (7)
2 — Keith Atherton, rhp; B: Mathews, VA; Mathews HS, Mathews, VA; 1983 OAK (4) (7)
4 — Mike Woodard, 2b; B: Melrose Park, IL; Proviso East HS, Maywood, IL; 1985 SFG (3) (4)
5 — Scott Meyer, c; B: Evergreen Park, IL; Western Michigan University; 1978 OAK (1) (1)
6 — Kelvin Moore, 1b; B: Le Roy, AL; Jackson State University; 1981 OAK (3) (3)

1979

June—Regular Phase
27 — Bert Bradley, rhp; B: Toledo, IL; BYU; 1983 OAK (1) (1)

1980

June—Regular Phase
3 — Rich Bordi, rhp; B: South San Francisco, CA; Fresno State University; 1980 OAK (3) (9)

1981

January—Regular Phase
1— Steve Kiefer, ss; B: Chicago, IL; Fullerton JC, CA; 1984 OAK (2) (6)

June—Regular Phase
1— Tim Pyznarski, 3b-of; B: Chicago Ridge, IL; Eastern Illinois University; 1986 SDP (1) (1)
2 — Mike Gallego, 2b; B: Whitier, CA; UCLA, CA; 1985 OAK (7) (8) (from White Sox for Jim Essian)
2 — Rick Rodriguez, rhp; B: Oakland, CA; University of California, Riverside, CA; 1986 OAK (2) (4)
4 — Curt Young, lhp; B: Saginaw, MI; Central Michigan University, MI; 1983 OAK (9) (10)
5 — Mickey Tettleton, c-of; B: Oklahoma City, OK; Oklahoma State University, OK; 1984 OAK (4) (9)
8 — Bill Bathe, c; B: Downey, CA; Pepperdine University; 1986 OAK (1) (3)

June—Secondary Phase
1— Donnie Hill, ss; B: B: Pomona, CA; ASU; 1983 OAK (4) (9)

1982

January—Secondary Phase
1— Dave Leiper, lhp; B: Whittier, CA: Fullerton JC, CA; 1984 OAK (3) (5)

June—Regular Phase
2 — Steve Ontiveros, rhp; B: Tularosa, NM; University of Michigan, MI; 1985 OAK (4) (6)
3 — Phil Stephenson, 1b; B: Guthrie, OK; Wichita State University; 1989 CHC (1) (4)

5 — Charlie O'Brien, c; B: Tulsa, OK; Wichita State University; 1985 OAK (1) (7)

10 — Jeff Kaiser, lhp; B: Wyandotte, MI; Western Michigan University, MI; 1985 OAK (1) (6)

13 — Jim Eppard, 1b; B: South Bend, IN; University of California, CA; 1987 CAL (3) (4)

15 — Jose Canseco, 3b; B: Havana, Cuba; Carol City HS, Miami, FL; 1985 OAK (9) (15)

1983

June — Regular Phase

7 — Jose Tolentino, 1b; B: Mexico City, Mexico; University of Texas; 1991 HOU (1) (1)

9 — Terry Steinbach, 3b; B: New Ulm, MN; University of Minnesota, MN; 1986 OAK (11) (13)

10 — Brian Dorsett, c; B: Terre Haute, IN; Indiana State University; 1987 CLE (1) (9)

11 — Greg Cadaret, lhp; B: Detroit, MI; Grand Valley State College; 1987 OAK (3) (9)

June — Secondary Phase

1 — Rob Nelson, 1b; B: Pasadena, CA; Mt. San Antonio JC, CA; 1986 OAK (2) (5)

1984

June — Regular Phase

1 — Mark McGwire, 1b; B: Pomona, CA; USC; 1986 OAK (12) (13)

7 — Todd Burns, rhp; B: Maywood, CA; Oral Roberts University; 1988 OAK (3) (6)

1985

June — Regular Phase

1 — Walt Weiss, ss; B: Tuxedo, NY; UNC; 1987 OAK (6) (12)

2 — Dave Otto, lhp-1b; B: Chicago, IL; University of Missouri; 1987 OAK (4) (8)

3 — Wally Whitehurst, rhp; B: Shreveport, LA; University of New Orleans; 1989 NYM (3) (6)

22 — Jeff Shaver, rhp; B: Beaver, PA; SUNY, Fedonia; 1988 OAK (1) (1)

26 — Larry Arndt, inf-of; B: Fremont, OH; Bowling Green State University; 1989 OAK (1) (1)

1986

January — Regular Phase

4 — Dave Veres, rhp; B: Montgomery, AL; Mount Hood CC, OR; 1994 HOU (2) (5)

June — Regular Phase

1 — Scott Hemond, c; B: Taunton, MA; University of South Florida, FL; 1989 OAK (6) (7)

2 — Kevin Tapani, rhp; B: Des Moines, IA; Central Michigan University, MI; 1989 NYM (1) (10)

10 — Lance Blankenship, 3b; B: Anaheim, CA; University of California, CA; 1988 ATL (1) (3)

13 — Rob Beck, rhp; B: Burbank, CA; Grant HS, Van Nuys, CA; 1991 SFG (7) (8)

18 — Dan Howitt, 1b; B: Battle Creek, MI; Cal State Fullerton; 1989 OAK (4) (6)

1987

1 — Lee Tinsley, of; B: Shelbyville, KY; Shelby County HS, Shelbyville, KY; 1993 SEA (1) (5)

14 — Ron Coomer, 3b; B: Crest Hill, IL; Taft JC, CA; 1995 MN (4) (4)

20 — Scott Brosius, 3b; B: Hillsboro, OR; Linfield College; 1991 OAK (7) (8)

1988

2 — Joe Slusarski, rhp; B: Indianapolis, IN; University of New Orleans; 1991 OAK (3) (4)

3 — John Briscoe, rhp; B: La Grange, IL; Texas Christian University; 1991 OAK (6) (6)

18 — Darren Lewis, of; B: Berkeley, CA; University of California, CA; 1990 OAK (1) (9)

23 — Bronswell Patrick, rhp; B: Greenville, NC; D.H. Conley HS, Greenville, NC; 1998 MIL (1) (1)

1989

2 — Scott Lydy, of; B: Mesa, AZ; South Mountain CC, AZ; 1993 OAK (1) (1)

8 — Craig Paquette, 3b; B: Long Beach, CA; Golden West JC, CA; 1993 OAK (3) (6)

15 — Kurt Abbott, ss; B: Zanesville, OH; St. Petersburg JC, FL; 1993 OAK (1) (6)

42 — Mike Mohler, lhp; B: Upland, CA; USC; 1993 OAK (6) (6)

1990

1 — Todd Van Poppel, rhp; B: Hillsdale, IL; Martin HS, Arlington, TX; 1991 OAK (5) (6)

2 — Eric Helfand, c; B: Erie, PA; ASU; 1993 OAK (3) (3)

6 — Creighton Gubanich, c; B: Belleville, NJ; Phoenixville, Area HS, PA; 1999 BOS (1) (1)

10 — Ernie Young, of; B: Chicago, IL; Lewis University; 1994 OAK (4) (5)

16 — Doug Johns, lhp; B: South Bend, IN; University of Virginia; 1995 OAK (2) (3)

22 — Izzy Molina, New York; B: New York, NY; Columbus HS, Miami, FL; 1996 OAK (3) (3)

23 — Tanyon Sturtze, rhp; B: Worcester, MA; Quinsigamond CC, MA; 1995 CHC (2) (3)

1991

1 — Brent Gates, ss; B: Grand Rapids, MI; University of Minnesota; 1993 OAK (4) (6)

2 — Mike Neill, of; B: Martinsville, VA; Villanova University; 1998 OAK (1) (1)

4 — Steve Wojciechowski, lhp; B: Blue Island, IL; St. Xavier College; 1995 OAK (3) (3)

8 — Scott Sheldon, ss; B: Hammond, IN; University of Houston; 1998 TEX (1) (1)

9 — Damon Mashore, of; Ponce, PR; University of Arizona; 1996 OAK (2) (3)

11 — Jason Wood, 3b; B: San Bernardino, CA; Fresno State University; 1998 OAK (1) (1)

12 — Miguel Jimenez, rhp; B: New York, NY; Fordham University; 1993 OAK (2) (2)
24 — George Williams, c; B: La Crosse, WI; University of Texas; 1995 OAK (3) (3)

1992

2 — Jason Giambi, 3b; B: West Covina, CA; Long Beach State University; 1995 OAK (4) (4)
4 — Don Wengert, rhp; B: Sioux City, Iowa; Iowa State University; 1995 OAK (3) (4)
22 — Gary Haught, rhp; B; Tacoma, WA; University of Southwestern Louisiana; 1997 OAK (1) (1)
25 — Brian Lesher, of; B: Antwerp, Belgium; University of Delaware;1996 OAK (3) (3)

1993

1 — John Wasdin, rhp; B: Fort Belvoir, VA; FSU; 1995 OAK (2) (4)
2 — Jeff D'Amico, 3b; B: St. Petersburg, FL; Redmond HS, WA; 1996 MIL (2) (2)
4 — Jason McDonald, of; B: Modesto, CA; University of Houston; 1997 OAK (2) (2)
6 — Scott Spiezio, 1b; B: Joliet, IL; University of Illinois, IL; 1996 OAK (3) (3)
7 — Tim Kubinski, lhp; B: Pullman, WA; UCLA; 1997 OAK (1) (1)
12 — Chris Michalak, lhp; B: Joliet, IL; University of Notre Dame; 1998 ARZ (1) (1)

1994

1 — Ben Grieve, of; B: Arlington, TX; Martin HS, Arlington, TX; 1997 (2) (2)
2 — Brad Rigby, rhp; B: Milwaukee, WI; Georgia Tech; 1997 OAK (1) (1)
6 — Emil Brown, of; B: Chicago, IL; Indian River (FL) CC; 1997 PIT (2) (2)

1995

1 — Ariel Prieto, rhp; B: Beverly Hills, CA; Western League, Palm Springs, CO; 1995 (4) (4)
2 — Mark Bellhorn, 3b; B: Boston, MA; Auburn University; 1995 OAK (2) (2)
10 — Ryan Christenson, rhp; B: Redlands, CA; Long Beach State University; 1998 OAK (1) (1)
24 — Steve Connelly, rhp; B: Long Beach, CA; University of Oklahoma; 1988 OAK (1) (1)

1996

1 — Eric Chavez, 3b; B: Los Angeles, CA; Mount Carmel HS, San Diego, CA; 1998 (1) (1)
3 — A.J. Hinch, c; B: Waverly, IA; Stanford University; 1998 OAK (1) (1)

Seattle Mariners

1977

June — Regular Phase
1— Dave Henderson, of; B: Merced, CA; Dos Palos (CA) HS; 1981 SEA (6) (14)
3 — Bud Anderson, rhp; B: Westbury, NY; Rutgers University; 1982 CLE (2) (2)
5 — Ron Musselman, rhp; B: Wilmington, NC; Clemson University; 1982 SEA (1) (3)
12 — Karl Best, rhp; B: Aberdeen, WA; Kent Meridian HS, Kent, WA; 1983 SEA (4) (5)

1978

January — Regular Phase
1— Jim Maier, 1b; B: New York, NY; Miami–Dade South CC; 1981 SEA (3) (3)

June — Regular Phase
2 — Dave Valle, c; B: Bayside, NY; Holly Cross HS, Bayside, NY; 1984 SEA (10) (13)
10 — Bob Stoddard, rhp; B: San Jose, CA; Fresno State University; 1981 SEA (4) (7)
11 — Vance McHenry, ss; B: Chico, CA; UNLV; 1981 SEA (2) (2)
21 — Dave Edler, inf.: B: Sioux City, Iowa; Washington State University; 1980 SEA (4) (4)

1979

June — Regular Phase
1 — Al Chambers, of; B: Harrisburg, PA; John Harris, HS, Harrisburg, PA; 1983 SEA (3) (3)
2 — Jamie Allen, inf; B: Yakima, WA; ASU; 1983 SEA (1) (1)
4 — Jim Presley, ss; B: Pensacola, FL; Escambia HS, Pensacola, FL; 1984 SEA (6) (8)
7 — Brian Synder, lhp; B: Flemington, NJ; Clemson University; 1985 SEA (1) (2)
13 — Mike L. Hart, of; B: Milwaukee, WI; University of Wisconsin; 1984 MIN (1) (2)
17 — Bud Black, lhp; B: San Mateo, CA; San Diego State University; 1981 SEA (1) (15)

June — Secondary Phase
1 — Carlos Diaz, lhp; B: Kaneohe, Hawaii; Hancock JC, CA; 1982 ATL (1) (5)

1980

January — Secondary Phase
2 — Dan Firova, c; B: Refugio, Texas; no school; 1981 SEA (2) (3)

June — Regular Phase
1 — Darnell Coles, ss; San Bernadino, CA; Eisenhower HS, Riaito, CA; 1983 SEA (3) (14)
2 — Matt Young, lhp; B: Pasadena, CA; UCLA; 1983 SEA (4) (10)
10 — Donell Nixon, of-3b; B: Evergreen, NC; West Columbus, HS, Evergreen, NC; 1987 SEA (1) (4)
13 — Ed Vande Berg, lhp; B: Redlands, CA; ASU; 1982 SEA (4) (7)

16 — John Moses, of; B University of Arizona; 1982 SEA (7) (11)

17 — Rusty McNealy, of; B: Sacramento, CA; Florida International University; 1983 OAK (1) (1)

June — Secondary Phase
1 — Harold Reynolds, ss; B: Eugene, CA; Canada JC, CA; 1983 SEA (10) (12)

1981

June — Regular Phase
1 — Mike Moore, rhp; B: Carnegie, OK; Oral Roberts University; 1982 SEA (7) (14)

2 — Mark Langston, lhp; B: San Diego, CA; San Jose State University; 1984 SEA (6) (15)

3 — Phil Bradley, of; B: Bloomington, IN; University of Missouri; 1983 SEA (5) (8)

4 — Ricky Nelson, of; Eloy, AZ; ASU; 1983 SEA (4) (4)

4 — Lee Guetterman, lhp; B: Chattanooga, TN; Liberty University; 1984 1984 SEA (5) (11)

5 — Brick Smith, lb; B: Charlotte, NC; Wake Forest University; 1987 SEA (2) (2)

1982

June — Regular Phase
1 — Spike Owen, ss; B: Clebume, TX; University of Texas; 1983 SEA (4) (13)

4 — Terry Taylor, rhp; B: Crestview, FL; Crestview (FL) HS; 1988 SEA (1) (1)

6 — Alvin Davis, 1b; B: Riverside, CA; ASU; 1984 SEA (8)(9)

1983

June — Regular Phase
1 — Darrel Akerfelds, rhp; B: Denver, CO; Mesa College; 1986 OAK (1) (5)

1 — Terry Bell, c; B: Dayton, OH; Old Dominion University; 1986 KCR (1) (2)

2 — Mike Brantley, of; B: Catskill, NY; Coastal Carolina College; 1986 SEA (4) (4)

3 — Dave Hengel, of; B: Oakland, CA; University of California; 1986 SEA (3) (4)

4 — Bill Wilkinson, lhp; B: Greybull, WY; Cherry Creek HS, Englewood, CO; 1985 SEA (3) (3)

6 — Scott Nielsen, rhp; Salt Lake City, UT; BYU; 1986 NYY (1) (4)

27 — Rick Luecken, rhp; B: McAllen, TX; Texas A&M University; 1989 KCR (1) (2)

1984

June — Regular Phase
1 — Bill Swift, rhp; B: Portland, MA; University of Maine; 1985 SEA (6) (12)

1985

June — Regular Phase
1 — Mike Campbell, rhp; B: Seattle, WA; University of Hawaii; 1987 SEA (3) (6)

1 — Bill McGuire, c; B: Omaha, NE; University of Nebraska; 1988 SEA (2) (2)

2 — Mike Schooler, rhp; B: Anaheim, CA; Cal State Fullerton; 1988 SEA (5) (6)

3 — Clint Zavaras, rhp; B: Denver, CO; Mullin HS, Denver, CO; 1989 SEA (1) (1)

15 — Clay Parker, rhp; B: Columbia, LA; LSU; 1987 SEA (1) (4)

1986

January — Secondary Phase
1 — Eric Fox, of; B: Lemoore, CA; Fresno State University; 1992 OAK (3) (4)

June — Regular Phase
1 — Patrick Lennon, of; B: Whiteville, NC; Whiteville (NC) HS; 1991 SEA (2) (5)

2 — Erik Hanson, rhp; B: Kinneion, NJ; Wake Forest University; 1988 SEA (6) (11)

3 — Jerry Goff, c; B; San Rafael, CA; University of California; 1990 MON (2) (6)

6 — Rich DeLucia, rhp, B: Reading, PA; University of Tennessee; 1990 SEA (4) (9)

12 — Jim Bowie, 1b; B: Tokyo, Japan; LSU; 1994 OAK (1) (1)

June — Secondary Phase
1 — Greg Briley, 2b; B: Greenville, NC; North Carolina State University; 1988 SEA (5) (5)

1987

1 — Ken Griffey, Jr., of; B: Donora, PA; Moeller HS, Cincinnati, OH; 1989 SEA (10) (10)

2 — David Burba, rhp; B: Dayton, OH; Ohio State University; 1990 SEA (2) (9)

18 — Mike Gardner, rhp; B: Sarnia, ON, Canada; Indiana State University; 1990 SEA (1) (7)

38 — Todd Haney, 2b; B: Galveston, TX; University of Texas; 1992 MON (5)

1988

1 — Tino Martinez, 1b; B: Tampa, FL; University of Texas; 1990 SEA (6) (9)

2 — Greg Pirkl, rhp; B: Long Beach, CA; Los Alamitos (CA) HS; 1993 SEA (4) (4)

4 — Lee Hancock, lhp; B: North Hollywood, CA; Cal Poly San Luis Obispo, CA; 1995 PIT (2) (2)

13 — Jeff Darwin, rhp; B: Sherman, TX; Alvin (TX) CC; 1994 SEA (1) (2)

17 — Scott Taylor, rhp; B: Topeka, KS; University of Kansas; 1995 TEX (1) (1)

29 — Kerry Woodson, rhp; B: Jacksonville, FL; San Jose CC; 1992 SEA (1) (1)

1989

1 — Roger Salkeld, rhp; B: Burbank, CA; Saugus (CA) HS; 1993 SEA (2) (3)

1990

1— Marc Newfield, of; B: Sacramento, CA; Marina HS, Huntington Beach, CA; 1993 SEA (3) (6)

3 — Dave Fleming, lhp; B: Queens, NY; University of Georgia; 1991 SEA (5) (5)

5 — Bret Boone, 2b; B: El Cajon, CA; USC; 1992 SEA (2) (7)

6 — Mike Hampton, lhp; B: Brooksville, FL; Crystal River (FL) HS; 1993 SEA (1) (6)

7 — Kevin King, lhp; B: Atwater, CA; University of Oklahoma; 1993 SEA (3) (3)

8 — John Cummings, lhp; B: Torrance, CA; USC; 1993 SEA (3) (5)

16 — Jim Converse, rhp; B: San Francisco, CA; Cass Roble HS, Orangeville, CA; 1993 SEA (3) (4)

1991

1— Shawn Estes, lhp; B: San Bernardino, CA; Douglas HS, Minden, NV; 1995 SFG (4) (4)

3 — Jim Mecir, rhp; B: Queens, NY; Eckerd College, FL; 1995 SEA (1) (3)

4 — Desi Relaford, ss; B: Valdosta, GA; Sandalwood HS, Jacksonville, FL; 1996 PHI (3) (3)

8 — Derek Lowe, rhp; B: Dearborn, MI; Ford HS, Dearborn, MI; 1997 SEA (1) (2)

22 — Darren Bragg, of; B: Waterbury, CT; Georgia Tech; 1995 SEA (3) (5)

25 — Matt Mantei, rhp; B: Tampa, FL; River Valley HS, Sawyer, MI; 1995 FLA (3) (3)

32 — George Glinatsis, rhp; B: Youngstown, OH; University of Cincinnati; 1994 SEA (1) (1)

63 — Charles Gipson Jr., of; B: Orange, CA; Cypress (CA) JC; 1996 SEA (1) (1)

1992

1— Ron Villone, lhp; B: Englewood, NJ; University of Massachusetts; 1995 SEA (1) (4)

2 — Bob Wolcott, rhp; B: Huntington Beach, CA; North HS, Medford, OR; 1995 SEA (3) (4)

3 — Chris Widger, c; B: Wilmington, DE; George Mason University; 1995 SEA (2) (4)

4 — Andy Sheets, ss; B: Baton Rouge, LA; LSU; 1996 SEA (2) (3)

23 — Ryan Franklin, rhp; B: Fort Smith, AR; Seminole Junior College, OK; 1999 SEA (1) (1)

34 — Tim Harikkala, rhp; B: West Palm Beach, FL; Florida Atlantic University; 1992 SEA (2) (2)

36 — Raul Ibanez, of; B: Manhattan, NY; Miami–Dade CC South; 1996 SEA (3) (3)

1993

1— Alex Rodriguez, 1994; B: New York, NY; Westminsiter Christian HS, Miami, FL; 1994 SEA (5) (5)

6 — Ken Cloude, rhp; B: Baltmore, MD; McDonough HS, Pomfret, MD; 1994 SEA (3) (3)

10 — Dean Crow, rhp; B: Garland, TX; Baylor University; 1998 DET (1) (1)

13 — Rafael Carmona, rhp; B: Rio Piedras, PR; Indian Hills (IA) CC; 1995 SEA (3) (3)

1994

1— Jason Varitek, c; B: Rochester, MI; Georgia Tech; 1997 BOS (2) (2)

2 — Trey Moore, lhp; B: Houston, TX; Texas A&M University; 1998 MON (1) (1)

3 — Matt Wagner, rhp; B: Cedar Falls, IA; Iowa State University; 1996 SEA (1) (1)

1995

2 — Shane Monahan, of; B: Syosset, NY; Clemson University; 1998 SEA (1) (1)

Tampa Devil Rays

As of June 1999, none of the Devil Rays draft picks had yet to make it to the majors.

Texas Rangers

Washington Senators:

1965

June — Regular Phase

1— Joe Coleman, Jr., rhp; B: Boston, MA; Natick HS, MA; 1965 WAS (6) (15)

3 — Gene Martin, of; B: Americus, GA; Edougherty HS, Albany, GA; 1968 WAS (1) (1)

15 — Tom Ragland, ss; B: Talladega, AL; North HS, Detroit, MI; 1971 WAS (2) (3)

18 — Bill Gogolewski, rhp; B: Oshkosh, WI; Oshkosh HS, WI; 1970 WAS (2) (6)

25 — Dick Billings, of; B: Detroit, MI; Michigan State University; 1968 WAS (7) (8)

August — Legion Phase
No selections

1966

January — Secondary Phase

8 — Dick Such, rhp; B: Sanford, NC; Elon College; 1970 WAS (1) (1)

June — Regular Phase

1— Tom Grieve, of-c; B: Pittsfield, MA; Pittsfield HS, MA; 1970 WAS (7) (9)

25 — Jerry Schoen, rhp; B: New Orleans, LA; Loyola University, LA; 1968 WAS (1) (1)

June — Secondary Phase

1— Del Unser, of-1b; B: Decatur, IL; Mississippi State University; 1968 WAS (4) (15)

1967

January — Secondary Phase

1— Jan Dukes, lhp; B: Cheyenne, WY; Santa Clara University; 1969 WAS (3) (3)

June — Regular Phase

3 — Michael Thompson, rhp; B: Denver, CO; Ponca City HS, OK; 1971 WAS (1) (4)

5 — Ike Brookens, rhp; B: Chambersburg, PA; Chambersburg HS, Fayetteville, PA; 1975 DET (1) (1)

11 — Rich Steimaczek, c; B: Chicago, IL; Mendel HS, Chicago, IL; 1971 WAS (2) (3)

36 — Bobby Jones, 1b; B: Elkton MD; Elkton HS, MD; 1974 TEX (7) (9)

42 — John Wockenfuss, 3b-rhp; B: Welch, WV; Dickinson HS, Wilmington, DE; 1974 DET (10) (12)

1968

June — Regular Phase

1 — Don Castle, lhp-1b; B: Kokomo, IN; Coldwater HS, MS; 1973 TEX (1) (1)

2 — Jimmy Mason, ss; B: Mobile, AL; Murphy HS, Mobile, AL; 1971 WAS (5) (9)

5 — Jeff Terpko, rhp; B: Sayre, PA; Sayre HS, PA; 1974 TEX (2) (3)

10 — Larry Bittner, lhp-1b; B: Pocahontas, LA; Buena Vista College; 1970 WAS (5) (14)

June — Secondary Phase

1 — Rick Henninger, rhp; B: Hastings, NE; University of Missouri; 1973 TEX (1) (1)

1969

January — Regular Phase

1 — Joe Lovitto, c; B: San Pedro, CA; 1972 TEX (4) (4)

June — Regular Phase

1 — Jeff Burroughs, of; B: Long Beach, CA; Woodrow Wilson HS, Long Beach, CA; 1970 WAS (7) (16)

4 — Pete Mackanin, 3b-ss; B: Chicago, IL; Brother Rice Catholic HS, Chicago, IL; 1973 TEX (2) (9)

5 — David Criscione, c; B: Dunkirk, NY; Dunkirk HS, NY; 1977 BAL (1) (1)

43 — Steve Foucault, 3b-rhp; B: Duluth, MN; South Georgia College; 1973 TEX (4) (6)

June — Secondary Phase

4 — David Moates, of; B: Great Lakes, IL; Florida State University; 1974 TEX (3) (3)

1970

January — Secondary Phase

1 — Bill Fahey, c; B: Detroit, MI; St. Clair County CC, MI; 1971 WAS (6) (11)

5 — Bill Madlock, ss-3b; B: Memphis, TN; Southeastern CC, IA; 1973 TEX (1) (15)

June — Regular Phase

5 — Rick Waits, lhp; B: Atlanta, GA; Terrell HS, Atlanta, GA; 1973 TEX (1) (12)

June — Secondary Phase

1 — Lenny Randle, inf; B: Long Beach, FL; ASU; 1971 WAS (6) (12)

1971

January — Secondary Phase

1 — Jim Kremmel, lhp; B: Belleville, IL; University of New Mexico; 1973 TEX (1) (2)

June — Regular Phase

6 — Gregory Pryor, 2b; B: Marietta, OH; Florida Southern College; 1976 TEX (1) (10)

June — Secondary Phase Delayed

1 — Pete Broberg, rhp; B: W. Palm Beach, FL; Dartmouth College; 1971 WAS (4) (8)

2 — Mike Cubbage, ss-3b; B: Charlottesville, VA; University of Virginia; 1974 TEX (3) (8)

Texas Rangers:

1972

June — Regular Phase

1 — Roy Howell, 3b; B: Lompoc, CA; Lompoc HS, CA; 1974 TEX (4) (11)

2 — Ron Pruitt, c-of; B: Flint, MI.; Michigan State University; 1975 TEX (1) (9)

4 — Brian Doyle, ss; B: Glasgow, KY; Caverna HS, Cave City, KY; 1978 NYY (3) (4)

19 — Bobby Thompson, ss; B: Charlotte, NC; Harding HS, Charlotte, NC; 1978 TEX (1) (1)

25 — Mike Hargrove, 1b; B: Perryton, TX; Northwestern Oklahoma State University; 1974 TEX (5) (12)

June — Secondary Phase

4 — Keith Smith, of; B: Palmetto, FL; Manatee JC, FL; 1981 TEX (1) (3)

1973

January — Secondary Phase

1 — Jim Sundberg, c; B: Galesburg, IL; University of Iowa; 1974 TEX (11) (16)

June — Regular Phase

1 — David Clyde, lhp; B: Kansas City, KS; Westchester HS, Houston, TX; 1973 TEX (3) (5)

3 — Len Barker, rhp; B: Fort Knox, KY; Neshaminy HS, Trevose, PA; 1976 TEX (3) (11)

5 — Ken Pape, ss; B: San Antonio, TX; University of Texas; 1976 TEX (1) (1)

30 — Dan Duran, 1b; B: Palo Alto, CA; Foothill JC, CA; 1981 TEX (1) (1)

1974

January — Regular Phase

1 — Roy Smalley, ss; B: Los Angeles, CA; USC; 1975 TEX (2) (13)

3 — Johnny Sutton, rhp; B: Dallas, TX; Plano JC, TX.; 1977 STL (1) (2)

June — Regular Phase

1 — Tommy Boggs, rhp; B: Poughkeepsie, NY; Lanier HS, Austin, TX; 1976 TEX (3) (9)

2 — Jeff Byrd, rhp; B: La Mesa, CA; El Capitan HS, Lakeside, CA; 1977 TOR (1) (1)

4—Jim Clancy, rhp; B: Chicago, IL; St. Rita HS, Chicago, IL; 1977 TOR (12) (15)

13 — Rick Lisi, 3b; B: Halifax, Nova Scotia, Canada; Pittsfield HS, MA; 1981 TEX (1) (1)

16 — Jim Umbarger, lhp; B: Burbank, CA; ASU; 1975 TEX (4) (4)

18 — Gary Gray, 3b; B: New Orleans, LA; Southeastern Oklahoma State University; 1977 TEX (3) (6)

29 — Bobby Cuellar, rhp; B: Alice, TX; University of Texas; 1977 TEX (1) (1)

1975

January — Secondary Phase

1— Bump Wills, 2b; B: Washington DC; ASU; 1977 TEX (5) (6)

June — Regular Phase

1—Jim Gideon, rhp; B: Taylor, TX; University of Texas; 1975 TEX (1) (1)

2 — Eddie Miller, of; B: San Pablo, CA; Ells HS, Richmond, CA; 1977 TEX (1) (7)

6 —John Poloni, lhp; B: Dearborn, MI; ASU; 1977 TEX (1) (1)

23 — Larue Washington, ss; B: Long Beach, CA; Cal State Dominguez Hills; 1978 TEX (2) (2)

June — Secondary Phase

1— Pat Putnam, 1b; B: Bethel, UT; University of South Alabama; 1977 TEX (6) (8)

1976

January — Secondary Phase

1— Paul Mirabella, lhp; B: Belleville, NJ; Montclair State College; 1978 TEX (1) (13)

June — Regular Phase

3 — Mike Griffin, rhp; B: Clousa, CA; Woodland HS, CA; 1979 NYY (3) (6)

4 — Brian Allard, rhp; B: Spring Valley, IL; Henry Senachwine HS, Henry, IL; 1979 TEX (2) (3)

10— Billy Sample, 3b-of; B: Roanoke, VA; James Madison University; 1978 TEX (7) (9)

1977

January — Regular Phase

1— Dave Righetti, lhp; San Jose CC, CA; 1979 NYY (11) (16)

June — Regular Phase

4 — George Wright, of; B: Oklahoma City, OK; Capitol Hill HS, Oklahoma City, OK; 1982 TEX (5) (5)

7 — Odie Davis, ss; B: San Diego, CA; Prairie View A&M University; 1980 TEX (1) (1)

9 — Bobby Johnson, c; B: Dallas, TX; Kimball HS, Dallas, TX; 1981 TEX (3) (3)

13 — Don Kainer, rhp; B: Houston, TX; University of Texas; 1980 TEX (1) (1)

22 — Ed Lynch, rhp; B: Brooklyn, NY; University of South Carolina; 1980 NYM (7) (8)

June — Secondary Phase

1—John Butcher, rhp; B: Glendale, CA; Yavapai JC, AZ; 1980 TEX (4) (7)

1978

June — Regular Phase

6 — Terry Bogener, of; B: Hannibal, MO; University of Oklahoma; 1982 TEX (1) (1)

8 — Wayne Tolleson, ss; B: Spartansburg, SC; Western Carolina University; 1981 TEX (5) (10)

11— Chris Smith, of-inf; B: Torrance, CA; USC; 1981 MON (2) (3)

29— Jimmy Farr, rhp; B: Waverly, NY; Penn State University; 1982 TEX (1) (1)

30— Gene Nelson, rhp; B: Tampa, FL; Pasco County HS, Dade City, FL; 1981 NYY (1) (13)

June — Secondary Phase

1— Mike Richardt, 3b; B: Los Angeles, CA; Fresno CC, CA; 1980 TEX (4) (4)

1979

June — Regular Phase

1— Jerry Don Gleaton, lhp; B: Brownwood TX; University of Texas; 1979 TEX (2) (12)

2 — Donnie Scott, c; B: Dunedin, FL; Tampa Catholic HS, FL; 1983 TEX (2) (4)

3 — Nick Capra, 2b; B: Denver, CO; University of Oklahoma; 1982 TEX (4) (5)

12 — Tony Fossas, lhp; B: Havanna, Cuba; University of South Florida; 1988 TEX (1) (9)

15 — Pete O'Brien, 1b; B: Santa Monica, CA; University of Nebraska; 1982 TEX (7) (12)

26 — Dave Schmidt, rhp; B: Niles, MI; UCLA; 1981 TEX (5) (12)

30— Jay Pettibone, rhp; B: Mt. Clemens, MI; Chapman College; 1983 MIN (1) (1)

34 — Ray Fontenot, lhp; B: Lake Charles, LA; McNeese State University; 1983 NYY (2) (4)

1980

January — Regular Phase

2 — Billy Taylor, rhp; B: Monticello, FL; Abraham Baldwin JC, GA; 1994 OAK (4) (4)

January — Secondary Phase

1— Tommy Dunbar, of; B: Graniteville, SC; Middle Georgia JC; 1983 TEX (3) (3)

June — Regular Phase

2 — Dwayne Henry, rhp; B: Elkton, MD; Middletown HS, Odessa, DE; 1984 TEX (5) (11)

4 — Curt Wilkerson, ss; B: Petersburg, PA; Dinwiddie HS, Sutherland, VA; 1983 TEX (6) (11)

33 — Walt Terrell, rhp; B: Jeffersonville, IN; Morehead State University; 1982 NYM (3) (11)

June — Secondary Phase

1— Mike Mason, lhp; B: Faribault, MN; Oral Roberts University; 1982 TEX (6) (7)

4 — Tom Henke, rhp; B: Kansas City, MO; East Central JC, MO; 1982 TEX (5) (14)

1981

January — Regular Phase
1— Greg Tabor, inf; B: Castro Valley, CA; Chabot JC, CA; 1987 TEX (1) (1)

June — Regular Phase
1— Ron Darling, rhp; B: Honolulu, HI; Yale University; 1983 NYM (9) (13)
1— Al Lachowicz, rhp; B: Los Angeles, CA; University of Pittsburgh; 1983 TEX (1) (1)
17 — Kevin Buckley, of; B: Quincy, MA; University of Maine; 1984 TEX (1) (1)
24 — Glen Cook, rhp; B: Buffalo, NY; Ithaca College; 1985 TEX (1) (1)

1982

June — Regular Phase
5 — Steve Buechele, 2b; B: Lancaster, CA; Stanford University; 1985 TEX (8) (11)
39 — Kenny Rogers, lhp-of; B: Savannah, GA; Plant City HS, Dover, FL; 1989 TEX (7) (10)

June — Secondary Phase
1— Randy Kramer, rhp; B: Palo Alto, CA; San Jose CC, CA; 1988 PIT (3) (4)

1983

June — Regular Phase
1— Jeff Kunkel, ss; B: W. Palm Beach, FL; Rider College; 1984 TEX (7) (8)
3 — Randy Asadoor, 3b; B: Fresno, CA; Fresno State University; 1986 SDP (1) (1)
5 — Bob Sebra, rhp; B: Ridgewood, NJ.; University of Nebraska; 1985 TEX (1) (6)

1984

June — Regular Phase
1— Oddibe McDowell, of; B: Hollywood, FL; ASU; 1985 TEX (4) (7)
7 — Scott Anderson, rhp; B: Corvallis, OR; Oregon State University; 1987 TEX (1) (3)
43 — Paul Kilgus, lhp; B: Bowling Green, KY; University of Kentucky; 1987 TEX (2) (6)

1985

June — Regular Phase
1— Bobby Witt, rhp; B: Arlington, MA; University of Oklahoma; 1986 TEX (11) (13)
4 — Steve Wilson, lhp; B: Victoria, BC, Canada; University of Portland; 1988 TEX (1) (6)
5 — Chad Kreuter, c; B: Greenbrae, CA; Pepperdine University; 1988 TEX (4) (11)
11— Kevin Reimer, 1b; B: Macon, GA; Cal State Fullerton; 1988 TEX (5) (6)
16 — Mike Stanley, 1b; B: Ft. Lauderdale, FL; University of Florida; 1986 TEX (6) (11)
26 — Gary Mielke, rhp; B: St. James, MN; Mankato State University; 1987 TEX (3) (3)

1986

June — Regular Phase
1— Kevin Brown, rhp; B: Macon, GA; Georgia Tech; 1988 TEX (8) (12)
2 — Roger Pavlik, rhp; B: Houston, TX; Aldine HS, Houston, TX; 1992 TEX (7) (7)
3 — Dean Palmer, ss; B: Milledgeville, GA; Florida HS, Tallahassee, FL; 1986 TEX (8) (12)
7 — Mike Loynd, rhp; B: St. Louis, MO; Florida State University; 1986 TEX (2) (2)
11— John Barfield, lhp; B: Pine Bluff, AK; Oklahoma City University; 1989 TEX (3) (3)
13 — Rey Sanchez, ss; B: Rio Piedras, PR; no school; 1991 CHC (7) (8)
19 — Bob Malloy, rhp; B: Arlington, VA; University of Virginia; 1987 TEX (1) (2)

1987

1— Brian Bohanon, lhp; B: Denton, TX; North Shore HS, Houston, TX; 1990 TEX (5) (9)
1— Bill Haselman, c; B: Long Branch, NJ; UCLA; 1990 TEX (2) (7)
1— Mark Petkovsek, rhp; B: Beaumont, TX.; University of Texas; 1991 TEX (1) (6)
2 — Barry Manuel, rhp; B: Mamou, LA; LSU; 1991 TEX (2) (5)
3 — Scott Coolbaugh, 3b; B: Binghamton, NY.; University of Texas; 1989 TEX (2) (4)
4 — Jonathan Hurst, rhp; B: New York, NY; Spartanburg Methodist JC, SC; 1992 MON (1) (2)
5 — Terry Mathews, rhp; B: Alexandria, LA; Northeast Louisiana University; 1991 TEX (2) (7)
31— Kevin Mmahat, lhp; B: Memphis, TN; Tulane University; 1989 NYY (1) (1)
32 — Robb Nen, rhp; B: San Pedro, CA; Los Alamitos HS, Seal Beach, CA; 1993 TEX (1) (6)

1988

3 — Darren Oliver, lhp; B: Kansas City, MO; Rio Linda (CA) HS; 1993 TEX (6) (6)
6 — Rob Maurer, 1b; B: Evansville, IN; University of Evansville; 1991 TEX (2) (2)
30— Jeff Frye, 2b; B: Oakland, CA; Southeastern Oklahoma State University; 1992 TEX (3) (5)

1989

1— Donald Harris, of; B: Waco, TX; Texas Tech University; 1991 TEX (3) (3)
4 — Joey Eischen, lhp; B: West Covina, CA; Pasadena (CA) CC; 1994 MON (1) (4)
21— Gerald Alexander, rhp; B: Baton Rouge, LA; Tulane University; 1990 TEX (3) (3)
47 — Danny Patterson, rhp; B: San Gabriel, CA; Cerritos JC, CA; 1996 TEX (3) (3)

1990

5 — Jon Shave, 2b; B: Waycross, GA; Mississippi State University; 1993 TEX (1) (2)

7 — Terry Burrows, lhp; B: Lake Charles, LA; Mc-Neese State University; 1994 TEX (2) (4)

8 — Steve Dreyer, rhp; B: Ames, IA; University of Northern Iowa; 1993 TEX (2) (2)

10 — Rusty Greer, of; B: Fort Rucker, AL; University of Montevallo, AL; 1994 TEX (5) (5)

13 — David Hulse, of; B: San Angelo, TX; Schreiner College, TX; 1992 TEX (3) (5)

25 — Matt Whiteside, rhp; B: Charleston, MO; Arkansas State University; 1992 TEX (6) (7)

1991

1 — Benji Gil, ss-of; B: Tijuana, Mexico; Castle Park HS, Chula Vista, CA; 1993 TEX (4) (4)

2 — Terrell Lowery, of; B: Oakland, CA; Loyola Marymount University; 1997 CHC (2) (2)

9 — Scott Eyre, lhp; B: Inglewood, CA; JC of Southern Idaho; 1997 CHW (2) (2)

15 — Kerry Lacy, rhp; B: Chattanooga, TN; Chattanooga State Technical CC; 1996 BOS (2) (2)

30 — Desi Wilson, 1b; B: Glen Cove, NY; Fairleigh Dickinson University; 1996 SFG (1) (1)

1992

1 — Rick Helling, rhp; B; Devils Lake, ND; Stanford University; 1994 TEX (5) (5)

24 — Rich Aurilia, ss; B: Brooklyn, NY; St. John's University; 1995 SFG (4) (4)

26 — Mark Bradenburg, rhp; B; Houston, TX; Texas Tech; 1995 TEX (2) (3)

1993

2 — Edwin Diaz, 2b; B: Bayamon, PR; Vega Alta (PR) HS; 1998 ARZ (1) (1)

13 — Marc Sagmoen, of; B: Seattle, WA; University of Nebraska; 1997 TEX (1) (1)

24 — Eric Moody, rhp; B: Greenville, SC; Erskine College, SC; 1997 TEX (1) (1)

41 — Mike Cather, rhp; B: San Diego, CA; University of California: 1993 ATL (2) (2)

1994

2 — Kevin Brown, c; B: Valparaiso, IN; University of Southern Indiana; 1996 TEX (2) (3)

8 — Mark Little, of; B: Edwardsville, IL; University of Memphis; 1998 STL (1) (1)

10 — Stephen Larkin, of; B: Cincinnati, OH; University of Texas; 1998 CIN (1) (1)

1995

1 — Jonathan Johnson, rhp; B: La Grange, GA; Florida State University; 1998 TEX (1) (1)

3 — Ryan Dempster, rhp; Sechelt, BC, Canada; Elphinstone HS, Gibsons, BC, Canada; 1998 FLA (1)

4 — Ryan Glynn, rhp; B: Portsmouth, VA; Virginia Military Institute, 1999 TEX (1) (1)

29 — Mike Venafro, lhp; B: Takoma Park, MD; James Madison University; 1999 TEX (1) (1)

Toronto Blue Jays

1977

June — Regular Phase

9 — Jesse Barfield, of; B: Joliet, IL; Central HS, Joliet, IL; 1981 TOR (9) (12)

15 — Danny Ainge, ss; B: Eugene, OR; North Eugene (OR) HS; 1979 TOR (3) (3)

1978

January — Regular Phase

3 — Gene Petralli, c; B: Sacramento, CA; Sacramento CC, CA; 1982 TOR (3) (12)

June — Regular Phase

1 — Lloyd Moseby, 1b; B: Portland, OR; Oakland (CA) HS; 1980 TOR (10) (12)

5 — Dave Stieb, of; B: Santa Ana, CA; Southern Illinois University; 1979 TOR (15) (16)

7 — Brian Milner, c; B: Fort Worth, TX; Southwest HS, Fort Worth, TX; 1978 TOR (1) (1)

11 — Dave Baker, 3b; B: Lacona, IA; UCLA; 1982 TOR (1) (1)

1979

January — Regular Phase

2 — Mark Eichhorn, ss-rhp; B: San Jose, CA; Cabrillo (CA) JC; 1982 TOR (6) (11)

June — Regular Phase

2 — Ron Shepherd, of; B: Longview, TX; Kilgore (TX) HS; 1984 TOR (3) (3)

4 — Andre Robertson, 2b; B: Orange, TX; University of Texas; 1981 NYY (5) (5)

1981

June — Regular Phase

1 — Matt Williams, rhp; B: Houston, TX; Rice University; 1983 TOR (1) (2)

1 — John Cerutti, lhp; B: Albany, NY; Amherst College; 1985 TOR (6) (7) (from Brewers for Roy Howell)

6 — Stan Clarke, lhp; B: Toledo, OH; University of Toledo; 1983 TOR (3) (6)

June — Secondary Phase

1 — Mike Sharperson, ss; B: Orangeburg, SC; DeKalb South (GA) CC; 1987 TOR (1) (8)

1982

June — Regular Phase

2 — David Wells, lhp; B: Torrance, CA; Point Loma HS, San Diego, CA; 1987 TOR (6) (13)

3 — Jimmy Key, lhp; B: Huntsville, AL; Clemson University; 1984 TOR (9) (15)

6 — Pat Borders, 3b-of; B: Columbus, OH; Lake Wales (FL) HS; 1988 (7) (11)

21 — Steve Davis, lhp; B: San Antonio, TX; Texas A&M University; 1985 TOR (2) (3)

1983

June — Regular Phase

1 — Matt Stark, c; B: Whittier, CA; Los Altos HS, Hacienda Heights, CA; 1987 TOR (1) (2)

2 — Webster Garrison, ss; B: Marrero, LA; John Ehret HS, Marrero, LA; 1996 OAK (1) (1)

3 — Jeff DeWillis, c; B: Houston, TX; Pearland (TX) HS; 1987 TOR (1) (1)

4 — Jeff Hearron, c; B: Long Beach, CA; University of Texas; 1985 TOR (2) (2)

9 — Glenallen Hill, of; B: Santa Cruz, CA; Santa Cruz (CA) HS; 1989 TOR (3) (10)

1984

January — Regular Phase

1 — Eric Yelding, of-inf; B: Montrose, AL; Chipola (FL) JC; 1989 HOU (4) (5)

June — Regular Phase

2 — Dane Johnson, rhp; B: Coral Gables, FL; St. Thomas University, FL; 1994 CWS (1) (3)

3 — Greg Myers, c; B: Riverside, CA; Polytechnic HS, Pasadena, CA; 1987 TOR (5) (11)

1985

June — Regular Phase

2 — Kevin Batiste, of; B: Galveston, TX; Ball HS, Galveston, TX; 1989 TOR (1) (1)

6 — Jeff Musselman, lhp; B: Doylestown, PA; Harvard University; 1986 TOR (4) (5)

June — Secondary Phase

1 — Todd Stottlemyre, rhp; B: Yakima, WA; Yakima Valley JC, WA; 1988 TOR (7) (11)

1986

January — Regular Phase

5 — Mark Whiten, of; B: Pensacola, FL; Pensacola JC; 1990 TOR (2)(9)

June — Regular Phase

2 — Steve Cummings, rhp; B: Houston, TX; University of Houston; 1989 TOR (2) (2)

4 — Xavier Hernandez, rhp; Port Arthur, TX; University of Southwestern Louisiana; 1989 TOR (1) (10)

5 — Pat Hentgen, rhp; B: Detroit, MI; Fraser (MI) HS; 1991 TOR (8) (8)

10 — Randy Knorr, c; B: San Gabriel, CA; Baldwin Park (CA) HS; 1991 TOR (5) (8)

11 — Willie Blair, rhp; B: Paintsville, KY; Morehead State University; 1990 TOR (1) (9)

27 — Tom Quinlan, 3b; B: St. Paul, MN; Hill Murray HS, Maplewood, MN; 1990 TOR (2) (4)

28 — Darren Hall, rhp; B: Marysville, OH; Dallas Baptist University; 1994 TOR (2) (5)

43 — Doug Linton, rhp; B: Santa Ana, CA; UC Irvine; 1992 TOR (2) (5)

1987

1 — Alex Sanchez, rhp; B: Concord, CA; UCLA; 1989 TOR (1) (1)

2 — Derek Bell, of; B: Tampa, FL; King HS, Tampa, FL; 1991 TOR (2) (8)

5 — Mike Timlin, rhp; B: Midland, TX; Southwestern University, TX; 1991 TOR (7) (8)

13 — Ryan Thompson, of; B: Rock Hall, MD; Kent County HS, Rock Hall, MD; 1992 NYM (4) (5)

1988

1 — Ed Sprague, 3b-c; B: Castro Valley, CA; Stanford University; 1991 TOR (8) (8)

3 — David Weathers, rhp; B: Lawrenceburg, TN; Motlow State CC, TN; 1991 TOR (2) (8)

28 — Woody Williams, rhp; B: Houston, TX; University of Houston; 1994 TOR (5) (5)

38 — Ray Giannelli, 3b; B: Brooklyn, NY; New York Tech; 1991 TOR (1) (2)

1989

1 — Eddie Zosky, ss; B: Whittier, CA; Fresno State University; 1991 TOR (2) (3)

2 — Brent Bowers, of; B: Bridgeview, IL; St. Laurence HS, Burbank, IL; 1996 BAL (1) (1)

3 — John Olerud, 1b; B: Seattle, WA; Washington State University; 1989 TOR (8) (10)

20 — Jeff Kent, 2b; B: Bellflower, CA; University of California; 1992 TOR (1) (7)

22 — Aaron Small, rhp; B: Oxnard, CA; South Hills HS, West Covina, CA; 1994 (1) (5)

1990

1 — Steve Karsay, rhp; B: Flushing, NY; Christ The King HS, Queens, NY; 1993 OAK (3) (4)

2 — Tim Hyers, of; B: Atlanta, GA; Newton County HS, Covington, GA; 1994 SDP (2) (3)

3 — Felipe Crespo, of; B: Rio Piedras, PR; Notre Dame HS, Caguas, PR; 1996 TOR (3) (3)

4 — Howard Battle, of; B: Biloxi, MS; Mercy Cross HS, Ocean Springs, MS; 1996 PHI (1) (1)

7 — Scott Brow, rhp; B: Butte, MT; University of Washington; 1993 TOR (3) (4)

8 — Paul Menhart, rhp; B: St. Louis, MO; Western Carolina University; 1995 TOR (1) (3)

9 — Huck Flener, lhp; B: Austin, TX; Cal State Fullerton; 1993 TOR (3) (3)

37 — Ricardo Jordan, lhp; B: Boynton Beach, FL; Miami–Dade CC South, FL; 1995 TOR (1) (4)

45 — Travis Baptist, lhp; B: Forest Grove, Ore.; Hillsboro (Ore.) HS; 1998 MIN (1) (1)

1991

1— Shawn Green, of; B: Des Plaines, IL; Tustin (CA) HS; 1993 TOR (6) (6) (from Giants for Bud Black)

1— Jeff Ware, rhp; B: Palm Harbor, FL; Old Dominion University; 1991 TOR (2) (2)

3 — Chris Stynes, of; B: Queens, NY; Boca Raton (FL) HS; 1995 KCR (2) (4)

5 — Rickey Cradle, of; B: Norfolk, VA; Cerritos (CA) HS; 1998 SEA (1) (1)

6 — Jose Silva, rhp; B: Tijuana, Mexico; Hilltop HS, Chula Vista, CA; 1996 TOR (1) (3)

10— Ken Robinson, rhp; B: Barberton, OH; FSU; 1995 TOR (1) (3)

13 — Alex Gonzalez, ss; B: Miami, FL; Killian HS, Miami, FL; 1994 TOR (5) (5)

28 — Steve Sinclair, lhp; B: Victoria, BC, Canada; Kwantien College, BC, Canada; 1991 TOR (1) (1)

1992

1— Shannon Stewart, of; B: Cincinnati, OH; Southridge HS, Miami; 1995 TOR (4) (4)

1— Todd Stevenson, of; B: Los Angeles, CA; ASU; 1996 DET (1) (2)

2 — Tim Crabtree, rhp; B: Jackson, MI; Michigan State University; 1995 TOR (3) (4)

4 — Tom Evans, rhp-3b; B: Kirkland, WA; Juanita HS, Kirkland, WA; 1997 TOR (2) (2)

7 — Anthony Sanders, 3b-of; B: Tucson, AZ; Santa Rita High School, Tuscon, AZ; 1999 TOR (1) (1)

1993

1— Chris Carpenter, rhp; B: Exeter, NH; Trinity HS, Manchester, NH; 1997 TOR (2) (2)

17 — Mike Johnson, rhp; B: Edmonton, ON, Canada; Salisbury Composite HS, Edmonton, ON, Canada; 1997 BAL (1) (2)

1994

1— Kevin Witt, 1b; B: High Point, NC; Bishop Kenny HS, Jacksonville, FL; 1994 TOR (1) (1)

1995

1— Roy Halladay, rhp; B: Denver, CO; West HS, Arvada, CO; 1998 TOR (1) (1)

AMERICAN LEAGUE

Arizona Diamondbacks

As of June 1999, none of the Diamondback draft picks had made it to the majors.

Atlanta Braves

Milwaukee Braves:

1965

June — Regular Phase

4 — Charles Vaughan, lhp; B: Mercedes, TX; Brownsville HS, TX; 1966 ATL (2) (2)

6 — Wayne Garrett, ss; B: Brooksville, FL; Sarasota (FL) HS; 1969 NYM (8) (10)

Atlanta Braves:

1966

June — Regular Phase

1— Al Santorini, rhp; B: Irvington, NJ; Union HS, NJ; 1968 ATL (1) (6)

5 — George Stone, lhp-1b; B: Ruston, LA; Louisiana Tech; 1967 ATL (6) (9)

47— Roe Skidmore, c-1b; B: Decatur, IL; Millikin University; 1970 CHI (1) (1)

June — Secondary Phase

1— Oscar Brown, of; B: Long Beach, CA; USC; 1969 ATL (5) (5)

2 — Gary Neibauer, rhp; B: Billings, MT; University of Nebraska; 1969 ATL (4) (5)

1967

January — Secondary Phase

3 — Ron Schueler, rhp; B: Catherine, KS; 1972 ATL (2) (8)

June — Regular Phase

3 — Ralph Garr, 2b; B: Monroe, LA; Grambling University; 1968 ATL (8) (12)

4 — Bob Didler, c; B: Hattiesburg, MS; Glen Oaks, HS; 1969 ATL (4) (6)

26 — Dusty Baker, of; B: Riverside, CA; Del Campo HS, Carmichael, CA; 1968 ATL (8) (19)

June — Secondary Phase

1— Garry Hill, rhp; B: Rutherfordton, NC; UNC; 1969 ATL (1) (1)

3 — Tom House, lhp; B: Seattle, WA; USC; 1971 ATL (5) (8)

1968

June — Regular Phase

1— Clint Compton, lhp; B: Montgomery, AL; Robert E. Lee HS, Montgomery, AL; 1972 CHC (1) (1)

4 — Mike McQueen, lhp; B: Oklahoma City, OK; Spring Branch HS, Houston, TX; 1969 ATL (4) (5)

11— John Fuller, 1b; B: Lynwood, CA; Lynwood (CA) HS; 1974 ATL (1) (1)

1969

June — Regular Phase

6 — Jimmy Freeman, lhp; B: Carlsbad, NM; Hale HS, Tulsa, OK; 1972 ATL (2) (2)

20— Bucky Guth, ss; B: Baltimore, MD; West Virginia University; 1972 MIN (1) (1)

June — Secondary Phase

2 — Mickey Rivers, of; B: Miami, FL; Miami–Dade North CC; 1970 CAL (6) (15)

1970

January — Regular Phase
2 — Jack Pierce, 1b; B: Laurel, MS; San Jose CC, CA; 1973 ATL (2) (3)

June — Regular Phase
2 — Adrian Devine, rhp; B: Galveston, Texas; no school; 1973 ATL (3) (7)

3 — Rod Gilbreath, ss-rhp; B: Laurel, MS, R.H. Watkins HS, Laurel, MS; 1972 ATL (7) (7)

4 — Rowland Office, of; B: Sacramento, CA; Mc-Clatchy HS, Sacramento, CA; 1972 ATL (7) (11)

1971

June — Regular Phase
1— Taylor Duncan, ss; B: Memphis, TN; Grant Union HS, Sacramento, CA; 1977 STL (1) (2)

2 — Jamie Easterly, lhp; B: Houston, TX; Crockett (TX) HS; 1974 ATL (6) (13)

11— Junior Moore, 3b; B: Waskom, TX; J.F. Kennedy HS, Richmond, CA; 1976 ATL (2) (5)

17 — Bill Pocoroba, c; B: Burbank, CA: Canoga Park (CA) HS; 1975 ATL (10) (10)

1972

June — Regular Phase
1— Preston Hanna, rhp; B: Pensacola, FL; Escambia HS, Pensacola, FL; 1975 ATL (8) (9)

June — Secondary Phase
2 — Don Collins, lhp; B: Lyons, GA; South Georgia JC; 1977 ATL (1) (2)

1973

January — Secondary Phase
1— Brian Asselstine, of-inf; B: Santa Barbara, CA; Hancock JC, CA; 1976 ATL (6) (6)

June — Regular Phase
1— Pat Rockett, 2b-ss; B: San Antonio, TX; Robert E. Lee HS, San Antonio, TX; 1976 ATL (3) (3)

16 — Terry Harper, rhp-of; B: Douglasville, GA; Douglas County HS, Douglasville, GA; 1980 ATL (7) (9)

19 — Larry Bradford, lhp; B: Chicago, IL; Clark HS, Chicago, IL; 1977 ATL (4) (4)

1974

January — Regular Phase
1— Larry McWilliams, lhp; B: Wichita, TX; Paris JC, TX; 1978 ATL (6) (13)

January — Secondary Phase
2 — Mike Davey, lhp; B: Spokane, WA; Gonzaga University; 1977 ATL (2) (2)

June — Regular Phase
1— Dale Murphy, c; B: Portland, OR; Wilson HS, Portland, OR; 1976 ATL (15) (17)

2 — Joey McLaughlin, rhp; B: Tulsa, OK; McLain HS, Tulsa, OK; 1977 ATL (2) (7)

7 — Rick Camp, rhp; B: Trion, GA; West Georgia College; 1976 ATL (9) (9)

10 — Mickey Mahler, lhp; B: Montgomery, AL; Trinity University; 1977 ATL (3) (8)

1975

June — Regular Phase
2 — Larry Whisenton, of; B: St. Louis, MO; Central HS, St. Louis, MO; 1977 ATL (5) (5)

3 — Gary Cooper, of; B: Savannah, GA; Grove HS, Garden City, CA; 1980 ATL (1) (1)

4 — Hank Small, of; B: Atlanta, GA; University of South Carolina; 1978 ATL (1) (1)

8 — Jerry Maddox, ss; B: Whittier, CA; ASU; 1978 ATL (1) (1)

12 — Duane Theiss, rhp; B: Zanesville, OH; Marietta College; 1977 ATL (2) (2)

20 — Glenn Hubbard, 2b; B: Hahn, West Germany; Ben Lomond HS, Ogden, UT; 1978 ATL (10) (12)

1976

January — Secondary Phase
1— Mike Macha, 3b; B; Victoria, TX; Rice University; 1979 ATL (1) (2)

June — Regular Phase
1— Ken Smith, 3b; B: Youngston, OH; Youngstown East HS, OH; 1981 ATL (3) (3)

3 — Dan Morogiello, lhp; B: Brooklyn, NY; Seton Hall University; 1983 BAL (1) (1)

5 — Bruce Benedict, c; B: Birmingham, AL; University of Nebraska–Omaha; 1978 ATL (12) (12)

6 — Jim Wessinger, ss; B: Utica, NY; LeMoyne College; 1979 ATL (1) (1)

14 — Rick Matula, rhp; B: Wharton, TZ; Sam Houston State University; 1979 ATL (3) (3)

1977

June — Regular Phase
2 — Tony Brizzolara, rhp; B: Santa Monica, CA; University of Texas; 1979 ATL (3) (3)

3 — Bob Porter, of; B: Yuma, AZ; Napa HS, CA; 1981 ATL (2) (2)

6 — Albert Hall, ss; B: Birmingham, AL; Jones Valley HS, Birmingham, AL; 1981 ATL (8) (9)

17 — Larry Owen, c; B: Cleveland, OH; Bowling Green State University; 1981 ATL (4) (6)

1978

June — Regular Phase
1— Bob Horner, 3b; B: Junction City, KS; ASU; 1978 ATL (9) (10)

2 — Matt Sinatro, c; B: Hartford, CT; Conrad HS, West Hartford, CT; 1981 ATL (4) (10)

3 — Steve Bedrosian, rhp; B: Methuen, MA; University of New Haven; 1981 ATL (5) (11)

4 — Rich Behenna, rhp; B: Miami, FL; South Ridge HS, Cutler Ridge, FL; 1983 ATL (1) (3)

8 — Jose Alvarez, rhp; B: Tampa, FL; University of Southwestern Louisiana; 1981 ATL (4) (4)

11 — Gerald Perry, of; B: Savannah, GA; McCracken HS, Hilton Head, SC; 1983 ATL (7) (10)

1979

January — Regular Phase

2 — Milt Thompson, of; B: Washington, DC; Gaithersburg, MD; 1984 ATL (2) (9)

7 — Brook Jacoby, of; B: Philadelphia, PA; Ventura JC, CA; 1981 ATL (2) (11)

June — Regular Phase

1 — Brad Komminsk, of-1b; B: Lima, OH; Lima, OH; 1983 ATL (4) (8)

6 — Mike Payne, rhp; B: Woonsocket, RI; Williston HS, FL; 1984 ATL (1) (1)

9 — Paul Runge, ss; B: Kingston, NY; Jacksonville University; 1981 ATL (8) (8)

23 — Brett Butler, of; B: Los Angeles, CA; Southeastern Oklahoma State University; 1981 ATL (3) (17)

1980

January — Regular Phase

1 — Craig McMurtry, rhp; B: Temple, TX; McLennon CC, TX; 1983 ATL (4) (7)

June — Regular Phase

1 — Ken Dayley, lhp; B: Jerome, ID; University of Portland; 1982 ATL (3) (11)

1 — Jim Acker, rhp; B: Freer, TX; University of Texas; 1983 TOR (4) (10) (from Expos for Rowland Office)

2 — Brian Fisher, rhp; B: Honolulu, HI; Hinkley HS, Aurora, CO.; 1985 NYY (2) (7)

15 — Paul Zuvella, 2b; B: San Mateo, CA; Stanford University; 1982 ATL (4) (9)

1981

No selections

1982

June — Regular Phase

1 — Duane Ward, rhp; B: Park View, NM; Farmington HS, NM; 1986 ATL (1) (7)

2 — Joe Johnson, rhp; B: Brookline, MA; University of Maine; 1985 ATL (2) (3)

3 — Zane Smith, lhp; B: Madison, WI; Indiana State University, IN; 1984 ATL (6) (13)

1983

June — Regular Phase

3 — Marty Clary, rhp; B: Detroit, MI: Northwestern University; 1987 ATL (3) (3)

4 — Ronnie Gant, ss; B: Victoria, TX; Victoria (TX) HS; 1987 ATL (7) (11)

8 — Steve Ziem, rhp; B: Milwaukeee, WI; Cal Poly Pomona; 1987 ATL (1) (1)

11 — Kevin Coffman, of-rhp; B: Austin, TX; Victoria (TX) HS; 1987 ATL (2) (3)

27 — Mark Lemke, 2b; B: Utica, NY; Notre Dame HS, Whitesboro, NY; 1988 ATL (10) (11)

1984

June — Regular Phase

1 — Drew Denson, 1b-of; B: Cincinnati, OH; Purcell Marion HS, Cincinnati, OH; 1989 ATL (1) (1)

2 — Tom Glavine, lhp; B: Concord, MA; Billercia HS, North Billercia, MA; 1987 ATL (12) (12)

June — Secondary Phase

1 — Jeff Blauser, ss; B: Los Gatos, CA; Sacramento CC, CA; 1987 ATL (11) (12)

1985

June — Regular Phase

1 — Tommy Greene, rhp; B: Lumberton, NC; Whiteville (NC) HS; 1989 ATL (2) (8)

4 — David Justice, 1b; B: Cincinnati, OH; Thomas More College; 1989 ATL (8) (10)

8 — Al Martin, of; B: West Covina, CA; Rowland HS, West Covina, CA; 1992 PIT (7) (7)

12 — Gary Eave, rhp; B: Monroe, LA; Grambling State University; 1988 ATL (2) (3)

21 — Jeff Wetherby, of; B: Granada Hills, CA; USC; 1989 ATL (1) (1)

1986

June — Regular Phase

1 — Kent Mercker, lhp; B: Dublin, OH; Dublin (OH) HS; 1989 ATL (7) (10)

29 — Jim Czajkowski, rhp; B: Cleveland, OH; University of North Alabama; 1994 COL (1) (1)

1987

1 — Derek Lilliquist, lhp; B: Winter Park, FL; University of Georgia, GA; 1989 ATL (2) (8)

4 — Keith Mitchell, of; B: San Diego, CA; Lincoln HS, San Diego, CA; 1991 ATL (1) (4)

8 — Brian Hunter, of; B; El Toro, CA; Cerritos JC, CA; 1991 ATL (3) (7)

13 — Mike Stanton, lhp; B: Houston, TX; Alvin CC, TX; 1989 ATL (7) (10)

14 — David Nied, rhp; B: Dallas, TX; Duncanville (TX) HS; 1992 ATL (1) (6)

1988

1 — Steve Avery, lhp; B: Trenton, MI; Kennedy HS, Taylor, MI; 1990 ATL (7) (9)

2 — Matt Murray (from Phillies for Dave Palmer)

5 — Turk Wendell, rhp; B: Pittsfield, MA; Quinnipiac College, 1993 CHC (5) (6)

8 — Mark Wohlers, rhp; B: Holyoke, MA; Holyoke (MA) HS; 1991 ATL (8) (8)

15 — Tony Tarasco, of; B: New York, NY; Santa Monica HS, CA; 1993 ATL (2) (6)

1989

1— Tyler Houston, c; B: Las Vegas, NV; Valley HS, Las Vegas, NV; 1996 ATL (1) (3)

5 — Ryan Klesko, lhp-lb; B: Westminister, CA; Westminster HS, CA; 1992 ATL (7) (7)

6 — Mike Mordecai, ss; B: Birmingham, AL; University of South Alabama; 1994 ATL (4) (5)

18 — Joe Roa, rhp; B: Southfield, MI; Hazel Park (MI) HS; 1995 CLE (2) (3)

1990

1— Chipper Jones, ss; B: Deland, FL; The Boiles School, Jacksonville, FL; 1993 ATL (5) (5)

5 — Joe Ayrault, c; B: Rochester, MI; Sarasota HS, FL; 1996 ATL (1) (1)

7 — Ed Giovanola, ss; B: Los Gatos, CA; Santa Clara University; 1995 ATL (3) (4)

9 — Brian Kowitz, of; B: Baltimore, MD; Clemson University; 1995 ATL (1) (1)

10 — Anthony Graffagnino, ss; B: Amityville, NY; East Islip (NY) HS; 1996 ATL (3) (3)

12 — Brian Bark, lhp-of; B: Baltimore, MD; North Carolina State University; 1995 BOS (1) (1)

18 — Michael Potts, lhp; B: Langdale, AL; Gordon JC, GA; 1996 MIL (1) (1)

1991

1— Mike Kelly, of; B: Los Angeles, CA; ASU; 1994 ATL (2) (5)

8 — Jason Schmidt, rhp; B: Kelso, WA; Kelso (WA) HS; 1995 ATL (2) (4)

14 — Kevin Lomon, rhp; B: Fort Smith, AR; Westark CC, AR; 1995 NYM (1) (1)

1992

1— Jamie Arnold, rhp; B: Dearborn, MI; Osceola HS, Kissimmee, FL; 1999 LAD (1) (1)

4 — Damon Hollins, of; B: Fairfield, CA; Vallejo (CA) HS; 1998 ATL (1) (1)

10 — Brad Clontz, rhp; B: Stuart, VA; Virginia Tech; 1995 ATL (3) (4)

11 — Bobby Smith, 3b; B: Oakland, CA; Fremont HS, Oakland, HS; 1998 TAM (1) (1)

12 — Chris Brock, rhp; B: Orlando, FL; FSU; 1997 ATL (1) (2)

46 — Darrell May, lhp; B: San Bernardino, CA; Sacramento CC, CA; 1995 ATL (1) (3)

1993

3 — Carl Schutz, lhp; B: Hammond, LA; Southeastern Louisiana University; 1996 ATL (1) (1)

10 — Rob Sasser, 3b; B: Philadelphia, PA; Oakland (CA) HS; 1998 TEX (1) (1)

11 — Kevin Millwood, rhp; B: Gastonia, NC; Bessemer City (NC) HS; 1997 ATL (2) (2)

15 — John LeRoy, rhp; B: Bellevue, WA; Sammamish HS, Bellevue, WA; 1997 ATL (1) (1)

17 — Jermaine Dye, rhp; B: Vacaville, CA; Cosumnes River CC, CA; 1996 ATL (1) (3)

18 — John Rocker, lhp; B: Statesboro, GA; First Presbyterian Day School, Macon, GA; 1998 ATL (1) (1)

20 — Roosevelt Brown, of; B: Vicksburg, MS; Vicksburg HS, MS; 1999 CHC (1) (1)

1994

2 — George Lombard, of; B: Atlanta, GA; The Lovett School, Atlanta, GA; 1998 ATL (1) (1)

10 — Wes Helms, ss-rhp; B: Gastonia, NC; Ashbrook HS, Gastonia, NC; 1998 ATL (1) (1)

1996

7 — Mark DeRosa, 3b; B: Passaic, NJ; University of Pennsylvania; 1998 ATL (1) (1)

Chicago Cubs

1965

June — Regular Phase

1— Rick James, rhp; B: Sheffield, AL; Coffee HS, Florence, AL; 1967 CHC (1) (1)

2 — Ken Rudolph, c; B: Rockford, IL; Los Angeles CC; 1969 CHC (5) (9)

4 — Ken Holtzman, lhp; B: St. Louis, MO; University of Illinois; 1965 CHC (9) (15)

7 — Gary Jestadt, ss; B: Chicago, IL; Fremont HS, Sunnyvale, CA; 1969 MON (1) (3)

9 — Joe Decker, rhp; B: Storm Lake, IA; Petaluma (CA) HS; 1969 CHC (4) (9)

20 — Jim Williams, of; Zachary, LA; Harry Ells HS, Richmond, CA; 1969 SDP (2) (2)

1966

June — Regular Phase

14 — Rich Nye, lhp; B: Oakland, CA; University of California; 1966 CHC (4) (5)

31 — Bill Stoneman, rhp; B: Oak Park, IL; University of Idaho; 1967 CHC (2) (8)

38 — Archie Reynolds, rhp; B: Glendale, CA; Paris JC, TX; 1968 CHC (3) (5)

June — Secondary Phase

2 — Jophrey Brown, rhp; B: Grambling, LA; Grambling University; 1968 CHC (1) (1)

3 — Joe Niekro, rhp; B: Martins Ferry, OH; West Liberty State College; 1967 CHC (3) (22)

1967

January — Regular Phase

1— Alec Distaso, rhp; B: Los Angeles, CA; Wilson HS, Los Angeles, CA; 1969 CHC (1) (1)

2 — James Dunegan, rhp; B: Burlington, IA; Bacone JC, OK; 1970 CHC (1) (1)

3 — Earl Stephenson, lhp; B: Benson, NC; Benson HS, NC; 1971 CHC (1) (4)

January — Secondary Phase
1— Gary Ross, rhp; B: McKeesport, PA; Portvue, PA; 1968 CHC (2) (11)
4 — Pat Jacquez, rhp; B: Stockton, CA; San Joaquin Delta JC, CA; 1971 CHW (1) (1)

June — Regular Phase
1— Terry Hughes, ss; Spartansburg, SC; Dorman HS, Spartanburg, SC; 1970 CHC (1) (3)
2 — Jimmy McMath, of; B: Tuscaloosa, AL; Druid HS, Tuscaloosa, AL; 1968 CHC (1) (1)

June — Secondary Phase
1— Randy Bobb, c; B: Los Angeles, CA; ASU; 1968 CHC (2) (2)
6 — Darcy Fast, lhp; B: Dallas, OR; Warner Pacific College; 1968 CHC (1) (1)

1968

June — Regular Phase
2 — Matt Alexander, 3b; B: Shreverport, LA; Grambling University; 1973 CHC (2) (9)
16 — Oscar Gamble, of; B: Montgomery, AL; 1969 CHC (1) (17)

June — Secondary Phase
1— Dave Lemonds, lhp; B: Charlotte, NC; University of North Carolina; 1969 CHC (1) (2)
3 — Chris Ward, of; B: Oakland, CA; Chabot JC, CA; 1972 CHC (2) (2)
4 — Paul Reuschel, rhp; B: Quincy, IL; Western Illinois University; 1975 CHC (4) (5)

1969

June — Regular Phase
Major League selection:
1— Roger Metzger, ss; B: Fredericksburg, TX; St. Edward's University; 1970 CHC (1) (11)
2 — Larry Gura, lhp; B: Joilet, IL; ASU; 1970 CHC (5) (17)
10— Jim Todd, rhp; B: Lancaster, PA; Millersville University, PA; 1974 CHC (2) (6)
12 — Bill North, of; B: Seattle, WA; Central Washington University; 1971 CHC (2) (11)
33 — Pat Bourque, of; B: Worcester, MA; Holy Cross College; 1971 CHC (3) (4)

1970

January — Regular Phase
1— Pete LaCock, 1b; B: Burbank, CA; Taft HS, Woodland Hills, CA; 1972 CHC (5) (9)

June — Regular Phase
1— Gene Hiser, of; B: Baltimore, MD; University of Maryland; 1971 CHC (5) (5)
3 — Rick Reuschel, rhp; B: Quincy, IL; Western Illinois University; 1972 CHC (12) (19)

June — Secondary Phase
1— Tom Lundstedt, c; B: Davenport, IA; University of Michigan; 1973 CHC (2) (3)

1971

June — Regular Phase
3 — Dennis Lamp, rhp; B: Los Angeles, CA; St. John Bosco HS, Los Alamitos, CA; 1977 CHC (4) (16)
5 — Rob Sperring, 3b-ss; B: San Francisco, CA; University of the Pacific; 1974 CHC (3) (4)
7 — Jim Tyrone, of; B; Alice, TX; Pan American University; 1972 CHC (3) (4)

June — Secondary Phase Delayed
1— Burt Hooton, rhp; B: Greenville, TX; University of Texas; 1971 CHC (5) (15)

1972

June — Regular Phase
3 — Mike Gordon, c; Brockton HS, MA; 1977 CHC (2) (2)
6 — Buddy Schultz, lhp; B: Cleveland, OH; Miami University, OH; 1975 CHC (2) (5)
17 — Ray Burris, rhp; B: Idabel, OK; Southeastern Oklahoma State University; 1973 CHC (7) (15)
20— Wayne Tyrone, 2b; B: Alice, TX; Pan American University; 1976 CHC (1) (1)

1973

January — Secondary Phase
1— Donnie Moore, rhp-of; B: Lubdock, TX; University of Tulsa; 1975 CHC (4) (13)

June — Regular Phase
1— Jerry Tabb, 1b; B: Altus, OK; University of Tulsa; 1976 CHC (1) (3)
5 — Dave Geisel, lhp-1b; Tonawanda HS, NY; 1978 CHC (3) (7)
6 — Joe Wallis, of; B: E. St. Louis, IL; Southern Illinois University; 1975 CHC (4) (5)
8 — Mike Krukow, rhp; B: Long Beach, CA; Cal Poly San Luis Obispo; 1976 CHC (6) (14)

1974

June — Regular Phase
1— Scot Thompson, of; B: Grove City, PA; Knox HS, Renfrew, PA; 1978 CHC (6) (8)
2 — Mike Sember, ss; B: Hammond, IN; University of Tulsa; 1977 CHC (2) (2)
4 — George Riley, lhp; B: Philadelphia, PA; South Philadelphia HS; 1979 CHC (2) (4)

1975

January — Secondary Phase
1— Ed Putman, c; B: Los Angeles, CA; USC; 1976 CHC (2) (3)

June — Regular Phase
2 — Lee Smith, rhp; B: Shreveport, LA; Northwestern State University, LA; 1980 CHC (8) (17)

1976

January — Regular Phase
3 — Ron Davis, rhp; B: Houston, TX; Blinn JC, TX; 1978 CHC (2) (11)

June — Regular Phase
1— Herm Segelke, rhp; B: San Mateo, CA; El Camino HS, South San Francisco; 1982 CHC (1) (1)
3 — Kurt Seibert, ss; B: Cheverly, MD; Clemson University; 1979 CHC (1) (1)
4 — Keith Drumright, 2b; B: Springfield, MO; University of Oklahoma; 1978 HOU (1) (2)
5 — Greg Keatley, c; B: Princeton, WV; University of South Carolina; 1981 KCA (1) (1)
14 — Steven Davis, ss; B: Oak, CA; Stanford University; 1979 CHC (1) (1)

June — Secondary Phase
1— Karl Pagel, 1b; B: Madison, WI; University of Texas; 1978 CHC (2) (5)

1977

January — Regular Phase
4 — Jim Tracy, of; B: Hamilton, OH; Fairfield, OH; 1980 CHC (2) (2)

June — Regular Phase
1— Randy Martz, rhp; B: Harrisonburg, PA; University of South Carolina; 1980 CHC (3) (4)
4 — Dan Rohn, 2b; B: Alpena, MI; Central Michigan University; 1983 CHC (2) (3)
5 — Steve Macko, 3b-2b; B: Burlington, IA; Baylor University; 1979 CHC (2) (2)
29 — Gary Krug, 1b; B: Garden City, KS; University of Oklahoma; 1981 CHC (1) (1)

1978

June — Regular Phase
1— Bill Hayes, c; B: Cheverly, MD; Indiana State University; 1980 CHC (2) (2)
2 — Mel Hall, of; B: Lyons, NY; Port Byron HS, Cayuga, NY; 1981 CHC (4) (13)
14 — Mark Gilbert, of; B: Atlanta, GA; FSU; 1985 CHC (1) (1)
30 — Mike Diaz, 1b; B: San Francisco, CA; Terra Nova HS, Pacifica, CA; 1983 CHC (1) (4)

1979

June — Regular Phase
1— Jon Perlman, rhp; B: Dallas, TX; Baylor University; 1985 CHC (1) (3)
10 — Dave Owen, ss; B: Cleburne, TX; University of Texas–Arlington; 1983 CHC (3) (4)
11— Ray Soff, rhp; B: Adrian, MI; Central Michigan University; 1986 STL (2) (2)
16 — Tom Grant, of; B: Worchester, MA; University of New Haven; 1983 CHC (1) (1)

June — Secondary Phase
1— Scott Fletcher, ss; B: Fort Walton Beach, FL; Georgia Southern College; 1981 CHC (2) (12)

1980

June — Regular Phase
1— Don Schulze, rhp; B: Roselle, IL; Lake Park HS, Roselle, IL; 1983 CHC (2) (6)
7 — Fritz Connally, 3b; B: Bryan, TX; Baylor University; 1983 CHC (1) (2)
9 — Craig Lefferts, lhp; B: Munich, West Germany; University of Arizona; 1983 CHC (1) (12)

1981

January — Regular Phase
6 — Billy Hatcher, of; B: Williams, AZ; Yavapai JC, AZ; 1984 CHC (2) (12)

June — Regular Phase
1— Joe Carter, of; B: Oklahoma City, OK; Wichita State University; 1983 CHC (1) (16)
1— Vance Lovelace, lhp; B: Tampa, FL; Hillsborough HS, Tampa, FL; 1988 CAL (2) (3) (from Reds for
2 — Darrin Jackson, of; B: Los Angeles, CA; Culver City HS, CA; 1985 CHC (4) (11)

1982

June — Regular Phase
1— Shawon Dunston, ss; B; Brooklyn, NY; Thomas Jefferson HS, Brooklyn NY; 1985 CHC (13) (14)
5 — Gary Varsho, 2b; B: Marshfield, WI; University of Wisconsin, Oshkosh, WI; 1988 CHC (3) (8)

1983

January — Secondary Phase
3 — Dave Martinez, of; B: New York, NY; Valencia CC, FL; 1986 CHC (3) (13)

June — Regular Phase
2 — Rich Amaral, of; B: Visalia, CA; UCLA; 1991 SEA (8) (8)
5 — Steve Engel, lhp; B: Cincinnati, OH; Eastern Kentucky University; 1985 CHC (1) (1)
7 — Jacob Brumfield, of; B: Bogalusa, LA; Hammond HS, Atlanta, GA; 1992 CIN (3) (6)
13 — Mike Capel, rhp; B: Marshall, TX.; University of Texas; 1988 CHC (1) (3)

1984

January — Regular Phase
1— Damon Berryhill, c; B: S. Laguna, CA; Orange Coast JC, CA; 1987 CHC (5) (9)

June — Regular Phase
1— Drew Hall, lhp; B: Louisville, KY.; Morehead State University; 1986 CHC (3) (5)
2 — Greg Maddux, rhp; B: San Angelo, TX; Valley HS, Las Vegas, NV; 1986 CHC (7) (13)
6 — Jamie Moyer, lhp; B: Sellersville, PA; St. Joseph's University; 1986 CHC (3) (12)
13 — Jeff Pico, rhp; B: Antioch, CA; Antioch HS, CA; 1988 CHC (3) (3)

June — Secondary Phase
3 — Dwight Smith, of; B: Tallahassee, FL; Spatanburg Methodist JC, SC; 1989 CHC (5) (8)

1985

June — Regular Phase
1 — Rafael Palmeiro, cf; B: Havana, Cuba; Mississippi State University; 1986 CHC (3) (13)
2 — Greg Smith, ss; B: Baltimore, MD; Gleneig HS, Sykesville, MD; 1989 CHC (2) (3)
5 — Rick Wrona, c; B: Tulsa, OK; Wichita State University; 1988 CHC (4) (6)
12 — Doug Dascenzo, of; B: Cleveland, OH; Oklahoma State University; 1988 CHC (5) (7)
16 — Joe Kraemer, lhp; B: Olympia, WA; Vancouver, WA; 1989 CHC (2) (2)
20 — Kelly Mann, c; B: Santa Monica, CA; Santa Monica HS, CA; 1989 ATL (2) (2)
24 — Mark Grace, 1b; B: Winston Salem, NC; San Diego State University; 1988 CHC (11) (11)

1986

January — Regular Phase
1 — Shawn Boskie, rhp; B: Hawthorne, NV; Modesto JC, CA; 1990 CHC (5) (9)
2 — Jerome Walton, of; B: Los Angeles, CA; Enterprise State JC, AL; 1989 CHC (4) (10)

June — Regular Phase
1 — Derrick May, of; B: Rochester, NY; Newark HS, DE; 1990 CHC (5) (9)
5 — Joe Girardi, c; B: Peoria, IL; Northwestern University; 1989 CHC (4) (10)
9 — Jimmy Bullinger, ss-rhp; B: New Orleans, LA; University of New Orleans; 1992 CHC (5) (7)
23 — Rick Wilkins, c; B: Jacksonville, FL; Florida JC; 1991 CHC (5) (8)

1987

1 — Mike Harkey, rhp; B: San Diego, CA; Cal State Fullerton; 1988 CHC (5) (7)
3 — Alex Arias, 3b; B: New York, NY; George Washington HS, NY; 1992 CHC (1) (7)
6 — Frank Castillo, rhp; B: El Paso, TX.; Eastwood HS, El Paso, TX; 1991 CHC (7) (8)
7 — Matt Franco, 3b; B: Santa Monica, CA; Westlake HS, Westlake Village, CA; 1995 CHC (1) (4)
8 — Matt Walbeck, c; B: Sacramento, CA: Sacramento (CA) HS; 1993 CHC (1) (6)
38 — Tom Thobe, lhp; B: Covington, KY; Edison HS, Huntington Beach, CA; 1995 ATL (2) (2)

1988

4 — Jessie Hollins, rhp; B: Conroe, TX; Willis (TX) HS; 1992 CHC (1) (1)
16 — Kevin Roberson, of; B: Decatur, IL.; Parkland JC, IL.; 1993 CHC (3) (4)

1989

2 — Gary Scott, 3b; B: New Rochelle, NY; Villanova University; 1991 CHC (2) (2)
9 — Dave Swartzbaugh, rhp; B: Middleton, OH; Miami University, OH; 1995 CHC (2) (2)
20 — Dave Stevens, rhp; B: Fullerton, CA; Fullerton CC, CA; 1994 MIN (4) (5)

1990

1 — Lance Dickson, lhp; B: Fullerton, CA; University of Arizona; 1990 CHC (1) (1)
2 — Ryan Hawblitzel, rhp; B: West Palm Beach, FL; Leonard HS, West Palm Beach, FL; 1996 COL (1) (1)
12 — Pedro Valdes, of; B: Fajardo, PR; Carlos Escobar Lopez, HS, Loiza, PR; 1996 CHC (2) (2)

1991

1 — Doug Glanville, of; B: Hackensack, NJ; University of Pennsylvania; 1996 CHC (2) (3)
4 — Terry Adams, rhp; B: Mobile, AL; Mary Montgomery HS, Semmes, AL; 1995 CHC (4) (4)
5 — Ozzie Timmons, of; B: Tampa, FL; University of Tampa; 1995 CHC (2) (3)
8 — Steve Trachsel, rhp; B: Oxnard, CA; Long Beach State University; 1993 CHC (6) (6)
33 — Robin Jennings, of; B: Singapore; Manatee JC, FL; 1996 CHC (2) (2)

1992

1 — Derek Wallace, rhp; B: Van Nuys, CA; Pepperdine University; 1996 NYM (1) (1)
3 — Brant Brown, 1b; B: Porterville, CA; Fresno State University; 1996 CHC (3) (3)
8 — Mike Hubbard, c; B: Lynchburg, VA; James Madison University; 1995 CHC (3) (4)
12 — Kennie Steenstra, rhp; B: Springfield, MO; Wichita State University; 1998 CHC (1) (1)

1993

1 — Brooks Kieschnick, of; B: Robstown, TX; 1996 CHC (2) (2)
1 — Kevin Orie, 3b; B: West Chester, PA; Indiana University; 1997 CHC (2) (2)
74 — Jason Maxwell, 2b; B: Lewisburg, TN; 1998 CHC (1) (1)

1994

3 — Javier Martinez, rhp; B: Bayamon, PR; Liceo HS, Bayamon, PR; 1998 PIT (1) (1)
37 — Rich Barker, rhp; B: Revere, MA; Quinsigamond CC; 1999 CHC (1) (1)
47 — Kyle Farnsworth, rhp; B: Wichita, KS; JC; 1999 CHC (1) (1)

1995

1— Kerry Wood, rhp; B: Irving, TX; Grand Prairie (TX) HS; 1998 CHC (1) (1)

55 — Justin Speier, rhp; B: Walnut Creek, CA; Nicholls State University; 1998 CHC (1) (1)

Cincinnati Reds

1965

June — Regular Phase

1— Bernie Carbo, 3b; B: Detroit, MI; Livonia HS, Garden City, MI; 1969 CIN (4) (12)

2 — Johnny Bench, c; B: Oklahoma City, OK; Anadarko HS, Binger, OK; 1967 CIN (17) (17)

6 — Hal McRae, ss; B: Avon Park, FL; Florida A&M University; 1968 CIN (1) (19)

1966

January — Secondary Phase

1— Dan McGinn, lhp; B: Omaha, NE; University of Notre Dame; 1968 CIN (1) (5)

4 — John Noriega, rhp; B: Ogden, UT; University of Utah; 1969 CIN (2) (2)

June — Regular Phase

1— Gary Nolan, rhp; B: Herlong, CA; Oroville (CA) HS; 1967 CIN (10) (10)

2 — Darrell Chaney, ss; B: Hammond, IN; Morton HS, Hammond, IN; 1969 CIN (7) (11)

1967

June — Regular Phase

1— Wayne Simpson, rhp; B: Los Angeles, CA; Centennial HS, Los Angeles, CA; 1970 CIN (3) (6)

4 — Fred Kendall, c; B: Torrance, CA; Torrance (CA) HS; 1969 SDP (10) (12)

29 — Dave Tomlin, lhp; B: Mayville, KY; West Union (OH) HS; 1972 CIN (5) (10)

June — Secondary Phase

1— Frank Duffy, ss; B: Oakland, CA; Stanford University; 1970 CIN (3) (6)

12 — Kurt Bevacqua, 2b; B: Miami Beach, FL; Miami–Dade North CC; 1971 CLE (2) (15)

1968

June — Regular Phase

2 — Milt Wilcox, rhp; Honolulu, HI; Crooked Oak HS, Oklahoma City, OK; 1970 CIN (2) (16)

June — Secondary Phase

1— Mel Behney, lhp; B: Newark, NY; Michigan State University; 1970 CIN (1) (1)

1969

January — Secondary Phase

1— Ross Grimsley, lhp; B: Topeka, KS; Jackson State CC, TN; 1971 CIN (3) (10)

1995

1— Don Gullett, lhp; B: Lynn, KY; McKell HS, Lynn, KY; 1970 CIN (7) (9)

3 — Rawly Eastwick, rhp; B: Camden, NJ; Haddonfield (NJ) HS; 1974 CIN (4) (8)

12 — Nardi Contreras, rhp; B: Tampa, FL; Tampa (FL) Catholic HS; 1980 CHW (1) (1)

29 — Ken Griffey, of; B: Donora, PA; Donora (PA) HS; 1973 CIN (9) (19)

1970

January — Regular Phase

2 — Joel Youngblood, c-ss; B: Houston, TX; Stephen F. Austin HS, Houston, TX; 1976 CIN (2) (14)

June — Regular Phase

6 — Tom Carroll, rhp; B: Utica, NY; North Allegheny HS, Pittsburgh, PA; 1974 CIN (2) (2)

8 — Will McEnaney, lhp; B: Springfield, OH; Springfield (OH) North HS; 1974 CIN (3) (6)

10 — Ray Knight, rhp-3b; B: Albany, GA; Dougherty HS, Albany, GA; 1974 CIN (6) (11)

19 — Pat Zachry, rhp; B: Richmond, TX; Richfield HS, Waco, TX; 1976 CIN (2) (10)

June — Secondary Phase

1— Pat Osburn, lhp; B: Murray, KY; FSU; 1974 CIN (1) (2)

1971

June — Regular Phase

5 — Don Werner, c; B: Appleton, WI; East HS, Appleton, WI; 1975 CIN (5) (7)

7 — Dave Revering, lb; B: Roseville, CA; Bella Vista HS, Fair Oaks, CA; 1978 OAK (4) (5)

1972

January — Secondary Phase

1— Tom Hume, rhp; B: Cincinnati, OH; Manatee (FL) JC; 1977 CIN (9) (11)

June — Regular Phase

21— Dan Dumoulin, rhp; B: Kokomo, IN; Kokomo (IN) HS; 1977 CIN (2) (2)

1974

January — Regular Phase

1— Mike Armstrong, rhp; B: Glen Cove, NY; University of Miami (FL); 1981 SDP (2) (8)

June — Regular Phase

2 — Mike Grace, 3b; B: Pontiac, MI; Waterford Mott HS, Pontiac, MI; 1978 CIN (1) (1)

3 — Mike LaCoss, rhp; B: Glendale, CA; Mt. Whitney HS, Visalia, CA; 1978 CIN (4) (14)

5 — Steve Henderson, ss-3b; B: Houston, TX; Prairie View A&M University; 1977 NYM (4) (12)

9 — Ron Oester, ss; B: Cincinnati, OH; Withrow HS, Cincinnati, OH; 1978 CIN (13) (13)

10 — Lynn Jones, of; B: Meadville, PA; Thiel College; 1979 DET (5) (8)

15 — Dan Norman, 1b-of; B: Los Angeles, CA; Barstow (CA) CC; 1977 NYM (4) (5)

1975

June — Regular Phase

2 — Frank Pastore, rhp; B: Alhambra, CA; Damien HS, Upland, CA; 1979 CIN (7) (8)

3 — Paul Moskau, rhp; B: St. Joseph, MO; Azusa Pacific University; 1977 CIN (5) (7)

4 — Scott Brown, rhp; B: DeQuincy, LA; DeQuincy (LA) HS; 1981 CIN (1) (1)

1976

January — Secondary Phase

1 — Duane Walker, lhp-of; B: Pasadena, TX; San Jacinto (TX) JC; 1982 CIN (4) (5)

June — Regular Phase

2 — Paul Householder, of; B: Columbus, OH; North Haven (CT) HS; 1980 CIN (5) (8)

7 — Bill Dawley, rhp; B: Norwich, CT; Griswold HS, Lisbon, CT; 1983 HOU (3)(7)

21— Eddie Milner, of; B: Columbus, OH; Central State University, OH; 1980 CIN (8) (9)

31— Jay Howell, rhp; B: Miami, FL; University of Colorado; 1980 CIN (1) (15)

June — Secondary Phase:

1 — Bruce Berenyl, rhp; B: Bryan, OH; Northeast Missouri State University; 1980 CIN (5) (6)

1977

January — Secondary Phase

1 — Bill Scherrer, lhp; B: Tonawanda, NY; Las Vegas, NV; 1982 CIN (3) (7)

June — Regular Phase

4 — Joe Price, lhp; B: Inglewood, CA; University of Oklahoma; 1980 CIN (7) (11)

7 — Tom Foley, ss; B: Columbus, GA; Palmetto HS, Miami, FL; 1983 CIN (3) (13)

8 — Tony Walker, ss; B: San Diego, CA; San Marcos HS, Martindale, TX; 1986 HOU (1) (1)

1978

January — Regular Phase

3 — Paul Gibson, lhp; B: Southampton, NY; Center Moriches (NY) HS; 1988 DET (4) (8)

June — Regular Phase

1 — Nick Esasky, ss; B: Hialeah, FL; Carol City (FL) HS; 1983 CIN (6) (8)

2 — Dave Van Gorder, c; B: Los Angeles, CA; USC; 1982 CIN (4) (5)

5 — Jeff Lahti, rhp; B: Oregon City, OR; Portland State Unversity, OR; 1982 STL (5) (5)

9 — Charlie Liebrandt, lhp; B: Chicago, IL; Miami (OH) University; 1979 CIN (4) (14)

15 — Gary Redus, ss; B: Tanner, AL; Athens State College; 1982 CIN (4) (13)

16 — Skeeter Barnes, 2b; B: Cincinnati, OH; University of Cincinnati; 1983 CIN (2) (9)

17 — Tom Lawless, ss-2b; B: Erie, PA; Penn State University; 1982 CIN (2) (8)

June — Secondary Phase

1 — Brad Lesley, rhp; B: Turlock, CA; Merced JC, CA; 1982 CIN (3)(4)

1979

January — Secondary Phase

1 — Bill Bordley, lhp; B: Los Angeles, CA; El Camino (CA) JC; 1980 SFG (1) (1)

June — Regular Phase

2 — Keefe Cato, rhp; B: Santa Monica, CA; Fairfield University; 1983 CIN (2) (2)

2 — Bob Buchanan, lhp; B: Ridley Park, PA; Riverview HS, Sarasota, FL; 1985 CIN (1) (2)

5 — Jeff Russell, rhp; B: Cincinnati, OH; Wyoming HS, Cincinnati, OH; 1983 CIN (2) (14)

20— Jeff Jones, of; B: Philadelphia, PA; University of Iowa; 1983 CIN (1) (1)

25 — Kurt Kepshire, rhp; B: Bridgeport, CT; University of New Haven; 1984 STL (3) (3)

1980

June — Regular Phase

1 — Ron Robinson, rhp-ss; B: Exeter, CA; Woodlake (CA) HS; 1984 CIN (7) (9)

3 — Danny Tartabull, 2b; B: San Juan, PR; Carol City (FL) HS; 1984 SEA (3) (14)

8 — Eric Davis, ss; B: Los Angeles, CA; Fremont HS, Los Angeles, CA; 1984 CIN (8) (14)

12 — Scott Terry, of; B: Hobbs, NM; Southwestern University, TX; 1986 CIN (1) (5)

1981

January — Secondary Phase

1 — Rob Murphy, lhp; B: Miami, FL; no school; 1985 CIN (4) (11)

June — Regular Phase

4 — Paul O'Neill, of; B: Columbus, OH; Brookhaven, HS, Columbus, OH; 1985 CIN (8) (14)

8 — Terry McGriff, c; B: Fort Pierce, FL; Westwood HS, Fort Pierce, FL; 1987 CIN (4) (6)

1982

June — Regular Phase

9 — Tom Browning, lhp; B: Casper, WV; Tennessee Wesleyan College; 1984 CIN (11) (12)

June — Secondary Phase

1 — Kal Daniels, of; B: Vienna, GA; Middle Georgia JC; 1986 CIN (4) (7)

1983

January — Secondary Phase

1 — Tracy Jones, 3b; B: Inglewood, CA; Hawthorne, CA; 1986 CIN (3) (6)

June — Regular Phase

1— Kurt Stillwell, ss; B: Glendale, CA; Thousand Oaks (CA) HS; 1986 CIN (2) (9)

2— Chris Sabo, 3b; B: Detroit, MI; University of Michigan; 1988 CIN (7) (10)

2— Joe Oliver, c; B: Memphis, TN; Boone HS, Orlando, FL; 1989 CIN (8) (10)

5— Lenny Harris, 3b; B: Miami, FL; Jackson HS, Miami, FL; 1988 CIN (2) (11)

9— Jeff Montgomery, rhp; B: Wellston, OH; Marshall University; 1988 KCR (11) (11)

June — Secondary Phase

1— Rob Dibble, rhp; B: Bridgeport, CT; Southington, CT; 1988 CIN (6) (8)

1984

January — Regular Phase

5— Michael Smith, rhp; B: Jackson, MS; Ranger (TX) JC; 1984 CIN (3) (5)

June — Regular Phase

1— Pat Pacillo, rhp; B: Jersey City, NJ; Seton Hall University; 1987 CIN (2) (2)

3— Chris Jones, of; B: Utica, NY; Liverpool (NY) HS; 1991 CIN (1) (8)

1985

June — Regular Phase

1— Barry Larkin, ss; B: Cincinnati, OH; University of Michigan; 1986 CIN (13) (13)

12— Marty Brown, of-3b; B: Lawton, OK; University of Georgia; 1988 CIN (2) (3)

17— Mike Roesler, rhp; B: Fort Wayne, IN; Ball State University; 1989 CIN (1) (2)

1986

January — Regular Phase

6— Chris Hammond, lhp; B: Atlanta, GA; Gulf Coast (FL) CC; 1990 CIN (3) (9)

11— Keith Lockhart, 2b; B: Whittier, CA; Oral Roberts University; 1994 SDP (1) (5)

June — Regular Phase

1— Scott Scudder, rhp; B: Paris, TX; Praireland HS, Blossom, TX; 1989 CIN (3) (5)

3— Reggie Jefferson, 1b; B: Tallahassee, FL; Lincoln HS, Tallahassee, FL; 1991 CIN (1) (8)

6— Ed Taubensee, c; B: Beeville, TX; Lake Howell HS, Casselberry, FL; 1991 CLE (1) (8)

7— Jeff Richardson, ss; B: Grand Island, NE; Louisiana Tech; 1989 CIN (1) (3)

9— Chuck Carr, of; B: San Bernardino, CA; Fontana (CA) HS; 1990 NYM (2) (8)

11— Keith Lockhart, 2b; B: Whittier, CA; Oral Roberts University; 1994 SDP (1) (5)

1987

1— Jack Armstrong, rhp; B: Englewood, NJ; University of Oklahoma; 1988 CIN (4) (7)

7— Reggie Sanders, ss-of; B: Florence, SC; Spartanburg Methodist JC, SC; 1991 CIN (8) (8)

14— Bill Risley, rhp; B: Chicago, IL; Truman JC, IL; 1992 MON (2) (7)

15— Butch Henry, lhp; B: El Paso, TX; El Paso (TX) HS; 1992 HOU (1) (6)

1988

2— Jeff Branson, ss; B: Waynesboro, MS; Livingtson (AL) College; 1992 CIN (6) (8)

19— Jerry Spradlin, rhp; B: Fullerton, CA; Fullerton JC, CA; 1993 CIN (3) (5)

32— Mo Sanford, rhp; B: Americus, GA; University of Alabama; 1991 CIN (1) (2)

1989

6— Tim Pugh, rhp; B: Lake Tahoe, CA; Oklahoma State University; 1992 CIN (5) (6)

11— Trevor Hoffman, ss; B: Bellflower, CA; University of Arizona; 1993 FLA (1) (6)

34— Scott Pose, of; B: Davenport, IA; University of Arkansas; 1993 FLA (1) (2)

1990

1— Dan Wilson, c; B: Arlington Heights, IL; University of Minnesota; 1992 CIN (2) (7)

2— Keith Gordon, ss; B: Bethesda, MD; Wright State University; 1993 CIN (1) (1)

6— Steve Gibralter, of; B: Dallas, TX; Duncanville (TX) HS; 1995 CIN (2) (2)

8— Larry Luebbers, rhp; B: Cincinnati; University of Kentucky; 1993 CIN (1) (1)

12— John Roper, rhp; B: Southern Pines, NC; Hoke County HS, Raeford, NC; 1993 CIN (2) (3)

1991

1— Calvin Reese, ss; B: Columbia, SC; Lower Richland HS, Hopkins SC; 1997 CIN (2) (2)

8— John Courtright, lhp; B: Marion, OH; Duke University; 1995 CIN (1) (1)

14— Brian Koelling, 2b; B: Cincinnati, OH; Bowling Green State University; 1993 CIN (1) (1)

21— Kevin Jarvis, rhp; B: Lexington, KY; Wake Forest University; 1994 CIN (4) (4)

1992

1— Chad Mottola, of; B: Augusta, VA; University of Central Florida; 1996 CIN (1) (1)

4— Eric Owens, of; B: Danville, VA; Ferrum College, VA; 1995 CIN (3) (4)

6— Curt Lyons, rhp; B: Greencastle, IN; Madison Central HS, Richmond, KY; 1996 (1) (1)

15— Tim Belk, 1b; B: Cincinnati; Lubbock Christian University, Texas; 1996 CIN (1) (1)

21— Will Brunson, lhp; B: Irving, TX; Southwest Texas State University; 1998 LAD (1) (1)

23 — Chad Fox, rhp; B: Coronado, CA; Tarleton State University; 1998 MIL (1) (1)

28 — Ricky Pickett, lhp; B: Fort Worth, TX; Northeastern State University, OK; 1998 ARZ (1) (1)

1993

1— Pat Watkins, of; B: Raleigh, NC; East Carolina University; 1993 CIN (2) (2)

2 — Scott Sullivan, rhp; B: Carrollton, AL; Auburn University; 1995 CIN (4) (4)

5 — Paul Bako, c; B: Lafayette, LA; University of Southwestern Louisana; 1998 DET (1) (1)

1994

1— C.J. Nitkowski, lhp; B: Suffern, NY; St. John's University; 1995 CIN (1) (3)

3 — Aaron Boone, 3b; B: La Mesa, CA; USC; 1997 CIN (2) (2)

9 — Eddie Priest, lhp; B: Boaz, AL; Southern Union State JC, AL; 1998 CIN (1) (1)

1995

2 — Brett Tomko, rhp; B: Cleveland, OH; Florida Southern College; 1997 CIN (2) (2)

1997

7 — Mike Frank, of; B: Pomona, CA; Santa Clara University; 1998 CIN (1) (1)

Colorado Rockies

1992

1— John Burke, rhp; B: Durango, CO; University of Florida; 1996 COL (2) (2)

2 — Mark Thompson, rhp; B: Russellville, KY; University of Kentucky; 1994 COL (5) (5)

3 — Roger Bailey, rhp; B: Chattahoochee, FL; FSU; 1995 COL (3) (3)

7 — Jason Bates, ss; B: Downey, CA; University of Arizona; 1995 COL (4) (4)

10— Garvin Alston, rhp; B: Mount Vernon, NY; Florida International University; 1996 COL (1) (1)

11— Craig Counsell, ss; B: South Bend, IN; University of Notre Dame; 1995 COL (2) (4)

14 — Juan Acevedo, rhp, B: Juarez, Mexico; Parkland (IL) JC; 1995 COL (1) (3)

17 — Angel Echevarria, of; B: Bridgeport, CT; Rutgers University; 1996 COL (3) (3)

25 — Quinton McCracken, of; B: Wilmington, NC; Duke University; 1995 COL (3) (4)

28 — Mark Strittmatter, c; B: Huntington, NY; Virginia Commonwealth University; 1998 COL (1) (1)

1993

1— Jamey Wright, rhp; B: Oklahoma City, OK; Westmoore HS, Oklahoma City, OK; 1996 COL (3) (3)

2 — Bryan Rekar, rhp; B: Oak Lawn, IL; Bradley University; 1995 COL (3) (4)

7 — John Thomson, rhp; B: Vicksburg, MS; Blinn JC, TX; 1997 COL (2) (2)

10— Edgard Velazquez, of; B: Santurce, PR; No school; 1998 COL (1) (1)

30— Mark Brownson, rhp; B: West Palm Beach, FL; Palm Beach (FL) CC; 1998 COL (1) (1)

40— Terry Jones, of; B: Birmingham, AL; University of North Alabama; 1996 COL (1) (2)

1994

12 — Mike Saipe, rhp; B: San Diego, CA; University of San Diego; 1998 COL (1) (1)

1995

1— Todd Helton, 1b; B: Knoxville, TN; University of Tennessee; 1997 COL (1) (2)

Florida Marlins

1992

1— Charles Johnson, c; B: Fort Pierce, FL; University of Miami; 1994 FLA (5) (5)

25 — Andy Larkin, rhp; B: Chelan, WA; South Medford HS, Medford, OR; 1996 FLA (2) (2)

1993

1— Marc Valdes, rhp; B: Dayton, OH; University of Florida; 1995 FLA (2) (4)

2 — John Roskos, 1b; B: Victorville, CA; Cibola HS, Rio Rancho, NM; 1998 FLA (1) (1)

7 — Todd Dunwoody, of; B: Lafayette, IN; Harrison HS, Evansville, IN; 1997 FLA (2) (2)

8 — Billy McMillon, of; B: Otero, NM; Clemson University; 1996 FLA (2) (2)

20— Bryan Ward, lhp; B: Bristol, PA; University of South Carolina; 1998 CHW (1) (1)

38 — Dave Berg, 2b; B: Rossville, CA; University of Maine; 1998 FLA (1) (1)

1994

1— Josh Booty, ss; B: Starkville, MS; Evangel Christian HS, Shreveport, LA; 1996 FLA (3) (3)

3 — Rusty Meacham, rhp; B: Montgomery, AL; Henderson HS, Troy, AL; 1998 FLA (1) (1)

7 — Ryan Jackson, 1b; B: Sarasota, FL; Duke University; 1998 FLA (1) (1)

12 — Rob Stanifer, rhp; B: Easley, SC; Anderson College, SC; 1997 FLA (2) (2)

1995

3 — Randy Winn, of; B: Los Angeles, CA; Santa Clara University; 1998 TAM (1) (1)

16 — Gabe Gonzalez, lhp; B: Long Beach, CA; Long Beach State University; 1998 FLA (1) (1)

19 — Mike Duvall, lhp; B: Warrentown, VA; Potomac State JC; 1998 TBD (1) (1)

1996

1 — Mark Kotsay, of; B: Whittier, CA; Cal State Fullerton; 1997 FLA (2) (2)

5 — Brent Billingsley, lhp; B: Downey, CA; Cal State Fullerton; 1999 FLA (1) (1)

Houston Astros

1965

June — Regular Phase

2 — Keith Lampard, of; B: Warrington, England; University of Oregon; 1969 HOU (2) (2)

10 — Danny Walton, of; B: Los Angeles, CA; Bishop Amat HS, La Puente, CA; 1968 HOU (2) (9)

1966

January — Regular Phase

Major League selection:

1 — Tom Griffin, rhp; B: Los Angeles, CA; Grant HS, Sun Valley, CA; 1969 HOU (8) (14)

June — Regular Phase

1 — Wayne Twitchell, rhp; B: Portland, OR; Wilson HS, Portland, OR; 1970 MIL (1) (10)

5 — Cliff Johnson, c; B: San Antonio, TX; Wheatley HS, San Antonio, TX; 1972 HOU (6) (15)

8 — Fred Stanley, inf; B: Farnhamville, IA; Monte Vista HS, Whittier, CA; 1969 SEA (1) (14)

22 — Robert Watkins, rhp; B: Los Angeles, CA; Compton HS, CA; 1966 HOU (14) (19)

1967

June — Regular Phase

1 — John Mayberry, 1b-of; B: Detroit, MI; North-western HS, Detroit, MI; 1968 HOU (4) (15)

2 — Jay Schlueter, of; Central HS, Phoenix, AZ; 1971 HOU (1) (1)

1968

January — Regular Phase

1 — Glenn Adams, of; B: Northbridge, MA; Spring-field College; 1975 SFG (2) (8)

June — Regular Phase

2 — Rich Chiles, of; B: Sacramento, CA; Winters HS, CA; 1971 HOU (3) (6)

3 — Bill Grief, rhp; B: Ft. Stockton, TX; Reagan HS, Austin, TX; 1971 HOU (1) (6)

5 — Larry Young, rhp; B: Houston, TX; Taft HS, Woodland Hills, CA; 1971 HOU (1) (1)

18 — Ken Forsch, rhp; B: Sacramento, CA; Oregon State University; 1970 HOU (11) (16)

June — Secondary Phase

1 — Buddy Harris, rhp; B: Philadelphia, PA; University of Miami, FL; 1970 HOU (2) (2)

1969

January — Regular Phase

1 — Derrel Thomas, ss; B: Los Angeles, CA; Dorsey HS, Los Angeles, CA; 1971 HOU (1) (15)

June — Regular Phase

1 — J.R. Richard, rhp; B: Vienna, LA; Lincoln HS, Ruston, LA; 1971 HOU (10) (10)

2 — Stan Papi, ss; B: Fresno, CA; Bullard HS, Fresno, CA; 1974 STL (1) (6)

14 — Mike Easler, 3b; B: Cleveland, OH; Benedictine HS, Cleveland, OH; 1973 HOU (3) (14)

1970

January — Regular Phase

3 — Greg Minton, rhp; B: Lubbock, TX; San Diego Mesa JC, CA; 1975 SFG (12) (16)

January — Secondary Phase

2 — Mike Cosgrove, lhp; B: Phoenix, AZ; Phoenix JC; 1972 HOU (5) (5)

June — Regular Phase

4 — Greg Gross, of; B: York, PA; Red Land HS, Et-ters, PA; 1973 HOU (4) (17)

1971

January — Secondary Phase

1 — Doug Konieczny, rhp; B: Detroit, MI; St. Clair County CC, MI; 1973 HOU (4) (4)

June — Regular Phase

2 — Art Gardner, lhp-of; B: Madden, MS; South Leake HS, Walnut Grove, MS; 1975 HOU (2) (3)

3 — Paul Siebert, lhp; B: Minnesota, MN; Edina HS, MN; 1974 HOU (3) (5)

1972

June — Regular Phase

14 — Jim Crawford, lhp; B: Chicago, IL; ASU; 1973 HOU (2) (5)

1973

January — Secondary Phase

1 — Mike Stanton, rhp; B: Phoenix City, AL; Miami–Dade South CC; 1975 HOU (1) (7)

June — Regular Phase

5 — Mike Mendoza, rhp; B: Inglewood, CA; Mc-Clintock HS, Tempe, AZ; 1979 HOU (1) (1)

17 — Joe Sambito, lhp; B: Brooklyn, NY; Adelpha University; 1976 HOU (8) (11)

1974

January — Regular Phase

1— Joe Cannon, of; B: Camplejeune, NC; Pensacola JC, FL; 1977 HOU (2) (4)

June — Regular Phase

3 — Alan Knicely, c-inf; B: Harrisonburg, VA; Turner Ashby HS, Bridgewater, VA; 1979 HOU (4) (8)

1975

June — Regular Phase

1— Bo McLaughlin, rhp; B: Oakland, CA; David Lipscomb College; 1976 HOU (4) (6)

5 — Joe Pittman, 3b; B: Houston, TX; Southern University; 1981 HOU (2) (3)

June — Secondary Phase

1— Bruce Bochy, c; B: Landes De Bussac, France; Brevard CC, FL; 1978 HOU (3) (9)

1976

January — Regular Phase

1— Gary Wilson, rhp; B: Camden, AK; Southern Arkansas University, AK; 1979 HOU (1) (1)

June — Regular Phase

1— Floyd Bannister, lhp; B: Pierre, SD; ASU; 1977 HOU (2) (15)

3 — Reggie Baldwin, c; B: River Rouge, MI; Grambline State University; 1978 HOU (2) (2)

4 — Jim Pankovits, 3b; B: Pennington Gap, VA; University of South Carolina; 1984 HOU (5) (6)

7 — Tom Wiedenbauer, of; B: Menomonie, WI; Sahuaro, HS, Tuscon, AZ; 1979 HOU (1) (1)

8 — Dave Smith, rhp; B: Richmond, CA; San Diego State University; 1980 HOU (11) (13)

11— Gary Rajsich, 1b-of; B: Youngstown, OH; ASU; 1982 NYM (2) (4)

17 — Bert Roberge, rhp; B: Lewiston, MA; University of Maine; 1979 HOU (3) (6)

1977

June — Regular Phase

1— Ricky Adams, ss; B: Upland, CA; Montclair HS, CA.; 1982 CAL (2) (3)

5 — Scott Loucks, of; B: Anchorage, AK; Southeastern Oklahoma State University; 1980 HOU (4) (5)

14 — Billy Smith, rhp; B: LeMarque, TX; Sam Houston State University; 1981 HOU (1) (1)

1978

January — Regular Phase

2 — Pat Perry, lhp; B: Taylorville, IL; Lincoln Land CC, IL; 1985 STL (3) (3)

June — Regular Phase

2 — Danny Heep, of-lhp; B: San Antonio, TX; St. Mary's University, TX; 1988 LAD (1) (2)

4 — Ron Meridith, lhp; B: San Pedro, CA; Oral Roberts University; 1984 CHC (2) (4)

11— Jack Lazorko, 3b-rhp; B: Hoboken, NJ; Mississippi State University; 1984 MIL (1) (5)

12 — Tim Tolman, of; B: Santa Monica, CA; USC; 1981 HOU (5) (7)

1979

June — Regular Phase

1— John Mizerock, c; B: Punxsutawney, PA; Punxsutawney HS, PA; 1983 HOU (3) (4)

2 — Ty Gainey, inf; B: Cheraw, SC; Cheraw (SC) HS; 1985 HOU (4) (3)

4 — Larry Ray, of; B: Madison, IN; Kentucky Wesleyan College; 1982 HOU (1) (1)

6 — Bill Doran, inf; B: Cincinnati, OH: Miami University, OH; 1982 HOU (9) (12)

7 — Mark Ross, rhp; B: Galveston, TX; Texas A&M University; 1982 HOU (3) (6)

12 — Johnny Ray, 2b; B: Chouteau, OK; University of Arkansas; 1981 PIT (7) (10)

25 — Chris Jones, of; B: Los Angeles, CA; San Diego State University; 1985 HOU (1) (2)

1980

June — Regular Phase

3 — Jeff Calhoun, lhp; B: LaGrange, GA; University of Mississippi; 1984 HOU (3) (5)

June — Secondary Phase

1— Jeff Heathcock, rhp; B: Covina, CA; Oral Roberts University; 1983 HOU (4) (4)

1981

January — Secondary Phase

1— Glenn Davis, 1b-of; B: Jacksonville, FL; Manatee JC, FL; 1984 HOU (7) (10)

June — Secondary Phase

1— Eric Bullock, of; B: Los Angeles, CA; Los Angeles Harbor JC; 1985 HOU (2) (7)

1982

June — Regular Phase

2 — Louie Meadows, 1b; B: Maysville, NC.; North Carolina State University; 1986 HOU (4) (4)

3 — Mark Knudson, rhp; B: Denver, CO; Colorado State University; 1985 HOU (2) (8)

6 — Mark Bailey, 2b; B: Springfield, MO; Southwest Missouri State University; 1984 HOU (5) (7)

June — Secondary Phase

1— Charlie Kerfeld, rhp; B: Knob Noster, MO; Yavapai JC, AZ; 1985 HOU (4) (4)

1983

June — Regular Phase

1— Robbie Wine, c; B: Norristown, PA; Oklahoma State University; 1986 HOU (2) (2)

10 — Roger Samuels, lhp; B: San Jose, CA; Santa Clara University; 1988 SFG (1) (2)

28 — Tom Funk, lhp; B: Kansas City, MO; North-west Missouri State University; 1986 HOU (1) (1)

1984

January — Regular Phase
6 — David Meads, lhp; Montclair, NJ; Middlesex County JC, NJ; 1987 HOU (2) (2)

January — Secondary Phase
1 — Rob Mallicoat, lhp; B: St. Helens, OR; Taft JC, CA; 1987 HOU (3) (3)

June — Regular Phase
1 — Don August, rhp; B: Inglewood, CA; Chapman College; 1988 MIL (4) (4)
3 — Ken Caminiti, 3b; B: Hanford, CA; San Jose State University, CA; 1987 HOU (8) (12)
7 — Chuck Jackson, of; B: Seattle, WA; University of Hawaii; 1987 HOU (2) (3)

1985

January — Secondary Phase
1 — Mel Stottlemyre Jr., rhp; B: Sunnyside, WA; Yakima Valley JC, WA; 1988 TOR (7) (11)

June — Regular Phase
1 — Cameron Drew, of; B: Boston, MA; University of New Haven; 1988 HOU (1) (1)
4 — Blaise Ilsley, lhp; B: Alpena, MI; Indiana State University, Terre Haute, IN; 1994 CHC (1) (1)
6 — Mike Simms, of; B: Whittier, CA; Esperanza HS, Yorba Linda, CA; 1990 HOU (6) (8)
9 — John Fishel, of; B: Fullerton, CA; Cal State Fullerton; 1988 HOU (1) (1)

1986

June — Regular Phase
1 — Ryan Bowen, rhp; B: Hanford, CA; Hanford (CA) HS; 1991 HOU (2) (5)
5 — Lou Frazier, of; B: St Louis, MO; Scottsdale (AZ) JC; 1993 MON (3) (5)
12 — Trent Hubbard, 2b; B: Chicago, IL; Southern University; 1994 COL (3) (5)
16 — Brian Meyer, rhp; B: Camden, NJ; Rollins College; 1988 HOU (3) (3)
18 — Ed Whited, 3b; B: Bristol, PA; Rider College; 1989 ATL (1) (1)
34 — Eric Anthony, of; B: San Diego, CA; Sharpstown HS, Houston, TX; 1989 HOU (5) (8)

1987

1 — Craig Biggio, c; B: Smithtown, NY; Seton Hall University; 1988 HOU (11) (11)
30 — Darryl Kile, rhp; B: Garden Grove, CA; Chaffey JC, CA; 1991 HOU (7) (8)

1988

2 — Dave Silvestri, 2b; B: St. Louis, MO; University of Missouri; 1992 NYY (4) (7)

3 — Scott Servais, c; B: Lacross, WI; Creighton University; 1991 HOU (5) (8)
4 — Luis Gonzalez, 1b; B: Tampa, FL; University of South Alabama; 1990 HOU (6) (9)
17 — Kenny Lofton, of; B: East Chicago, IN; University of Arizona; 1991 HOU (1) (8)

1989

1 — Jeff Juden, rhp; B: Salem, MA; Salem HS, MA; 1991 HOU (2) (7)
1 — Todd Jones, rhp; B: Marietta, GA; Jacksonville, FL; 1993 HOU (4) (6)
2 — Brian L. Hunter, of; B: Portland, OR; Fort Vancouver HS, Vancouver, WA; 1994 HOU (3) (5)
3 — Shane Reynolds, rhp; B; Bastrop, LA; University of Texas, TX; 1992 HOU (7) (7)
17 — Mark Small, rhp; B: Portland, OR; Washington State University; 1996 HOU (1) (1)
18 — Donne Wall, rhp; B: Potosi, MO; University of Southwestern Louisiana; 1995 HOU (3) (4)

1990

1 — Brian Williams, rhp; B: Lancaster, SC; University of South Carolina; 1991 HOU (4) (7)
3 — Chris Hatcher, of; B: Anaheim, CA; University of Iowa; 1998 KCR (1) (1)
12 — Jeff Ball, 3b; B: Merced, CA; San Jose State University; 1998 SFG (1) (1)
13 — Ray Montgomery, of; B: Bronxville, NY; Fordham University; 1996 HOU (3) (3)
26 — Jim Dougherty, rhp; B: Brentwood, NY; University of North Carolina; 1995 HOU (2) (3)

1991

7 — James Mouton, of; B: Denver, CO; St. Mary's College; 1995 HOU (3) (4)
39 — Alvin Morman, lhp; B: Rockingham, NC; Wingate College, NC; 1996 HOU (1) (3)

1992

3 — Chris Holt, rhp; B: Dallas, TX; Navarro JC, TX; 1996 HOU (2) (2)
5 — Sean Runyan, lhp; B: Fort Smith, AR; Urbandale (IA) HS; 1998 DET (1) (1)
10 — Jamie Walker, lhp; B: McMinnville, TN; Austin Peay State University; 1997 KCR (2) (2)
19 — Mike Grzanich, rhp; B: Canton, IL; Parkland JC, IL; 1998 HOU (1) (1)

1993

1 — Billy Wagner, lhp; B: Tannersville, VA; Ferrum College, VA; 1995 HOU (4) (4)

1994

1 — Scott Elarton, rhp; B: Lamar, CO; Lamar (CO) HS; 1998 HOU (1) (1)

1— Russ Johnson, 3b; B: Baton Rouge, LA; LSU; 1997 HOU (2) (2)

23 — John Halama, lhp; B: Brooklyn, NY; St. Francis College, NY; 1998 HOU (1) (1)

Los Angeles Dodgers

1965

June — Regular Phase

2 — Alan Foster, rhp; B: Pasadena, CA; Los Altos HS, Hacienda Heights, CA; 1967 LAD (4) (10)

15 — Leon Everitt, rhp; B: Marshall, TX; Pemberton HS, Marshall, TX; 1969 SDP (1) (1)

28 — Gary Moore, of; B: Tulsa, OK; University of Texas; 1970 LAD (1) (1)

1966

January — Secondary Phase

3 — Jim Hibbs, c; B: Kiamath Falls, OR; Stanford University; 1967 CAL (1) (1)

June — Regular Phase

2 — John Gamble, ss; B: Reno, NV; Carson City (NV) HS; 1972 DET (2) (2)

8 — Charlie Hough, inf-rhp; B: Honolulu, HI; Hialeah HS, FL; 1970 LAD (11) (25)

9 — Bill Russell, of; B: Pittsburg, KA; Pittsburg HS, KA; 1969 LAD (18) (18)

12 — Billy Grabarkewitz, 3b; B: Lockhart, TX; St. Mary's University, TX; 1969 LAD (4) (7)

15 — Ted Sizemore, c; B: Gadsden, AL; University of Michigan; 1969 LAD (2) (12)

40— Ray Lamb, rhp; B: Glendale, CA; USC; 1969 LAD (2) (5)

June — Secondary Phase

1— Bob Stinson, c-of; B: Elkin, NC; Miami–Dade CC; 1969 LAD (2) (12)

1967

June — Regular Phase

4 — Steve Yeager, c; B: Huntington, WV; Meadow Dale HS, Dayton, OH; 1972 LAD (14) (15)

63 — Bruce Ellingsen, lhp; B: Pocatello, WI; Lakewood HS, CA; 1974 CLE (1) (1)

June — Secondary Phase

3 — Larry Burchart, rhp; B: Tulsa, OK; Oklahoma State University; 1969 CLE (1) (1)

1968

January — Secondary Phase

2 — Davey Lopes, of; B: Providence, RI; Washburn University; 1972 LAD (10) (16)

5 — Geoff Zahn, lhp; B: Baltimore, MD; University of Michigan; 1973 LAD (3) (13)

June — Regular Phase

1— Bobby Valentine, of; B: Stamford, CN; Rippowam HS, Stamford, CT; 1969 LAD (3) (10)

2 — Bill Buckner, 1b; B: Vallejo, CA; Napa HS, Vallejo, CA; 1969 LAD (8) (22)

5 — Tom Paciorek, of-1b; B: Detroit, MI; University of Houston; 1970 LAD (6) (18)

8 — Joe Ferguson, c; B: San Francisco, CA; 1970 LAD (11) (14)

9 — Doyle Alexander, rhp; B: Cordova, AL; Woodlawn HS, Birmingham, AL; 1971 LAD (1) (19)

17 — Bob Gallagher, of; B: Newton, MA; Stanford University; 1972 BOS (1) (4)

June — Secondary Phase

1— Steve Garvey, 3b; B: Tampa, FL; Michigan State University; 1969 LAD (14) (19)

2 — Sandy Vance, rhp; B: Lamar, CO; Stanford University; 1970 LAD (2) (2)

3 — Ron Cey, 3b; B: Tacoma, WA; Washington State University; 1971 LAD (12) (17)

1969

January — Regular Phase

2 — Lee Lacy, 3b; B: Longview, TX; Laney JC, CA; 1972 LAD (7) (16)

4 — Bob O'Brien, lhp; B: Pittsburgh, PA; Frenso CC, CA; 1971 LAD (1) (1)

June — Regular Phase

1— Terry McDermott, c; B: Rockville, NY; St. Agnes HS, West Hempstead, NY; 1972 LAD (1) (1)

6 — Stan Wall, lhp; B: Butler, MO; Raytown South HS, MO; 1975 LAD (3) (3)

22 — Royle Stillman, of; B: Santa Monica, CA; North Torrance HS, CA; 1975 BAL (2) (3)

June — Secondary Phase

2 — Bobby Randall, ss; B: Norton, KS; Kansas State University; 1976 MIN (5) (5)

1970

June — Regular Phase

3 — Lance Rautzhan, lhp; B: Pottsville, PA; Blue Mountain HS, Pottsville, PA; 1977 LAD (3) (3)

Class A (Bakersfield and Daytona Beach) selections:

33 — Greg Shanahan, rhp; B: Eureka, CA; Humboldt State University; 1973 LAD (2) (2)

June — Secondary Phase

1— Doug Rau, lhp; B: Columbus, TX; Texas A&M University; 1972 LAD (8) (9)

1971

June — Regular Phase

1— Rick Rhoden, rhp; B: Boynton Beach, FL; Atlantic HS, Boynton Beach, FL; 1974 LAD (5) (16)

5 — Rex Hudson, rhp; B: Tulsa, OK; Hale HS, Tulsa, OK; 1974 LAD (1) (1)

14 — John Hale, of-3b; B: Fresno, CA; Wasco (CA) HS; 1974 LAD (4) (6)

29 — Kevin Pasley, c; B: Bronx, NY; Chaminade HS, Bethpage, NY; 1974 LAD (3) (4)

1972

January — Secondary Phase
1— Dennis Lewallyn, rhp; B: Pensacola, FL; Chipola JC, FL; 1975 LAD (5) (8)

June — Regular Phase
3 — Bobby Detherage, rhp-of; B: Springfield, MO; Hillcrest HS, Springfield, MO; 1980 KCA (1) (1)
17 — Glenn Burke, of; B: Oakland, CA; D: San Leandro, CA.; Merritt HS, CA; 1976 LAD (3) (4)

1973

June — Regular Phase
3 — Joe Simpson, of; B: Purcell, OK; University of Oklahoma; 1975 LAD (5) (9)
6 — Mike Dimmel, of; B: Albertlea, MN; Logansport (IN) HS; 1977 BAL (2) (3)

1974

June — Regular Phase
1— Rick Sutcliffe, rhp; B: Independence, MO; Van Horne HS, Kansas City, MO; 1976 LAD (5) (18)
2 — Steve Shirley, lhp; B: San Francisco, CA; Terra Nova HS, Pacitica, CA; 1982 LAD (1) (1)

1975

June — Regular Phase
1— Mark Bradley, ss; B: Elizabethtown, KY; Elizabethtown (KY) HS; 1981 LAD (2) (3)
2 — Myron White, of; B: Long Beach, CA; Santa Ana (CA) HS; 1978 LAD (1) (1)
16 — Dave Stewart, rhp; B: Oakland, CA; St. Elizabeth HS, Oakland, CA; 1978 LAD (4) (16)
17 — Brad Gulden, c; B: Newlum, MN; Chaska HS, Carver, MN; 1978 LAD (1) (7)

1976

January — Regular Phase
2 — Dave Patterson, rhp; B: Springfield, MO; Cerritos JC, CA; 1979 LAD (1) (1)

June — Regular Phase
1— Mike Scioscia, c; B: Upper Darby, PA; Springfield HS, Morton, PA; 1980 LAD (13) (13)
3 — Max Venable, of; B: Phoenix, AZ; Cordova HS, Rancho Cordova, CA; 1979 SFG (5) (12)
5 — Ted Power, rhp; B: Guthrie, OK; Kansas State University; 1981 LAD (2) (13)
6 — Mike Howard, of-3b; B: Seattle, WA; Sacramento HS, CA; 1981 NYM (3) (3)
15 — Keith MacWhorter, rhp; B: Worcester, MA; Bryant College; 1980 BOS (1) (1)
16 — Jack Perconte, 2b; B: Joliet, IL; Murray State University; 1980 LAD (2) (7)

1977

June — Regular Phase
1— Bob Welch, rhp; B: Detroit, MI; Eastern Michigan University; 1978 LAD (10) (17)
2 — Joe Beckwith, rhp; B: Opelika, AL; Auburn University; 1979 LAD (5) (7)
5 — Mickey Hatcher, of; B: Cleveland, OH; University of Oklahoma; 1979 LAD (6) (12)
7 — Bobby Mitchell, of; B: Salt Lake City, UT; USC; 1980 LAD (2) (4)
23 — Mitch Webster, of; B: Larned, KS; Larned (KS) HS; 1983 TOR (3) (13)

June — Secondary Phase
1— Ron Roenicke, of; B: Covina, CA; UCLA; 1981 LAD (3) (8)

1978

January — Regular Phase
1— Brian Holton, rhp; B: McKeesport, PA; Louisburg JC, NC; 1985 LAD (4) (6)

June — Regular Phase
6 — Mike Marshall, lb-rhp; B: Libertyville, IL; Buffalo Grove (IL) HS; 1981 LAD (9) (11)
9 — Steve Sax, ss; B: Sacramento, CA; Marshall HS, West Sacramento, CA; 1981 LAD (8) (14)
19 — Gary Weiss, inf; B: Brenham, TX; University of Houston; 1980 LAD (2) (2)

June — Secondary Phase
1— Dann Bilardello, c; B: Santa Cruz, CA; Cabrillo JC, CA; 1983 CIN (3) (8)

1979

June — Regular Phase
1— Steve Howe, lhp; B: Pontiac, MI; University of Michigan; 1980 LAD (5) (12)
3 — Don Crow, c; B: Yakima, MI; Washington State University; 1982 LAD (1) (1)
13 — Greg Brock, lb; B: McMinnville, OR; University of Wyoming; 1982 LAD (5) (10)
17 — Orel Hershiser, rhp; B: Buffalo, NY; Bowling Green State University; 1983 LAD (12) (16)
24 — Morris Madden, lhp; B: Laurens, SC; Spartanburg Methodist JC, SC; 1987 DET (1) (3)

1980

January — Regular Phase
2 — R.J. Reynolds, of; B: Sacramento, CA; Sacramento JC, CA; 1983 LAD (3) (8)

January — Secondary Phase
1— Ricky Wright, lhp; B: Paris, TX; University of Texas; 1982 LAD (2) (5)

June — Regular Phase
1— Ross Jones, ss; B: Miami, FL; University of Miami; 1984 NYM (1) (3)

1981

June — Regular Phase

1— David C. Anderson, ss; B: Louisville, KY; Memphis State University; 1983 LAD (8) (10)

2 — Sid Bream, 1b; B: Carlisle, PA; Liberty University; 1983 LAD (3) (12)

2 — Lemmie Miller, of; B: Dallas, TX; ASU; 1984 LAD (1) (1) (from Astros for Don Sutton)

3 — Sid Fernandez, lhp; B: Honolulu, HI; Kaiser HS, Honolulu, HI; 1983 LAD (1) (14)

5 — John Franco, lhp; B: Brooklyn, NY; St. John's University; 1984 CIN (6) (13)

9 — Stu Pederson, of; B: Palo Alto, CA; USC; 1985 LAD (1) (1)

June — Secondary Phase

1— Ralph Bryant, of; B: Fort Gaines, GA; Abraham Baldwin Agricultural JC, GA; 1985 LAD (3) (3)

1982

June — Regular Phase

1— Franklin Stubbs, 1b; B: Richlands, NC; Virginia Tech; 1984 LAD (6) (10)

3 — Ken Howell, rhp; B: Detroit, MI; Tuskegee Institute; 1984 LAD (5) (7)

13 — Reggie Williams, of; B: Memphis, TN; Southern University; 1985 LAD (3) (4)

29 — Jeff Hamilton, ss-of; B: Flint, MI; Flint Carman HS, Davison, MI; 1986 LAD (6) (6)

1983

January — Regular Phase

13 — Wayne Kirby, B: Williamsburg, VA; Newport News (VA) Apprentice School; 1991 CLE (6) (8)

June — Regular Phase

6 — Scott May, rhp; B: West Bend, WI; University of Wisconsin, Oshkosh; 1988 TEX (1) (2)

1984

January — Secondary Phase

1— Shawn Hillegas, rhp; B: Dos Palos, CA; Middle Georgia JC; 1987 LAD (2) (7)

June — Regular Phase

2 — Tim Scott, rhp; B: Hanford, CA; Hanford (CA) HS; 1991 SDP (3) (7)

3 — Tracy Woodson, 1b; B: Richmond, VA; North Carolina State University; 1987 LAD (3) (5)

16 — Darren Holmes, rhp; B: Asheville, NC; T.C. Roberson HS, Skyland, NC; 1990 LAD (1) (9)

22 — Jeff Nelson, rhp; B: Baltimore, MD; Catonsville HS, Baltimore, MD; 1992 SEA (4) (7)

1985

January — Secondary Phase

2 — John Wetteland, rhp; B: San Mateo, CA; College of San Mateo, CA; 1989 LAD (3) (10)

June — Regular Phase

1— Chris Gwynn, of; B: Los Angeles, CA; San Diego State University; 1987 (7) (10)

5 — Mike Devereaux, of; B: Casper, WY; ASU; 1987 LAD (3) (12)

8 — Jack Savage, rhp; B: Louisville, KY; University of Kentucky; 1987 LAD (1) (2)

16 — Mike Huff, of; B: Honolulu, HI; Northwestern University; 1989 LAD (1) (7)

1986

June — Regular Phase

2 — Dave Hansen, ss; B: Long Beach, CA; Rowland HS, Rowland Heights, CA; 1990 LAD (7) (8)

3 — Mike Munoz, lhp; B: Baldwin Park, CA; Cal Poly Pomona; 1989 LAD (2) (10)

5 — Kevin Campbell, rhp; B: Marianna, AR; University of Arkansas; 1991 OAK (3) (5)

1987

3 — Chris Nichting, rhp; B: Cincinnati, OH; Northwestern University; 1995 TEX (1) (1)

6 — Darren Fletcher, c; B: Elmhurst, IL; University of Illinois; 1989 LAD (2) (10)

7 — Tony Barron, 3b-of; B: Portland, OR; Willamette (OR) University; 1996 MON (1) (2)

19 — Rafael Bournigal, inf; B; Azua, DR; Florida State University; 1992 LAD (3) (6)

21— Dennis Springer, rhp; B: Fresno, CA; Fresno State University; 1995 PHI (1) (4)

43 — Mike James, rhp; B: Fort Walton Beach, FL; Lurleen B. Wallace State JC, AL; 1995 CAL (4) (4)

1988

3 — Billy Ashley, 1b; B: Taylor, MI; Belleville (MI) HS; 1992 LAD (6) (7)

6 — Eric Karros, 1b; B: Hackensack, NJ; UCLA; 1991 LAD (8) (8)

9 — Jim Poole, lhp; B: Rochester, NY; Georgia Tech; 1990 LAD (1) (8)

10 — Eddie Pye, 2b; B: Columbia, TN; Middle Tennessee State University; 1994 LAD (2) (2)

12 — Jerry Brooks, of-3b; B: Syracuse, NY; Clemson University; 1993 LAD (1) (2)

35 — Hector Ortiz, c; B: Rio Piedras, PR; Ranger JC, TX; 1998 KCR (1) (1)

62 — Mike Piazza, 1b-c; B: Norristown, PA; Miami–Dade North CC; 1992 LAD (7) (8)

1989

1— Jamie McAndrew, rhp; B: Williamsport, PA; University of Florida; 1995 MIL (2) (2)

34 — Matt Howard, 2b; B: Fall River, MA; Pepperdine University; 1996 NYY (1) (1)

43 — Eric Young, 2b; B: Brunswick, NJ; Rutgers University; 1992 LAD (1)(7)

44 — Garey Ingram, of; B: Columbus, GA; Middle Georgia JC; 1994 LAD (3) (3)

1990

4 — Mike Busch, 1b; B: Davenport, IA; Iowa State University; 1995 LAD (2) (2)

17 — Steve Mintz, rhp; B: Leland, NC; Mount Olive College, NC; 1995 SFG (1) (1)

24 — Mike Mimbs, lhp; B: Macon, GA; Mercer University; 1995 PHI (3) (3)

54 — Todd Williams, rhp; B: Syracuse, NY; Onodaga CC; 1995 LAD (1) (2)

1991

3 — Todd Hollandsworth, of; B: Dayton, OH; Newport HS, Bellevue, WA; 1995 LAD (4) (4)

11 — Chris Latham, of; B: Coeur D'Alene, ID; Basic HS, Henderson, NV; 1991 MIN (2) (2)

19 — Rick Gorecki, rhp; B: Evergreen Park, IL; Oak Forest (IL) HS;1997 LAD (1) (2)

41 — Carlos Castillo, rhp; B: Boston, MA; Cypress JC, CA; 1997 CHW (1) (1)

1992

9 — Ryan Henderson, rhp; B: Arcadia, CA; USC; 1998 MIL (1) (1)

1993

1 — Darren Dreifort, rhp; B: Wichita, TX; Wichita State University; 1994 LAD (4) (4)

25 — Paul LoDuca, c; B: Brooklyn, NY; ASU; 1998 LAD (1) (1)

1994

1 — Paul Konerko, 1b; B: Providence, RI; Chaparral HS, Scottsdale, AZ; 1997 LAD (2) (2)

2 — Gary Rath, lhp; B: Gulfport, MS; Mississippi State University; 1998 LAD (1) (1)

3 — Mike Metcalfe, 2b; B: Quantico, VA; University of Miami; 1998 LAD (1) (1)

22 — Adam Riggs, 2b; B: Steubenville, OH; University of South Carolina; 1997 LAD (1) (1)

1996

3 — Alex Cora, ss; B: Caguas, PR; University of Miami; 1998 LAD (1) (1)

38 — Jeff Kubenka, lhp; B: Weimar, TX; St. Mary's University, TX; 1998 LAD (1) (1)

Milwaukee Brewers

Seattle Pilots:

1968

June — Regular Phase

7 — Bill Parsons, rhp; B: Riverside, CA; Riverside CC, CA; 1971 MIL (3) (4)

8 — Tom Kelly, of; B: Graceville, MN; St. Mary's HS, South Amboy, NJ; 1975 MIN (1) (1)

19 — Wilbur Howard, of; B: Lowell, NC; Holbrook HS, Lowell, NC; 1973 MIL (1) (6)

1969

January — Regular Phase

2 — Jerry Bell, rhp; B: Madison, TN; Southwestern College, TN; 1971 MIL (4) (4)

January — Secondary Phase

1 — Ray Peters, rhp; B: Buffalo, NY; Harvard University; 1970 MIL (1) (1)

7 — Rick Auerbach, ss; B: Woodland Hill, CA; Los Angeles Pierce JC; 1971 MIL (3) (11)

June — Regular Phase

1 — Gorman Thomas, ss-rhp; B: Charleston, SC; James Island HS, Charleston, SC; 1973 MIL (10) (13)

5 — Gary Martz, rhp; B: Spokane, WA; West Valley HS, Spokane, WA; 1975 KCA (1) (1)

15 — Jim Staton, rhp; B: Seattle, WA; Antelope Valley JC, CA; 1972 DET (2) (2)

17 — Bobby Coluccio, inf; B: Centralia, WA; Centralia HS, WA; 1973 MIL (3) (6)

21 — Bob Hansen, 1b; B: Boston, MA; University of Massachusetts; 1974 MIL (2) (2)

Milwaukee Brewers:

1970

June — Regular Phase

1 — Darrell Porter, c; B: Joplin, MO; Southeast HS, Oklahoma City, OK; 1971 MIL (6) (17)

6 — Bill Travers, lhp; B: Norwood, MA; Norwood HS, MA; 1974 MIL (7) (9)

1971

June — Regular Phase

1 — Tommy Bianco, ss; B: Rockville Centre, NY; Sewanhaka HS, Elmont, NY; 1975 MIL (1) (1)

2 — Larry Anderson, rhp; B: Maywood, CA; El Rancho HS, Pico Rivera, CA; 1974 MIL (2) (3)

5 — Charlie Moore, c-3b; B: Birmingham, AL; Minor HS, Birmingham, AL; 1973 MIL (14) (15)

June — Secondary Phase Delayed

1 — Rob Ellis, inf; B: Grand Rapids, MI; Michigan State University; 1971 MIL (3) (3)

1972

June — Regular Phase

1 — Danny Thomas, 1b; B: Birmingham, AL; Southern Illinois University; 1976 MIL (2) (2)

15 — Roger Miller, rhp; B: Connellsville, PA; Uniontown HS, Mill Run, PA; 1974 MIL (1) (1)

22 — Bob Sheldon, ss; B: Montebello, CA; Loyola Marymount University; 1974 MIL (3) (3)

24 — Joe Erardi, rhp; B: Syracuse, NY; Liverpool HS, NY; 1977 SEA (1) (1)

1973

June — Regular Phase

1— Robin Yount, ss; B: Danville, IL; Taft HS, Woodland Hills, CA; 1974 MIL (20) (20)

1974

June — Regular Phase

1— Butch Edge, rhp; B: Houston, TX; El Camino HS, Sacramento, CA; 1979 TOR (1) (1)

2 — Moose Haas, rhp; B: Baltimore, MD; Franklin HS, Owings Mills, MD; 1976 MIL (10) (12)

4 — Barry Cort, rhp; B: Toronto, Ontario; King HS, Tampa, FL; 1977 MIL (1) (1)

5 — Gary Beare, rhp; B: San Diego, CA; Cal State Long Beach; 1976 MIL (2) (2)

7 — Steve Bowling, of; B: Tulsa, OK; University of Tulsa; 1976 MIL (1) (2)

12 — Jim Gantner, ss; B: Fond Dulac, WI; University of Wisconsin, Oshkosh, WI; 1976 MIL (17) (17)

15 — Jerry Augustine, lhp; B: Kewaunee, WI; University of Wisconsin, La Crosse, WI; 1975 MIL (10) (10)

1975

January — Secondary Phase

1— Lenn Sakata, 2b; B: Honolulu, HI; Gonzaga University; 1977 MIL (3) (11)

1976

June — Regular Phase

8 — Lary Sorensen, rhp; B: Detroit, MI; University of Michigan; 1977 MIL (4) (11)

9 — George Frazier, rhp; B: Oklahoma City, OK; University of Oklahoma; 1978 STL (3) (9)

13 — Gary Holle, 1b; B: Albany, NY; Siena College; 1979 TEX (1) (1)

1977

June — Regular Phase

1— Paul Molitor, ss; B: St. Paul, MN; University of Minnesota; 1978 MIL (15) (21)

2 — Kevin Bass, of; B: Menlo Park, CA; Menlo HS, Menlo Park, CA; 1982 MIL (1) (14)

10 — Dave LaPoint, lhp; B: Glen Falls, NY; Glens Falls HS, NY; 1980 MIL (1) (12)

1978

January — Regular Phase

2 — Doug Loman, of; B: Bakersfield, CA; Bakersfield JC, CA; 1984 MIL (2) (2)

3 — Doug Jones, rhp; B: Lebanon, IN; Central Arizona JC; 1982 MIL (1) (10)

June — Regular Phase

3 — Rickey Keeton, rhp; B: Cincinnati, OH; Southern Illinois University; 1980 MIL (2) (2)

1979

June — Regular Phase

5 — Andy Beene, rhp; B: Freeport, TX; Baylor University; 1983 MIL (2) (2)

8 — Bill Schroeder, c; B: Baltimore, MD; Clemson University; 1983 MIL (6) (8)

13 — Bob Skube, of; B: Northridge, CA; USC; 1982 MIL (2) (2)

1980

June — Regular Phase

Major League selection:

1— Dion James, of; B: Philadelphia, PA; McClatchy HS, Sacramento, CA; 1983 MIL (3) (9)

6 — Randy Ready, 2b; B: Mesa, CO; Mesa College, CO; 1983 MIL (4) (13)

1981

January — Regular Phase

2 — Tim Crews, rhp; B: Tampa, FL; Valencia CC, FL; 1987 LAD (6) (6)

3 — Mike Felder, 2b; B: Vallejo, CA; Contra Costa JC, CA; 1985 MIL (6) (10)

January — Secondary Phase

3 — Ernest Riles, ss; B: Cairo, GA; Middle Georgia JC; 1985 MIL (4) (9)

June — Regular Phase

5 — Bill Wegman, rhp; B: Cincinnati, OH; Oak Hills HS, Cincinnati, OH; 1985 MIL (11) (11)

7 — Bryan Clutterbuck, rhp; B: Detroit, MI; Eastern Michigan University; 1986 MIL (2) (2)

1982

January — Secondary Phase

2 — Chris Bosio, rhp; B: Carmichael, CA; Sacramento CC, CA; 1986 MIL (7) (11)

June — Regular Phase

1— Dale Sveum, ss; B: Richmond, CA; Pinole Valley (CA) HS; 1986 MIL (5) (11)

6 — Billy Joe Robidoux, 1b; B: Ware, MA; Ware (MA) HS; 1985 MIL (4) (6)

8 — Jim Paciorek, of; B: Detroit, MI; University of Michigan; 1987 MIL (1) (1)

10 — Jay Aldrich, rhp; B: Alexandria, LA; Montclair State College; 1987 MIL (2) (4)

17 — Chuck Crim, rhp; B: Van Nuys, CA; University of Hawaii; 1987 MIL (5) (8)

1983

January — Regular Phase

1— LaVel Freeman, of; B: Oakland, CA; Sacramento CC, CA; 1989 MIL (1) (1)

June — Regular Phase

1— Dan Plesac, lhp; B: Gary, IN; North Carolina State University; 1986 MIL (7) (13)

2 — Glenn Bragg, of; B: Bernardino, CA; University of Hawaii; 1986 MIL (5) (7)

4 — Mike Birkbeck, rhp; B: Orrville, OH; University of Akron; 1986 MIL (4) (5)

5 — Joey Meyer, 1b; B: Honolulu, HI; University of Hawaii; 1988 MIL (2) (2)

9 — Jeff Parrett, rhp; B: Indianapolis, IN; University of Kentucky; 1986 MON (3) (8)

15 — Mark Ciardi, rhp; B: New Brunswick, NJ; University of Maryland; 1987 MIL (1) (1)

June — Secondary Phase

2 — Alex Madrid, rhp; B: Springerville, AZ; Yavapai JC, AZ; 1987 MIL (1) (3)

1984

June — Regular Phase

14 — John Jaha, 3b-ss; B: Portland, OR; Douglas HS, Portland, OR; 1992 MIN (7) (7)

1985

January — Secondary Phase

1 — Randy Veres, rhp; B: Sacramento, CA; Sacramento CC, CA; 1989 MIL (2) (5)

June — Regular Phase

1 — B.J. Surhoff, ss-c; B: Bronx, NY; University of North Carolina; 1987 MIL (9) (12)

4 — Bill Bates, 2b; B: Houston, TX; University of Texas; 1989 MIL (2) (3)

8 — Doug Henry, rhp; B: Sacramento, CA; ASU; 1991 MIL (4) (8)

June — Regular Phase

1 — Gary Sheffield, ss; B: Tampa, FL; Hillsborough HS, Tampa, FL; 1988 MIL (4) (11)

3 — Tim McIntosh, c; B: Crystal, MN; University of Minnesota; 1990 MIL (4) (5)

6 — George Canale, 1b; B: Memphis, TN; Virginia Tech; 1989 MIL (3) (3)

11 — Darryl Hamilton, of; B: Baton Rouge, LA; Nicholls State University; 1988 MIL (7) (10)

June — Secondary Phase

1 — Greg Vaughn, of; B: Sacramento, CA; University of Miami, FL; 1989 MIL (8) (10)

1987

1 — Bill Spiers, ss; B: Orangeburg, GA; Clemson University; 1989 MIL (6) (10)

3 — Jamie Navarro, rhp; B: Bayamon, Puerto Rico; Miami–Dade New World Center CC; 1989 MIL (6) (10)

13 — Troy O'Leary, of; B: Compton, CA; Cypress HS; CA; 1993 MIL (2) (6)

1988

5 — Pat Listach, ss; B: Natchitoches, LA; ASU; 1993 MIL (2) (6)

1989

1 — Cal Eldred, rhp; B: Cedar Rapids, IA; University of Iowa; 1991 MIL (8) (8)

1990

5 — Duane Singleton, of; B: Staten Island, NY; McKee Vocational Tech, Staten Island, NY; 1994 MIL (2) (3)

6 — Tom McGraw, lhp; B: Portland, OR; Washington State University; 1997 STL (1) (1)

12 — Marshall Boze, rhp; B: San Manuel, AZ; Southwestern CC, CA; 1996 MIL (1) (1)

1991

8 — Mike Matheny, c; Reynoldsburg, OH; University of Michigan; 1994 MIL (5) (5)

11 — Jeff Cirillo, 3b; B: Pasadena, CA; USC; 1994 MIL (5) (5)

1992

2 — Bobby Hughes, c; B: Burbank, CA; USC; 1998 MIL (1) (1)

6 — Scott Karl, lhp; B: Riverside, CA; University of Hawaii; 1995 MIL (4) (4)

1993

1 — Jeff D'Amico, rhp; B; St. Petersburg, FL; Northeast HS, St. Petersburg, FL; 1996 MIL (2) (2)

1 — Todd Dunn, of; B: Tulsa, OK; University of North Florida; 1996 MIL (2) (2)

2 — Brian Banks, c-of; B: Mesa, AZ; BYU; 1996 MIL (3) (3)

2 — Danny Klassen, ss; B: Leamington, ON, Canada; John Carroll HS, Fort Pierce, FL; 1998 ARZ (1) (1)

7 — Mark Loretta, 2b; B: Santa Monica, CA; Northwestern University; 1995 MIL (4) (4)

19 — Sean Maloney, rhp; B: South Kingston, RI; Georgetown University; 1997 MIL (1) (2)

24 — Greg Martinez, of; B: Las Vegas, NV; Barstow JC, CA; 1998 MIL (1) (1)

1994

8 — Ronnie Belliard, ss; B: Miami, FL; Central HS, Miami, Fla.; 1998 MIL (1) (1)

1995

1 — Geoff Jenkins, of; B: Olympia, WA; USC; 1998 MIL (1) (1)

9 — Mike Kinkade, 3b; B: Livonia, MI; Washington State University; 1998 NYM (1) (1)

Montreal Expos

1969

June — Regular Phase
1— Balor Moore, lhp; B: Smithville, TX; Deer Park (TX) HS; 1970 MON (4) (8)
39 — Terry Humphrey, c-1b; B: Chickasha, OK; Los Angeles CC; 1971 MON (4) (9)
71— Tony Scott, of; B: Cincinnati, OH; Withrow HS, Cincinnati, OH; 1973 MON (3 (12)

1970

June — Regular Phase
1— Barry Foote, c; B: Smithfield, NC; Selma HS, Smithfield, NC; 1973 MON (5) (10)
2 — Chip Lang, rhp; B: Pittsburgh, PA; North Hills HS, Pittsburgh; PA; 1975 MON (2) (2)
5 — Pat Scanlon, 3b; B: Minneapolis, MN; Richfield (MN) HS; 1974 MON (3) (4)
9 — Joe Gilbert, lhp; B: Jasper, TX; Newton HS, Jasper, TX; 1972 MON (2) (2)
14 — Jerry White, of; B: Shirley, MA; Washington HS, San Francisco, CA; 1974 MON (10) (11)
18 — Dale Murray, rhp; B: Cuero, TX; Blinn JC, TX; 1974 MON (5) (12)

1971

June — Regular Phase
2 — Dan Warthen, lhp; Omaha, NE; Omaha (NE) North HS; 1975 MON (3) (4)
6 — Larry Lintz, ss-2b; B: Martinez, CA; San Jose State University; 1973 MON (3) (6)

June — Secondary Phase Delayed
1— Steve Rogers, rhp; B: Jefferson City, MO; University of Tulsa, OK; 1973 MON (13) (13)

1972

January — Secondary Phase
1— Jim Cox, ss; B: Bloomington, IL; University of Iowa; 1973 MON (3) (4)

June — Regular Phase
2 — Ellis Valentine, c-of; B: Helena, AR; Crenshaw HS, Los Angeles, CA; 1975 MON (7) (10)
3 — Gary Carter, c; B: Culver City, CA; Sunny Hills HS, Fullerton, CA; 1974 MON (12) (19)
5 — Dennis Blair, rhp; B: Middletown, OH; Eisenhower HS, Riaito, CA; 1974 MON (3) (4)
11— J. Michael Hart, 1b-of; B: Kalamazoo, MI; Kalamazoo Valley CC, MI; 1980 TEX (1) (1)

June — Secondary Phase
1— Craig Caskey, lhp; B: Visalia, CA; University of Puget Sound; 1973 MON (1) (1)

1973

June — Regular Phase
1— Gary Roenicke, ss; B: Covina, CA; Edgewood HS, West Covina, CA; 1976 MON (1) (12)

25 — Tim Ireland, 2b; B: Oakland, CA; Chabot JC, CA; 1981 KCR (2) (2)

June — Secondary Phase
1— Warren Cromartie, of; B: Miami Beach, FL; Miami–Dade North CC; 1974 MON (9) (10)

1974

January — Regular Phase
1— Joe Kerrigan, rhp; Philadephia, PA; Temple University; 1974 MON (2) (4)

June — Regular Phase
2 — Jerry Fry, ss; Salinas, CA; Springfield (IL) HS; 1978 MON (1) (1)
7 — Bobby Ramos, c; Havana, Cuba; Jackson HS, Miami, FL; 1978 MON (5) (6)

June — Secondary Phase
2 — Shane Rawley, lhp; B: Racine, WI; Indian Hills CC, IA; 1978 SEA (4) (12)

1975

June — Regular Phase
11— Andre Dawson, of; B: Miami, FL; Florida A&M University; 1976 MON (11) (21)

1976

June — Regular Phase
1— Bob James, rhp; B: Glendale, LA; Verdugo Hills HS, Sunland, CA; 1978 MON (5) (8)
3 — Dan Schatzeder, lhp-of; B: Elmhurst, IL; University of Denver; 1977 MON (8) (15)
4 — Bobby Pate, of; B: Los Angeles, CA; ASU; 1980 MON (2) (2)
9 — Jack O'Connor, lhp; B: Twentynine Palms, CA; Yucca Valley (CA) HS; 1981 MON (1) (6)
21— David Palmer, rhp; B: Glen Falls, NY; Glen Falls (NY) HS; 1978 MON (6) (10)

1977

June — Regular Phase
1— Bill Gullickson, rhp; B: Marshall, MN; Joliet Catholic HS, Orland Park, IL; 1979 MON (7) (14)
3 — Scott Sanderson, rhp; B: Dearborn, MI; Vanderbilt University; 1978 MON (6) (19)
5 — Tim Raines, ss; B: Sanford, FL; Seminole HS, Sanford, FL; 1979 MON (12) (20)
26 — Anthony Johnson, of; B: Memphis, TN; LeMoyne-Owen College; 1981 MON (1) (2)

1978

January — Secondary Phase
1— Tony Phillips, ss-2b; B: Atlanta, GA; New Mexico Military Institute; 1982 OAK (8) (17)

June — Regular Phase
4 — Dave Hostetler, 1b; B: Pasadena, CA; USC; 1981 MON (1) (5)

9 — Charlie Lea, rhp; B: Orleans, France; Memphis State University; 1980 MON (6) (7)

10 — Tom Wieghaus, c; B: Chicago Heights, IL; Illinois State University; 1981 MON (2) (3)

18 — Razor Shines, c; B: Durham, NC; St. Augustine HS, Durham, NC; 1983 MON (4) (4)

20 — Pat Rooney, of; B: Chicago, IL; Eastern Illinois University; 1981 MON (1) (1)

1979

June — Regular Phase

1 — Tim Wallach, 1b; B: Huntington Park, CA; Cal State Fullerton; 1980 MON (13) (17)

6 — Wallace Johnson, 2b; B: Gary, IN; Indiana State University; 1981 MON (9) (9)

7 — Mike Gates, 2b; B: Culver City, CA; Pepperdine University; 1981 MON (2) (2)

17 — Brad Mills, 3b; B: Exeter, CA; University of Arizona; 1980 MON (4) (4)

1980

January — Secondary Phase

1 — Mike Stenhouse, of; B: Pueblo, CO; Harvard University; 1982 MON (3) (5)

June — Regular Phase

1 — Terry Francona, of; B: Aberdeen, SD; University of Arizona; 1981 MON (5) (10)

2 — Joe Hesketh, lhp; B: Lackawanna, NY; SUNY, Buffalo, NY; 1984 MON (7) (12)

3 — Greg Bargar, rhp; B: Inglewood, CA; University of Arizona; 1983 MON (2) (3)

4 — Tom Gorman, lhp; B: Portland, OR; Gonzaga University; 1981 MON (2) (8)

5 — Roy Johnson, of; B: Parkin, AR; Tennessee State University; 1982 MON (3) (3)

9 — Bryan Little, ss; B: Houston, TX; Texas A&M University; 1982 MON (3)(6)

1981

June — Regular Phase

2 — Mike Fuentes, of; Miami FL; Florida State University; 1983 MON (2) (2)

June — Secondary Phase

1 — Al Newman, 2b; B: Kansas City, MO; San Diego State University; 1985 MON (2) (8)

1982

June — Regular Phase

2 — John Dopson, rhp; B: Baltimore, MD; Delore Catholic HS, Finksburg, MD; 1985 MON (2) (8)

5 — Rene Gonzales, ss; B: Austin, TX; Cal State Los Angeles; 1984 MON (2) (8)

June — Secondary Phase

1 — Nelson Santovenia, c; B: Pinar Del Rio, Cuba; University of Miami (FL); 1987 MON (5) (7)

1983

June — Regular Phase

1 — Brian Holman, rhp; B: Denver, CO; North HS, Wichita, KS; 1988 MON (2) (5)

5 — Cliff Young, lhp; B: Willis, TX; D: 11/4/93; Willis (Texas) HS; 1990 CAL (2) (3)

6 — Bill Moore, of-1b; B: Los Angeles, CA; Cal State Fullerton; 1986 MON (1) (1)

1984

June — Regular Phase

1 — Norm Charlton, lhp; B: Fort Polk, LA; Rice University; 1988 CIN (5) (6)

4 — Gary Wayne, lhp; B: Dearborn, MI; University of Michigan; 1989 MIN (4) (6)

1985

June — Regular Phase

1 — Pete Incaviglia, 3b; B: Pebble Beach, CA; Oklahoma University; 1986 TEX (5) (13)

2 — Randy Johnson, lhp; B: Walnut Creek, CA; USC; 1988 MON (2) (12)

7 — Jeff Fischer, rhp; B: West Palm Beach, FL; University of Florida; 1987 MON (1) (2)

8 — Mark Gardner, rhp; B: Los Angeles, CA; Fresno State University; 1989 MON (4) (11)

23 — Frank Bolick, 3b; B: Ashland, Pa.; Georgia Tech; 1993 MON (1) (1)

June — Secondary Phase

1 — Jim Hunter, rhp; B: Jersey City, NJ; University of Georgia; 1991 MIL (1) (1)

1986

June — Regular Phase

2 — Jeff Tabaka, lhp; B: Barbarton, OH; Kent State University; 1994 PIT (1) (5)

4 — Kent Bottenfield, rhp, Madison HS, Portland, Ore.; 1992 MON (2) (6)

5 — Gene Harris, rhp; B: Sebring, FL; Tulane University; 1989 MON (1) (7)

10 — Mike Blowers, ss; B: Wurzburg, Germany; University of Washington; 1989 NYY (3) (10)

1987

1 — Delino DeShields, ss; B: Seaford (DE) HS; 1990 MON (4) (9)

2 — Nate Minchey, rhp; B: Austin, TX; Pflugerville (TX) HS; 1993 BOS (3) (4)

2 — Richie Lewis, rhp; B: Muncie, IN; FSU; 1992 BAL (1) (7)

3 — John Vanderwal, of; B: Grand Rapids, MI; Western Michigan University; 1991 MON (3) (8)

5 — Arci Cianfrocco, ss; B: Rome, NY; Purdue University, 1992 MON (2) (7)

6 — Greg Colbrunn, 3b; B: Fontana, CA; Fontana (CA) HS; 1992 MON (2) (7)

7 — Howard Farmer, rhp; B: Gary, IN; Jackson State University; 1990 MON (1) (1)

13 — Rob Natal, c; B: Long Beach, CA; University of California; 1992 MON (1) (7)

29 — Kevin Foster, 3b; B: Evanston, IL; Evanston (IL) HS; 1993 PHI (1) (5)

1988

1— Dave Wainhouse, rhp; B: Toronto, ON, Canada; Washington State University; 1991 MON (1) (5)

2 — Chris Nabholz, lhp; B: Harrisburg, PA; Towson State University; 1990 MON (4) (6)

3 — Marquis Grissom, of-rhp; B: Atlanta, GA; Florida A&M University; 1989 MON (6) (10)

4 — Scott Davison, rhp-ss; B: Inglewood, CA; Redondo Union HS, Redondo Beach, CA; 1994 SEA (2) (2)

6 — Tim Laker, c; B: Encino, CA; Oxnard (CA) JC; 1992 MON (3) (6)

7 — Bret Barberie, ss; B: Long Beach, CA; USC; 1991 MON (2) (6)

11— Reid Cornelius, rhp; B: Thomasville, AL; Thomasville (AL) HS; 1994 MON (1) (2)

18 — Darrin Winston, lhp; B: Passaic, NJ; Rutgers University, 1997 PHI (2) (2)

1989

2 — Glenn Murray, c; B: Manning, SC; Manning (SC) HS; 1996 PHI (1) (1)

4 — Brian Barnes, lhp, B: Roanoke Rapids, NC; Clemson University; 1990 MON (4) (5)

6 — Pete Young, rhp-3b; B: Meadville, MS; Mississippi State University; 1991 MON (3) (3)

9 — Doug Bochtler, rhp; B: West Palm Beach, FL; Indian River (FL) CC; 1995 SD (3) (4)

20— F.P. Santangelo, ss; B: Livona, MI; University of Miami; 1995 MON (4) (4)

1990

1— Shane Andrews, 3b; B: Dallas, TX; Carlsbad (NM) HS; 1995 MON (4) (4)

1— Rondell White, of; B: Baldwin, GA; Jones County HS, Gray, GA; 1994 MON (6) (6)

1— Gabe White, lhp; B: Sebring, FL; Sebring (FL) HS; 1994 MON (2) (4)

1— Stan Spencer, rhp; B: Vancouver, WA; Stanford University; 1998 SDP (1) (1)

1— Ben VanRyn, lhp; B: Fort Wayne, IN; East Noble, HS, Kendallville, IN; 1996 CAL (1) (2)

2 — Tavo Alvarez, rhp; B: Obregon, Mexico; Tuscon (AZ) HS; 1995 MON (2) (2) (from Yankees for Perez)

2 — Chris Haney, lhp; B: Baltimore, MD; UNC Charlotte; 1991 MON (2) (8)

4 — Jeff Barry, of; B: Medford, OR; San Diego State University; 1995 NYM (1) (2)

16 — Jim Converse, rhp; B: San Francisco, CA; Casa Roble HS, Orangevale, CA; 1992 SEA (3) (4)

1991

1— Cliff Floyd, 1b; B: Chicago, IL; Thornwood HS, South Holland, IL; 1993 MON (4) (6)

6 — Derrick White, of; B: San Rafael, CA; University of California; 1993 MON (1) (3)

10— Brian Looney, lhp; B: New Haven, CN; Boston College; 1993 MON (2) (3)

11— Mark Grudzielanek, ss; B: Milwaukee, WI; Trindad State (CO) JC; 1995 MON (4) (4)

18 — Kirk Rueter, lhp; B: Centralia, IL; Murray State University; 1993 MON (4) (6)

1992

2 — Rod Henderson, rhp; B: Greensburg, KY; University of Kentucky; 1992 MON (1) (1)

3 — Everett Stull, rhp; B: Fort Riley, KS; Tennessee State University; 1997 MON (1) (1)

6 — Jose Vidro, 2b; B: Mayaguez, PR; Blanca Morales HS, Sabana Grande, PR; 1997 MON (2) (2)

10— Steve Falteisek, rhp; B: Mineola, NY; University of South Alabama; 1997 MON (1) (1)

41— Curt Schmidt, rhp; B: Miles City, MT; University of Kansas; 1995 MON (1) (1)

1993

2 — Brad Fullmer, 3b; B: Los Angeles, CA; Montclair Prep, Van Nuys, CA: 1997 MON (2) (2)

8 — Neil Weber, lhp; B: Newport Beach, CA; Cuesta JC, CA; 1998 ARZ (1) (1)

1994

1— Mike Thurman, rhp; B: Corvallis, OR; Oregon State University; 1997 MON (2) (2)

4 — Jeremy Powell, rhp; B: Bellflower, CA; Highlands HS, North Highlands, CA; 1998 MON (1) (1)

5 — Javier Vazquez, rhp; B: Ponce, PR; Colegio Ponceno HS, Ponce PR; 1998 MON (1) (1)

1995

1— Michael Barrett, ss; B: Atlanta, GA; Pace Academy, Atlanta, GA; 1998 MON (1) (1)

1996

19 — Tim Young, lhp; B: Gulfport, MS; University of Alabama; 1998 MON (1) (1)

New York Mets

1965

June — Regular Phase

1— Les Rohr, lhp; B: Lowestaft, England; West HS, Billings, MT; 1967 NYM (3) (3)

3 — Joe Moock, ss; B: Plaquemine, LA; LSU; 1967 NYM (1) (1)

4 — Ken Boswell, 2b; B: Austin, TX; Sam Houston State University; 1967 NYM (8) (11)

11 — Jim McAndrew, rhp; B: Lost Nation, IA; University of Iowa; 1968 NYM (6) (7)

12 — Nolan Ryan, rhp; B: Refugio, TX; Alvin (TX) HS; 1966 NYM (5) (19)

24 — Steve Renko, 1b-rhp; B: Kansas City, KS; University of Kansas; 1969 MON (8) (10)

35 — Don Shaw, lhp; B: Pittsburgh, PA; San Diego State University; 1967 NYM (2) (5)

44 — Joe Campbell, of; B: Louisville, KY; Morehead State University; 1967 CHC (1) (1)

47 — Barry Raziano, rhp-of; B: New Orleans, LA; East Jefferson HS, Kenner, LA; 1973 KCR (1) (2)

1966

June — Regular Phase

4 — Mike Jorgenson, 1b-of; B: Passiac, NY; Francis Lewis HS, Queens, NY; 1968 NYM (3) (8)

20 — Ernie McAnally, rhp; B: Mt. Pleasant, TX; Paris (TX) JC; 1971 MON (4) (4)

June — Secondary Phase

1 — Duffy Dyer, c; B: Dayton, OH; ASU; 1969 NYM (7) (14)

3 — Dan Frisella, rhp; B: San Francisco, CA; Washington State University; 1967 NYM (6) (11)

1967

January — Regular Phase

1 — Ken Singleton, of; B: New York, NY; Mt. Vernon, NY; 1970 NYM (2) (15)

June — Regular Phase

1 — Jon Matlack, lhp; B: West Chester, PA; Henderson HS, West Chester, PA; 1971 NYM (7) (13)

10 — Charles Hudson, lhp-of; B: Ada, OK; Tupelo (OK) HS, 1972 STL (1) (3)

38 — David Schneck, lhp-of; B: Allentown, PA; White Hall (PA) HS; 1972 NYM (3) (3)

50 — Tom Robson, 1b; B: Rochester, NY; Utah State University; 1974 TEX (2) (2)

June — Secondary Phase

1 — Rich Folkers, lhp; B: Waterloo, IA; Parsons College; 1970 NYM (1) (7)

2 — Rod Gaspar, of; B: Long Beach, CA: Cal State Long Beach, CA; 1969 NYM (2) (6)

3 — Gary Gentry, rhp; B: Phoenix, AZ; ASU; 1969 NYM (4) (7)

8 — Rich Hacker, ss; B: Belleville, IL; Southern Illinois University; 1971 MON (1) (1)

1968

June — Regular Phase

1 — Tim Foli, ss; B: Culver City, CA; Notre Dame HS, Canoga Park, CA; 1970 NYM (2) (10)

7 — Charlie Williams, rhp; B: Queens, NY; Parsons College; 1971 NYM (1) (8)

10 — Hank Webb, rhp; B: B: Copaigue, NY; Copaique (NY) HS; 1972 NYM (5) (6)

11 — Dan Rose, rhp; B: Covine, CA; Stanford University; 1971 NYM (1) (3)

14 — John Milner, of; B: Atlanta, GA; South Fulton HS, East Point Point, GA; 1971 NYM (7) (12)

1969

June — Regular Phase

1 — Randy Sterling, rhp; B: Key West, FL; Key West (FL) HS; 1974 NYM (1) (1)

2 — Joe Nolan, c; B: St Louis, MO; Southwest HS, St. Louis, MO; 1972 NYM (1) (11)

21 — Lute Barnes, 2b; B: Forest City, IA; Oregon State University; 1972 NYM (2) (2)

27 — Buzz Capra, rhp; B: Chicago, IL; Illinois State University; 1971 NYM (3) (7)

31 — George Theodore, 1b-of; Salt Lake City, UT; University of Utah; 1973 NYM (2) (2)

June — Secondary Phase

3 — Larry Fritz, 1b; B: East Chicago, IL; ASU; 1975 PHI (1) (1)

1970

January — Secondary Phase

1 — Roy Staiger, ss; B: Tulsa, OK; Bacone (OK) JC; 1975 NYM (3) (4)

June — Regular Phase

20 — Bruce Boisclair, of; B: Putnam, CA; Killingly HS, Danielson, CT; 1974 NYM (5) (5)

June — Secondary Phase

1 — Bret Strom, lhp; B: San Diego, CA: USC; 1972 NYM (1) (5)

1971

January — Regular Phase

5 — Frank Estrada, rhp; B: Navojoa, Mexico; Cuesta (CA) JC; 1971 NYM (1) (1)

June — Regular Phase

1 — Rich Puig, 2b; B: Tampa, FL; Hillsborough HS, Tampa, FL; 1974 NYY (1) (1)

9 — Rick Baldwin, of-rhp; Fresno, CA; Downey HS, Modesto, CA; 19775 NYM (3) (3)

23 — Mark DeJohn, 3b; B: Middletown, CT; Wilson HS, Middletown, CT; 1982 DET (1) (1)

1972

January — Regular Phase

5 — Randy Tate, rhp; B: Florence, AL; John C. Calhoun (AL) CC; 1975 NYM (1) (1)

January — Secondary Phase

2 — Ron Hodges, c; B: Rocky Mount, CA; Appalachian State University; 1975 NYM (1) (1)

June — Regular Phase

3 — Craig Swan, rhp; B: Van Nuys, CA; ASU; 1973 NYM (12) (12)

6 — Brock Pemberton, 1b; B: Tulsa, OK; Marina HS, Huntington Beach, CA; 1974 NYM (2) (2)

9 — Craig Cacek, of; B: Hollywood, CA; Monroe HS, Sepulvada, CA; 1977 HOU (1) (1)

1973

June — Regular Phase

1 — Lee Mazzilli, of; B: New York, NY; Lincoln HS, Brooklyn, NY; 1976 NYM (6) (14)

2 — Jackson Todd, rhp; B: Tulsa, OK; University of Oklahoma; 1977 NYM (1) (4)

21 — Mardie Cornejo, rhp; B: Wellington, KS; University of Tulsa; 1978 NYM (1) (1)

1974

June — Regular Phase

1 — Cliff Speck, rhp; B: Portland, OK; Beaverton (OR) HS; 1986 ATL (1) (1)

2 — Dwight Bernard, rhp; B: Mount Vernon, IL; Belmont College; 1978 NYM (2) (4)

4 — John Pacella, rhp; B: Brooklyn, NY; Connetquot HS, Oakdale, NY; Brooklyn, NY; 1977 NYM (3) (6)

20 — Bob Myrick, lhp; B: Rockford, IL; Mississippi State University; 1976 NYM (3) (3)

June — Secondary Phase

1 — Ned Yost, c; B: Eureka, CA; Chabot (CA) JC; 1980 MIL (4) (6)

1975

January — Regular Phase

4 — Marshall Brant, 1b; B: Garberville, CA; Santa Rosa (CA) JC; 1980 NYM (1) (2)

June — Regular Phase

1 — Butch Benton, c; B: Tampa, FL; Godby HS, Tallahassee, FL; 1978 NYM (2) (4)

1976

January — Regular Phase

3 — Jody Davis, 1b-c; B: Gainesville, GA; Middle Georgia JC; 1981 CHC (8) (10)

January — Secondary Phase

4 — Kim Seaman, lhp; B: Pascagoula, MS; Mississippi Gulf Coast JC; 1979 STL (2) (2)

June — Regular Phase

2 — Mike Scott, rhp; B: Santa Monica, CA; Pepperdine University; 1979 NYM (4) (13)

11 — Neil Allen, rhp; B: Kansas City, KC; Ward HS, Kansas City, KS; 1979 NYM (5) (12)

17 — Dave Von Ohlen, lhp; B: Queens, NY; Flushing HS, College Point, NY; 1982 MIN (8) (14)

1977

June — Regular Phase

1 — Wally Backman, ss; B: Hillsboro, OR; Aloha HS, Beaverton, OR; 1980 NYM (9) (14)

2 — Mookie Wilson, of; B: Bamberg, SC; University of South Carolina; 1980 NYM (10) (12)

5 — Fred Martinez, rhp; B: Los Angeles, CA; Cal State Los Angeles; 1980 CAL (2) (2)

6 — Brent Gaff, rhp; B: Fort Wayne, IN; Churubusco (IN) HS; 1982 NYM (3) (3)

1978

8 — Jamie Nelson, c; B: Clinton, OK; Orange Coast JC, CA; 1983 SEA (1) (1)

June — Regular Phase

1 — Hubie Brooks, of; B: Los Angeles, CA; ASU; 1980 NYM (5) (15)

3 — Brian Giles, 2b; B: Manhattan, NY; Kearny HS, San Diego, CA: 1981 NYM (3) (6)

6 — Mike Fitzgerald, c; B: Long Beach, CA; Lakewood (CA) HS; 1983 NYM (2) (10)

11 — Randy Johnson, ss; B: Escondido, CA; San Jose State University; 1982 ATL (3) (3)

24 — Rick Anderson, rhp; B: Everett, WA; University of Washington; 1987 NYM (1) (2)

1979

January — Regular Phase

10 — Rusty Tillman, of; B: Jacksonville, FL; Florida JC; 1982 NYM (1) (3)

June — Regular Phase

1 — Tim Leary, rhp; B: Santa Monica, CA; UCLA; 1981 NYM (3) (13)

2 — Jeff Bettendorf, rhp; B: Lompoc, CA; Lompoc (CA) HS; 1984 OAK (1) (1)

6 — Ron Gardenhire, inf; B: Butzbach, Germany; University of Texas; 1981 NYM (5) (5)

27 — David W. Smith, rhp; B: Tomball, TX; Lamar University; 1984 CAL (2) (2)

1980

June — Regular Phase

1 — Darryl Strawberry, of; B: Los Angeles, CA; Crenshaw HS, Los Angeles, CA; 1983 NYM (8) (16)

1 — Billy Beane, of; B: Orlando, CA; Mt. Carmel HS, Rancho Bernardo, CA; 1984 NYM (2) (6)

1 — John Gibbons, c; B: Great Falls, MT; MacArthur HS, San Antonio, TX; 1984 NYM (2) (6)

2 — Jay Tibbs, rhp; B: Birmingham, AL; Huffman HS, Birmingham, AL; 1984 CIN (2) (7)

5 — Ronn Reynolds, c; B: Wichita, KS; University of Arkansas; 1982 NYM (3) (6)

7 — Jeff Bitiger, rhp; B: Jersey City, NY; Secaucus (NJ) HS; 1986 PHI (1) (4)

8 — Lloyd McClendon, c; B: Gary, IN; Valparaiso University; 1987 CIN (2) (9)

13 — Rick Ownbey, rhp; B: Coronas, CA; Santa Ana (CA) JC; 1982 NYM (2) (4)

1981

January — Regular Phase

1— Randy Milligan, of; B: San Diego, CA; San Diego Mesa JC; 1987 NYM (1) (8)

June — Regular Phase

1— Terry Blocker, of; B: Columbia, SC; Tennessee State University; 1985 NYM (1) (3)

2 — John Christensen, of; B: Downey, CA; Cal State Fullerton; 1984 NYM (2) (4)

4 — Dave Cochrane, rhp-3b; B: Riverside, CA: Troy HS, Yorba Linda, CA; 1986 CHW (1) (5)

8 — Mark Carreon, of; B: Chicago, IL; Salpointe HS, Tucson, AZ; 1987 NYM (5) (10)

13 — Len Dykstra, of; B: Santa Ana, CA; Garden Grove (CA) HS; 1985 NYM (5) (12)

19 — Louis Thornton, 3b; B: Montgomery, AL; Jefferson Davis HS, Hopehull, AL 1985 TOR (3) (5)

1982

June — Regular Phase

1— Dwight Gooden, rhp; B: Tampa, FL; Hillsborough HS, Tampa, FL; 1984 NYM (11) (16)

2 — Floyd Youmans, rhp; B: Tampa, FL; Fontana (CA) HS; 1985 MON (4) (5)

3 — Roger McDowell, rhp; B: Cincinnati, OH: Bowling Green State University; 1985 NYM (5) (12)

5 — Gerald Young, ss; B: Tele, Honduras; Santa Ana (CA) Valley HS; 1987 HOU (6) (8)

7 — Greg Olson, c; B: Marshall, MN; University of Minnesota; 1989 MIN (1) (5)

9 — Joe Redfield, ss; B: Doylestown, PA; UC Santa Barbara; 1985 CAL (1) (2)

12 — Mickey Weston, rhp; B: Flint, MI; Eastern Michigan University; 1989 BAL (2) (5)

15 — Barry Lyons, c; B: Biloxi, MS; Delta State University; 1986 NYM (7) (8)

22 — Wes Gardner, rhp; B: Benton, AR; University of Central Arkansas; 1984 NYM (2) (8)

June — Secondary Phase

1— Randy Myers, lhp; B: Vancouver, WA; Clark (WA) JC; 1985 NYM (5) (14)

1983

January — Secondary Phase

2 — Jeff McKnight, ss; B: Conway, AR; Westark (AR) CC; 1989 NYM (1) (6)

June — Regular Phase

1— Eddie Williams, 3b; B: Shreveport, LA; Hoover HS, San Diego, CA; 1986 CLE (3) (9)

1— Stan Jefferson, of; B: New York, NY; Bethune-Cookman College; 1986 NYM (1) (7)

1— Calvin Schiraldi, rhp; B: Houston, TX; University of Texas; 1984 NYM (2) (8)

2 — Dave Magadan, 1b; B: Tampa, FL; University of Alabama; 1986 NYM (7) (12)

3 — Rick Aguilera, rhp; B: San Gabriel, CA; BYU; 1985 NYM (5) (14)

4 — David West, lhp; B: B: Memphis, TN; Craigmont HS, Memphis, TN; 1988 NYM (2) (9)

6 — Marcus Lawton, ss; B: Gulfport, MS; Harrison Central HS, MS; 1989 NYM (1) (1)

13 — Jeff Innis, rhp; B: Decatur, IL; University of Illinois; Decatur, IL; 1987 NYM (7) (7)

36 — Joe Klink, lhp; B: Johnstown, PA; Biscayne College; 1987 MIN (1) (5)

1984

January — Regular Phase

2 — Kevin Elster, ss; B: San Pedro, CA; Golden West JC, CA; 1986 NYM (7) (12)

7 — Scott Little, of; B: East St. Louis, MO; Mineral Area JC, MO; 1989 PIT (1) (1)

June — Regular Phase

1— Shawn Abner, of; B: Hamilton, OH; Mechanicsburg (PA) HS; 1987 SDP (5) (6)

13 — Mauro Gozzo, rhp-ss; B: New Britain, CT; Berlin (CN) HS; 1989 TOR (1) (6)

1985

June — Regular Phase

1— Gregg Jefferies, ss; B: Burlingame, CA; Serra HS, Millbrae, CA; 1988 NYM (4) (11)

1986

June — Regular Phase

4 — Kip Gross, rhp; B: Scottsbluf, NE; University of Nebraska; 1990 CIN (2) (4)

10 — Curtis Pride, of; B: Washington DC; Kennedy HS, Silver Spring, MD; 1993 MON (2) (6)

16 — Archie Corbin, B: Beaumont, TX; Charlton Pollar HS, Beaumont, TX; 1991 KCR (1) (2)

1987

1— Chris Donnels, inf; B: Los Angeles, CA; 1991 NYM (2) (2)

2 — Todd Hundley, c; B: Martinsville, VA; Fremd HS, Palatine, IL; 1990 NYM (9) (9)

2 — Pete Schourek, lhp; B: Austin, TX; Marshall HS, Falls Church, VA; 1991 NYM (3) (8)

8 — Tim Bogar, ss; B: Indianapolis, IN; Eastern Illinois University; 1993 NYM (4) (6)

16 — Eric Hillman, lhp; B: Gary, IN; Eastern Illinois University; 1992 NYM (3) (3)

18 — Denny Harriger, rhp; B: Kittanning, PA; Ford City (PA) HS; 1998 DET (1) (1)

20 — John Johnstone, rhp; B: Liverpool, NY; Bishop Ludden HS, Liverpool, NY; 1993 FLA (1) (6)

38 — Anthony Young, rhp; B: Houston, TX; University of Houston; 1991 NYM (3) (6)

1988

3 — Doug Saunders, 3b; B: Lakewood, CA; Esperanza HS, Yorba Linda, CA; 1993 NYM (1) (1)

7 — Kevin Baez, ss, B: Brooklyn, NY; Dominican (NY) College; 1990 NYM (3) (3)

1989

3 — Brook Fordyce, c; St. Bernards HS, Old Lyme, CT; 1995 NYM (1) (4)

7 — Butch Huskey, 3b; B: Anadarko, OK; Eisenhower HS, Lawton, OK; 1993 NYM (5) (5)

23 — Mike Thomas, lhp; B: Sacramento,CA; Labette (KS) JC; 1995 MIL (1) (1)

24 — Joe Vitko, rhp, St. Francis College, NY; 1992 NYM (1) (1)

31 — Dave Telgheder, rhp; B: Middletown, NY; University of Massachusetts; 1993 NYM (3) (6)

1990

1 — Jeromy Burnitz; of; B: Westminster, CA; Oklahoma State University; 1993 NYM (2) (6)

2 — Aaron Ledesma, ss; B: Union City, CA; Chabot JC, CA; 1995 NYM (1) (3)

3 — Micah Franklin, of; B: San Francisco, CA; Lincoln HS, San Francisco, CA; 1997 STL (1) (1)

7 — Pete Walker, rhp; B: Beverly, MA; University of Connecticut; 1995 NYM (1) (2)

8 — Raul Casanova, c; B: Humacao, PR; Ponce (PR) HS; 1996 DET (3) (3)

17 — Brian Daubach, 1b; B: Belleville, IL; Belleville Township (IL) HS; 1998 FL (1) (1)

45 — Ricky Otero, of; B: Vega Baja, PR; Lino Padron Rivera HS, PR; 1995 NYM (1) (3)

1991

1 — Bobby Jones, rhp; B: Fresno, CA; Fresno State University, CA; 1993 NYM (6) (6)

2 — Bill Pulsipher, lhp; B: Fort Benning, GA; Fairfax (VA) HS; 1995 NYM (3) (3)

2 — Marc Kroon, rhp; B: Bronx, NY; Shadow Mountain HS, Phoenix, AZ; 1995 SDP (3) (3)

12 — Jason Jacome, lhp; B: Tulsa, OK; Pima CC, AZ; 1994 NYM (2) (5)

17 — Joe Crawford, lhp; B: Gainesville, FL; Kent State University; 1997 NYM (1) (1)

44 — Jason Isringhausen, rhp; B: Brighton, IL; Lewis & Clark JC, IL; 1995 NYM (3) (3)

1992

1 — Preston Wilson, ss; B: Bamberg, SC; Bamberg Ehrhardt HS, Bamberg, SC; 1998 NYM (1) (1)

20 — Allen McDill, lhp; B: Greenville, MS; Arkansas Tech; 1997 KCR (2) (2)

1993

2 — Eric Ludwick, rhp; B: Whiteman AFB, MO; UNLV; 1996 STL (2) (3)

3 — Mike Welch, rhp; B: Haverhill, MA; University of Southern Maine; 1998 PHI (1) (1)

30 — Benny Agbayani, of; B: Honolulu, Hawaii; Hawaii Pacific University; 1998 NYM (1) (1)

1994

1 — Paul Wilson, rhp; B: Orlando, FL; FSU; 1996 NYM (1) (1)

1 — Jay Payton, of; B: Zanesville, OH; Georgia Tech; 1998 NYM (1) (1)

Philadelphia Phillies

1965

June — Regular Phase

2 — Larry Hisle, of; B: Portsmouth, OH; Portsmouth (OH) HS; 1968 PHI (4) (14)

3 — Billy Champion, rhp; B: Shelby, NC; Shelby HS, Shelby NC; 1969 PHI (4) (8)

5 — Terry Harmon, ss; B: Toledo, OH; Ohio University; 1967 PHI (10) (10)

1966

January — Regular Phase

1 — John Vukovich, 3b-ss; B: Sacramento, CA; American River JC, CA; 1970 PHI (7) (10)

January — Special Phase

1 — Lowell Palmer, rhp; B: Sacramento, CA; American River JC, CA; 1969 PHI (3) (6)

June — Regular Phase

4 — Ken Reynolds, lhp; B: Trevose, PA; New Mexico Highlands University; 1970 PHI (3) (6)

June — Secondary Phase

1 — Steve Arlin, rhp; B: Seattle, WA; Ohio State University; 1969 SDP (6) (7)

1967

June — Secondary Phase

2 — Scott Reid, of; B: Chicago, IL; ASU; 1969 PHI (2) (2)

1968

June — Regular Phase

1 — Greg Luzinski, 1b; B: Chicago, IL; Notre Dame HS, Prospect Heights, IL; 1970 PHI (11) (15)

1969

June — Regular Phase

1 — Mike Anderson, 1b; B: Florence, SC; Timmonsville (SC) HS; 1971 PHI (5) (9)

2 — Mike Rogodzinski, of; B: Evanston, IL; Southern Illinois University: 1973 PHI (3) (3)

4 — Mike Wallace, lhp; B: Gastonia, NC; James Madison HS, Vienna, VA; 1973 PHI (2) (5)

6 — Bob Boone, 3b; B: San Diego, CA; Stanford University; 1972 PHI (10) (19)

16 — Ron Diorio, rhp; B: Waterbury, CT; University of New Haven; 1973 PHI (2) (2)

1970

June—Regular Phase
6—David Downs, rhp; B: Logan, CT; Viewmont HS, Bountiful, UT; 1972 PHI (1) (1)
8—Fred Andrews, ss; B: Lafayette, LA; Lincoln Heights HS, OH; 1976 PHI (2) (2)
11—Craig Robinson, ss; B: Abington, PA; Wake Forest University; 1972 PHI (2) (6)
22—Erskine Thomason, rhp; B: Laurens, SC; Erskine College; 1974 PHI (1)(1)
28—Bob Beall, 1b; B: Portland, OR; Oregon State University; 1975 ATL (3) (4)

1971

June—Regular Phase
1—Roy Thomas, rhp; B: Quantico, VA; Lompoc HS, CA; 1977 HOU (1) (8)
2—Mike Schmidt, ss; B: Dayton, OH; Ohio University; 1972 PHI (18) (18)
8—Mac Scarce, lhp; B: Danville, VA; Florida State University; 1972 PHI (3) (5)

June—Secondary Phase Delayed
1—Dane Iorg, ss; B: Eureka, CA; BYU; 1986 SDP (1) (1)

1972

June—Regular Phase
1—Larry Christenson, rhp; B: Everett, WA; Marysville HS, WA;1973 PHI (11) (11)
2—Tom Underwood, lhp; B: Kokomo, IN; Kokomo HS, IN; 1974 PHI (4) (11)
6—Bill Nahorodny, c; B: Hamtramck, MI; St. Clair County CC, MI; 1976 PHI (1) (9)

1973

January—Regular Phase
1—Alan Bannister, ss; B: Monte Bello, CA; Arizona State University; 1974 PHI (2) (15)
7—Rick Bosetti, 2b; B: Redding, CA; Shasta JC, CA; 1976 PHI (1) (7)

January—Secondary Phase
1—Dick Ruthven, rhp; B: Sacramento, CA; Fresno State University; 1973 PHI (9) (11)

June—Regular Phase
1—John Stearns, c; B: Denver, CO; University of Colorado; 1974 PHI (1) (11)
2—Todd Cruz, ss; B: Highland Park, MI; Western HS, Detroit, MI; 1978 PHI (1) (8)
5—Jim Wright, rhp; B: St. Joseph, MO; Benton HS, St. Joseph, MO; 1981 KCA (2) (2)
6—Manny Seoane, rhp; B: Tampa, FL; Tampa Catholic HS, FL; 1977 PHI (1) (2)
8—Randy Lerch, lhp; B: Sacramento, CA; Rancho Cordova HS, CA; 1975 PHI (6) (13)

June—Secondary Phase
1—Dan Boitano, rhp; B: Sacramenton, CA; Fresno CC, CA; 1978 PHI (1) (5)

1974

January—Secondary Phase
4—Warren Brusstar, rhp; B: Oakland, CA; Fresno State University; 1977 PHI (6) (10)

June—Regular Phase
1—Lonnie Smith, of; B: Chicago, IL; Centennial HS, Compton, CA; 1978 PHI (4) (17)
2—Kevin Saucier, lhp; B: Pensacola, FL; Escambia HS, Warrington, FL; 1978 PHI (3) (5)
4—Don McCormack, c; B: Omak, WA; Omak HS, WA; 1980 PHI (2) (2)
5—Jim Morrison, 3b; B: Pensacola, FL; Georgia Southern College; 1977 PHI (2) (12)
8—Mark Clear, rhp; B: Los Angeles, CA; Northview HS, Covina, CA; 1979 CAL (2) (11)

1975

January—Secondary Phase
1—Barry Bonnell, of; B: Clermont Co., OH; Ohio State University; 1977 ATL (3) (10)

June—Regular Phase
4—Dickie Noles, rhp; B: Charlotte, NC; Harding HS, Charlotte, NC; 1979 PHI (3) (13)
7—Keith Moreland, 3b; B: Dallas, TX; University of Texas; 1978 PHI (4) (13)

1976

January—Regular Phase
2—Derek Botelho, rhp; B: Long Beach, CA; Miami–Dade South CC; 1982 KCA (1) (2)

June—Regular Phase
5—Lee Matuszek, of; B: Toledo, OH; University of Toledo; 1981 PHI (4) (8)
6—Ozzie Virgil, c; B: Mayaguez, Puerto Rico; Moon Valley HS, Glendale, AZ; 1980 PHI (6) (11)

June—Secondary Phase
2—Joe Charbonneau, of; B: Belvidere, IL; West Valley JC, CA; 1980 CLE (3) (3)
3—Bob Walk, rhp; B: Van Nuys, CA; College of the Canyons, CA; 1980 PHI (1) (14)

1977

June—Regular Phase
1—Scott Munninghoff, rhp; B: Cincinnati, OH; Purcell HS, Cincinnati, OH; 1980 PHI (1) (1)
4—George Vukovich, of; B: Chicago, IL; Southern Illinois University; 1980 PHI (3) (6)
20—Greg Walker, c; B: Douglas, GA; Coffee HS, Douglas, GA; 1982 CHW (9) (10)
22—Jerry Reed, rhp; B: Bryson City, NC; Western Carolina University; 1981 PHI (2) (10)

1978

June — Regular Phase
4 — Ed Hearn, c; B: Stuart, FL; Fort Pierce Central HS, FL; 1986 NYM (1) (3)
20 — Ryne Sandberg, inf; B: Spokane, WA; North Central HS, Spokane, WA; 1981 PHI (1) (15)

1979

January — Secondary Phase
1 — Mark Davis, lhp; B: Livermore, CA; Chabot JC, CA; 1980 PHI (3) (15)

June — Regular Phase
3 — Roy Smith, rhp; B: Mt. Vernon, NY; Mt. Vernon HS, Mt. Vernon, NY; 1984 CLE (2) (8)
4 — Jay Baller, rhp; B: Stayton, OR; Canby HS, OR; 1982 PHI (2) (6)
26 — Kelly Downs, rhp; B: Ogden, UT; Viewmont HS, Bountiful, UT; 1986 SFG (7) (9)

1980

January — Regular Phase
1 — Tony Ghelfi, rhp; B: La Crosse, WI; Iowa Western CC; 1983 PHI (1) (1)

June — Regular Phase
9 — Steve Jeltz, ss-2b; B: France; University of Kansas; 1983 PHI (7) (8)
21 — Rocky Childress, rhp; B: Santa Rosa, CA; Santa Rosa HS, CA; 1985 PHI (2) (4)
23 — Marty Decker, rhp; B: Upland, CA; Point Loma Nazarene College; 1983 SDP (1) (1)
25 — Darren Daulton, c; B: Arkansas City, KS; Arkansas City HS, KS; 1983 PHI (14) (14)

June — Secondary Phase
3 — Ken Dowell, ss; B: Sacramento, CA; Sacramento CC, CA; 1987 PHI (1) (1)
5 — Ed Wojna, rhp; B: Bridgeport, CN; Indian River CC, FL; 1985 SDP (3) (4)

1981

January — Secondary Phase
1 — Kevin Gross, rhp; B: Downey, CA; Oxnard JC, CA; 1983 PHI (6) (14)

June — Regular Phase
1 — Johnny Abrego, rhp; B: Corpus Christi, TX; Mission HS, San Jose, CA; 1985 CHI (1) (1)
12 — Charles Hudson, rhp; B: Ennis, TX; Prairie View A&M University; 1983 PHI (4) (7)

1982

January — Regular Phase
20 — Rick Surhoff, rhp; B: Bronx, NY; St John's River CC, FL; 1985 PHI (1) (2)

June — Regular Phase
1 — John Russell, c-of; B: Oklahoma City, OK; University of Oklahoma; 1989 ATZ (1) (1)

2 — Lance McCullers, rhp; B: Tampa, FL; Tampa Catholic HS, FL; 1985 SDP (4) (8)
5 — Mike Maddux, rhp; B: Dayton, OH; University of Texas, El Paso, TX; 1986 PHI (4) (13)
22 — Greg Legg, ss; B: San Jose, CA; Southeastern Oklahoma State University; 1986 PHI (2) (2)

June — Secondary Phase
1 — Kenneth Jackson, ss; B: Shreveport, CA; Angelina JC, TX; 1987 PHI (1) (1)

1983

June — Regular Phase
1 — Ricky Jordan, lb; B: Richmond, CA; Grant HS, Sacramento, CA; 1988 PHI (7) (8)
24 — Tom Newell, rhp; B: Monrovia, CA; Lassen JC, CA; 1987 PHI (1) (1)

1984

January — Secondary Phase
2 — Mike Jackson, rhp; B: Houston, TX; Hill JC, TX; 1986 PHI (2) (11)

June — Regular Phase
1 — Pete Smith, rhp; B: Abington, MA; Burlington HS, MA; 1987 ATL (7) (9)
2 — Marvin Freeman, rhp; B: Chicago, IL; Jackson State University; 1986 PHI (4) (10)
13 — Todd Frohwirth, rhp; B: Milwaukee, WI; Northwest Missouri State University; 1987 PHI (4) (9)
16 — Keith Miller, ss; B: Dallas, TX; Lubbock Christian College; 1988 PHI (2) (2)
25 — Bob Scanlan, rhp; B: Beverly Hills, CA: Harvard HS, North Hollywood CA; 1991 CHC (3) (7)

1985

June — Regular Phase
2 — Bruce Ruffin, lhp; B: Lubbock, TX; University of Texas; 1986 PHI (2) (2)
4 — Wally Ritchie, lhp; B: Glendale, CA; Glendale JC, CA; 1987 PHI (4) (4)
10 — Jason Grimsley, rhp; B: Cleveland, TX; Tarkington HS, Cleveland, TX; 1989 PHI (3) (7)
16 — Rick Parker, of; B: Kansas City, MO; University of Texas; 1990 SFG (2) (6)

1986

January — Regular Phase
2 — Steve Scarsone, inf; B: Anaheim, CA; Rancho Santiago JC, CA; 1992 PHI (1) (5)

June — Regular Phase
8 — Chuck McElroy, lhp; B: Galveston, TX; Lincoln HS, Port Arthur, TX; 1989 PHI (2) (10)

1987

4 — Rick Trlicek, rhp; B: Houston, TX; La Gange (TX) HS; 1992 TOR (1) (5)

7 — Donnie Elliott, rhp; B: Pasadena, TX; San Jacinto (TX) JC; 1994 SDP (2) (2)

27 — Toby Borland, rhp; B: Quitman, LA; Quitman (LA) HS; 1994 PHI (4) (5)

36 — Greg McCarthy, lhp; B: Norwalk, CT; Bridgeport (CT) HS; 1996 SEA (3) (3)

1988

1 — Pat Combs, lhp; B: Newport, RI; Baylor University; 1989 PHI (4) (4)

5 — Mickey Morandini, ss; B: Kittanning, PA; Indiana University; 1990 PHI (8) (9)

40 — Paul Fletcher, rhp; B: Gallipolis, OH; West Virginia State College; 1993 PHI (3) (3)

1989

5 — Steve Parris, rhp; B: Joliet, IL; College of St. Francis, IL; 1995 PIT (2) (3)

18 — Matt Whisenant, lhp; B: Los Angeles, CA; Glendale CC; 1997 FLA (1) (2)

32 — Steve Bieser, of-c; B: Perryville, MO; Southeast Missouri State University; 1997 NYM (1) (2)

1990

1 — Mike Lieberthal, c; B: Glendale, CA; Westlake HS, Westlake Village, CA; 1994 PHI (5) (5)

7 — Joel Adamson, lhp; B: Lakewod, CA; Cerritos JC, CA; 1996 FLA (1) (2)

11 — Gary Bennett, c; B: Waukegan, IL; Waukegan (IL) East HS; 1995 PHI (3) (3)

14 — Mike Williams, rhp; B: Radford, VA; Virginia Tech; 1992 PHI (5) (7)

1991

1 — Tyler Green, rhp; B: Springfield, OH; Wichita State University; 1993 PHI (4) (4)

2 — Kevin Stocker, ss; Spokane, WA; University of Washington; 1993 PHI (5) (6)

4 — Gene Schall, of; B: Abington, PA; Villanova University; 1995 PHI (2) (2)

10 — Mike Grace, rhp; B: Clearwater, FL; Bradley University; 1995 PHI (4) (4)

1992

5 — Larry Mitchell, rhp; B: Flint, MI; James Madison University; 1996 PHI (1) (1)

12 — Jon Zuber, of; B: Encino, CA; University of California; 1996 PHI (2) (2)

23 — Bobby Estella, c; B: Hialeah, FL; Miami–Dade CC South; 1996 PHI (3) (3)

1993

1 — Wayne Gomes, rhp; B: Hampton, VA: Old Dominion University; 1997 PHI (2) (2)

2 — Scott Rolen, 3b; B: Jasper, IN; Jasper (IN) HS; 1996 PHI (3) (3)

14 — Rich Hunter, rhp; B: Pasadena, CA; The Linfield School, Temecula, CA; 1996 PHI (1) (1)

27 — Dave Doster, 2b; B: Fort Wayne, IN; Indiana State University: 1996 PHI (1) (1)

33 — Kevin Sefcik, of; B: Oak Lawn, IL; St. Xavier College, IL; 1995 PHI (4) (4)

1994

1 — Carlton Loewer, rhp; B: Lafayette, LA; Mississippi State University; 1998 PHI (1) (1)

2 — Ryan Ney, rhp; B: Biloxi, MS; Texas Tech; 1997 PHI (2) (2)

12 — Wendell Magee, of; B Hattiesburg, MS; Samford University; 1996 PHI (3) (3)

14 — Robert Dodd, lhp; B: Kansas City, KS; University of Florida; 1998 PHI (1) (1)

37 — Bronson Heflin, rhp; B: Clarksville, TN; University of Tennessee; 1996 PHI (1) (1)

1995

2 — Marlon Anderson, 2b; B: Montgomery, AL; University of South Alabama; 1998 PHI (1) (1)

Pittsburgh Pirates

1965

June — Regular Phase

18 — Bob Moose, rhp; B: Export, PA; D: Martins Ferry; Franklin Area HS, Export, PA; 1967 PIT (10) (10)

20 — Gene Garber, rhp; B: Lancaster, PA; Elizabethtown HS, PA; 1969 PIT (3) (19)

22 — Fred Patek, ss; B: Seguin, TX; 1968 PIT (3) (14)

30 — Lou Marone, lhp; B: San Diego, CA; San Diego Mesa JC, CA; 1969 PIT (2) (2)

31 — Jim Nelson, rhp; B: Birmingham, AL; Burbank HS, Sacramento, CA; 1970 PIT (2) (2)

1966

June — Regular Phase

1 — Rickie Hebner, ss; B: Boston, MA; Norwood HS, MA; 1968 PIT (11) (18)

2 — James Minshall, rhp; B: Covington, KY; Newport Catholic HS, Melbourne, KY; 1974 PIT (2) (2)

5 — Dave Cash, ss; B: Utica, NY; Proctor HS, Utica, NY; 1969 PIT (5) (12)

6 — Gene Clines, 2b-of; B: San Pablo, CA; Ells HS, Richmond, CA; 1970 PIT (5) (10)

7 — Bill Laxton, lhp; B: Camden, NJ; Audubon HS, NJ; 1970 PHI (1) (5)

June — Secondary Phase

1 — Frank Brosseau, rhp; B: Dayton, ND; University of Minnesota, MN; 1969 PIT (2) (2)

1967

June — Regular Phase
3 — Richie Zisk, of; B: Brooklyn, NY; Parsippany HS, NJ; 1971 PIT (6) (13)

1968

January — Secondary Phase
3 — Tom Dettore, rhp-c; B: Canonsburg, PA; Juniata College; 1973 PIT (1) (4)

June — Regular Phase
1 — Dick Sharon, of; B: San Mateo, CA; Sequola HS, Redwood City, CA; 1973 DET (2) (3)
11 — Milt May, ss; B: Gary, IN; St. Petersburg (FL) HS; 1970 PIT (4) (15)
14 — Bruce Kison, rhp; B: Pasco, WA; Pasco (WA) HS; 1971 PIT (9) (15)

1969

January — Secondary Phase
1 — John Morlan, of-rhp; B; Columbus, OH; Ohio University; 1973 PIT (2) (2)

June — Regular Phase
3 — Fred Cambria, rhp; B; Cambria Heights, NY; St. Leo College; 1970 PIT (1) (1)
4 — James McKee, rhp; B: Columbus, OH; Otterbein College; 1972 PIT (2) (2)

1970

June — Regular Phase
14 — Dave Parker, c-of; B: Calhoun, MS; Courter Tech HS, Cincinnati, OH; 1973 PIT (11) (19)
23 — Ed Ott, 3b-c; B: Muncy, PA; Muncy HS, PA; 1974 PIT (7) (8)

1971

June — Regular Phase
1 — Craig Reynolds, ss; B: Houston, TX; Regan HS, Houston, TX; 1975 PIT (2) (15)
2 — Doug Bair, rhp; B: Defiance, OH; Bowling Green State University, OH; 1976 PIT (3) (15)

1972

January — Secondary Phase
7 — Larry Demery, rhp; B: Bakersfield, CA; Los Angeles CC, CA; 1974 PIT (4) (4)

June — Regular Phase
2 — John Candelaria, lhp; B: New York, NY; LaSalle Academy, Brooklyn, NY; 1975 PIT (12) (19)
4 — Tim Jones, rhp; B: Sacramento, CA; Ponderosa HS, El Dorado Hills, CA; 1977 PIT (1) (1)
6 — Ken Macha, 1b-3b; B: Monroeville, PA; University of Pittsburgh, PA; 1974 PIT (3) (6)
7 — Willie Randolph, ss-c; B: Holy Hill, SC; Tilden HS, Brooklyn, NY; 1975 PIT (1) (18)
28 — Butch Alberts, 3b; B: Williamsport, PA; University of Cincinnati, OH; 1978 TOR (1) (1)

1973

June — Regular Phase
1 — Steve Nicosia, c; B: Paterson, NJ; North Miami Beach HS, FL; 1978 PIT (6) (8)
3 — Mitchell Page, of; B: Los Angeles, CA; Cal Poly Pomona, CA; 1977 OAK (7) (8) PIT (1)

1974

January — Regular Phase
3 — Fred Breining, rhp; B: San Francisco, CA; College of San Mateo, CA; 1980 SFG (4) (5)

June — Regular Phase
1 — Rod Scurry, lhp; B: Sacramento, CA; Proctor Hug HS, Sparks, NV; 1980 PIT (6) (8)
2 — Gary Hargis, inf; B: Minneapolis, MN; Cabrillo HS, Lompoc, CA; 1979 PIT (1) (1)
6 — Ed Whitson, rhp; B: Johnson City, TN; Unicoi County HS, Erwin, TN; 1977 PIT (3) (15)
7 — Mike Edwards, inf; B: Fort Lewis, WA; UCLA, CA; 1977 PIT (1) (4)
10 — Bryan Clark, lhp; B: Madera, CA; Madera HS, CA; 1981 SEA (4) (8)

1975

June — Regular Phase
1 — Dale Berra, ss; B: Ridgewood, NJ; Montclair HS, NJ; 1977 PIT (8) (11)
3 — Don Robinson, rhp; B: Ashland, KY; Ceredo-Kenova HS, Kenova, WV; 1978 PIT (10) (15)

1976

January — Secondary Phase
1 — Larry Littleton, of; B: Charlotte, NC; University of Georgia, GA; 1981 CLE (1) (1)

June — Regular Phase
2 — Dorian Boyland, of; B: Chicago, IL; University of Wisconsin–Oshkosh, WI; 1978 PIT (3) (3)
17 — Rick Honeycutt, 1b-lhp; B: Chattanooga, TN; University of Tennessee, TN; 1977 SEA (4) (20)
24 — Bob Long, rhp-of; B: Jasper, TN; Shorter College; 1981 PIT (1) (2)

1977

June — Regular Phase
4 — Stew Cliburn, rhp; B: Jackson, MS; Delta State University; 1984 CAL (3) (3)
11 — Rich Lancellotti, of; B: Providence, RI; Glassboro State College; 1982 SDP (1) (3)

1978

June — Regular Phase
18 — John Stuper, rhp; B: Butler, PA; Point Park College; 1982 STL (3) (4)
21 — Dave Dravecky, lhp; B: Youngstown, OH; Youngstown State University, OH; 1982 SDP (6) (8)

27 — Jeff Zaske, rhp; B: Seattle, WA; Meadowdale HS, Lynwood, WA; 1984 PIT (1) (1)

39 — Vance Law, ss; B: Boise, ID; BYU; 1980 PIT (2) (11)

1979

June — Regular Phase

3 — Jose DeLeon, rhp; B: Rancho Viejo, DR; Perth Amboy, NJ; 1983 PIT (4) (13)

4 — Chris Green, lhp; B: Los Angeles, CA; Dorsey HS, Los Angeles, CA; 1984 PIT (1) (1)

16 — Ron Wotus, ss; B: Colchester, CT; Bacon Academy HS, Colcheser, CT; 1983 PIT (2) (2)

37 — Joel Skinner, c; B: LaJolia, CA; Mission Bay HS, San Diego, CA; 1983 CHI (4) (9)

June — Secondary Phase

1 — Mike Bielecki, rhp; B: Baltimore, MD; Valencia CC, FL; 1984 PIT (4) (13)

1980

June — Regular Phase

1 — Rich Renteria, ss; B: Harbor City, CA; South Gate HS, CA; 1986 PIT (1) (3)

2 — Tim Burke, rhp; B: Omaha, NE; University of Nebraska, NE; 1985 MON (7) (8)

6 — Joe Orsulak, of-1b; B: Glenridge, NJ; Parsippany Hills HS, Parsippany, NJ; 1983 PIT (4) (13)

1981

June — Regular Phase

1 — Jim Winn, rhp; B: Stockton, CA; John Brown University; 1983 PIT (4) (6)

2 — Lee Tunnell, rhp; B: Tyler, TX; Baylor University; 1982 PIT (4) (6)

June — Secondary Phase

1 — Ray Krawczyk, rhp; B: Pittsburgh, PA; Oral Roberts University; 1984 PIT (3) (5)

1982

January — Secondary Phase

2 — Benny Distefano, 1b; B: Brooklyn, NY; Alvin CC, TX; 1984 PIT (4) (5)

June — Regular Phase

1 — Sam Khalifa, ss; B: Fontana, CA; Sahuaro HS, Tucson, AZ; 1985 PIT (3) (3)

14 — Shawn Holman, rhp; B: Sewickley, PA; Ambridge HS, Sewickley, PA; 1989 DET (1) (1)

June — Secondary Phase

1 — Bip Roberts, ss; B: Vicksburg, MI; Chabot JC, CA; 1974 DET (2) (11)

4 — Scott Bailes, lhp; B: Chillicothe, OH; St Louis CC, Meramec, MO; 1986 CLE (7) (7)

1983

January — Regular Phase

12 — Tim Drummond, rhp, B: LaPlata, MD; Charles County CC, MD; 1987 PIT (1) (3)

June — Regular Phase

2 — Stan Fansler, rhp; B: Elkins, WV; Elkins HS, WV; 1986 PIT (1) (1)

12 — John Smiley, lhp; B: Phoenixville, PA; Perkiomen HS, Trappe, PA; 1986 PIT (6) (12)

June — Secondary Phase

5 — Rich Sauveur, lhp; B: Arlington, VA; Manatee JC, FL; 1986 PIT (1) (5)

1984

January — Secondary Phase

2 — Jay Buhner, of; B: Louisville, KY; McLennan CC, TX; 1987 NYY (2) (12)

4 — Tom Prince, c; B: Kankakee, IL; Kankakee CC, IL; 1987 PIT (7) (12)

June — Regular Phase

3 — Barry Jones, rhp; B: Centerville, IN; Indiana University, Centerville, IN; 1986 PIT (3) (8)

1985

June — Regular Phase

1 — Barry Bonds, of; B: Riverside, CA; ASU, AZ; 1986 PIT (7) (13)

6 — Brett Gideon, rhp; B: Ozona, TX; University of Mary Hardin–Baylor; 1987 PIT (1) (3)

7 — Tommy Gregg, of; B: Boone, NC; Wake Forest University; 1987 PIT (2) (8)

1986

January — Regular Phase

1 — Moises Alou, of; B: Atlanta, GA; Canada JC, CA; 1990 PIT (1) (8)

June — Regular Phase

1 — Jeff King, ss-3b; B: Marion, IN; University of Arkansas, AK; 1989 PIT (8) (10)

8 — Tony Longmire, of; B: Vallejo, CA; Hogan HS, Vallejo, CA; 1993 PHI (3) (3)

10 — Stan Belinda, rhp; B: Huntington, PA; Allegheny CC, PA; 1989 PIT (5) (8)

11 — Keith Sheperd, rhp; B: Wabash, IN; Wabash (IN) HS; 1992 PHI (1) (4)

26 — Rick Reed, rhp; B: Huntington, PA; Marshall University; 1988 PIT (4) (10)

1987

4 — Wes Chamberlain, of; B: Chicago, IL; Jackson State University; 1990 PHI (5) (6)

17 — Steve Carter, of; B: Charlottesville, VA; University of Georgia, GA; 1989 PIT (2) (2)

1988

6 — Blas Minor, rhp; B: Merced, CA; ASU; 1992 PIT (3) (6)

7 — John Wehner, 3b; B: Pittsburgh, PA; Indiana University, IN; 1991 PIT (6) (8)

8 — Tim Wakefield, 1b; B: Melbourne, FL; Florida Institute of Technology, FL; 1992 PIT (2) (6)

11 — Joe Ausanio, rhp; B: Kingston, NY; Jacksonville, University; 1994 NYY (2) (2)

19 — Mandy Romero, c; B: Miami, FL; Brevard CC, FL; 1997 SDP (2) (2)

1989

1 — Willie Greene, ss; B: Milledgeville, GA; Jones County HS, Gray, GA; 1992 CIN (7) (7)

2 — Rich Aude, 3b; B: Van Nuys, CA; Chatsworth (CA) HS; 1993 PIT (3) (3)

2 — John Hope, rhp; B: Fort Lauderdale, FL; Stranahan HS, Fort Lauderdale, FL; 1993 PIT (4) (4)

12 — Paul Wagner, rhp; B: Milwaukee, WI; Illinois State University, IL; 1992 PIT (6) (7)

35 — Steve Cooke, lhp; B: Kauai, HI; JC of Southern Idaho; 1992 PIT (5) (6).

1990

1 — Kurt Miller, rhp; B: Tucson, AZ; West HS, Bakersfield, CA; 1994 FLA (3) (4)

7 — Kevin Young, 3b; B: Alpena, MI ; University of Southern Mississippi; 1992 PIT (6) (7)

9 — Rich Robertson, lhp; B: Nacogdoches, TX; Texas A&M University; 1994 PIT (1) (5)

13 — Brian Shouse, lhp; B: Effingham, IL; Bradley University; 1990 PIT (1) (2)

14 — Jeff McCurry, rhp; B: Bellaire, TX; San Jacinto JC, TX; 1995 PIT (1) (4)

15 — Rick White, rhp; B: Springfield, OH; Paducah CC; 1994 PIT (2) (3)

20 — Mark Johnson, 1b; B: Worcester, MA; Dartmouth College; 1990 PIT (3) (4)

24 — Keith Osik, c; B: Port Jefferson, NY; LSU; 1996 PIT (3) (3)

1991

3 — Matt Ruebel, lhp; B: Cincinnati, OH; University of Oklahoma; 1996 PIT (2) (2)

7 — Tony Womack, 2b; B: Danville, VA; Guilford College; 1993 PIT (5) (5)

19 — Marc Pisciotta, rhp; B: Edison, NJ; Georgia Tech; 1997 CHC (2) (2)

1992

1 — Jason Kendall, c; B: San Diego, CA; Torrance (CA) HS; 1996 PIT (3) (3)

2 — Danny Clyburn, of; B: Lancaster, SC; Lancaster (SC) HS; 1997 BAL (2) (2) (from Mets for Bonilla)

2 — Trey Beamon, of; B: Dallas, Texas; WT White HS, Dallas; 1996 PIT (1) (3)

6 — Sean Lawrence, lhp; B: Oak Park, IL; College of St. Francis, IL; 1998 PIT (1) (1)

18 — Gary Wilson, rhp; B: Arcata, CA; Cal State Sacramento; 1995 PIT (1)(1)

27 — Chance Sanford, 2b; B: Houston, TX; San Jacinto JC, TX; 1998 PIT (1) (1)

30 — Kevin Polcovich, ss; B: Auburn, NY; University of Florida; 1987 PIT (2) (2)

31 — Lou Collier, ss; B: Chicago, IL; Triton (IL) CC; 1997 PIT (2) (2)

47 — Marc Wilkins, rhp; B: Mansfield, OH; University of Toledo; 1992 PIT (3) (3)

48 — Adrian Brown, of; B: McComb, MS; McComb (MS) HS; 1997 PIT (2) (2)

1993

1 — Jermaine Allensworth, of; B: Anderson, IN; Purdue University; 1996 PIT (3) (3)

37 — Chris Peters, lhp; B: Fort Thomas, KY; Indiana University; 1996 PIT (3) (3)

St. Louis Cardinals

1965

June — Regular Phase

4 — Harry Parker, rhp; B: Highland, IL; Collinsville (IL) HS; 1970 STL (3) (6)

27 — Jerry Robertson, rhp; B: Winchester, KS; Washburn University; 1969 MON (1) (2)

1966

June — Regular Phase

1 — Leron Lee, inf-of, B: Bakersfield, CA; Grant HS, Sacramento, CA; 1969 STL (3) (8)

3 — Clay Kirby, rhp; B: Washington DC; Washington HS, Arlington, VA; 1969 SDP (5) (8)

June — Secondary Phase

1 — Jerry DaVanon, 2b; B: Oceanside, CA; Westmount College; 1969 SDP (1) (8)

1967

June — Regular Phase

1 — Ted Simmons, c-of; B: Highland Park, MI; Southfield (MI) HS; 1968 STL (13) (21)

2 — Jerry Reuss, lhp; B: St. Louis, MO; Ritenour HS, Overland, MO; 1969 STL (3) (22)

June — Secondary Phase

5 — Bobby Chlupsa, rhp; B: New York, NY; Manhattan University, NY; 1970 STL (2) (2)

1968

January — Secondary Phase

4 — Skip Jutze, c; B: Queens, NY; Central Connecticut State University; 1972 STL (1) (6)

June — Regular Phase

7 — Tom Heintzelman, 2b; B: St. Charles, MO; Parsons College; 1973 STL (2) (4)

26 — Bob Forsch, 3b-rhp; B: Sacramento, CA; Hirman Johnson HS, Sacramento, CA; 1974 STL (15) (16)

33 — Tom Plodinec, rhp; B: Aliquippa, PA; University of Arizona; 1972 STL (1) (1)

1969

January — Regular Phase
1— Al Hrabosky, lhp; B: Oakland, CA; Fullerton JC, CA; 1970 STL (8) (13)
2 — Ed Crosby, 2b; B: Long Beach, CA; Long Beach CC, CA; 1970 STL (3) (6)

January — Secondary Phase
3 — Ray Bare, rhp; B: Miami, FL; Miami–Dade North CC, FL; 1972 STL (3) (6)

June — Regular Phase
3 — Mick Kelleher, ss; B: Seattle, WA; University of Puget Sound, WA; 1972 STL (3) (11)
4 — Bill Stein, ss; B: Battle Creek, MI; Southern Illinois University; 1972 STL (2) (14)
31— Ken Reitz, ss; B: San Francisco, CA: Jefferson HS, Daly City, CA; 1972 STL (4) (11)

1970

January — Regular Phase
3 — Mike Tyson, ss; B: Rocky Mount, NC; Indiana River CC, FL; 1972 STL (8) (10)

January — Secondary Phase
Class A (Modesto, St. Petersburg, Cedar Rapids and Lewiston) selections:
4 — Rudy Arroyo, lhp; B: New York, NY; Foothill CC, CA: 1971 STL (1) (1)

June — Regular Phase
5 — Greg Terlecky, rhp; B: Culver City, CA; West Covina (CA) HS; 1975 STL (1) (1)
7 — Don Durham, rhp-of; B: Yosemite, KY; Western Kentucky University; 1975 STL (1) (1)
10— Marc Hill, c; B: Elsberry, MO; Elsberry (MO) HS; 1973 STL (2) (14)
29— John Denny, rhp; B: Prescott, AZ; Prescott (AZ) HS; 1974 STL (6) (13)
37— Bake McBride, lhp-of; B: Fulton, MO; Westminster College, MO; 1973 STL (5) (11)

1971

January — Secondary Phase
4 — Mike Vail, ss; B: San Francisco, CA; San Jose, CA; 1975 NYM (3) (8)
6 — Mike Potter, of; B: Montebello, CA; Mt. San Antonio JC; CA; 1976 STL (2) (2)

June — Regular Phase
3 — Larry Herndon, of; B: Sunflower, MS; Douglas HS, Memphis, TN; 1974 STL (1) (14)
4 — Jerry Mumphrey, ss-of; B: Tyler, TX; Chapel Hill HS, Tyler, TX; 1974 STL (6) (15)
11— Jim Dwyer, of; B: Evergreen Park, IL; Southern Illinois University; 1973 STL (5) (6)
42 — Keith Hernandez, 1b; B: San Francisco, CA; Capuchino HS, Millbrae, CA; 1974 STL (10) (17)

1972

June — Regular Phase
1— Dan Larson, rhp; B: Houston, TX; Alhambra (CA) HS; 1976 HOU (2) (7)
9 — Mike Proly, rhp; B: Queens, NY; St. John's University; 1976 STL (1) (7)

1973

June — Regular Phase
1— Joe Edelen, 3b; B: Durant, OK; Gracemont (OK) HS; 1981 STL (1) (12)
5 — Randy Wiles, lhp; B: Fort Belvoir, VA; LSU; 1977 CWS (1) (1)
6 — John Tamargo, c; B: Tampa, FL; Georgia Southern College; 1976 STL (3) (5)
32 — Eric Rasmussen, rhp; B: Racine, WI; LSU; 1975 STL (4) (8)

1974

January — Regular Phase
1— John Urrea, rhp; B: Los Angeles, CA; Rio Hondo (CA) JC; 1977 STL (4) (5)

June — Regular Phase
1— Garry Templeton, ss; B: Russellton, PA; Santa Ana (CA) Valley HS; 1976 STL (6) (16)
8 — Bill Caudill, rhp; B: Santa Monica, CA; Aviation HS, Redondo Beach, CA; 1979 CHC (3) (19)

1975

June — Regular Phase
2 — Kelly Paris, ss; B: Encino, CA; Taft HS, Woodland Hills, CA; 1982 STL (1) (5)
3 — Mike Ramsey, ss; B: Roanoke, VA; Appalachian State University; 1978 STL (5) (6)
9 — Andy Replogle, rhp; B: South Bend, IN; Kansas State University; 1978 MIL (2) (2)
12 — Jim Lentine, of; B: Los Angeles, CA; University of LaVerne; 1978 STL (3) (3)
13 — Alan Olmstead, lhp; B: St. Louis, MO; Hazelwood East HS, St. Louis; 1980 STL (1) (1)

1976

January — Secondary Phase
3 — Dan O'Brien, rhp; St. Petersburg, FL; FSU; 1978 STL (2) (2)

June — Regular Phase
1— Leon Durham, 1b-lhp; B: Cincinnati, OH; Woodward HS, Cincinnati, OH; 1980 STL (2) (10)
12 — Gene Roof, ss; B: Paducah, KY; St. Mary's Paducah, KY; 1981 STL (3) (3)
22 — Ray Searage, lhp; B: Freeport, NY; West Liberty State College; 1981 NYM (1) (7)
30— John Littlefield, rhp; B: Covine, CA; Azusa Pacific University; 1980 STL (1) (2)

June — Secondary Phase
1— John Fulgham, rhp; B: St. Louis, MO; Yavapai JC, AZ; 1979 STL (2) (2)

1977

January — Regular Phase
4 — Tye Waller, 3b; B: Fresno, CA; San Diego CC; 1980 STL (1) (4)

June — Regular Phase
1 — Terry Kennedy, c; B: Euclid, OH; FSU; 1978 STL (3) (14)

3 — Joe DeSa, 1b; B: Honolulu, HI; Damien HS, Honolulu, HI; 1980 STL (1) (2)

4 — Jim Gott, of-rhp; B: Hollywood, CA; San Marino (CA) HS; 1982 TOR (3) (14)

5 — Andy Rincon, rhp; B: Monterey Park, CA; St. Paul HS, Pico Rivera, CA; 1980 STL (3) (3)

6 — Jeff Doyle, ss; B: Harve, MT; Oregon State University; 1983 STL (1) (1)

32 — Neal Fiala, inf; B: St. Louis, MO; Southern Illinois University; 1981 STL (1) (1)

1978

June — Regular Phase
4 — George Bjorkman, c; B: Ontario, CA; Oral Roberts University; 1983 HOU (1) (1)

1979

June — Regular Phase
1 — Andy Van Slyke, of; B: Utica, NY; New Hartford (NY) HS; 1983 STL (4) (13)

11 — Tom Dozier, rhp; B: San Pablo, CA; Richmond (CA) HS; 1986 OAK (1) (1)

18 — Mark Salas, c; B: Montebello, CA; Nogales, HS, LaPuente, CA; 1984 STL (1) (8)

23 — Terry Clark, rhp; B: Los Angeles, CA; Mt. San Antonio JC, TX; 1988 CAL (2) (6)

June — Secondary Phase
1 — Ralph Citarella, rhp; B: East Orange, NJ; Florida Southern College; 1983 STL (2) (3)

1980

January — Regular Phase
4 — Kevin Hagen, rhp; B: Renton, WA; Bellevue CC, WA; 1983 STL (2) (2)

June — Regular Phase
4 — Ricky Horton, lhp; B: Poughkeepsie, NY; University of Virginia; 1984 STL (4) (7)

7 — Jim Adduci, of; B: Chicago, IL: Southern Illinois University; 1983 STL (1) (14)

1981

June — Regular Phase
1 — Bobby Meacham, ss; B: Los Angeles, CA; San Diego State University; 1983 NYM (6) (16)

3 — Tom Nieto, c; B: Downey, CA: Oral Roberts University; 1984 STL (2) (7)

4 — Curt Ford, 2b; B: Jackson, MS; Jackson State University; 1985 STL (4) (6)

7 — Jeff Keener, rhp; B: Pana, IL; University of Kentucky; 1982 STL (2) (2)

13 — Danny Cox, rhp; B: Northampton, England; Troy State University; 1983 STL (6) (11)

June — Secondary Phase
1 — Randy Hunt, c; B: Prattville, AL; University of Alabama; 1985 STL (1) (2)

1982

June — Regular Phase
1 — Todd Worrell, rhp; B: Arcadia, CA; Biola University; 1985 STL (6) (11)

7 — Terry Pendleton, of; B: Los Angeles, CA; Fresno State University; 1984 STL (7) (15)

10 — Vince Coleman, of; B: Jacksonville, FL; Florida A&M University; 1985 STL (6) (13)

1983

June — Regular Phase
1 — Jim Lindeman, 3b; B: Evanston, IL; Bradley University; 1986 STL (4) (9)

8 — Tom Pagnozzi, c; B: Tucson, AZ; University of Arkansas; 1987 STL (12) (12)

24 — John Costello, rhp; B: Bronx, NY; Mercyhurst College; 1988 STL (3) (4)

1984

June — Regular Phase
1 — Mike Dunne, rhp; B: South Bend, IN; Bradley University; 1987 PIT (3) (5)

2 — Matt Kinzer, rhp; B: Indianapolis, IN; Purdue University; 1987 STL (1) (2)

5 — Scott Arnold, rhp; B: Lexington, KY; Miami (Ohio) University; 1988 STL (1) (1)

6 — Lance Johnson, of; B: Cincinnati, OH; University of South Alabama; 1988 CWS (10) (1)

10 — Greg Matthews, lhp; B: Harbor City, CA; Cal State Fullerton; 1986 STL (4) (5)

20 — Craig Wilson, ss-2b; B: Annapolis, MD; Anne Arundel (Md.) CC; 1989 STL (4) (5)

22 — Jeff Fassero, lhp; B: Springfield, IL; University of Mississippi; 1991 MON (6) (8)

June — Secondary Phase
1 — Mike Fitzgerald, c-of; B: Savannah, GA; Middle Georgia JC; 1988 STL (1) (1)

1985

January — Regular Phase
2 — Alex Cole, of; B: Fayetteville, NC: Manatee JC, FL; 1990 CLE (3) (7)

June — Regular Phase
1 — Joe Magrane, lhp; B: Des Moines, IA; University of Arizona; 1987 STL (6) (8)

2 — Tim Jones, ss; B: Sumter, SC; The Citadel; 1988 STL (6) (6)

5 — Steve Peters, lhp; B: Oklahoma City, OK; University of Oklahoma; 1987 STL (2) (2)

6 — Ray Stevens, c; B: Houston, TX; Troy State University; 1990 STL (2) (3)

22 — Howard Hilton, rhp; B: Oxnard, CA; University of Arkansas, 1990 STL (1)(1)

1986

June — Regular Phase

1 — Luis Alicea, 2b; B: Santurce, PR; FSU; 1988 STL (5) (8)

2 — Todd Zeile, c; B: Van Nuys, CA; UCLA; 1989 STL (7) (10)

5 — Bien Figueroa, ss; B: Santo Domingo, DR; FSU; 1992 STL (1)(1)

10 — Larry Carter, rhp; B: Charleston, WV; West Virginia State College; 1992 SF (1)(1)

12 — Mike Perez, rhp; B: Yauco, PR; Troy State University; 1990 STL (5)(8)

23 — Mark Grater, rhp; B: Rochester, PA; Florida International University; 1991 STL (1)(2)

1987

1 — Cris Carpenter, rhp; B: St. Augustine, FL; University of Georgia; 1988 STL (5) (8)

2 — Jeremy Hernandez, rhp; B: Burbank, CA; Cal State Northridge; 1991 SDP (5)

3 — Ray Lankford, of; B: Modesto, CA; Modesto JC, CA; 1990 STL (9) (9)

5 — Rodney Brewer, 1b-of; B: Eustis, FL; University of Florida; 1990 STL (4)(4)

18 — Tim Sherrill, lhp; B: Harrison, AR; University of Arkansas; 1990 STL (2)(2)

1988

1 — John Ericks, rhp; B: Tinley Park, IL; University of Illinois 1995 PIT (3) (3)

1 — Brian Jordan, of; B: Baltimore, MD; University of Richmond; 1992 STL (7) (7)

6 — Rheal Cormier, lhp; B: Moncton, New Brunswick, Canada; CC of Rhode Island; 1991 STL (4) (7)

9 — Mark Clark, rhp; B: Bath, IL; Lincoln Land CC, IL; 1991 STL (2) (8)

10 — Joe Hall, 3b; B: Paducah, KY; Southern Illinois University; 1994 CWS (1) (2)

1989

2 — Mike Milchin, lhp; B: Knoxville, TN; Clemson University, 1996 MIN (1)(1)

3 — Tripp Cromer, ss; B: Lake City, SC; University of South Carolina; 1993 STL (3) (5)

20 — Bill Hurst, rhp; B: Miami Beach, FL; Central Florida CC; 1996 FLA (1) (1)

31 — Steve Dixon, lhp; B: Cincinnati, OH; Paducah CC, KY; 1993 STL (2) (2)

37 — Frank Cimorelli, rhp; B: Poughkeepsie, NY; Dominican College, NY; 1994 STL (1) (1)

1990

1 — Donovan Osborne, lhp B: Roseville, CA; UNLV; 1992 STL (6) (6)

1 — Aaron Holbert, ss; B: Torrance, CA; Jordan HS, Long Beach, CA; 1998 STL (1) (1)

3 — Marc Ronan, c; B: Ozark, AL; FSU; 1993 STL (1) (1)

7 — Scott Baker, lhp; B: San Jose, CA; Taft JC; 1995 OAK (1) (1)

9 — Terry Bradshaw, of; B: Franklin, VA; Norfolk State University; 1995 STL (2) (2)

13 — Tom Urbani, lhp; B: Santa Cruz, CA; Long Beach State University; 1993 STL (4) (4)

24 — Duff Brumley, rhp; B: Cleveland, TN; Cleveland State CC, TN; 1994 TEX (1) (1)

1991

1 — Dmitri Young, of; B: Vicksburg, MS; Rio Mesa HS, Oxnard, CA; 1996 STL (2) (3)

1 — Allen Watson, lhp; B: Brooklyn NY; New York Tech; 1993 STL (3) (6)

1 — Brian Barber, rhp; B: Hamilton, Ohio; Dr. Phillips HS, Orlando, FL; 1995 STL (2) (3)

5 — DaRond Stoval, of; B: St. Louis, MO; Althoff HS, East St. Louis, IL; 1998 MON (1) (1)

6 — John Mabry, of; B: Wilmington, DE; West Chester University, PA; 1994 STL (5) (5)

7 — Doug Creek, lhp; B: Winchester, VA; Geogia Tech; 1995 STL (1) (3)

10 — Allen Battle, of; B: Grantham, N.C.; University of South Alabama; 1995 STL (1) (2)

11 — Mike Difelice, c; B: Philadelphia, PA; University of Tennessee; 1996 STL (2) (3)

14 — Mike Busby, rhp; B: Lomita, CA; Banning (CA) HS; 1996 STL (3) (3)

24 — John Frascatore, rhp; B: Queens, NY; C.W.Post University; 1994 STL (4) (4)

26 — Rigo Beltran, lhp-1b; B: Tijuana, Mex.; University of Wyoming; 1997 STL (1) (2)

1992

1 — Sean Lowe, rhp; B: Dallas, TX; ASU; 1997 STL (2) (2)

2 — Mike Gulan, 3b; B: Steubenville, OH; Kent University; 1997 STL (1) (1)

3 — Steve Montgomery, rhp; B: Westminster, CA; Pepperdine University; 1996 OAK (2) (2)

10 — Scarborough Green, of; B: Creve Coeur, MO; St. Louis CC; 1997 STL (1) (1)

20 — Brady Raggio, rhp; B: Los Angeles, CA; Chabot JC, CA; 1997 STL (2) (2)

28 — Joe McEwing, of; B: Bristol, PA; JC of Morris, NJ; 1992 STL (1) (1)

32 — Kirk Bullinger, rhp, B: New Orleans, LA; Southeastern Louisiana University; 1998 MON (1) (1)

36 — T.J. Matthews, rhp; B: Belleview, IL; UNLV; 1995 STL (3) (4)

1993

1—Alan Benes, rhp; B: Evansville, IN; Creighton University; 1995 STL (3) (3)
2—Jay Witasick, rhp; B: Baltimore, MD; University of Maryland; 1996 OAK (3) (3)
3—El Marrerok, c; B: Havana, Cuba; Coral Gables (FL) HS; 1997 STL (2) (2)
7—Jeff Berblinger, 2b; B: Wichita, KS; University of Kansas; 1997 STL (1) (1)

1994

5—Curtis King, rhp; B: Philadelphia, PA; Philadelphia College of Textiles; 1997 STL (2) (2)
6—Blake Stein, rhp; B: McComb, MS; Spring Hill College, AL; 1998 OAK (1) (1)
19—Placido Polanco, ss; B: Santo Domingo, DR; Miami–Dade CC Wolfson; 1994 STL (1) (1)
42—Keith Glauber, rhp; B: Brooklyn, NY; Montclair State College, NJ; 1998 CIN (1) (1)

1995

1—Matt Morris, rhp; B: Middletown, NY; Seton Hall University; 1997 STL (2) (2)
34—Kerry Robinson, of; B: St. Louis, MO; Southeast Missouri State University; 1998 TAM (1) (1)
54—Cliff Politte, rhp; B: Kirkwood, MO; Jefferson JC, MO; 1995 STL (1) (1)

1996

1—Braden Looper, rhp; B: Weatherford, OK; Wichita State University; 1999 STL (1) (1)

1998

1—J.D. Drew, of; B: Valdosta, GA; Florida State University; 1998 STL (1) (1)

San Diego Padres

1968

June— Regular Phase
7—David Robinson, of; B: Minneapolis, MN; San Diego State University; 1970 SDP (2) (2)

June— Secondary Phase
5—Bob O'Brien, lhp-1b; B: Pittsburgh, PA; University of Arizona; 1971 LAD (1) (1)

1969

June— Regular Phase
1—Randy Elliott, 1b; B: Oxnard, CA; Camarillo HS, CA; 1972 SDP (2) (4)

1970

January— Regular Phase
1—John Scott, inf; B: Jackson, MS; Centennial HS, Los Angeles, CA; 1974 SDP (2) (3)

June— Regular Phase
1—Mike Ivie, c; B: Atlanta, GA; Walker HS, Decatur, GA; 1971 SDP (5) (11)
2—Dan Spillner, rhp; B: Casper, WY; Federal Way HS, WA; 1974 SDP (5) (13)
4—Steve Simpson, rhp; B: St. Joseph, MO; Washburn University; 1972 SDP (1) (1)
6—Bob Davis, rhp-ss; B: Pryor, OK; Locust Grove HS, OK; 1973 SDP (5) (8)
18—Ralph Garcia, rhp; B: Los Angeles, CA; UNLV; 1972 SDP (2) (2)
23—Larry Hardy, rhp; B: Goose Creek, TX; University of Texas; 1974 SDP (2) (3)

1971

January— Regular Phase
1—Dave Hilton, 3b; B: Vualde, TX; Southwest Texas JC; 1972 SDP (4) (4)

January— Secondary Phase
1—John Grubb, of; B: Richmond, VA; Florida State University; 1972 SDP (5) (16)

June— Regular Phase
1—Jay Franklin, rhp; B: Arlington, VA; James Madison HS, Vienna, VA; 1971 SDP (1) (1)
5—Dave Freisleben, rhp; B: Coraopolis, PA; Sam Rayburn HS, Pasadena, TX; 1974 (5) (7)
7—Frank Snook, rhp; B: Somerville, NJ; Grand Canyon College; 1973 SDP (1) (1)
8—Joe Goddard, c; B: Beckley, WV; Marshall University; 1972 SDP (1) (1)
12—Mike Caldwell, lhp; B: Tarboro, NC; North Carolina State University; 1971 SDP (3) (15)

1972

January— Secondary Phase
1—Rich Troedson, lhp; B: Paco Alto, CA; Santa Clara University; 1973 SDP (2) (2)

June— Regular Phase
1—Dave Roberts, 3b; B: Lebanon, OR; University of Oregon; 1972 SDP (6) (10)
5—Randy Jones, lhp; B: Fullerton, CA; Chapman College; 1973 SDP (8) (10)
10—Jerry Turner, of; B: Texarkana, AK; Venice HS, Culver City, CA; 1974 SDP (9) (11)
12—Rusty Gerhardt, lhp; B: Baltimore, MD; Clemson University; 1974 SDP (1) (1)

1973

January— Regular Phase
1—Dave Wehrmeister, rhp; B: Berwyn, IL; Northeast Missouri State University; 1976 SDP (3) (6)
4—Mike DuPree, rhp; B: Kansas City; Fresno CC, CA; 1976 SDP (1) (1)

June — Regular Phase

1— Dave Winfield, rhp; B: St. Paul, MN; University of Minnesota; 1973 SDP (8) (22)

2— Mike Champion, ss-3b; B: Montgomery, AL; Foothill HS, Santa Ana, CA; 1976 SDP (3) (3)

13— Joe McIntosh, rhp; B: Billings, MT; Washington State University; 1976 SDP (2) (2)

1974

January — Regular Phase

1— Tucker Ashford, 3b-ss; B: Memphis, TN; Shelby State CC, TN; 1976 SDP (3) (7)

June — Regular Phase

1— Bill Almon, ss; B: Providence, RI; Brown University; 1974 SDP (6) (15)

7— Jim Wilhelm, 1b; B: San Rafael, CA; Santa Clara University; 1978 SDP (2) (2)

1975

January — Regular Phase

1— Gene Richards, of; B: Monticello, SC; South Carolina State College; 1977 SDP (7) (8)

January — Secondary Phase

1— Juan Eichelberger, rhp; B: St. Louis, MO; University of California; 1978 SDP (5) (7)

2— Chuck Baker, ss; B: Seattle, WA; Loyola Marymount University; 1978 SDP (2) (3)

3— Rick Sweet, c; B: Longview, WA; Gonzaga University; 1978 SDP (1) (4)

June — Regular Phase

3— Tony Castillo, c; B: San Jose, CA; James Lick HS, San Jose, CA; 1978 SDP (1) (1)

6— Vic Bernal, rhp; B: Los Angeles, CA; Cal Poly Pomona; 1977 SDP (1) (1)

18— Don Reynolds, of; B: Arkadelphia, AK; University of Oregon; 1978 SDP (2) (2)

1976

January — Secondary Phase

1— Bob Shirley, lhp; B: Cushing, OK; University of Oklahoma; 1977 SDP (4) (12)

June — Regular Phase

1— Bob Owchinko, lhp; B: Detroit, MI; Eastern Michigan University; 1976 SDP (4) (10)

2— Steve Mura, rhp; B: New Orleans, LA; Tulane University; 1978 SDP (4) (7)

5— Jim Beswich, of; B: Wilkinsburg, PA; East Allegheny HS, North Versailles, PA; 1978 SDP (1) (1)

9— Craig Stimac, c; B: Oak Park, IL; University of Denver; 1980 SDP (2) (2)

11— Tom Tellmann, rhp; B: Warren, PA; Grand Canyon College; 1979 SDP (2) (5)

13— Mark Lee, rhp; B: Inglewood, CA; Pepperdine University; 1978 SDP (2) (4)

15— Broderick Perkins, 1b; B: Pittsburg, CA; St. Mary's College, CA; 1978 SDP (5) (7)

19— Gary Lucas, lhp; B: Riverside, CA; Chapman College; 1980 SDP (4) (8)

1977

June — Regular Phase

1— Brian Greer, of; B: Lynwood, CA; Sonora HS, Brea, CA; 1977 SDP (2) (2)

2— Barry Evans, ss; B: Atlanta, GA; West Georgia College; 1978 SDP (2) (2)

4— Ozzie Smith, ss; B: Mobile, AL; Cal Poly San Luis Obispo; 1978 SDP (4) (17)

10— Ron Tingley, of; B: Presque Isle, MA; Ramona HS, Riverside, CA; 1982 SDP (1) (9)

1978

January — Secondary Phase

Class A (Walla Walla) selections:

1— Mike Martin, c; B: Portland, OR; Mt. Hood CC, OR; 1986 CHC (1) (1)

June — Regular Phase

Major League selection:

1— Andy Hawkins, rhp; B: Waco, TX; Midway HS, Waco, TX; 1982 SDP (7) (11)

Class AAA (Hawaii) selection:

2— Doug Gwosdz, c; B: Houston, TX; Madison HS, Houston; 1981 SDP (4) (4)

Class AA (Amarillo) selection:

3— George Stablein, rhp; B: Inglewood, CA; Cal State Dominguez Hills; 1980 SDP (1) (1)

Class A (Reno) selections:

5— Floyd Chiffer, rhp; B: Glencove, NY; UCLA; 1982 SDP (3) (3)

6— Tim Flannery, 2b; B: Tulsa, OK; Chapman College; 1979 SDP (11) (11)

7— Steve Fireovid, rhp; B: Bryan, OH; Miami University, OH; 1981 SDP (2) (6)

18— Eric Show, rhp; B: Riverside, CA; UC Riverside; 1981 SDP (10) (11)

1979

June — Regular Phase

Major League selections:

1— Joe Lansford, 1b; B: San Jose, CA; Wilcox HS, San Jose, CA; 1982 SDP (2) (2)

1— Bob Green, c; B: San Diego, CA; Clairemont HS, San Diego; 1988 SDP (4) (5)

4— Mark Parent, c; B: Ashland, OR; Anderson HS, Cottonwood, CA; 1986 SDP (5) (9)

5— Mark Thurmond, lhp; B: Houston, TX; Texas A&M University; 1983 SDP (4) (8)

8— James Steels, of; B: Jackson, MS; Santa Maria HS, CA; 1987 SDP (1) (3)

1980

June — Regular Phase

6— Gerry Davis, 3b; B: Trenton, NJ; Howard University; 1983 SDP (2) (2)

11— George Hinshaw, of; B: Los Angeles, CA; University of LaVerne; 1982 SDP (2) (2)

19 — Mike Couchee, rhp; B: San Jose, CA; USC; 1983 SDP (1) (1)

1981

June — Regular Phase

1— Kevin McReynolds, of; B: Little Rock, AK; University of Arkansas; 1983 SDP (4) (12)

2 — Bill Long, rhp; B: Cincinnati, OH; Miami University, OH; 1985 CHW (6) (7)

3 — Tony Gwynn, of; B: Los Angeles, CA; San Diego State University; 1982 SDP (17) (17)

10— Greg Booker, rhp; B: Lynchburg, VA; Elon College; 1983 SDP (7) (9)

14 — Paul Noce, ss; B: San Francisco, CA; Washington State University; 1987 CHC (1) (2)

June — Secondary Phase

3 — John Kruk, of; B: Charleston, WV; Allegany CC, PA; 1986 SDP (4) (10)

1982

June — Regular Phase

1— Jimmy Jones, rhp; B: Dallas, TX; Thomas Jefferson HS, Dallas, TX; 1986 SDP (3) (8)

3 — Mark Wasinger, 2b; B: Monterey, CA; Old Dominion University; 1986 SDP (1) (3)

4 — Mark Williamson, rhp; B: Corpus Christi, TX; San Diego State University; 1987 BAL (8) (8)

8 — Mitch Williams, lhp; B: Santa Ana, CA; West Linn HS, OR; 1986 TEX (3) (10)

21— Bob Patterson, lhp; B: Jacksonville, FL; East Carolina University; 1985 SDP (1) (9)

29 — Gene Walter, lhp; B: Chicago, IL; Eastern Kentucky University; 1985 SDP (2) (5)

1983

June — Regular Phase

1— Ray Hayward, lhp; B: Enid, OK; University of Oklahoma; 1986 SDP (2) (3)

3 — Ed Vosberg, lhp; B: Tucson, AZ; University of Arizona; 1986 SDP (1) (2)

1984

January — Secondary Phase

1— Randy Byers, inf; B: Bridgeton, NJ; CC of Baltimore; 1987 SDP (2) (2)

June — Regular Phase

1— Shane Mack, of; B: Los Angeles, CA; UCLA; 1987 SDP (2) (9)

1— Gary Green, ss; B: Pittsburgh, PA; Oklahoma State University; 1986 SDP (2) (5)

1985

June — Regular Phase

1— Joey Cora, ss; B: Caguas, Puerto Rico; Vanderbilt University; 1987 SDP (3) (7)

3 — Jim Tatum, of; B: San Diego, CA; Santana HS, Santee, CA; 1992 MIL (1) (5)

6 — Eric Nolte, lhp; B: Canoga Park, CA; UCLA; 1987 SDP (4) (5)

10— Greg Harris, rhp; B: Greensboro, NC; Elon College; 1988 SDP (6) (8)

12 — Jerald Clark, 3b; B: Crockett, TN; Lamar University; 1988 SDP (5) (6)

1986

January — Regular Phase

1— Doug Brocail, rhp; B: Clearfield, PA; Lamar CC, CO; 1992 SDP (3) (7)

4 — Warren Newson, of; B: Newnan, GA; Middle Georgia JC; 1991 CWS (5) (8)

June — Regular Phase

1— Thomas Howard, of; B: Middletown, OH; Ball State University; 1990 SDP (3) (9)

6 — James Austin, rhp; B: Farmville, VA; Virginia Commonwealth University; 1991 MIL (3) (3)

1987

2 — Roger Smithberg, rhp; B: Elgin, IL; Bradley University; 1993 OAK (2) (2)

6 — Dave Hollins, 3b; B: Buffalo, NY; University of South Carolina; 1990 PHI (5) (9)

1988

1— Andy Benes, rhp; B: Evansville, IN; University of Evansville; 1989 SDP (7) (10)

3 — Ray Holbert, ss; B: Torrance, CA; Jordan HS, Long Beach, CA; 1994 SDP (2) (3)

5 — Bryce Florie, rhp; B: Charleston, SC; Hanahan HS, SC; 1994 SDP (3) (5)

10— A.J. Sager, rhp; B: Columbus, OH; University of Toledo; 1994 SDP (1) (5)

15 — Mike Humphreys, of; B: Dallas, TX; Texas Tech University; 1991 NYY (3) (3)

1989

5 — Dave Staton, 1b; B: Seattle, WA; Cal State Fullerton, 1993 SDP (2) (2)

6 — Darrell Sherman, of; B: Los Angeles, CA; Long Beach State University 1993 SDP (1) (1)

12 — Kevin Higgins, 2b; B: San Gabriel, CA; ASU, 1993 SDP (1) (1)

20— Tim Worrell, rhp; B: Pasadena, CA; Biola University; 1993 SDP (5) (6)

1990

1— Robbie Beckett, lhp; B: Austin, TX; McCallum HS, Austin, TX; 1996 COL (2) (2)

1— Scott Sanders, rhp; B: Hannibal, MO; Nicholls State University; 1993 SDP (5) (6)

14 — Scott Frederickson, rhp; B: Manchester, NH; University of Texas; 1993 COL (1) (1)

17 — Matt Mieske, of; B: Midland, MI; Western Michigan University; 1993 MIL (5) (6)

25 — Lance Painter, lhp; B: Bedford, England; University of Wisconsin; 1993 COL (4) (6)

1991

1— Joey Hamilton, rhp; B: Stateboro, GA; Georgia Southern University; 1994 (5) (5)

4 — Sean Mulligan, c; B: Lynwood, CA; University of Illinois; 1996 SDP (1) (1)

5 — Joey Long, lhp; B: Sidney, OH; Kent University; 1997 SDP (1) (1)

7 — Homer Bush, ss; B: East St. Louis, IL; East St. Louis (IL) HS; 1997 NYY (2) (2)

19 — Charlie Greene, c; B: Miami, FL; Miami–Dade CC South; 1996 NYM (1) (3)

38 — Rich Loiselle, rhp; B: Neenah, WI; Odessa JC, TX; 1996 PIT (3) (3)

1992

9 — Todd Erdos, rhp; B: Washington, PA; Meadville (PA) HS; 1997 SDP (1) (2)

1993

1— Derrek Lee, 1b; B: Sacramento, CA; El Camino HS, Sacramento, CA; 1997 SDP (1) (2)

3 — Matt Clement, rhp; B: McCandless Township, PA; Butler (PA) Area HS; 1998 SDP (1) (1)

6 — Greg Keagle, rhp; B: Corning, NY; Florida International University; 1996 DET (3) (3)

9 — Jason Thompson, 1b; B: Orlando, FL; University of Arizona; 1996 SDP (1) (1)

1994

1— Dustin Hermanson, rhp; B: Springfield, OH; Kent University; 1995 SDP (2) (4)

San Francisco Giants

1965

June — Regular Phase

1— Alan Gallagher, 3b; B: San Francisco, CA; Santa Clara University; 1970 SFG (4) (4); 1973 CAL (1)

5 — Rich Robertson, rhp; B: Albany, CA; Santa Clara University; 1966 SFG (6) (6)

11— Chris Arnold, ss; B: Long Beach, CA; Arcadia (CA) HS; 1971 SFG (6) (6)

22 — Ron Bryant, lhp; B: Redlands, CA; Davis HS, CA; 1967 SFG (7) (8)

1966

June — Regular Phase

1— Bob Reynolds, rhp; B: Seattle, WA, Ingraham HS; 1969 MON (1) (6)

11— Bernie Williams, of; B: Alameda, CA; St Elizabeth HS, Oakland, CA; 1970 SFG (3) (4)

13 — Gary Ryerson, lhp; B: Los Angeles, CA; Rolling Hills HS, Palos Verdes, CA; 1972 MIL (2) (2)

17 — Don Hahn, of; B: San Francisco, CA; Campbell HS, San Jose, CA; 1969 MON (2) (7)

31— John Harrell, c; B: Long Beach, CA; West Valley JC, CA; 1969 SFG (1) (1)

1967

June — Regular Phase

1— Dave Rader, c; B: Claremore, OK; South Bakersfield HS, CA; 1971 SFG (6) (10)

3 — Don Carrithers, rhp; B: Lynwood, CA; Lyndale HS, Lynwood, CA; 1970 SFG (4) (8)

11— Jim Willoughby, rhp; B: Salinas, CA; Gustine (CA) HS; 1971 SFG (4) (8)

20— Gary Lavelle, lhp; B: Scranton, PA; Liberty HS, Bethlehem, PA; 1974 SFG (11) (13)

June — Secondary Phase

1— Bob Fenwick, ss; B: Okinawa, Ryukyu Island; University of Minnesota; 1972 HOU (1) (2)

3 — James Johnson, lhp-of; B: Muskegon, MI; Western Michigan University; 1970 SFG (1) (1)

1968

January — Regular Phase

2 — Garry Maddox, of; B: Cincinnati, OH; San Pedro HS, CA; 1972 SFG (4) (15)

3 — George Foster, of; B: Tuscaloosa, AL; El Camino JC, CA; 1969 SFG (3) (18)

June — Regular Phase

1— Gary Matthews, of; B: San Fernando, CA; San Fernando HS, Pacoima, CA; 1972 SFG (5) (16)

8 — Jim Howarth, of; B: Biloxi, MI; Mississippi State University; 1971 SFG (4) (4)

June — Secondary Phase

1— Ed Goodson, ss; B: Pulaski, VA; East Tennessee State University; 1970 SFG (6) (8)

1969

January — Secondary Phase

4 — Steve Stone, rhp; B: Euclid, OH; Kent State University; 1971 SFG (2) (11)

June — Regular Phase

1— Mike Phillips, ss; B: Beaumont, TX; McArthur HS, Irving, TX; 1973 SFG (3) (11)

3 — Horace Speed, of; B: Los Angeles, CA; Banning HS, Compton, CA; 1975 SFG (1) (3)

6 — Steve Ontiveros, 3b; B: Bakersfield, CA; Bakersfield HS, CA; 1973 SFG (4) (8)

7 — Gary Thomasson, of; B: San Diego, CA; Oceanside HS CA; 1972 SFG (6) (9)

11— Skip Pitlock, lhp; B: Chicago, IL; Southern Illinois University; 1970 SFG (1) (3)

June — Secondary Phase

1— Jake Brown, c; B: Sumrall, MA; Southern University; 1975 SFG (1) (1)

1970

January — Regular Phase
1— Randy Moffitt, rhp; B: Long Beach, CA; Cal State Long Beach; 1972 SFG (10) (12)

January — Secondary Phase
1— Chris Speier, ss; B: Alameda, CA; Laney JC, CA; 1971 SFG (7) (19)

June — Regular Phase
1— John D'Acquisto, rhp; B: San Diego, CA; St. Augustine HS, San Diego, CA; 1973 SFG (4) (10)
2 — Butch Metzger, rhp; B: Lafayette, IN; Kennedy HS, Sacramento, CA; 1974 SFG (1) (5)
25 — Doug Capilla, lhp; B: Honolulu, HI; Westmont HS, Campbell, CA; 1976 STL (2) (6)

June — Secondary Phase
1— Dave Kingman, rhp-of; B: Pendleton, OR; USC; 1971 SFG (4) (16)
3 — Jim Barr, rhp; B: Los Angeles, CA; USC; 1971 SFG (8) (13)

1971

June — Regular Phase
1— Frank Riccelli, lhp; B: Syracuse, NY; Christian Brothers HS, Syracuse, NY; 1976 SFG (1) (3)
3 — Willie Prall, lhp; B: Hackensack, NJ; Upsala College; 1975 CHC (1) (1)
5 — Skip James, lb-of; B: Elmhurst, IL; University of Kansas; 1977 SFG (2) (2)
32 — Greg Thayer, rhp; B: Cedar Rapids, IA; St. Cloud State University; 1978 MIN (1) (1)

June — Secondary Phase Active
1— Steve Strougher, of; B: B: Visalia, CA; College of the Sequoias, CA; 1982 SEA (1) (1)

1972

January — Regular Phase
2 — Reggie Walton, 1b; B: Kansas City, MO; Compton JC, CA; 1980 SEA (2) (3)

January — Secondary Phase
2 — Gary Alexander, c; B: Los Angeles, CA; Los Angeles Harbor JC, CA; 1975 SFG (3) (7)

June — Regular Phase
1— Rob Dressler, rhp; B: Portland, OR; Madison HS, Portland, OR; 1975 SFG (2) (5)
2 — Bob Knepper, lhp; B: Akron, OH; Calistoga HS, CA; 1976 SFG (7) (15)
24 — Ed Halicki, rhp; B: Newark, NJ; Monmouth College; 1974 SFG (7) (8)

June — Secondary Phase
4 — Terry Cornutt, rhp; B: Roseburg, OR; Linn-Benton CC, OR; 1977 SFG (2) (2)

1973

January — Secondary Phase
1— Dave Heaverlo, rhp; B: Ellensburg, WA; Central Washington University; 1975 SFG (3) (7)

June — Regular Phase
1— Johnnie LeMaster, ss; B: Portsmouth, OH; Paintsville HS, KY; 1975 SFG (11) (12)
3 — Jeff Little, lhp; B: Fremont, OH; Woodmore HS, Woodville, OH; 1980 STL (1) (2)
6 — Tommy Toms, rhp; B: Charlottesville, VA; East Carolina University; 1975 SFG (3) (3)
10 — Eddie Plank, rhp; B: Chicago, IL; University of Nevada–Reno; 1978 SFG (2) (2)
13 — Jack Clark, rhp-of; B: New Brighton, PA; Gladstone HS, Covina, CA; 1975 SFG (10) (18)

June — Secondary Phase
1— Pete Falcone, lhp; B: Brooklyn, NY; Kingsborough CC, NY; 1975 SFG (1) (10)

1974

June — Regular Phase
3 — Alan Wirth, rhp; B: Mesa, AZ; St. Mary's HS, Mesa, AZ, 1978 OAK (3) (3)
10 — Guy Sularz, of-rhp; B: Minn, MI; North Hollywood HS, CA; 1980 SFG (4) (4)
15 — John Henry Johnson, lhp; B: Houston, TX; Somona HS, CA; 1978 OAK (2) (8)

1975

June — Regular Phase
3 — Jose Barrios, 1b; B: New York, NY; South Miami HS, FL; 1982 SFG (1) (1)
6 — Rich Murray, 1b; B: Los Angeles, CA; Locke HS, Los Angeles, CA; 1980 SFG (2) (2)
12 — Greg Johnston, of; B: Los Angeles, CA; Citrus JC, CA; 1979 SFG (1) (3)
22 — Mike Rowland, rhp; B: Chicago, IL; Millikin University; 1980 SFG (2) (2)

1976

January — Secondary Phase
1— Dennis Littlejohn, c; B: Santa Monica, CA; USC; 1978 SFG (3) (3)

June — Regular Phase
26 — Jeff Stember, rhp; B: Elizabeth, NJ; Westfield HS, NJ; 1980 SFG (1) (1)

1977

June — Regular Phase
2 — Phil Huffman, rhp; B: Freeport, TX; Brazoswood HS, Lake Jackson, TX; 1979 TOR (1) (2)
11— Chili Davis, of; B: Kingston, Jamaica; Dorsey HS, Los Angeles, CA; 1981 SFG (7) (18)
12 — Bob Tufts, lhp; B: Medford, MS; Princeton University; 1981 SFG (1) (3)
14 — Bob Kearney, c; B: San Antonio, TX; University of Texas, TX; 1979 SFG (1) (8)

1978

June — Regular Phase
4 — Rob Deer, of; B: Orange, CA; Canyon HS, Anaheim, CA; 1984 SFG (2) (11)
5 — Jeff Ransom, c; B: Fresno, CA; Berkeley HS, CA; 1981 SFG (3) (3)
11 — John Raab, c; B: Los Angeles, CA; Washington HS, Los Angeles, CA; 1982 SFG (3) (5)
21 — Mark Calvert, rhp; B: Tulsa, CA; University of Tulsa; 1983 SFG (2) (2)

1979

June — Regular Phase
1 — Scott Garrelts, rhp; B: Urbana, IL; Buckley-Loda HS, Buckley, IL; 1982 SFG (10) (10)
2 — Chris Brown, 3b; B: Jackson, MS; Crenshaw HS, Los Angeles, CA; 1984 SFG (4) (6)
4 — Randy Kutcher, ss; B: Anchorage, AK; Palmdale HS, CA; 1986 SFG (2) (5)
11 — Frank Williams, rhp; B: Seattle, WA; Lewis-Clark State College; 1984 SFG (3) (6)
16 — Tom O'Malley, 2b-inf; B: Orange, NJ; Montoursville HS, PA; 1982 SFG (3) (9)

1980

June — Regular Phase
1 — Jessie Reid, 1b; B: Honolulu, HI; Lynwood HS, CA; 1987 SFG (2) (2)
10 — Alan Fowlkes, rhp; B: Brawley, CA; Cal Poly Pomona; 1982 SFG (1) (2)
26 — Mark Dempsey, rhp; B: Dayton, OH; Ohio State University, OH; 1982 SFG (1) (1)

1981

June — Regular Phase
1 — Mark Grant, rhp; B: Aurora, IL; Catholic HS, Joliet, IL; 1984 SFG (3) (8)
2 — Kelvin Torve, 1b; B: Rapid City, SD; Oral Roberts University; 1988 MIN (1) (3)
20 — Matt Nokes, c; B: San Diego, CA; Patrick Henry HS, San Diego, CA; 1985 SFG (1) (11)

1982

June — Regular Phase
1 — Steve Stanicek, 1b; B: Lake Forest, IL; University of Nebraska; 1987 MIL (1) (2)
34 — Randy Bockus, of; B: Canton, OH; Kent State University; 1986 SFG (3) (4)

1983

June — Regular Phase
2 — Jeff D. Robinson, rhp; B: Santa Ana, CA; Cal State Fullerton; 1984 SFG (4) (9)
4 — Charles Hayes, 3b; B: Hattiesburg, MS; Forrest County Agricultural HS, Hattiesburg, MS; 1988 SFG (2) (11)

6 — John Burkett, rhp; B: New Brighton, PA; Beaver HS, PA; 1987 SFG (6) (10)
7 — Mike Aldrete, 1b-of; B: Carmel, CA; Stanford University; 1986 SFG (3) (10)

June — Secondary Phase
1 — Robby Thompson, ss; B: West Palm Beach, FL; University of Florida, FL; 1986 SFG (11) (11)

1984

January — Regular Phase
1 — Greg Litton, 2b; B: New Orleans, LA; Pensocola JC, FL; 1989 SFG (4) (6)
5 — Mackey Sasser, c; B: Fort Gaines, GA; Dothan, AL; 1987 SFG (1) (9)

June — Regular Phase
1 — Terry Mulholland, lhp; B: Uniontown, PA; Marietta College; 1986 SFG (4) (12)
3 — Tony Perezchica, ss; B: Mexicali, Mexico; Palm Springs HS, CA; 1988 SFG (3) (4)
8 — Stu Tate, rhp; B: Huntsville, AL; Auburn University; 1989 SFG (1) (1)

1985

June — Regular Phase
1 — Will Clark, 1b; B: New Orleans, LA; Mississippi University; 1986 SFG (8) (13)
6 — Jeff Brantley, rhp; B: Florence, AL; Mississippi State University; 1988 SFG (6) (11)
8 — Trevor Wilson, of-lhp; B: Torrence, CA; Oregon City, OR; 1988 SFG (7) (8)
10 — Joe Kmak, c; B: Napa, CA; UC Santa Barbara; 1993 MIL (1) (2)
15 — Randy McCament, rhp; B: Albuquerque, NM; Grand Canyon College; 1989 SFG (2) (2)
18 — Dennis Cook, of-lhp; B: LaMarque, TX; University of Texas, TX; 1988 SFG (2) (11)

1986

June — Regular Phase
1 — Matt Williams, 3b; B: Bishop, CA; UNLV; 1987 SFG (10) (12)
2 — Kirt Manwaring, c; B: Elmira, NY; Coastal Carolina College; 1987 SFG (10) (12)
9 — Russ Swan, lhp; B: Fremont, CA; Texas A&M University; 1989 SFG (2) (6)
20 — Craig Colbert, 3b; B: Iowa City, Iowa; Oral Roberts University; 1992 SFG (2) (2)

1987

1 — Mike Remlinger, lhp; B: Middletown, NY; Dartmouth College; 1991 SFG (1) (6)
2 — Eric Gunderson, lhp; B: Portland, OR; Portland State University, OR; 1990 SFG (2) (8)
3 — Mike Benjamin, ss; B: Euclid, OH; ASU; 1989 SFG (7) (10)
9 — Gil Heredia, rhp; B: Nogales, AZ; University of Arizona; 1991 SFG (2) (7)

35 — Jimmy Myers, rhp; B: Oklahoma City, OK; Crowder (OK) HS; 1996 BAL (1) (1)

1988

1— Royce Clayton, ss; B: Burbank, CA; St. Bernard HS, Plays del Rey, CA; 1991 SFG (5) (8)

9 — Kevin Rogers, lhp; B: Cleveland, MS; Mississippi Delta JC; 1992 SFG; 1988 SFG (3) (3)

21— Steve Decker, c; B: Rock Island, IL; Lewis-Clark State College; 1990 SFG (4) (5)

23 — John Patterson, 2b; B: Key West, FL; Grand Canyon College; 1992 SFG (4) (4)

25 — Reggie Williams, of; B: Laurena, SC; University of South Carolina; 1992 CAL (1) (3)

1989

1— Steve Hosey, of; B: Los Angeles, CA; Fresno State University; 1992 SFG (2) (2)

9 — Rafael Nova, lhp; New York, NY; Villanova University; 1990 SFG (1) (2)

11— Greg Brummett, rhp; B: Wichita, KS; Wichita State University; 1993 SFG (1) (1)

15 — Pat Rapp, rhp; B: Los Angeles, CA; University of Southern Mississippi; 1992 SFG (2) (7)

33 — Dan Carlson, rhp; B: Portland, OR; Mount Hood (OR) CC; 1996 SFG (2) (3)

1990

1— Marcus Jensen, c; B: Oakland, CA; Skyline HS, Oakland, CA; 1996 SFG (2) (3)

3 — Rick Huisman, rhp; B: Oak Park, IL; Lewis University, IL; 1995 KCR (2) (2)

4 — Mike Myers, lhp; B: Arlington Heights, IL; Iowa State University; 1995 FLA (1) (4)

8 — Kevin McGehee, rhp; B; Alexandria, LA; Louisiana Tech; 1993 BAL (1) (1)

1991

5 — William Van Landingham, rhp; B: Columbia, TN; University of Kentucky; 1994 SFG (4) (4)

8 — Dax Jones, of; B: Pittsburgh, PA; Creighton University; 1995 SFG (1) (1)

53 — Ken Grundt, lhp; B: Melrose Park, IL; Missouri Southern State University; 1996 BOS (2) (2)

1992

5 — Doug Mirabelli, c; B: Kingman, AZ; Wichita State University; 1996 SFG (3) (3)

10— Jamie Brewington, rhp; B: Greenville, NC; Virginia Commonweath University; 1995 SF (1) (1)

11— Chad Fonville, ss; B: Jacksonville, NC; Louisburg (NC) JC; 1995 MON (1) (3)

1993

4 — Jay Canizaro, ss; B: Beaumont, TX; Blinn (TX) JC; 1996 SFG (1) (1)

7 — Keith Williams, of; B: Bedford, PA; Clemson University; 1993 SFG (1) (1)

15 — Bill Mueller, 3b; B: Maryland Heights, MO; Southwest Missouri State University; 1996 SFG (3) (3)

21— Steve Bourgeois, rhp; B: Lutcher, LA; Northeast Louisiana University; 1996 SFG (1) (1)

1994

1— Dante Powell, of; B: Long Beach, CA; Cal State Fullerton; 1997 SFG (2) (2)

1— Jacob Cruz, of; B: Oxnard, CA; ASU; 1996 SFG (3) (3)

5 — Bobby Howry, rhp; B: Phoenix, AZ; McNeese State University; 1998 CWS (1) (1)

9 — Keith Foulke, rhp; B: San Diego, CA; Lewis-Clark State (ID) College; 1997 SFG (1) (2)

1995

1— Joe Fontenot, rhp; B: Lafayette, LA; Acadiana HS, Lafayette, LA; 1998 FLA (1) (1)

4 — Russ Ortiz, rhp; B: Encion, CA; University of Oklahoma; 1998 SFG (1) (1)

6 — Joe Nathan, ss; B: Houston, TX; SUNY–Stony Brook; 1999 SFG (1) (1)

1996

2 — Mike Caruso, of; B: Queens, NY; Stoneman Douglas HS, Parkland, FL; 1998 CWS (1) (1)

Index